BENJAMIN HARSHAV

Marc Chagall and His Times

A DOCUMENTARY NARRATIVE

With translations from Russian, Yiddish, French, German, and Hebrew by

BENJAMIN AND BARBARA HARSHAV

Stanford University Press   Stanford, California 2004

Stanford University Press
Stanford, California

Printed in the United States of America
on acid-free, archival-quality paper.

Library of Congress Cataloging-in-Publication Data

Harshav, Benjamin, 1928– .
    Marc Chagall and his times : a documentary narrative / Benjamin Harshav ;
translations from Russian, Yiddish, French, German, and Hebrew by
Benjamin and Barbara Harshav.
        p.   cm.
    Includes bibliographical references and index.
    ISBN 0-8047-4213-8 (alk. paper) — ISBN 0-8047-4214-6 (pbk. : alk. paper)
    1. Chagall, Marc, 1887–1985.   2. Artists—Russia (Federation)—Biography.
3. Chagall, Marc, 1887–1985—Correspondence.   4. Artists—Russia (Federation)—
Correspondence.   5. Artists—Belarus—Biography.   6. Artists—Belarus—
Correspondence.   I. Chagall, Marc, 1887–1985.   II. Harshav, Barbara, 1940– .
III. Title.
N6999.C46H37   2003
709'.2—dc21   2003007566

Original Printing 2003
Last figure below indicates year of this printing:
12   11   10   09   08   07   06   05   04   03

Designed by Janet Wood
Typeset by James P. Brommer in 11/14 and 11/21 Filosofia

Frontispiece: Marc Chagall at twenty, 1907

CONTENTS

PREFACE

This book tells the story—through narrative, correspondence, original documents, and illustrations—of the remarkable life of Marc Chagall, an artist and a Jew, thrown into the excitement and turmoil of the twentieth century. It is a large volume, reflecting the immense range of Chagall's ninety-eight years of creative life and wanderings (1887–1985). He had three wives and three cultural identities: Jewish, Russian, and French. He was influenced by Fauvism, Russian Neo-Primitivism, and avant-garde painting, by Yiddish literature, Russian poetry, and the Hebrew Bible; he was attracted to Surrealism and Expressionism, Zionism and Communism, yet always recoiled from groups and ideologies and retreated into his own private world. Chagall was, in his own perception, a Wandering Jew, who carried his home on his back around the globe. The major stations of his life were the Jewish Pale of Settlement in Russia, the Tsarist capital St.-Petersburg, post-Cubist Paris, Russia in World War I, the Revolutionary Soviet Union, Berlin, again Paris, Palestine, Vichy France, New York City and upstate New York, again France, Israel, and his final home in the French Riviera.

The book offers a new reconstruction of Marc Chagall's life and consciousness, based on hundreds of letters and original documents found in many pri-

"Remembrance," gouache, India ink, and pencil on paper. A Jew goes into exile, tears in his eyes, carrying not a peddler's sack but the memory of his home with him. To represent Chagall's own Jewish experiences, he uses the icon of a religious Jew, not of the young generation: elderly, with hat and beard. Drawing with Chagall's whimsical asymmetries. It is the small, minimal version of a house, with mother or grandmother in the door (see the image of his grandfather on the roof in Chapter 2). In the lower right corner is a penciled date: 914 (with Chagall's typical omission of the "1" for one thousand). The signature in ink above it seems to be renewed on top of an earlier penciled signature. To the left of it is an inscription in German: Erinnerung 1914; this must have been added when Chagall was in Berlin in 1922–1923. The painting is ascribed to ca. 1918, but Chagall's date sends us back to the experience of exile in 1914–1915, when Vitebsk was flooded by refugees and to other paintings of the Wandering Jew of that period.

vate and public archives. It is written on two interrelated levels: (1) the voices of Marc Chagall and his contemporaries, as recorded in Chagall's autobiographical writings, private letters, official documents, and other texts, all annotated and translated into English; and (2) my own narrative voice, connecting the original documents and telling the story of the major stages in Chagall's life and their historical and cultural contexts; these portions are set off typographically.

Most of the original texts presented here have never been published before. The book contains Chagall's own autobiographical writings of various years, as well as hundreds of letters written in several languages by Chagall or by his contemporaries and companions.

I wrote the Introduction and Chapter 1, as well as many passages—a kind of narrative "voice-over" running throughout the book. It is a story quite different from the well-known Chagall biography, repeated in many books and catalogues. It is based on a rethinking of all available documentary material, both known and hitherto unknown. Yet in most cases, I have tried not to interpret the documents or analyze the motivations of their protagonists; I let them speak for themselves, leaving a great deal open to the reader's impressions and interpretations.

The book can be read as a nonfictional novel, written by an omniscient author who presents the characters and lets them speak for themselves. It is not just a book about Marc Chagall, but a book about the times and places he lived in; large chunks of modern history, and particularly Jewish history, are reflected in it.

*

The scope of Chagall's written legacy, mostly unknown, required a division of the material into two books. This volume contains his autobiographical writings, a selection of the correspondence, and my narrative outline of his life. His public statements, lectures, essays, and interviews are included in a separate volume, *Marc Chagall on Art and Culture*. For interpretations of Chagall's paintings and iconography, the reader may turn to my forthcoming book *The Art of Marc Chagall*.

The letters and documents are inevitably of a double selection. First, a great deal of material has been preserved for some periods and with some correspondents, yet for others little or nothing survived. Second, we have many written utterances on some topics, while others remained oral, painterly, intuitive, and not articulated in language. For reasons of space, I selected only about a third of the original letters available to us; many letter exchanges had to be excerpted, and other correspondents not included. Nevertheless, I have tried to represent each kind of issue and, even when curtailed, every correspondence has been represented with sufficient continuity for the scattered letters to echo and respond to each other.

Thus, for the first time, we have a well-documented image of Chagall's stormy activities as "commissar" (actually, "Plenipotentiary for Matters of Art in Vitebsk Province"). It is a vivid example of the involved yet precarious role of the revolutionary artist in molding the culture of the Russian Revolution. And for the first time, Chagall's pro-Zionist and pro-Communist sentiments and disappointments of various years are openly exposed. Above all, the sources of his art, his apprenticeship, his struggles and successes, his explorations of a range of different artistic media, and the religious problematic of his church art are illuminated from within. Furthermore, in many letters we can see his incessant, anxious, yet ambivalent attachment to the Jewish world, and the central place it occupied in Chagall's consciousness throughout his life.

An especially interesting period was the seven years (1945–1952) in the prime of his life, when Chagall lived with Virginia Haggard. Between his two official marriages—with Bella (Berta) Rosenfeld (1915–1944) and Vava (Valentina) Brodsky (1952–1985)—the common-law marriage with Virginia, blessed by their son David, occurred at a critical time in Chagall's life, when he moved from the American haven back to post-Holocaust Europe. During this time, he was sympathetic to Soviet Russia and bitterly defeated by Stalin's anti-Semitism; admired the new

State of Israel and contemplated working for Christian churches; recovered his prewar engravings, published them, and received First Prize in the Venice Biennale of 1948; bought houses and pondered his homelessness; and was accepted as a major European artist. We have hundreds of letters written by Virginia in English or French to many friends and collectors, notably their close friends, the Yiddish writer Yosef Opatoshu and his wife Adele, describing daily events, little joys, and big worries; as well as many letters from Chagall to Virginia, the Opatoshus, the art chronicler Pavel Ettinger in Moscow, and others. Even personal and business letters not written by Marc himself reflect his responses to a large extent. Virginia told me that Marc would "dictate" such letters to her, though, no doubt, her style and personality dominated the text. These letters raise a curtain on Chagall's daily life, exploits, loves, and ambitions, whose like we do not have for any other period.

Of particular interest is the correspondence with Chagall's collectors and friends, notably Louis Stern, Bernard Reis, Chagall's dealer Pierre Matisse in New York, and Professor John Ulric Nef in Chicago, conducted by Marc, his daughter Ida, Virginia, or Vava; as well as his correspondence with friends in Israel, notably Meir Dizengoff, first Mayor of Tel Aviv; Kadish Luz, Speaker of the Knesset; and Abraham Sutzkever, anti-Nazi partisan, Yiddish poet and editor. And last but not least, Chagall's letters to Charles Marq, the master artist who for twenty-seven years collaborated with Chagall and produced all his stained glass windows, and to Charles Sorlier, the master printer of his lithographs.

I have also recovered the complete early version of Chagall's autobiography from a manuscript of 1924 (see Chapter 2). Later, this autobiography was expanded and reworked in a French translation by Bella Chagall (whose French at the time was a few years old) and published in 1931 as *Ma vie*, from which the well-known English *My Life* and all translations in other languages were made. The published version is prodigiously quoted in books on Chagall, but the earlier version is more authentic and precise, and includes many details that were later suppressed or omitted. Furthermore, I have included several additional autobiographical chapters, scattered in long-forgotten Russian and Yiddish journals between 1922 and 1939, as well as Chagall's poems, written in Yiddish on specific occasions and contributing to the story of his life.

*

Preparing Chagall's multilingual letters and texts for a contemporary reader involved international detective work, seeking and finding letters and manuscripts in dozens of public and private archives; retrieving publications in old and marginal journals; and translating them all into English. In addition, I tried to identify the dates and events; place the texts in their chronological context, where they responded to and complemented each other; decipher allusions to persons or events mentioned in them; and provide hundreds of annotations. Thus, I tried to reconstruct the world in which Chagall moved—a large chunk of the twentieth century.

In principle, all texts appear in this book in their chronological order. As a result, and as in real life, Chagall's relations with a variety of persons and topics are interlaced with no system. For the reader's convenience, the flow of time has been divided into chapters; their titles take off from some event or theme, but other themes flow in and out and the title topic may continue in later chapters.

Several memoirs, however, written after the events but mainly describing an earlier period are placed in the earlier time frame. Thus, a memoir on Chagall's work in the Moscow Yiddish Theater, published in 1928, is placed in the period of his work there (1920). Essays containing recollections of his Russian teachers Yury Pen and Léon Bakst, his early mentors and friends Maxim Vinaver, Yakov Tugendhold, and Dr. Isidore Elyashev, or his visit with Max Liebermann in Berlin, all written in Paris during the 1920s and 1930s, are placed in the time frame of their main focus. Similarly, Chagall's second French period, starting in 1923, is introduced by an interview given in 1927, centering on his adoption of France as his "Second Vitebsk"; and the FBI surveillance of Chagall in the United States is given in the summary Report of the FBI, placed at the beginning of his American period.

Persons and events are briefly described the first time they become relevant to the text. Names mentioned in passing are merely identified, whereas key events and historical and biographical contexts are introduced either in the narrator's essay or in a margin note. There is an obvious exception: The many names mentioned in Chagall's autobiography (Chapter 2) are merely identified there, while more substantial descriptions are given when the person actually appears on the scene, from Chapter 3 onward. Important clarifications of the text and its connotations are provided in margin notes, whereas references and other annotations are in the endnotes.

I have indicated in each text the language from which it was translated (French, Yiddish, Russian, German, or Hebrew) or transcribed (English). The date, whenever available, is registered in the exact form of the original. Therefore, if the full date is given in numbers, we must distinguish between the European way, writing day first and month second; and the American way, starting with the month. For example, "3.12" can mean either December 3 in a European context, or March 12 in an American context, respectively. From an analysis of the content, in most cases it was possible to reconstruct the correct date. Whenever the numbers are unclear, I indicated the correct month in words, or added a reconstructed date in brackets.

The word *rébe* in Yiddish (from the Hebrew *rábi*) has several distinctly different meanings, disambiguated by native speakers in each context. In English we shall distinguish as follows: *Rebbe* is the hereditary head of a Hasidic dynasty; *rebbe* is a religious schoolteacher in *Heder* (also used metaphorically, for someone's teacher, if the person was a pupil and follower of his); *Reb* followed by a name is equivalent to "Mr." ("Reb Alter"); *Rov* (Hebrew *Rav*) is a clearly defined title of a religious authority, a person with a rabbinical degree and a hired religious head of a Jewish community, similar to the contemporary American concept of "Rabbi." It is important to note that the word *Yidish* in Yiddish, or *Evreysky* in Russian, means both the nation (Jewish) and the language (Yiddish). In the English translation we could use only one meaning, depending on the context, yet the other should be kept in mind. Another ambiguity.

An interesting detail is the fact that in many letters and paintings, Chagall wrote the year without the "1" for one thousand; thus, "928" means "1928." This reflected Chagall's primarily spoken knowledge of Russian: For the English "nineteen twenty-eight" the Russian says "nine hundred twenty-eight," omiting the thousand. He knew languages mainly by talking.

A caution: We must not use our contemporary modes of judgment about Chagall's discourse. He was a cosmopolitan and liberal man, and yet, when addressing other Jews in Yiddish, he often used the same clichés as his parents or the "folk" in the Pale of Settlement. Thus, people belonged to categories: You don't encounter a "man" but either a "Goy" or a "Jew," and a woman is either a "Goya" or a "Jewess." There is nothing necessarily pejorative about such expressions, though they may carry stereotypical connotations, it was simply part of his language and social categorization. For example, when describing his work in Mexico, he refers to the Mexicans as "the black-yellow Goyim. Something sings out of their souls." And a "Goy" could also be an assimilated Jew or any Jew illiterate in Judaism, like Chagall himself.

social categorization: The usage is somewhat like that in African-American novels, referring to a "brother" or a "sister," just as an indication that they are black.

*

I have not preserved all awkward spellings, but I have retained some colorful idioms or disjointed syntax. In letters written in English, I left the language as is, even when it is not quite idiomatic or correct, as in Ida Chagall's English letters. Parentheses are often used by Chagall and other authors; brackets indicate my own insertions—providing either complementary information [   ] or explanatory information [=]. Many ellipses are used in the original; ellipses in brackets [. . .] indicate my deletion of text.

The structure of this book is as follows: In Chapter 1, "Imagining Chagall's Childhood and Youth" I set the cultural and political context of Chagall's early life. Chapter 2, "Chagall's First Autobiography," contains the early version of Marc Chagall's own mythologized story. Chapters 3–25 resume Chagall's life story, through letters and texts, starting with his earliest experiences in learning art, around 1900, and continuing through his death in 1985. My own introductions and interventions are always indented.

Abbreviations

Marc Chagall and His Times   Benjamin Harshav, *Marc Chagall and His Times: A Documentary Narrative*, Stanford, Calif.: Stanford University Press, 2004.

Marc Chagall on Art and Culture   Benjamin Harshav, editor, *Marc Chagall on Art and Culture*, Stanford, Calif.: Stanford University Press, 2003.

Marc Chagall and the Jewish Theater   *Marc Chagall and the Jewish Theater*, New York: Guggenheim Museum, 1992 (pp. 15–204 by B. Harshav).

Marc Chagall: Les années russes   *Marc Chagall: Les années russes, 1907–1922*, Paris: Musée d'Art Moderne de la Ville de Paris, 1995 (two essays and twenty interpretations by B.H.).[1]

The Meaning of Yiddish   *The Meaning of Yiddish*, Berkeley: University of California Press, 1990; paperback edition: Stanford, Calif.: Stanford University Press, 1999.

Language in Time of Revolution   *Language in Time of Revolution*, Berkeley, University of California Press, 1993; paperback edition: Stanford, Calif.: Stanford University Press, 1999.

Ma vie   Marc Chagall, *Ma vie*, Traduit de russe par Bella Chagall, Préface d'André Salmon, Paris: Librairie Stock, 1931.

My Life   Marc Chagall, *My Life*, Translated from the French by Elisabeth
Abbott, New York: Orion Press, 1960.

My Own World   Marc Chagall, *My Own World*, Chapter 2 in this volume.

Acknowledgments

I encountered the legendary Marc Chagall in my childhood, when he came with
Bella to my native Vilna in the summer of 1935 to inaugurate a Jewish Art Museum, which he had initiated. We had a *dacha* next to a summer colony for
"weak" (actually, tubercular) Jewish city children, directed that summer by my
father, Dr. Abraham Hrushovski, who hosted a visit by the great historian Shimon Dubnov and Marc Chagall (see the photo in Chapter 12). Sixty years later, I
was fortunate to talk and correspond with members of the family: Marc Chagall's
daughter Ida Chagall, still impressive in her last days; her ex-husband and dean
of Chagall studies Franz Meyer; the artist's son, songwriter and novelist David
McNeil; and Chagall's granddaughters Bella Meyer and Meret Meyer-Graber,
who spend a great deal of time and energy on the Chagall legacy.

My special thanks and admiration go to the foremost Chagall specialist and indefatigable researcher Meret Meyer-Graber, granddaughter of Marc Chagall and
daughter of his ground-breaking biographer Franz Meyer, who opened to me her
mother's large collection of documents, letters, and photographs. Of special
value are the many letters, reviews, and documents, copied for Ida Chagall on
a typewriter by the prominent Jewish Russian literary scholar Ilya Samuilovich
Zilbershteyn in Moscow in 1959.

A most unusual role in this book was played by Virginia Haggard-Leirens, Chagall's common-law wife for seven years. She generously shared with me Chagall's
personal letters to her and allowed me to use the hundreds of letters she wrote to
friends and business relations during their life together, which I found in various
archives fifty years later. Our vivid picture of Chagall's private life owes a great

deal to Virginia's intelligent and prolific letter writing, describing it in all its colorful details from within. Though she had not seen her own letters in half a century, they support and supplement her own book of memoirs.[2] Virginia answered dozens of my queries in writing, clarifying many forgotten issues, and made many photographs available to me. Her presence in this book speaks for itself.

The book benefited from the contributions of the Moscow art historian Dr. Alexandra Shatskikh, who put at my disposal her annotated edition of Chagall's letters to Pavel Ettinger and responded to many queries, based on her extensive knowledge of the period.

The book was enriched by material from the files on Chagall in the archives of the FBI and the U.S. Department of State, released according to the Freedom of Information Act (FOIA). The material was obtained by the Public Citizen Litigation Group in Washington, D.C., directed by David Vladeck, whose grandfather B. Vladeck was a friend of Chagall and a Yiddish poet, as well as a prominent political leader in New York City under Mayor LaGuardia. I owe special thanks to Attorneys Lucinda Sykes and Douglas Stevick, who applied their indefatigable effort and professional devotion to the cause of uncovering the truth.

Barbara Harshav, as always, gave the translations a precise and vivid shape in English. My gratitude to her has no words I care to say in public.

*

I thank the Lucius N. Littauer Foundation in New York for their support of this research, as well as the Griswold Fund at the Whitney Humanities Center, the Rifkind Fund at the Jewish Studies Program, both at Yale University, and the research fund of Tel Aviv University. Warm thanks to Judith Hibbard for her love and devotion to this project.

*

I am most grateful to the Comité Chagall in Paris for their general permission to publish all Chagall's letters, texts, and photographs; to the YIVO Jewish Research

Institute in New York and the Archives of American Art, now part of the Smithsonian Institution in Washington D.C., who opened their archives for this project and gave me permission to publish the selected texts.

In addition, the following institutions allowed me to research and publish from their archival materials: Art Institute of Chicago; Beinecke Rare Book and Manuscript Library at Yale University; Bibliothèque d'art et d'archeologie (Fondation Jacques Doucet) in Paris; Bibliothèque Nationale de France; "Genazim" Archives of the Israel Writers Union in Tel Aviv; Solomon R. Guggenheim Museum Archives in New York; Historical Archive of Tel Aviv-Jaffa Municipality; Israel Museum in Jerusalem; Knesset of Israel; National and University Library in Jerusalem; Musée national d'Art moderne, Centre Georges Pompidou; Archives of the Museum of Modern Art in New York; J. Pierpont Morgan Library in New York; Rare Books and Manuscripts Library of Columbia University; Special Collections of the University of Chicago Library; U.S. Holocaust Memorial Museum in Washington, D.C. I thank them all.

*

Of special value in this Chagall odyssey were Anthony Calnek, Director of Publications of the Solomon R. Guggenheim Museum in New York, who commissioned my first text on Chagall; Susanne Pagé, Director of the Musée d'Art moderne de la Ville de Paris, who invited me to participate in the catalogue of their Chagall retrospective in 1995; Daniel Marchesseau, curator of the Chagall exhibition in Paris, with whom I had the most warm and fruitful relationship, and his collaborators Dominique Gagneux and Marianne Sarkari, as well as the fine translator into French Dennis Collins; my late friend Professor Chone Shmeruk in Jerusalem, who always shared with me his vast knowledge of the Yiddish world; Annette R. Fry, who gave me the Chagall files of her late husband, Varian Fry; and my research assistant at the time, the lawyer Shari Motro, who contributed her alert precision, devotion to the project, and knowledge of English,

Hebrew, and Word for Windows. I am grateful to my research assistants of various times, including Dan Friedman, Ilya Kliger, and Ravit Reichman. Daniel Feldman prepared the index of names and paintings mentioned in the book.

My sincere thanks to all those who were instrumental in this search, provided information, or loaned me their documents; only a few can be listed here: Jacob Baal-Teshuva, who included many translations made by Barbara Harshav and myself in his comprehensive book, *Chagall: A Retrospective*; Chana Bar-Ner, Director of the archives of the Israel Museum; Zachary Becker, former Librarian of the YIVO Jewish Research Institute in New York; Elizabeth Berman, U.S. Holocaust Memorial Museum in Washington, D.C.; Nikolay Borodulin at the YIVO Jewish Research Institute in New York; Miriam Cendrars, writer and editor, daughter of Blaise Cendrars; Sylvie Forestier, former director of the Musée National Message Biblique Marc Chagall, Nice; David Giladi, Tel Aviv journalist and author of a Hebrew book on Chagall; Vincent Giroud, Curator of the Beinecke Library at Yale University; Susan Goodman, Curator of the Jewish Museum in New York; Shulamit Harel, daughter of the writer A.Z. Ben-Yishay in Tel Aviv; Eberhard W. Kornfeld, publisher of the catalogue raisonné of Chagall's engravings; Yves Lebouc, Bouquinerie de l'Institut in Paris, who gave me original photographs and Chagall's correspondence with Charles Sorlier; André Leleup, who kindly sent me some materials by Gustave Coquilot; Professor Zvi Luz and the archivist of Kvutsat Degania B, who opened the Chagall correspondence with the Speaker of the Knesset Kadish Luz; Rivka Marcus, Director of the Knesset archives in Jerusalem; Charles Marq, master of stained glass windows, who worked with Chagall for a quarter of a century, shared with me his memories and allowed me to use his correspondence; Walter Meyerhof, Varian Fry Foundation Project; Nina Mokady Hayon in Ra'anana, daughter of the Israeli artist Moshe Mokady; Lilyan and Daniel Opatoshu, daughter-in-law and grandson of Yosef Opatoshu; Bella Rosenfeld Zelter, niece of Bella Chagall in Paris; Yosef Schein in

Paris, painter and former actor of the Moscow Yiddish State Theater; Didier Schulman at the Musée national d'Art moderne, Centre Georges Pompidou; Dvora Stavi at Genazim, the archives of the Hebrew Writers Union in Tel Aviv; Abraham Sutzkever, Yiddish poet and editor of *Di Goldene Keyt* in Tel Aviv, who published Chagall's poems, essays, and letters in Yiddish; Viviane Tarènne at the Musée national d'Art moderne, Centre Georges Pompidou, who was generous in opening their Chagall possessions to me; Judith Throm, Head of Reference at the Archives of American Art at the Smithsonian Institution in Washington, D.C.; Mordekhai Tsanin, Yiddish writer and editor of the main Yiddish newspaper in Tel Aviv; Marek Webb, archivist of YIVO Jewish Research Institute, New York; Rafi Weiser and his colleagues at the National and University Library in Jerusalem.

All private and public owners of letters published here were marvelously forthcoming. They deserve my thanks and the gratitude of Chagall scholars and readers of this book. Unfortunately, there are still many inaccessible letters in various collections; their eventual availability will surely add to our knowledge, as well as to the value of the documents themselves.

The author would be most grateful for any additional letters or other texts and memoirs, as well as corrections of my inevitable mistakes—to be used for my work in progress on Chagall's life and art: Benjamin Harshav, J. & H. Blaustein Professor of Hebrew and Comparative Literature and Professor of Slavic Languages and Literatures, Yale University. Department of Comparative Literature, Yale University, New Haven, CT 06520-8299, USA . E-Mail: Benjamin.Harshav @yale.edu

—B. H.

MARC CHAGALL AND HIS TIMES

Introduction

Marc Chagall (1887–1985) was one of the prominent artists of the modern age—sometimes admired, sometimes disparaged, always present. He stood out as a different artist, one who determines for himself the nature of art and representation, responding to—yet outside of—any modernist trend. His unique place has been recognized through numerous major exhibitions held from 1914 to this day in the great museums of the world, always intriguing, provoking, and seen by mass audiences.

Chagall's paintings are intimately related to his personal biography. Typically, several disconnected figures and objects appear side by side on one canvas and create an associative ensemble, a "poetic" or "dreamlike" world, repeated in many variations. The connections between such modular units are not sustained by any realistic logic but rather motivated by their coexistence in the artist's life and mind. Hence, Marc Chagall's life story is indispensable to the reading of his art. Chagall understood very early that he had to "explain" his paintings, to tell the story behind the "Surrealist" impression, and began writing his autobiography when he was about thirty years of age.

Chagall was influenced and challenged by the stylistic questions and formal innovations of various modernist trends of his time, borrowing from them yet not joining any of them. With the avant-garde, he shared the contempt for realism and for "psychologism." He emphasized the autonomy of the color areas and geometrical forms, and favored a non-mimetic composition of the figures and objects on a canvas. Yet he situated such modernist features in counterpoint to a network of cultural representations. And he was a multicultural person indeed: Elements of Jewish, Russian, and French culture, the great tradition of Christian art, as well as fictional worlds from great literature, informed his paintings and illustrations. If his was an eclectic art, it was so vis-à-vis the "pure," exclusive, and clearly defined styles—yet most art in history is never "pure." Chagall's style included a deliberate, demonstrative eclecticism, or—to use a positive term—a well-orchestrated polyphony.

Chagall lived in the most exuberant and turbulent age, at the heart of the twentieth century. He experienced the outcast status of Jews in the Russian Empire and the enthusiastic Russian reception of French art; the excitement of Fauvism and Cubism, and the provocations of the artistic avant-garde; the utopia of the Russian Revolution and the haunting Holocaust; French culture and American life; the revival of the State of Israel and the myth of the Bible. How did he perceive it and respond to it all?

The main outlines of Chagall's life have been told many times, notably in the monumental and comprehensive biography written by Chagall's son-in-law Franz Meyer in the late 1950s.[1] Meyer's experience combined the solidity of a European art historian and the humanistic traditions of art interpretation with a close knowledge of Chagall's life story. At his disposal, he had the family archives and a vast store of information provided by his wife, Ida Chagall, and the artist himself. Meyer compiled a detailed, exhaustive bibliography and catalogue raisonné, which are the foundation of all Chagall scholarship.

The most important interpretations of Chagall's work were written in Western

"'One for all and all for one'—United Bundist Artists of Vitebsk, 1906." (Photo published in *Forverts*, New York, April 1, 1928, under the title "Jewish Revolutionary Groups—from Olden Days.") Some biographers of Chagall claimed he was the first to break the taboo of painting human figures, yet a secular painters movement was alive in Vitebsk. Here are just members of the illegal Jewish Socialist party, the Bund; all atheists—they wear no hats.

Europe and reflected Chagall's reception there—the best he ever had. One weakness of that criticism, however, was its rudimentary or secondary knowledge of Eastern Europe and its Jewish culture. Furthermore, many sources in Russian, Yiddish, and Hebrew concerning the economic and cultural renaissance of Vitebsk Jewry remained untapped. Thus, Chagall and his biographers emphasized his daring violation of the religious ban on making graven images, yet that "violation" clearly preceded Chagall. It was self-evident in the realistic Jewish art in Germany and Poland in the nineteenth century. And in his native Vitebsk, Yury Pen, Chagall's own art teacher, "raised several generations of Jewish artists" (as

Chagall put it) in his private art school, which opened in 1896–1897. A published photograph survived, showing twenty artists in 1906, members of the Jewish Socialist Bund—just in Vitebsk alone (and not counting all other political trends).

Like many painters who speak the language of color and form, Chagall was not an analytical thinker or a master of words. He was, in his own words, "an unconsciously conscious artist." His early fantasies of becoming a singer or a violinist and his later love of classical music, which he liked to play while painting, underlined his affinity with nonverbal art. Yet there is a vast body of hitherto unpublished texts—speeches, essays, poems, and letters that he wrote on many occasions and to many addressees—and they reveal a great deal about his innermost, immediate, and changing affiliations, situations, and responses.

Chagall biographies written in Western languages rarely deal with his lifelong and highly emotional concerns with Jewish culture and destiny, on the one hand, and his flirtation with Communist cultural circles, especially between 1937 and 1952, on the other hand. To some extent this was due to the lack of authentic sources and, to a large extent, to Chagall's own obfuscations when he presented himself to the "external" world. The two topics—the persecuted Wandering Jew regaining his dignity and the Communist Revolution in Russia—had been intertwined in his consciousness since the days of the Revolution. The rhetoric of both domains permeated his writings and paintings from the very formation of his ideological discourse: beginning with his artistic responses to the mass expulsions of Russian Jews from the front areas in World War I (see his painting "The Red Jew," 1915) and merging with his subsequent activity as commissar of art in Vitebsk. Indeed, the concepts of *folk* ("the people") and *folkstimlekh* ("in a popular manner") that he used in Yiddish speeches and letters cover both the simple people of "the masses," as used in Communist parlance, and the Jewish nation.

A special example of cultural-ideological influence is Chagall's ambitious painting "Revolution," created in France on the 20th anniversary of the October

Revolution, at the same time as Picasso's "Guernica," and probably intended for the World Exhibition in Paris in 1937. The painting was prominently displayed in Chagall's exhibition at the Pierre Matisse Gallery in New York in 1942, on the 25th anniversary of the October Revolution. Though relatively small in size, it continued the genre of huge, political murals, massively populated and accessible to the masses, which he had envisioned in 1918, as commissar of art in Vitebsk, and first executed in his mural, "Introduction to the Jewish Theater" in the new Moscow Yiddish theater in 1920.

Though a finished oil painting, "Revolution" is a mere blueprint for such a mural; but it has all the ingredients of a massive presentation of the historical world upheaval and the Jewish element in it. Center stage is shared by Lenin standing on his head (Chagall wrote: "Lenin would turn Russia upside down, the way I turn a picture upside down"—as if Lenin was influenced or foreshadowed by Chagall) and the sad, Eternal Jew with his Torah. The joyful brigade on one side is clearly Jewish, but the Revolutionary masses with red banners on the other side also have many Jews in their traditional garb, participating in the armed uprising. This last image appeared in a drawing Chagall made for Lyesin's Yiddish poetry in the 1930s and was inspired by Lyesin's poem. (A selection of these illustrations appears in the section starting on page 394.)

Chagall never made a huge mural based on this sketch (when he lived in America during the 1940s, who would want a mural celebrating the Russian Revolution?). But later he divided the ambitious composition into three paintings, which he called "Resistance," "Resurrection," "Liberation."[2] He worked on this triptych during World War II and completed two parts in 1948; he finished the last one in 1952. In the new version, Lenin's place in the center was taken by a crucified Jesus Christ wearing a Jewish prayer shawl as a loincloth—an image of the eternal suffering Jew, which Chagall borrowed from Yiddish poetry and used in his own "White Crucifixion," painted in France in 1938, shortly after "Revolution."

Although the triptych is clearly a response to the Holocaust, it cannot be understood unless we read the Jewish Communist rhetoric of the first years after the Holocaust and Chagall's own writings in the Communist press. Instead of the prevalent religious and Zionist narrative: Diaspora leads to persecution and annihilation, hence the solution is a Jewish state; he uses the Communist narrative: Resistance leads to the Resurrection of the Jews and their Liberation by the Red Army, as part of the victory of Communism in Eastern Europe.

In the first panel, there is a total eclipse of the Jewish *shtetl* represented in the painting; it fell into the dark. Yet the emphasis is not on victimhood but on resistance: the revolutionary fighters of 1917 are transformed into Jewish partisans of 1941–1944 in Eastern Europe. The fusion of the anti-Fascist cause and Jewish collective memory was already central to Chagall's responses to the Spanish Civil War in the late 1930s and repeated time and again in his speeches to leftist audiences in America during the 1940s.[3]

The second step in this narrative was the belief in the resurrection of Jewish life in Eastern Europe under the wings of the victorious Red Army, indicated by the generally accessible Christian symbol of the resurrected Christ in the second panel—though it is a Jewish Jesus, in a Jewish prayer shawl and coming from Yiddish literature. The third panel represents the third step—the joyful liberation of Jewish popular culture under the red banner.[4]

Thus, the emphasis was on Liberation rather than Holocaust. But for Chagall, the major issue was the survival of the Jewish people rather than the victory of Communism.

*

Chagall often presented himself as a Russian or a French painter. The Chagall album of the journal *Der Sturm*, published in Berlin in 1923, opens thus: "*Marc Chagall ist Russe*"—"Marc Chagall is a Russian." It was written by the editor Herwarth Walden (whose real name was Georg Lewin, a Jew himself). In the perspective of that time, it is understandable: If Jewishness is just a religion, and we live in a secular society, why stress a painter's religion if he doesn't even believe in it? Why open a door to discrimination? And in a letter to the art chronicler Pavel Ettinger in Moscow (October 4, 1936), Chagall wrote: "Though in the world I am considered an 'international' [artist] and the French take me into theirs, but I think of myself as a Russian artist and this is very pleasing to me." Yet a year later, in a questionnaire for the Art Institute of Chicago, he indicates: "Nationality: French," apparently referring to his recently acquired French citizenship, rather than an ethnic or cultural identity.

On the other hand, in his autobiography, written in Russian, he pointed out: "Had I not been a Jew (with the full content I put into this word), I would not have been an artist, or I would be entirely different." And his old friend André Salmon wrote, in his introduction to the French translation of *Ma vie* (1931): "Chagall is a Jew, and only a Jew could achieve this art which no Jew before Chagall had produced."

A telling example of his longing for a Russian identity appears in a letter Chagall wrote in 1933 to Isaac Israelevich Brodsky in Moscow. In the Soviet period, Brodsky became the painter of several famous and canonized portraits of Lenin and a pillar of Socialist Realism. He even received the Great Prize of the International Exhibition of Technology and Art in Paris, 1937, for his painting "V.I. Lenin's Speech at a Meeting of Workers at that Putilov Factory in May 1917"—a recognition of Socialist Realism as a legitimate style. Chagall writes: "I was happy to get a word from you. For only rarely do I get regards from [my] homeland. They don't write to me, why? Am I not a Russian?" The irony lies in that Brodsky himself was a Jew and took part in organizing exhibitions of Jewish artists and sculptors in Moscow and Petrograd during 1915–1919.

Inwardly, in his private life and letters, however, Chagall always maintained he was a Jew—even when he was a self-critical Jew, like most active or upwardly mobile Jews in that period—and throughout his life he kept in touch with Jewish cultural affairs, Yiddish writers, and Israel. He understood very well that the Jewish sources of his art were not merely thematic but have a profound relationship with his emotional attitudes, irrespective of theme, and even with the "technical" aspect, the nature of his associative compositions. Thus, in a letter to his old friend, the Yiddish art critic Leo Kenig in London (April 27, 1948), he writes: "True, my art is Jewish, i.e., emotionally, and even 'technically'"; and in the same breath he continues: "Please do not emphasize that I was especially inspired by the 'Lubok' [Russian narrative folk paintings] or, as Venturi[5] thinks, by 'icons.' I was inspired by everything, even the pig who scratched his back on the fence in Vitebsk." This is the point: everything—stylistic, thematic, cultural elements—could serve as materials for his polyphonic fictional canvasses.

*

Chagall was a typical child of the Modern Jewish Revolution at the end of the nineteenth and beginning of the twentieth century.[6] Millions of Jews moved out of the old *shtetl* world to the cities and to the capitals of culture outside the Jewish Pale of Settlement, both West and East. Many such individuals took a visible place in the general culture. Those who used the medium of language—Franz Kafka or Sigmund Freud, Saul Bellow or Philip Roth—needed two generations for this transition: They had to be born into the new language to be able to use it in art. Painters, however, like Marc Chagall or Chaim Soutine, and philosophers like Emanuel Levinas, could accomplish the shift in one generation. Parallel to this trend, a vigorous secular Jewish culture emerged, modeled on the modern cultures of Europe and using the internal Jewish languages, Hebrew or Yiddish. Eventually, this intrinsic trend resulted in the creation of a Hebrew-speaking society and the modern state of Israel, whereas the major, Yiddish-language branch dwindled in the Diaspora or was destroyed by Hitler and Stalin.

Yet in Chagall's time, especially during the first half of the twentieth century, a rich and multifarious Yiddish culture was still active around the globe, producing thousands of books, modern poetry, novels, a library of translations, as well as school networks, newspapers, Jewish political parties, theaters, and so on. As an artist, Chagall lived mostly in a non-Jewish world, yet emotionally and personally he was attached to this Jewish culture in Yiddish and its speakers. The themes and ideologies of his paintings drew on it. Chagall was also drawn emotionally to the new Jewish society in Palestine, but, not knowing any Hebrew, he was a mute outsider there. Vis-à-vis both Yiddish and Hebrew modern culture, he was always ambivalent, sitting on the fence, judging it from the standards of the "Goyim."

*

Chagall's basic language was Yiddish; over time, he learned to speak Russian and French fluently (though with a Yiddish accent). While he learned to read Hebrew in his childhood, his real first language of culture, reading, and writing was Russian. He began speaking it in his teens and probably spoke Russian with his peers in Vitebsk and with the assimilated Jews in St.-Petersburg. With his first wife Bella he spoke the language of their youth, Russian, but Yiddish as well. Bella herself wrote two volumes of her memoirs in Yiddish during the 1940s. Their daughter Ida mainly spoke Russian, but she understood Yiddish stories when read aloud and received a Yiddish literary journal in the 1930s. Marc spoke French with his second (common-law) wife Virginia, but—as she reveals in her autobiography—also Russian with Ida, Raïssa Maritain, or Louis Stern, and Yiddish with various neighbors and visitors.

Chagall had many genuine friends among French intellectuals; his house was open to them, and he illustrated many of their books. He spoke French with Picasso (Picasso in his Spanish accent); with his partners the artisans Fernand Mourlot, Charles Marq, Charles Sorlier, and Georges Ramié; with his dealers Pierre Matisse and Aimé Maeght; and with his friends Blaise Cendrars, Jacques

Maritain, André Lhote, Jacques Prévert, Paul Eluard, Tériade, and many more.
No doubt, French was the language of Chagall's life in the art world, but he did
not need to write it. Jean-Louis Prat, Director of the Maeght Foundation in
France, which has handled Chagall's art since the 1950s, informed me that they
have no Chagall letters. The reason is simple: Chagall lived nearby and could
communicate orally, or through intermediaries. Charles Marq, the master of
stained glass windows, has many letters by Chagall, mostly short notes, announcing a visit and professing his friendship. As Marq told me, their collaboration was expressed in "oral conversations and short reflections during our
work together."

Indeed, Chagall's written French was marred by spelling errors, as we can see
from the letters he wrote in longhand, to his love Virginia Haggard and to a few
others. Here, for example, is a complete letter from Paris in 1946 to the art critic
Emily Genauer in New York:

> Chers ami!
>
>> Comment alez Vous?
>>
>> Souvenirs de Pariss.
>>
>> le Mussee d'Art Modern de Paris projette de faire un grand exposition
>> retrospective de moi le ceson prochaine et peut-etre aussi le musse de Londres
>> Je espere rentrer bientot
>> Je espere Vous alles biens?
>> A Vous
>>
>>> Marc Chagall

It sounds like a child's exercise riddled with mistakes—and it was written by a
French artist and citizen who by that time had lived in France for 22 years. Indeed, most of Chagall's French, Russian, or English letters were handwritten or
typed by the women around him: his wives Bella, Virginia, or Vava, and signed
by Marc Chagall; or written by daughter Ida or Virginia in his name. Even his

letters to the first mayor of Tel Aviv, Meir Dizengoff, were written at first in Russian by Bella and signed by Marc Chagall, until he became close to his correspondent and they switched to their real mother tongue, Yiddish. And when Chagall resorted to his own pen, he ended almost every letter with an apology for his spelling mistakes, in Yiddish as in French.

Chagall's first language of culture was Russian. In his twenties, his instinctive recourse to writing was in Russian. But his Russian education was minimal: he spent five years in a city high school, a four-class *uchilishche*, without graduating,[7] and for several years attended art schools conducted in Russian. He was apparently exposed to some Russian literature, especially Symbolist poetry. In 1909–1910, he wrote a book of poetry in Russian (never published),[8] which shows a certain mastery of Russian meters and poetic clichés of classical and Symbolist poetry. Chagall's written Russian was fluent and mostly correct. After the Revolution, he conducted his Art College in Vitebsk in Russian, published several articles in Russian, and wrote his autobiography in Russian. He talked or corresponded in Russian throughout the years, but there is no evidence of poetry originally written in Russian after he left Russia in 1910. (Later he translated, however, some of his Yiddish poems into Russian, from which the French translations were made.) When he was commissioned to illustrate Gogol's *Dead Souls*, Bella read the book aloud to him in Russian.

Chagall's truly spontaneous, intimate language was Yiddish; he had an intense affinity with the world and mentality of Yiddish speakers from Eastern Europe and was bemoaning the state of Yiddish/Jewish culture. It was so easy for Chagall to deliver dozens of lectures in Yiddish (all written out in his own hand) and respond to many hundreds of Yiddish letters: to the speaker of the Israeli Knesset Kadish Luz; to the Yiddish writers Yosef Opatoshu, Leo Kenig, A. Lyesin, Sh. Nigger, A. Sutzkever, Mendl Man, Leo Leneman, Avrom Reizin, Zalman Shneur; and to many casual correspondents. He often spontaneously wrote to Yiddish writers

See the details in note 7.

congratulating them on their anniversaries. Over eighty percent of his surviving handwritten letters and lectures are in Yiddish. Chagall never revealed in public, and no critic noticed, that he illustrated the Bible not from the Hebrew original but from a modern Yiddish translation—which gave the interpretation an altogether different tone. Even in the mock-ups he made in 1960 for the Hadassah synagogue windows in Jerusalem, devoted to the biblical twelve tribes, he jotted down words in Yiddish inside the painting—though in the final windows he inserted, of course, the original biblical names only in Hebrew.[9]

Chagall's Yiddish spelling was also outlandish; he simply recorded the spoken language.[10] He acquired Yiddish as an oral language at home, and it is not clear whether he wrote anything at all in Yiddish before the 1920s. Yet, notwithstanding his weak performance in literary Yiddish, we must not forget that spoken Yiddish was the language of his parents, with whom he lived for the first twenty years of his life and for four more years in 1914–1918. Subsequently, he lived in a Yiddish cultural milieu in Moscow during 1920–1922, and (not knowing German) he certainly spoke Yiddish in Berlin in 1922–1923 with Chaim-Nakhman Bialik and Dr. Elyashev. During the 1930s, living in France, he wrote Yiddish poetry and some articles in Yiddish. And the language was revitalized again during his seven years in America, 1941–1948, where he knew no English, read Yiddish newspapers, was connected to a Yiddish cultural milieu, and wrote and lectured in Yiddish.

Only during his first four years in Paris, 1910–1914, did he have some French-speaking friends and must have communicated in French, rudimentary as it was. When Chagall recollects a day he spent with the French poet Max Jacob, he adds: "What did we talk about? In what language?" (*My Life*, p. 112). And even upon his return to France in 1923, he spoke Yiddish and Russian to Ossip Zadkine, Jacques Lipchitz, and other friends in the cafés of Montparnasse.[11]

I am stressing this point because Chagall's personal Jewish consciousness, continuing to the very end, is overlooked in most books about him—except as a point of origin. And we are talking not about the Jewish sentiments of Albert Einstein, a physicist, but of Marc Chagall, the very substance of whose art depended on his cultural affinities and attitudes. Thus, his poems were published in French, without disclosing their Yiddish origin. They even appeared in French (untranslated!) in an English edition of his writings,[12] as if those were French poems, without as much as mentioning in what language they were originally created. Indeed, many of those poems are segments of his autobiographical long poem, "My Distant Home" (1936–1937), published in four versions in Yiddish journals. It was written in Yiddish meter and rhyme, in precise iambic tetrameters (which Chagall could not have done in translation); yet in Franz Meyer's otherwise meticulous bibliography, its first, Yiddish publication appears as "translated from the Russian."[13] Of course, at that point Chagall himself would have presented himself as a Russian rather than a Yiddish poet. Yet, in a letter of 1937 to his editor, the Yiddish poet A. Lyesin, Chagall announces: "Here is my first *Poema* (long poem) in Yiddish. (I used to write in Russian, but I lost it all)." And there is correspondence about details of the text in Yiddish poems with his other editors, which leave no doubt about their original language.

Furthermore, the semiotics of Eastern European Yiddish discourse influenced his discourse and behaviour,[14] which was often either perceived as "cute" and "childish," joking and entertaining, or seemed cunning and devious in the eyes of people used to Western norms of communication. Thus, a year after Virginia left him and he married Vava Brodsky, while he is worried about his son David and pities himself, Chagall wrote in a letter in Yiddish on July 12, 1953, to his friend Yosef Opatoshu (the question marks are Chagall's):

> Dear Opatoshu, thank you for your letters. I'm sitting at the desk, quite tired. And today is my day, our day, the 12/7 when Valya became my wife—and it seems she is happy and I have a very nice friend for my life. Though only God knows how my life

is twisted, and it seems, tortured, and when you imagine, through such a false (?) human being[15] without any soul (?) and a pity for the little Dovid'l,[16] you have to have a lot of strength not to see it (just recently I saw him for the first time), that who knows whether he remained a Jew in that dark village school. How are you? And how is Adelye? Well, I became a grandfather.

This associative style, moving from good to bad and back again, mixing up everything and involving God in the mess of his world, is pure Sholem-Aleichem: Tevye the Milkman's rambling monologues.[17]

By now, Yiddish culture as the language of a society has dwindled and cannot defend itself, but it still carries a stigma in certain circles. Chagall was one of its last witnesses, and though he lived outside it and saw its cultural poverty, he often made forays into its center. Quite possibly, Marc Chagall himself was often guilty of the clumsy cover-up, "ghetto-Jew" or "chameleon" that he was. Many Jews of his generation (Bakst, Walden, Raïssa Maritain, Sonia Delaunay) were happy not to flaunt their Jewishness, or subdue it, for fear of being marred by the negative stereotypes they themselves believed in. And Yiddish speech was a stigma within a stigma.

This is not to minimize Chagall's recurring ambivalence about the Jewish/cosmopolitan and Jewish/Christian tensions that informed his creative work and his social relations—as it preoccupied the minds of many creative Jews in modern culture. Chagall knew he was a Jew, but always wanted to be accepted as a universal "Artist" rather than a "Jewish" painter.

I have no intention of underestimating Chagall's place in general twentieth-century art (as, for example, Miró's place is in it, despite his strong Catalan consciousness). Chagall's thinking about art certainly derived from a wide knowledge of European art and strong, intuitive judgments about what he called its "chemistry." As an artist, he lived in the world of the Western art establishment —its museums, exhibitions, collectors, and art histories. Furthermore, his attitudes toward the Russian Revolution and Communism were also an important component in his cosmopolitan consciousness and discourse, as they were in the lives of many of his European contemporaries. This book reflects all of those. Yet we must also listen to what Chagall said and wrote to friends and audiences inside his native culture, even when he himself lived outside it.

In a painting called "Cubist Landscape," inside an immaculate Cubist composition he depicts the Art College he founded in Vitebsk, with a happy Chagall walking toward it, protected by fate (with an umbrella above his head). On the left, climbing upward, he surveyed his languages in their chronological order, in a multilingual recording of his name:

שאגאל шагал шагал шагал шагал шагал // шагал шагал шагал шагал chagall chagall chagall chagall шагал шагал шагал шагал художественное училище

Since the word *Shagal* in Russian means "he walked" (which Chagall always represented as striding upwards on a diagonal), it could also be interpreted as: "Chagall walked and walked, through many languages, until he got to his triumph: the Art College." Apparently, Chagall wrote the number of repetitions in each language as the number of years spent there. The basis is Yiddish (in small letters), then eight (ten?) years in Russian (1900–1910), then four years in French (1910–1914), then again four years in Russian (1914–1918), culminating in the Art College.

Chagall was not alone in this multilingual confusion. Another artist of that generation, David Shterenberg, who was appointed after the Revolution by the Minister of Culture, A. Lunacharsky, to be the "boss" of art in Soviet Russia, was thus described by a contemporary critic: "Shterenberg was born in Zhitomir [Ukraine], studied in Paris and became an artist in Moscow. He doesn't speak any of the three languages, but can explain himself in all. What is lacking in words, he substitutes by interjections and gestures."[18] Chagall was a similar

"Cubist Landscape," 1918

multilingual dilettante; his language was the language of art. And in art, he was part of the French art establishment, certainly in the last third of his century.

*

In sum, we cannot reduce Chagall's complex world to one essential attitude or identity. His mind contained a cluster of identities and relationships, and his letters and speeches were highly addressee-oriented: Not only the language of the text, but also its ideology, discourse, jokes, and beliefs, were targeted to the special channel he had with any given particular correspondent or audience. His was a multicultural cluster of communications about the complex and contra-dictory world he experienced. Chagall's messages are channel-dependent, and each message needs to be supplemented by other languages and channels. All that makes for a polyvalent personality and renders the individual expressions partial but no less authentic.[19]

PART ONE

Roots

CHAPTER ONE   **Imagining Chagall's Childhood and Youth**

Origins

As all biographers tell us, Marc Chagall was born on the lucky day of 7/7/1887 (or was he?)[1] in the city of Vitebsk, the capital of a province (*guberniya*) in Tsarist Russia. He was the first child, the beloved son of his diminutive sixteen-year-old mother, followed by his brother David and six sisters. Marc's mother was the oldest of many siblings; her own mother had died when she was fifteen, and she kept an eye on her sisters until they married. She was also the "boss" in her hard-working husband's home—keeping a store, building houses for rent, and taking care of her children's education.

On the day of Chagall's birth, a fire broke out in the poor Jewish neighborhood and mother and child were carried with bed and mattress to another part of the city. Like Pablo Ruiz (later known as Picasso) a few years earlier and at the other end of Europe, Moyshe Shagal (later known as Marc Chagall) was born dead. "Imagine," Chagall wrote in his autobiography, "a pale bladder that doesn't want to live in the world . . . As if it were glutted with Chagallian pictures." They threw him into a trough filled with cold water and revived him; when he opened his eyes, the first thing he saw was a trough, such as we see in several of his paintings called "The Birth." "But," says Chagall, "what's important is that I was born

Prerevolutionary postcard of Vitebsk: Zamkovaya [Castle] Street and Cathedral. The Rosenfelds lived on this street.

dead." Like Picasso, Chagall was driven all his life—he lived for ninety-eight years!—by an incessant creative urge, but since he asked us not to draw any psychological conclusions, we shall leave the issue alone.

Like Pablo Picasso, F. T. Marinetti, Gertrude Stein, Chaim Soutine, and many other modern artists, Chagall was an outsider, a person from the periphery who made it in the center. Usually the rise of a prominent artist proceeded in three stages: First, he studied art in his home context; then he became an artist in a cultural center away from home; and eventually, as a recognized artist, he conquered a prominent place in a major center of art. Marinetti, for example, was born in Egypt of Italian parents, became a French poet in Paris, and then came to dictate a new norm of art to the Italian center, as an Italian poet and theoretician of Futurism in Milan. For Chagall, those stations were Vitebsk and the capitals of Russia and France: St.-Petersburg and Paris. All his life, Chagall felt like a provincial who wants to make it in the center. He absorbed the norms and ideals of that center; yet his strength lay in bringing to the center the marvelous, "thick" world of his provincial past.

Both his parents came from Lyozno, or Lyezhne, a Jewish town in the Russian Pale of Settlement. As was common among newcomers to a city, they lived in a poor, unpaved, peripheral neighborhood of Vitebsk called Peskovatik (meaning "in the sands"). They would be nicknamed "Lyezhner," by their place of origin, and would be considered provincial. Sometimes Chagall himself indicated that he was born in Lyozno, and so did the art critic Abram Efros, who was in close contact with Chagall during World War I, when Efros coauthored the first book about Chagall and Chagall himself illustrated it. In 1937, responding to a questionnaire for the Art Institute of Chicago, Chagall still hesitated and wrote both places: "Born: Liozno, Vitebsk." Nevertheless, the story about the fire in Vitebsk, which is corroborated by documents on that precise day, proves that the actual birthplace was indeed the provincial capital Vitebsk.[2] His grandfather David Shagal went from Lyozno to the burgeoning city of Vitebsk (60 km by train), where he lived in an unpaved suburb and eked out a living as an elementary Hebrew teacher. He took his eldest son Hatskl (short for Yikhezkel, Yiddish for Ezekiel) with him and found a place for him as an apprentice to a herring merchant. When a woman relative died in Lyozno, her eldest daughter, Feyge-Ite, age fifteen, was married to Hatskl and joined him in Vitebsk, where their son Moyshe (later Marc) was born.

Chagall often went back to his large clan in Lyozno, where his grandfather was an honorable Jew, a butcher; here he liked to draw images of the authentic *shtetl*, its characters and professions, and to court its girls—times were changing! In Vitebsk he was a Jewish poor boy who was exceptionally admitted to a Russian city school (his mother gave a heavy bribe to the teacher), and there he met Viktor Mekler, the son of an industrialist and Jewish community leader. Viktor, himself a budding painter, pestered him at first. But he began to admire Marc's painting talent and introduced him to youth "from the city" (i.e., from the center of town)— young Jews of well-to-do homes, children of professionals or merchants, who spoke Russian, had ambitions about Russian culture, and adopted cosmopolitan modes of behavior. Among them were such modern girls as Thea Brachman, daughter of a doctor, who posed in the nude for Chagall (a poor artist, who cannot pay for a model) and her friend Basha, renamed Berta Rosenfeld, daughter of a rich jeweler, who would become Chagall's first wife. A beautiful, curly haired boy with blue eyes and a pale face, who often painted his lips and cheeks (unheard of at the time[3]), Marc attracted both Mekler and the young women for whom he represented the natural prodigy steeped in folk culture, the artistic genius.

As a child, according to Chagall, at the age of thirteen he was admitted to Yury Pen's School of Art, which defied the biblical commandment, "Thou shalt not make unto thee any graven image, or any likeness of any thing." Typically for that time, it was his pious yet pragmatic mother who helped him overcome the barriers of admission in both cases, thus opening a road for her son out of the confined Jewish domain. Early in 1907, Mekler asked Chagall to join him and go to St.-Petersburg to study art. Normally, Jews could not get a Right of Residence permit in the capital, but Mekler's father was a merchant of the First Guild and apparently provided Chagall with a letter, sending him on a business trip to the capital for two months. Chagall failed the admissions test at Stieglitz's School of Art, but when he was admitted to the school of the Imperial Society for the Encouragement of the Fine Arts, he was protected from expulsion. Yet when he left the school on a whim, in the summer of 1908, trouble ensued. Once he was arrested and kept in jail for coming to the capital without a Right of Residence permit; later, he was taken into the household of a lawyer Goldberg, a patron of art, and allowed to stay either in the capital as Goldberg's servant or in the town of Narva, close to the Baltic Sea, in the summer house of Goldberg's in-laws Gormant.

He attended several art schools, until he reached the most "European" art school of all, owned by E. N. Zvantseva, with the famous teachers Léon Bakst and Mstislav Dobuzhinsky. In St.-Petersburg, he sold his first truly "Chagallian" pictures, and in 1910, with the aid of some assimilated and influential Jews, he went to Paris. As a painter, he brought to St.-Petersburg the world of the Jewish Pale of Settlement, and to Paris, the world of provincial Russia. In the summer of 1914, at the age of twenty-seven, this poor Russian artist in Paris was offered a large, one-man show in the influential avant-garde gallery Der Sturm in Berlin. And when he arrived in Russia that same summer, he came as an internationally acclaimed artist.

Facts and Stereotypes

We know very little about Chagall's early life, except for what he relates in his own imaginative and imaginary autobiography. But we can reconstruct the cultural world in which he grew up. Chagall lived at the crossroads of three empires. He shared in all three, and frequently crossed their boundaries: the powerful yet backward prerevolutionary Russian Empire; the separate, extraterritorial Jewish cultural "empire within an empire"[4]; and the metaphorical "empire" of European art. His was the situation of millions of Jews moving out of the Jewish small towns, the so-called "ghetto," and into the European and American secular world.

On the face of it, we know the basic facts of Chagall's background; they are repeated from book to book. Yet even those facts were much more complex and contradictory than may appear. Let us mention a few essential problems.

First, Vitebsk, where Chagall grew up, was neither a village nor a small town (a *shtetl*), as it is often described, and as Chagall saw it from the distance of Paris. It was legally a city, quite large for that time, the capital of a province, headed by a governor, and growing fast in industry and population. It was close to the rich forests, used for building railroad tracks and ship masts, producing paper, and

Prerevolutionary postcard of Vitebsk: the Circuit Court and Smolensk Street with tramway.

export. It had river shipping leading to the Baltic Sea and the West, and a major railroad junction, with lines leading from Moscow to Riga and the West and from St.-Petersburg to Kiev and Odessa. Moving from the Jewish town of Lyozno to the multicultural Vitebsk meant getting out of the stagnant, "eternal" culture of a Yiddish-speaking small town to the opportunities of a bilingual, growing city, open to the new winds of capitalism, urbanization, Russian literature, and Europe. That first step was taken by Chagall's grandfather, the Torah teacher David Shagal. The trains, built in the 1860s, opened that movement out of the *shtetl*.

Second, the Jewish world of Chagall's youth was not simply the orthodox religious milieu, often depicted in his paintings. Indeed, Moyshe himself sang for a while in the synagogue, but he abruptly abandoned religion at the age of thirteen, never to return, and so did all his siblings and peers. It was the ambiance of the Modern Jewish Revolution,[5] when an entire generation shed the old religious

(*above*) Postcard of prerevolutionary Vitebsk: the City Theater.

(*below*) Prerevolutionary Vitebsk: the Governor's Mansion.

Prerevolutionary Vitebsk: the Great Synagogue.

garb and ritual and embraced Russian literature and the professions, ideologies, and ideals of European secular culture. When Chagall moved out of the "ghetto" to the general, cosmopolitan world, he was part of a whole generation of Jews, ripe for their active role in the implementation of the Russian Revolution and their contributions to Western culture and science. What was "Jewish" about him was his participation in this radical move—much more so than his knowledge of traditional Jewish learning (which was rudimentary). Moreover, Chagall's looking back to depict the traditional world, when he did, was part of a movement of some assimilated yet populist Jewish intellectuals at the beginning of the twentieth century who looked back from their new, secular Russian and European position to discover the values and folk art of their grandparents. Both the grotesque and the sentimental stereotypes of Jews in his paintings represented a "lost world" (as the poet O. Mandelshtam called it) already for Chagall and his generation. Such looking back was a very Jewish phenomenon in the twentieth century.

Third, Hasidism was indeed the dominant form of Jewish religion in the area, yet its use in many books on Chagall is misleading. For one, the Byelorussian CHaBaD (or "Lubavich") Hasidic sect was very different from Polish or Galician Hasidism—and it was the dominant Jewish trend in the area, without any competing sects. Outside of vague generalizations about mentality and behavior, no specific Hasidic influences can be detected in Chagall's work. He was quite ignorant in religious matters, did not understand and could not read or write the simplest words in Hebrew—and there was no other source of Hasidic learning. The Marxist scholar Isaac Deutscher, son of a learned Rabbi himself, was right in his criticism of Franz Meyer's biography of Marc Chagall (which he highly praised on the whole):

> Again and again Mr. Meyer refers to Chassidism, the religious romanticism of Eastern European Jewry, and even to the medieval Cabbala, as the sources of the painter's inspiration. Chagall's Jewishness is undeniable—he is steeped in Jewish folklore. But his alleged indebtedness to the Cabbala and to the Jewish theological heritage is hardly credible. Least of all can it be said that his Surrealism "accords" in any way with Judaism.[6]

The myth of Chagall's Hasidic background was promoted when the Romantic ethos of Hasidism became fashionable among some secular Jewish populists and in the young Yiddish literature at the beginning of the twentieth century (notably Y. L. Peretz). Of course, it was only the spirit of Hasidism, without the religious garb and daily ritual performance, that the secular intellectuals admired. They embraced it as an optimistic, emotional, and spiritual alternative to dry learning, "rationality," and the proverbial Jewish sadness. Indeed, Yakov Tugendhold and Abram Efros, both assimilated Jews and Russian art critics, were the first to suggest the Hasidic source of Chagall's art in their book of 1918, *The Art of Marc Chagall* (in Russian).[7] However, Chagall's first teacher Yury Pen, who himself painted Jewish types and ceremonies, was a *Misnaged* (opponent of Hasidism); and the religious types in Chagall's paintings may represent any traditional Jewish society, Hasidic or not. For Chagall, the opposition, *Hasid/Misnaged*, was equivalent to *illogical/academic* art, and he regarded only the first as really creative. When he dubbed the Berlin painter Max Liebermann a *"Misnaged*," he placed him in a lesser rank of creativity.[8]

Fourth, it is true that most Jews in Tsarist Russia were poor and oppressed, had no civil rights, and were not allowed out of the infamous Pale of Settlement. Yet an ever-growing stratum of individual Jews were enterprising and successful, and they exerted a conspicuous influence in the building of Russian railroads, banks, trade, industry, culture, and Revolutionary activities. The poor boy Moshka Shagal also benefited from and participated in that upward movement. Russian-speaking Jewish intellectuals in Vitebsk and St.-Petersburg helped him survive, overcome the obstacles of being a novice artist, and reach Paris.

The Jewish World in the Russian Empire

In the nineteenth century, Russia was an immense empire that dominated dozens of nations in one uninterrupted Euro-Asian territorial mass, stretching from the German border to Japan and from the North Pole to the approaches of Iran and India. It was governed by the Tsar, an absolutist Emperor, aided by a huge army and a formidable network of bureaucracy and police. Russian literature, carried by a small stratum of intelligentsia, became a significant force in European culture. A network of railroads and modern industry in the big cities was developed toward the end of the nineteenth century, and a process of urbanization began. Yet the overwhelming majority of the Russian population were peasants, that is, former slaves ("serfs"), who could be bought and sold, until they were emancipated in 1861. In Chagall's youth, a generation or two later, the more enterprising peasants moved to the big cities and formed the base of a new Russian proletariat, but those who remained in the villages were still predominantly poor, uneducated,

The Pale of Settlement in 1835.

Map labels:

St Petersburg

The Pale of Settlement in 1835

Volga River

Riga

Moscow

Dvinsk

Polotsk · Vitebsk

Vilna

Grodno · Minsk · Mohilev

Lomza · Bialystok · Bobruisk

Plock · Wegrow · Slutzk · Gomel

Warsaw · Brest-Litovsk

Kalisz · Lodz

Piotrkow · Radom · Pinsk

Chernigov · Lublin · Vladimir

Kielce · Zamosc · Lutsk

Dubno · Zhitomir · Kiev

Ostrava · Poltava

Berdichev · Kremenchug

Kamenets · *Dnieper River* · Yekaterinslav

Uman · Elisabetgrad

Bug River

Kishinev · Nikolaev · Melitopol

Odessa · Kherson

Simferopol

Svestopol · Yalta

Danube River

Provinces in which settlement in villages was forbidden

Area of 50 versts along the western border, where new settlement of Jews was forbidden

★ City forbidden to Jewish settlement

⊛ City forbidden to new Jewish settlement

0   100   200
km

© **carta**, JERUSALEM

passive; they owned little or no land and depended on rich landowners or the Village Council. Legally, however, the most powerless social group were the Jews.

Until the end of the eighteenth century, Jews were officially barred from entering the Russian Empire. The majority of world Jewry lived in the large united Kingdom of Poland-Lithuania. Between 1772 and 1794, Poland was dismantled by its neighbors, and the largest chunk was taken by Russia. The Jews came with the territory, yet they were barred from moving out of the occupied provinces and were thus enclosed in a huge geographic ghetto, the so-called Pale of Settlement, where they lived among other minorities, far from Russia proper and separated from its language and culture. The Pale of Settlement encompassed what is all of modern-day Belarus (Byelorussia), most of Ukraine, central Poland, Lithuania, and chunks of Latvia. In time, only several thousand Jews— mostly merchants of the "First Guild" and university-educated professionals— could get Right of Residence permits outside the Pale, including such forbidden cities as Moscow, St.-Petersburg, and Kiev.

The northern part of the Pale, separated from Ukraine by the Polesye swamps, was considered Lithuania in Jewish geography. It encompassed today's Lithuania, all of Byelorussia, and some Latvian and Russian areas. In Yiddish this large domain was called *Litah* and its Jews the *Litvaks*—quite a separate Jewish tribe. Indeed, Jewish *Litah* was six or seven times larger than modern Lithuania, for it preserved the old boundaries of the medieval Grand Duchy of Lithuania before it merged with Poland in the sixteenth century. It was a Jewish identity of a lost kingdom. The Lithuanian language was still spoken by some peasants in the far western corner of that domain, in today's Lithuania. However, the former Lithuanian aristocracy was assimilated to Polish culture (e.g., aristocrats such as Radziwil and Count Potocki and Polish writers such as Adam Mickiewicz and Czeslaw Milosz), the peasants spoke East Slavic dialects (today's Byelorussian), and the administration was conducted in Russian.

Jewish *Litah* had its own Yiddish dialect, culinary traditions, and "mentality." It was famous for its admiration for learning and intensive Jewish education, especially as launched by the Gaon of Vilna in the eighteenth century and his disciples in the nineteenth, who instituted many *yeshivas* (talmudic academies) in small towns. In the eastern part of this large domain, however, in the forests of Byelorussia, a Hasidic movement developed, appealing to both the learned and the simple people. Typically for *Litah*, this movement combined emotional religiosity with the ideals of learning, as indicated by the name of the movement, CHaBaD, an acronym of "wisdom, insight, knowledge." In young Chagall's mentality, we can discern this combination of emotional warmth and optimism with the aspiration toward high culture, even though now it was the culture of Russia and Europe.

Empire within Empire

The Jews in Russia had their own social and cultural empire within the empire of power. They had a dense network of Jewish social, educational, religious, and cultural institutions, unified by one religion, the myth of their own, different history and worldwide dispersion, and the charismatic authority of their scholars and sages. They had a library of sanctified texts, a universe of folklore, and—in modern times—political ideologies and Jewish parties, secular literature, books, and newspapers. This unique world of the Jews operated in their own three private languages, separating them from the rest of the population: Yiddish—for home, social communication, and education, and later, for modern books and newspapers; Hebrew—for the Bible, prayers, and other traditional texts that every male child studied in *Heder*; and Aramaic—for talmudic literature, the main vehicle of religious law, studied in *yeshiva* and used in all rabbinical judgments.

Traditionally, each Jewish town had its own power structure. Its legal, religious head was the Rov (like the American Rabbi), appointed by the local Community

Rebbe: For the distinction between four different variants of this word—Rebbe, rebbe, Reb, Rov— see page xiii.

Council (*Kehila*) on the basis of an earned rabbinical degree, and subject to no outside religious hierarchy. The emergence of Hasidism in the eighteenth century caused a shift of power: from the local Rov, to the Hasidic spiritual leader, the princely Rebbe, the son of a dynasty with extensive influence over a wide territory.[9] In addition to the local organization of each Jewish community and its legal arbiter, the Rov, now a voluntary, countrywide network was created, unified by one authority and spiritual fraternity. This Hasidic network prepared the groundwork for the modern, statewide Jewish political parties of a secular world.

In 1909, Vitebsk had two synagogues and sixty prayer houses, almost all of them CHaBaD Hasidic; three Jewish graveyards (one had been closed for some time); a Jewish hospital with an old people's home and a maternity ward; several Jewish religious schools and three Jewish colleges for women; soup kitchens, philanthropic institutions, and adult education courses.

This autonomous world was situated in the social and linguistic context in which the Jews lived. The peasants in the surrounding villages spoke Byelorussian dialects and were mostly illiterate. Many landowners were Poles, aloof and barely accessible. In general, aristocrats would not mix with Jews or members of other classes. Russia proper was far away and barred to most Jews; it was present in the Pale mainly through the bureaucracy, the army, the schools, and the Orthodox church. Only the local Russian power elite and a few bourgeois intellectuals in the city could be approached by rich and intelligent Russian-speaking Jews. For example, Chagall's teacher Yury Pen painted portraits of the provincial governor and of Baron Karpf and his wife, a typical Russian bureaucrat of German origin, but he would hardly mix with them socially. Thus, Jews encountered the stereotypically ignorant peasant—the proverbial Yiddish "Goy"—on his visit to the weekly market, where he sold his merchandise, got some money, and often got drunk, as well as the brute policeman, or the soldier of peasant origin, or the young peasant girl—the proverbial "shikse"—who worked and lived as a maid in rich Jewish homes. A Russian society on the same level as the new Jewish middle class, and open to dialogue with it, was barely available in the Pale of Settlement.

Elementary education for Jewish boys began at the age of three or four, when the child spent a long day in *Heder* (elementary school), learning to read (but not to write or speak) basic Hebrew texts—mainly passages of the Pentateuch and the prayers—and socializing. He would be taken to *Heder* by his Mama early in the morning and carried a lantern to return home in the dark. *Heder* means "room," and teaching was conducted in the living room (or only room) of the teacher's house. In Vitebsk Province, the average teacher, called rebbe or *melamed*, had eight pupils, and was poorly paid. He was a babysitter as well as a teacher. When the child exhausted the knowledge of one teacher, he moved to a more advanced *Heder*. Chagall's last teacher, "Dyadkin the Melamed," would take him to the bath on Fridays, flog him in the steamroom, and prepare him for his bar mitzvah sermon; Chagall depicted him in his autobiography.

Little Moshka Shagal went to *Heder* from age three or four until his bar mitzvah at thirteen. We have a corroboration in Chagall's case: Once, when Moshka was sent by his mother to his rebbe on a Saturday to do some additional study, he was bitten by a mad dog, taken to St.-Petersburg, recovered, and returned to witness his brother's birth—when he himself was less than four years old. This traumatic experience, as seen with the eyes of a bewildered four-year-old, was depicted in the fantasmagoric painting "Birth" of 1911.

His head did not seem to retain much of this learning, and in later years he could not correctly spell the simplest Hebrew words contained in Yiddish. At the age of thirteen, with his mother's help (and a bribe to the teacher), he entered the third grade of a Russian school, where he had to learn an altogether new language. No wonder he was made to repeat a year and studied for five years (1900–1905, until he was eighteen) without graduating. At one point, he tore up and scattered several hundred pages of a textbook: "Let the wind read it in Russian!"

But eventually he did learn Russian—probably in his late teens and early twenties, when he befriended the rich kids in the center of Vitebsk and lived in St.-Petersburg. He had an intuitive sense for some of the highlights of Russian literature, and when he wrote poetry in Russian during 1909–1910, he was able to recreate Russian meters, rhymes, and poetic diction. He was even commissioned to make stage sets for a Russian experimental cabaret in St.-Petersburg, directed by the famous Nikolay Evreinov. Yet in Paris, when invited to illustrate Gogol's *Dead Souls*, Bella read the book aloud to him.

The Year 1897

It was a crucial time in Jewish history. The wave of pogroms of 1881–1882 in Russia, at that time the largest Jewish community in the world, shook the consciousness of Jewish society, in Russia as in the West. The first response was panic and mass emigration. Yet economically and culturally, the new Jewish middle class in Russia was rapidly moving upward. Barely a generation after the pogroms, various political and cultural solutions for the Jewish problem crystalized. Furthermore, young Jewish intellectuals participated in the revolutionary fermentation that swept the Russian intellectual class. The mood of fin-de-siècle and Decadence that was dominant in Western Europe at the time also permeated Russian literature and art. Yet paradoxically, public consciousness, social fermentation, and the emerging ideologies were mostly idealistic, utopian, and future-oriented.

To have an idea about the range of alternatives opened in the Jewish world at the time, we may list a series of cultural and political events that occurred in 1897 and ushered in a new era in the history of the Jews:

1. The World Zionist Organization was founded by Dr. Theodor Herzl in Basel. Zionism as an ideology preceded Herzl's organization (The Lovers of Zion group

was founded in Odessa in 1881) and was implemented later by an idealistic move-ment among Eastern European Jews (the Second and Third Aliya, in 1903–1921).

2. Shimon Dubnov began the publication of his *Letters on the Old and New Judaism*, proclaiming the ideology of Jewish cultural Autonomism in the Diaspora, based on a Jewish "Community, language, and school." Dubnov became the great historian of the Jews as a World Nation.

3. The General Jewish Workers' Union in Lithuania, Poland, and Russia" (the Bund) was founded in Vilna in the underground and became a Jewish mass party, promoting Democratic Socialism and secular culture in Yiddish.

4. Six months later, in March 1898, the Russian Social-Democratic Workers' Party (R.S.D.R.P) was founded in Minsk with the help of the Bund (the Bund Central Committee resided there). Five of the nine delegates of the founding conference of the Russian Party were Jews, and with time the Party included a large contingent of Jews in its leadership, especially in its Menshevik (Social-Democratic) wing. Eventually its radical wing led to the Russian Revolution of 1917.

5. In the beginning of the Jewish year 1896–1897, the Hebrew journal *HaShiloah* appeared, edited by the ideologue of Spiritual Zionism, Ahad-Ha'am. It became the crown journal of modern Hebrew literature.

6. *The Daily Forward*, the Yiddish mass-circulation newspaper, appeared in New York, which signaled the emergence of a new historical center of Jewish existence and promoted Socialism, Yiddish literature, and rapid Americanization.

7. Solomon Shaechter discovered the Cairo Genizah, a trove of manuscripts hidden in an ancient Cairo synagogue where Jewish documents (in Hebrew, Arabic, and even Yiddish) covering a span of ten centuries were preserved. The interest in the Genizah symbolized the quest to reconstruct two millennia of Jewish history in the Diaspora.

8. In the beginning of the Jewish year 1896–1897, Yury (Yehuda) Pen founded in Vitebsk the first school of art that broke with the religious tradition and raised dozens of Jewish artists.

9. In 1897, Karl Luger was elected mayor of Vienna on a platform of political anti-Semitism, an omen of things to come.

10. Sigmund Freud joined not the new World Zionist Organization but the Bnei Brith in Vienna—the symbolic Jewish identity of an assimilated Jew.

11. Walther Rathenau, son of the head of AEG (General Electrical Company) in Berlin, called for the total assimilation of the Jews. He became the German Foreign Minister and was assassinated in 1922.

12. The great census of the Russian Empire brought to consciousness the precise demographic and professional situation of the Jews in Russia and, a decade later, served as the factual foundation for the comprehensive sixteen-volume Russian *Evreyskaya Entsiklopediya* (*Jewish Encyclopedia*), which consolidated the state-of-the-art knowledge of the Jews, their culture, history, and self-awareness.

All those new frameworks offered options either for the building of a Jewish secular nation and culture or for the participation of Jews in general culture and politics. Thus, in the beginning of the twentieth century, the distinction was debated between a "Jewish Artist" or "Jewish art" on the one hand, and a "Jew-artist," that is, an artist of Jewish origin who contributes to general "Art," on the other. Chagall as a painter with a place in culture could join either direction; indeed, he hovered all his life between the two.

It is amazing how Chagall managed to avoid the fermentation of political parties and movements—Socialist, Zionist, and others—and social and cultural organizations that swept Vitebsk during the years of his youth. He was a self-centered truant, protecting his private domain as an artist, and he reached out beyond the political world—to a naively cosmopolitan notion of "art" as identity. After the Holocaust, when a book on Vitebsk was being prepared in Tel Aviv by his compatriots, Chagall complained that "they want to turn the city into three-fourths activists of Judaism, while socially the city was three-fourths mystical, poetic, and artistic."[10] The latter was his city, the Vitebsk of imagination. Yet he did absorb—and carried all his life—the general sentiments of that revival: Socialist, Zionist, Populist, and Russifying, however in a folklorized, nonideological version, matching the ethos of his parents' home.

Demographics

The striking—and decisive—fact about Jewish life in the Pale of Settlement was the peculiar demographic situation of the Jews in Russia. In the significant year of 1897, a very detailed census of the Russian population was taken, providing precise data for every town and village. At the time, there were in Russia well over five million Jews, living mostly in the Pale of Settlement; 97.8 percent of them declared Yiddish as their language[11]—that is, most were still immersed in the traditional Jewish social and cultural world.

In writings about the Jews in Eastern Europe, Western authors often confuse the three very different demographic and administrative concepts: village, town (in Yiddish: *shtetl*), and city (*shtot*).[12] A village was an agricultural settlement or hamlet of Christian peasants (until recently, serfs) toiling on the land; they were legally defined as a separate class. A town (*shtetl*) was a small city; it can be described in modern terms as a shopping center. It provided the marketplace and administrative center of the region, the central location of artisans and commerce, often a railroad station, linking the villages with the larger world, as well as churches and a synagogue. A city is an even higher administrative entity; headed by a mayor, it is the capital of a province or one of its constituent districts.[13]

On the confusion between these three concepts, see note 13.

According to the 1897 census, close to a million and a half inhabitants of Vitebsk Province lived in 26,590 named places. Over 92 percent of the population lived in villages. Only forty-three locations had a population of 500–10,000 inhabitants, and only three cities had more than 10,000 residents each. There were officially twelve cities, including Vitebsk and Dvinsk, and twenty-eight towns in Vitebsk Province.[14]

But the Jewish demographic structure was the exact opposite to that of the general population. Typical of the whole Pale of Settlement, the Jews in Vitebsk Province constituted about 12 percent of the total population, but they were unequally distributed. On the one hand, only 1.9 percent of the village inhabitants were Jews (mostly nonfarmers: tavern owners, traders, or artisans). On the other hand, the Jews made up 66.3 percent of the population of all towns and 52.7 percent of all cities in Vitebsk Province. Thus, the towns were really a Jewish country—predominantly Jewish settlements strewn over the map of Byelorussia, though dominated politically by a Christian administration and police, and physically by the cross and cupola of the tallest *shtetl* building: the Russian Orthodox Church.[15] Those Jewish islands were surrounded by a sea of Slavic-speaking villages, but they maintained a dense cultural and social network among themselves.

This Jewish "empire" was not always there. It is the result of an immense explosion of the Jewish population in the nineteenth century (it grew at least fourfold in eighty years). Whereas German medieval towns had a "Jewish street" (*Judengasse*), in Eastern Europe the town itself, and especially its center, was predominantly Jewish. To this demographic situation we must add the unifying force of the railroad network, built in the second half of the nineteenth century, especially in the Pale, which served as a bridge between Russia and Western Europe. Instead of a centrifugal movement of individual Jews, reaching out and scattered in a wide area and half-illiterate in their Jewishness, what now emerged was a centralized nation based on a network of towns and cities that dominate the whole map. This shift fed both emigration and urbanization in Russia itself.

The language criterion illustrates this change palpably: There was a Yiddish literature in Venice in 1508, in Amsterdam in the seventeenth century, and in New York in the twentieth century, but usually such flourishing survived for a generation or two, until the children of the Yiddish speakers assimilated to the dominant language. Only in Eastern Europe did Yiddish become the social base of a national culture (in which other languages were embedded) that survived from the sixteenth to the twentieth century, separated from its German source. This was due to the predominantly Jewish territory in the Pale of Settlement, the polka-dotted map of Jewish-majority towns.

While the small towns were the base and main reservoir of the Jewish empire, steeped in a religious society, the cities were the meeting point between the Jewish and Russian cultures, and many individuals shared both or moved back and forth between them. The new literature, as well as the new political and cultural trends, were based in the cities, though supported by people who still remembered the *shtetl*.

And if we realize that the mass of peasants were recent slaves and had little power in the economic and cultural life of Russia (unless they moved to the cities and became proletarians), we can understand the importance of the network of Jewish towns and their descendants in the Russian economic and cultural world itself. Indeed, after the October Revolution, several leaders of the Jewish Section of the Communist Party in Byelorussia proposed to build a Jewish Soviet State in part of Byelorussia (and were shot for Jewish "nationalism").

The Move to the City

Moyshe Shagal's uncle Leybe lived in a real village, raising his cows and his daughters in nature, as Chagall put it. The rest of the family, on both his mother's and his father's side, lived in Lyozno (Russian: Liozno; Polish: Łozniany; Yiddish: Lezne, or "Lyezhne" in the local Yiddish dialect). This was a town in the nearby Mohilev (Mogilev) Province, with 1665 Jews (67.3 percent of the total population). Lyozno was a station on the Vitebsk-Moscow railway line, 60 km east of Vitebsk, hence easily accessible. Marc's uncle Zusya Shagal had a barbershop in the center of town, as seen in the painting "The Barber of Lyozno." Chagall's maternal grandfather was a butcher in Lyozno and had an honorable "seat" in the synagogue; his sons would travel to the villages to buy cattle, and the choice cut of meat would go to the estate of the lord of the manor—the former serf owner and still dominant force in the village world.

Lyozno was an aristocratic place in Jewish geography: The Rebbe Shneur-

Zalman, founder of the CHaBaD Hasidic sect, was born there in 1745. And not in vain did Shneur-Zalman Rubashov (who changed his name to ShaZaR), the President of Israel (himself a former CHaBaDnik from Byelorussia, as his name betrays), greet Chagall as "our brother from Lyozno and Paris!" After Napoleon's campaign in Russia, the CHaBaD dynasty moved its capital to Lubavich, a similar town in Mohilev Province with 1660 Jews (also exactly 67.3 percent of the population), where they ruled their countrywide movement between 1813 and 1915. Chagall himself was proud of his Lyozno origins, even though he mythologized Vitebsk as the wellspring of his art and mind.

The network of small towns in the Pale of Settlement was closely connected to the cities. Rabbis, teachers, artisans, merchants, and political agitators moved back and forth from city to the *shtetls*, from the center to the places of local roots and back. Unlike the general population, Jews were highly mobile and moved around the map; relatives and townspeople supported these ties. Indeed, the small towns were satellites of the big city, and when a Jew emigrated to America or elsewhere and said he came from Vitebsk or Vilna, in most cases he was born in a *shtetl* in those respective provinces.

In the big cities, the Jews constituted a somewhat smaller percentage of the population, though still an absolute majority. In the provincial capital of Vitebsk, there was a considerable Christian population representing the power structure of the Russian Empire: administration officials of the city and province, police, army, schoolteachers, and railroad employees—all professions practically closed to Jews; as well as urbanized peasants and soldiers, and landowners who kept their city houses along with their country manors. Still, the Jews made up 52.4 percent of the population of Vitebsk, while Russians and Byelorussians combined had only 39.9 percent, and the rest were Poles, Germans, and Latvians.

In 1897, the city of Vitebsk had 34,420 Jews—a typical figure for a city at that

A prerevolutionary postcard of Vitebsk: "Gogol Street and Jean-Albert pastry Shop." The official card does not mention the big sign under the pastry shop, on the right: "Sh. N. Rosenfeld"—the jewelry store of Bella's father. See Chagall's drawing, "A String of Pearls II," page 152.

time.[16] However, they were closely related to the rest of the 175,586 Jews in the province as well as to those in the neighboring provinces, notably the 204,000 Jews in Mohilev Province, including the town of Lyozno. Some 39 percent of all Jews in Vitebsk Province were engaged in trade, 36 percent in manufacturing, mostly individual artisans. Characteristically, 80 percent of all artisans in the city of Vitebsk were Jews—and half of them couldn't read or write Russian; that is, they lived in their own culture. Jews were predominant in trade on all levels. As early as in 1855, there were twelve Jewish merchants of the First and Second Guild in Vitebsk, and only four Christians; and in the whole Province fifty-eight Jews and six Christians. All the great trade and export of wood, grains, and even hog bristles from Vitebsk Province, mostly shipped by river to the Baltic Sea, were in Jewish hands. Indeed, most of the industry, trade, shops, and banking in Vitebsk were developed and owned by Jews. A retrospective report on Vitebsk recounts:

> If I were a stranger and not a Vitebskite, and after having read the signs on stores and the names of tenants and offices, recorded on the lists of tenants in every yard along all the streets, I would have said that Vitebsk was a purely Jewish city, built by Jews, with their initiative, energy, and money. The sense that Vitebsk is a Jewish city is felt especially on Sabbath and Jewish holidays, when all the stores, offices, factories are closed and silent. And when the streets are empty, a physical calm is pervasive along all the streets. Even in government offices, such as the Government Bank, the Notary, the Courthouse, Post and Telegraph Offices, and so on.[17]

Thus, Jews were the major force in the urbanization of Vitebsk, their flourishing economy and vigorous cultural and political life inspired them with energy and optimism, especially during the years 1905–1914. The city population grew from 10,000 in 1815 to over 100,000 in 1914, and the role of the Jews in this development was disproportionately high.[18] The move to the city was especially enhanced after the railroad was built, traversing Vitebsk in the 1860s. It is the train that grandfather David Shagal took from Lyozno to the big city. Yet the constant influx of Jews from the small towns to the city was compensated for by emigration to the Russian capitals, abroad, and overseas.

Nevertheless, legally defined and confined by their religion, Jews had no civil rights, no right to move to the capital cities and Russia proper, almost no representation in the local City Council and power structure. They were exposed to chicanery by any policeman or official, and were helpless in the face of pogroms (Chagall tells how, as a child, he would hide under the bed when the policeman on the beat passed by their windows). There was a *numerus clausus* (limited admittance) for Jews in Russian schools and universities, and very few were allowed to attend; rich Jews often hired private teachers for their children at home and sent them to universities abroad.

Привѣтъ изъ Витебска.   Общій видъ и мостъ.

The bridge with pedestrians, and a view of the poorer side of town.

The Map of Vitebsk

The city of Vitebsk spread out on both sides of the Western Dvina River. On its eastern bank, the Viterba River flows into the Dvina, and parallel to it, the negligible Dvina Stream did the same. Between those two tributaries and the Dvina River lies the center of the city. The Jews called it *af der greyser zayt* ("on the big side") to distinguish it from the western bank, *af der kleyner zayt* ("on the small side").

On the Big Side, the large shops and wholesale stores were concentrated. Here was the Zamkovaya (Castle Street), the major street of Vitebsk, where Berta Rosenfeld lived, as well as Chagall's Russian City school and Pen's art school. On the Small Side were the railroad station and the large exporters and warehouses, of flour, sugar, "colonial" wares, paper, oil, iron, fur, clothing, dry fruit, and herring.

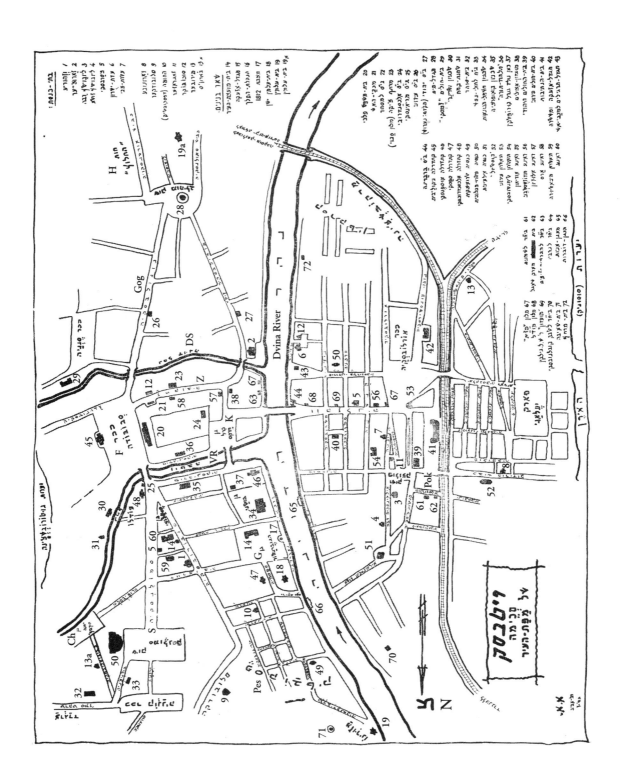

The Map of Vitebsk

This map was reconstructed from memory in 1957 by Vitebsk-ites in Israel who left Vitebsk after the Revolution. It reflects the year 1918: there is already a Freedom Square and a Karl Marx Square, as well as a Zionist "HeHalutz" farm, but not yet Chagall's Art College.

Ch	Chana Horwitz Square	N	North
DS	Dvina Stream	Pes	Peskovatik
F	Freedom Square		(where Chagall was born)
Gog	Gogol Street	Pok	Pokrovskaya Street
G	Governor's Square		(where Chagall grew up)
H	HeHalutz Farm	S	Smolenskaya Street
	(Socialist-Zionist Pioneers)	VR	Vitba River
K	Karl Marx Square	Z	Zamkovaya Street

1–13a: Synagogues		37	Here General Kropotkin was born
3	Big Lubavich Synagogue	38	Nobility Club
4	Little Lubavich Synagogue	39	Jewish Hospital
10	"Wall" Synagogue of Peskovatik	40	City Hospital
14	City Hall	41	Railroad Station
16	District Administration	45	Nikolay Cathedral
17	Monument to 1812	46	Uspensky Cathedral
	(the defeat of Napoleon)	47	Spassky Cathedral
18	Old Jewish Cemetery	48	Alexander Cathedral
19	Jewish Cemetery	49	Troyitsky Cathedral
19a	Jewish Cemetery	50	Peter-and-Paul Church
20	District Court	52	Catholic Church
21	Fire Brigade	*53–54, 59: theaters*	
22	Mercantile School	55	cinema Odeon
	(where Viktor Mekler studied)	56	Art Cinema
23	Cellars of the CheKa	57	cinema Illusion
	(secret police), former Hotel Savoy	58	cinema Ars
24–27: Schools		59	Miniature theater
26	City School	61	Oil factory on Pokrovskaya Street
27	Jewish School		(Chagall used it as a metaphor)
29	Hospital	62	Chagall's home on Pokrovskaya Street
30	Veterinary College	63	factory for hog-bristle brushes
32	prison	65	dock for ships
33	madhouse asylum	66	dock for barges
34	Electric-Mechanical College	*67–68: hotels*	
35	Cooperative College	70	Tobacco factory
36	Talmud Torah	72	public bath

The brick house of Chagall's family on Pokrovskaya Street in Vitebsk, where he lived from age three to twenty-eight.

Chagall was born in the northwestern suburb of Peskovatik, where small huts were built, probably for newcomers from the provinces. This area was paved and developed only after 1904–1905. But in 1890, when grandfather died, the Chagalls sold the hut and moved to Pokrovskaya Street on the Small Side of Vitebsk, next to the railroad line. Thus, Moyshe had to cross the bridge to get to school or to his fiancée's house on the Big Side. Chagall's father was a store manager[19] in Yakhnin's herring warehouse and worked hard, carrying herring barrels. His mother was a business woman. In 1902, she built a brick house for the family; next to it was her grocery store (on three steps, as seen on many paintings); and in the yard, four wooden houses, rented out to eight tenants. She also took care

Yury (Yehuda) Pen with neighbors in Chagall's courtyard, next to the wooden houses built for rent. Marc had a room in a tenant's apartment.

of the education and well-being of her eight children, particularly, her first-born Moshka.

The Lure of Russian Culture

Both the power and the lure of modern culture were in Russian; and Jews, especially the relatively rich, young, or intelligent, embraced Russian language and literature. Initially, they fostered Russian culture among themselves, read Russian literature, and spoke Russian mainly with other Jews. But after the Revolution, integration ensued: Those Jews who remained in the city provided the major contingent for the general Russian and Soviet political institutions and cultural movements, of which Vitebsk was for a few years a conspicuous center, including the People's Art College founded by Chagall. Most of the young generation left in the early 1920s for the real centers of Russian culture, education, and industrial progress, Moscow and Leningrad, as did Marc and Bella Chagall and all their siblings.

Jews in the Vitebsk Art
College: see note 21.

Why would a small city like Vitebsk become a center of culture, albeit for a few years?[20] This phenomenon cannot be understood without the considerable participation of Jews in that cultural revival.[21] Vitebsk was in the extreme northeastern corner of the Jewish Pale of Settlement, at the border of Russia proper, a railroad junction closest to both Russian capitals, Moscow and St.-Petersburg. It was incorporated into Russia and Russified twenty years earlier than the rest of the Pale, and the expulsion of most Jews from Moscow in 1891 brought a stratum of Russian-speaking Jews to the city, who served as a social base for Russian culture in Vitebsk. During World War I, important Russian politicians and writers were invited to speak in Vitebsk to largely Jewish audiences: Aleksandr Kerensky (the future Prime Minister), Professor P. N. Milyukov (leader of the KaDet Party), V. Nabokov (the father of the novelist), the poet Fedor Sologub, and others. In 1919, Granovsky's new Yiddish theater came from Petrograd, and before that, Sholem-Aleichem had given a memorable reading.

In the 1890s, a conspicuous group of rich Vitebsk Jews abandoned religion, and the same trend infiltrated all layers of society. Chagall's father—relatively poor, uneducated, and traditional—diligently went to the prayer house every morning, but, like most fathers of his generation, did not impose religious behavior on his children. Religious practice at home was rudimentary and consisted mainly of Mother's trying every Saturday evening to make the children hum the "Rebbe's tune"—a wordless melody, that is, a minimalist Hasidic expression of devotion—as the weary father dozed off. Indeed, most young Jews in the Pale abandoned religion overnight, around the beginning of the twentieth century, even before the Bolshevik Revolution sanctified this change.

Joining Russian culture seemed a natural act. The Chagall siblings are regis-

Berta Rosenfeld in Vitebsk.

tered in the official Russian birth certificate by their Yiddish names only, but among themselves they used Russian names—the reverse of what one might expect. Thus, the Russian family birth certificate lists Zislya and Lia; Chagall himself (in the mural for the Yiddish theater) calls them Zisle and Leyke in Yiddish, but Franz Meyer lists them by their Russian names: Zina and Liza, which the siblings used among themselves when they grew up.[22] Moyshe Chagall's future fi-

(*left*) Berta Rosenfeld's mother, Alte (Levyant) Rosenfeld. Inscription of photographer's studio in prerevolutionary Russian spelling: "A.M. Makovsky/Vitebsk."

(*right*) Berta Rosenfeld's father Shmuel Noah Rosenfeld, jewelry store owner and Hasid of Lubavich.

ancée was called by her parents Basha; outside the family she was Berta, and thus she was called by the employees of her parents' household and by Chagall's mother. Indeed, she signed "Berta" in Russian on the back of photographs (in the spelling of both before and after the Revolution), and a postcard from around 1920 has Berta's inscription: "We wish you rest and happiness, Berta, Moysey [Chagall] and daughter." Chagall still records her name as Berte in Yiddish in the Moscow theater mural in December 1920. When she became Bella Chagall is not clear; I found no evidence for the name Bella before Paris in the 1920s.[23]

Berta's father, the owner of three jewelry-and-watches stores, was an active Lubavich Hasid, maintained a warm, religious home centering on celebrations of the Sabbath and holidays, and had a live-in Rabbi with whom he studied every morning. Yet Berta and her circle of friends recited Russian poetry and performed Russian plays. Photographs of her five brothers show them in European garb and without hats—at the time, a conclusive sign of atheism. In June 1907, after Marc left for St.-Petersburg, Berta went to Moscow, presumably to study Russian literature at the University.[24] Nevertheless, when she began writing her autobiography in France in 1939, she deliberately used her native language, Yiddish.

Another example for the role of Russian is Shmaryahu Mekler, the father of Chagall's best friend Viktor and a rich paper manufacturer, who owned a stationery store and several houses in the center of Vitebsk. He was a Merchant of the First Guild and could freely go to the capital cities. In his youth, he became an atheist; but after his mother died, he turned into an enthusiastic Lubavich Hasid, studied Talmud every day, attended prayers at the prayer house, and was a prominent Jewish community leader. Nevertheless, at home the family spoke Russian, and he employed a private teacher of modern Hebrew for his children.

From this position of Russian—and through it, of Western European culture—as an ideal standard, some Jewish intellectuals turned back to Jewish society and helped create a modern, secular, European-type culture in Yiddish and Hebrew.

Berta Rosenfeld and her brothers (from left to right:) Abrasha, Aharon, Yakov, Israel, Mendel. All are secular.

Among them in Vitebsk were Sh. An-sky (Rapaport), scholar, collector of folk-lore, and author of the famous play *The Dybbuk*; his best friend Dr. Chaim Zhit-lovsky, former Russian S.R. (Socialist-Revolutionary) who emigrated to the United States and became the ideologue of Yiddishism as a cultural renaissance; An-sky's nephew, the folklorist Sh. Yudovin; and Chagall's teacher, the painter Yury (Yehuda) Pen. The fictional worlds created in Yiddish prose in the late nine-teenth and early twentieth centuries by the triumvirate of Classical writers Men-dele, Sholem-Aleichem, and Y. L. Peretz served as a base for the self-awareness of this renaissance, soon inundated by waves of Modernism. The dense traditional culture of the Jewish religious world was now seen as folklore, a source of vitality, imagery, and folk wisdom that can be recycled into the modern, secular world, as Chagall tried to do in his murals for the Moscow Yiddish Theater. For a while,

Marc Chagall's parents: Yikhezkel/Zakhar and Ite-Feyge Shagal. Mother with the rich shawl she got as a wedding gift from her husband. Yikhezkel Shagal without a hat, in a secular gait, posing for a "modern" photograph. The photographer's logo is in French.

Chagall participated in this revival; he even restored his presumed original family name, and signed several paintings "Moyshe Segal." His was not a crisis of identity; Chagall embraced Jewish, Russian, and Western European culture in one consciousness—as did, in various proportions, his entire generation.

Sh. An-sky (Rapaport) and Chaim Zhitlovsky, Russian S.R. (Socialist-Revolutionary party) turned to their own people, became leaders of the Yiddishist cultural movement, Vitebsk, 1882.

Some Basic Concepts of Chagall's Consciousness

Throughout Chagall's life—in his paintings, letters, and other texts—we find recurrent images, basic perceptions of the world, derived from Jewish folk semiotics and literature. Later he added some notions of Communist and even Zionist discourse. We shall introduce three concepts of the former category; further examples are strewn throughout this book.

DATES AND MEMORY: THE PERCEPTION OF TIME, SPACE, AND LOGIC

Chagall had a remarkable knack for confusing dates. Many of his paintings were backdated by several years. This in itself happened also to other painters, who wanted to show that they had arrived, for example, at abstract painting earlier than others. But in Chagall's work, many dates are unreliable. Sometimes, perhaps, he intended to indicate the time of the first conception of a painting, before he actually executed it. But at other times, it makes no sense; for example, he dates a portrait of a religious Jew ("The Pinch of Snuff") 1912, when he was in Paris and could not have painted such a type before his return to Vitebsk in 1914. He writes that he worked for the Moscow Yiddish Theater in 1918 and dates drawings for it 1918 or 1919, while the theater arrived in Moscow only in November 1920, as everyone knew. This kind of habitual "lying" about time, which one encounters in autobiographies of Eastern European Jews, can be seen in a benevolent light if we understand that a date in this perception is not a precise point in a chronological sequel but an emotive marker with a contextual function. Sholem-Aleichem understood it and mocked it in his fiction. Thus, his character Tevye the Dairyman remembers an event that took place some time ago: *a-yor-mit-a-mitvokh* ("a-year-and-a-Wednesday" or literally a year and half a week), but he goes on to explain: "that is, precisely [sic] nine, or ten years, and perhaps with a tail too."

Jewish folk semiotics represents a different kind of mind than the one promoted by the European Enlightenment; a mind of associations that perceives events as situations and images parallel to one another in one global universe, rather than as points in a causal chain, a narrative sequel with precise, rational chronologies. This traditional Jewish folk semiotics derives from the perception of postbiblical Judaism, that after the destruction of the Jewish state and the close of the Bible, history was over; that theirs is a totality of beliefs above all and any history and geography; that the Jews are a chosen and persecuted nation irrespective of the changing powers and politics, and nothing changes until the Messiah comes. Therefore, in traditional Judaism, the Bible is read not as the historical narrative it was, but as a source of legend and law; "there is no earlier or later in the Bible," according to a basic talmudic precept: All stories are parallel to each other.

This perception of time entails a basic principle of composition: Most traditional Jewish texts lack a narrative direction (except for short stories embedded in them); that is, every detail is not a link in a chain of events, but is significant outside of its context, in a total universe of meaning. Hence, it needs interpretation rather than counting. And this atemporal world perception and signification of every detail was internalized in Jewish folklore and behavior.

To be sure, modern Jewish political movements wanted to join history and interfere in it, to break the perception of the "Eternal" or Wandering Jew, and participate in actions related to the contemporary, specific time and place. But Chagall's world perception was molded by the folk ethos of his "primitive" parents; therefore, he rarely remembered the sequel of events and returned, time and again, to the basic images of his paintings and his self-constructed biography. He just couldn't care less when exactly on the calendar a certain piece was done, or what preceded what, or how old he was when he first came to Paris. His autobiography itself is structured by persons (with parts devoted to mother, grandfather, Pen, etc.) rather than chronologically.

The same holds for the attitudes toward a consistent logical argument and a mimetic perception of space. In this world view, every existential detail is significant and needs interpretation within a higher, ideological order—though it may remain an enigmatic parable; but it does not have to be placed in a logical chain of argument, or in a "realistic" order of space. We cannot argue a theory, we can only see and believe. Chagall's work, and even his private letters, are informed by this mode of thinking; each figure and object may be a representation, even a distorted one, but the composition of the whole has no realistic coherence of time, space, or logic.

CRAZY ARTIST

When the French poet Blaise Cendrars[25] returned from America to Paris, as his daughter tells it, he went to see the "crazy Russian artist" in La Ruche. And when Max Liebermann appraised Chagall to Paul Cassirer, he said: "Talented but *meshuge*." *Meshuge* ("crazy") was a puzzlement from the outside, but a title of honor for Chagall.

The connection between madness and creativity is a familiar Romantic and modern topos, from Hölderlin's poetry written in a mental institution to Salvador Dali's theory of "Creative paranoia." When Chagall talks about van Gogh or boasts about his own craziness, he tries to fit into that honorable category. But his source is in the wealth of connotations of the Yiddish word *meshuge* (pronounced *mishúge*) and its derivatives: *mishugás* ("craziness, madness"), *mishúgener* ("crazy person"), *mishugóyim* ("crazy people"). *Mishúge* is widely used in Yiddish discourse, and it may mean anything and everything. It may be literal: a clinical description of an insane person, or just a pejorative epithet, when applied to some unreasonable people or person the speaker disapproves of. It may

apply to all the Jews as a nation, or to the Israelis, implying irrational, erratic behavior, yet often with affection and an emphasis on their uniqueness. It may apply to an unusual person, "madly" devoted to some goal without rational calculations. Often it is said with admiration for a person who pursues an unrealistic
or absurd idea, and it is also used as a warm, affectionate epithet, connoting
idiosyncracy, unpredictability, and creativity.

This polysemy, conflating craziness and creativity, derives from the biblical
meshuga ish ha-ruah ("crazy is the man of spirit," the inspired person, the
prophet), or in the King James version: "The prophet is a fool, the spiritual man
is mad" (Hos. 9:7). It is reinforced by the sound qualities of the word: words with
sh + *m* + a third consonant are strongly expressive in Yiddish: *mishúge* ("crazy"),
mishúne ("strange, outlandish"), *shlimázl* ("a bungler, a luckless poor devil"),
shmegége ("jerk"), *shmok* ("prick"), and so on. They shade into each other with
mutual, hovering connotations. Furthermore, *GÓEN* ("genius") is even phonetically embedded in *shiGÓEN* ("madness"), both deriving from Hebrew, thus carrying a special stylistic weight and higher sanction. In an early drawing of 1907,
Chagall stands on his head in bed, with the Russian inscription: *Ya sumaskhazhu*
("I am going out of my mind").

A popular Yiddish idiom is *Mishugener, arop fun dakh!* ("You're crazy, get off
the roof!"). This is a phrase said to a person who neither sits on a roof nor is
clinically insane, but who has unrealistic or fantastic ideas. Chagall made a "realization" of this metaphor (to use a Russian Formalist term), transferring the
image from the level of style to the fictional reality of the painting. He actually
placed a fiddler on a roof (in "The Dead Man," 1908), combining lunacy with
music, a nonverbal art.[26] In his memoirs, written in 1922–1924, Chagall quotes
his mother's story about her father, who disappeared on one holiday: "It turned
out that in the nice weather he climbed on the roof, sat on the chimney and ate
tsimmes [sweet carrot stew]." Chagall appraised it: "Not a bad picture," and

added: "And perhaps I dreamt it all." Indeed, the painting of 1908 preceded the story, and the story may be a way of rationalizing the absurd quality of his painting. In his memoirs, Chagall identifies with that grandfather, and in his early paintings we can often see the ladder with the pot on the roof, while the lunatic went off the roof to play his violin.

Chagall's memoirs and letters are filled with the word *crazy* and its synonyms: He was born near a crazy house, he was bitten by a "mad" dog—and telling about it, he adds: "Are you [the critics] happy, you found the secret [of his madness]"; mother calls him "madman," assumes that his wish to be an artist is "surely a madness" (of course it was!), and so on.

WANDERING JEW

The famous image of a Jew flying with sack and stick over Vitebsk is the embodiment of the *luftmenchn* ("air-people") created in classical Yiddish literature by Mendele and Sholem-Aleichem: people who have no productive work and live "on air" as well as "in the air," with no ground under their feet, unlike a normal nation rooted in its own soil. This image of self-criticism of the Jewish Diaspora existence served both Zionists and Jewish Socialists, who wanted to change the relation of the people to the soil or to productive work, and the very class structure of the Jews. Chagall accepted it as a fact and, as a Populist, rather stressed the beauty and power in this Jewish existence. The concrete prototype was a Jew who would come begging at his mother's door, carrying a sack and wearing the hat of a discharged Tsarist soldier, as depicted in Chagall's early drawings.

This figure, however, has much more to it. It includes the Christian anti-Semitic image of the Eternal or Wandering Jew, appropriated by Jewish literature in modern times as a self-described existential reality. Apparently influenced by the expulsion of a million Jews "within 24 hours" from the border areas during World War I, many of whom flooded Vitebsk during 1914–1915, Chagall's painting "Above Vitebsk" also has something transcendental about it,

For the origin of this
idiom, see note 27.

an existence above the mundane, transient cities. Furthermore, the picture is a realization of an idiom: *er geyt iber di hayzer*, which means in Yiddish, "he is a beggar"; literally, the words mean "he walks above [= over] the houses"[27]—and this meaning was realized in the painting. Yet this figure is not just a beggar, he is the prototypical Jewish peddler, who must make a living by walking over villages. It is also the image of a "sinner," who abandoned his home and family to "perform Diaspora" (*praven goles*). As Mendele philosophized: "All of Israel— one sack"; and that beggar's or nomad's sack (called *tórbe* or *pekl*) contains a mishmash of food, peddler's merchandise, prayer books, and what not. It was epitomized in the popular song *"Goles Marsh"* ("March of Exile") by the American Yiddish poet Morris Rosenfeld (1861–1923):

> With the wanderer's staff in hand,
> With no home and with no land,
> No friend or savior on the way,
> No tomorrow, no today,
> Chased, not suffered in our plight,
> Ne'er a day where spent a night,
> Always pain will knock, knock, knock,
> Always walk, walk, walk,
> Always stride, stride, stride,
> While your strength can still abide.[28]

In July 1948, when Chagall leaves America with his young Christian wife Virginia Haggard to return to Paris, he writes in a letter to Opatoshu: "I am toiling on the *peklakh* [wanderer's packages] together with the thin, young Virginia, who must also taste a bit of what it means to be a Jew with the sack on your back." Surely, this was no exile but a triumphant return of a famous artist to France, but in his self-perception, and in his internal Jewish correspondence, Chagall often saw himself as a homeless Jew.

Notes on a Personal Profile

WHAT'S IN A NAME?

Marc Chagall's Jewish name at birth was *Móyshe Shagal*; his parents referred to him as *Móshka*.[29] The official Russian birth certificate, listing the whole family,[30] registered him as *Movsha Khatskelev*: *Movsha*, son of *Khatskel*. *Khatskel* is his father's name Yikhézkel (the biblical Ezekiel). *Movsha* is a Russian equivalent to the biblical Moses, yet his friends in St.-Petersburg, and still in Paris, as well as his family members when speaking Russian, used the more elevated name *Moysey*.[31]

Chagall's favorite name *Marc* was influenced by his St.-Petersburg Jewish mentors, who hoped he would become a "second Marc Antokolsky." Antokolsky (1843–1902) was a prominent Russian sculptor, who was born in Vilna and lived in St.-Petersburg, where he sculpted the heads of famous Russians and Jesus Christ. He was an early model of a ghetto Jew who "made it" in Russian society, even though he spoke Russian with a Yiddish accent. In any case, Chagall's *Marc* was firmly established in Paris after 1910. It appeared on a painting ("Homage to Apollinaire") in 1911–1912; he signed his letters "Marc Chagall," and his reviewers refered to him by this name.

Since his first return from Paris, he was addressed in Russian as *Mark Zakharovich*, "Mark, son of Zakhar"—his father's adopted Russian name. Yet on family photos, Bella refers to him as *Moysey* and to herself as *Berta*, even after the Revolution.

On top of the family list in that certificate appears the name *Shagalov*, a Russified form of the Hebrew last name *Shagal*. Another Russian document has both versions: *Moysey (Movsha) Shagal (Shagalov).*"[32] This confusion gave him trouble when he applied for French citizenship in 1937.[33]

During World War I in Russia, a movement of "Jewish art" evolved. The artists El Lissitzky and Nathan Rybak discovered a synagogue in Mohilev with beautiful

"primitive" paintings on the walls by the eighteenth-century painter Chaim Ben
Yitskhak Segal from Slutsk.[34] Chagall claimed that Chaim Segal was his great-
grandfather and signed several of his own paintings *Moyshe Segal*. This is plausible, because Lithuanian Jews confused *s* and *sh* and collapsed them into one
sound. In western Lithuania, it all became *s*; in eastern Lithuania, especially in
Mohilev Province (where the Shagals came from), it all became *sh*. Thus, if a
registration clerk asked for his client's name, he would pronounce *Segàl* as
Shegàl, which was easily fixed in a Russian manner as *Shagàl*.

The story that Chagall's own father changed the name from *Segal* to *Shagal*
cannot be true: He did not have such intellectual ambitions, and his brother Uncle Zusya in Lyozno was also *Shagal*, as the sign on his barbershop in Marc's
painting can attest. If it was an intentional change, it could have been done by
the learned grandfather, modeled upon such Hebrew acronyms as the writers
Yalág, *Shadál*, the last name *Shabád*, the movement *Chabád*, etc.—all with an ultimate accent, conspicuous in Ashkenazi Hebrew. *Segal* is not a casual Yiddish
word but a Hebrew acronym: SGL (SGan Levy = "assistant Levy"). Changing
names was not an easy matter with the Russian bureaucracy.

As for referring to the Mohilev synagogue painter as his "great-grandfather,"
Chagall could have simply meant "forefather" or "ancestor." It is, however, not
impossible, for Lyozno was a *shtetl* in Mohilev Province. Yet we have no independent evidence that there was a name *Segal* in Chagall's family.

The French spelling *Marc Chagall* was a stroke of genius: *Moyshe Segal* could
hardly become a unique, French, and international artist. Indeed, the un-
friendly French police insisted in 1937, when he was accorded French citizenship, on calling him *Moïse*.

WHEN AND WHERE WAS CHAGALL BORN?

The October Revolution, which raised such exuberant excitement about the
birth of a new world, took place on October 25, 1917. The Bolsheviks abolished

the old, Julian calendar, still accepted in Russia at the time, and introduced the common European, Gregorian calendar, running thirteen days later. Thus, the anniversary of the Revolution, which occurred on October 25, was moved to November 7.

Chagall made a similar move. According to the official family birth certificate, Movsha Shagal was born on June 24, 1887.[35] He added thirteen days to June 24, and got the magic figures 7/7/87. This could have occurred when he arrived in Paris in 1910. Indeed, his "Self-Portrait with Seven Fingers" (1913) conveys the sense that 7 was his lucky, magic number. What he apparently did not realize was that in the nineteenth century, when he was born, the difference between the two calendars was only twelve days, and he was actually born on July 6 according to the general European calender.

In her memoirs, Bella Chagall[36] tells how she tried to get Marc's birthdate during their courtship. He didn't know it and didn't care, quite in keeping with his fuzzy perception of time: "Who knows? Who can know it outside of mother? —and mother surely forgot. She had so many children."[37] His sisters claimed he was born in Tamuz (roughly July), in the heat of the summer, and therefore was crazy. But how did they know; they were all younger! No specific date was available until Bella invented one, she says. Yet the birth certificate proves it was a very precise invention.

What about the year 1887? In several private letters, on different occasions, Chagall feels guilty about his age, presumably doctored by his father, as was often done by Jews in Tsarist Russia to avoid military service; that is, Father, who registered the whole family, added two years to create a four-year gap between the two brothers, thus helping Moyshe avoid the draft (as if he were an only son). Believing that story, Chagall often assumed he was actually born in 1889, and calculated his age accordingly. J. J. Sweeney accepted this date in the catalogue of the Museum of Modern Art in New York in 1946,[38] and so did other biographers.

THE OFFICIAL REGISTRATION DOCUMENT

The document, written out in longhand on stationery, enumerates the whole Shagalov family as of January 1, 1908, yet almost four years later, an addition was made and the paper was signed and stamped on November 9, 1911.[39] In the first column, the precise birth dates of the male members are given, while in the second column, the names of Mother and all the daughters are enumerated, recording their ages in years only, probably as reported in one summary list by the head of the family. A stamp and signature close the list on January 1, 1908; yet after the signature, "Rachel, 3 years old" is added, obviously in 1911.

Since for the women, all ages were given at the same time and without any dates, we must be careful about them. Mother is listed as forty-one years old in 1908. Chagall himself tells in his formal Soviet résumé written in 1921 that she was forty-five at her death (in 1916). If that is true, she was thirty-seven in 1908. It means that she was only fifteen when she married and sixteen when Marc was born—quite usual for Jews in that period.

On the other hand, the men have their exact dates listed by year, day, and month. The reason is clear. Both dates in which the document was signed occurred just a week short of half a year before the respective twenty-first birthdays of the boys, the draft age of the Russian army. The dates of the registration are January 1, 1908, for Movsha's twenty-first birthday on June 24, 1908; and November 9, 1911, for David's birthday on May 1, 1912. Thus, the document was written twice: for Marc's and for David's draft into the army. Indeed, after Movsha's name, an explanation follows that, for reasons of education, his conscription was postponed until 1910 (when he actually left Russia), and the 1911 document is issued for David's school, for a similar deferment of service.[40]

But more importantly, there is a decisive argument against 1889: A. Shatskikh's finding that a great conflagration enveloped parts of Vitebsk, as described in Chagall's autobiography, on June 24, 1887 (and none in 1889). That would also

The Chagall family before Marc's departure for Paris in 1910. Top row from left: Marc, Zina, Uncle Noah, Lisa, Manya. Bottom row: Anyuta, Marussya, Mother, Father, Rosa.

fix the place of birth as Vitebsk, in spite of Chagall's own hesitations about Lyozno. Pity, Chagall could have been two years younger, as he often wished.

BELLA CHAGALL'S AGE

A puzzling issue is Bella Chagall's age. According to Chagall's obituary, published in 1945, she was born in 1895. The same date was given in her American death certificate,[41] based on her daughter Ida's information, and was inscribed by Chagall on her tombstone. Yet that would make her eight years younger than Chagall, whereas as teenagers they shared the same youth circles in Vitebsk. Moreover, her friend and classmate Thea Brachman knew Marc earlier and

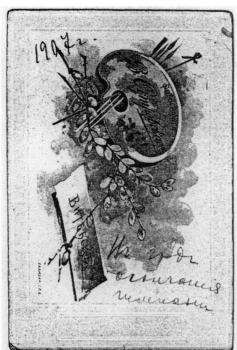

Two portraits of Berta Rosenfeld, 1907.

At bottom, the reverse side of the two portraits. Berta's handwritten inscription in Russian: "For Thea—for a long long memory of the days of our youth/Berta/June 1907" and: "In the year of our finishing the Gymnasium/1907." Important evidence of Berta's age (see text).

posed for him in the nude in his own room—which would hardly be possible for a twelve-year old from "a good family" at the time; indeed, "The Red Nude" painting represents a full-bodied, mature woman. Furthermore, Berta's photos of 1907 show her as a young woman rather than a twelve-year-old girl. A daughter of a strictly religious father, she could hardly be Chagall's fiancée, the subject of his paintings, and climb out of his window late at night to walk home at age twelve or even fourteen (if they got engaged in 1909). In his autobiography, he tells: "Berta brings flowers, blue, greenery. All in white, with black gloves, and I paint her portrait"—that is "My Fiancée in Black Gloves" of 1909 and then, he adds, he painted "The Dead Man" of 1908—was she thirteen?—the portrait and photograph of the same appearance seem to belie it.

The decisive evidence is found in two photo portraits of Berta, preserved in Ida Chagall's archives. On the reverse side there are inscriptions in Berta's own handwriting in Russian (as corroborated in her Russian letters from Paris): "For Thea—for a long long memory of the days of our youth / Berta / June 1907" and "In the year of our finishing the Gymnasium/1907." In the year she finished gymnasium, said farewell to her youth, and went to university in Moscow, she had to be at least eighteen or nineteen (admission to gymnasium at eleven, for eight years). Thus, she was born in 1889 or 1888, a year or two younger than Chagall and six or seven years older than was assumed until now.

CHAPTER TWO

Chagall's First Autobiography

A Self-Constructed Life at Thirty

Marc Chagall indulged in autobiographical story telling early on. The Marxist exile Anatoly Lunacharsky, in a review written in Paris for a Kiev paper in 1914, wrote: "A small picture. A man sits on a roof and eats, another man walks in a mere shirt in the street. 'You see, says Chagall in his childish language, here is my whole biography: They used to find my grandpa on a roof, he loved eating *tsimmes* there. And my uncle loved walking the street in just a nightshirt to his body'."[1] The same stories turned up eight years later in Chagall's autobiography.

Chagall began writing his memoirs when he was in his early thirties. Several motivations contributed to this unusual move. The disjointed, puzzling, and un-realistic figures and events in his paintings needed an explanation, and one was that they all stemmed from one life and one "crazy" mind. Guillaume Apollinaire dubbed Chagall's art "Surnaturalism" even before he coined the term Surrealism. Yet there was a cardinal difference between them: The Surrealists claimed that they created from their subconscious, from their dream world, which they did not care to explain, whereas Chagall, producing similar paintings, had a need to claim that all this was real, that he "really" experienced those strange images. Instead of de-scribing his paintings as a private mythology, he mythologized his own biography.

Furthermore, his paintings could be seen as an attempt to understand himself and to go back to his roots, to show the world where he came from, the Jewish and Russian provincial life (with shifting emphases between the two). Chagall himself was amazed at the unbelievable road he had traveled from his origins to international acclaim. And, in spite of his protestations that he was not a "literary" artist, all his life he wanted to tell a story, which he did, both in art and in words. More precisely, he never told a consecutive narrative, but evoked typical or unusual situations, as fragments from such a narrative, "pregnant moments" (to use Lessing's term). Those situations, unusual to a Peterburgian or Parisian eye, attracted attention precisely because they represented an exotic yet authentic world in the midst of Europe.

Some critics classified the early Chagall as a Russian Neo-Primitivist, which in a sense he was. But his art was more complex than that. During 1909–1910 in St.-Petersburg he encountered the Fauve revolution of color—through a Russian prism; and during 1910–1914 in Paris, he was influenced by the Paris avant-garde in its days of searching, after the first breakthrough of Cubism. Chagall shared some basic stylistic features of those post-Cubist days (such as the Delaunays' circles and Eiffel Tower), and combined them with his own idiosyncratic fantasies. He was straddling a deep cultural divide—between the provincial, "primitive" world of his parents, ignorant even in matters Jewish, and the most sophisticated refinements of postcultural Europe—and he was shifting back and forth between the two. He would show the exotic and vital world of his origins to the baffled modernist culture, on the one hand, and bring the new stylistic features of modern art to the representation of the culture of his origins, on the other hand.

The moment was right: European Modernism was prepared to move beyond formal problems and raise again the horizon of representation, albeit in various modes of "deformation" of the depicted figures and objects, and away from the central, post-Renaissance heritage. It was eager to reach out beyond the solid tradition of mimetic art and psychological portraiture—toward the "expressive" or "surreal." Hence the interest in "primitive" art of exotic cultures, as well as in prerational, childish, dreamlike, or poetic expressions. Chagall responded to several of those needs and evoked many of those labels.

The gap between the two worlds was laid bare when Chagall came back from avant-garde Paris to provincial Vitebsk in 1914, with no museum or modern artist in sight. Chagall himself attacked the situation head-on and produced some sixty paintings and drawings in a series he called "documents," as if recording the world of his family, Vitebsk and Lyozno, the bygone days of religious Jewry, while preparing concrete material for new, imaginative paintings. He renewed his friendship with his first art teacher Yury Pen and went out with him to paint the "fences, fences, fences" of Vitebsk. That was an important move, renewing Chagall's contact with his world of origin and enriching the store of his "realistic" images. On the one hand, he wanted to be an avant-garde artist or a "Revolutionary artist" (as he called it after the Bolshevik Revolution), carrying out a revolution in the style and concept of art; and on the other hand, he felt the compulsion of an authentic, associative, "poetic," or "crazy" genius.

The changes in Chagall's verbal dedications reflect in a nutshell his retreat from the avant-garde to a kind of pan-historical stance in art and to his private roots. The painting "Homage to Apollinaire" (Paris, 1911–1913) was dedicated to his peers "Apollinaire, Canudo, Cendrars, Walden"—the radical innovators in his Parisian milieu.[2] Yet in 1925, he already dedicated his first autobiography (published in this chapter) to "Rembrandt, Cézanne, My mother, My wife," going back to two pivotal points of art history, and placing the two women central to his life on the same level. And in 1931, the dedication to the published book *Ma vie* (*My Life*) is entirely devoted to his roots: "to my parents, to my wife, to my native city."

Appollinaire et al.: discussed more fully in note 2.

During most of World War I, Chagall served as a clerk in an office of the Central War-Industrial Committee in Petrograd, directed by his brother-in-law Yakov Rosenfeld. When two young art critics, Yakov Tugendhold (whom he had befriended earlier in St.-Petersburg and Paris) and Abram Efros, wrote *The Art of Marc Chagall* (published in Russian in 1918),[3] Chagall collaborated with them, provided illustrations for the book, and must have given them some information about his origins. It was the first book about Chagall's art, was soon translated into German (1921), and, to a large extent, defined the terms of the discourse about Chagall, exploring both the fantastic nature of his art and his cultural roots. This book apparently provoked Chagall himself to try to understand and explain his personal origins. It was only after the book was published that Chagall wrote and published any text of his own.

The Art of Marc Chagall summed up the essential characteristics of the artist and his achievement; it was a stock-taking for the critics and for Chagall himself, and thus closed a chapter and raised a question about the direction of his future work—when he was only thirty-one years old. The intelligent and shrewd critic Abram Efros already noted the impasse in the artist's development, and indicated that illustrations for literature might be Chagall's way out—as, indeed, they were in the future. Chagall's autobiography, too, would be the stock-taking of the life of an internationally renowned artist.

An additional motivation came from the early Soviet situation. Chagall's first published articles, in 1918–1919, were tools in his struggle for the artistic autonomy of the People's Art College, which he established in Vitebsk. They fulfilled a political and pragmatic function and discussed the question of "Revolutionary Art."

Moreover, Chagall had to prove that he himself was a real proletarian and came "from the people." He exaggerated his humble origins and claimed that his father was "almost a proletarian" or even both a worker and a peasant—the two classes that nominally ruled Soviet Russia. The Jewish lower middle class, however, did not really fit such categories: His father worked in commerce, and his mother built houses for rent and kept a shop—both considered "asocial" classes in the early Soviet regime, with no voting rights.

There may have been some other apologetic elements, conditioned by his situation in the Soviet Union, such as the grotesque and hostile description of his religious in-laws and their family, and his keeping his distance from them. Indeed, his in-laws were considered bourgeois in Vitebsk—a search for jewelry was conducted in their home by the Bolsheviks, walls were torn up—and it is very plausible that this contributed to his wish to leave Vitebsk.

During the writing itself, however, a transformation occurred. What began as an account of his life as a son of the people in a Soviet context culminated in putting an end to his Soviet experience and saying farewell to Russia. Indeed, his style betrayed the very opposite of ideological consistency or class consciousness: it was ironic, whimsical, associative, capricious, and self-centered.

When and Where Was the Autobiography Written?

The text published here concludes with the dates: "Vitebsk 14 . . . Moscow 22 . . . " Those were the dates of Chagall's second Russian period. It is plausible, indeed, that the impulse to write his autobiography was part of his search for roots in 1914, when he was hurled from the peaks of artistic Paris and Berlin to backward Vitebsk, cut off by the chasm of an apocalyptic world war and revolution. The "documents" series of drawings and paintings of that time is akin in spirit to the autobiography, and expresses a similar affirmation of the vitality of the old world. In view of his collaboration with Efros and Tugendhold in wartime Moscow, he could have felt that the hatching period of his autobiography stretched from 1914 on.

Yet there is no evidence that Chagall actually wrote anything in this vein before 1921 or 1922. His resumé, written in Russian in March 1921,[4] is a short, dry, and factual document and still a far cry from the autobiography. The first published text later included in the autobiography, "Leaves from My Notebook,"[5] appeared in the first issue of the Yiddish literary almanac *Shtrom* in Moscow in 1922. It was written as a response to the editors' question of what is "Jewish art," and continued the combination of personal bravado and manifesto style used in Chagall's articles as a Commissar of Art in Vitebsk. Although there is no indication that this text was planned as part of any larger framework or even of an autobiography, it was later included in *Ma vie*.

The year 1921 was a year of endings for Chagall. He lost his job with the Yiddish avant-garde theater in Moscow (for which he was never paid) because the director could not bear the artist's domination of the performance; his father was killed by "the only truck in Vitebsk" and his family in Vitebsk dispersed; the famous artists left the People's Art College he founded, and Vitebsk was "over" for him. "Enough of Vitebsk," he wrote. "The city died. My Vitebsk road is finished and my family died out."[6] He worked as a teacher in a colony for Jewish homeless children in Malakhovka, a village 100 km from Moscow; he could not buy paint, was destitute, unhappy as an artist, and unrecognized by the avant-garde dominating Russian art at the moment (when "everybody was a professor").

While in Paris in 1910–1914, even as a foreigner who barely spoke the language, Chagall was part of the general art scene and exhibited in the Salon des Indépendants; and in Communist Vitebsk, he was a moving force in Soviet Revolutionary art; but now, in Moscow, he became confined to the narrow Jewish sphere. He worked in the Yiddish theater but had no commissions on the Russian stage; and he exhibited his recent work, together with Nathan Altman and David Shterenberg, in a show organized in Moscow by *Kultur-Lige*, the Yiddish Culture League, in 1922, that is, as a "Jewish artist" (a definition he deplored). At that time, he made the graphic design and illustrations for David Hofshteyn's Yiddish long poem "Troyer" ("Grief"), expressing the paradoxical birth of "twins": a "New World" and the slaughter of the Jews in the towns of Ukraine in 1919.[7]

The text of the autobiography has several indications that it was first written in 1922.[8] But it was not ready for publication with Cassirer in Berlin in 1923. (Cassirer despaired of it and published the illustrations without a text.) As we learn from his correspondence, the entire first version was completed only in 1924–1925, when Chagall worked intensively on its first publication in Yiddish.

The Style of the Memoirs

Chagall's memoir begins as an evocation of his early life in Russia, and concludes with a farewell to Russia and a nostalgic appeal to his friends, the artists in Paris—for help and recognition that would, perhaps, bring him recognition in Russia as well. The ending of the book, which Russian critics see to this day as a patriotic cry of love for Russia, is actually an indictment of Russia, which did not recognize or love him. The original text reads: "I grew thin . . . I even want to eat. I want to see you, Gleizes, Cendrars, magician Picasso. I am tired. I will come with wife and child. I will spread like a river among you. Europe will love me and perhaps Russia too, my Russia."[9]

The memoirs are written in a peculiar style: elliptical, abbreviated, associative, an emotional variant of the "telegraphic style" of prose in fashion at the time. Most of the text is presented in poignant, painterly vignettes, accompanied by emotive valuations. He recalls something in the past, reflects on the observation, apostrophizes the long-dead characters, and simultaneously issues whimsical asides to the contemporary reader. There is no chronological narrative, but a series of segments devoted to specific persons (members of his family, his teachers) or to particular situations (Commissar of Art, Yiddish theater). Yet all this is written with an eye to his contemporary, urban reader who must be enlightened about this provincial, exotic world of the past. He sometimes glides into the pose of a sincere clown, who entertains his audience with funny, and endearing anecdotes.

Chagall often describes his characters and situations in terms of the classical art he learned much later, when he roamed the halls of the Louvre: the Vitebsk buildings look like Giotto's frescoes, Father looks like a "marginal character" in Florentine paintings, and the bare-assed uncle parading in the streets of Lyozno is as if a painting by Masaccio or Piero della Francesca had come to life in the *shtetl*. We may assume that the observation itself, in its own time in the past, was not informed by such knowledge of art history on the part of the observer; yet it is reflected in the present from the sophisticated point of view of a modern, cultural narrator and reader.

Surprising metaphors are sprinkled throughout. Their little house in 1887 looks like both the bump on the head of the "Green Jew" (painted in 1913) and a potato washed in brine in a herring barrel of his father's cellar. And even the most unrealistic moves of his paintings are realized in the actual life of his family; thus, the yellow color actually slides down Uncle Leyba's face to the window molding, and spreads over the cupola of the church—not just in his painting, but in reality.

A Continuous Project

Chagall was always interested in the interaction of media: painting and theater, art illustrating literature, and texts embedded in art. The autobiography was planned in two voices, text and illustrations, while the text itself sheds light on some of his major paintings, and vice versa. It is amazing to what extent Chagall, ostensibly drawing on a fantastic imagination, was precise in the details of his constructed myth: They appear both in writing and in images throughout his life. Indeed, the illustrations are an integral part of the autobiography. In this book, we include some of the etchings made in Berlin in 1922, drawings of his family home presumably made in Paris in 1911, and several illustrations Chagall made for his wife Bella's memoirs in the United States during 1944–1946.

Chagall's memoirs were to be published in German by Paul Cassirer in Berlin, where Chagall stayed in 1922–1923. As Fernand Mourlot, the French producer of Chagall's lithographs and editor of their catalogue raisonné, wrote: "At that time, Chagall was working [in Berlin] in the atelier of Hermann Struck, a famous engraver of the epoch, and he was much absorbed by the possibilities of graphic expression. [. . .] Chagall did not work in a lithographic print-shop, but handed his drawings directly to the publisher."[10] Yet only twenty of the engravings made in Berlin were published as an album by Cassirer in a small edition and without the text that explains them.[11] One reason may have been the difficulty of translating Chagall's "crazy" text from Russian; but there were enough Russians in Berlin at the time who could have done it, if there was a written text. A more cogent reason was Chagall's own recognition that the text was unfinished. Only after he found a Yiddish publisher in New York in 1924 did Chagall work seriously on this text in its Yiddish version, in collaboration with his translators.

Though as early as 1924, he claimed that German and French editions were imminent, Chagall's autobiography was first published only in Yiddish in 1925 (the original Russian was apparently lost). As his letters to the Yiddish writers Sh. Nigger and A. Lyesin in New York show, he worked on the Yiddish version for over a year (in 1924–1925), changing many details in the process, until it was published in five installments in 1925, in the prominent New York Yiddish social and literary journal *Di Tsukunft* (*The Future*), edited by A. Lyesin.[12] The French version appeared only in 1931, translated by Bella Chagall and introduced by André Salmon, a theoretician of Cubism and prewar friend of Chagall. Unfortunately, the German, English, and Hebrew translations were made from the French and followed only after World War II. The Russian version, retranslated from the French, appeared only after the Cold War was over, in 1994.

Peretz Markish en 1923 Paris Chagall

Perets Markish, Yiddish Expressionist poet and translator of Chagall's autobiography. Inscription in French: "Peretz Markish in 1923/Paris/Chagall." The date should be 1924, when Markish, age twenty-nine, was in Paris and worked with Chagall on his translation from Russian into Yiddish.

Chagall's original Russian manuscript was translated into Yiddish by the brilliant Yiddish poet Perets Markish (1895–1952). It was then edited to the last detail by Marc Chagall himself, in collaboration with Markish and the innovative Yiddish fiction writer Oyzer Varshavski (Ozer Warszawski, 1898–1944). Bella was not involved in either the Russian or the Yiddish text. In the early 1920s, Markish and Varshavski belonged to an original "Expressionist" group of young

Yiddish writers, *Khalyastre* ("happy gang"),[13] moving from Warsaw to Berlin and Paris. Both were residing at the moment in Paris and published one issue of a journal each—*Khalyastre* No. 2, 1924, edited by Markish, and *Pariz Revi* (*Paris Review*), 1926, edited by Varshavski—to which Chagall contributed many illustrations, notably the hilarious front page of *Khalyastre* No. 2, as well as a chapter from his autobiography.

Markish had a thorough command of both Russian and Yiddish, and Chagall worked on the text with him. Indeed, Chagall authorized the Yiddish version and published it as his own text, not mentioning any translators. Thus, there can be no doubt as to the precision and superior quality of the Yiddish version over all others. It is of one piece, one rhythm running through it all, rather than the disjointed, additive composition of the better known *My Life*. And it contains many authentic anecdotes and details, written closer to the time of the events, which later became blurred, distorted, or deleted.[14]

Yet on top of this typescript (version A), many changes, deletions, and additions were made, as well as stylistic corrections, often sentimentalizing Chagall's restrained tone or "smoothing" rough surfaces. The corrections were made in ink, mostly in Oyzer Varshavski's handwriting, and toward the end, Markish's as well.[15] This edited text (version B) was published in Yiddish in *Di Tsukunft* in 1925.[16] However, there is no reason to doubt that all the additions in version B were either added or approved by Chagall himself. Indeed, he insisted on going over the whole text carefully with his translators, even though the process took more than a year.

In the process of editing the Yiddish version, Chagall became involved in reworking the text, and even after the last installment was published, he wrote to his editor Lyesin: "I am changing and adding a lot," and as late as November 26, 1937, he wrote to Opatoshu: "I want to publish my little book on my life in Yiddish (it still needs some work)." Various additional chapters (version D) were published in Russian and Yiddish journals between 1926–1939. Some of them were included, often in abbreviated form, in the French edition of 1931 (version C). All these scattered texts have been translated in this volume and independently placed in their chronological order. We did not want to disturb the authentic scope and mood of the first autobiography by inserting later texts in it, or integrate into one book what Chagall had no time to do. Yet the scope in Chagall's mind was clearly larger than the published book.

Even after the publication of *Ma vie*, Chagall continued writing his memoirs. During 1936–1937, he wrote a new version, "My Distant Home," this time in meter and rhyme and in Yiddish. The structure of this long poem follows that of *My Life*: It is a cycle of segments devoted to key figures of his family and city and some basic situations of his past. Yet, after the rise of Hitler, the Nazi burning of Chagall's painting in Mannheim, and the murder of Yury Pen in Soviet Vitebsk, it is much more pessimistic. When a new Yiddish literary journal was launched by A. Sutzkever in Tel Aviv in 1948, Chagall eagerly suggested sending Yiddish poems, essays, and chapters of *eygns* (*My Own World*), which he claimed he continued to write. The memoirs were always called *eygns* in Yiddish by Chagall himself; it means literally: "[some of] my own," or "what belongs to me," or "from my own [world]," and is best translated as *My Own World*. This title focuses more on his milieu, his relatives, teachers, and encounters than on his own life, as the later title *My Life* would suggest.

My Own World *(1924)* and My Life *(1931)*

The French translation (version C[17]) was somehow made from Russian by Bella Chagall, aided by her daughter's French teacher—without Chagall's corrections in the Yiddish version. Bella's active French at the time was probably not sufficient to convey all the concrete details and the precision of Chagall's observations, hidden behind his "crazy," associative style. And perhaps she wanted to

smooth some hard edges and was not so attentive to all the subtleties.[18] The
French writer André Salmon, a friend of Chagall's from his earlier French period, who was supposed to edit the translation with Bella, grappled with it and
gave up. In his introduction he wrote: "Chagall is untranslatable," and added: "It
is possible that Chagall's Russian is no Russian at all" [sic].[19] The French version
(C) does contain many additional passages and anecdotes, or parts of later articles, but it also wants to make it "proper," suppresses some Jewish elements, and
"corrects" undesired impressions. For example, when his father's image was
rough and coarse, a sentimental story was added, in which he would come from
work with cakes and frozen pears in his pockets (didn't they smell of herring?).

Yet the main problem is that version C—in French and all other languages
translated from it—is often fuzzy, imprecise, and even mistaken in many details.
Clearly, Chagall's French was not sufficient to edit it himself, as he did the Yiddish, nor did he trust his sense of a different readership. The attentive reader
will discover many authentic details and expressions in our version that were
later obscured in *My Life*. Here is one example offered by Franz Meyer: A chapter from *My Life*, about Léon Bakst, was published in Chagall's Russian original
text (a year before the book appeared) in the Paris Russian Zionist journal
Razsvet. According to *My Life*, viewing a painting by the student Chagall, Bakst
said, "a few casual words, the way one makes polite conversation."[20] "Polite conversation" would hardly make the student flee the expensive art school for three
months. But in the original Russian, Bakst utters "words one is ashamed to use
in good society"—a different story altogether.

Other details are simply misleading. For example, Lyozno and Lyubavich
were not suburbs of Vitebsk but independent towns in another province, 60 and
80 km from Vitebsk.

Already the first paragraph exposes the problem: Why should the first thing
he ever saw be a market trough? *My Life* says: "Once inside, I filled it completely"

(p. 1); apparently he was so big. But the original says the exact opposite: "I was entirely immersed in it"; that is, he did not fill all of the trough, but rather all of him disappeared in it! For he was thrown into it at birth, to revive the stillborn infant, which explains why the first thing he ever saw was a trough—not clear from the text at all.

A similar case: In *My Life* (p. 116) we read: "I even thought of putting my picture on my calling card"—strange! But the original version A is quite specific: "I often said I was not an artist but some kind of cow" (in Yiddish: *beheyme*, an idiot, a mindless animal); "I thought of placing her [the cow] on my calling card." Indeed, the cow is his intimate friend; in the painting "I and the Village," it is a metonymy for Chagall, and that painting became his identity card. When invited by Varian Fry to flee Nazi Europe in 1941, he asked: "Are there cows in America?" which Fry, not understanding the Jewish joke, read as a hesitation to leave (see Chapter 13), whereas what he meant was: Are there idiots in America such as me [who stayed in Nazi Europe for so long]? Or: Will they accept such an idiot? In his country homes in High Falls, New York and in Orgeval, near Paris, he took photographs of a cow in a field, beside his own figure.

A more "sexy" example: *My Life* (pp. 103–104) reads: "But perhaps Cendrars will come and take me out to lunch. Before my friends entered the studio, they always had to wait. That was to give me time to tidy up, to put on my clothes, for I worked in the nude." But in the original text, it was not Cendrars coming at noon, but the chambermaid coming up to him at dawn, after a night of painting, to make love ("I love French blood . . . I wanted to savor the taste of a French body"), and it is her he kept waiting to tidy up his bed and dress—which may have not been to Bella's taste when she translated the passage. Similarly, in the wings of the Russian Ballet in Paris, the Italian poet d'Anunzio was originally flirting with the male dancer Nijinsky—and not with Ida Rubinstein, as "corrected" later.

Perhaps the most striking example for how censored some of the published parts of *My Life* were is the essay on Bakst, which was published separately in 1930 in Chagall's original Russian with a note announcing that this was a chapter from the forthcoming book.[21] Yet in the book, published in 1931, the chapter was shortened and the whole ending dealing with Bakst's and Chagall's own Jewishness deleted.

True, Chagall himself often presented the published *My Life* as his authoritative book, and he must have contributed new anecdotes to it, some clearly apocryphal, like the stories he tells to explain the "realism" of various paintings. But he was not involved in actually making the French version. He did not know the language well enough or would not dare to contradict his "intelligent" spouse. The critics keep quoting it as if it represented either the author or the real facts. And a charming book it is.[22]

With no publisher in sight, Chagall began transcribing Bella's French translation in longhand, accompanied by illustrative drawings, perhaps for an edition in handwriting, in the tradition of the Russian Futurists. That would seem to indicate that he approved the translation. Yet he copied the French text as is, not daring to change a thing, even making basic mistakes in French and correcting them (*ces* corrected to *ses*). The first illustration, however, shows a tiny infant all but disappearing in the trough, as in the Yiddish version.

In sum, *My Life* is an expanded version of *My Own World* and adds various episodes or anecdotes absent in the first version; in detail and precision, however, the earlier version, as published here, is closest to Chagall's original autobiography. Moreover, the additional memoirs (D), published in this volume, are either new or more comprehensive than the added sections of *My Life*.

My Own World covers a large span of time (1887–1922). We shall have to revisit those events in Chapters 3–9. I did not feel that breaking up the autobiography and merging it with the later material was justified, and it is presented in its entirety in this chapter.

We (the translators) have tried to attain the most precise translation possible. We took as our basic text the original manuscript A, rather than the published, somewhat smoothed out Yiddish version B. Yet we indicate all significant changes and additions of B and C, disregarding some stylistic editing. The following symbols are used:

A—the Yiddish typescript of 1924, never before published.

B—the edited version, as published in Yiddish in 1925.

C—*Ma vie/My Life*, the French version of 1931, later translated into English and other languages; here quoted from the English.

D—individual chapters, published before or after the publication of C, yet never fully translated into Western languages.

{In braces}—parts of A, deleted in B.

/Between slashes//—parts not in A, added in B.

** (begin) and *** (end)—parts published elsewhere

Marc Chagall: My Own World

For Rembrandt
Cézanne
My mother
My wife[a]

I

The first thing that struck my eye was a trough. A simple, rectangular, half-eroded[b] trough. A trough you can buy in the market. My whole body disappeared in it.[c]

I don't remember who—my mother, I think—told me that when she was giv-

---

[a]The typewritten manuscript (A) and the corrections in ink (B) are in Yiddish, yet the dedication in Chagall's longhand is in Russian.

[b]B: "half-deep, half-flat"—i.e., longer than it is high, an added explanation, to distinguish it from a high and round trough, used for kneading bread.

[c]In Yiddish: *ikh bin in ir arayn ingantsn*. Such a trough can be seen at the mother's bed in several paintings titled "The Birth." The vivid recollection is apparently from the birth of Chagall's only brother David, born when Moshka was four years old, as described below. The trough appears elsewhere and is part of Chagall's repertory; see, e.g., "The Trough" in Louis Stern's collection, now in the Philadelphia Museum of Art: a woman and a pig, similarly shaped figures, both bent over a trough.

"The Birth": The midwife sinks the baby in a trough, to bring it to life. From the album *My Life,* 20 *Etchings with Drypoint* (Berlin: Cassirer, 1922/1923).

ing birth to me in Vitebsk, on the "Pyeskovatik,"[a] behind the prison, in a little hut next to the highway—there was a big fire in the city. The town was in flames. The section inhabited by the Jewish poor. The bed and mattress, with me at Mama's feet, was carried off to safety in another part of the city.

But first of all, I was born dead . . .

I didn't want to be alive. Imagine a pale bladder that doesn't want to live in the world . . . As if it were glutted with Chagallian pictures. They pricked it with pins, revived it, threw it into a bucket of water, and finally it gave out a squeal. But what's important is that I was born dead. I certainly don't want the psychologists to draw any unfavorable interpretation for me . . . Please![b]

But the fire didn't touch the little house of my father and grandfather in Piskovatik on the highway. I recently saw it there. When things began to go a bit better for my father, he sold it. That little house reminds me of the bump on the head of the Green Preacher ["The Green Jew"] which I painted in Vitebsk in 1914; and it also reminds me of a potato tossed into a herring barrel and washed in brine.

[a]Alternatively, he spells: "Piskovativke," "Peskovativke." The name of the neighborhood means "in the sands," i.e., outside the paved city center. This neighborhood was developed only in the beginning of the twentieth century.

[b]Literally: "Forgive me!" B: "Take pity!"

"Fire in the City," from *My Life*. "The town was in flames. The bed and mattress, with me at Mama's feet, was carried off to safety in another part of the city."

When I regarded the cottage from the height of my current "greatness"—I shrank back and asked myself: "Where could I possibly have been born here? . . . Where could I catch my breath here?"

But when my black-bearded, tall grandfather died in ripe old age, my father bought another piece of property for a pittance, which was no longer near a Crazy House, as in Piskovatik. All around were churches, fences, shops,[a] and Jewish prayer houses. Simple, elementary, eternal—like the buildings in Giotto's frescos. Past me, running back and forth in circles, or just walking aimlessly—a variety of Jews: old, young: Yaviches and Beylins.[b] Beggars are running home, rich

[a]In A: "benches"—a bad translation from Russian: *Lavka* is both a bench and a small shop. Corrected in B.

[b]"Yavich" is the Hebrew *Yavets* (or *Javitz*), as pronounced in Chagall's dialect. B, for some reason, changed it to: "Lifshitzes and Gureviches" (perhaps not to offend the neighbors, still in the Soviet Union). But *My Life* has the names as in A; which indicates that Bella translated from the earlier Russian version, without the editorial corrections in B. Yavich was the real name of one of the Chagalls' tenants, where Moshka had a room to himself.

Grandfather's little house in the unpaved Peskovatik suburb, where Chagall was born and spent three years of his life. On the right, Father peeing; in the doorway, Grandfather (above him, in Russian: Shagal); in the outhouse, Moshka. The chicken has laid an egg (Yiddish proverb, implying "big deal," from all that effort, all she did was lay an egg). Upon his return from France, Chagall was shown the house and asked himself: "Where could I have possibly be born here?" The answer, on the lower left: TUT ("here" in Russian). From *My Life*.

men go home. A little boy walks home from *Heder*.[a] My father strolls home. For in those days there was no cinema! So you walked, either home or to the store.

This is what I remember after my period of the trough.

I'm not talking about the sky or about my childhood stars. For those were my stars—my quiet stars—they went with me to *Heder*, waited for me outside in the street until I went back home . . . Poor things, forgive me. I left you alone at such a terrific height . . .

My joyful, gloomy city. As a child, I watched you fearfully from the little gate in our fence. And in my child's eyes, you were so intelligible and clear. When the fence blocked the view—I stood on a stump. If I still couldn't see you—I climbed on the roof. That didn't matter—my grandfather also used to climb on the roof.

[a]A Jewish religious elementary school, conducted as a class in the teacher's home.

The parents' house on Pokrovskaya Street, where Chagall lived from age three to twenty-eight. On the right, the family brick house; to the left of the gate, Mother's grocery store and Mother inviting customers. On the sign, in a mirror image and in postrevolutionary Russian spelling: lavka Shagal ("store/Shagal"). From *My Life*.

A carter and wagon "flying by" the Chagalls' brick house. Through the side door, one can see the courtyard with the wooden houses for rent; in the window, probably Marc's room. From *My Life*.

And you lay before my eyes.

Here, on Pokrovska[a] Street, I was born a second time.

II

Have you ever seen one of the "marginal characters" in Florentine paintings, with a beard never shaved, eyes ashen and brown at the same time, a face the color of burnt ochre with wrinkles and pimples—that is my father.

Or have you seen a figure in the Passover Hagadah, kosher-for-Passover and simple-minded[b] . . . "Forgive me, father!" Remember, I drew a sketch of you. Your portrait was to give the impression of a flickering candle, and at the same time, a candle going out[c] . . . Its smell is the smell of a dream. A fly was buzzing incessantly, it put me to sleep . . .

Does it make sense to talk about my father? What is the worth of a person who has no worth: an inestimable personality. And precisely because he was of no value, I have a hard time finding suitable words for him.

My grandfather, a pious teacher by profession, knew nothing better for his oldest son—my father—than to place him as a clerk[d] in a herring cellar[e] while he was still a child. And his younger son—as a barber.[f] But no—for thirty-two years, he wasn't a clerk, just a simple laborer.[g] He would hoist heavy barrels of four and five *poods* [120–160 pounds], and my heart would shrink like a Turkish bagel as I watched my father lift the loads while the potbellied boss[h] stood by, or as he rummaged around in the herring with frozen hands . . .

[a]In Russian: Pokrovskaya; yet the manuscript spells as in Yiddish: Pokrovske (which we transcribe as Pokrovska).

[b]One of the four sons in the Passover Hagadah, a naïve person, who asks: "What does this mean?"

[c]An allusion to Leonid Andreev's play "The Life of Man," in which the candle symbolizes Man's life and the death of the candle symbolizes Man's death.

[d]In Yiddish: *mishores*—a translation of the Russian *podryadchik*—a store manager or contractor. The original Hebrew word, *mesharet*, means servant, but in Yiddish it can be used for a clerk (as in the English "public servant") or a store manager. Chagall puts the meaning back to the literal "servant," to show both his "proletarian" origins and his father's lowly status, a positive asset in the Soviet context. A document issued on July 5, 1935, by the City Council of Vitebsk for Maria Chagall's application to a Planning Institute certifies that her father was indeed a worker for the employer Yakhnin, yet it also states that he was a member of the Union of Store Managers between 1905 and 1918. After the October Revolution he became a salesman in a city cooperative.

[e]B: "herring shop." It was both, of course.

[f]Uncle Zusya, the barber in Lyozno.

[g]From 1885 (a year before his marriage) until 1917, the October Revolution.

[h]A Soviet stereotype of the bourgeois.

"My Father." Father (with religious hat and beard) dropped the heavy herring barrel and holds a samovar to cook tea. Mother milking the goat. From *My Life*.

By the way, I understood too well this poetic folk-heart, numbed by silence. Almost to his last years, he earned only around twenty Rubles. The six-kopek and ten-kopek tips he got from the customers increased his pocket money. Yet my father was not a poor Jew. Not at all. The photo from his younger years and an exploration of our wardrobe indicated that my father married my mother provided with a bit of money and a fine physical strength. He gave his bride an

мои отец, мать и я. Шагал. Paris. 1911 года.

"My Father, my Mother and I. Shagal. Paris. 1911" in Russian; "Paris" in French. Religious Father is wearing a hat; Mother is wearing a wig and the fancy hat of a married woman. Marc has a twisted face, reproduced in the first book about him (1918); this drawing was probably made for that book. The Russian inscription is in the postrevolutionary spelling.

exquisite shawl. She was a short little girl,[a] who grew bigger only after she was married.

After the wedding, father stopped giving grandfather his week's wages and ran his own household.

But first I want to finish the story of my black-bearded grandfather. I don't know how long he taught children. People say he was a fine, honorable Jew. Some ten years ago,[b] when I visited his grave with my grandmother and discovered his tombstone, I was convinced that he was a good Jew.[c] An invaluable Jew, a holy Jew. He lies close to the river, at the black fence, where the turbid water runs off . . . He lies below, behind a hill, near the long-dead scholars and geniuses.[d] The carved Jewish letters on the tombstone are worn, but still legible:

Here Lies a "Sage"

My grandmother pointed: "*That* is your grandfather's grave. Your father's father and my first husband."[e]

Her lips mumbled something, she couldn't cry. She muttered unintelligible words, that came either from herself or from the prayer book. As she bent over the tombstone, I heard her speak something, as if the tombstone and the mound of the grave was my grandfather. As if she were appealing to the entrails of the earth or to some kind of cupboard where some object was hidden forever:

"David, I beg you, David, intervene for us[f]; for your children, I—your Basheve

---

[a]According to Chagall's resumé, she was forty-five years old at her death, i.e., no more than fifteen when she got married, as was the custom of the time among Jews.

[b]The earliest this could have happened was 1914, when Chagall came back to Russia, lived in Vitebsk for the first time as an adult, and got interested in his roots. This is another indication that the text was finished not in Russia in 1922, but in France in 1924.

[c]Pious, or studying daily, versed in Jewish religious matters, as indicated on the tombstone. Chagall is playing naive.

[d]Chagall is being ironic: The grave was in the worst part of the cemetery, set aside for the poor, while the tombstone aggrandized his learning, as was the custom of tombstone inscriptions, with no relation to reality. Thus, in the painting "Cemetery" of the same period, all of the half-submerged tombstones on a slope announce in Hebrew: Rabani ("the rabbinical"), an honorific title for a sage and learned man, inscribed equally on all the graves.

[e]The painting "Cemetery Gate" commemorates the discovery of his grandfather's grave, as pointed out to Chagall by his Lyozno grandmother after his return from Paris. The gate of the cemetery prominently carries the dates not of a cemetery, but of a person's life: 1818–1890, and the Star of David on top of the gate jubilantly announces again: 1890. If so, his paternal grandfather died when Chagall was three years old.

[f]The folk belief that a deceased, hence "saintly," person can intervene in heaven to improve the lot of their relatives on earth.

"My Grandfathers." On the right, probably the learned grandfather David Chagall (who died when Marc was three); tefilin straps on his arm, philactery box on his forehead, he reads a prayer book. On the left, the butcher from Lyozno makes an argument. The geometrical L-shaped form with the axe suggest the Hebrew letter H, implying God's name. From *My Life*.

[Bath-Sheba]. Intervene for your frail son, Khatsi,[a] your skinny Zuske,[b] and their children. Pray that they grow up good human beings, pious with God and humane with people."

With my grandmother, my father's mother, I felt more intimate.[c] The old woman consisted of only a kerchief on her head, a dress, and a wrinkled face. A little figure, four and a half feet tall. In her heart was devotion and love for a few chosen children and for the women's prayer book, *korbn minkha.* When she was widowed, she obtained the Rebbe's permission to marry my grandfather, my mother's father, whose wife had also died. The first spouses died the year my parents were married.[d]

My mother ascended the throne.

My heart will always shrink: either in a dream, or at an accidental recollection, or on the anniversary of her death, when we visit her grave—mother's grave.[e] I see you in my mind's eye, mother, walking so slowly toward me, so slowly I want to stop you. You smile my smile. Oh, that smile is mine.

My mother was born in that same Lyezne where I painted the priest's house, and next to it—a fence, and next to the fence—pigs . . . She was the oldest[f] daughter of my grandfather, who spent half his life lying on the oven, a quarter of his life in the study house, and the other quarter—in the butcher shop. At that time, as he lay on the oven, my grandmother couldn't stand it and died in her prime. Then my grandfather stirred. And so did the cattle and the calves.

Was my mother really so short? My father took her "sight unseen."[g] But that's wrong. In our eyes, mother was a person of rare expressiveness, as far as possible in her small-town milieu. But I don't want to praise my mother, who is no more. How can I speak? Sometimes it's not only speech, but weeping . . . At the cemetery, toward the gates, lighter than a flame, airier than a shadow, I rush there to shed a tear . . .

[a]A Slavicized and intimate form of the Yiddish name Khatskl, derived from the Hebrew Yihezkel (Ezekiel); in Russian: Zakhar, Chagall's father.

[b]A diminutive form of Zusya, Chagall's uncle, the barber in Lyozno.

[c]The use of "more" is strange here, unless he means more intimate than with his dead grandfather David Chagall.

[d]This is only true about his mother's mother; when she died, Chagall's mother, Feyge-Ite, as the oldest daughter, "ascended the throne." She was fifteen years old and was married off to Ezekiel Shagal, who lived with his father in Vitebsk.

[e]Died in 1916.

[f]In A and B: "last" = youngest; probably a typographical error, for she was like a mother to her other sisters. In Yiddish, the words are very similar: the text reads *letste* (last) instead of *eltste* (oldest). Here corrected from C.

[g]What a gap between the generations: Marc Chagall's marriage followed a long courtship, love, hesitations, and rivalry.

"My Grandmother": "The old woman consisted of only a kerchief on her head, a dress, and a wrinkled face. A little figure, four and a half feet tall." In her hand, the woman's prayer book. From *My Life*.

I see the river flowing into the distance, even farther—the bridge, and nearby—the eternal fence.[a] Graveyard earth and graves. Here is my soul. Look for me here, this is where I am, here are my pictures, my creation. My gloom, gloom. Here is her picture. What's the difference—it is I. Who am I? (You may smile, passerby, you'll wonder and laugh.) A lake of suffering. Prematurely gray hair, eyes with a city of tears inside them; a soul that is almost no more, a brain that is no more. So what is there?

I remember her managing the house and managing my father, inexhaustibly building houses,[b] setting up a small grocery store, hiring carters, bringing a wagonload of merchandise, without money, on credit.

What are words? What means can I use to describe her standing at the door with a smile, or sitting at the table for a long while, waiting for a customer to come in—to show her wisdom in conversation and in sadness. And on Friday evening, after the Sabbath meal, when father, without fail, would doze off at the table, always in the same place, in the middle of the blessing (on my knees to You![c])—her eyes would grow sad and she would say to her eight children:

"Children, let us sing the Rebbe's tune.[d] Lend me your voices!"

The children sang along as they dropped off. She burst into tears and I said:

"You're starting again?" . . .

"Well, I'm stopping."

I wanted to say that somewhere in her was my talent, that she gave me everything, perhaps except for her wisdom.[e] Now she is coming to my room (in Yavich's courtyard), she knocks and asks:

"My child, are you here? What are you doing? Was Berta[f] with you? Do you want to eat?"

"Look, Mama, do you like this?" She looks deep into my painting with God knows what eyes. I wait for the verdict. Finally, she says pensively: "Yes, my son, I see. You have talent. But, my child, listen to me: maybe you'd rather be a clerk? I pity you. What can you do with those shoulders? And where did we [our family] get such shoulders?" . . .[g]

[a]In Yiddish, "the eternal place" is a euphemism for cemetery.

[b]In 1902—twelve years after they moved to Pokrovskaya St.—she built a brick house for the family, a mark of status. To the left of the gate was her store; and in the yard she built four wooden houses, rented to eight families.

[c]Chagall asks forgiveness for "slandering" his hard-working father.

[d]A Rebbe, the head of a Hasidic dynasty, would compose a tune of his own, like a hymn, for Hasidim need no words to express their love for God (and their solidarity with their Rebbe).

[e]"Wisdom"—an erased gap in A, amended in B.

[f]Berta Rosenfeld, later Bella Chagall.

[g]Unlike his father's shoulders, which could carry heavy herring barrels. In *My Life* (C) the shoulders are omitted: "I'm sorry for you. Where do you get that in our family?"—which makes no sense.

"Our Dining Hall." Signed in French: "1911/Chagall." Moyshe is drawing; one sister is flirting behind the curtain; the other sister stands at the samovar, preparing tea. Mother is "humanizing" her traditional husband, who wouldn't trim his beard.

"My Parents." Signed in Russian: "My parents" and in French: "Chagall 1911." The three steps of mother's store; sign in Russian: "Bakaleyn[aya lavka]," (grocer[y store]). It seems that Mother is calling in a customer (he doesn't look like Father).

The family dining room: Father dozing off; Marc, close to Mother, in his Russian, "Tolstoyan" shirt and student hat. From *My Life*.

It has been many years since she died. The first time I was at the cemetery, they put up her tombstone near the fence. Next to her lie women like her, from Mohilev or from Lyezne.[a] Hearts lie here. Strokes. Catarrhs. I know them well. It is all the same heart that killed my young, blond, rosy-cheeked grandmother. Ruptured from hard work, beyond her strength, while my grandfather constantly lay on the oven or went to the study house. The same heart that killed the "marvellous butcher" in the study house on Yom Kippur, after the fast, on a moonlit evening, at the beginning of the New Year.

Dear, young old man.[b] How much I loved you when I was in Lyezne, in your rooms redolent with the smell of tanned cattle hides. I loved your sheepskins. Yes. Your whole wardrobe was always hanging in the hall at the doorway, and the

[a]Apparently, people from the provinces are buried near the fence. The fence is an important social marker, outcasts are buried beyond the fence. When he says Mohilev he means Mohilev Province, next door to the city of Vitebsk. Lyezne was closer to Vitebsk than to Mohilev, but was in Mohilev Province.

[b]Marc's grandfather, the "marvelous butcher" of Lyozno.

rack with the clothes, the hats, the whip, and similar treasures formed such a modern silhouette on the gray background of the wall, which even now I haven't fully fathomed. That was my grandfather. Every day, two or three cattle were slaughtered, and the fresh meat would be offered to the Lord of the Manor and other notables.

In grandfather's stables stood a young cow, with a little bulging belly, gazing somewhere stubbornly. Grandfather goes to her and says: "Well, listen, give me your legs. We have to tie them. We need merchandise, meat, you hear?"

She falls down with a sigh. I stretch my hands to her, stroke her chin, whisper a few words to her, tell her not to be afraid—I won't eat any meat . . . What else could I do . . . She hears the waves passing through the rye and beyond the fence is a blue sky. But the black-and-white butcher with the slaughtering knife is already rolling up his sleeves. You barely hear a blessing. He stretches her head and jerks the steel into her throat . . . A gush of blood.

Then it's quiet. They separate the intestines, remove the cuts of meat, the hide falls off. Pink colors flow, bleeding colors . . . Steam rises. What a professional skill is in his hands! I like that. I want to eat meat. My second Lyezne grandmother[a] fed me such strange, large pieces of meat, strange fried, steamed, and roasted pieces. What kind of meat it was I don't know. Maybe it was the stomach, the neck, the ribs, a fetus, lung-and-liver, I didn't understand. At that time, I was a great fool, and apparently happy.

Grandfather, let me think about you a bit longer. Once, the old man, coming across the picture of a nude woman, turned away, as if it didn't concern him. Or as if it were an alien star in the marketplace that the shopkeepers had disregarded, as if it were none of their business. Then I understood that both my grandfather and my tiny grandmother with the tiny wrinkles, and almost all my family didn't think much of my art (What kind of painting is this that doesn't look like anything?) and did think very much of meat.

Or another story my mother told me about her father, my Lyezne grandfather. Or maybe I dreamed it. It was on the holiday of Succoth or Simhath Torah—they search for grandfather.

"Where is he?"

It turned out that, in nice weather, he clambered up to the roof, sat on the chimney, and ate *tsimmes* [carrot stew]. Not a bad picture.

I don't mind if people are pleased or relieved to find the secret of my work in those innocent events of my family. Oh, it doesn't bother me. Dear citizens,[b] as much as you like.

---

[a]He means the second wife of his maternal grandfather, the butcher of Lyozno. She has been Moshka's father's mother, but after the death of David Shagal, she moved back to Lyozno and married the other, widowed grandfather.

[b]A typical Soviet form of address, i.e., written still in Soviet Russia.

And now I shall tell you [readers] something more, if you don't have enough facts for the future and proof of your rightness and my guilt in the court of common sense—what my mother told me about my good Lyezne relatives . . . One of them found it more expedient to appear in the streets of the *shtetl* in a mere undershirt. So what, is that so terrible? Memories of that bare ass will always fill my heart with a sunny joy. Just as if a painting by Masaccio or Piero della Francesca had come to life in broad daylight on the streets of Lyezne. I would have been their friend.

I don't mean the joke of a prankster. If my art didn't play any role in the lives of my family, their lives and creations, on the contrary, were very significant in my work. You know? I was overwhelmed by Grandfather's "Eastern Seat" in the synagogue . . .[a] Poor, unhappy, how I would whirl around until I crept to my grandfather's "Eastern Place" on the Sabbath, to face the window, prayerbook in hand, looking up at the panorama of Lyezne, the *shtetl*.[b] Behind me they're starting the *Musaf* [early evening] prayer, my grandfather is called to the podium. He prays, he sings, he trills, and then starts all over again, overflowing in song. As if there was an oil factory in my heart. Such newly gathered honey flows inside me. And as he bursts into tears, I recall an unsuccessful sketch I made, and ponder:

"Will I become a great artist?"

But I've forgotten to mention you, Uncle Noah.[c] I used to travel to the villages with you for cattle. How happy I was when he consented to take me along to the villages in his rickety cart. Never mind, you could ride in it. And you could see a lot on both sides.

Road-in and road-out. Fine sand. My Uncle Noah prods the horses: "Gidi-yup! Come on!"

On the way back, I decided to show my extreme nimbleness and skill: I dragged a cow by the tail in back of the wagon, arguing with her not to fall behind . . .

When we crossed the wooden bridge of the small town [Lyozno], I always

---

[a]Yiddish: *Shtot* (literally: city), a permanent "Seat," as close as possible to the Eastern wall of the synagogue, was bought by respectable citizens and reflected social prestige.

[b]There is a pun between grandfather's *shtot* (synagogue seat) and Marc's smaller yet more attractive *shtetl* (diminutive of *shtset*—small town) in the window.

[c]In Chagall biographies, he is mentioned by the strange name of Neuch. This is a mistake. The biblical Noah (spelled in consonants: *NH* or *NUH*) is pronounced in Yiddish: *Noyakh* (Lithuanian: *Neyakh*) or *Noykh*, which was transcribed by Franz Meyer in German as *Neuch*, but it makes no sense in French or English. Berta Rosenfeld wrote in Russian, on the back of her father Shmuel-Noah's photo: *Shmuel-Neukh* (in two syllables: *Ne-ukh*), instead of the correct Russian *Noy*.

There is a Yiddish proverb: *Noyakh mit zibn grayzn*—"[he spells] Noah with seven mistakes." The Hebrew word has only two letters, and it takes some ingenuity to produce seven mistakes in its Yiddish transcription.

Grandfather's house in Lyozno. Grandfather disappeared, Mother was looking for him everywhere, while he sat on the chimney and ate sweet carrot *tsimmes*. From *My Life*.

"Not a bad picture," wrote Chagall upon recounting the above story, perhaps a figment of his imagination—as shown in this 1947 framing, with the artist inside and outside of the frame.

thought several wooden cutlets were bouncing in my stomach . . . The wheels squeaked differently. My uncle wasn't interested in the bridge or the reeds[a] at the river, or the fences stretching on the bank up to the mill, and farther on: the one little church, the small houses on the market square where everything was steeped in darkness. We returned tired and God knows what was in our soul . . .

It would be interesting to paint my sisters and my brother. How lovingly I'd treat the texture of their hair, their skin. How swiftly I would leap inside them, intoxicating my canvases and you too[b] with the breathing of my thousand-year-old colors.[c] But to write about them—

I won't undertake to say even a few words about my aunts. One of them had a long nose, a good heart, and a dozen children. The other was snub-nosed, had half a dozen children, and loved herself best. Why not? The third had a nose like in a Morales painting, three children—one stuttered, the second was deaf, and the third was still growing. I also have uncles, half a dozen and more. All of them good Jews: one with a big belly and an empty head, one with a black beard, and one with a yellow beard. In short: this is painting.

Every Sabbath, Uncle Noah /still a bachelor// would put on someone's *tallis* and read the Torah, year after year, he played the violin like a cobbler,[d] and my grandfather would listen and ponder . . . Only Rembrandt knows what my old grandfather—butcher, shopkeeper, cantor—was thinking while his son played to the window. It felt like falling asleep. I know it too, but I can't convey it.

In the village, next to his little cottage, Uncle Leyba sits on a bench. A lake. His daughters graze like red cows. Uncle Yuda always lies on the oven, doesn't even go to the prayer house, he prays at home at the window. He mumbles something quietly, and the yellow color slides down his face to the window molding, flows outside and spreads over the dome of the church . . .

He looks like a wooden house with a transparent roof . . . I can paint him quickly . . .

Uncle Israel is sitting in the prayer house in one place in back of the oven. His hands behind his back, warming himself, eyes closed, while the lamp burns on the table. A dark, thick shadow has spread on the floor and on the Holy Ark. He reads and sways, swings and sings, murmurs and sighs. Stands up: it's time for evening prayer.

Evening. Blue stars. Lilac earth. Shops are closed. Supper is served. Cheese, plates. Why didn't I die in your house under the table? My uncle is afraid to

---

[a]B: "willows."

[b]The spectators.

[c]"Two thousand years" is the proverbial span of the Jewish exile; i.e., carrying the weight of the Jewish Diaspora. Such was Chagall's cultural perception of color and form in his art.

[d]The Yiddish idiom "like a cobbler" means "incompetently" or "coarsely."

shake my hand. People say I am a painter. All of a sudden, I may paint him up. God forbade it, a sin . . .

May God forgive me for not including in my self-portrait my great calf's love[a] for men in general—and my relatives are holier than others. That's my wish.

I have an uncle, a barber, Zuske. He cut my hair and shaved me with a heartless love and he boasted of me (the only one who boasted!) all over the area, even to the Lord of the Manor. Well, enough about them. Farewell.

III

Day in and day out, at about six o'clock, winter or summer, my father would get up and go to the prayer house. He simply had to say *Kaddish* [prayer for the dead] for somebody. He set up the samovar, drank tea, and went to work. Work—hell, slave labor. Why should I hide it? And how to tell it? No words will make my father's fate easier. (I am talking about empathy, not pity.) There was butter and cheese on the table. Bread-and-butter,[b] like an eternal symbol, never left my child's hands. Wherever I went—to the house next door, to the street, to the toilet—I went everywhere with bread-and-butter, like all my family. Were we hungry? Never! . . . It was a kind of itch: to eat and think, yawn and chew. We especially liked every evening to empty ourselves at the fence, forgive my coarseness.[c] (Everything is called literature! . . . Forgive my rudeness.) Am I coarse? Not in the least. It can be worse. Simple: in the moonlight, when it is scary to go far away, we children just couldn't go far, our little legs didn't bend. True, the next morning, my father would curse endlessly: {What children pranksters! (He would have cursed even more had he seen how the "emptied stuff" was served as a dish to the dear "modern" teacher . . .)}[d]

[a]A play on the Yiddish idiom *kelberne hispayles* ("a calf's excitement") = naïve, wholehearted. We kept the idiom literally because, in this context, Chagall's identification with a calf is significant.

[b]The Yiddish idiom "bread-and-butter" has a literal meaning, or it can mean "sandwich," or "food." If you have bread *with* butter, you aren't starving. A child would take a slice of bread-and-butter and run out in the street.

[c]This was not a joke, but a major problem in the life of children without a toilet indoors. You want to do it in the dark, yet in the dark you are afraid to go too far. And even if there is an outhouse, it is dangerous—you may fall in. Chagall inserted the image of a child defecating near a fence as a little counterpoint in several of his quite "romantic" paintings, "Above the City" (1914–1918) and "Music" (the fiddler in the theater murals, 1920).

[d]"Modern" is ironic, referring to the "medieval" teacher in Heder. The text in braces was vigorously crossed out in the manuscript. The correction B, in Varshavski's hand, reads: /father, spade in hand, wouldn't stop cursing with no particular aim: 'N-na! Children, pigs!' . . . /

"Man at the Fence." Actually: boy defecating under the fence. From *My Life*.

I like to sleep. Not at night—in the morning I like to sleep. When a sunbeam creeps under the roof and into the window. Flies are already buzzing and aiming at my nose. Oh, how much longer—I imagine my father coming in with a belt in his hand and saying: "It seems to me it's time to go to school?"

I study the blue wallpaper, the ceiling with cobwebs, the window with the houses, and think: true, everybody is apparently up, enough scratching. Finally the door opens and a housewife comes into the room. "Give me," she says, " a good herring for three kopecks, but a really *good* one! You must have good herrings, don't you? . . . " I wake up: I don't know how late it is.

In the morning: tea on the table. I feel incapable of conveying its color, its aroma. And such a sweet fluid pours into me from my hand, right through the bagel.

On Friday, when my father began his "general wash" for the Sabbath, mother would take a hot pot out of the oven and father would somehow wash his head, chest, and black hands. He would groan: "Why is there no order, why no soda.[a] A whole family of eight, sitting on my shoulders—and no help from anyone." I swallowed tears and thought about my poor art and my future. The steam from

[a]Washing soda.

the hot water blended with the smell of soap and soda annoyed me especially. And the fire of the Sabbath candles cut through me just like [the blood of] that cow in /grandfather's/ barn. Holy blood! It was warm and . . . annoying.

The Sabbath meal. Clean hands. Father's face and white shirt would calm us. Everything felt good. Dinner was served. Oh, my appetite!—if only the stomach allowed, herring and gefilte fish, carrots with meat, *pecha* [calves' foot jelly], compote soup, *bilke* [chicken breast]. The temperature rose. Father dozed off. The last piece of meat flies from father's plate to mother's and—back. "Eat it yourself." "No, you eat it." And father was snoring even before the blessing. (What could one do?) And mother at the stove was already singing the Rebbe's tune with all of us.

I mentioned my grandfather, the cantor.[a] I mentioned my prayer house oil factory. And I wept in my heart behind the curtain of the big oven, at mother's side, when she ended the tune in straightforward weeping, crying aloud, singing aloud . . . What kind of heart (not mine) wouldn't tremble on the Sabbath night knowing there was no one outside.[b] Just cross-eyed lanterns and riffraff fooling around . . .

The candles in our room flicker and die out—in the sky the lights go out. It smells. My head hurts. I'm afraid to go out into the front hall, into the courtyard. (Once late at night, I caught a woman thief. She asked me: "Where's there a tavern here? I'm coming from the cemetery." . . .[c])

Everybody goes to sleep. Only from the market place do I hear distant music. They're playing in the park. They're strolling there. Caressing each other. Trees bend in the dark. Leaves rustle.

On weekdays, among other things, I was raised on buckwheat kasha.[d] For me, there was no more hellish cereal than kasha, the barley food. The awareness that little pellets were in my mouth upset me as if my mouth was filled with buckshot. Only now, in the Soviet time, have I become a special expert, even a lover of millet and kasha. Especially when a sack of millet was riding on my shoulders.[e]

At dinner I would usually fall asleep in my clothes and mother would shuffle over and wake her firstborn son:

"I don't know why, as soon as it's dinnertime, he falls asleep. Go eat, my son."

"Eat what?"

"Kasha."

[a]The butcher, moonlighting as a cantor.

[b]All families were at their homes for the Sabbath meal.

[c]Apparently a prostitute, plying her trade in the cemetery field.

[d]A cooked cereal, a staple of Russian and "Jewish" Eastern Europe cuisine.

[e]Clearly, this part was still written in Soviet Russia. He refers to the hunger in Moscow in the first Soviet years and Chagall carrying either a monthly ration or a sack of millet from the black market.

"Our Dining Room." Signed in French: "Chagall 911" and in Russian: "our dining room." Father is rolling cigarettes from cut-up tobacco. Behind him, perhaps a portrait of Herzl (indicating Father's Zionist leanings). In the left window, a retired Russian soldier-cum-Jewish beggar, knocking at the window (see figures on the next two pages); in the right window, a lit window across the yard (perhaps Moyshe's room). The boy drawing is probably brother David. At left is Moyshe's notebook.

"Which kasha?"

"Buckwheat with milk."

"I want to sleep."

"Go eat."

"I don't like it."

"Go try it. If you choke on it or you faint—you won't have to eat."

I admit that I often prayed and wished to be overcome by a swoon. Sometimes it saved me! Yet that fainting happened at another time, for other reasons, and in another place.[a]

Winter. My feet stand and my head is flying off. I often stand at the black iron oven, and just warm myself. In front, mother sits on a little bench, full, a big belly—imperial. Father sets the samovar, sits down, and rolls cigarettes.

My God, the sugar bowl! How glad I am. Mother talks and talks, drums her fingers on the stool, adjusts her wig,[b] and her tea grows cold. And father listens, looks at the cigarette wrapper. A mountain of cigarettes piles up.

Every illness of one of us children was foretold in mama's dream. At night. A

[a]He refers to a later date, when he fainted of starvation in St.-Petersburg.

[b]A religious married woman had her hair shaved and wore a wig, or hat-cum-wig, as in Chagall's drawing.

"My Mother at the Baking Oven." Signed in French: "Chagall 1911." Mother is shoving loaves of bread into the oven. At the door is a beggar, the Wandering Jew, in the hat of a retired soldier. There is a modern faucet, yet the sister washes in a bucket. To the right of the table, a Russian *lubok* (popular wall illustration) with the inscription *Moskva* (Moscow) and a nostalgic gesture, as in Chekhov's *Cherry Orchard*. The *lubok* on the left perhaps reads: *ognem* in Russian ("with fire").

winter frost. The house is sleeping. But suddenly—from the street comes the figure of Grandma Hannah from The Other World, shuts the little opening in the window with a thud, and says: "Daughter, dear, why do you keep the little window open in such cold weather in the middle of the night?"

Another time, a white old man from The Other World[a] comes into our house, one of my uncles with a long beard. He comes in and holds out his hand for alms. I give him a piece of bread. He doesn't say a word and gives me a smack on the hand. The bread falls out of my hand.

"Khatsi," says mama, waking up; "go take a look: what's going on with the children."

That's how we would get sick.

Palings and roofs, logs and fences, and what was behind the fences—all that you can see in my picture "Above the City." Or I can tell you:

A bunch of outhouses, houses with windows, gates, chickens, an idle factory, a church, a mound (the old Jewish cemetery, where no one lies anymore).

More details I saw from the little window in our roof, looking down . . . lower . . .

Sometimes, I stick my head out and breathe the fresh, blue air. Birds fly past

[a]A corpse in a white shroud.

"An Old Jew." On his back, the sack of a peddler-cum-beggar, symbol of the Wandering Jew.
From *My Life*.

my head. I hear—Sara is splashing around.[a] I see socks and legs. She sprayed my
beloved toys, pieces of broken pottery, my pebbles . . . She is hurrying to a wedding. She's a barren woman. She will cry there over the bride's lot . . .

I love *klezmers*,[b] I love the sound of their polkas and waltzes. I too am running
to the wedding and cry along with mama. I love to cry. When the wedding jester

[a]Apparently: urinating.
[b]*Klezmers* are a band of Jewish musicians.

"Lovers above the City." We can see the "fences, fences, fences" and the boy defecating.
From *My Life*.

sings at the top of his lungs and screams: "Bride, bride, cry,[a] remember that
you're going to the marriage canopy. Think of what awaits you . . . "

Awaits you. What awaits her? At these words, my head slowly separates from
my body and bursts into weeping somewhere in the kitchen where the fish is being prepared for the table. Cried to your heart's content—enough. Everybody
wiped their noses—and like a storm, the confetti rose out of many-colored wrap-
ping papers.

"Mazel-tov!"[b]

And who should I kiss? I have to choose somebody to kiss. I can't kiss grand-
mothers or bearded men.

In awe of God, I looked at the girls around me, {the childish craziness went so
far that a little girl, as if bewitched, followed me to the stable; and after a short
time of torture, we emerged from there and went back to freedom.}[c] I don't
know how old I was then, ten or twelve. {Playing with a girl, I didn't consent to

[a]Typical influence of Slavic folklore on Jewish mores. In a Russian folk wedding ritual,
the bride conventionally cries, lamenting the imminent loss of her virginity, the separation
from her mother, and the move to a new family clan. We can see this scene in the mural
painting "Drama" (in Yiddish: "The Wedding Jester") for the Moscow Yiddish Theater.

[b]Hebrew and Yiddish: "Congratulations!" Literally, "Good luck!"

[c]Crossed out and omitted in B.

give her back the ball until she gave me her legs as a prize: "Give me a leg} and I'll return your ball."

{Such frolicking amazes me now and offends me with its failure and negligible results.} But there were days when I played not just with sticks, buttons, bones, and pens. Either I would climb into the neighbors' yard with my friend {who would bang his member on the beams} . . . That scared me a lot. Or, on other days, I would spend all my time on the rafts on the Dvina River, bathe, strip naked, and leap again and again into the water. Just one thing: I was embarrassed to walk into the water. My schoolmate Tsirlson pestered me too much, laughed, and pointed at me: "See what a little one he has . . . " Nothing annoyed me as much as such comments by this yellow thief. Always the same thing. Is he better off, this long idiot, the nasty boor, the pervert, the masturbator . . .

But outside of the talent for sticks, playing with pens, swimming in the river, and climbing on the roofs during city fires—I was graced with many other talents. Didn't you ever hear in Vitebsk about my boyish voice? I joined the cantor as a singer. On the High Holy Days, the whole synagogue crowd and myself clearly heard my hovering descant. I thought: I'll become a singer, a cantor. I'll go study in a conservatory.

A *klezmer* taught me to play the violin. I whittled something . . . and thought: I'll become a violinist. I'll enter a conservatory.

In Lyezne, in every house, my women relatives and neighbors invited my sister and me for a dance. I was graceful. Had a head of curly hair. And I thought: I'll become a dancer. I'll apply to . . . —I don't know where.

Day and night I wrote poetry. They praised it. I thought: I'll be a poet. I'll enter . . . I didn't know where to turn.

IV

The years moved on. I'll have to start imitating other people. To be like everybody else. One fine day, I saw before my eyes a tiny teacher [rebbe] from Mohilev. He leaped out of one of my paintings or escaped from a circus. You don't have to call him. He comes all by himself, like a matchmaker appearing in your house or a gravedigger for a corpse.

[I study with him] one term, two terms. How nimble he is. I look straight into his beard. I know already: an *Alef* א [A] with a *Kometz* ָ is א (O).[a] On top of the

---

[a]The proverbial mode of Jewish education: the first letter of the alphabet, the consonant A (א), is given a vowel-sign: a small kometz (ָ) under the letter: א, which makes it: "O" in Ashkenazi Hebrew. Indeed, it was the first syllable in *Heder* teaching, as the popular song announces: "*Kometz alef O*" ("A + Kometz = O").

Kometz I will fall asleep and on the *Alef* I will . . .[a] And just at that moment, the teacher fell asleep. It looks grotesque to me.

Quick as a wink I would walk to the *Heder.* And lantern in hand,[b] I would return home every evening. On Fridays he would take me to the bath, spread me on the bench, leaf through my body with a wet branch, as if he were leafing through the Talmud.

I had three such little teachers. The first one was the tiny flea from Mohilev. The second, Uri the Melamed[c] (a nothing; I remember nothing). The third one—an important personage, died young, Dyadkin the Melamed. He is the one who taught me the famous sermon I memorized and delivered at my Bar-Mitzva ceremony, standing on a stool—a sermon about tefillin. I admit I forgot the sermon (I felt it to be my duty) half an hour later, or half an hour earlier.

But it seems to me that my first, tiny demon, the little Mohilev teacher, influenced me more than all the others. How could it be otherwise? Instead of going to swim in the river every Sabbath, my mother insisted I go to him, to study a chapter.[d] But I know well: at that hour (Sabbath after *cholent*), the teacher sleeps soundly with his wife, the *Rebbetzin*[e]—in honor of the Sabbath—entirely naked. Wait till he puts on his pants. Knocking on the closed door, I woke up the landlord's dog, a mean old yellow bitch[f] with fangs. Without a sound, determined, he went down the stairs, straight to the boy, and . . .

I don't remember anything that happened to me next. I only know that I got up at the gate of the yard. My hand was bleeding. My legs too. The dog bit me hard.

"Don't undress me yet. Put ice right here."

"We have to take him to his mother as fast as possible."

The same day, city guards chased the dog, and only the twelfth bullet hit him under a porch. That day I rushed with my uncle to Petersburg to be healed. Doctors said /I would die on the fourth day.

---

[a]The child Chagall overlooks the signification and immediately sees the letters as shapes and forms: he can sleep on the upper surface of the T-shaped *Kometz* (ָ) and squat on top of the *Alef* as in an outhouse: א.

[b]Little boys would study all day and walk home in the dark, carrying a kerosene lantern.

[c]*Melamed* or rebbe is Hebrew and Yiddish for "teacher."

[d]In Yiddish, *Perek*, "a chapter," usually refers to *Pirkey oves* (*Pirkey avot*), the "Ethics of the Fathers," i.e., the child should be exposed to moral teaching and learn to honor his father and mother.

[e]The wife of the rebbe, teacher of the *Heder.* The children were small, studying at the rebbe's home, and she played an important, albeit secondary role in their education.

[f]Possible connotations: Yellow connotes a prostitute; a "yellow house" is a madhouse, like the color of the madhouse in St.-Petersburg.

דיאדקין דער מעלאמד

Dyadkin the teacher (pronounced "Dyatkin"). Yiddish inscription: "Dyatkin the melamed," the Torah teacher closest to Moyshe Shagall. The usual title for this image, "Talmud Teacher," is wrong: Chagall never studied the Aramaic Talmud and a melamed teaches no Talmud. The confusion derives from "Talmud Toyre," which means elementary school or teaching of the Hebrew Torah. His title: *MelaMD* is spelled half Hebrew (consonants only: *MLMD*) and half Yiddish (with all vowels: *melamed*). Chagall the gymnasium student steps on Dyadkin's shoulders and moves on. From *My Life*.

Swell! Every day I'm closer to death. They all tiptoe around me. I'm the hero. It turns out the dog was mad. (Are you happy, you found the secret!)//[a]

With every passing year, I felt that some mysterious will was leading me to strange thresholds. It started when my father growled over my thirteen-year-old body wrapped in a tallis: "Blessed is He who released me!"[b]

/What shall I do? Should I remain an innocent boy? At dawn, in the evening, always praying. And wherever I go, whatever I put in my mouth, whatever I hear (all sounds are like thunder), I have to make a blessing? Or should I run out of *shul*, throw away the prayerbook, the tallis, run through the streets to the river!

I was scared at the idea that I was already an adult//, and would have all the signs of an adult man, even a beard . . . And mother drags me to the Russian city school.[c] At first glance at the school from the outside, the idea occurred to me: "Here I shall probably have hearty stomach aches—and the teacher won't let me /out." In fact, I wanted a cockade very much.[d] If you wear a cockade and an officer walks by you, do you salute him? Officials, soldiers, policemen, gymnasium students—we are all like one family.//

But they didn't take Jews. Mother goes confidently to the teacher. Our savior, he's the only one who is on the take . . . Fifty Rubles isn't much. I enter straight into third grade, just because it is his class. I adorned myself with the cockade and with great courage began to look into the open windows of the women's Gymnasium. My body stood on its hind legs. Wearing a black class uniform, I probably became a few pounds sillier. First of all, I immediately started stammering (a strike) and though I didn't memorize, instinctively I knew the lessons. But atrociously I refused to answer them. It was quite funny and tragic too. Devil take the "2's."[e] But the sea of heads on all the school benches mortally upset me. I was shaken out of my skin. And moving up to the blackboard I got black as soot, as some put it, and red—according to others. And—stop! Often I even smiled, but that was the ecstasy of my dumbness. Naturally, the prompting by the students in the first row was superfluous. /I knew the lesson. But I stammered. I imagined a dog, a bitch as yellow as the proverb,[f] covered with blood.

[a]"Mad," in Yiddish: *meshuge*, "crazy." Chagall claimed "craziness" as the source of his artistic originality. Here is an additional source: he was bitten by a mad dog in childhood.

[b]"Blessed be God who released me" (from having to feed a child). At thirteen, a boy is bar mitzvah, an independent man, off his father's shoulders.

[c]It was a four-year city high school. According to the school records, Chagall studied there for five years (1900–1905), but his name does not appear among those of the graduating students.

[d]A cockade, worn on a uniform hat; he must mean the hat itself, as depicted in many of Chagall's paintings, e.g., "I and the Village."

[e]A 2 in the Russian system was a failing grade.

[f]A realization of the proverbial "yellow dog," an allusion to the incident when he passed out after being bitten by a rabid dog.

Marc Chagall with his school uniform hat, 1907. "If I wear a hat with a cockade, does it mean I get to salute all policemen and officers?" (*My Own World.*)

And maybe she barked over my prone body. My mouth was covered with dust and my teeth barely white . . .

What do I need the lessons for? I don't mind tearing out a hundred, two hundred, three hundred, four hundred pages of my books. Scatter them to the wind, to the expanses of air. Let them whisper by themselves in the air, in Russian,[a] about countries and seas. But let me alone. I want to be wild. Cover myself with greenery, rustle, and cry.

But on the one hand, my stammer at that time;// on the other hand, the heads of the third grade—my youth. I don't know what brought me to this reactionary mood[b], stubborn and closed in myself.

"Well, Chagall, today you'll answer the lesson?"

I am silent, or I start: "Ta-Ta-Ta-Ta-Tartar occupation . . . "

I imagined they would throw me out of the fourth floor. My life in uniform trembled like a leaf in early autumn. Naturally, except for going back to my place, nothing happened. But from the distance, I saw the teacher's hand clearly draw a "2." That I still saw. Through the classroom window I could see trees and the building of the women's Gymnasium. "Permit me to go out, Nikolay Antonovich, I badly need . . . "

I forgot how they call the days before the High Holy Days when crowds of Jews and lonely figures walk to the cemeteries.[c] In some two hours Pauline appeared, like a naked body in the street among clothed people. I used to go there by myself with my books. Came, sat down, groped along the fence. "Are you sad?" Only you and I know how easy it is to stray, recognize names you know, walk in, wander into the [dead] rabbis' huts, sort out little notes.[d] Who asked for what favor. They would be piled up like a dungheap.

An autumn wind.

Only on a day when no one was called on, and the students were in a good mood, we didn't know what to do with ourselves. Not we, I—usually sitting on the bench, shot at from all sides with fillips—I already knew what to do with myself.

/I looked for crumbs of bread in my pockets. I move, I fidget, I get up, I sit back down. And suddenly, I move my head and hand out the window to blow a kiss to the delicate, distant figure.

The inspector is coming. He catches my arm and squeezes. Caught, I am red,

[a]An indication of the child's alienation from the language of instruction, Russian, and the reason for his stammer when he was called to the blackboard.

[b]A Soviet label for non-cooperation or individualism.

[c]Days of Awe. "I forgot" is, of course, a mannerism, to distance the writer from his long-forgotten religious past.

[d]Notes that people stick in the tombs or tomb-huts of the righteous dead, especially on the Days of Awe, to ask the dead to intercede for them in The Other World.

I am pink, pale. "Remind me, bastard, to give you a '2' for Conduct tomorrow!" . . .

Then I steeped myself in my painting. I didn't know what it was.// Spitballs flew over our heads, pieces of paper, often hitting the teacher. And my benchmate, Skorikov, devoted himself to his beloved entertainment: knocking under the bench. His knocking was half-loud and joyful. At moments, he roused the attention of the whole class. They grow silent. They laugh. "Skorikov!"

The teacher calls on Skorikov, who turns red, and catching a "2," sits back down.

But more than anything I loved geometry. In this, no one could get the better of me. Lines, angles, triangles, and squares enchanted me and beckoned to some hopeful distances. And in drawing classes there were not enough thrones for me. Here I was the center of the class's attention, the model. I would come alive until the next lesson. Finally, when I played enough with sticks before the exams and trained with heavy weights[a]—I stayed behind in the same class for another year. What that meant for me, I don't remember clearly. What is the rush? If I am to be a store clerk or an accountant, it's not too late. Let time flow. Let it stretch. I would sit through the nights and hold my hands in my pockets as if I'm studying, and hear my mother from the bedroom:

"Enough burning kerosene, go to sleep. I told you: do your lessons in the daytime, madman."

On the other hand, in the fifth grade,[b] the following happened to me: in a drawing class, one of the diligent students of the front benches who very often tapped my head, suddenly opened a drawing on tracing paper (a copy from the *Niva*).[c]

And . . . chaos. Let me! I don't remember, but the drawing and the fact that it was made by this tapper and not by me immediately kindled a fire in me. A jackal awoke in me. I went to the library, took out the thick volume of *Niva*, and began copying it—Rubenstein's portrait[d]—for his stern look and wrinkled face.

---

[a]To develop muscles like his father.

[b]Since Chagall went to school at the age of thirteen and entered the third grade, then stayed twice in the same class, this would indicate that he was fifteen or sixteen years old when he discovered art. Yet in his essay on Bakst, he mentions that he was thirteen when he first came to Pen's art school—which would be closer to his self-image as a child.

[c]A literary and cultural "thick" journal.

[d]Apparently Anton Rubenstein (1829–1894), world-famous virtuoso pianist and composer, born in the Pale of Settlement and converted to Christianity in his childhood. Rubenstein was admired by Jews as one who made it in the general world. The choice of Rubenstein could hardly have been an accident, a name simply encountered in any issue of a high cultural Russian journal.

Oh, this is not a Greek woman, or the like,[a]—it is something of my own, invented. I hung it all in our bedroom.

I knew all the [Russian] curses of the street[b]—and some respectable and modest words as well. But such a fantastic, bookish word, such an unreal word: *khu-dózh-nik* ["artist" in Russian]—I never heard. That is, I did hear it, but in our city it was never used. How would we rise to that? By my innate—I don't know what[c]—I would never allow myself to pronounce such a word even in my thoughts. If not for my schoolmate who, after several visits in our room, seeing my paintings hung on the wall, blurted out:

"Hey, listen, you are a real *khudozhnik*!"

"What does it mean, *khudozhnik*? Who *khudozhnik*? Could I really be sss . . . uch?"

He left and didn't answer. And I remembered that somewhere in the city of Vitebsk I had really seen a big sign, as on store fronts, that said:

"School of Painting and Drawing of the *Khudozhnik* Pen."

And I thought: My destiny is set. I just have to go there and finish that school, and I'll be a *khudozhnik*. And I shall forever part from mother's dreams about a future of a store clerk, an accountant, or, at best, a photographer with furniture.[d]

V[e]

One fine day (there are no others!), when my mama put the bread in the oven, I stole up to the shovel and to her, grabbed her flour-covered elbow, and blurted out:

"Mama, I want to be an artist!

That's it!

I don't want to be a store manager, or an accountant.

I want to be an artist!"

My heart whispered to me that it wouldn't go very smoothly, so I continued

[a]A typical inversion of times in the autobiography: At the time of writing, in retrospect, he evokes the Greek plaster figures that served as models in Pen's art school and in the art school in St.-Petersburg, which Chagall attended at a later time.

[b]Yiddish had no pornographic curses of its own and borrowed them from Russian; thus, he knew some Russian.

[c]Modesty; Chagall saw himself as a shy person.

[d]Mother placed Moshka as an apprentice with a photographer in Vitebsk to do the retouching, a profession he later practiced in St.-Petersburg for a while.

[e]Chapter V was published in version A, i.e., in Perets Markish's original translation, unedited by Chagall, in the Yiddish avant-garde journal *Khalyastre*, No. 2, Paris, 1924, edited by Markish.

"Mother and Son." Mother takes him to the art teacher Pen or to the Russian school. From *My Life*.

arguing with my mother: "See, mother, tell me yourself: am I a *mench*? Am I good for anything?

I beg you: save me, come with me, come! Come! There is a place in the city, if I could get in there, study and finish it—I'll be an accomplished artist. And I'll be happy!"

"What? An artist? Are you, God forbid, out of your mind? Please, my child, let me put the bread in the oven and—don't disturb me. For my bread sits in the oven!"

"Mama, I don't want to. Come with me!"

"Get lost!"

In the end, I got what I wanted. My mother and I are going to Pen.[a] If he says I have talent, it will be worth making a big fuss; if not—I shall be an artist anyway, I thought, but on my own.

You can easily imagine that my destiny lay in the hands of the artist Pen—at least, that's how it seemed to my mother, which means: to the ruler of our house. For my father didn't give me the five-piece for monthly tuition, but rather rolled it over the whole herring-yard, so I had to chase it until I caught it. But now we're going.

I rolled all my drawings up in a scroll, trembling with great joy,[b] and with my mama, went to the atelier in Pen's school.

As soon as we got to the stairs, I was struck by the intoxicating smell of paint and paintings. Portraits on all sides: Mrs. Province Governor and the Governor himself; Madame Levinson and himself; Baron Karpf and the Baroness; and what do you know—who can list them all? Certainly not me. And at the same time, I felt that somehow this was not the place—it was somehow not my way—though which way was mine, I didn't know, but at that moment, I felt strongly that something here was irrelevant to me.[c]

Meanwhile, everything surprised me: the pictures, the vivid impact, the smell. Climbing the stairs, I touched furtively, groped here a nose, there a cheek.[d]

The Maestro was not home at the moment.

There is no way I can convey something of my mama's attitude in the artist's atelier. Her eyes wandered over all the corners, climbed up the canvases, and, after considerable amazement, she suddenly turns to me and says, almost begging, with so much love and adult understanding: "Well, my child, see for yourself—you will never be able to make it like this. Come home."

"Mama, wait!" Deep in my heart, I too was convinced that I would never be able to do it like this. So what. One shouldn't even do it like this!

Different! But how?

I don't know.

And we're waiting for *him*. Now he has to decide our destiny.

[a]Yury Moyseevich Pen (1854–1937), artist and director of his own Art School in Vitebsk; Chagall's first art teacher (see Chapter 3).

[b]The manuscript A is clear: *freyd* ("joy"), though spelled as pronounced: *freyt*; but B misread it as *pakhad*, "fear." Chagall usually overcorrects his dialect and spells: *froyd* פֿרױד, which in writing looks similar to *pakhad* פֿחד, fear.

[c]Chagall admired Pen and was grateful to him all his life, yet Pen's meticulously descriptive style of painting was alien to him. Here, Chagall projects his subsequent revolt against the naturalist and academic style onto his first encounter with it.

[d]Of the plaster figures.

God Almighty! What will happen if, by my luck, he is not in his right mind. And he'll interrupt my mother: "Nonsense!"

My heart pounds: "Everything is possible. Be prepared. If not with mama, then without mama."

There is nobody in the atelier. But in the other room, one of Pen's students bustles about. We walk in. He hardly notices us.

"Good day!"

"Good day, if you please."

He sits astride a chair and makes a sketch. I liked it.

My mother addresses a question to him: "Tell me, I beg your pardon, can you somehow make a living with this 'painting' thing, Hah?"

"Ach, what! Miserable: neither a store nor merchandise."

Naturally you couldn't expect a more precise and vulgar answer. In any case, this was more than enough to convince my mother that she was right—and to pour some drops of gloom in the stammering boy, me.

But here comes the *cher Maître*—short with a prickly little beard—Pen! He will surely finish what his pupil began. He will shut the case for good. He walks in. Mechanically says Hallo (how can he as much as glance at a dweller-in-the-dust, I thought, while he is used to the rich and provincial governors!) and blurts out: "What did they want?"

"Here he is. I don't know myself. He's taken it into his head to become a *khu-dozhnik*.[a] Do I know?—Surely a madness. Take a look, that's what he's done. If it's worth anything, let him study; if not . . . Let's go home!"

Pen didn't even blink. Murderer, I think to myself, blink!

Mechanically, as out of habit, he takes my copies from the *Niva* and mumbles something like "yes—there is talent" . . .

Ach, may the devil take you . . . —I said to myself.

Naturally, mama hardly understood anything.

But for me it was enough.

Somehow, I scraped out a five-piece from my father every month, and for a month-and-a-half[b] I studied in Pen's school—in Vitebsk.

What I actually did there—I don't know.

In front of me hung a piece of plaster. I was told to paint it, like everyone else. I sat down diligently, pressed the pencil to my eyes and—measured and measured.

---

[a]Chagall's mother speaks to Pen in Yiddish but uses a technical term in Russian.

[b]"Some one-and-a-half months," an expression meaning: some negligible period of time, counted in months not in years, but not necessarily the precise number. If it were literal how would father pay "every month"? And just two pages later, he writes: " . . . ever after I studied in his school for free, for such a long time, until I really sensed that 'it is neither a store nor merchandise.'" It is clear that Chagall's connection with Pen did last for years, not months.

But somehow, everything was off, not precise. Voltaire's nose pulls me off the mark, draws me ever lower—

So Pen himself walks up to me.

At Blokh's they sold paints. I had my own: a small cupboard, little bottles lay in it like children's corpses. There was no money.

For sketches I went out of town. The farther away from the city—the more scary to paint. Fearing that if I went beyond the Sabbath boundary,[a] near the soldiers' barracks, my paints themselves would turn blue, and the painting would turn sour.

Where are the sketches that used to hang at the oven, on thick canvases? It turns out that as soon as there were thick canvases, they were put on the floor instead of a carpet.

It is even prettier. For you have to wipe off your shoes when the floor was washed. The children [his siblings] found that that was why paintings were painted on thick canvases.

And I almost choked to death with that discovery.

And at Pen's, on the side, I painted with violet colors. "What is this? Where did it come from?" This was such a daring move on my part that ever after I studied in his school for free, for such a long time until I really sensed that "it is neither a store nor merchandise," as Pen's pupil said at the beginning.

The environs of Vitebsk and Pen. The soil with the remnants of my family and relatives, who are so close and dear to me now.

I love Pen. I often felt like begging him at the door, on the threshold of his vestibule: "I don't need to be famous—to be a poor, quiet worker in our own city, just like you. Just like your paintings hanging on the walls, I would hang myself in the street, near you, at your place. Let me!"

VI

On the banks of the river I walked around with girls. And in the lumberyards, on rooftops and attics, I hung around with boys. One of them walks by our fence gate. We sit. A neighbor woman raises a fuss and curses. I hide behind the gate, stick out my head and say: "Yosl, tomorrow is the exam." So I stay at his home overnight and observe his curly head. We shall prepare the lessons together.

Fokin[b] with his toys, Yakhnin with his earrings, Matzenko with his locomotive. All of them excited me. Turned everything upside down inside me. Such is my nature.

---

[a]The limit a religious Jew may walk in a city on a Sabbath, marked by a wire (*eruv*), i.e., within the city boundaries.

[b]Or "Pokin." However, B and C read: "Paykin."

Once a pupil of Pen's came over to my house. He was the son of a city merchant.[a] A classmate in my school, until he left to change this proletarian school
for a more bourgeois one, a Mercantile School. Because of some special "achievements" of his,[b] he was asked to leave there. Black-haired, pale, he somehow kept
his distance from me, like his whole family. Meeting me on the bridge, his face
would turn red and he would walk up to me determinedly with a question about
the sky or the clouds, and a proposal to prepare the lessons together.

/"Wouldn't you assume, Marc, that the cloud over there—far away, near the
river, is too blue? When it is reflected in the river, it turns into violet colors.
You, like me, value the violet color. Don't you?"//[c]

I would curb the emotions that gathered inside me all the time of my shlemiel
studies in school, where this aristocrat would observe me like a wooden antique.
I must confess that this youth was endowed with a charming exterior. Often I
didn't know to whom or to what to compare his head.

Forgetting how rich and abundant his life was, it was with him that I spent my
childhood years in a special way.

"OK, I said, in a few months I'll be your teacher. But I don't want any tuition
from you—instead, let us be friends."

I stopped staying at my parents' home and spent more and more time at Viktor's summer home ["Datcha"], where we would roam the fields and lose ourselves. Why do I write about this? Because only the big-city attitude[d] of my
friends gave them the courage to think I was worth more than just Moska
/Moshka// from Pokrovska Street. As a person who already was in the great
world outside the city of Vitebsk, Viktor let me know he was preparing to go to
Petersburg to continue his art studies.

"So, listen, shall we go together?" What else could I do? I, the son of a store
clerk, and not the son of a Merchant of the First Guild.[e] I had been apprenticed
to the city photographer, so I started sitting at the retouching table and lost my
gaze in the hole of the camera. The boss, the photographer, promised me a
splendid future if I didn't cheat, and—if I agreed to work for a year without pay.

[a]Viktor Mekler.

[b]Perhaps revolutionary activities.

[c]That may be inspired by the admired Russian proto-Symbolist painter Vrubel (see
Chagall's dream about Vrubel and note on p. 134). Pen praised Chagall for his original
violet color, yet the influence came apparently from Viktor, who was more knowledgeable
and traveled to St.-Petersburg. Chagall's quick intuition adopted this new move.

[d]"Big-city attitude" meant unprejudiced, generous, rational; as opposed to small-town,
shtetl mentality, primitive and narrow-minded.

[e]Jewish Merchants of the First Guild had the right to live outside the Pale of Settlement,
or send their representative for several months to the capital. Hence Mekler was free to live
in St.-Petersburg and apparently helped Marc to get there.

"Art is a very important thing, but it won't go away. And on the other hand, what is art?—See how I live."

Suddenly something erupted. I grabbed the only twenty Rubles my father ever gave me to study and travel—and went with my friend to St.-Petersburg. With determination.

With how many tears and with what dignity did I collect the paper Rubles father threw on the table for me (I forgive him, that's how it's given here). He had the highest intentions, and the Rubles flew over the other side of the table. I bent down and collected them. To my father's questions of what, actually, it was and why I was going, I answered that I was going to study in a *khu-dó-zhest-ven-no-e* [art] school. I don't remember my father's answer or the expression on his face. As usual, he got up right away to set the samovar, warning me on the way that, in general, he had no money, and there was nothing to send me. Don't hope for any. Now I remember that there was not a day or an hour when I didn't tell myself: "I am still a child."

No. I shuddered. How will I start and how will I begin to support myself, if I am good for nothing except painting. I couldn't even be a clerk like my father. You need tremendous strength to lift an eighty-kilo barrel. But I was happy that it was my destiny to be a painter. It is an excellent excuse for me not to have to make a living.

Well, of course, by becoming an artist,—I thought to myself,—I am a full-fledged adult.

Somehow I scraped up a merchant's "Patent" for the "Right of Residence" in Petersburg, and in 1907 I left for a new life in that city.

VII

Nevertheless, while playing with sticks or walking over the roofs during city fires, swimming, or painting, nothing prevented me from ruthlessly pursuing girls on the river banks at the same time. Some unbearable fever gripped me when I saw the Gymnasium girls, their panties and their braids. I must confess to you that, according to some persons and the probable confirmation of the mirrors, my fourteen- or fifteen-year-old youthfulness was a blend of Passover wine and pale matzo meal with dry, pink leaves found in books. Now you can understand how I carried around my own self. My family would often see me standing before the mirror. But in truth I looked at the mirror thinking of how hard it would be to paint my self-portrait. (Found a way out.)

On the other hand, why not? Some of it was my self-love. I confess that I was not averse to starching my cheeks a bit and reddening my lips, though even so they didn't need any paint. And yes, yes. I wanted to please those . . . on the banks of the river.

I did have success. But of all the successes, I couldn't get anything useful for myself. Here I am with her, in Lyezne. A stroll is not forbidden. I feel something and tremble, or vice versa. We are under the bridge, or under the roof of an old stable. On a bench. At night. Alone. Only a pig stopped naïvely in the middle of the market place, enchanted by the moon. At a distance, you see a carter driving to the railroad station. And no one else. You can do what you want. And what do I want? I kiss. (I kiss today, I kiss the next day,[a] everything has a limit.) Soon dawn will break. I am dissatisfied.

Thus we walk into her parents' Sabbath home, the air is stuffy. All the children are asleep. Tomorrow is the Sabbath. And when they see me in the morning, they'll all be glad: a fitting bridegroom . . . Congratulations will fly to her and me.

To stay? What kind of night is it? Hot.

Where are you?

I am an ignoramus in questions of diligent romantics. I strolled around and circled around with Anyuta for four years—only to answer her at the end of the fourth year with the same—a stubborn kiss. A kiss at the gate, at the entrance of the fence. At night. Just at the time when acne covered her face. How many golden mountains and castles did this wicked Gymnasium student build to catch me in her net. How many intimate, familiar rendezvous, especially staged by her and her girlfriends. I don't know what went on with me, where did my daring disappear.

I was a totally worthless man. And she felt that things could have been altogether different if I had been a bit more fresh. No, no. I was scared to death of her bursting corset /which she wore on purpose//. I understood nothing, but I did understand that I was wasting time. In vain did she accompany me to my sketching outside the city, on Yuryev Hill. Neither the forest calm, nor the valleys, nor the empty spaces sufficiently stirred my masculine energy to overcome my fear. And yet . . . Once I was sitting like this on the river bank with Anyuta at the very end of the city, near the old, stone-built bath, late in the evening. The river below was melting. I hear it whispering—"Dare!" I thought to myself.

Sitting like that, my cap somehow wandered off to her head. I bend over to her shoulders. And suddenly someone is walking. A gang is moving on us, on me, and I beg her for my hat.

But then, beyond the bridge, on a barrel, I got friendly with another girl. A square face, snub nose, and half-squinting eyes. Again two or three years lost. She used to swing disgustingly. I cannot watch a girl fall.

When I saw her, I suffered the pains of a pregnant woman. Various drives

---

[a]Yiddish idiomatic pattern: "[do something] today, [do it] tomorrow"—meaning, to no avail, nothing will come out of it.

"Before the Gate." From *My Life*.

plowed me up, and she wanted nothing less than eternal love—otherwise she wouldn't budge.

I wanted to go to another room at once and mess her up, but her soft little hands and her short little legs provoked my pity. Wasn't she starved for eternal love? And this was not my profession. But when I left her, I sent Polya a farewell poem with this comment:

"On the Bridge," an illustration for the second volume of Bella Chagall's memoirs, *The First Encounter* (in Yiddish; New York, 1947). Moyshe Shagal is courting Berta Rosenfeld on the bridge between the rich and poor sides of Vitebsk. No trace of Jewish religious behavior: The boy takes off his hat for the girl.

"I was not yet created just for eternal love."

/Does it make sense to torment you and myself with my childish loves? For every year, the evenings died out in vain. And the barely awakened love dissolved behind the fences. In the orchard, in the garden, on the benches, the kisses have melted long ago. Rains chased us out. And no one recalls your names. I shall walk through your streets. And the bitterness of unfulfilled encounters I shall transfer to my canvases. Let the mists of our days glimmer and turn pale. And a stranger will look and laugh . . . //

I moved into a new house.//[a]

Every year a series of lost opportunities crystallizes in my memory. I ache and regret. But on my third romance, I lost my timidity. I kissed left and right. I wasn't shy.

Then I was immediately shown the unique limits of my daring.

Weighing in the memory all my love events, I regret to say that I want to mention them. For, except for my last encounter [with Bella], I combined in my imagination the same dreams that took me nowhere, for I was a terrible coward. They wearied me and teased me, and I chase away those stubborn memories. It all went on as if by inertia. I became a kind of skirt-chaser. This self-esteem was reflected in my works: "Birth,"/"The Barber,"// "On the Floor," and other early paintings of 1909.

"The Bridge and the Boat," an illustration for the second volume of Bella Chagall's memoirs, *The First Encounter*. A simpler version was published in the book. The river is overflowing, people cross by boat, but the lovers fly over on the wings of love.

[a]Probably refers to his moving to a room in the parents' courtyard, where Berta visited him.

VIII [In St.-Petersburg]

Many rooms, corners too [for rent]. Many green notes and much humidity. I moved in with a budding sculptor, whom Sholem-Aleichem had called a future Antokolsky. (He would sooner become a doctor.) He neighed like a young animal and sprayed [water] so the clay wouldn't dry out.

What am I doing here? I am just a human being—and I cannot wake up at 1 in the morning because he neighed again. Once I threw the lamp at him and told him:

"Go to Sholem-Aleichem . . . I'll stay alone."

When I arrived with my friend in Petrograd [sic],[a] we went to take an exam in Baron Stieglitz's *Gewerbschule*, Graphic Arts School. Solyanka.[b]

Well, here is where you can get the Right of Residence and a stipend. But I was scared of their occupations and the painting of long ornaments, that seemed to me like whole magazines.

Those ornaments are especially intended to scare you, so you wouldn't know where to begin, maybe especially for Jews, so that they wouldn't get residence permits. Those premonitions didn't let me down. I failed the exam. I was left with no rights and no stipend.

Nothing doing. I had to get admitted to a more accessible school of the Society for the Encouragement of Fine Arts, where I was immediately admitted to the third year. What I did there, I couldn't tell you. Plaster heads of Roman and Greek citizens spun before my eyes, and I, a poor provincial, had to dig and look deep into the unfortunate nostrils of Alexander the Great or some other plaster idiot. Sometimes I walk up to a nostril and flip it with my finger. And from a distant corner of the class I send a long gaze to the breasts of the dusty Venus.

They even praised my inventions, but that could have been an endless tale. I couldn't look at those carter-boy[c] students without some special feeling, as they worked with rubber and sweat as with shovels, on paper.

Actually they were pretty nice guys. My Semitic countenance roused their curiosity. I was advised to take all my sketches (not even one survived) to a competition. When I was one of the four who received a fellowship, I sensed that the past would not return. For a year, I got ten Rubles a month. I was rich and almost every day ate my supper entrée in a public kitchen on Zhikovskaya St., and afterward fainted once or twice a month, and always in the small toilet.

---

[a] When Chagall got to the city, it was called St.-Petersburg. Yet at the time he wrote the memoirs, the city was called Petrograd. Clearly, he writes in retrospect, from the position he is at the time of writing.

[b] Solyanka is an intimate or dismissive nickname for Solyany Pereulok ("Salt Alley"), where Stieglitz's Art School stood.

[c] Proverbially coarse, uneducated.

My situation was saved by the sculptor Ginzburg,[a] a tiny, skinny little Jew, but an excellent person. I recall him with much gratitude. His atelier in the Art Academy, packed with relics of his teacher Antokolsky and his own little statues of all the famous figures of his time, seemed to me to be the center where the chosen one lived, one who had had a hard road. Indeed, this little character kept in touch with Count Lev Tolstoy, Stasov, Gorky, Repin, and Shalyapin.

His popularity in the center. And I—a nothing, with no Right of Residence, and an income of twenty Rubles a month. I don't know whether the sculptor Ginzburg saw, or could have seen any artistic merit in my early work. In any case, as he did with everybody, he sent me off with a letter to Baron Ginzburg.[b] The Baron, seeing that such a personage existed, and that there was, in his view, a chance for "a future Antokolsky" (how many destroyed dreams!), also gave me a stipend of ten Rubles a month, for a few months . . . and you have to live. This learned Baron, Stasov's friend,[c] apparently understood very little about art. Yet he felt it was his duty, just in case, and very amiably, to make conversation with me and by the way to tell me a parable with a moral, warning how careful an artist must be.

"For example, Antokolsky's wife was not a good woman," he said. "She wouldn't let a poor person cross her threshold . . . Watch out, be careful . . . A wife in the life of an artist can be very meaningful . . . " Very politely, I thought of something else.

At this time, I was barely eating and was working in the School for the Encouragement of Fine Arts, I was introduced to a whole group of art benefactors, in all their parlors I felt as if I had just come from a bath, after being whipped with branches, red, pink . . .

Oh, Right of Residence. Now I am the indentured servant of a sworn attorney and must live with him (a dear man).[d]

---

[a]Ilya Yakovlevich Ginzburg (also Guenzburg, 1860 [?]–1939), Russian sculptor. (No relation to Baron Guenzburg.) He was born in Vilna and came to St.-Petersburg at age eleven with his teacher Mark Antokolsky; there he became a sculptor, sculpting heads of prominent people. In 1908, he published his memoirs, *Iz moyey zhizni* (*From My Life*), which Chagall must have known. Surely, Ginzburg must have seen a great deal of affinity between his own background and Chagall's.

[b]Baron David Ginzburg (also Guenzburg, 1857–1910) headed the Jewish community in St.-Petersburg and the Society for the Promotion of Culture Among the Jews of Russia. A prolific scholar of Jewish and Oriental studies, he assembled one of the most important private collections of books and manuscripts in Judaica in the world.

[c]Vladimir Vasilyevich Stasov (1824–1906), prominent Russian literary and art critic. Baron David Guenzburg and Stasov published together a book on ancient Jewish ornaments, *L'ornement Hébreu* (1903).

[d]Chagall's patron Attorney Goldberg, a privileged Jew, in whose house Chagall lived formally as a servant, to have Right of Residence permit in St.-Petersburg.

Then, for unforeseen reasons, I moved to the editorial offices of a journal,[a] next to the apartment of the [Duma] Deputy Vinaver.[b] But until I met them [the Jewish benefactors], I had no idea where to stay. My material situation didn't give me much freedom and I was forced to rent a "corner" with workers and women traders in the same room. All I could do was lie on my cot and think about myself. What else? And dreams surrounded me:

An empty, rectangular room. One bed in the corner. I on top of it. Dark. Suddenly, the ceiling bursts and a wingèd creature descends with a white commotion, flooding the room with movement and clouds. A rustle of fluttering wings. I thought—an angel. I cannot open my eyes—light, bright. Smelling all around the room, it roams high up through the ceiling and sucks out all the light and the blue air. Dark again. Then I woke up.

My painting "Apparition" recalls that dream.

Another time. I rent half a room, somewhere on Panteleymonova Street. But at night I cannot understand why there is such a turmoil in the other half-room, separated by a sheet. Why are they breathing so heavily . . . It keeps me awake. And once, when the drunkard—a harmonica player in the parks at night and a typesetter in the daytime—who owned the other half of the room came home at night to his wife, and full of acid, "demanded" his wife—She didn't agree to his demands and came into my part of the room. And from the room into the corridor, in her sheer nightie.

And he—after her with a knife: "How did she dare refuse her lawful husband?"

Then I understood that it wasn't just Jews who had no Right of Residence in Russia—many Russians had no rights either and lived like lice in a head, My God!

I moved to another room. My neighbor was a Persian, of dubious pedigree, a refugee from his country, or a revolutionary, or someone close to the retired Shah. Hard to know. He loved me like a bird, thinking of his Persia and some secret dealings.

Later on, in Paris, I heard that he put a bullet through his head on one of the prettiest boulevards.

At the time, the torments of the "kind" of Residence Rights,[c] on the one hand, and the call to army service,[d] on the other, renewed their claims on me. One nice day, when I returned to Petrograd after a vacation in Vitebsk, with no documents, the Liteyny District police captain himself scolded me, and the passport officer,

[a]The editorial offices of *Voskhod* (*Dawn* or *Orient*), a Russian journal of Jewish Enlightenment. The journal ceased publication in 1906; thus, Chagall could stay and work in the office. It was in the same house as the editor Vinaver's apartment.

[b]Maksim Vinaver (1862–1926), influential lawyer and politician and Chagall's mentor; the last editor of *Voskhod*, (see Chapter 3, p. 193).

[c]His inferior status as a Jew.

[d]He was due for the draft at age twenty-one, i.e., in July 1908.

"The Apparition," 1924–1925, is based on a similar painting of 1917–1918. The composition and the folds of the angel's wings are reminiscent of Mikhail Vrubel's painting "Princess Swan," 1900.

who got nothing "in hand" from me on time (I didn't realize), blessed me with "Yid," and ordered: "Hey, who is it? He came willfully by himself to the [Tsar's] Residence and without a Right of Residence—arrest him, put him in the can with the thieves and put him in jail with the others."

That's what they did.

Thank God. I calmed down. Here, surely, I have a right of residence and can be free and sated, live a little and paint a little. I would like to say that nowhere before the prison, where they undressed me and gave me new clothes, did I feel so good and free. The language of the thieves and prostitutes was impressive. They did not touch or curse me, on the contrary: they even respected me. Afterward, I was transferred to a separate room with a fantastic old man. I often liked to indulge in the latrine, reading the graffiti, or to sit at the long kitchen table with a bowl of water . . . And here, in the cell for two, where the electricity was shut off at nine p.m., and I couldn't paint or read—here I slept my fill. Dreams crowded my head. Here is one:

We, the children of one father,[a] live somewhere at the seashore. Except for me, all are locked up in a cage for animals—a high and wide cage. The father, an orang-utang, black as tar, stands with a whip at the cage and neither threatens nor scolds us children . . . Suddenly we all felt like bathing. So did our older brother Vrubel, the Russian artist, who became one of my many brothers.

Mikhail Vrubel (1856–1910) was considered the great precursor of Russian modern painting. His "Demon Downcast" inspired the Symbolists, who saw his work as a response to academic Realism. His use of blue, violet, and purple colors, and his insanity, would appeal to Chagall. The "mad genius" had the greatest influence on Bakst's illustrations. In a prominent place in the round workshop of Bakst's school stood an enormous easel, covered in brown velvet—it was Vrubel's. It is amazing how this Jewish boy from an illiterate home in the Pale of Settlement aspires to become the heir to Russia's most revered artist.

Vrubel was the first one allowed out to bathe. I recall, I see: he undressed, our beloved brother. And in the distance I see his golden legs, spreading like scissors. He swam far away. The sea is seething, roaring, such white, roiling waves, camels running, water like tar, a honeycomb, flowers of honey, thick, slowly, noisily flowing.

[a]This cosmopolitan slogan was used against the anti-Semites, including Jews and Gentiles in one humankind, thus legitimizing Chagall as an heir to the throne of Russian art.

Where is my poor brother? We are all worried. In the distance, we see just his head. His legs do not shine like scissors anymore, and finally the head is also lost from sight. An arm popped out—and no more.

All the children wailed: "Our older brother Vrubel drowned."

The father's bass voice joined in: "Our son Vrubel drowned. Only one son, an artist, remained with us—you, my son."

That means me . . .

What kind of dream is it?—I woke up.

IX

But no matter how much I studied in the School for the Encouragement of the Fine Arts, I couldn't sense where the limit of my discontent actually was. Or why, no matter how much I painted, I was left with nothing but a sediment of bitter-ness? And between us, all I heard now was praise. I felt that it could drag on like this endlessly, but it made no sense. Sometimes the long-legged overseer of the nature class cursed me in public . . .[a]

The problem was that painting from . . . hollow models and then drawing in their heels and muscles in a cold classroom—brought me into a strange, tran-scendent state of mind.

Russian peasants sat there for several years. I didn't know what to do or how to do it: should I press the paper with the charcoal and my finger, or follow with my ears along with them.

The overseer considered my painting as some senseless daubing. And when I heard such criticism as for example: "What kind of behind do you have?[b] And a scholarship boy at that . . . "—I left for good.

A famous school in Petrograd was Bakst's school.[c] It was the only school, far from the academy and from "encouragement of art," that smelled of Europe.

But the thirty-Ruble tuition each month scared me. Where could I get it?

I took courage, as well as all my works from school and a few from home—and went to Bakst's apartment on Sergeyevskaya Street.

**[d] "The master is still asleep," answered Lev Bakst's secretive maid. One o'clock—and still asleep. Quiet. No noise of children, no scent of a wife.

Walls. Reproductions of Greek gods. A Curtain of a synagogue Holy Ark.

---

[a]In reversed language, i.e., praised him public.

[b]This is rather ambiguous: does it refer to the painted behind, or to Chagall's own? The published *My Life* turned it into an innocuous painted "knee."

[c]Actually, the school of Zvantseva, directed by Léon Bakst.

[d]The text between these double asterisks and triple asterisks (several pages later), was published in an expanded and changed version as an essay, "My Teachers: Bakst" (see in Chapter 3, p. 185).

Strange.

His apartment enchanted me. I had never been so feverish as when waiting for him. I shall never forget—whether it was just a smile or a smile of pity he welcomed me with . . .

"How can I serve you?" On Bakst's lips, the individual sounds drawled out unusually. And this unusual accent gave him a non-Russian character.[a]

His fame at the Russian Season[b] abroad turned my head.

"Show me your work," he mumbled.

I . . . Well. No point refusing. Or being ashamed.

I felt quite unlike that first time, when my thirteen-year-old's short pants hung on my body,[c] and I came to Pen in Vitebsk with mama's question: Am I talented, and if not, I must become a clerk, as mama thinks.

As little as I was worried during that first visit, which was so meaningful to my mother, this second visit with Bakst had a decisive significance for me, and his answer, however it went, seemed to decide my destiny.

I wished only that there should be no mistake.

Will he recognize a talent in me, or not?

As he went over my works, which he lifted from the floor, he tapped out words in his aristocratic accent: "*Da-a—Da-a-a* [Yes], there is talent. But you are spo-o-oiled, you are going in a *wrong direction*, you are damaged." Enough.

My God, my God, that is me. The scholarship boy of the School for the Encouragement of the Arts, the one on whom the director Roerich lavished his (somewhat mechanical) smiles, flashing his white teeth, the one whose "manner" (may it be cursed) was praised over there, but also the one who really did not know when this endless, unsatisfying daubing would finally come to an end . . .

And only after Bakst's voice, came his words, qualifying: "Spoiled, but not entirely."

That remark saved me.

Had the same words been uttered by someone else, I would have spat and calmed down. But Bakst's authority was too great for me not to listen to his verdict. I stood there unsettled, believing every word of his, and shyly gathering and rolling up my drawings.

I will always remember meeting him in his school. I, who had no idea that somewhere in the world there was an artistic Paris, discovered Europe in miniature here.

[a] In *My Life*, this was "corrected" to: "a special accent that made him appear more European than ever." The opposite is true; it was, of course, the accent from Grodno.

[b] The Russian Season, when Diaghilev's Ballets Russes performed in Paris. Bakst was the troupe's chief decorator.

[c] According to this, he was thirteen when his mother first brought him to Pen.

With more or less talent, the students knew the road they were taking. And I, firmly convinced that the past must be forgotten, sat down to make a sketch.

A woman model stood there. Thick, pink legs, a bare background, a regular, hired model. In the atelier, among the students, Countess T. [Tolstoy][a], the dancer Nijinsky.[b] I am shy again.

The sketch is done.

Friday Bakst arrives. He used to come once a week.

Everyone drops his work. The easels line up in a row. Waiting.

He walks, observes, not knowing whose work it is, only later does he ask: "Who painted it?" He says little. Just [remarking on] this and that.

But the magic, the fear, and the smell of Europe prevailed. He comes closer to me. I'm lost. About my work, not knowing (or pretending not to know), he utters words not used in polite society.

Everyone looks at me with pity.

"Whose work is this," he asks.

"Mine!"

"I thought so," he answers.

Well, naturally. I mentioned earlier all the "corners" of my dwellings, my half rooms, but nowhere did I feel so uncomfortable as here, after Bakst's review.

I felt that this could not last much longer. I did the second sketch.

Friday. Bakst's visit. No praise.

I leave the atelier and for three months my tuition of thirty Rubles is paid[c] and I am absent. It was more than I could endure.

Actually, I cannot learn anything. More correctly, no one can teach me anything. Not in vain did I study in the city school, according to public opinion: badly. I grasp things only with my inner ear. You understand? The general methods of schools do not stick to me. My attendance in the schools had the character of general attitudes and getting acquainted [with topics] rather than enforced learning.

After my failure in the new school with Bakst during the first two sketches and not understanding (really not wanting to understand) why Bakst actually scolded me, I fled, to find my own way in freedom, to shake a burdensome weight off my shoulders.

Three months later I returned to Bakst's school,[d] deciding to give in and force recognition from him and from the distinguished students.

[a]Sofia Dymshits-Tolstoy, the Jewish wife of the writer Count Aleksey Tolstoy.

[b]A: "among the students of Countess T.—the dancer Nijinsky."—A mistake; here, corrected from C and the essay on Bakst (see Chapter 3, p. 185).

[c]By his benefactor, Alicia Berson.

[d]More like a month and a half. In the meantime, he was in Vitebsk and Lyozno, steeped in love and writing love poetry in Russian.

And that's what happened. I forgot the whole past and drew a sketch. Next Friday Bakst *distinguished it as a "model"* and hung it on the wall. After that, I moved upward, and entered the road you can't get off.

From now on, the essence wasn't in doubt, for this road and no other is the road of art. Branching out and searching can come in various forms.

To get to this transitional boundary I wasted 4 or 5 years.[a] I soon sensed that I had no more reason to stay in Bakst's school. Furthermore, Bakst himself, in connection with the Russian Season abroad, left his school in Petrograd for good.

I began to stammer. "Perhaps it may be possible, Lev Samoylovich,[b] you know, Lev Samoylovich, I want . . . to Paris."

"*Pozhaluysta!* [By all means!] Listen, can you paint decorations?"

"Sure." (Didn't even know how to begin.)

"Here's a hundred Francs!"

Nevertheless our roads parted, and I went to Paris by myself.***

X

I appealed to my father to revolt.

"Papa," I said. "Listen, you have a grown-up son, an artist. How long will you wallow in forced labor? And toil for your boss? Look, didn't I faint enough in Petrograd? Didn't I eat enough chopped cutlets? What will happen to me in Paris?"

He retorted: "So what, leaving? You will feed me? We know that."

Mama clutched her heart. "My child, aren't we your parents. Write more often. Ask us for something."

My home ground [Vitebsk] slid from under my feet, but the river was flowing—clouded, not the same at whose banks I kissed you . . . The Uspensky church, the Kosciol[c] on the hill—rose higher, sharper.[d] The Dvina River was flowing into the distance, I am no longer a boy. Everything curbs me. And in Petersburg—the State Duma.

Meetings. A newspaper—*Rech*.[e]

Serious.

[a]This occured probably in the fall of 1909. Obviously, Chagall includes his studies with Pen, since about 1904 or 1905.

[b]Bakst's Russian name and patronymic.

[c]The Polish Catholic Church.

[d]On his paintings.

[e]"The Word" (or: "prophetic sermon"), a viciously anti-Semitic newspaper.

The memory of Vitebsk joys is fading. This and the next sentence are cryptic and short, Chagall was always careful when talking about Jewish problems in a language other than Yiddish. The atmosphere in the Third Duma and the overt threats to annihilate the Jews in the newspaper *Rech* shook the confidence of Russian Jewry, including the popular mood. The Third, or Black Duma, elected in 1907, was a stage for anti-Jewish laws and vicious anti-Semitic speeches. Under heavy political pressure, only two Jewish candidates and a weak liberal opposition were elected to this Duma. Vinaver was out, and being close to him, Chagall felt the full pressure of those menacing days. As the historian Shimon Dubnov puts it: "The hirelings of [Tsar] Nicholas II danced like a horde of savages over the dead body of the emancipation movement, singing hymns in praise of slavery and despotism."[a] Toward the beginning of 1910, wholesale expulsions of Jews from the cities outside the Pale and from the villages within the Pale, severe restrictions on education, and other measures, were implemented. The Jewish Deputy Friedman, in a courageous speech in the Duma in February 1910, declared: "during the most terrible time which the Jews had to live through under [Interior Minister] Plehve no such cruelties and barbarities were practiced as at the present moment." For the Jewish masses it was a signal of no hope in Russia. For Chagall, who lived in the capital—under threat of expulsion and close to Vinaver who was thrown out of the new Duma—it was an additional incentive to leave Russia.

> And I paint such paintings, almost like Leonardo (who will say no?) and mama watches over my painting. She finds, for example, that in the picture "Birth," the woman's belly has to be covered. Right. The body comes to life.
> Berta brings flowers, blue, greenery. [She is] all in white, with black gloves,

[a] S.M. Dubnow, *History of the Jews in Russia and Poland*, New York: Ktav Publishing House, 1975, p. 155.

"Visiting"—illustration for the second volume of Bella Chagall's memoirs, *The First Encounter*. Bella, at home called Basha, with her parents Shmuel-Noah and Alte Rosenfeld in Vitebsk. The women walk behind the man.

"Morning," an illustration for the second volume of Bella Chagall's memoirs, *The First Encounter*, not published in the book. Shy Basha, her brother Abrashka, and father Rosenfeld the watchmaker (his body becomes a clock), emerging with fresh wisdom from the morning study of Talmud with his live-in Rabbi.

and I paint her portrait.[a] I counted all the fences in town and I paint "Death"[b] I took the pulse of my family and I paint "The Wedding."[c]

I feel good with you, but . . . have you heard of traditions, of Aix . . . the artist with his ear cut off, of cubes and squares, of Paris?[d]

Vitebsk, I abandon you!

"Remain alone, herring merchants!"

XI

To tell the truth, I cannot say for sure that I was swept up by a spontaneous urge[e] to go to Paris. I didn't have that feeling when I went from Vitebsk to Petersburg either. I just knew I had to go.

I could hardly determine what I really wanted. It would sound too "provincial" if I had confessed it openly. Enamoured of wandering, I still dreamed of being satisfied with a much smaller cage. I would always say that a tiny cell with a hole in the door, through which food and other things would be given to me— would satisfy me forever.[f]

With such a feeling I travelled to Petrograd and Paris.

But I really had no means at all for a trip to Paris. And, so that I wouldn't become one of the thirty thousand artists of all countries and nations that fill the city, I had to secure some means for study and work in advance.

Around that time I was introduced to Vinaver. Enriched with my painting "The Wedding," Vinaver appointed a monthly stipend for me. I went.

Four days later I was in Paris.

It was precisely this long, four-day distance [by train] from Paris to Russia that prevented me from returning—right away, or a week or a month later.

I wanted to dream up some vacation, just to be able to visit home.

All those thoughts and ideas about returning home were cut off by the Louvre.

Wandering about the round hall of Veronese and below, in the halls of Manet, Delacroix, Courbet, Millet—I wanted nothing more.

[a]"My Fiancée in Black Gloves," 1909.

[b]"The Dead Man," 1908.

[c]His sister's wedding.

[d]Allusions to Cézanne and van Gogh.

[e]Russian: *Stikhiyny*, i.e., spontaneous, elemental, by an irrational force.

[f]An allusion to the legendary Hasidic Rebbe, Menakhem Mendel of Kotsk (1787–1859), who decided to "leave the world" in search of Truth. He secluded himself for the last twenty years of his life in a room, where food was passed through an aperture in the door, to think and meditate, to the amazement and admiration of his followers. This image stayed with Chagall throughout his life.

Russia rose in my imagination as a basket hanging under a flying balloon. The inflated balloon remained hanging, frozen in one place; with the years, it slowly sinks down. Thus I imagined Russian art.

Or what else? Every time I think or talk about Russian art—I experience all the same turgid and nebulous feelings of grief and bitterness. It seemed condemned—in the course of its historical destiny—to be connected to the West.

And if Russian artists were condemned to be students of the West—you could no longer accuse them of being imperfect students. Perhaps because by nature they could not be different. Because the best Russian Realist was an offense to the realism of Courbet. The best Russian Impressionist appeared as a monster, a profanation of Manet and Pissarro. I cannot talk about it!

For I love Russia . . .

Next day I went to the Salon des Indépendants.

My friend who accompanied me warned me that going through the whole Salon was exhausting. He himself was breathless after surveying such enormous halls. Pitying him in my heart, and armed with my own method of looking at Salons, I went through the front halls as if chased by a downpour—and burst into the central halls.

Thus I saved my strength.

I burst into the heart of French painting of 1910.

I clutched its very body. No academies or schools of any city could give me what I bit off and gnawed at the heart of the French exhibits, display windows, and museums. Everything, from the French market, where, in my poverty, I bought only a chunk of a long cucumber; a laborer in a blue shirt; up to the diligent followers of Picasso, Gleizes,[a] or the tall Delaunay—all spoke of the authentic French taste, measure, lucidity, and form. Of painting even more painterly on the canvases even by second-rate French painters.

And I didn't know: did anyone have a clearer conception of the almost unsurpassable mark separating French painting before 1914 from the painting of other nations. In Russia they seem to think very little about this difference. But in Paris, I thought about it all the time. It is, apparently, not because any individual or nation has more or less talent. Here, more psychophysiological forces are operative, forces in your blood that move peoples toward music, or painting, or literature, or dreaming.

For some time, I lived in an atelier in Montparnasse next to the sculptor Bourdelle[b]; from there I moved to a modest atelier, more appropriate for my situation,

[a]Albert Gleizes (1881–1953), French painter, coauthor (with Jean Metzinger) of the first book on Cubism, *Du cubism*, 1912. Chagall knew him during his first stay in Paris.

[b]Émile-Antoine Bourdelle (1861–1929), French sculptor, influenced by Rodin.

in La Ruche.[a] That was the name of a hundred or so ateliers, unified in one framework and surrounded with little gardens and city slaughterhouses, where the artistic bohemia of all nations lived. At that time, when a model was wailing in Russian ateliers, songs and guitars were heard from the Italians, curses from the Jews; and there I was, with my little kerosene lamp, in my study . . .

The sky is blue. Dawn.

Further down, they slaughtered cattle.[b] In the slaughterhouses, cows mooed. I painted cows. Didn't sleep at night. A week passed and nobody cleaned my atelier. Paintings. Eggshells. Little cubes of "two-sous bouillon" everywhere. The lamp burned. And so did I. It burned so long that the corridor blue began to glimmer. Then I ascended the sofa . . . Though you could already go out to the street and buy fresh croissants, I went to sleep. Later, the *femme de menage* came and I didn't know if she really wanted to clean my atelier (it is absolutely necessary, but please don't touch my desk!) or intended to get upstairs to me. I love French blood. While gnawing at French painting, trying to overcome it, I wanted to savor the taste of a French body.

It took some time to walk into my atelier. To wait outside the door half an hour. That was enough time for me to put things in order and dress. I worked naked . . . In general, I cannot stand the weight of any clothes. I have no taste for suits, and dress most tastelessly.

While visiting the schools and academies of the Boulevard Saint-Parnasse, I also very diligently prepared for the Salon. How could I carry my screaming canvases [from] La Ruche through Paris by myself?

The agile immigrants clutched at anything. Especially when you could laugh at it. On the way, my rickshaw encountered other "Rembrandts" transporting their pictures to the Salon. Everyone drove to the canvas barracks. There I would soon see clearly what separated me from traditional French painting. The pictures are hung. The exhibition preview is in an hour. The French censor approaches and condemns one [of my paintings] to be taken down: "The Ass and the Woman."[c] Tarkhov[d] and I persuade him: "Monsieur, it's nothing." Corrected —it remained.

[a]La Ruche ("beehive"), a building complex with some 140 studios for painters, where Chagall lived and had a studio on the top floor in 1911–1914.

[b]La Ruche was near the slaughterhouses in Vaugirard, Paris.

[c]He refers to the painting of 1911–1912, later renamed (tongue-in-cheek): "To My Fiancé," where a man/ass sits inside the open legs of a woman.

[d]Nikolay Aleksandrovich Tarkhov (Moscow 1871–Orsey 1930), Russian painter, lived in France after 1899. During 1901–1914, he exhibited every year in the Salon des Indépendants in Paris. He also exhibited in Russia, as well as other countries, including the 1913 Armory Show in New York.

My early painterly tendencies were, no doubt, strange to the French. And didn't I look so carefully at their art? I was truly offended.

Does this nation have the right of uniqueness forever? Could another nation, at least for a while, usurp the right to uniqueness along with them? I don't know any nation that would think like the French that only they are the salt of the earth in art. They are mostly right. But still it is ruthless.

The irony vis-à-vis a foreigner is unbearable and unjustified. And I must admit that lying in Paris with such ideas, I often thought about a plot against this tradition, against the confidence of their artistic consciousness.

My appearances in the Salon did indeed have such a character.

For a while, I left the fences of my hometown and moved straight into the circles of French poets and artists. Here is Canudo, the editor of *Monjoie!*. On Fridays here you meet Gleizes, Metzinger, Léger with Delaunay, Valentine de Saint-Point with the three lover boys.[a] One shorter than the other. Warm and hot.

/Truly, I'm telling you," says Canudo. "Your face reminds me of Christ's head. To hell with the newspaper, it says nothing about me," and he drops it right here.

"Hard to remember who your face reminds me of," I answer. "Italy, rue de Dante, and along with you I swim on the waves of *Monjoie!*, as if beaming splinters were floating near and around you. A flock of white seagulls hovering, as if rolled up white spots rose on wires to the sky."

Here is Apollinaire's garret. The sweet Zeus. In poems of figures and familiar letters, he engraves a new way . . .[b]

Like a rain,[c] unexpected, crossed through, the meaning of your words whips us. You surely dream of watercolors! A new face of pictures, poets, bitter destinies. All of us, about whom you ever said a word.

He's gone. What stayed, or withered over the dead face—his smile! . . .

Here, the white flame, the sonorous Blaise—my friend; Cendrars, a yellow sweater and multicolored socks.[d]

Wells of sun, poverty in nets of rhythm and color, art—flaming fluid, the impetus of newborn canvases, heads, cows, flying pieces,—all this I remember.

"And you?"

It's enough for me.//

[a]According to C, they were his friends Dunoyer de Segonzac, André Lhote, and Luc-Albert Moreau (*My Life*, p. 111).

[b]The graphic arrangements of letters on a page in Apollinaire's *Calligrammes*; its early poems were written in December 1912 and in early 1913.

[c]An allusion to Apollinaire's poem, "Il Pleut" ("It's Raining"), arranged graphically in the form of strings of descending rain.

[d]An allusion to the performances of the Russian Futurists and Mayakovsky's provocative readings in a yellow sweater, thus identifying Cendrars as an avant-garde poet.

And my days wandering in the Place de la Concorde, lovely garden. I look at Danton and Watteau. I pluck leaves.

Oh if, riding the stone chimera, I could only engrave with my hands and feet my road in the sky. Paris, You, my second Vitebsk.

XII

I often said that I was not an artist, but some kind of a cow.[a] What's the difference. I thought of placing her [the cow] on my calling card. At the time it seemed: a silly cow was making world politics.

Cubism chopped itself up, Futurism swirled, and suddenly these premonitions were realized in the East.[b]

I saw with my own eyes how in Kahnweiler's galleries,[c] pictures of Derain and others were tightly packed, the colors leaping off . . . At the end of 1914, I seemed to take with me from Paris to Berlin the beginning of the dreamed-up epoch before the storm.[d] My pictures were flaunted on the Potsdammerstrasse while armaments were prepared nearby.

What can we do if world events appear to us only on canvases, through colors, through texture that grows dense and vibrates like pillars of suffocating mustard gas.

Europe, start a war.[e] Picasso, finish Cubism.

Who cares about Serbia?[f]—

Attack the *muzhiks* in burlap sandals! Ignite Russia and everyone after her!

XIII

While in Berlin, I did not sense that a month later that bloody comedy[g] would begin; that comedy in which the whole earth, along with Chagall, would be

[a]In Yiddish: *beheyme*, a cow; also a stupid, unthinking person.

[b]Chagall reflects the widespread notion that avant-garde art had a premonition of the breakup of forms and the upheaval of World War I and the Russian Revolution.

[c]Daniel-Henri Kahnweiler (1884–1976) was a major dealer of modern art in Paris, who promoted Picasso.

[d]A pun on Der Sturm (The Storm), Walden's famous gallery on Potsdammerstrasse 75 in Berlin, where Chagall had a one-man show in June–July 1914; and the "storm" of World War I that embroiled all of Europe in August 1914, as if foreshadowed by modern art, including that of Chagall.

[e]Perhaps an echo of T.F. Marinetti's slogan: "War—the only hygiene of mankind."

[f]Russia entered the war in defence of its Slavic ally Serbia.

[g]World War I.

turned upside down on a brand new stage where such mass acts are performed in a ballet.

My premonitions did not worry me enough to keep me from travelling to Russia for three months, where I planned on the one hand to attend my sister's wedding, and on the other hand—to meet her . . .[a]

This fourth and last love [with Bella] could have come to nought in my four years in France. At the end of my stay in Paris, all that remained of it was a heap of letters, which didn't even have a sign of an ending. One more letter with a few interesting words, and I decided everything was over between us.

After two months in Berlin, I left for Russia.[b]

I reached Vilna with a fellow passenger, a French woman. I told her: "You see, this is Russia. Especially since the porter almost disappeared with my luggage. Even more so, since the Tsar has consented to travel to Odessa and is receiving a delegation at the [Vilna] railroad station. Such a *kielbasa*[c] city this is . . . And we remained on the platform. We both deserve pity, especially you . . . But never mind, I shall put you in a [train] car and you will get to *Tsarskoe Selo*,[d] to the Senator, you'll be a governess . . . "

But this is not really Russia. I didn't even see Russia well enough. Did I see it at all? Where is Novgorod, Rostov, Kiev, where, where? All my life, to this very day, I have seen only Petrograd, Moscow, the small town of Lyezhne and Vitebsk. Vitebsk is a different country altogether. An unusual city—an unfortunate city. A sad city. A city filled with girls, young girls I had no chance (or no sense) to even touch. A city with dozens, even hundreds of prayer houses, butcher shops, passersby . . . What kind of Russia is this. It is only my city, mine, a city I found myself.

In those days I painted my Vitebsk series of 1914. I painted everything that popped into my eyes. I was satisfied with anything, fences, posts, a floor, a table. I painted from a window (I never walked around the city with my box). I painted beggars in prayer shawls. For twenty Kopeks.[e] And tradesmen. No matter how

---

[a]His former "fiancée" Berta Rosenfeld (later: Bella Chagall), whom he hadn't seen in four years.

[b]According to the documents in Chapter 4 he could have left Paris on May 1, after collecting the first monthly payment from the Malpel Gallery, and he left Berlin for Russia on June 15.

[c]A stereotypical Polish sausage; the majority of the Vilna population was Polish.

[d]Literally, "Tsar's Village," a suburb of St.-Petersburg where the Tsar's palace was located; a kind of Russian Versailles.

[e]The price Chagall paid for sitting for him as a model. The famous painting "The Rabbi" was originally called "The Praying Jew," showing an orthodox Jew in his regular praying garb, in this case, worn by a beggar. Chagall changed the name to accommodate his Western audience.

"The Train," an illustration for the second volume of Bella Chagall's memoirs, *The First Encounter*.
Marc left for Paris by train, his fiancée's love flying after him. In "Paris Through the Window" (1913),
part of the train is turned upside down—he cannot return.

much I resisted, no matter how stubborn I was, one rainy evening, I stood under the wedding canopy, in the proper way, as in my painting.[a]

The wedding was conducted by the rules.

The ceremony was preceded by a small comedy and somber tones. This is what happened. The parents and the large family of my—yes-yes—wife, didn't like my—yes-yes—"pedigree," my *Yikhes* (you know what that means). How come my father is no more than a simple clerk. My grandfather (it's a shame to admit [a butcher]). Whereas her father—not a trifling matter—he trades on Zamkovaya Street, selling watches and teaspoons of silver and gold. What do you know! In their home, every morning they serve tea with dozens of strudels, and each member of their abundant family of Abrashkas[b] gulped it down. While in our home—a simple, coarse "still-life" by Chardin. Poor papa: just like me, right before the wedding, he preferred to go to sleep. Does it make sense to cook up a brew with people of such high pedigree.

Arrived late at my bride's house—there I encountered a whole Sanhedrin.[c] Regrettably, I am no Veronese. Around the table the wise, prankster Rov sits expansively, and next to him a tiny merchant of the First Guild. And all around a host of well-endowed, well-to-do Jews, their eyes rummaging around at me and at the meal, for without me there would be no meal . . . I knew it and teased their appetites. Some sit, some stand, the sisters-in-law bustle about. Maids with ripe breasts. Tears, smiles, candy. Everything proper. Enough to cover the bride-groom with it. They were waiting for me and in the meantime gossiping . . . It wasn't proper to admit he's a painter. On the other hand, they say he's famous and gets a lot of money for his paintings. You know. On the other hand, what kind of living is that. What do you say: neither honor nor respect. But who is his father . . . Ah, what's the point . . .

It seems to me that if I was put into a grave, my features would look more supple than this mask sitting next to my future wife. But at the same time, I regretted that, because of some stupid shyness, I had no courage to touch the heaps of grapes, fruit, and other delicacies.

Half an hour later (What am I saying—much sooner—the Sanhedrin was in a

[a]The paintings "The Russian Wedding," "The Wedding," and "The Canopy" were made from his sister's wedding a few years earlier, thus foreshadowing in art Marc and Berta's actual wedding.

[b]An anti-Semitic label for typical, "ugly" Jews; it was a shibboleth, for Jews from the Pale could not pronounce the proper Russian *R*. Chagall, writing in Soviet times, dissociates himself from the behavior of the rich orthodox family.

[c]Originally, a learned assembly of seventy Jewish sages; here, a negative image of so many religious "Yids" arguing with each other. Again, he mockingly conflates the orthodox with the rich, in good Soviet style.

"Wedding." Under the canopy are Berta and Moyshe Chagall. Next to Berta is her mother, ritually crying. Behind Berta is her rich father in a top hat. To the right of the groom is his father in a working apron. Idle religious relatives look on and celebrate. From *My Life*.

hurry), something whispered over my head under the canopy: either a blessing or wine or a curse. I didn't understand. We turned in circles. In a special way, I pressed the thin bones of my wife's little hands. I felt like fleeing with her as soon as possible to some summer house, embracing her, and bursting into laughter. Indeed, that's what we did a few days later.

I won. I chased a mouse and killed it. My wife thought I was capable of murder . . . (No, just a mouse.) The honeymoon was not made of honey, but of milk.[a] Herds of military cows grazed all around us. Every morning, soldiers sold us a bucket of milk for twenty Kopeks. My wife, raised exclusively on cakes, fed me only milk. In short, by autumn, I could barely button my top button. By

[a]An allusion to the biblical "land flowing with milk and honey."

"A String of Pearls I," an illustration for the second volume of Bella Chagall's memoirs, *The First Encounter*. A simpler version was published in the book. Father Rosenfeld is in his jewelry store. Bella writes: "The aristocratic women of the city liked to buy from my pious, quiet father. Especially one woman who was brought to our city, I don't know from where, by a rich Director of an Insurance Company."

"A String of Pearls II," an illustration for the second volume of Bella Chagall's memoirs, *The First Encounter*. This version was not published in the book. On the left, a Russian sign: "Store of watches/ Rosenfeld"; on the right: "Fruit"; second level: "Pastry shop Jean Albert"; upper left, edge of sign, as seen in full on a postcard: "[khudozhestvennaya fotog]rafiya" ("Artistic photography"), where Chagall apprenticed.

twelve in the morning the room looked like the ceiling of a Parisian Grand Salon painted by a genius.

Then the war broke out, and Europe was closed for me. Nothing doing. Still, I needed to move somewhere. Petrograd, or someplace. To tell the truth, I didn't think right away about going to Peter [Petrograd]. In that summer place of Zaolshe[a] lived Shneurson, the Rebbe of Lubavich.[b] The residents of the towns all around crawled to him for advice. This one didn't have enough. That one was in pain. One thing or another. This one doesn't feel like going to the army so he comes to the Rebbe for advice. That one has no children so he travels to the Rebbe—to pray for him. This one doesn't quite understand a phrase in the Talmud, so he too goes to the Rebbe for an intepretation. That one travels to the Rebbe with no particular reason, hasn't seen him in a while, no reason. Who knows what may happen?

But in the lists of the Rebbe's faithful, there certainly never was a painter. Forgive me, Master of the Universe, it's a bit awkward. But at a certain moment, at the end of autumn and at the beginning of the war,[c] when I actually didn't know where to turn—we decided to set out to visit the learned Rebbe to ask him for advice. (I remembered the Rebbe's tune which mama would sing on the Sabbath.)

Is he indeed such a holy man. The Rebbe always spent his summers in Zaolshe, in his permanent summer home that looked like an old synagogue with little courtyards and side yards, little buildings, with janitors and women cooks. On reception days, the hall was filled with people. Crowding, screaming, squeaking, a herd. But in truth, for an extra Ruble to the janitor, you could get in faster.

The Rebbe doesn't talk much to simple mortals. You have to write it all up and submit the note at the entrance. Not to speak. Finally, the door opened and I went from the noisy commotion of the hall straight into a green, empty square room, where the Rebbe sits alone at a long table. And on the table are heaps of paper, coins, petitions, notes, prayers, questions, advice . . . A candle burns. His gaze . . .

"So, you want to go to Petrograd, my son. You say, it is more comfortable for you there. Well, why not, my son. I bless you, go, my son, to Petrograd."

"Rebbe," I say, "in Vitebsk I would feel better, there, you know, are my wife's parents and my own . . . there."

[a]A recreation town at a railroad station, about 20 km east of Lyozno, just outside the Pale of Settlement.

[b]The Rebbe of Lubavich was the head of the ChaBaD Hasidic dynasty. Apparently, Berta's father, a rich supporter of the Rebbe, arranged for this honeymoon and the Rebbe's audience.

[c]Chagall confuses the dates: World War I started in August 1914, while he married Berta only the next summer, on July 25, 1915, a year after he returned from the West.

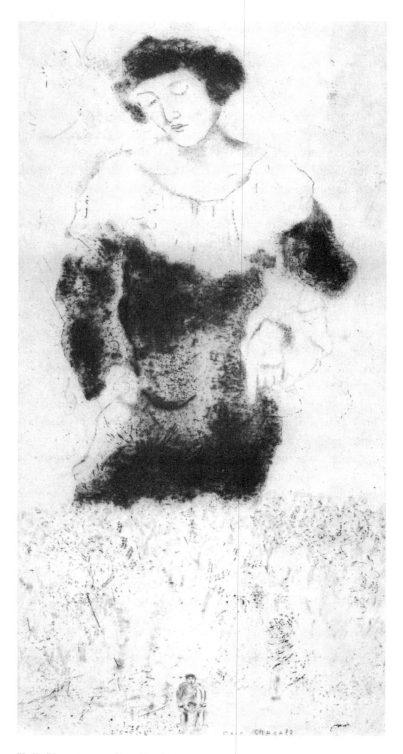

"Bella," looming over Chagall and Ida, 1924.

"Well, why not, my son, if you want to go to Vitebsk, I bless you—go to Vitebsk."[a]

I didn't turn around, but shuffled backward to the door and left. I fled to my wife. It was evening. Dogs. And nothing was better than . . . My God, what kind of Rebbe do you have?—Rebbe Shneurson.

In spite of the mice that disturbed my honeymoon, running up on my easel, I would have stayed in the summer place of Zaolshe, or, if worse came to worse, I would have left with the Rebbe to his capital of Lubavich. But the war called and my year was called up to the army. What shall I do: my wife pulls me to the capital, she likes big cities (and how right she is!); and I like a hole, some Godforsaken hole, I would have been happy there too. Well, I would have sat in the synagogue and watched. Nothing else. Or I would have visited people and painted pictures that would shake the world. No.

One nice—and how nice!—and unfortunate evening, I climbed into a railroad car and went to Petrograd. Because that pleased my wife. She loves culture. (And how right she is!) Doesn't she suffer enough because of me?

Over there, my savior was waiting—the office.[b] And soon enough I was writing papers, and far away they were fighting a war . . . My manager struggled with me for two years until he bestowed a new talent on me: from now on I understand a great deal about incoming and outgoing papers. And I write reports that aren't bad at all.

The Germans won victories. Their repeated mustard gas attacks [on the front] choked me at 46 Liteynaya Street [in Petrograd], and my painting was suffocated. I begged [Kaiser] Wilhelm: "Please be happy with [conquering] Warsaw, with Kovno, but don't move on Dvinsk,[c] don't push into Vitebsk . . . There I sit and draw sketches."[d]

Fortunately for him, the Russian soldiers were bad fighters. That is, they were good fighters, but—they'd see the Germans but couldn't reach them with their fists.[e] And without fists, the war was no war. The soldiers went to battle. Nikolay

[a]This kind of advice, first agreeing with the supplicant's proposal, then agreeing with its opposite, and back again, comes directly from Sholem-Aleichem's story, "The Advice."

[b]Berta's brother, Yakov Rosenfeld directed a war economy office in Petrograd during World War I. He gave Chagall a clerical position, where he served throughout the war; he had plenty of time to paint and exhibit.

[c]Dvinsk, the second largest city of Vitebsk Province, was in the western corner of the province. In 1915, when the German army closed in, Jewish refugees from Dvinsk fled to Vitebsk, in the far eastern part of the province.

[d]Apparently, Chagall had plenty of opportunities to go back to Vitebsk during the war.

[e]An allusion to the lack of far-reaching weapons in the Russian army.

Chagall in military service, working in an office, during World War I. The official stationery is marked: "No. 24. Moscow. Typo[graphy] of Distr[ict] Headquarters." The date should be later than "1914–15," for he did not serve before the fall of 1915. The signature on the left is "Marc" in French and "Lagash" in Yiddish (if read from left to right, as in Russian, it reads: "Shagal"). Chagall bends unnaturally backwards, to fit the official frame; his head is upside down (in Yiddish: *kop arop*, head upside down, means "butter-side down," topsy-turvy, failure, irrational world). The animal metonymy is *"a fiksl,"* a smart, thin little fox, that can get through the fences of the system.

Nikolayevich commanded,[a] and recognized that it was all *their* [the Jews'] fault. "Expel in 24 hours and shoot to kill, expel and shoot!"

The Russian army rolled back and the Jewish population of the cities and towns rolled out. Fists were raised to the sky. And I was writing the same military papers, registering them all, until thunder roared—the February Revolution.[b]

[a]The Tsar's uncle was commander-in-chief of the Russian army during the war; noted for his anti-Semitic actions, especially the drastic expulsion of over a million Jews from the front areas ("within twenty four hours—or to be shot"), as the front swiftly retreated eastward.

[b]The democratic centrist Revolution that deposed the Tsar, February 24–28, 1917 (according to the old calender).

XIV

In this chapter, Chagall describes the turmoil that engulfed Petrograd in the period between the two revolutions of 1917. He uses some slogans he remembered from the time, as well as echoes of A. Blok's poem "Twelve," along with the Communist narrative of the Revolution. But, above all, he reflects the chaotic confusion of the Revolutionary days and thus conveys the spirit of the time more authentically than the official, neat narratives of the historians.

The main points are: Strikes began in Petrograd on February 22, 1917. On February 27, a regiment of the Volyn Guards mutinied, and by the evening 70,000 joined the mutiny. The Duma decided to form a Provisional Government until the election of a Constituent Assembly; and on March 2, Tsar Nicholas II abdicated. In April, Lenin returned to Russia in a sealed wagon traveling through Germany. In July, Aleksandr Kerensky became Prime Minister. In August, Chief of Staff General Kornilov attempted a march on Petrograd to "Save Russia" and failed. The Bolsheviks were given arms to stop Kornilov, yet on October 25, they stormed the Winter Palace and captured the ministers of the Provisional Government. The first freely elected Russian parliament, the Constituent Assembly, met for one day, and was dispersed by the Bolsheviks.

> The first thing I realized was that my business with the passport people had come to an end.[a] The Volin Regiment revolted. I went to Znamensky Square, from there to Liteynaya, from Liteynaya to Nevsky Prospekt—and back.
> Shots were fired, attacks were prepared, weapons were laid down, people surrendered. Machine-gun units decided: "They are for the Regiment." The machine-guns were put on their carriages. "Forward—March!" Regiments go to take the oath. Along with the officers and sailors. And at the Duma, Rodzyanko[b] thunders: "Remember, brothers, the enemy is at the gates,[c] swear, swear!" "We swear. Hurrah!" And so on. Your throat got sore.

[a]The Jews were given equal civil rights after the February Revolution, and didn't need any "passport" to live in the capital.

[b]Mikhail V. Rodzyanko (1859–1924), a leader of the Duma, who attempted to save the monarchy during the February Revolution.

[c]The German army was moving toward Petrograd.

Something was happening. Revolution. Real freedom. I fell into a languid mood and didn't hear Kerensky.[a] The Cadet ["Constitutional Democrats"] government was supplanted by a half-democratic cabinet. The half-democratic—by a democratic. Coalitions were formed and re-formed. It didn't work. Then Kornilov[b] wanted to save Russia. Deserters attacked the whole Russian railroad network. "Enough sucking our blood like leeches!—Now we go home!"

It happened in June. The S.R. were in. Chernov[c] spoke in the circus: "Constituent Assembly! Constituent Assembly!" On Znamenskaya Square, where the coarse monument for Alexander the Third stands, rumors circulated that Lenin had arrived. "Lenin himself? To us? Down with him! Long live the Provisional Government! All power to the Constituent Assembly!"

"Is it true that he arrived [by train] from Germany in a sealed car?"

Russia was covered with glass. Lenin would turn Russia upside down, the way I turn a picture upside down.[d] Kshesinskaya left.[e] He speaks from her balcony. Everybody is there. The letters R.S.F.S.R.[f] were flaming. The factories stopped. The horizons opened. Wasteland, and there is no bread. And the black typographic paper of the morning posters cut your heart. Lenin, Chairman of the Sovnarkom [Council of People's Commissars, i.e., government]. Trotsky[g] is

[a]Aleksandr F. Kerensky (1881–1970), lawyer, orator, Minister of Justice in the first Provisional Government; became Prime Minister and head of the Provisional Government during July–October 1917; deposed by the Bolsheviks.

[b]L.G. Kornilov, a white general who marched on Petrograd in August 1917 with the slogan, "Save Russia!," intending to depose the Provisional Government from the right, without success.

[c]Viktor M. Chernov (1873–1952), a founder of the S.R. (Socialist-Revolutionary Party). In 1917, the S.R. won the only free general elections in Russia, and Chernov was elected President of the Constituent Assembly on January 18, 1918; the next day, the Bolsheviks dispersed the Assembly by force.

[d]Chagall kept this image for years; in 1937, on the twentieth anniversary of the October Revolution, he painted "Revolution" with Lenin standing on his head next to masses of Jews with Torah Scrolls and red banners.

[e]The tsar's mistress. When she fled, Lenin resided in her palace. Later, in Paris, she was the ballet teacher of Chagall's daughter.

[f]Russian Soviet Federation of Socialist Republics, the name of Soviet Russia at the time.

[g]Lev (Leon) Trotsky (1879–1940), charismatic orator, switched to Lenin's side and headed the Petrograd Soviet during the Bolshevik Revolution. Under Lenin, he led the October insurrection, organized the Red Army, and led it to victory in the Civil War. He was Commissar of Foreign Affairs and Commissar of War, 1917–1924. After Lenin's death, Trotsky was pushed out of power by Stalin, expelled from the Soviet Union in 1927, and killed in Mexico by Stalin's agents in 1940.

there too. And Zinovyev.[a] Uritsky[b] bans the Constituent Assembly. Everybody is there and I—in Vitebsk.

[In Vitebsk] I can survive without dinner for several days in a row. And to sit there outside, behind the mill, watch the bridge, the beggars, the shleppers carrying something. I can sit near a house, watch soldiers walking out of a bath and Gentile women sweeping with brooms. I can sit at the river. At the graveyard. I can forget you, Vlidimir Ilyich, you—Lenin, and Trotsky I can also forget . . . But instead of sitting and painting pictures, instead of all that—I opened an Art School [in Vitebsk] and became its Director. Then everybody loved me. I became a celebrity of Vitebsk the city. And I sired dozens of painters. That was not enough. I began inviting other professors from the center, so that all trends would be represented in the Art School, and the professors began to "love" one another and—me too.[c]

I shall be silent about my friends and foes. All their masks are piled up in my heart like lumber. They expel me and my family within 24 hours.[d] They tear down the signs.[e] Stammer.[f] Don't worry, I shall not mention you. Then I thought:

"No one is a prophet in his own country."[g]

And I left for Moscow.

XV

Moscow, surrounded by the Kremlin. Or the Kremlin surrounded by Moscow, by Soviets. Hunger in your mouth. And the scream of October.

[a]Grigory Zinovyev (1883–1936), one of the Russian socialist leaders close to the Bolsheviks. In 1919, he was First President of the Communist Internationale, the Comintern, liquidated by Stalin.

[b]Moysey S. Uritsky (1873–1918), Chairman of the Petrograd Cheka (political secret police), dispersed the Constituent Assembly. He was assassinated in Petrograd. All three—Trotsky, Zinovyev, and Uritsky—were Jews.

[c]Tongue in cheek; they quarrelled and actually pushed Chagall out of the school.

[d]Here, "twenty-four hours" is not a precise figure; it is derived from the order expelling Jews from their towns in the front areas during World War I, literally "within 24 hours." Thus, it is a hint at Malevich's anti-Semitism, rather than a short-term ultimatum. In a later interview, and in his essay on Bakst (see Chapter 3), Chagall ascribes the cold treatment he received from both the Symbolists and the avant-garde to anti-Semitism.

[e]In Chagall's absence, the Malevich forces tore down the sign of the school and raised their own banner: Unovis, "Affirmers of the New Art."

[f]As always, stammering indicates Chagall's sensibility as a Jew, speechless in a foreign culture.

[g]Hebrew proverb: "There is no Prophet in his own city."

Every day I go to the Narkomopros [People's Commissariat of Enlighten-ment]. I live in Malakhovka.[a] I bring [food] rations.

What am I, a writer or something? How can I describe how our muscles stood on their hind legs in those years. Flesh turned into color. The body was a brush. And the head was a tower.

Crazily, I attacked the ceiling and the walls of the theater, where my painting sighs in the dark.[b] You saw it? You may fume, people of my time! My first theatrical-artistic alphabet is anyway in your belly. And it is not described. So I send all modesty to my little grandma.[c] I had enough of it. You may hate me, re-fuse to see [my art]. Yesterday, M.[d] delivered his first speech in the theater of R.S.F.S.R.: "The whole Komercheskaya Alley[e] must be blown up." I jumped up. "We shall see who will break whose back." The sweet theater director on Tversky Boulevard[f] says with a smile: "Sit down,[g] it won't work."

And you are still asking me to write and speak about Jewish art. I am prepared for the last time [to do so].

**h"What is it?"

Not long ago, in Jewish artistic circles an argument raged about the so-called Jewish art. In the fever and commotion, a group of Jewish artists was promoted, including Marc Chagall. I was still in Vitebsk when this calamity occurred—just returned from Paris, I smiled in my heart. I was busy with something else.

—My small town streets, hunchbacked, herring-like residents, green Jews, uncles, aunts with their questions: "Thank God, you grew up, became big!" And I kept painting them . . .

On the other hand, I was then a hundred years younger and I loved them, simply loved them . . .

[a]A village 100 km east of Moscow, where Chagall worked as a teacher in a colony for Jewish orphans.

[b]The Yiddish Chamber Theater, opened in Moscow on January 1, 1921. Chagall painted his famous murals in November–December 1920. When the theater moved to a larger hall in 1921, Chagall's paintings remained in their old place, which was turned into a teaching studio; the paintings were no longer exhibited, "sighing in the dark."

[c]A coarse Russian curse, meaning: "to Hell."

[d]Probably the avant-garde theater director Vsevolod Meyerhold.

[e]The theater district; literally: "business street."

[f]The theater director Aleksander Y. Taïrov (Kornfeld, 1885–1950), founder of the Moscow Chamber Theater ("Kamerny").

[g]"Calm down," "don't get agitated."

[h]The text between these double asterisks and the triple asterisks after "Kill me if not" was published in the Yiddish literary journal *Shtrom* in 1922 as "Leaves from My Notebook" (see the translation in *Marc Chagall on Art and Culture*). Several minor changes were made in this later and shorter text. The question "What is Jewish Art?" was adressed to Chagall by the editors.

So I was busier with that, it preoccupied me more than the thought that they anointed me as a Jewish artist.

Once upon a time, back in Paris, while working in my room in La Ruche, through the Spanish partition, I overheard Jewish immigrant voices quarrelling. "Well, what do you finally think: is Antokolsky not a Jewish artist? Or Israels? Or Liebermann?"

The lamp burned darkly, lighting my painting that stood on its head (that's how I work—are you happy?). And at the end, when dawn began to break in the Parisian sky, I laughed joyfully at my neighbors' idle ideas about the destiny of Jewish art:

"OK, you talk, and I will work."

Representatives of all countries and nations, to you I appeal. (I don't demand, I remember Spengler[a].) Please confess: now, when Lenin sits in the Kremlin, there is no piece of wood, [the stove] smokes, the wife is not in her right mind, now you have a "national art?"

You wise B. [Blaise Cendrars] and you various others preaching international art, finest Frenchmen. And (if they are still alive) they will answer me: "Chagall, you're right!"

Jews, if they feel like it (I do), may bemoan the fact that the painters of small town wooden synagogues (why am I not in one grave with you?) and the carvers of wooden synagogue-gavels—"Hush!"—(I saw it in An-sky's collections, got scared) are deceased.

But what is, indeed, the difference between my crippled great-grandfather Segal from Mohilev, who painted the walls of the Mohilev synagogue, and me, who painted the Yiddish theater (a good theater) in Moscow? Believe me, we both had plenty of lice, wallowing on the floor, in workshops, in synagogues, in the theater.

I am also certain that if I stopped shaving, you would see his likeness precisely . . .

By the way, my father.

Believe me, I put in a lot of effort, and no less love (and what love!) have we both expended. The difference is only that he [Segal] got commissions from synagogues and I studied in Paris. He knew something about that too.

And still, both I and he, and others (there are such) are still not Jewish art as a whole.

And why not tell the truth? Whence could it come to me? God forbid, if it should come from some commission or from an article by Efros,[b] or because they give me an "academic ration!"

---

[a]An allusion to the decline of the West. Oswald Spengler (1880–1936) made a tremendous impression at the time with his book *Der Untergang des Abendlandes* (*The Decline of the West*), Vol. I, 1918; Vol. II, 1922.

[b]Abram Efros was an influential art critic who wrote about Chagall.

There was Japanese art, Egyptian, Persian, Greek; but ever since the Renaissance, national arts have begun to decline. The contours disappeared. Individual artists arrived on the scene, citizens of this or that country, born here or there (blessed be you, my Vitebsk), and you'd need a good registration or even a passport specialist (of the Jewish desk) to classify all arts by "nationality."

And still it seems to me: Had I not been a Jew (with the full content I put in this word), I would not have been an artist, or I would be entirely different.

Some news! I myself know very well what this little nation can accomplish.

Unfortunately, I am shy and cannot say aloud what it can accomplish.

It is not for words to say what this little nation has accomplished!

If it wished—it showed Christ and Christianity.

If it wished—it gave Marx and Socialism.

Could it be that it won't show the world some art?

Kill me if not.***

W. [Herwarth Walden] is sorry I am alive. All my paintings were left with him. They say what is waiting for me in Berlin is a finger, not my works.[a] I am a fool. Soviet snot running from my nose.[b] I am only longing for the Paris sky I saw through the window of my atelier. It was he [Walden] who came up with the idea that I was an "Expressionist." Not on your life. I'm a painter. I am quiet. I don't know who I am. I am a good person. Look at me. No eyes can see in one's own lifetime. I think with more joy about my family: Rembrandt, Leonardo, Manet, Cézanne, Picasso, and my wife.

I'd like to go to Holland, Southern Italy, Provence, and taking off my clothes, I'd say: "Dear ones, you see, I came to you. I am sad here. The only thing I want is—to paint pictures and something else.[c] Forgive me." I am convinced that Rembrandt loves me. I shall go mad.

XVI

The city died. My Vitebsk road is finished and my family died out. (I want to write a few words for myself—you may not read them. Turn away.) "Children,[d] it's an outrage not to put a gravestone for Father, for Rosa, for David. Please write

---

[a]This was clearly written in Soviet Russia, before Chagall went to Berlin in the summer of 1922. Herwarth Walden, assuming Chagall was dead, sold most of his painting from the exhibition of 1914. Because of the severe German inflation, the money lost its value, or so argued Walden.

[b]A Russian and Yiddish idiom meaning "I am still a naïve child." Here, it is also an allusion to the Soviet state in its infancy, inexperienced in capitalist matters.

[c]Apparently, making love with French women.

[d]He appeals to his younger sisters.

"At Mother's Gravestone." Mother died in 1916. Their last name is spelled in Hebrew, consonants only: *ShGL*. The inscription is in longhand or in "women's typeface." From *My Life*.

to me immediately. We shall agree on something. We may forget where he lies."[a]

My memory is burning. I painted you, David, with the mandolin. You sit blue in the picture. You lie in the Crimea, in an alien place. And mama, whom you imagined so sadly through the window of the tuberculosis sanatorium—take my heart.

Papa, nobody is home. I would have cut all my art in half—so hard is it to remember, to think about you. It's not you, not the little white hands and not myself, gritty white. The son of an almost proletarian.[b] And a painter, who grew noble (and how!)—refined—the flourish of our last years and my belly and my canvases are covered with the breath of their dying. He loaded a truck, barely making enough for bread. It crushed him. It threw him down and—he died. Just like that. Later, I shall see your grave. From mama to you—two steps. I shall stretch out on the ground the length of your grave, but you won't get resurrected anyway. And when I get old (perhaps sooner), I shall lie down not far from you.

Enough of Vitebsk. Its road is finished and its art came to an end.[c]

You[d] alone are with me, you, my soul won't say a superfluous word about you. When I observe you for a long time, it seems to me that you are my creation and our daughter is with us in our paintings.

More than once have you saved my canvases from unknown destiny. I don't understand people. I don't understand my canvases. Whatever you say is true. Lead me. Take the brush and like an orchestra conductor lead me to mysterious territories.

Let my dead father and mother bless the seed of our painting. And let black—be blacker, and white—whiter.[e]

Forgive me [Ida] for not mentioning you sooner and not coming to mother in the hospital until four days after you were born. A shame, I thought of a boy and it turned out the opposite . . . and at night, when you screamed for no reason, I

[a]Chagall's father was run over by a truck and died in 1921, when Chagall was in Moscow; his brother David died of consumption in the Crimea; his sister Rosa (Rachel) died in childhood. He doesn't mention his mother, who died in 1916, when Chagall was in Petrograd; a tombstone was erected for her. The other siblings also abandoned Vitebsk by 1922.

[b]Officially, the ruling classes in Soviet Russia were then the proletariats and the peasants; children of other classes had no voting rights and had difficulty getting accepted at universities, etc. The irony was that poor Jews, no matter how hard working, were neither peasants plowing the field nor proletarians working in big factories. Chagall tries his best to "fit in."

[c]Chagall was no longer there; his sisters left the city; the "bourgeois" Rosenfelds' property was confiscated; Malevich left in May 1922, and other artists left by the fall of that year.

[d]His wife Berta/Bella.

[e]An allusion to the painting "My Fiancée with Black Gloves."

"Father's Tombstone." Father died in 1921, after the Revolution, hence the last name is in Soviet Yiddish spelling, including all the vowels, yet his given name (a biblical name) is spelled in Hebrew: YHZKEL (Shagal). The letters are simplified, "geometrical" Hebrew. From *My Life*.

hurled you in the bed . . . It's terrible . . . Afterward, a few years later, in Mala-khovka, do you remember, child, what happened?

I had a dream: A dog bit Idochka.[a]

Night. Through the window of my room I can see the balloon of the sky, criss-crossed by gigantic colorful squares, radii, circles, meridians, engraved with words. Moscow—a dot. Berlin—a dot. New York—a dot. Rembrandt, Vitebsk, mil-lions suffering. All colors are burning and burning out, except for ultramarine.

I turn around and see my painting where people are "outside themselves" [= beside themselves].

It is hot, and so green. I sleep between those two worlds and look in the win-dow. For me the sky is not blue, and at night it buzzes like a turtle and shines sharper than the sun.

Is there a connection between this dream and my running over fields the next morning, when my daughter fell and ran to me, covered with blood, with a stick in her cheek.

[a]The Russian diminutive of Ida. The story is parallel to Chagall's own mad dog episode at the age of four.

And I feel again that inside me everything is turning upside down. I walk strangely, alone over the earth. If I could write—the lumps of my words would be more insipid than the earth, than the meadow where you fell down, my daughter. It seems that after me there will be something else altogether. Who knows whether this world will still live.

All this has some textural meaning. If there was a little closet inside my paintings, I would have hidden this text in it . . . And perhaps it would lie entirely on the back of some hero, or in the pants of a klezmer of my theater images.

But who needs to know what is written on his back. In the age of R.S.F.S.R., I scream: "Do you feel how the electrical stages are floating under our feet, and were not my painterly premonitions right that we are truly floating in the air. And we are sick with a disease: 'Thirst for embodiment.'"

For five years,[a] fountains have been gushing in our souls. I grew thin . . . I even want to eat.—I want to see you, Gleizes, Cendrars, magician Picasso. I am tired. I will come with wife and child. I will spread like a river among you. Europe will love me and perhaps Russia too, my Russia.

Vitebsk 14 . . .

Moscow 22 . . .

[a]Clearly, this was written in 1922, five years after the Revolution.

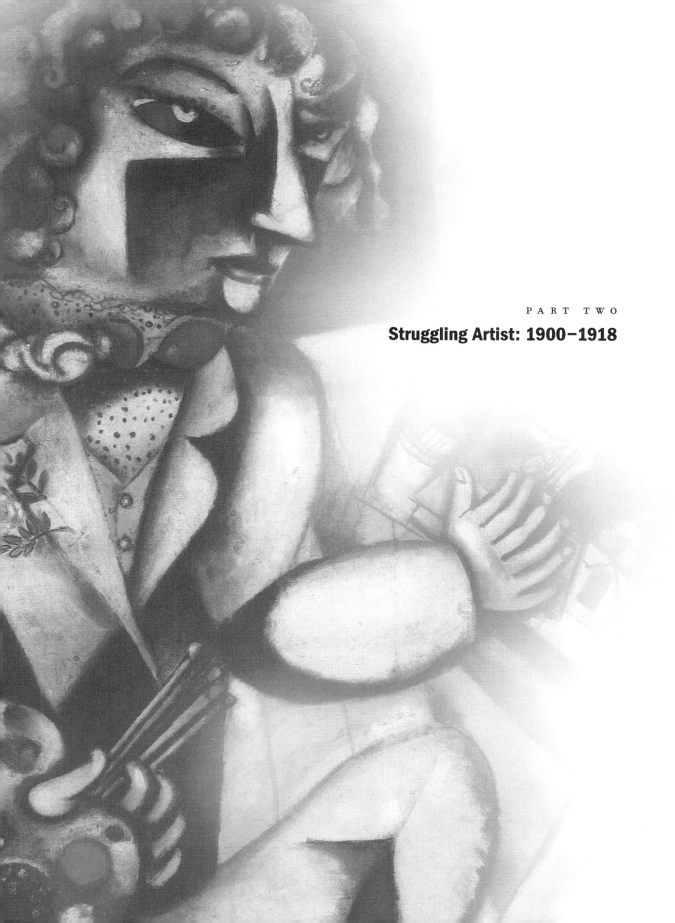

CHAPTER THREE

First Teachers: 1900–1910

School for Jewish artists

Chagall's memoirs of his early teachers, Yury Pen and Léon Bakst, and his mentor Maksim Vinaver, published in this chapter, were written during the 1920s and 1930s in Paris, from a more relaxed and self-confident position. Yet they do tell us something about those "father figures" (as Chagall himself saw them) who were so crucial to the course his life assumed. He did not follow any one of them, but rather used their support and recognition to assert his own contrary and independent personality.

Marc Chagall began drawing at an early age, apparently before his Bar-Mitzva. At thirteen, he went to a Russian school, and when a classmate proclaimed that Moysey was a *khudozhnik* (an artist), he already had paintings hanging on the walls of his parents' home. The matter became serious when the boy coaxed his mother to take him to a real art school to test his talent.

Chagall's first art teacher, Yury Moyseevich Pen, or Yehuda Pen (1854–1937), was born in Lithuania into a poor Jewish family with ten children. After overcoming many obstacles, he did get into the Art Academy and graduated with distinction. Then he settled in Vitebsk and established an art school in 1896–1897, where he taught children from the city and neighboring provinces. Though the art school was not openly defined as Jewish, all the pupils seem to have been Jews, and Pen was a consciously Jewish artist. "You have raised a great generation of Jewish artists," wrote Chagall in 1921, in one of several published tributes to Pen, and Chagall proposed to place his paintings in the future Museum of Jewish Art.

Art was one avenue of modern expression for Jews emerging from the ghetto and embracing the modes of discourse of general European culture. Defying the Commandment "Thou shalt not make unto thee any graven image" (especially in its purist interpretation), many young Jews who did not master the languages of the dominant cultures expressed their artistic drive in painting.

Chagall's biographers tend to boast that he was the first to defy that Commandment, but actually he was participating in a widespread trend. As soon as the religious framework fell in one radical move, a whole generation swept away all barriers and embraced all forms of European civilization and culture, including modern art. Thus, in 1906, a year before Chagall finished his studies with Pen and left for St.-Petersburg, a photo was taken of no less than twenty artists, members of the underground Jewish socialist-democratic party, the Bund, in Vitebsk. At about the same time, the Bezalel Art School was founded in Jerusalem in 1906, and the first modern Jewish artists of Eastern European origin emerged in New York. Jacob Epstein went from the Lower East Side to Paris in 1902 and eventually became a distinguished sculptor in England, where he was knighted; Max Weber and Abraham Walkowitz went from New York to Paris in 1905 and brought Cubism back to New York. Although Chagall was not alone in this move, he became its most prominent artist.

In his style, Yury Pen was a *Peredvizhnik* ("Itinerant") artist[1]—an adherent of a Russian national and realist school of art, interested in social issues and in depicting the mores and manners of provincial Russia. He was also a Jewish populist in his art and attitudes. His early pupils included such famous names as Ossip Zadkine, Marc Chagall, Oskar Meshchaninov, and El Lissitzky. Chagall and

Zadkine were classmates both in the city high school and in Pen's art school, and they saw each other often in Montparnasse cafés during the 1920s.

Pen impressed Chagall with his total devotion to his art and his diligent professionalism. He imbued in the young Chagall the self-confidence of a Jew, a second-class citizen, who can become a real artist, and master a non-Jewish language—the language of art—that competes with the highest Russian standards. He taught Chagall to paint the humble houses and fences of his environment as heroic and colorful objects, as well as Jewish types and religious, folklorized iconography. Chagall clearly was not a follower of Pen's style, nor was he capable of the detailed precision of Pen's naturalism or "academism." Yet precisely in this failure he found his own "primitive" and expressionist style.

Chagall despised everything about his own father—his ignorance, his low status at work, his coarse behavior, his smell of herring, his very mode of existence—and yet he was overwhelmed by sympathy and emotion whenever he mentioned him in later years ("I understood too well this poetic folk-heart, numbed by silence"). He transferred the same attitude to his adopted father figures: Pen, Vinaver, Bakst. He admired the artists and teachers Pen and Bakst as genuine authorities, who influenced his life in his formative years and, however grudgingly, accepted and encouraged his deviant art. Yet he could not appreciate their work and saw them not as models for imitation but as negative models, showing what path not to take. He revered the artists and moved away from their art.

The length of time Chagall studied with Pen is not clear. In any case, it was not just for two months before he left for St.-Petersburg in 1907, as some biographers have assumed.[2] In his original autobiography (see Chapter 2 in this book), he says he studied with Pen for "a month-and-a-half," but in the same breath, he tells us that he had to beg his father "every month" for 5 Rubles for tuition; then he adds that when Pen liked his colors, he let him study for free ever after. "A month-and-a-half" in colloquial Yiddish may simply mean a long time,

"Marc Chagall in Rembrandt Hat," a portrait of the painter by his teacher Yury Pen, 1907 or 1908. On the right is the signature, Yu. M. Pen.

whose precise span the speaker is dismissing. Such expressions of time in Yiddish are not objective statements of fact but subjective valuations (see Chapter 1, p. 57).[3]

In the same early version of his memoirs, Chagall mentions that he was thirteen when he first came with his mother to Pen (i.e., in 1900); in a letter to Pen of September 14, 1921, he says: "I remember myself as a boy climbing the stairs of your workshop"; and in his essay on Pen he writes: "In my childhood, I heard, smelled, and touched his paintings." That could hardly be true in 1907, when Chagall was twenty years old and Pen made a Rembrandt-style portrait of him as a serious artist. In one text he mentions that he was in fifth grade when he went to Pen—fifteen or sixteen years old—which may be closer to the truth, though that would not quite match the childhood images he remembered from his first visit.

Chagall had a fuzzy (or, better, a "functional") sense of time; all times were parallel in his mind, and he identified rather with a series of timeless images and anecdotes. He also often mystified time to minimize the role of his teachers in his growth as an artist. Furthermore, he was in contact with Pen even after he left Vitebsk in 1907, wrote letters to him and articles about him (Chagall was not usually generous with praise of others), and appointed Pen as Professor in his Art College after the Revolution, even though Pen had nothing to do with Leftist avant-garde art. All this is not likely the result of "a month-and-a-half" of studies. Thus, Chagall probably worked under Pen's supervision on and off between 1900 and 1907, or at least between 1903 and 1907.

When Chagall left the Soviet Union, the borders of Russia were closed, and Pen stayed in Vitebsk, teaching in the Art College established by Chagall. In 1927, Pen was awarded the Soviet title of People's Artist of Vitebsk Province. The same year, Chagall published in Paris an essay on his "first teacher" (reproduced on the next page).

On March 1, 1937, the eighty-three-year-old Pen was brutally murdered in his home, ostensibly by robbers, but apparently by the NKVD. The murder was lamented in Chagall's autobiographical poem in Yiddish, *My Distant Home* (see Chapter 12, p. 462). In 1939, Pen's home and workshop were turned into a memorial Picture Gallery in the Name of Yu. M. Pen. During World War II, when Vitebsk was occupied by the German army, Pen's paintings were evacuated to the hinterland and were returned after the war to the State Art Museum of Belarus, in its capital of Minsk. Pen's home and gallery were demolished in the early 1970s. In June 1992, about 150 of Pen's paintings were returned to Vitebsk and are exhibited in its Art Museum. (Pen's portrait of Marc Chagall, however, was left in Minsk.)

Marc Chagall: My First Teachers: Y. Pen[4]

[Russian] Pen was my first teacher. He has always lived in Vitebsk. Vitebsk is alive and Pen lives there permanently. If I am jealous of anything, if I am nostalgic about anything—it is that Pen still lives in Vitebsk, and I always, always live in the Parises. He doesn't understand my letters to him full of questions: "How are my fences, fences, and fences?"

I learned about Pen when the streetcar rolling downhill slowed to climb the hill of Sobornaya [Cathedral] Square, and from the running-board, I discerned a piece of white inscription on a blue background: " . . . Pen's Art School."

Blue and white are the Zionist colors and could not be accidental in the colorless Russian environment. See also the blue and white sky in Chagall's painting "Cemetery Gate," where the Hebrew text promises resurrection of the Jews and a return to the Land of Israel—signed "1917," the year of the Balfour Declaration.[5]

"Oh," I thought, while moving away. "It's an intelligent city, our city of Vitebsk." And I decided to get better acquainted with that sign.

It turns out to be a big, blue tin sign, the kind they hang outside of shops. In our city, little calling cards, wooden planks on doors, mean nothing, no one pays attention to them . . .

"Gurevich's Bakery and Pastry Shop," "Tobacco, Variety of Tobaccos," "Fruit and Vegetables," "Warsaw Tailor," "School of Painting and Drawing of the Artist Pen"—all this looks from the outside like *a shtikl gesheft* [Yiddish: "a serious business"].

This sign seemed to be from another world. Its blue color like the blue color of the sky. It trembles under the sun and the rain. Incidentally, today this sign has melted away like all the snows of yesteryear and I do not insist on anything . . . Have you heard of Pen, my first teacher, the artist, the laborer, who still lives on Gogol Street?

I have lived 38 years[6] and at no other artist's [place] have I seen an atelier so filled with the atmosphere of art. His atelier is overflowing with paintings from floor to ceiling. On the floor, heaps of papers and canvases. The ceiling is free. The ceiling is covered with spiderweb and total freedom. People don't use their ceilings yet. That's why I like to paint people on ceilings . . . Let them sit there. You don't need to go out to the field or out of town, or to pay attention to people, go to the theater, to the synagogue. All this is here. All this is complaining and sighing on Pen's walls—daily, hourly, on Sabbath and holidays, day and night . . . Here and there, between the paintings, are sprinkled some educational Greek plaster heads—arms, legs, ornaments. White objects covered with dust. Wiping our noses, we pupils looked up to the plaster and down to the paper.

And the artist himself? I would lack all talent if I couldn't show you how he looks. Let him be short—that only makes his figure more intimate. The corners of his jacket hang down to his feet, move right, left, down, and with them his watch chain. A bright little beard—sharp, flexible, swiftly painting either sadness or a greeting: *"a gut morgn."*[7]

No beautiful lady in our city reached her twentieth spring without being invited by Pen to pose for him—however she liked. If possible down to the breasts —so much the better.

Pen walks out on the balcony—his hand would get tired from the greetings.

If I write about all this, it is because when I sat in his atelier, I had plenty of free time. I observed everything. I cannot describe Pen's paintings. In my childhood, I heard, smelled, and touched his paintings. I cannot see them from a distance. That is why I am a bad critic, thank God. Incidentally, you like one thing, I another. It's a matter of taste.

Twenty years have passed since I left Pen.[8] My destiny hurled me far from my familiar ruins. But all my life, no matter how different our art is from one another, I remember his trembling figure. He lives in my memory as a father. And often, when I think of the deserted streets of the city, he appears now here, now there . . . And I cannot refrain from entreating you: remember his name.

field: In Yiddish, "field" is also a euphemism for a cemetery, which is apparently the case here.

wiping our noses: Russian and Yiddish expression (*smarkatsh*) indicating that they were still infants in the matter; naïve and ignorant.

From Periphery to Center

From his earliest conscious self-assertion, Chagall strove to break out of the periphery into whatever center appeared on his horizon—and he pushed that horizon ever further. He embraced the new ideals of the center, but rather than being an epigone of trends reigning there, he looked back to the strength of his family and tribe and startled the new center by the whimsy and idiosyncratic images he drew from his past and his periphery. The first step was made by his grandfather and his parents, who moved from the small town of Lyozno to the capital of a province, Vitebsk. Time and again, Chagall would go back to his large family in Lyozno to be in touch with its concrete, tangible world. In Vitebsk, he ventured out of his poor, Yiddish-speaking neighborhood and befriended a group of rich youths in the city center, children of influential Jews who spoke Russian, were interested in Russian literature and culture, traveled abroad, and admired the handsome boy with his unconventional artistic power.

He moved from the primitive, religious *Heder* to a Russian high school; beyond that, to the art school of Yury Moyseyevich Pen; from the old-fashioned "academic" painter Pen to the capital of St.-Petersburg; from a populist school of the Imperial Society for the Encouragement of the Fine Arts to that most Parisian art teacher in Russia, Léon Bakst; from St.-Petersburg to Paris; from a "Beehive" (La Ruche) in Paris, filled with immigrant artists in 1911, to a one-man show in the most influential avant-garde gallery in Berlin, Der Sturm, in 1914.

The social journey started in his teens, the geographic journey when he was twenty. In the spring of 1907, Chagall went to St.-Petersburg to study art on the invitation of his best friend Viktor Mekler. Jews were not permitted to live in the capital unless they were Merchants of the First Guild or academics with a Right of Residence permit, or their legitimate servants. In his first autobiography (see Chapter 2), Chagall writes: "Somehow I scraped up a merchant's 'Patent' for the

'Right of Residence' in Petersburg." Mekler's father was a Merchant of the First Guild and Viktor probably helped Chagall obtain a document stating that he was on an errand for some authorized enterprise. Later, after he had quarreled with Mekler in Paris, Chagall minimized his friend's role in his life. Such a document could not have been obtained by Chagall's father, who smelled of herring, had no power, and didn't understand about studying art in the first place.

In Roerich's School

Between the spring of 1907 and the fall of 1908, Chagall studied in the Drawing School of the Imperial Society for the Encouragement of the Fine Arts (Imperatorskoye Obshchestvo Pooshchreniya Khudozhestv). Soon after his arrival, the painter Nikolay Konstantinovich Roerich (in Russian: Rerikh; St.-Petersburg 1874–India 1947), scion of a distinguished family, became Director of the school. Roerich designed theater sets in Moscow and St.-Petersburg, was a full member of the Salon d'Automne in Paris and the Viennese Secession, and designed sets for Diaghilev. Later, he lived in the United States, established Roerich Museums in New York and other cities, and was active in international peace initiatives.

Chagall donned a long-dreamed-of uniform and studied in the third grade of the class for out-of-town students of this selective school, whose standards had recently improved when painting "from nature"—that is, from human models—was introduced.[9] At the teachers' meeting of April 17, 1907, Chagall received a commendation, along with a group of other students, and was given 6 Rubles for travel expenses. He was awarded a stipend of 15 Rubles a month for the period from September 1, 1907 to September 1, 1908, sharing second and third place (the first stipend was 25 Rubles). In the ballot, all 19 teachers voted for him (whereas even the first student had fewer votes). The Russian intellectual class

Marc Chagall in the uniform of the Imperial School for the Promotion of Art, 1907.

often treated Jews quite differently from the official authorities and police. The stipend for May, June, and July was given in a lump sum of 45 Rubles in advance, allowing him to spend a vacation in Vitebsk. Yet for August, he did not sign the receipt of 15 Rubles, because in July he quarreled with a teacher and left the school.[10]

At the age of mandatory military service, twenty-one,[11] humble and afraid of being conscripted, Chagall appealed to the distinguished director for help.

Marc Chagall in St.-Petersburg to Nikolay Roerich in St.-Petersburg

[Russian] Most esteemed N.K. Roerich,

Reluctantly, I apologize for disturbing your serenity. Shattered by the course of my fate, I am forced to take the unusual step of asking you the following. As I mentioned to you one day, I have been called for military service this year; this has disrupted my work last semester at Bobrovsky's, and will deprive me of artistic training for another three years. My situation is desperate and the expiration date is approaching. I have decided to send a request for deferment to the Highest authority; possibly a highly placed person may intercede on my behalf; but your artistic authority is indispensable to testify to my participation in school, my success, etc.

on my behalf: Apparently, his benefactor Maksim Vinaver, a prominent lawyer and leader of the Russian KaDet (Constitutional Democratic) party.

I appealed to the administration of our school; they replied that they couldn't do anything without you and that they didn't know me . . . And they gave me your address. Perhaps you know me? I am your scholarship student, weary (by the draft) in this insoluble situation which forces me to stay in this Peter [St.-Petersburg] of stifling granite, when the sun draws me and calls me to non-urban nature, to draw! I hope you will not refuse me and expedite the note necessary for my request, and perhaps you will advise me on this personal matter? I love art too much, I have lost too much and am losing more, to accept the idea of wasting three years on military service. The deferment of my military service is absolutely indispensable as long as I have not yet found a solid base [in art] and haven't received a serious preparation in school.

Your devoted,/Your student, Shagal/10 June 908

Zakharyevskaya: The address of Maksim Vinaver and the journal *Voskhod*, where Chagall lived at the time.

My address:
Saint Petersburg, Zakharyevskaya, House 25, Apartment 13

Ministry of the Interior to N.K. Roerich in St.-Petersburg

[Russian] Ministry of the Interior
Office of Military Draft/ IIIrd Department
30 September 1908—no. 29462

To the Director of the Drawing School of the Imperial Society for the
Encouragement of the Fine Arts,

The Office asks you, dear Sir, to send us as quickly as possible information con-
cerning the request for deferment of military service no. 19962, of July 9 this year.
Until what time is the deferment of service needed by the student of your school,
Moysey (Movsha) Shagal (Shagalov) for the full completion of his education.

For the Director of the Office

For the Administrator

K. Roerich in St.-Petersburg to the Ministry of the Interior

[Russian] In response to your request, I have the honor to communicate that the
student Shagal showed outstanding success in school. He does indeed need a
military deferment of at least two years for sufficient perfection in matters of art.

Studies with Léon Bakst

We don't know what exactly Chagall did in 1908–1909; he was mainly in St.-
Petersburg and painted. Once, returning from a vacation in Vitebsk, he was arrested for entering the capital illegally, and was eventually saved by being registered as a servant to a legally privileged Jew. (Moses Mendelssohn in his time
was also allowed to stay in Berlin as a servant to a privileged Jew.) In dire need,
he gave about a hundred paintings of 1907–1908 to a frame maker for sale, but
on his next visit the man denied receiving anything, and thus Chagall experienced his first major loss. In a letter of February 2, 1961, to Ilya Zilbershteyn
in Moscow, Chagall wrote: "Unfortunately, there are also 'false' paintings and
drawings. It is best for me to see the photos. And one must not forget that 'Epic
story,' when a certain Antokolsky[12]—a framemaker etc.—took from me a *hundred*

pieces of the period 907–908 (before Bakst). Where are they? Or do they carry signatures of other, 'famous' Russian artists? In that case, I can identify them myself . . . "

Some circles of privileged St-Petersburg Jews discovered Chagall and helped him in his studies. Probably in the fall of 1909, a generous scholarship of 30 Rubles a month, awarded him by Alisa Berson, paid Chagall's tuition in the Paris-oriented art school of Elizaveta Nikolaevna Zvantseva. This was known as "Bakst's school" (which it certainly was), with the two teachers, Léon Bakst and Mstislav Dobuzhinsky, both prominent figures in the World of Art movement, whose legacy they both tried to overcome at the time.

The famous Russian artist Léon Bakst (in Russian: Lev Samuyilovich Bakst, 1866–1924) was born as Leyb son of Shmule Rosenberg in Grodno, Jewish *Litah*; he grew up in St.-Petersburg (he often claimed he was born there). He studied in the Academy of Art, yet was censored for a wrong treatment of "The Lamentation of Christ" and had to leave the Academy. Between 1891 and 1899 he lived mostly in Paris, where he befriended the Russian artist and critic Aleksandr Benois, and in 1898 they launched the World of Art aesthetic movement in the Russian capital.

Bakst returned to St.-Petersburg and became the graphic editor of the journal *World of Art* (published in 1898–1905). He designed many books and journals, painted portraits, historical paintings, and sets for the ballet. The style Bakst developed together with K.A. Somov and Aleksandr Benois dominated the design of books and journals in Russia for twenty years. In 1906–1910, Bakst was Director of the E.N. Zvantseva School of Art, where he and Mstislav Dobuzhinsky developed new teaching methods.

In 1903, Bakst married the daughter of Pavel M. Tretyakov (the founder of what is now the major Moscow art museum, the Tretyakov Gallery) and converted to Lutheranism (the religion of choice for Russian Jews converting to

Chagall's teacher Léon Bakst, Director of the Zvantseva School of Art in St.-Petersburg, 1907.

Christianity). Yet in 1910 he divorced his wife, returned to Judaism, and settled in Paris. On a visit to St.-Petersburg in 1912, Bakst was officially expelled from the capital as a Jew, and he never returned to Russia.

Bakst was famous as the chief decorator of Diaghilev's Ballets Russes in Paris. "The uninhibited splendor of his spectacles revolutionized European stage design with their combination of Oriental magnificence and the gaudy color of Russian peasant art."[13] He had a crucial impact on Art Deco.

We can imagine that Bakst would find young Chagall unruly, wild, and primitive. Bakst's style was colorful, "oriental," and decorative, composed of a large mosaic of particles, precisely delineated and minutely executed. Chagall could hardly keep precise boundaries or observe symmetrical designs. From the beginning, he felt the clash between his desires and the teacher's style. But once again, he used the teacher as a beloved yet "negative model," as a springboard from which to take off. Bakst's open and provocative style of teaching encouraged Chagall's innate tendencies. What was remarkable about Bakst's teaching was his critical attitude toward the "World of Art," the trend he himself helped create. Bakst's key words reappear in Chagall's Revolutionary manifestos: "academic" and "routine" are the enemy; "searching" is creative. And inadvertently he learned from Bakst the importance of French Fauvism, the autonomy and beauty of exuberant colors; the value of ornament—minute details, off center in any composition; and the lure of Paris.

Yuliya Leonidovna Obolenskaya: The School of Bakst[14]

Graphism: A tendency to prefer graphic design over spontaneous expression.

[Russian] No one would have guessed that under the directorship of Bakst the youth were raised on principles totally opposed to the foundations of "The World of Art": to its Retrospectivism—they opposed the naïve eye of a savage; to its Stylization—the immediacy of a child's painting; to its Graphism—the tempestuous, bright mishmash of colors; and, finally, to its Individualism—conscious collectivism. [. . .]

[Zvantseva had studied at the Art Academy but did not finish and went to Paris; when she returned, she decided] to create in Russia a similar school "against routine." [. . .]

Classes were conducted between 10.30–3.00: two days drawing, the third day from memory; two days a study for a painting, a third from memory. Dobuzhinsky would come on Wednesdays to supervise drawing, Bakst on Fridays—for painting. On Saturday—sketches. [. . .]

Bakst would approach a study, the first from the door, he demanded everybody's attention and, placing the unfortunate author before him, began to unmask all his secret intentions and failures. Thus Bakst's Fridays used to pass: the whole class formed a circle around Bakst, the study, and the accused, whose right ear was burning at the beginning of the investigation and the left ear at the end, after which he would join the general circle for the mutual dismantling of other colleagues. [. . .]

Bakst taught as they used to teach swimming, by throwing you into the water and letting you scramble out on your own. He deliberately refused to give us any ready examples for imitation, any helpful theories. [. . .] Though directing his students to the common goal, Bakst never curbed their innate tendencies, and the variety of those tendencies became clear from the beginning. [. . .]

Beautiful models were not in favor, because they left little space for evolving characteristic features. Nature was selected for its character, for the significant contours. A favorite model was a brown, stocky woman with shortened proportions, bulging belly, and simplified, strongly put-together forms. [. . .]

In sketches from nature, we looked first of all for an absolute combination of colors, a dialogue, even an argument between colors. [. . .] Black contours were totally forbidden: they misleadingly enhanced the power of individual colors but separated the colors from each other. [. . .] Often we were given the colors and themes for a poster of color combinations, e.g., blue, red, and sandy; yellow, green, and orange. [. . .] The ability to juxtapose contrasting colors, balancing their mutual influences and embodying them in the simplest forms—all that helped especially those of us who later worked on murals. [. . .] Marc Chagall's debut was a study done at home: roses on a yellow background. His studies made in class were insignificant, but his works at home constantly served for analysis on Fridays. Bakst valued him (he himself paid Chagall's tuition) but criticized severely. [. . .]

In his analysis of [students'] works Bakst was amazingly subtle in judgments and coarse in expressions. But no real student ever deemed of being offended: on the contrary, a good thrashing gave ammunition for a whole week. [. . .]

So what, after all, did Bakst's school give its students? [. . .] We trained not so much our hand as our sensibility. [. . .] We were preoccupied with the world of bright, sonorous, contrasting colors, the life of a color in its unfolding, in its clashes with other colors. We were interested in the simple and important silhouettes of objects and figures, with the unique, typical features of each object, alien to all schematism. The school gave us a childish immediacy in approaching nature. [. . .] In the dark workshops of Petersburg we had to heighten the color by juxtaposing it with the contrasting colors of the draperies. [. . .]

Our model was nature: an artist was defined as a person who sees objects for the first time. [. . .] With unbelievable vigilance, Bakst warned us against routine, he destroyed bad habits, approximate and insincere approaches, shook up unreceptive impressionability, he disturbed, attacked from all sides, didn't let you catch your breath. [. . .]

Bakst wrote: "I tried not so much to teach as to stir up the desire to search, carefully protecting the young, searching eye from any falsehood and routine."

Chagall's essay on Bakst (on the next page) is a typical example of how modified, often fuzzy, his published autobiography *My Life* is. A short sketch of his encounter with Bakst appeared in Chagall's early autobiography, *My Own World* (see p. 135). Chagall changed it and considerably expanded it here, and also announced it as a chapter of his forthcoming book. Yet the book in French translation, which appeared the next year, lost some concrete descriptions and suppressed various Jewish sentiments; the first two and the last five pages, dealing with Bakst's and Chagall's own Jewishness, were deleted.

An interesting case is the motif of stammering, repeated in many texts. The earliest recorded case of Marc being paralyzed by stammering occurs in the Russian school, when he is called to the blackboard, knows it all, but cannot utter a word. He was a child from an exclusively Yiddish-speaking home who suddenly had to answer in a foreign language, Russian, to a Russian teacher and before a predominantly Russian class. This was a cultural rather than a psychological barrier, but it took on a psychological expression as well as a self-conscious identity signal. Indeed, he hoped that Bakst would understand him because he too was "a stammering boy like me." Stammering becomes a code word for the Jew as outsider. Chagall perceived it as part of a Jewish ghetto syndrome when facing the Russian culture of power; combined it with a vision of unseen sidelocks ("peyes"), hidden behind Bakst's ears, and hoped for Bakst's Jewish solidarity.

Marc Chagall and his close friend Viktor Mekler, "Photographie Parisienne," Léon & Co., Nevsky 63, St.-Petersburg.

Marc Chagall: My Teachers: Bakst[15]

[Russian]** "The Master is still asleep,"—tells me secretively the chambermaid.

1 in the afternoon—and still asleep.

Silence. Neither children's noise, nor traces of a wife. On the walls, reproductions of Greek Gods, a Curtain of a synagogue Holy Ark.***[16]

I am standing thus in Bakst's entrance hall with a roll of my works, and wait. I stand exactly as I stood earlier in Vitebsk, waiting for Pen. Then I mumbled: "I—Mos'ka, my stomach is weak, no money, I want to be an artist." The same now, in Bakst's entrance hall, excited, I whisper: "Soon he comes out of the bedroom. I must think what and how to tell him." To be accepted in his school, to take a look at him. Maybe he will understand me, will understand why I stammer, why I am so often sad and why I paint with purple colors. Maybe he'll explain to me, unravel the meaning of those secrets, which from childhood block the street for me, veil the sky . . .

those secrets: His Jewishness in a foreign world.

—"Why is it? . . . You tell me."

I shall never forget his—perhaps just a smile, perhaps a smile of pity—with which he met me. He stood before me, barely showing a row of shining pink and gold teeth. I imagined I saw reddish *peyes* [sidelocks] curl slightly behind his ear. He could have been my uncle, a distant cousin. He was born, maybe, near my ghetto, and was also a pink and pale child, a stammering boy like me . . .

**"How could I be at your service?" uttered Bakst.

In his mouth, the individual letters seemed to stretch. His different accent gave him an unrussian characteristic, while his fame, in connection with the Russian Season abroad, turned my head too.

"Show your works."***

OK, I'm not shy. I felt that if Pen's judgment was significant only for my Mama, my visit with Bakst, his opinion, seemed to me fateful. I wanted only that no mistake be made—whether a talent is recognized in me or not . . .

Looking at my works, which I, excitedly, picked up from the floor and showed him,[17] he muttered through his teeth like a lord:

**"Y-yes, yes . . . There is talent here, but . . . You're spo-oi-led. You're on the wrong road. You're cor-rup-ted."

Enough! My God, is that me? The stipend bearer of the Imperial School for the Encouragement of the Arts; I, to whom the Director Roerich would mechanically throw smiles with bright teeth, whose "manner" was praised over there; but the same one who really didn't know when this endlessly unsatisfactory daubing would come to an end?

And only Bakst's voice, his words: "Corrupted, but not entirely" saved me.

If those words where uttered by anybody else, I would have spat and got calm . . . But to Bakst I listened standing, excited, believing every word, bashfully picking up and rolling up my drawings and canvases.

What I found in his school will forever be engraved in my memory. I, who had no idea that there was in the world an artistic Paris, discovered here Europe in miniature. The pupils, some more talented, some less, knew the road they were taking. I understood that I must forget my past. I set down to draw a sketch. A naked model stood there: thick, rosy legs, blue background.

In the atelier, among the students, Countess D. Tolstoy, the dancer Nijinsky . . . I am shy again. My sketch is finished. Friday Bakst arrives. He used to appear once a week. Everybody left their works. The easels stood in a row. Waiting. He comes. Looks closely without knowing whose work it is, then he asks: "Who drew it?"

He talks little—a word here, a word there—but the hypnosis and the fear and the smell of Europe made their impact.

He approaches me. I'm lost. He says about me, i.e., about my work, without knowing (or pretending not to know) that it is mine—"words uncomfortable in polite society."

They all look at me, empathize.

"Whose work?"—asks Bakst.

"Mine."

"I knew it," he says, "well, of course."

Countess Tolstoy: Sophia Dymshitz-Tolstoy, the Jewish wife of the writer Count Aleksey Tolstoy.

Nijinsky: Vaclav Nijinsky (Nizhinsky, 1890–1950), one of the great ballet dancers, the male star of Diaghilev's Ballets Russes.

In a flash, I remembered all my half-rooms, all the "corners," nowhere did I feel so awkward as here, after Bakst's remark. I felt that it cannot go on like this.

I draw another sketch. Friday. Bakst arrives, Doesn't praise. I flee from the school. For three months, dearest Alisa Berson, who treated me with such sensitivity, is paying thirty rubles per month to the school, and I am not there.

Berson: One of Chagall's mentors in St.-Petersburg.

Ambitious Chagall overreacted. As Obolenskaya tells it, that was Bakst's usual manner, probably enhanced by his love for Marc (and perhaps she generalized it from Chagall's case). For Marc, those were his first weeks with Bakst, and he fled to his home and his pursuit of love in Vitebsk and Lyozno for a month and a half in September—October 1909, as evidenced by the dates of his Russian poems. On November 8, he was already in St.-Petersburg.

This was beyond my strength. The truth of the matter is, I cannot learn. Or, more precisely, no one can teach me. Not by accident was I a lousy student in the city schools (from the conventional point of view). I absorb only with my internal sense. You understand? I do not fit into the general school theories.

My attendance in school had the character of joining and getting acquainted, rather than enforced study. Having failed with my first two sketches in Bakst's new school, and not quite understanding (not wanting to understand) why, actually, Bakst cursed me—I fled, in order to find my bearings, some orientation, to try to shed some disturbing burden off my shoulders. Then I returned to his school, determined not to surrender and to extort recognition from him and his distinguished pupils. And that is what happened.

I drew a sketch, and on the next Friday Bakst selected it as a "model," that was hung in the school as a sign of excellence.

I lost four or five years to get to this transitional boundary. After a short while, I felt that in Bakst's school too I have nothing more to do. Especially since, because of the establishment of the Russian Ballet abroad, he himself left the school and Petrograd [sic] for ever.***

My meeting with Bakst will stay in my memory for ever. But why should I deny it? Something in his art was foreign to me. Perhaps the fault was not with him but with that society, "The World of Art," where stylization, graphism, society manners flourished, and where the revolution of European art with Cézanne, Van Gogh, and others, seemed a passing French fashion.

Stasov: The Russian critic V.V. Stasov praised ethnicity as an authentic expression and encouraged Jews to treat "Jewish" themes, which would be a lesser kind of art in Chagall's eyes.

Isn't it the same way Stasov and his contemporaries, advocating national and ethnic subjects, derailed Antokolsky?

**Stammering, I said to Bakst:

"Couldn't I, Lev Samoylovich . . . you know, Lev Samoylovich, I want . . . to Paris."

"Ah? Of course! Listen, can you paint stage decorations?"

"Naturally" (couldn't do a thing).[18]

"Here are a hundred Rubles. Learn some techniques of making decorations, and I shall take you with me."

Our roads, however, parted, and I left for Paris by myself.*****

*

When I arrived in Paris, I went to a performance of Diaghilev's ballet, to see Bakst. As soon as I opened the door to the wings, I saw him from a distance. Reddish-pink color, smiled friendly. Nijinsky also went up to me, hugged my shoulders. He must run to the stage. Bakst tells him in a fatherly tone: "Vatsya, come here," and straightens his tie. D'Annunzio stands nearby and flirts languidly.[19]

"You came nevertheless [to Paris]"—says Bakst to me.

I felt awkward. He had warned me not to go to Paris, that among the 30,000 artists there, I could die of starvation, and that he won't be able to help me . . .

So what, should I have stayed in Russia?

But I, even as a child, felt at every step that I am a Jew. If you meet an artist from the society of the [early Futurist] "Union of Youth"—they will hide your paintings in the last and darkest room; and if you encounter an artist from the "World of Art," they simply don't exhibit your things, and leave it in the apartment of one of their members.[20] Everybody was invited to that society long ago, only you are left at the side, and you think: this is certainly because you are a Jew and you have no fatherland . . .

Paris! There was no word more endearing for me. At that moment, I didn't care any longer whether Bakst will visit me or not. He said it himself: "Where do you live, I shall visit you—I'll see what you are doing."

"Now your colors are singing," he said, visiting me.

Those were the last words of Professor Bakst to his former pupil. What he saw, surely told him that I cut myself off from my ghetto for ever, and that here, in "La Ruche," in Europe, I am a human being.

Now Bakst is in the grave. Is he the same who walked out on the stage to bow to the audience; the same who suddenly, 15 years later, walked into my studio on the birthday of my daughter, kissing with me? Bakst died, which means he is a human being. The flowers on his grave withered, and my modest wreath, on whose leaves remained many of my sad thoughts about the fate of an artist. Tears fell on his leaves. I barely put flowers on top of the big, black velvet pedestal in his atelier. The atelier is empty. An easel stands, with a painting turned to the wall. Candles burning. With him, a pillow with a cross and a medal, and nearby, on the sofa, hunchbacked, dozing off, old Jews sit in *yarmulkes* [skullcaps]. A psalm book in their hands, they mumble *tehilim* [psalms]. I felt like chasing out all the Goyim who stood at a distance, in the hall, hats down, and even Ida Rubinstein in a false tragical pose . . . For here a Jew is lying . . . He just ostensibly walked in black tie, chased fame . . . There is no longer fame . . . I looked at my wreath, the most modest of all, sought it out, not to lose it from my sight, and thought about my own fate . . . Couldn't I think [about it] when my heart beats so fast, and my head is flying. But those whom we loved—even if they are no longer with us—it seems to me, they protect us everywhere.

Rubinstein: Ida Rubinstein (1885–1960), a beautiful, Jewish-Russian actress-dancer in Diaghilev's Ballets Russes, a close friend and model of Bakst.

protect us: A Jewish folklore belief that the dead in heaven protect us. "May she protect us in heaven . . ." is a formulaic expression for praising the dead one as a saintly person.

The First Book of Poetry

Miriam Cendrars kept a notebook in Chagall's handwriting that had been in the possession of her father Blaise Cendrars.[21] It contains a collection of poetry written by Chagall in Russian during 1909–1910, neatly copied and precisely dated, as well as some very messy drafts of letters in Russian.[22] Clearly, Cendrars found his friend's notebook, along with Chagall's paintings, "under the bed" in Chagall's studio, which remained unlocked when Chagall went to Berlin and disappeared in Russia during World War I. Assuming Chagall was dead, Cendrars sold the remaining paintings to Gustave Coquiot, who wrote about Chagall and made him famous. But when Chagall returned to Paris in 1923 and did not find them, he refused to talk to his former friend. Thus, the poetry and some sketchbooks remained with Cendrars. Chagall assumed that he lost it: In a letter from Paris to A. Lyesin in 1937, he wrote: "Here is my first long poem in Yiddish (in the past, I sometimes wrote [poems] in Russian, but I lost them)." And in his autobiography: "And I threw away, abandoned or lost, the one copy-book that contained my juvenile poems" (*My Life*, p. 93).

The poems are titled "1909–910, my poems of my childhood, my love, my streets and familiar sky." Most were written in Vitebsk and Lyozno during Chagall's self-banishment from Bakst's school for a month and a half (he says three) in the fall of 1909.[23] Another reason for this flight from Bakst could have been his great, desperate, and unattainable love (was it for Bella, or somebody in Lyozno?), as expressed in the poems (though they are filled with clichés, Christian imagery, and suicidal overtones, in the vein of Symbolist poetry). The poems are most interesting for the understanding of Chagall's early personality and deserve an academic publication.

It is amazing how Chagall, whose Russian education was minimal, mastered the Russian system of precise meters and rhymes, and even wrote a sonnet. It was surely triggered by the aura poetry had in Chagall's surroundings: Bakst's school was located on the first floor of Vyacheslav Ivanov's "Ivory Tower," one of the strongholds of Symbolist poetry. And Chagall once claimed that Aleksandr Blok himself read and liked his poetry.

Yet the poems are filled with a thick fog of Symbolist and Romantic clichés; their language is eclectic and derivative; they seem to convey strong, yet stereotypical, emotions, and their realistic context is seldom clear. Typically, an innovative artist in one medium is a generation behind in another.

The Revolutionary years swept away this kind of poetry. Soon Chagall was separated from daily contact with the Russian language and stopped writing poetry altogether. Only after his visit to Vilna in 1935, where Chagall encountered a vibrant secular Yiddish culture, did he write poems again—truly personal poems in the intimate language he knew from his mother's home, Yiddish—which were later translated into French and other languages (translations from the original are included in this book).

The Russian poems are filled with metaphors of nature and religion: the temple of love or of life; the mood is decadent: he writes of death and suicide, her silences, their nights till dawn. And there are obvious traces of his love (in a literal translation):

When I meet my ennui,
I will tell everybody about you:

Your parting words,

And that you were mine.

And tomorrow you will betray me

And I know—you'll say: go away!

You will curse love forever

In my leave-taking heart.

In several poems he presents himself in the image of Christ:

I walk towards you [my beloved]

Through the thread of [your] yesterday's silence

On the path of momentary hesitations

Here I am sad.

The blue cupolas

As above Christ

I am his high pupil

[Hanging] in tandem, we are lonely

Forever.

From the morning I was assigned

My early destiny on the Cross.

This sentiment of a Chagall/child identifying with Jesus on the Cross was clearly influenced by Aleksandr Blok, especially his poem "Autumn Love" ("Osennyaya lyubov,"October 1907).[24] Indeed, Chagall's unusual painting "Golgotha" (1911?) is almost an illustration of Blok's poem:

When above the leaden ripple of rivers,

In the humid and grey height,

Before the countenance of my terse homeland

I shall swing on the Cross,—

Then—far and wide

I look through the blood of tears before dying,

And I see: in a wide river

Christ sails to me in a boat.

Christ! The homeland expanses are sad!

I grow faint on the Cross!

And your boat—will it moor

at my Crucified height?[25]

Chagall's painting has all those images (without an overtly tragic tone), but they are veiled in oriental garb, representing his "oriental" parents, Bakst's oriental imagery, and his interest in imprecise geometrical circles intercutting with triangular segments, which he developed in dialogue with Robert Delaunay.

Chagall's self-image as Christ was echoed both in Canudo's observation that Chagall looked like Christ (quoted by Chagall himself) and in Cendrars' poem about him: "He's Christ/He spent his childhood on the Cross/he commits suicide every day" ("Portrait")—which clearly came from the same source. Chagall's later Christ images in his Holocaust paintings are quite different—Christ is now the suffering Jew, wrapped in a loincloth made of a Jewish prayer shawl—and is inspired by internal, Jewish sources.

Maksim Vinaver

The two-year deferment from military service obtained for him by Nikolas Roerich expired: Chagall was twenty-three and no longer in Roerich's governmental school. In 1910, Chagall left St.-Petersburg for Paris with a fellowship for a year awarded him by Attorney Maksim Vinaver (1863–1926) and his brother-in-law Leopold Sev. Vinaver was a prominent lawyer, editor of *Vestnik Prava* (*The Law Herald*), a leader of the Russian KaDet (Constitutional Democratic) Party, a member of the Duma (Russian parliament), also prominent in Jewish affairs, and an early collector of Chagall paintings. Vinaver fled from the Bolshevik Revolution, was foreign minister of the White government in the Crimea during the Civil War, and was active in the Russian emigration in Paris.

Thus Chagall avoided conscription into the Russian army, fled the ominous anti-Semitic atmosphere, and reached what the avant-garde considered the center of modern art. When Vinaver died in Paris, Chagall wrote this memoir about his benefactor.

Marc Chagall: In Memoriam Maksim Vinaver[26]

[Russian] Do not be astonished that, leaving aside my brush for a while, I take up the pen—to write about Maksim Moyseevich Vinaver. Do not think that only politicians and public activists had relations with him.

In deep sadness, I shall say today, that with him died a man close to me, almost a father.

Did you closely observe his iridescent eyes, his eyelashes, rhythmically rising and falling, his thinly defined lips, the light chestnut color of his beard fifteen years ago, the oval of his face, which, alas, I was too shy to draw.

And though the difference between my father and him was that my father used to go only to the synagogue and Vinaver was elected by the people [a Representative in the Duma]—they were nevertheless similar to each other. My father begot me, and Vinaver made me into an artist. If not for him, I would surely be a photographer in Vitebsk and would have no idea about Paris.

In 1907, I, a curly-haired nineteen-year-old, left my home forever—to become an artist. In the evening, before the train left, my father asked me for the first time what I planned to do, where I was going, and why. My father, who was recently crushed to death by the only car in Vitebsk, was a holy Jew. In the synagogue, he shed copious tears—and he would leave me alone, if I held the prayerbook and looked in the window . . . In the noise of the prayers, the sky seemed bluer to me. Houses are resting in space and you can clearly see every passerby. Father scraped up 27 Rubles from all his pockets, and holding it in his hand, he said: Never mind, go, if you want, but I'll tell you one thing—I have no more money (you can see it yourself)—here is all that I saved up, and I have nothing more to send you—don't hope for it.

I left for Petersburg. No Right of Residence, no corner, no cot . . . my capital is at an end.

I often watched the kerosene lamp with envy. See, I thought, the lamp burns freely on the table and in the room, drinks the kerosene, and I? . . . I barely sit on the corner of a chair. It is not my chair. A chair without a room. I cannot sit freely. I wanted to eat. I thought of a package with sausage that a friend received. For many hours, I imagined sausage and bread.

And I wanted to paint crazy pictures. Sitting somewhere and waiting for me,

noise of the prayers: East European Orthodox Jews used to pray aloud in the synagogue, each man at his own pace; hence a noisy cacophony emerged.

waiting for me: This list enumerates paintings he will do in subsequent years, after 1914.

green Jews, peasants in bathhouses, red Jews, good and wise, with walking sticks and sacks on their back, in houses and even on roofs. Waiting for me, I am waiting for them, we are waiting for each other.

But suddenly, policemen in the street, janitors at the gates, passport checks in the police station.

Wandering in the streets, at the doors of restaurants, I read the menu like poetry: what they offer today and what is the price of a dish.

At that time, I was introduced to Vinaver. He settled me close to him, on Zakharyevskaya Street, in the editorial offices of the journal *Voskhod*. Vinaver, along with [the co-editors] M. N. Syrkin and L. A. Sev, thought I might become a second Antokolsky.

Voskhod (*Dawn*) was a Jewish journal in Russian, published in St.-Petersburg, 1881–1906. Vinaver was its last editor. Chagall could live in the offices because the journal had ceased publication.

Levitan: Isaac Levitan (1861–1900), Lithuanian-born Jew, was an admired Russian landscape painter in the Impressionist vein.

my painting: "Russian Wedding" (1909), acquired by Vinaver.

Korovin: Konstantin A. Korovin (1861–1939), Russian painter, member of the "World of Art" and Professor at the Moscow School of Painting, Sculpture and Architecture.

Prophet Elijah: At the Passover *Seder*, a goblet is set aside and the door left slightly open for the prophet Elijah. In Jewish folklore, Elijah is a miracle-maker, and surely had conjured up Chagall's trip to Paris—in the next sentence!

Every day on the staircase, Maksim Moyseevich would smile at me and ask: "Well, how?" [= How is it going?]

The editorial office was overflowing with my pictures and drawings. It was not an editorial room, but an atelier. My thoughts about art mingled with the voices of the editorial board: Slyozberg, Sev, Goldberg, Goldshteyn, Pozner, and others. After the meeting, many passed through my atelier, and I would hide behind the mountains of the journal *Voskhod* that took up half a room.

Vinaver had a small collection of paintings. Among others, you could see on his walls two paintings by Levitan. He was the first in my life who bought two paintings from me—the head of a Jew and the Wedding.

A famous lawyer, a representative in parliament, and still, he loves poor Jews, descending a hill with the bride, the bridegroom, and the musicians in my painting.

Once, panting, he came running to me in the editorial office *cum* atelier, and said: "Fast, gather up your best works and come upstairs to me. The art collector Korovin saw your paintings in my place and got interested in you."

Excited that Vinaver himself came running to me, I couldn't find any "best" . . . Once I was invited for dinner on Passover. Reflecting the burning candles and vapors, dark ochre was shimmering—Vinaver's color. Roza Georgyevna [= Mrs. Vinaver] smiled and gave orders, it seemed as if she had descended from a fresco by Veronese.

That meal and that evening sparkled, waiting for the Prophet Elijah.

In 1910, Vinaver granted me a stipend and sent me to Paris.

I worked in Paris, I went out of my mind, watched the Eiffel Tower, wandered

1910 – 1911 ....

Paris

Seule la grande distance qui sépare Paris de ma ville natale m'a retenu d'y revenir immédiatement ou du moins après une semaine, ou un mois. Je souhais même inventer des vacances quelconques, rien que pour pouvoir revenir. C'est le Louvre, qui mit fin à toutes ces hésitations.

A page from Chagall's handwritten autobiography in French. What kept him in Paris was the Louvre. Though the text has been expurgated by Bella, the drawing reflects the authentic version of his autobiography (as in this book): to know France, he has to love French women. The flaccid Eiffel Tower is bending over the city like a Jewish Shofar (ram's horn), heralding the new world. The date reflects the event, not the time of writing (in the late 1920s).

in the Louvre and on the boulevards. And at night, I painted pictures—pink cows, flying heads. The sky grew blue, the colors green, the canvases grew longer, were rolled up and sent to the Salon [des Indépendants]. They laughed, cursed, I got red, pink, white, couldn't understand a thing . . . He came to visit Paris, was looking for me, smiled and asked: "Well, how?" I was afraid to show him my paintings—perhaps he wouldn't like them. Didn't he say himself that he was not an expert in art. But those who don't understand are my beloved critics. Do I have to say that Vinaver's life itself is art?

Recently in Paris, at the wedding of his son, where I came with my family, he patted my back and said: "You justified, justified my hopes," and I was happy again, as nineteen years ago, when he sheltered me in the editorial office of *Voskhod* and later sent me to Paris, without which I would have been a regular green Jew.

Far from Paris, I learned that Vinaver died. An eagle flew down the mountains in those years and was quietly watching. We rarely heard his calm speech. I am sending you, dear Maksim Moyseevich, flowers painted on canvas, grateful flowers.

With your courageous voice, pray to the Almighty for all of us. He will hear you.

CHAPTER FOUR **Paris and Berlin: 1910–1914**

Confusion

Chagall wrote in his autobiography that what had kept him in Paris was the discovery of the Louvre. Yet he was a twenty-three year-old alien, without a word of French, and his early days in the big city were also a period of frustration and confusion, fraught with sexual, artistic, and religious ambivalences. The Cendrars Notebook contains fragments and drafts of letters, written in Russian, exulted, confused, heavily crossed-out, rewritten, unfinished, hardly decipherable. They relate to Marc's love/hate relationship with Viktor Mekler, the close friend of his youth in Vitebsk. The beginning was written in St.-Petersburg, after their emotional farewell at the railroad station, when Viktor left for Paris before Moysey (as he clearly called him). The last fragment was written in Paris. It is not clear whether the letters were ever fully written or mailed.

Fragments of Letters (1910)

[Russian] [. . .] It seems to me—no, my friend, I did not "change." I guarantee you, no one among us, in general, among all people, no one can essentially change. I find in myself terribly much of "such, you know," feminine. And though I know that there is much of "such, you know," feminine in you too, I am still afraid to send you so much written trash [the book of his poetry]. In Paris there are so many misfortunes along with all the best. I am already scared of the many misfortunes that (I read) have befallen the immigrants there . . .

*

[. . .] How do you live? Do you have a good and comfortable place? Is it true that you have a glass roof—a lot of light. I am happy (God knows about what). In part, because I shall certainly be in Paris. It will soon become clear. Good. [. . .] At what boundary did our strength expire, where did it end, the last resonance of our smoke-filled kiss at the railroad station. I only feel that for me (and I am not that important) you are a dear, from the past (you were necessary), you have passed, you are almost nonexistent. This feeling may be also in Paris. But I know—and this is *forever* (I am never disposed differently)—I will love you, perhaps did love and love now. I prostrate myself to a worthy person (in his own way, entirely in his own—in general), I demean myself, wherever and however I stand. I shall not conceal one word and shall humble myself before him.

Shoot me right after the first line for daring to write to you (so many times I started and did not finish). Death sentence. What else could I do? If I had done it at least out of deep hatred. I feel that at this moment my lines would not flow for anyone as freely as for you. But for you too this is exclusively the first thing and the further I move the more I feel this "indisposition"—inside me it becomes desolate and withers away, like fainting in a lukewarm bath (no harm in recalling Marat here). I don't want to write to you about anything, anything, but do you want my soul? It doesn't exist. And you cannot see it (and there is nothing to see). One must know [. . .]

*

I shall not invoke any curses. They have no impact on you. I only want to tell you, perhaps for the last time, that you treat me unjustly as a swine. After 6–7 years of our friendship, you could have been softer.

I left the café on St.-Michel then because my self-esteem was offended.

You told Kozlov[1] (that fallen man of St.-Michel), among other things: "Watch out that I don't abandon you as I left Moysey" [Chagall] [. . .]

Marc Chagall: In Memory of Ya. A. Tugendhold[2]

Yakov Aleksandrovich Tugendhold (1883–1928), scion of a prominent, assimilated Jewish family, was a Russian art critic and art historian, who lived in Paris between 1905 and 1913 and wrote the first reviews of Chagall's work for Russian journals. In 1918, he and Abram Efros coauthored the first book on *The Art of Marc Chagall*, published in Russian in 1918 and translated into German in 1921.

In the early Soviet period he was appointed Plenipotentiary for Art in Simferopol, Crimea, the same title as Chagall had in Vitebsk, and, according to Chagall,
he became an ardent advocate of "Proletarian Art." This memoir tells of Chagall's first days in Paris in 1910, without a friend or a language, yet it was written
two decades later, and naturally, reflects also later events as well as the fact that
it was written for a Soviet journal.

[Russian] I am sending these lines to my homeland. (Where do I get the
strength to overcome the meaning of this word.) Now, when Yakov Aleksandrovich lies in the field, under the Russian sky, my beloved sky—I would like to
say a few words about him who was the first, 20 years ago, to smile at me, who
was the first to open the door of his home, sit me down at a table, who observed
with empathy and a smile my first, crazy works.

"I cannot see his smile anymore?"

Many years have passed since the day I "came" to him for the first time in
Paris with a roll of my canvases and a suitcase left behind the door. I knew no
one in Paris. No one knew me. Going down from the railroad station, I looked
timidly at the rooftops, at the gray horizon, and thought about my lot in this city.
On the fourth day I wanted to return home. My Vitebsk, my fences . . . But Tugendhold took my canvases in his hands. What? What's the matter? Hurriedly,
he began to call one person, another, to call me to go here, or there, and I was
filled with joy just reading my stories . . . Tugendhold became my friend.[3] Many
times I asked him how I should work, and often, I admit, I whimpered (my spe-
cialty) to him. He comforted me, dispatched bundles of my works to exhibits in
Russia (in vain), made efforts to get a stipend. We wandered through Paris for
long hours, and many times, at the end, he stayed overnight in one terrible cot
with me in my poor atelier in La Ruche. And later, during the war, in Russia,
where I too was stranded—he was the first one to talk about me . . . —I even
asked him: should I get married? And he answered: "Yes, but no children" . . .
He pestered Morozov to buy paintings from me, and for the first 300 Rubles, I
boldly got married.

Revolution. In Vitebsk, I am director and commander of anything you like,
and he does the same in the south. Later I saw him in Moscow in a heavy peasant's coat—so tired, he fell asleep on a chair . . . I saw how he expired of love for
us artists, surrounding him in the name of [our] Renaissance.

Tugendhold—is my youth. Had not my heart been in pain anyway, it would
have pinched my heart now in a special way . . .

It is sad to get used to the idea that those years, those landscapes, and those

Morozov: Ivan Morozov (1871–1921), a major Russian collector of Russian and French art and member of a family of prominent art collectors.

our Renaissance: The Jewish secular cultural revival at the beginning of the twentieth century.

joys which I mumble about now—are gone . . . And he lies in the ground, that is close to my heart as my own blood. He lies there, and I am here . . .

Had he only known that I am writing these lines . . .

I don't care: death doesn't mean anything to me. I never believe in it. It's all the same—I see my beloved and dear ones in the sky, in the air, everywhere, persistent.

When I come to my homeland, somewhere I will also see Yakov Aleksandrovich. It must be.

Regards to all of you

Marc Chagall

Paris, 1928, December

The Urge to Exhibit

In Paris, Chagall received a monthly allowance from Maksim Vinaver. He worked on a series of paintings begun in Russia and searched desperately for a place to exhibit. At first, he sent several paintings to Russia, to the Symbolist-inspired World of Art exhibition in St.-Petersburg and to the radical avant-garde exhibition "The Donkey's Tail" in Moscow in 1912. The first did not exhibit Chagall's work at all; the latter took one painting, the significant early "The Dead Man," and put it in a remote corner. Chagall, naturally, attributed both actions to anti-Semitism.[4]

Marc Chagall in Paris to Aleksandr Benois in St.-Petersburg

In October 1911, Chagall was rejected by the Salon d'Automne, and applied to the World of Art exhibition to be held in St.-Petersburg in February 1912. Aleksandr Benois (St.-Petersburg 1870–Paris 1960), the son of a Russian member of the Academy of Architecture, was one of the founders of the Symbolist-Aestheticist World of Art movement in St.-Petersburg. He was a painter, an art critic, and a prolific set designer.

Impasse du Maine 18 Paris 911 [October or November]

[Russian] Very honorable Aleksandr Nikolayevich,

I wrote a few words and stopped, as if I wondered how I would dare write to you. Moreover, it is hard to write to you. To write to you in a lighter spirit, I should have a certain right, and for me, this is a great, complicated, and painful question. This is why I can sometimes be accused of timidity with people, especially with regard to you on this occasion. A thousand pardons. Allow me to tell everything frankly.

I am working in Paris. Not a day goes by that I don't think that there is something essential still alive [in me], and having lost everything (thank God, it is lost all by itself), I am trying to preserve everything by remaining dissatisfied. In a word, I am working. But I must—what else?—exhibit (which I want as much as possible). Furthermore, I have to, for it is my duty to some persons to whom I am materially obliged at the moment, as it will always be, and who themselves may not know why I am such a burden for them, and this feeling is painful to me. During the time spent in Paris, I was not accepted to the Salon d'Automne,[5] even though I was pushed there reluctantly (from that failed exhibit, two canvases were shipped back to Moscow just recently with Tarkhov).

I admit it. Why conceal it? It hurt. But later, Bakst consoled me, scolding me for not telling him sooner, when he was supporting several foreigners he didn't know. And I must say that "connections" are always necessary. I remember that at the Union of Youth, they also hurt me, and what's more, they offended me by not taking what should have been exhibited. But it is enough to torment myself in time of need, in moments when I ask other people (or when someone asks for me) for bread. When I work and address myself to painters, I think I can be freed from these superfluous demands. So here, I am not accepted at the exhibitions, perhaps for a long time—aside from my own indispensable artistic concerns, I must also torment myself and often for something else.

Union of Youth: A Futurist exhibiting society in 1910 in St.-Petersburg hung Chagall's painting in a dark corner (see the essay on Bakst in Chapter 3).

Addressing you, I rejoice first for writing sincerely to a man who knows me and understands me so profoundly that he even grasps what I can't express.

Moreover, your artistic integrity will give you a sure judgment. [. . .] Thanks to you, I may receive a very useful additional lesson. Forgive me for the disturbance and thanks—it seems to me that something has become lighter despite the great cold that prevails in my room.

Your devoted / Chagall

Marc Chagall in Paris to Mstislav V. Dobuzhinsky in St.-Petersburg

Chagall was also seeking connections in his homeland. Mstislav Valeryanovich Dobuzhinsky (1875–1957), a Russian-speaking Lithuanian aristocrat, whose father, a Lieutenant General in the Russian artillery, founded the Lithuanian Society for Preservation of Antiquities, was an artist, art teacher, prolific set designer, and a leading figure in the Symbolist group The World of Art. In 1909–1910, Chagall was his student in the private art school of E.N. Zvantseva in St.-Petersburg ("Bakst's school"). After the Revolution, Dobuzhinsky designed some stage sets for the new Yiddish Chamber Theater in Petrograd and its Yiddish logo. When Chagall founded an Art College in Soviet Vitebsk, he invited Dobuzhinsky to teach, offering him the post of Director of the school, which he held for a brief period, December 1918–March 1919. In 1924, he emigrated to Lithuania, and in 1939 to the United States; he spent his last five years in Western Europe.

912 Paris Passage de Dantzig 2 [La Ruche] Chagall [1911][6]

[Russian] Highly esteemed Mstislav Valeryanovich

In response to your kind invitation to participate in the "World of Art" exhibition conveyed to me by Mr. Tugendhold, I am sending several works. I did them in Paris in my desire to remember Russia. These works are not entirely typical of me; for the Russian exhibition I selected the most modest ones.[7] Let me thank you from the bottom of my heart for your attention to me, which, as I am fully aware, I do not deserve.

Your admiring and devoted/   Chagall

P.S. Please mention these works in your catalogue under the title:
From the cycle "Impressions of Russia"
NN (drawings) (No. 1 on the cover is not my property)

Marc Chagall in Paris to Mstislav V. Dobuzhinsky in St.-Petersburg[8]

Paris 1911 [?[9]]

[Russian] Highly esteemed Mstislav Valeryanovich,

I received your cable and send my works today (in the same box as the works of Mr. Tarkhov). I informed Bakst. Now I would like to ask you a favor: it is very important for me to be sure that all my works will be exhibited.

I remember the arguments with the censors at our exhibition in *Apollon*,[10] and therefore am very worried about the fate of the present works; I can rely only on you to defend my works with the censors, if possible. I have doubts about the piece called "Home Interior (The Birth)." The censor may dislike the title "Birth" —in that case, please keep only the first part [of the title] and explain it as a purely decorative exercise. I am sorry to disturb you, for I know how busy you are, but I don't know anybody in Moscow. Also, concerning the hanging of the pictures, I would think it advisable to hang them in a certain lighting (following the custom of the French Salon, where the hanging is always enhancing the paintings). I would like to hang them half-tilted, not facing a window with strong light; but neither in a place that is too dark. It is best to hang [the pictures] next to a window. You must also be careful about the distance: they have no place in a small room. Finally, I would like to ask you to ask the Exhibition Committee to send me the account of all expenses credited to me, including my part of the expenses for sending the works together with Tarkhov, or give it to the person who will come to pay my fee.

That is all I wanted to ask you and I hope you will take all measures, so I will remain sincerely grateful and obliged to you

M. Chagall

Names of the Works
No. 1 Home Interior, The Birth
No. 2 The Room
No. 3 Dead Man in the Street (but you can change all those names as you like, according to your own judgment)

Bakst: Chagall's teacher Léon Bakst resided in Paris and was a member of the jury of the St.-Petersburg exhibition.

decorative: Rather naïve; the painting centers on a naked woman, who just gave birth to a baby.

La Ruche

In late 1911, Chagall moved to La Ruche (The Beehive), a settlement of some 140 artists, mostly immigrants, including many Eastern European Yiddish-speaking Jews (several of whom became known as The School of Paris.) Among them were

The rotunda in La Ruche, where Chagall lived and worked during 1911–1914. (This photo was taken much later.)

the Russian Jews Chaim Soutine, Jacques Lipchitz, Moïse Kissling, Pinkhas Kremegne, David Shterenberg, Nathan Altman, the Italian Jew Amadeo Modigliani, the Ukrainian Archipenko, Léger, and the future Soviet Commissar of Enlightenment, Anatoly Lunacharsky. Chagall's relatively high stipend enabled him to rent a large studio on the upper floor; he met several French poets and artists, and had liaisons with French women.

Blaise Cendrars (1887–1961) was a close friend and promoter of Chagall. He was born in Switzerland as Frédéric Sauser, changed his name, became a French poet, adventurer, world traveler, and a major force on the French avant-garde scene. He spent three years in Russia and wrote his long poem, "Prose of the Transsiberian Train and of Little Jeanne of France." Later he spent several years

Inside the rotunda, Chagall climbing up to his old studio.

The French avant-garde poet Blaise Cendrars.

in America and upon his return to Paris in 1912, discovered "the crazy Russian." Cendrars married Fella Poznanski, a Jewish woman from Russia, whom he met as a student in Bern in 1907 (and whom Chagall wooed before his return).

Another friend and promoter of Chagall was Ricciotto Canudo, an Italian who founded and edited *Monjoie!*, a bimonthly journal in French that appeared between February 1913 and June 1914. Canudo also and published a "Manifesto of Cerebrist Art" both in his journal and in *Figaro* of February 9, 1914. The manifesto advocated an art that would merge the cerebral and the sensual and investigate character through deformation—a principle that appealed to Chagall.

On Friday evenings at Canudo's home, Chagall met the best artists of his generation, including Sonia (a Russian Jew herself) and Robert Delaunay, André Lhote, and other friends who supported him throughout his life.

About the same time, Chagall was discovered by the avant-garde poet and influential art critic Guillaume Apollinaire (1880–1918, born in Rome to a mother of Polish origin). Both Cendrars and Apollinaire wrote poems about Chagall; Apollinaire reviewed his paintings and helped promote his name.

Blaise Cendrars: from "Nineteen Elastic Poems"[11]

[French] I. Portrait

He is sleeping
He is awake
Suddenly, he paints
He takes a church and paints with a church
He takes a cow and paints with a cow
With a sardine
With heads, hands, knives
He paints with a bull's pizzle
He paints with all the foul passions of a little Jewish city
With all the heightened sexuality of provincial Russia
For France
Without sensuality

He paints with his thighs
He has eyes in his ass
And all of a sudden it's your portrait
It's your reader
It's me
It's him
It's his fiancée
It's the corner grocer
The milkmaid
The midwife
There are buckets of blood
The newly born are washed in them
Skies in torment
Modernistic mouths
The Tower spiraling
Hands
Christ
He's Christ
He spent his childhood on the Cross
He commits suicide every day
Suddenly, he's no longer painting
He was awake
he's asleep now
he is choking himself with his tie
Chagall is surprised he's still alive

II. Studio

The "ruche"
Stairs, doors, stairs
And his door opens like a newspaper
Covered with visiting cards
Then it closes.
Disorder, wild disorder
Photographs of Léger, photographs of Tobeen, which you can't see
And on the back
On the back
Frenzied drawings
And paintings . . .
Empty bottles
"We guarantee absolute purity of our tomato sauce"
Says one label

The window is an almanac
When the lightning like gigantic storks brawling empties the sky barges and
    tumbles out hampers of thunder
Out fall

Pell mell

Cossacks Christ a sun decomposing
Roofs
Sleepwalker goats
A werewolf
Petrus Borel
Madness winter
A genie split open like a peach
Lautréamont
Chagall
Poor kid beside my wife
Morose delight
His shoes are rent
An old pot filled with chocolate
A lamp casting its own shadow
And my drunkenness when I visit him
Empty bottles
Bottles
Zina
(We've talked a great deal about her)
Chagall
Chagall
In rungs of light

    October 1913

With the Cubists

Finally, in March 1912, Chagall was accepted into the Salon des Indépendants, where he also exhibited in 1913 and 1914, along with Archipenko, Brancusi, Delaunay, Gleizes, and Rivera—the second generation of Cubists, who were pronouncing new artistic trends, such as Orphism, Simultanism, and Synchronism. In October 1912, he was admitted to the Salon d'Automne, but for one year only.

    The early Russian reception of this Parisian generation and Chagall's place in it can be seen in two reviews of 1914, by Yakov Tugendhold (under the pseudo-nym Sillart[12]) and Anatoly Lunacharsky—both living in Paris at the time. Sillart's report was published in the prestigious Russian Post-Symbolist journal *Apollon* in St.-Petersburg.

Sillart [Tugenhold]: The Salon of the "Independents" (1914)

[Russian] The exhibition of the "Independents" opened very early this spring. As before, the hastily-erected wooden barracks remind you of the camp of a warring tribe, taking a position in enemy country. 3o years of existence could not soften the disfavor it has encountered from the government and the Paris city authorities. The Salon of the "Independents" discovered some of the major artists of our time: Gauguin, van Gogh, Toulouse-Lautrec, Matisse, Vuillard . . . who determined the whole face of modern art, and yet it sets up its tent as before, accompanied by the whistles of the firemen and the laughter of the idlers. To this day, original talents are huddled in that famous tent, and their presence determines the historical significance of this Salon.

After the recent refusal of the Salon d'Automne to admit the Cubists, it was to be expected that they would take revenge and go to the "Independents." Indeed, they appear here with a whole army, with pomp and noise, so that no one could conclude that they don't exist any longer. From the first step, in the front halls, where the most unassuming paintings were once located, in the style of the Society of French Artists, you now encounter immense Cubist canvasses, screaming wildly with saturated colors in the whirl of cylinders, spirals and trumpets. Picasso and Braque are absent, as always keeping their distance, in their proud isolation. Their unapproachable silence befits their role of enigmatic priests, who pre-determine the fate of art . . . Let us not bother them. As for their disciples, they have procreated more than ever, and in their daring initiatives they often leave their teachers behind. Their creations abound with posters, newspapers clippings, cinema tickets . . . and it is rumored that in the near future we shall be able to see real candlesticks and pipes inserted into the paintings. Bluff that has been practiced so far only in business increasingly begins to permeate the sphere of art, infecting the young, who seek quick success and noisy fame. "Breaking the record" has become the general slogan, and for this purpose everything is permitted, including the absurd and obfuscation. Every day new "Isms" emerge, with noisy manifestoes that destroy not just yesterday's "discoveries" but all the art that has existed till now. After Cubism and Futurism, Orphism appeared last year, and barely did this formula resound, when in its place, Delaunay promoted "Simultaneism" and Morgan Russel announced "Synchronism."

Orphism was coined by Apollinaire 1912–1913 to describe nonrepresentational color abstraction, especially as developed in the work of Robert Delaunay at the time. Simultanism was Robert Delaunay's term, indicating the use of color to create virtual space in a picture. Apollinaire widened its scope, to include all kinds of simultaneity and the expression of multiple awareness in the arts. Russel was an American working in Paris. Synchronism indicates the centrality of color in creating both the form and the content of a painting.

It would be superfluous to analyze these novelties of the season in the fashion of the Cubist critics, who discover in them profound truths, that can subvert the whole universe. I shall only say that I am struck by the agility of the contemporary innovators in finding ever new "Isms," ever new resounding words, for there is nothing new except for these words. Monet, Cézanne and Gauguin did not seek new words and yet created truly new works, whereas now, on the contrary, everyone thinks only about new labels. By the way, one cannot especially chastise them for it, because the artists adapt themselves to the spirit of the time, where advertising rules with absolute power. The old Cubism, as presented by Gleizes and Metzinger [in their defining book *Cubism*], appears pale in comparison to the "realizations" of the young.

The reader will permit me to dwell in passing on one feature that the Academic painters and the Cubists share: a negation of life. The former, instead of observing nature, study the techniques of the old masters; while the latter, unable to grasp the organic laws of creativity and the vital rhythm of nature, erect a world based on their own fantasy, choosing the moment of chaos as their point of departure. A natural concomitant of such an attitude toward art is, of course, the cult of the formal, which is expressed, particularly by the Cubists, in the search for a phantom "fourth dimension," in their play with volumes and planes. (If you wish, you could find here an analogy to the fantastic verse of Mallarmé). The Cubists strive to show all the material essence of objects, uncovering even its unseen sides, but they forget the most important (what most interests us): the spiritual side of things and creations,—thus one critic.

Here Sillart describes the work of the most prominent young painters: Dunoyer de Segonzac, Luc-Albert Moreau, André Lhôte, Moïse Kisling; most of them were in the orbit of Chagall's activity.

Most interesting are the works of the Russian artist Chagall. He loves the art of the Russian *Lubok* [colorful narrative folk paintings], the naïveté of its composition, the wild and chaotic, drunken life of the peasants in the remote villages of Lithuania [Byelorussia]. On the background of toy huts and exotic, nonsensical scenes of village life, an immense figure of a peasant rises, strumming on a fiddle in drunken despair. Chagall invests this figure with some higher, symbolic significance. It speaks with a more lucid and expressive power than long stories about dead boredom and longing, about the dark and oppressed peasant existence. Chagall feels deeply the mystery of daily life, the abhorrent aspects of the people's life. His disheveled compositions are magnificently accompanied with bright and teasing colors, florid as a handicraft, which sometimes attains a great and suggestive power. As a colorist, he occupies a special place in the Salon of the Independents, and his influence on the younger artists is palpable. But, what makes his painting especially valuable for us, is the presence of its psychological justification. Chagall has his own world, he gives us the truth, which sheds an original light on reality. A naïve and vivid sense of life have become quite rare in our time of soulless formalism, when art becomes mathematics. Just look at Chagall's neighbors in the Salon of the Independents —all those "Simultaneous Suns," "Electrical Prisms" and other mechanics—and your soul is chilled. This is why an artist for whom reality is something new and intimate, worth telling the world about it—and Chagall is such an artist—is infinitely precious to us.

Anatoly Lunacharsky: Marc Chagall (1914)[13]

After the Revolution of 1917, the People's Commissar of Enlightenment Anatoly Lunacharsky (1875–1933) played an important role in Chagall's life and career by promoting him to "Tsar" of all art activities in Vitebsk Province and financing Chagall's avant-garde Art College. But before the Revolution, he was a Marxist exile in the West. In Paris, Lunacharsky lived in La Ruche and befriended the painter David Shterenberg (whom he later appointed head of all art in Soviet Russia). From Shterenberg he learned about the fermenting art scene and wrote reviews for Russian papers.

> [Russian] In the same colorful and poor La Ruche, that huge collective nest of artists, where Shterenberg lives, so does young Marc Chagall. He is already well-known in Paris. His crazy canvasses with their intentionally childish manners, their capricious and rich fantasy, their typical grimace of horror and considerable share of humor, unwittingly provoke the spectators' attention in the salons—an attention that is, by the way, not always favorable.

Cendrars, who recently became famous with his invention of "Simultane-ism," i.e., accompanying a text with a range of colors, devoted two amazing po-ems to Chagall, published in the German journal *Der Sturm*.

Chagall—a young man, some twenty-four years, colorful himself, with strange, wide eyes, peeping out under tempestuous curls—gladly shows me a countless quantity of his canvasses and drawings, hastily adding that he has more in St.-Petersburg, in Berlin, in the Salon. Obviously, he works a lot. But his work is not that difficult. After all, those are fleeting fantasies, and his art lacks serious technical support.

Chagall was born in Vitebsk. Somewhere in a suburb, his parents traded in fish, or something like that. Then he got into the School for Encouragement of the Fine Arts. Even there, his paintings were strange in their enigmatic psycho-logical substance and their tendency toward deformation; yet they lacked color. His excited love for variegated, colorful canvasses came to Chagall from his later teacher, Bakst.

But now Chagall feels that he went beyond Bakst long ago. The genre he chose for himself—is madness. And what justifies this choice is the fact that he chose it unwittingly. His head is filled with curious anecdotes, nightmares and carica-tures. He cannot work otherwise.

When at work, his caprices or tastes, in a manner incomprehensible to him-self (if you wish, subconsciously), prod him: "Why is it forbidden? Why not? Why not make a purple cow? Why not paint a man walking on the ceiling? Why not break up the sky into several unequal triangles, and color each as the soul pleases?"

Chagall is capricious and playful, but it seems to him that he has no choice. Why do you have this or that?—you ask. In haste, the artist mumbles: "For me, you see, it was necessary to do it like this." At first sight—unrestrained capri-ciousness. But actually, he is possessed.

Here is a small painting. A man sits on the roof of a house and eats; another man, wearing only a nightshirt, walks in the street. "You see," says Chagall in his childish words, "here is my whole biography: they used to find my grandfather on top of the roof, where he loved to eat *tsimmes* [carrot stew]. And my uncle loved to walk the streets dressed only in a nightshirt."

"Our family," "Our living room," "Our dining room," "Our street"—Chagall repeats it often. All the elements of his fantasy come from the boring, crest-fallen, awkward life of the lower class people of a Lithuanian suburb. As if cut-ting himself off from the pressures of those gray people, Chagall mixed it and confused it all: then, he claims, it was funny and entertaining. But sometimes, horrifying. Black windows, half covered with curtains, twisted faces, strange, crooked lamps, gesticulating monuments, awkward positions, prosaic life mixed with nightmare.

A satirical and drunken spirit hovers over Chagall's almost chaotic compositions.

Among the unusual variety of curious incidents invented by him are also some compulsive ideas. Calves always appear, a soldier with a maiden, unnaturally steep mountains, traversed by horses and wagons, a he-goat in the sky, and the like.

The love for beautiful ornament, the love of a folktale can be felt in some branch covered with flowers or fruit, and mainly just in colors. Entirely oblivious of the realistic colors of objects, Chagall paints raspberry streets, brown sky, blue carpets. Mostly he chooses almost pure colors, beautiful in themselves, and strives to juxtapose them in new ways.

His reality fantasy sometimes is drawn to various attractive Cubist elements, but they are typical, and Chagall does not understand them: "Here I indulged in little squares, at that time I had to, it was a necessity, I had such a period."

There is, of course, a certain pretension there, a certain coquettry, a wish to amaze. If there was only this, Chagall's art would have been disgusting. But no. Through all the infantility, the absurdity of the simplified and, at the same time, fuzzy and confused picture, suddenly a great talent for observation, a great expressivity, peeps through sharply. This sudden illumination of a bright psychological talent in a childish manner of painting strikes us with special force, like old people's wisdom on the lips of a child.

Chagall is an interesting soul, though, no doubt, a sick one, both in its joy and its gloom. A young [E.T.A.] Hoffmann from a slum around Vitebsk. More precisely: a Remizov of the brush, a Remizov of the Pale of Settlement. And yet, he is not a great painter. His composition is torn up into small fragments, constantly falling apart into separate scenes, separate inventions, breaking up the viewers attention. His coloring is also reduced to such fragments. Every corner of the painting presents some scherzo, some "invention." It is not fused all together.

Observing Chagall's pictures and drawings is an entertaining endeavor, for they contain a hallucinating, bright imagination. Their *Lubok*-like character does not interfere with it. But for content it is as interesting to look at as at the colored etchings of the great Utamaro. There too, the artist strikes you at every step unexpectedly with the inspired dance of his fantasy. But what a difference! There—a painter, a man with an extraordinary culture of sensibility, dominating the painting, which is known to the painter in all its details, as well as the unmatched sense of the color tone; there—a virtuoso, who mastered it all and subordinated it all to the immense freedom of his invention.

Here . . . Perhaps Chagall could have drawn and painted somewhat better. Of course, he wants a certain naïveté on purpose. But to draw well, to paint *well* with colors—this he cannot do. You can see that he has little knowledge. His taste is also problematic, for, while pursuing his anecdotes, helpless before the visions

Remizov: Aleksey Remizov (1877–1857), a highly admired Russian Symbolist writer; often grotesque, weird, or whimsical; born to a poor family and known for his stories of Russian provincial life.

Utamaro: Kitagawa Utamaro (1753–1806), Japanese painter and printmaker.

of his excited imagination, Chagall doesn't know how to make all ends meet, how to harmonize his works.

Nevertheless, he remains an interesting artist. First of all, he is interesting as an original poet. A poet who strives to express his exceptional soul in graphic forms and colors, and attains it in a unique manner.

Had others joined the same path, it would have been a calamity. Unfortunately, eccentricity without the mastery of the craft, riding on sheer talent, unsupported by powerful means of expression—this is a disease of many young people. But Chagall is forgiven for it. His paintings are curious, absurd, and yet they make you laugh and scare you in turn, and you feel that he himself is like this, that, after all, it is all profoundly sincere.

Yes, you forgive Chagall, no doubt, you even look with interest at this hallucinating splendor, at those individual, prickly, sharp observations, at this naïve play of the brush, and at the same time . . . you feel sorry for the artist. He wants to fly, but he flies like a tamed bird, like a bird with cut wings: in a funny way, leaping up over the ground, sometimes tumbling and falling. Nevertheless, he likes this flight. And you laugh and are interested how he leaps into the air, how this semi-winged being wants to clap with its wings. And suddenly you come to, and sense disease and deformity in all of this . . .

However, if we exclude the wonderful knowledge of the language, I could have said almost the same about Aleksey Remizov. And he is famous! Chagall is from the same family of artists. And he is very young. Maybe his fame will rise even higher than the fame of Remizov?

Breakthrough

Herwarth Walden (pseudonym of Georg Lewin, 1878–1941), an Expressionist theoretician, was influential in presenting the international avant-garde in art and literature to a German audience. In 1910 he founded a journal in Berlin, *Der Sturm* (*The Storm*), and in 1912 he began exhibiting the new artists in his gallery of the same name. With Hitler's rise to power, Walden—as both a Jew and a promoter of "Degenerate Art"—fled Germany to the Soviet Union, where he was liquidated in Stalin's purges.

As Walden described it, when he visited Paris in March 1913, he met his friend Guillaume Apollinaire, as well as Canudo, Blaise Cendrars, Robert and Sonia Delaunay, Juan Gris, Fernand Léger, and Marc Chagall. "This young man with strange, bright eyes and curly hair is admired by his Parisian friends who consider him a genius, which he is after all."[14] The same year, he exhibited three of Chagall's key paintings in the First German Autumn Salon, featuring seventy-five artists from twelve countries. And in June 1914, Walden organized Chagall's first comprehensive one-man show in the Der Sturm gallery in Berlin, including forty oil paintings and 160 gouaches, which made a strong impression on the German Expressionists.

Chagall went to Berlin for the opening, and on June 15, 1914, he took the train to Russia. But before he left Paris he had received his first contract with a gallery, signed by its owner Charles Malpel. The first payment was made on May 1. According to Chagall, no more payments were made, because he was away from Paris.

Contract Between Charles Malpel and Marc Chagall in Paris

The document is hand-written by Malpel, signed and stamped.

[French] Between the Undersigned

Charles Malpel residing in Paris rue de Clichy, no. 26 on the one hand, and Mr. Chagall, artist, painter, residing in Paris Passage de Dantzig, on the other hand.

The following has been agreed:

Mr. Chagall agrees to deliver to Mr. Malpel, who accepts, his entire production for one and a half years, renewable by tacit agreement unless there is prior notice by either party by registered letter three months before the expiration of the first period. Consequently, Mr. Chagall will not have the right to sell or give any work without the agreement and consent of Mr. Malpel.

In exchange, Mr. Malpel agrees to provide Mr. Chagall a monthly salary of two hundred fifty francs corresponding to six canvases of more than 15 and less than 31 each [inches?] (those of larger dimensions counting as two), as well as the drawings and watercolors relating to the specified canvases.

Payment of the monthly salary will take place on delivery of the canvases and will be made by means of a check drawn on a Banque de Paris.

Mr. Chagall's currently existing canvases will be shown to Mr. Malpel on their return to Paris, and Mr. Malpel will have the right to choose which of them he likes. Payment for those canvases will be based on the above mentioned monthly salary.

Mr. Malpel may not influence Mr. Chagall in relation to his artistic aspirations and development. It is already agreed between them that Mr. Chagall trusts the tastes of Mr. Malpel, which he knows and appreciates.

The present contract will take effect on 1 May 1914 and the first monthly salary concerning the month of May has been paid on this day to seal the present contract.

Made in Paris, 30 April 1914

Charles Malpel [signature]

Marc Chagall [signature]

Marc Chagall in Paris to Jacques Doucet in Paris

In *My Life*, Chagall tells of a letter of recommendation which Riccioto Canudo wrote for him to Jacques Doucet (1853–1929), the foremost fashion designer of his time and a major art collector. Canudo praised Chagall as "the best colorist of our day." Chagall brought about fifty watercolors to Doucet and accompanied Canudo's letter with his own.

[May 1914] Passage de Dantzig 2, La Ruche

[French] Monsieur,

I know that you have an intelligent interest in the works of modern art for which new artists suffer and struggle while working with all their heart. The exceptional encouragement which the press has lavished on my work, especially at this time of the Salon des Indépendents, gives me the courage to address you directly in the hope of drawing your desired attention to my work. I am impelled particularly by my very wretched life which overwhelms me and shakes the little bit of health I have.

In a few days (toward the end of the week), my paintings and drawings are to leave for the one-man exhibition that is being organized in Berlin for me. May I hope that your genuine love of art will give you a desire to see my works before their departure and that if you like them, you will not refuse me the help that I expect from an enlightened and expert art collector like you. I take the liberty of attaching the copy of a letter that one of the most important figures of the modern art world, Mr. Canudo, did me the honor of writing. And I dare to await your reply with confidence.

My deepest respect,

Marc Chagall

But Doucet responded through a servant: "We don't need 'the best colorist of our day'." Embarrassed, Chagall hastened to respond with a little note of humble modesty.

Marc Chagall in Paris to Jacques Doucet in Paris

[French] Sir,

The spirit in which Mr. Canudo's letter was written is far from my character, I have no pretensions.
  I beg you to believe that I am a most modest fellow—
  Please accept, Sir, the assurance of all my respect

Marc Chagall

Sunday noon

Passage de Danzig, 2.

Marc Chagall in Paris to Robert Delaunay in Paris

Passage de Dantzig 2 [La Ruche]

[French] Dear Mr. Delaunay

I received your letter. Thank you. I shall take it to Berlin.
  My greetings

In a hurry   Chagall

Marc Chagall in Berlin to Leo Kenig in Paris

Leo Kenig (or Koenig, pseudonym of Leyb Yaffe, 1889–1970), a fellow Byelorussian Jew, was a painter and intellectual art critic, essayist, and journalist in Yiddish and Hebrew. In 1907–1908, he studied art in the Bezalel Art School in Jerusalem (founded in 1906); during 1910–1912, he studied art in Munich. He was a contemporary of Chagall in La Ruche in 1912–1914. Kenig was promoting the notion of "Jewish art," and tried to dissuade Chagall from avant-garde nonsense. In an article published in a Warsaw Yiddish newspaper, he wrote a devastating attack on Blaise Cendrars' poem about Chagall; when Cendrars heard about it, he went to the Yiddish kiosk in Paris and bought up all copies of the paper. During 1914–1952, Kenig lived in London and was the representative of world Yiddish literature in the International PEN club. He immigrated to Israel in 1952, lived in Haifa, and wrote essays in Hebrew. Chagall corresponded with him through the years.

Postcard: First German Autumn Salon, Berlin / Potsdamerstr. 75. "Marc Chagall: Dedicated to My Fiancée." Published by *Der Sturm*.

[French] To Mr. Kenig
Chagall
914 Paris

The painter Kurt Schwitters wrote a poem describing the absurd composition of Chagall's painting "The Drunkard," which sounds like a veritable Dada manifesto:

Kurt Schwitters: On a Painting by Marc Chagall[15]

Playingcard drones fish, head in the window.
Animal head yearning for the bottle.
On the bouncing mouth.
Man without head.
Hand wags sour knife.
Playingcard fish squander dumpling bottle.
And a table drawer.
Imbecile.
And a button on the table encircled introvert.
Fish presses the table, the stomach nauseous with swordscar.
A drunkard shaft leers dumb the clever animal.
Eyes thirst for the smell of the bottle.

Marc Chagall in Berlin to Sonia and Robert Delaunay in Paris

Postcard of the journal *Der Sturm* with image: Marc Chagall: Der Viehändler ("The Cattle Dealer").
Address: Kurfürstendam 76, Berlin. Stamped: 15.6.14.

[French] Bonjour à Mr et Mme Delaunay! Marc Chagall/Berlin 914

Miss Goldberg: A typical
Yiddish coded hint:
"gold" is sick, i.e.,
I have no money,
and the waistcoat
pocket is empty.

[Obverse, in Russian] Hot. Raining. Sauerkraut. Miss Goldberg is sick. Waistcoat? Exhibition open. The German women not very pretty. Today I am leaving [by train]: Vitebsk, Pokrovskaya St., Private House [Chagall's parents' home]. Marc Chagall. Regards!

CHAPTER FIVE

Back to Russia: 1914–1918

World War I

On June 15, 1914, after the opening of his Berlin exhibition, Chagall took a train to his parents' home in Vitebsk, to attend his sister's wedding. World War I broke out in August, and, very reluctantly, he got stuck in Russia. He resumed his friendship with Berta Rosenfeld, and they were married on July 25, 1915.

Contrary to some Russian patriotic notions, Chagall was quite ambivalent about his "homeland" and was unhappy about getting trapped there. In a letter to Sonia Delaunay in Paris of November 20, 1914, he refers to "our home-land . . . where I got stuck involuntarily"; and on October 1, 1917, he wrote to A. Benois: "If fate preserves me, I and my family may not be Russia's guests much longer." Of course, during World War I and the subsequent Civil War, it was impossible to go to the West and Chagall tried to make the best of it. After the Revolution, he may have been tempted by the openings for modern art and for himself, which the October Revolution seemed to provide, and was swept up by the revolutionary elan and rhetoric. But as soon as he could, he left for Paris.

Marc Chagall in Vitebsk to Aleksandr Benois in Petrograd

[Autumn 1914]

[Russian] Most honorable Aleksandr Nikolayevich,

May I send you some pictures (studies done in Russia) for your prestigious exhibition? Finding myself here because of the war, I am quite bored (oh, horror of our age!), and I would be happy about it.

You may be interested in a brief history of my life. I recently arrived from Berlin where, thank God, my exhibition was organized in June–July (200 works: 40 paintings and 160 drawings). I cannot express my grief. Everything got stuck there. Whatever happens, I cherish my previous works, I will answer for them before the "Terrible" Judgment. God knows if I will ever see them again, not to mention the money for works sold there.

got stuck there: Because World War I broke out between Germany and Russia, Chagall had no access to his work left in Berlin.

In addition, three big pictures (you may not like them, but I have lost my head over them) are stuck in Amsterdam in the Salon. Just before the war, the Committee informed me they were sold, but I had no time to receive [the payment] before the war broke out.

Two other pictures remained in Brussels. All other works I have left are in the gallery of my patron Charles Malpel [in Paris], who signed a contract with me this May—wasn't he killed?

So that's enough. Let us wait for news about the advances of the Russian generals from the Commander in Chief (I love him and will definitely do his portrait).

Commander in Chief: Chagall refers to the initial advances of the Russian army at the beginning of World War I. The Commander in Chief was the Tsar's uncle Nikolay Nikolayevitsh, who soon after became infamous for his expulsion of a million Jews from the front regions before the retreating Russian army.

If you could shelter me at the exhibition, I would come in person. If only you recognized in me the artistic quality, and this is the "only" thing. For the rest, allow my curly head to respond to it sooner or later.

Respectfully, Marc Chagall

Vitebsk, Pokrovskaya, private house [his parents' home]

Marc Chagall in Vitebsk to Sonia Delaunay in Paris

Postcard sent at the beginning of World War I from Russia to France. Stamped: "Vitebsk/Railroad Station" (near his parents' house) 20.11.14. Stamped: "War Censorship." The postcard was addressed to Paris and forwarded to "Poste restante à Fontarabie (Espagne)" where the pacifist Robert Delaunay spent the war years.

[Russian] Dear Mrs. Delaunay, I do not know the fate of your husband respected and loved by me but I know that you are safe in Paris with your son. Hence I am writing you a few words from our homeland where I somehow got from Berlin and where I got stuck involuntarily. I would be happy to get a word from you: how are you, where is Robert, how is the fate of our friends contemporaries acquaintances artists and writers? What happened to all our impulses and aspirations? . . . I send you my regards from Russia, from its depths, where the Russian people rose so beautifully to defend its future. And this gives me joy. I am longing for Paris. As to my exhibition [in Berlin], alas, against its will it became a prisoner of war. I squeeze your hands. Regards   Chagall

In Petrograd

At the end of 1914, Chagall was conscripted into the army, but apparently did not serve before his marriage in July 1915. After the honeymoon in Zaolshe (the summer residence of the Lubavich Rebbe), Moysey and Berta Chagall left for Petrograd (as St.-Petersburg was renamed during the war). He claimed that his new wife wanted "culture" in a big city, while he preferred to stay in quiet nature. Berta's brother Yakov Rosenfeld, who headed an army economics department in the Central War-Industrial Committee, arranged a convenient, clerical position in army service in the capital for Chagall, who could thus go on painting and exhibiting in Petrograd and Moscow. Strictures against Jews residing in the capitals were apparently relaxed during the war, and there were even special exhibitions of Russian Jewish artists in Moscow, where nominally they were forbidden to live. Furthermore, the radical left in art, which had snubbed him just four years earlier, now accepted Chagall and granted him plenty of exhibition room (forty-five works in the Jack of Diamonds exhibition in Moscow, November 1916).[1]

Several reviews of Chagall's exhibited work were published, some praising, some scoffing, but always spirited and argumentative. One Russian reviewer wrote

> No writer of the [anti-Semitic] Black Hundreds described the Jews in such an ugly form as Marc Chagall from Vitebsk. Why do the Jews have to be so dirty, with such idiotic and animal looks! Odessa anecdotes are disgusting, but these Vitebsk anecdotes are even more intolerable. And a whole Hall [of the exhibition] was given over to them! This is what the most modern art is like![2]

Bella and Marc Chagall in Petrograd, during World War I.

Yakov Tugendhold: A New Talent (1915)[3]

[Russian] In the exhibition "The Year 1915" [Moscow, March 1915], there are works by a young artist, almost unknown in Moscow but famous abroad, Marc Chagall. Among the unbridled bacchanalia of "Plastic Rayonism"[4] and painterly bric-a-brac, they seem to be modest, intimate, almost "retrograde." But this is the characteristic of any authentic art, that is moved not by the demands of an aesthetic fashion, but by the inner and timeless necessity of an artistic soul. This does not mean that Chagall is separated from our troubled present—there is much more of it in his works than in all the surrounding "Isms." Chagall was in Paris and absorbed all that is in the air. But he was born in Vitebsk, and the naïve, almost childish sincerity of the provinces, combined in him with the formal mastery of Paris, has endowed his creative work with something profoundly convincing, moving, spiritual. In Chagall, the "holy simplicity" of a true primitive has been preserved, and at the same time, there is in him already the cruel and sharp "strain" [*nadryv*] of Dostoevsky's adult children.

This premature complexity is reflected in the extraordinary variety of Chagall's works, which are so different from each other in their manner, sometimes lovingly following "nature" and sometimes transforming it with an irrational capriciousness. But this irrational and absurd element in Chagall is not forced but is psychologically fully acceptable, as all the nonsense and fantasy of Remizov and Sologub is acceptable. With extraordinary keenness, far beyond the work of Kustodeyev and Dobuzhinsky, Chagall senses the barely perceptible but eerie mysticism of Russian life. Such are his Vitebsk pictures: a sleepy and gray province, with a cheap barbershop, houses like toys, a turbid-lunar tryst of awkward lovers and a street sweeper, a dusty apparition of a provincial street [in "The Dead"]. Chagall takes a coarse and pale piece of life and creates his beautiful legend. The sweeper becomes a dusty-silvery figure, the ironing woman is painted in the colors of exquisite, Velasquez-type nobility, and so is the old Jew, whose stern solemnity is expressed through a combination of black and white. Chagall's palette can be restrained or bright and florid, depending on an inner necessity. His drawing can be lyrical and fanciful or realistic and expressive, as in the "Barbershop," which has so much truth of life, light and air—a study worthy of the Tretyakov gallery.

But Chagall feels not just the provinces, he responds also to European contemporaneity. His soldiers holding loaves of bread, brave bread bakers, the stomach of the army, are painted with amazing mastery and agility. His "sister" with scarlet lips and underlined femininity of her clothes—like a symbol of all that healthy, encouraging and life-awakening element, which a woman brings into the weary business of war. On the contrary, his "Prussians" have something miserable, dull, earthy, condemned to the soil. Some may not like Chagall's

Remizov: Aleksey Remizov (1877–1857), a highly admired Russian Symbolist writer; often grotesque, weird, or whimsical; born to a poor family and known for his stories of Russian provincial life.

Sologub: Fedor K. Sologub (1863–1927), a Russian poet and writer of the first Symbolist generation, born to a poor family. In his poetry and prose, he intermingled the grotesque, eroticism, and fantasy, and juxtaposed dream with reality.

"war" paintings, but they are valuable in that, where other painters hail the iron and wooden beauties, he senses the human face. In our days, when mechanical culture challenges the whole world, and artists still don't want to understand that their painterly bric-a-brac derives from the same Futurist devil—art that has love for the world and man, that has lyricism, is important.

In his "Clock," Chagall rises to grasp something more abstract. When you see this gigantic and relentless monument to time and this bottomless night in the window, and such a small man facing eternity, you recall Baudelaire and Edgar Poe and Tyutchev's poem: "The monotonous beat of a clock, the tedious tale of the night." Yet Chagall's "Clock" is not an illustration to a symbolical tale, but an independent work of painting, the "insomnia" of an artist who, somewhere in a gray province, can have "world-wide" dreams.

Perhaps precisely from this untouched, naïve provincial backwoods, a desired light will pour upon our metropolitan art, which performs a feast in time of plague; and produce fresh strength that a renovated Russia will pave the way for. In any case, Chagall is one of the great hopes of Russian art, for in his studies there is that thing that endures.

Benois: Concerning the "Jewish" Exhibition (excerpts) (1916)[5]

[Russian] I take this occasion to share with the reader my impressions of the works of Chagall, who was given his own room at the exhibition in Dobychina's gallery. Here is the most typical Jew. But I hasten to qualify my words: even in this case, I do not assume that Chagall's art is good because it is nationally Jewish. Not at all. The young artist knew how to preserve his immediacy; in spite of his years abroad, he remained the sincere, whimsical and impressionable child that grew up in the poverty of his native land. His charm is, of course, not in the national, but in the artistic element—that strange organization of any authentic artist, which enables him to see in the ugliest objects their soul, that thing which is "God's smile."

This smile is the more startling when it is revealed in the most unfortunate circumstances. It is understandable when Sorrento, luxuriating in the sun at the azure waters, is smiling, when the monuments of Athens and Rome are smiling, when the colorful crowds on Avenue du Bois are smiling, when exquisite objects or heroic, or even tragic things are smiling,—all this is understandable. It is also understandable that the Russian song, the Russian spreading landscape, [Turgenev's] *Memoirs of a Hunter* or [Tolstoy's] *Childhood and Adolescence*—are full of elevating beauty and true poetry. But that the dirty, stinking "Yids' Hole" with its crooked streets, its blind little huts, its outrageous population, depressed by poverty, appears to the eye of the artist full of splendour and beauty and poetry, that even this horror can be illuminated by a smile of beauty—this amazes with its unexpectedness, amazes and rejoices the heart.

What can be more rejoicing than the recognition that the rays of inner beauty, when emanating from an artistic talent, have no barriers! What is especially valuable in Chagall's art is that, in spite of his attraction to symbol and style, it remains true and sincere through and through. Chagall does not embellish what he sees, he just loves it. Suddenly, in the warmth of this love, everything takes on a different countenance, becomes endearing and riveting. The most awful and sick does not lose its awfulness and sickness, yet it somehow beckons and charms, becomes near and dear. I never actually saw such a miserable hole, as Chagall describes, I would have choked with anguish if I had to spend even one day shuffling along those fences, if I had to socialize with all those somber people. And all of a sudden, because of the charms of art, this "underground" becomes almost intimate. As if you reread your own diaries of childhood and adolescence, relive your own love affairs. All that is ugly and abhorrent collapses into an enchanting dream.

Chagall is still very young, and some negative aspects of his art can be excused. Sometimes he succumbs to what we call "literariness." Sometimes he begins to behave affectedly (which can hardly be avoided in this age of buffoonery and lies). Finally, Chagall has many traits that can be described as levity. But in his essence, he is a true artist, an artist to his very fingertips, capable of abandoning himself to the elements of painting creativity, full of bright and sharp images, and an artist who to a large extent has mastered the craft of his art, who can "speak" not just eloquently but also precisely, elegantly, supply.

And that Paris, where he went some five years ago as a complete ignoramus and "simpleminded primitive"—Chagall knew how to use it successfully, as only very gifted and perspicacious people can. All that was fashionable passed by him almost without a trace. On the other hand, without losing any of his freshness, he developed his sensibility for the exquisite and attained a charming fluency of style and the necessary mastery of colors. A propos the colors. In my opinion, one of his delights lies in his ability to scorn the bright and the colorful. The general impression of his paintings is rather gray and monochrome. But in this time of total "screaming," such restraint speaks in favor of the artist. Moreover, every painting, every study reveals in the effect of its colors a delicate and original harmony.

Marc Chagall in Petrograd to Aleksandr Benois in Petrograd

This letter was written in the tense days before the October Revolution, described in Chapter XIV of Chagall's autobiography (see Chapter 2), when Chagall was dismissed from the army and he and his family were floating with no support un-der the disintegrating "Temporary" regime. In March 1917, the influential Benois organized a powerful Committee for Matters of Art to negotiate with the tempo-rary government about the preservation of art and antiquities in time of turmoil. After the Bolshevik Revolution, in November 1917, he was appointed Director of the Hermitage Art Gallery in Petrograd, and was severely attacked as a "reac-tionary" by major figures of "Leftist" art (Meyerhold, Mayakovsky, Shklovsky). In 1926 he left the Soviet Union for Paris, where he lived until the end of his life, very active in painting, set design, and exhibitions.

1/X 1917 [October 1]

[Russian] Most Esteemed Aleksandr Nikolayevich,

First of all, I would like to say that, for some reason, I never was fortunate enough (in our, or just my melancholy moments of life) to talk with you at least a little, simply to meet. Are you surprised? How would a "young" person want to talk to an "old" man, to unburden his heart? Yes! Aleksandr Nikolayevich, you know perfectly well what "young" and "old" mean, especially in our Russia.

Please do not think that I am "flattering" you. For you perhaps know my ex-treme sincerity. I am not afraid of words, reproaches easily cast. Alas, and for-tunately, I have known this inside-out in the eternally grateful "abroad," may God bless her sinful soul—my second homeland [France].

Amazing: why the same dear, true people over there—are as close to you as on the palm of your hand and get closer, and here, the opposite. So what! Our Rus-sian moves are of the opposite nature. Well, forgive me, I talk too much. In this case, I have some business.

I admit, an unpleasant business for me and who knows, maybe not just for me—why conceal it? I shall be brief. External circumstances, which I cannot sympathize with from any aspect, forced me to do something, for the last tedious three years to serve in one of the departments of the War-Industrial Committee.

Naturally, in those three years I did almost no work (I do not count the Vitebsk series made in the middle and end of 1914, before my [army] service). No matter how hard and fruitless my plight may be (not just mine), I would have reconciled myself to it (for how long?), but the Committee was evacuated from Petrograd, departments and positions of the staff were reduced, and I became a superfluous person.

Recently I was told that the honor of exhibiting with your group [the World of

Art] or, even more so, to be on your list, as well as the "Union [of the Young]" justly frees one from "self-destructing," brings a person back from an abnormal milieu to his direct responsibilities. Miserable as my appeal to you is, especially, I think, in this written form (true?), I have allowed myself to talk from my heart only to you, and ask for advice.

"Is it possible?" It seems to me that, if we discard this forced and *temporary* motivation, my plea can't be realized because . . . I don't know myself. And you don't need to bother with me, for if fate preserves me, I and my family may not be Russia's guests much longer. And even after that, I would not like to interfere with the natural process of overcoming doubts and distrust about my modest person—on the part of your respectable colleagues, including my own teachers.

I would like, a propos, to tell you, Aleksandr Nikolayevich, a few words about our *young* [avant-garde] Russian societies and their "Unions" and "energy." It is at least an amusing phenomenon and I am *"happy"* that their last remnants have disintegrated, dissipated, that the power is *yours*. The "young" should not exist if it doesn't have in its heart a little true and pure blood, traditions, artistic nonadaptability, modesty. And no matter how I see "The World of Art"—the very fact that sometimes you could hear a human language there, that the task was posed once and resolved, according to the spirit of the time and the talents—for that it will always be respected.

Again I chatted away "not to the point." So here we are, Aleksandr Niko-layevich: either condemn or "hesitantly" propose. For three years I did nothing, for long days I was busy with office work, and now—very soon—I lose even this "blessing."

To become exclusively an artist, I am prepared to do anything. If you can, extend me a helping hand, if not—I won't be offended.

Perhaps you could write to me (Perekupnoy Pereulok 7, apt. 20) or let me know by telephone 575-20 (10 a.m.–5 p.m., except Sundays). We could meet and talk.

With deep admiration and love

Chagall

Dr. Elyashev: the Link to Yiddish Literature

Young Chagall was a famous, though controversial, artist and befriended various prominent Russian and Jewish cultural figures. His close friend in Moscow and Petrograd was Dr. Israel Elyashev (in Russian: Isidore Zakharyevich Elyashev, 1873–1924), who had served as a physician in the Russian army during the war. Under the pseudonym Baal-Makhshoves (The Thinker), he was one of the most

Chagall's friend, Yiddish literary critic Baal-Makhshoves (Dr. I.Z. Elyashev). Drawing made in Petrograd. Inscription in Russian: "Baal-Makhshoves in Russia/1918" and in Hebrew: "Baal Makhshoves" ["The Thinker"].

intelligent Yiddish literary critics, stressing literature as art in the European sense, and promoting the critical essay as a thinkpiece. In wartime Petrograd, Dr. Elyashev shared lodgings for some time with Chagall. His wife left him and he raised their son by himself. He talked to Chagall at length about his personal plight and about literature and literary criticism.

Baal-Makhshoves, fifteen years older than Chagall and an intelligent reader with a university education, steeped in the knowledge of Yiddish literature and questions of aesthetics, had a strong influence on the young Chagall. They saw each other often later, in Moscow and Berlin. Chagall's memoir was written on the fifteenth anniversary of Baal-Makhshoves's death. As a native Lithuanian, he was allowed to leave the Soviet Union when it recognized Lithuanian independence. He died in Berlin and was buried in his native Kovna/Kaunas, then the capital of Lithuania.

In Memory of My Friend Baal-Makhshoves[6]

[Yiddish] Dr. Elyashev was my friend, but in truth, wasn't he everybody's friend?

For he was a man of perpetual intimacy, whose eyes attracted you. But I don't think there were many artists among his many friends. His personality was magnetic; before you could figure out his opinions, he was already looking at you, not thinking about himself at all. Isn't this the best sign of friendship?

I don't know what internal flaws of my Diaspora mentality disturb me, but I always have difficulties until I get attached to a person. But Dr. Elyashev met me for the first time as an old acquaintance, as if we had just interrupted a long conversation.

It was a day when I left Vitebsk for the wide world, to see my exhibition in Moscow.[7]

It was my luck that Jews thought I might be the "future Antokolsky."

I don't remember who introduced me to Baal-Makhshoves.

"You know," he addressed me immediately, "at a meeting of the Jewish Society for Art, I suggested to Kagan-Shabshay that he buy as many of your paintings as possible for his future Jewish Museum." Kagan-Shabshay was a confused genius, an engineer without money but with plans. He wanted to found his own Jewish Museum in Moscow.

Kagan-Shabshay: Kagan-Shabshay bought thirty of Chagall's early paintings, but then gave them back when Chagall left Russia in 1922.

But I was drawn to the person of Elyashev himself, not just to what he was talking about. We would stroll day and night. Several times he would accompany me to my home and I would go with him to his. And we talked about everything. Especially about art and literature. Elyashev tried to clarify for himself many of his positions on questions of art.

It was "a happily calm" war time.

Often Baal-Makhshoves would look at his watch and say: "I am a doctor, am I not, I must see if there is a patient in my office."

He was a nerve-doctor of the psychoanalytical school of Dr. Freud, Steckel and others, who were not yet in fashion at the time. But no matter how long we would sit and wait—on that day no sick people would show up. Sometimes I thought Dr. Elyashev was interested in investigating me; he asked about my father, mother, grandmother, especially when I became talkative and excited. "Well, if so, it is already late and nobody is coming—so, let's go to a café. There we will meet Frishman. Do you know him?

Frishman: David Frishman (Frischmann, 1859–1922), a major Hebrew and Yiddish writer and literary critic—was in Moscow at the time. After the Revolution of February 1917, he became editor in chief of the Hebrew publishing house of A.J. Shtybel (Stybel) in Moscow and edited the prestigious "thick" journal of Hebrew literature, *HaTekufa*, closed down by the Soviets in 1919.

Truthfully, I didn't care about getting to know Frishman. In his own personality, Elyashev was closer to me as a type of a Yiddish literary critic. Though at the time I was actually quite alienated from all "kosher" and well-circumscribed trends in Jewish cultural and social questions. I was still too busy overturning artistic "worlds," but I rarely spoke about that to Elyashev. Even so, his eyes swirled and darkened and often scared me in the dark of the night, and even in daytime. I didn't talk about political and social issues with Elyashev either. Essentially, a man like him should have had no enemies, if he had remained a pure literary critic. But today, when I read some of his articles on other topics, I am upset that he was often mistaken in the complicated issues, in which, by the way, even stronger and more professional politicians than he were also mistaken.[8] But on the whole, his charm and trepidation were so conspicuous, his education and his free world view—which used to be called "European"—had almost no "Jewish" aspect . . .

And still he was considered correctly as the leading Jewish [= Yiddish] literary critic and his influence on the young writers and critics we can be proud of today was not in vain.

*

Later, in the revolutionary years of [1917–]1918, we often lived together in Petersburg. We would sit in the only warm room—the kitchen. In the corner, the maid would wash the laundry and we would drink the eternal tea with one piece of hard sugar. His little son, Alya, stood on the side, apparently didn't have enough to eat, and was always so gloomy, with his head down and his shirt sticking out of his short pants . . .

The father would look at his son and ask: "Did you do your homework? Look at him, he plays all day in theater, wants to become a theater director, who knows . . . "

Dr. Elyashev's son, Alya, during the Revolutionary years in Petrograd. Inscription in Russian: "A souvenir for Dr. I.Z. Elyashev and Alya/Shagal/February 919." Eliyahu Elyashev became a Zionist activist, Hebrew writer, and Israeli Ambassador to Moscow.

I would sit and draw him, the doctor with rare patients, expiring like Don Quixote of various sorrows.

His divorced wife visits. White as a statue, cold as a stone. Not a gaze, not a caress from her. But in a hurry, somewhat excited, he would say to me: "You, as an artist, look at her, watch her behavior, look at her profile, her black hair and eyes . . . "

But I was indifferent and thought about my half paralyzed friend who had very little joy in his life. Half frozen, in a greenish, faded and somewhat spat on jacket, he would wander around from room to room, looking for something, dragging his right leg and shoulder. And when a piece of horsemeat would appear on the table—that was a holiday.

for eternity: Elyashev lived in Berlin but died and was buried in Kovna.

Finally he left for Kovna, from Kovna to Berlin, and from Berlin back to Kovna for eternity. In Berlin in 1922 I met a different Elyashev, whose vivacity had vanished, with a different smile—once in the Romanisches Kaffee, and once in my apartment.

The last years of Germany's freedom and the last years of Elyashev's life.

world shame: The Nazi regime in Germany.

But he was lucky not to die alive, and not to see the greatest world shame. A time when the Jew, whose worries and trouble concerned Elyashev, cannot even get a piece of soil for his grave.

piece of soil: Jews put some soil of the Holy Land at the head of a dead man. This is an allusion to the British (MacDonald) White Paper of May 1939, banning the Jewish acquisition of land in Palestine.

Elyashev had the luck and the honor to die in the city of his birth, where all the Jews closed their houses and stores and went to accompany him to the garden where holy people rest, covered with grass and stones.

I wish I could see his Jewish Kovna and his eternal home and tell him better news about us Jews, and that he may rest in peace: he is appreciated and will be appreciated as the classical writer of Yiddish criticism.

Marc Chagall in Vitebsk to Nadezhda Dobychina[9] in Petrograd

In October 1917, cuts in the army department where Chagall worked made him "redundant." Shortly after, the "October Revolution" (actually, November 7) took place, Lenin called on the millions of soldiers to leave the front and go home. The Russian army disintegrated, and Chagall was no longer bound by his military service. In the great anarchy, Petrograd was starving and freezing. Chagall took his family back to the safety of their parents' home in Vitebsk, near the countryside, where there was some food, and didn't even say goodbye to his gallery owner.

[Russian] Director of the Dobychina Gallery in Petrograd, 1918.

12/III 1918, Vitebsk

Dear Nadezhda Evseevna!

I am writing from here. I didn't have time to see you before I left [Petrograd]. I was in a hurry, excited—I could have gone on foot . . . Now I am here [in Vitebsk]. This is my town and my tomb . . . Here I open like the tobacco flower at night . . . I am working. May God help me!

After all, it seems to me that He exists. He won't leave us, and at the last minute, save us. How are you? Say hello to Petr Petrovich, regards from my wife. Write someday.

I imagine that the times are awful and you probably have a hard time. But don't get discouraged. I am learning to live on "the holy spirit," it is so easy!

"the holy spirit": On spirit alone, without bread.

Regards,

Your Chagall

Vitebsk, Smolenskaya St. store of Sh.N. Rosenfeld [Berta's father's store]—

for M. Chagall

Marc Chagall in Vitebsk to Aleksandr Benois in Petrograd

May 1918. Since Chagall's last letter, the October Revolution took over Russia.

[Russian] Most Esteemed Aleksandr Nikolayevich,

I received your letter in Petrograd. But for almost two months I have been here [in Vitebsk]. All the time I wanted to express my thanks to you. I was happy that you, especially you, are talking simply and in a friendly language.

I am so tired of (forgive the expression) the "corset," which I personally never wore, but people think it is mandatory to wear it sometime in life. And when you hear (and see!) all this—you get so angry, that you undress "entirely" and work "as God made you."

the "corset": He refers, apparently, to the pressures of political ideology on the artist.

My dear, is it "morbidity"? Or, as you once jokingly accused me of "literariness." Deep inside I knew that you did not mean that. Here it is—the slightest deviation with us is accused of literariness. But I am not afraid of it; for, thank God, I was raised in France. I don't know one artist in the history of art, who would not seem "literary" when all is said and done. Not one. And if they don't seem to be "literary," I don't know them and you at least don't remember them, because there is nothing to remember. If one does not have a "critical" attitude to one's work—does it mean being "literary"? What is the fault of Manet, if he is after all "literary," though he didn't have an especially critical mind. And Odilon

Redon perhaps did have it, and both of them, like dozens of others, are equally literary. And their heritage, outside of the historical "sensation" provoked by the former, is equally valuable. Or couldn't you yourself get stuck in the "literariness" of Leonardo da Vinci, the "poetry" of Raphael, the "gesticulations" of Masaccio.

It is only a pity if all that has no foundation. One day I would really like to see a "pure" artist, but even in France I did not find him. The trouble, apparently, derives from the fact that objects are approached "from the wrong side," and the word "theme" obstructed the meaning of the object. Yet, even the most beautiful and non-narrative "theme" (an apple, grapes, or some "Objectless painting") will not help you, if you don't have *foundations*, either innate or acquired by hard work.

Objectless painting: Usually translated as "Non-Objective painting" (misleading).

And something else I don't understand in our "Russian history"—what is "Itinerary art" [Peredvizhnichestvo] (even in the sense of generalizing this definition). If it is 3/4 Surikov, then I am all excited about Itinerary art, and all the rest may be blamed as "Itinerary," for it is not artistic. But then, are only Itinerary artists thrown up by the sea? There are plenty of them even . . . in Sweden[10] . . . or perhaps they all are "literary" rather than "itinerary" artists?

So why don't we get the freedom to live? We aggravate and devour each other. Why don't we say clearly: "Here is freedom, and here is a prison, and every tree will have its own berries, but be a tree not a jackass." Or is this whole "commotion" needed for the "History of Art"?

Oh, no, never. If objects were made only through "competition," it wouldn't be worth living—as accidental, whimsical toys among them. Apparently there is a more sublime and more indifferent and modest force, but we are either lazy or have no time or are "hurt" too much to live under its laws.

Dear Aleksandr Nikolayevich, forgive my speechifying, forgive me from your heart and do not see me as an eccentric. God forbid. If I were, I wouldn't have liked to be. I simply use the opportunity (and in part, your friendly permission) to speak with an artist for a moment, closing your face with my hand, for I am still . . . shy.

In these long, starry nights (there are no farther stars than here), when you relax from your work and don't quarrel even with your wife (It's impossible to quarrel—she agrees in advance), you are unsettled—and I must apologize for my letter, in which I just meant to thank you for your attention, and it has become drawn out and endless.

But I hope that, when I return, perhaps, to Petrograd after doing some works with God's help and some "recreation" for the new year, I shall respond not with words but with a wordless request that you love what you see entirely. For I never had intended to measure up to the "Titans." I bow to them especially, I wish sometimes even to sing with an adolescent, ingratiating voice, so that I can once make the impression not of an "artist," but of a passer by. But those who got close to me once, I would like not to let them retreat, I'll repeat to them with my last strength: "believe, believe, believe."—

How is your life? You're starving, probably . . . Here it is a little easier. Come to our neighborhood to get fed.

Regards to your family. What do you do in the art worlds? Newspapers don't arrive here ([they are] bourgeois). That's how it is.

Your devoted Chagall

Vitebsk, Pokrovskaya St., IIId District, private home.

to get fed: After the Revolution, there was starvation in the capitals, whereas Vitebsk had an agricultural hinterland nearby.

they are bourgeois: In the eyes of the local Communist powers.

private home: The house of Chagall's parents. Apparently it was not comfortable (or was politically dangerous) to live in the rich house of Berta's parents.

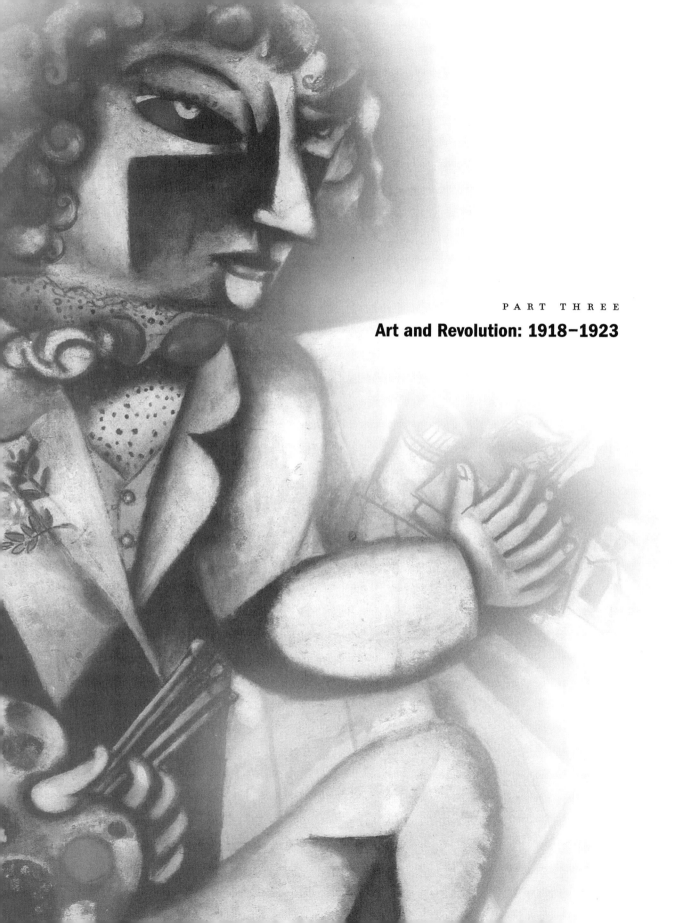

PART THREE

Art and Revolution: 1918–1923

CHAPTER SIX

Commissar of Art in Vitebsk: 1918–1920

The Artist and the Revolution

The October Revolution of 1917 promoted a new language of hope, even exuberance, about the unlimited possibilities now open to the people. This mood was embraced by many of the intelligentsia who stayed in Russia, and was especially supported by the avant-garde trends in all the arts. The Revolutionary discourse could be read as cognate to the discourse of the avant-garde; both were on the "Left" and both radically discarded the past. Furthermore, the new situation granted young artists and intellectuals a sense of importance and positions of power, as well as, simply, bread. Many old intellectuals left for the West, and all cultural and academic positions, expanding rapidly, opened up for supporters of the new system.

A special sense of freedom and participation as equals in the new regime was felt by young Jews, who were liberated from their isolation and second-class citizenship, and from the need to be trapped in the category "Jewish"; since religion was abolished (and they rejected religion altogether), they were now "Russians," sanctioned by the regime. For a while, Chagall shared that excitement. The screams of Revolutionary slogans drowned out the harsh daily realities. The selected documents published here show the enthusiasm, power, infighting, and confusion of the early days of the Revolution.

After the Revolution, Lenin appointed Anatoly Lunacharsky (1875–1933) as People's Commissar of Enlightenment (Minister of Education and Culture). At the beginning of the century, Lunacharsky had belonged to a group of intellectual "God-seekers," was arrested as a Marxist Revolutionary, and joined the Bolsheviks in exile. During the second decade of the century, he lived in Paris, wrote reviews for Russian newspapers, and befriended the painter David Shterenberg in La Ruche, who helped him understand the young art scene. When Lunacharsky returned to Russia and became People's Commissar of Enlightenment, he appointed Shterenberg Director of IZO (the Division of Graphic Arts of the People's Commissariat of Enlightenment).

In the first years of the Revolution, Lunacharsky was an influential literary and cultural critic of a Marxist-humanist bent who exerted a great deal of power in matters of centralized culture. He knew Chagall from Paris (where he reviewed Chagall's art quite ambivalently—see p. 213). Now, on receiving Chagall's proposal for an Art College in August 1918, he appointed the young painter to the position of Plenipotentiary for the Affairs of Art in the Province of Vitebsk. Vitebsk was unique in its achievements, yet similar Plenipotentiaries were appointed elsewhere: Yakov Tugendhold in Simferopol and Aleksandra Ekster in Kiev, while Nathan Altman took charge of the first anniversary celebrations of the October uprising in Petrograd. The high proportion of Jews in such activities reflected both the rise of a young, Russian-speaking, antitraditional, critical, and bright intelligentsia among the Jews, and the new regime's sense that the Jews, who were the most oppressed minority in Tsarist Russia, were now devoted supporters of Communist power.

Chagall plunged into all kinds of initiatives. He quickly built an Art College and an Art Museum in Vitebsk and launched a variety of artistic activities in the city and province. When no means were available, he went to Moscow for supplies and money and was thus relatively independent of the young and inexperienced local party bosses. It was Chagall's first and last actual public function ever.

On November 6, 1918, the eve of the first anniversary of the Bolshevik October Revolution, Chagall organized the decorating of the city with colorful posters painted by several artists, including himself, copied by their pupils and hung all over Vitebsk. A. Efros recalled: "In Vitebsk, Marc Chagall (Commissar Marc Chagall!) painted Chagallesques on all banners and raised a flag above the city, showing him, Chagall, riding a green horse, flying above Vitebsk and blowing a horn: 'CHAGALL—TO VITEBSK'."[1]

the eve of the first anniversary: Vitebsk was a Jewish city, and Jews begin the celebration of every holiday on the eve of the day.

The former mansion of the Jewish banker Israel V. Vishnyak at Voskresenskaya ("Resurrection") St. 10, now renamed after one of the leaders of the Revolution Bukharin St.,[2] was turned over to the new People's Art College[3] and Art Museum by decree of the City Management Department of October 18, 1918. The house was officially nationalized on November 10, 1918. We have no evidence about Chagall's role in the confiscation of Vishnyak's house, but as the Plenipotentiary on Matters of Art in Vitebsk Province, he must have been involved in it. The college opened classes on January 28, 1919. The professors lived on the third floor of the mansion, and Chagall moved into two rooms there with his wife and daughter. The official name of the school has changed several times during its existence.

Vitebsk was close to the front of the Civil War, which rolled westward and back. For some time, the Germans were in Polotsk, a city in Vitebsk Province, but they moved north and threatened the capital Petrograd itself. A Theater of Revolutionary Satire, TeRevSat, was established in Vitebsk to disseminate dramatized propaganda to the Red Army soldiers. During its first year, it presented 300 performances for 200,000 spectators. Commissar of Art Marc Chagall made all the decorations for the ten plays of its first season, 1919–1920, some of which were staged in Vitebsk and some on the front. The opening performance, on

The People's Art College, founded by Chagall in the former mansion of Israel Vishnyak, now renamed Bukharin Street 10, Vitebsk.

February 7, 1919, was mounted on the square of the dilapidated Vitebsk railway station, to the festive accompaniment of cannon fire.

In April 1919, Chagall exhibited twenty-three works in a separate room granted him in the great First Free Exhibition of Art, held in the magnificent former Winter Palace of the Tsar in Petrograd. That was probably one reason for his absence from Vitebsk during February and early March 1919, and his wish to resign from the school in April.

The Story of Israel Vishnyak

The story of Israel Vishnyak (c. 1860–1924)[4] illustrates the Revolutionary destruction and transformations of the time. A man of initiative and culture, Vishnyak built a bank in Vitebsk and was a philanthropist. He hosted concerts in his new neoclassical mansion, built prior to World War I, and was also involved in

Jewish community activities. In the early twentieth century, a modern, three-story Jewish school, with toilets and a kitchen, was built in Vitebsk. Subsequently, a wealthy St.-Petersburg woman, born in Vitebsk, left the huge sum of 140,000 prerevolutionary Rubles to the Jewish community of her native city. It was decided to use the funds to build a large professional school, adjacent to the new school, with modern workshops for many kinds of arts and crafts. The committee overseeing the project was chaired by the banker Israel Vishnyak. But when World War I broke out, the school was confiscated by the Tsarist authorities for an army hospital. Restored to the Jewish community after the February 1917 Revolution, it was nationalized again by the Bolsheviks, who also confiscated the heritage money and Vishnyak's own home.

Israel Vishnyak was one of ten siblings; his nephews included the photographer Roman Vishniac and the historian and member of Kerensky's government Marc Vishniak. After the Revolution, Israel fled to Vilna and Riga. After his sixth son was born, the family hoped for a daughter but were blessed with twin boys. He died destitute in Riga.

Chagall showed no scruples about using the "bourgeois" Vishnyak's house (and disparaging the former owner in writing). He surely must have known about such a major project of the Jewish community to build a vocational training school for the "productivization" of the Jewish masses, and might have borrowed the idea of teaching workshops for arts and crafts from the deposed owner of the mansion. Thus, he proclaims that the Art College must be constructed on "the principles of a professional school," which was, in his words, a "long-felt need" in the city. Behind the great ideals of avant-garde painting, there was a very practical social and professional purpose, which contributed to the great success of the College.

Now, however, it was not confined to the Jewish community but was a general Soviet school conducted in Russian, sanctioned by the state.[5] Still, the majority

Chagall's master class, 1919. From left to right: L. Khidekel, M. Chagall, M. Kunin, I. Chashnik, Kh. Zeldin. Standing: M. Veksler, L. Tsiperson. Sitting: L. Zevin. Most of them moved to Malevich's artistic trend, UNOVIS. All were Jews and all became artists.

of the students and most teachers were Jews, as was the population of this northern capital of the former Pale of Settlement and its Soviet Mayor Margolin. Chagall himself, in his first proposal for the Art College, addressed to the Commissar of Enlightenment Lunacharsky, pointed out that Vitebsk was a Jewish city and the College must especially emphasize the development of artistic talents among the Jewish masses, with whom he personally identified.

An Art School (August 23, 1918)[6]

[Russian] The Art Section of the Division of People's Enlightenment [headed by David Shterenberg] is considering a project for organizing an Art school in Vitebsk, proposed by the artist M. Chagall. The project is already in the Commissariat of People's Enlightenment and has been approved in principle by Comrade

Lunacharsky. According to the project, the school set its goal on artistic education through the theoretical and practical study of painting, sculpture, and the
applied arts.

Report by the Artist Marc Chagall Concerning the Art College (August 1918)

[Russian] The People's Art College in Vitebsk, fulfilling the needs of the whole
Western Land, is a ripe necessity, especially since our Revolutionary time com-
pels us with unusal force to undertake the authentic development and education
of the people's knowledge and talents that have been dormant till now.

Outside of the capital cities, there are at present no art colleges in Russia, especially since we were cut off from Vilna, Odessa, Kiev, and other cities, where
such colleges existed in the past. Because of that and because of material reasons, many talents of the people are totally shut up. This must not happen today,
when the people itself is its own master.

The Goals and Rights of the College

The main goals of the People's Art College are the following:

1. The foundation of the College will be based on the genuine artistic and Revolutionary trend in art, without any admixtures of academism and routine. Thus,
the provincial masses of the people, still innocent in their taste, will have an opportunity open to all to develop their artistic tendencies in general. In particular,

academism and routine:
Bakst's nemeses.

2. To open right here the possibility of picking up any accidental and rare
prominent talent of a beginner from the people and directing it on the right path,
a talent that for lack of proper conditions of education would perish for good.

In short, we refuse to take as our example other colleges that have existed so
far in various cities of Russia with their deadening stagnation and routine; they
have died a natural death together with Tsarism. Instead, we shall create an exclusively revolutionary and truly artistic nest in the provinces, the Art College in
Vitebsk, especially for the needs of the poorest classes of the city and the whole
Western Land.

3. One equally important task is the artistic education of workers and persons
from the people in the field of applied art. It is as significant for the truly artistic development of various handicrafts, works, tastes, and conceptions of the
workers in their own daily work.

Admissions

Admission to the College is open to all regardless of age, but first of all for workers and peasants and the poorest of the people *free of charge*, while others will pay
tuition.

Rights

After finishing the College, having spent a minimum of 2 and a maximum of 4 years there, the students will have an opportunity to enter one of the higher workshops of the Academy of Art in the capital for the perfection and crystallization of their artistic education, and, according to the future determinations of the emerging Academy, will receive their further dynamics and maturity.

Division by Classes

The College is divided into classes: 3 classes of drawing and painting, the first two of them are subdivided into two.

The 4th class of sculpture, and, finally,

The 5th class for applied arts, subdivided into architecture, decorations, painterly class, etc. Furthermore, a workshop will be established in this class for the fulfillment of decorative and modelling works—in sculpture, wood, the interior and exterior ornamentation of governmental, public, and private buildings, city streets and squares, painting of signs, posters, decorations for city theaters and all other artistic and artisan needs of the whole city. All this will be executed exclusively by the students and the teachers of the working elements and by no other routine craftsmen. Eventually, this will have to be approved as a mandatory regulation. Through this, the Art College will get a certain income and, most important, will give the needy working elements a certain material support for their life and studies, and at the same time, will tear out of the hands of unusually talentless artisans and contractors the work which will now become artistically acceptable and will decorate the city. Therefore, in due time we propose to eliminate all stereotypical and artless signs, posters, monuments, etc., from the face of the main streets of the city, and instead of all that kitschy and impersonal stuff, to create the new and artistic works, made with the hands of the working cooperative, by the students-artists from the people.

The Pedagogical and Administrative-Economic Personnel

The People's Art College is headed by 1) An Artistic Soviet, composed of the teachers and the Director/Chairman of the Artistic Soviet/and individual appointees; and 2) An Administrative-Economic Soviet. Every of those Soviets includes a certain number of members of the Artistic Soviet and of the Administrative-Economic Soviet.

The number of teachers/according to the number
of classes and subdivisions

3 teachers, including the Director, for the 3 basic classes of drawing and painting with their subdivisions; 1—for the class of sculpture; 3—for the class of applied and industrial arts and for the management of the workshop at the College.

1 lector-teacher of art history, anatomy, perspective, etc.—altogether 8 persons.

The Administrative-Economic Soviet, in addition to those members of the Artistic Soviet that participate in it and several appointees, includes at least 3 paid positions, depending on the distribution of responsibilities of an administrative-economical nature.

The junior personnel includes at least 3 service people. Stuff, altogether:

1/ Pedagogical personnel and Director	8 persons
2/ Administrative-Economic	3 "
3/ Lower employees	3 "

Financial-Material Aspect

Annual expenses

1/ 8 teachers /including the Director/	100,000 Rubles
2/ 3 administrative-economical employees	25,000
3/ 3 lower employees	20,000
Total	145,000
4/ Local	—
5/ Heating	—
6/ Lighting etc.	—
7/ Models, nature, plaster and other expenses	—
Total	40,000
SUM TOTAL	175,000–190,000 Rubles

One-time expenses

1/ 20,000–25,000 Rubles—expenses for the initial furnishing of the Art College and the preparation of the proper quantity of easels, tables, benches, shelves, pedestals, acquisition of figures or heads of plaster etc., ornaments, various materials, background planes, and other teaching tools.

2/ 15,000–20,000—expenses for buying the necessary materials for drawing, painting, sculptures, decorations, and painterly mural needs; for the organization of storage space at the College—in order to distribute such materials primarily to the neediest students, then for sale to others at accessible prices for the artistic tasks of the city. At present, a monopoly of one or two merchants in the city speculate with this material.

Total one-time expenses	40,000–50,000 Rubles.

Organization of a City Art Museum at the College

The First City Museum has to be organized at the Art College, temporarily in the same building. It would serve as a model of art for the students and represent the History of Russian Art for the city.

For that purpose, the Departments of Art in the capital and the art societies and organizations will be invited to send to Vitebsk a certain quantity of truly-artistic pictures, sculptures and other works of art of historical value, and to add new works of art from time to time. For the same purpose, here in Vitebsk and in the whole Province, valuable objects of art are to be given to the Art Museum and not hidden in private apartments and mansions or sold at auctions.

The City Museum will be headed by a Commission, consisting of members of the Artistic and Administrative Soviets of the College and persons invited and appointed by the Division of People's Education and the economic establishment of the city.

Regular Appointments in the City Museum

In addition to the Museum Commission, the positions of a Responsible Curator and a junior employee must be appointed.

Minimal expense for the museum

Museum Curator	9,000 Rubles
Junior employee	6,000
	———
Total	15,000–20,000

2/ 30,000 Rubles—annual sum for the acquisition of art objects initiated by the Museum Commission/apart from those that must be sent free of charge from the center/and the acquisition of art objects of the local past which may be not only of an artistic nature, but also characterize the ethnographic and typical local conditions of the city's life and the whole Western Land.

Total, for the first period of the City Museum at the People's College 45,000–50,000 R.

For the time being, those are the few most important cultural enterprises of enormous significance for raising the cultural level of the city of Vitebsk, the [Western] Land in general, and the masses in particular.

Participation of the Jewish Commissariat for National Affairs

Chagall's stress on the Jewish aspect may also have to do with his hope of getting money from the Jewish Commissariat or the American Jewish philanthropy, the "Joint."

Since the Art College will be functioning in a Jewish city, where most of the inhabitants are artisans-workers, the College must stress especially the development of artistic talents of the Jewish masses in general and the workers' sections in particular.

Therefore, though the Vitebsk Art College is a general state institution, it must also become one of the main concerns of the Jewish Commissariat for National Affairs.

The training of every young Jew in the class of applied arts especially—must be mandatory. For that purpose, the Jewish Commissariat must systematically utilize the free time of the Jewish working person and endeavor to combine the worker's studies in general educational topics with studies of industrial arts—which is advantageous for him too.

Finally, it must be of essence to the Jewish Commissariat, in connection with the Art College, to care for and support the especially talented beginners from the people in the field of art. For that purpose, if possible, it would be more radical to establish general educational courses for workers in general and for Jews in particular at the Art College.

Jewish talents have too often perished in dire need.

At the Art College a dormitory must be established for those who are in need, yet are prominent or beginners from the people—with a kitchen, a library, etc.

The question of the participation of the Jewish Commissariat, in this and in the following field, is open.

A Jewish Division in the City Museum

A City Museum in a mostly Jewish city must naturally establish a Division of Jewish Art, which would include, as far as possible, objects of the Jewish tradition in general, on the one hand, and on the other hand, works by Jews-artists, reflecting the short history of Jewish art.

Since Jewish societies for the encouragement of the arts in the capital cities are by nature and spirit not very productive, and are even reactionary, they cannot contribute to supplying objects and works of art to a Museum Division free of charge, for the simple reason that they themselves don't have such and have no material means for that purpose. The Jewish Commissariat in the center must itself undertake the collection of truly artistic Jewish objects of art in general and supply them to the Vitebsk Division in particular, as well as to other cities, where such a need arises.

No expenses are large enough for such high cultural goals of a deeply national character. Only our time—the time of unfolding popular initiative, liberated from all bourgeois-patronizing and other philanthropic guardianships—can and must build its internal and external life generously and authentically.

Temporary School—The Workshop

In advance of opening the main College to give an opportunity to all who wish to study and work, a temporary preparatory school-workshop must immediately be opened.

At the opening of the People's Art College, such a temporary school with all its students will eventually merge with the College according to the assigned classes and according to the level of preparadness of each student. To achieve this urgent goal the Section of the Division of People's Education must immediately take such a temporary school under its wing, provide it with a minimal subsidy, and appoint a Director of the temporary school.

The expenses are minimal

1 / The Director is also the teacher.
2 / the second teacher—is an assistant /for drawing/
3 / a junior employee.
4 / expenses for the building etc.
————————————————

Total: 2,500–3,000 Rubles per month.

The Director submits a monthly statement of all expenses.

On September 12, 1918, Chagall went to Petrograd (where the Soviet government was still located) to get final approval for his project. He returned after a week, bringing his official appointment.

Marc Chagall—Plenipotentiary of the Collegium on Matters of Art in Vitebsk (September 20, 1918)[7]

[Russian] The Division of Graphic Arts of the People's Commissariat of Enlightenment informs the population of the city of Vitebsk that according to the decision of the Collegium for Matters of Art and Industrial Art at the People's Commissariat of Enlightenment, the artist Mark Chagall is hereby appointed Plenipotentiary of the said Collegium on Matters of Art in Vitebsk Province. Comrade Chagall is accorded the right to organize art schools, museums, exhibitions, lectures, and presentations on art and all other artistic enterprises within the boundaries of the city of Vitebsk and its Province. All Revolutionary authorities in Vitebsk are requested to grant Comrade Chagall full cooperation in fulfilling the abovementioned goals.

To the Artists of the City of Vitebsk and Vitebsk Province (September 26, 1918)[8]

[Russian] All artists, decorators, and drawing masters, inspired by the idea of the great Revolution—are to prepare a series of large, expressive, and bright posters.

The best will be remunerated, the most original ones will get a prize and will be preserved for the Vitebsk City Museum.

The deadline for submitting posters to the Dept. of People's Enlightenment is October 15.

Plenipotentiary on Matters of Art in Vitebsk Province   Mark Chagall

From the Plenipotentiary on Matters of Art in Vitebsk Province (October 8, 1918)[9]

[Russian] Since, to successfully accomplish all works for the decoration of the city of Vitebsk at the impending celebration of the October Revolution, all artistic forces of the city must be mobilized, the Subdivision of Graphic Arts informs all artists and decorators of the city of Vitebsk that they are required: 1) immediately to stop all work on orders for signs, decorations, etc., and place themselves at the disposal of the artistic commission for the decoration of the city of Vitebsk toward the October celebrations; 2) within 3 days of the issue of this resolution to report to the Subdivision of Graphic Arts (between 10 and 3 pm) for registration and acceptance of the immediate task.

Plenipotentiary on Matters of Art in the Vitebsk Province   Mark Chagall

Let Us Not Be Ridiculous (October 19, 1918) [Excerpts][10]

[Russian] The pomp and circumstance that accompanied bourgeois festivities is alien to the spirit of the laborers. [. . .] But that is apparently not understood by all who join the ranks of the proletariat today. A striking proof of this is provided by the plans of the Commission for the organization of the celebrations of the October Anniversary in Vitebsk. Thus far, this Commission has not tended to the preparation of the Vitebsk workers for the celebration, has not held even one workers' assembly to that effect, has not thought of any improvements of the daily life of the workers for their holiday, has not taught them even one proletarian song.

But, knowing that the Socialist Revolution is conducted under the red proletarian banner, this Commission, at a time of extreme shortage of cloth in the country, has contrived to rub in the eyes of the working class with red ribbons, for which they plan to spend 20 thousand *Arshins* of cloth to be painted in red for the city of Vitebsk alone! Did the organizers of the festivities consider that 5 thousand pairs of underwear could be made from this cloth?

Arshin: A Russian measure equal to 71 cm or 28 inches; the precise figure hardly matters. Does one need 10 feet of cloth for one pair of underwear?

This argument echoes Aleksandr Blok's immensely popular revolutionary long poem, *Twelve*, presenting twelve Red Army soldiers like twelve apostles marching in a storm, with Jesus Christ leading them, in a wreath of red roses. The poem was read at October assemblies in Vitebsk, as elsewhere. One episode gives voice to an old woman, facing a huge political banner, complaining: "how many foot bindings could be made for the children, and all are naked, barefoot." Ten years later, Yakov Tugendhold wrote: "The celebration of the first anniversary of the October Revolution, that attempt at dyeing tens of thousands of meters of cloth to cover whole buildings (Altman himself spent 20,000 meters! [In Petrograd]), may have shocked the unsophisticated with its obtrusiveness and wastefulness. But this does not mean that we should denigrate the enormous and interesting decorative work which Altman, Shterenberg, Punyi, Lebedev, Kozlinsky executed at the festivities of May 1, 1918, November 7, 1919 [First Anniversary of the October Revolution], and the First Anniversary of the Red Army in 1919, and furthermore, the work of Chagall in Vitebsk, Ekster in Kiev, etc. On the contrary, it was in these street festivities that our Leftist art was most impressive. It did not just 'decorate' the streets but fulfilled a Revolutionary mission—it covered up the 'holy temples,' the palaces and monuments, destroying their habitual faces with new forms (as, for example, Altman did with the Aleksandr Column on Palace Square [in Petrograd]), it *exploded* and *undermined* the old feelings of slavery. It was that destructive work which was required by the psychology of the moment . . . "[11]

From the Plenipotentiary on Matters of Art (October 22, 1918)[12]

[Russian] All artists, decorators and painters are required to appear every day at the commission for the decoration of the city of Vitebsk for the October festivities to register and be assigned various tasks as requested by the commission. Those who do not appear will be considered conscious evaders.

Plenipotentiary on Matters of Art in Vitebsk Province   Mark Chagall

Secretary Ya. Maltsin

Posters (October 28, 1918)[13]

[Russian] At present, all artists of Vitebsk are working on artistic posters. There will be about 350 posters altogether. In addition, 7 arches and tribunes will be erected in the squares. All Soviet and workers' buildings will be decorated with artistic posters, wreaths of greenery, and illuminated at night . . .

Registration of Art Objects (November 2, 1918)[14]

[Russian] The Subdivision of Graphic Arts of the Department of People's Enlightenment decided to hold a registration of art objects in the city of Vitebsk and Vitebsk Province, and to concentrate the most valuable objects in the Vitebsk Province Museum. In view of this, the Subdivision submitted for approval to the Gubispolkom [= Province government] the proper mandatory resolution, forbidding all auctioneers, merchants, and other individuals to sell paintings, sculptures, tapestries, miniatures, stylish antique furniture, valuable books on art, engravings, etc., without special permission by the Subdivision.

The Red Holiday in Vitebsk (November 11, 1918) [Excerpts][15]

[Russian] More than anything, the artistic posters displayed around the city evoked arguments. The bright, unusual hues, the new manner of painting and combinations of colors, the unintelligible conception—all this struck the masses, who stood in disbelief before the pictures and demanded explanations. Passing by a poster "Regards to Lunacharsky!" [by M. Chagall], near the Proletarian Club, girls turned their heads, exclaiming: an amoral picture! It was curious to see this protest by the self-satisfied petit-bourgeois, who consider everything they don't understand as ridiculous and absurd, become indignant, foam at the mouth, and scream that it is not art if they don't understand and approve it.

Marc Chagall: The People's Art College (November 16, 1918)[16]

[Russian] The Art School that will soon open in Vitebsk is designed to fulfill the long-felt need for an artistic cultural-educational center, whose existence will make it possible right here, in our city, to direct a novice artist from the people on the right road. The revolutionary people will give full space for the unfolding of all talents among the people, inhibited so far by both the old, outmoded academic school and the social conditions of the bourgeois world. The task of the Art School opening in Vitebsk is first of all to execute in reality the foundations of a true Revolutionary Art, that breaks with the old academic routine. At the same time, the principles of a professional school will be implemented in the construction of the College. The Applied Art class will have a workshop to carry out various decorative works—in painting, ceramics, wood, etc., writing signs, posters, etc. The activity of such a workshop will aid the embellishment of the city—at the same time, it will give the students an opportunity to apply their talents practically, to provide them with a livelihood now and in the future. Now that the work of decorating the city on the October anniversary, which had mobilized all the artistic forces of Vitebsk, is over, it is possible to enhance the work on the organization of the College. Teaching will soon begin—before the arrival of the invited teachers and the opening of the planned classes, studies will be conducted in 2 groups: an advanced class (painting from nature) and evening courses of drawing. Work in the decorative workshop will begin in the very near future to fill orders for new artistic signs for schools, reading rooms, etc.

Mandatory Resolution (November 22, 1918)[17]

[Russian] All institutions, both private and governmental, are requested to return all posters, display boards, and similar decorations to the Subdivision of Graphic Arts (Bukharin St. 10) within three days of this date.

Institutions wishing to leave the abovementioned objects for themselves, are to submit a proper application to the office of the Subdivision of Graphic Arts between 10 and 3 p.m.

Chairman of the Commission   Krylov

Province Representative on Matters of Art   Mark Chagall

Public Debate (December 5, 1918)[18]

[Russian] The Subdivision of Fine Arts in the City Department of People's Enlightenment organizes a public debate on the topic "The Minority in Art," to be held in the District Court on Saturday, December 7. Comrade Chagall will read an address about art. Its theses are: What is Art? Art in Russia and in Western Europe, Revolutionary Art. After the address, an open debate with the participation of the Comrades Margolin [Mayor], Krylov [Party], Medvedev [Dept. of Culture], Tsshchokher [Music], Okunev, Sheydlina [City Dept. of Enlightenment], Romm [Art College], and others. Entrance free. Beginning at 7.00 p.m.

Chagall discussed the issue of "the minority in art" in his address on the Anniversary of the October Revolution,[19] arguing that "Art lived and will continue to live by its own laws." Now, "when Humanity has taken the road of ultimate Revolution," Art can also be "Revolutionary in essence." "But some will object to us and say: So why are you a minority? No one, at least in our city, literally no one understands you, we are baffled by your works—while our political Revolution is supported by a majority." Chagall concedes the point: "Yes, the creators of Revolutionary Art always were and are now a minority," but: "The majority will come with us when two Revolutions, the political and the spiritual, systematically uproot the heritage of the past with all its prejudices." "No matter how embarrassed many are by the radical edge of Leftist Art, we have to say to our friends and our foes: Down with prejudices! Plunge head first into the sea of the people's Revolutionary Art!" Of course, Chagall couldn't see that the so-called political "majority" was achieved only after a tiny minority had taken total power; the Leftist artists expected a similar turn in art.

G. Grilin, "The Right to Solitude" (December 8, 1918)[20]

On today's address by Marc Chagall [Excerpts]

[Russian] The talented artist Marc Chagall has finally decided to present not just his works but also his views on art to the court of public opinion. Today he will read a public address on "The Minority in Art," accompanied by a debate.

For a sensitive artist it is hard and stifling to live in our commonplace atmosphere, among the coarse and vulgar tastes of the citizenry. But it is even harder to live among us for Marc Chagall, still barely understood and explained by the art connoisseurs and critics. The narrow-minded and coarse citizenry demands that an artist "open his soul," provide an arithmetical key to his work; it doesn't recognize any sphinxes, and whatever it deems unintelligible it considers absurd, unworthy, buffoonery.

Yes. It is so. Remember the posters hung all over our city on the anniversary of the October Revolution. With what irony was it met by our citizenry, how they scoffed and spurned the same Marc Chagall, who is admired by the best specialists on art, whose pictures have evoked such an uproar, so many interesting articles, even books, in Paris, Berlin, Holland, and Russia.

Today Marc Chagall will expound his views on art, today he will throw a glove to our Vitebsk "society," to his homeland, whose love permeates most of his works of art.

Marc Chagall will lecture on "The Minority in Art." But actually it is a matter not of a minority but of "solitude" in art. Marc Chagall is truly alone, surrounded by coarse and vulgar tastes and ignorance. This is the tragedy of the artist's soul. [. . .]

But the people of Vitebsk [whom he painted]—the Rabbis, the Talmudists and the paupers, see Chagall, apparently, as a renegade from Judaism, an iconoclast. And not only those people [. . .] but, we may say, all of Vitebsk, including its intelligentsia, sees Chagall as a renegade and even a buffoon. Strange as it may be, so it is. [. . .]

"The Minority in Art" or "The Solitude of Chagall"—this is the theme of today's debate. But what can we answer the artist, we, coarse provincials, who have almost no idea about true, great art. Every word of ours wounds the artist, because it is coarse, vulgar and worthless.

Nevertheless we will be "right." Because we are the majority and Chagall is alone. And if he decides to come to us, if he makes an attempt to bring us closer to him, if he hopes to get the right to "solitude" from us, he takes a risky step. They will not give him that right.

Marc Chagall: Letter to the Editor (December 9, 1918)[21]

[Russian] Comrade Editor!

Allow me to announce in your paper that, for unforeseen reasons and not my fault, the address-and-debate in the Circuit Court on December 7 could not be held.[22]

Marc Chagall

Marc Chagall: Letter from Vitebsk (December 1918)[23]

[Russian] The city of Vitebsk stirred.

In this provincial "hole" with a population of almost a hundred thousand, where once upon a time, some Yury Klever stagnated and the *Itinerant* artists [*Peredvizhniki*] still continue their miserable existence—today, in the days of October, the wide-ranging Revolutionary Art is in full swing.

From the moment of our arrival in Vitebsk, we succeeded in mobilizing all the hidden meager art forces of the city and province.

Our hearts rejoiced at the sight of several beginning artists and especially workers—painters. With how much love, with what childish devotion did they follow our big-city, "sophisticated" studies.

On the anniversary of October, Vitebsk Province was adorned with 450 large posters, numerous flags for workers' organizations, rostrums, and arches.

The Committee for Decorating the City and the Province divided its work in sections: for painting, architecture, and lighting (electrical illumination of buildings, arches, rostrums, fireworks, torches, etc.)

At the end, the evening of November 6 burned with an unforgettable fire.

This was also a holiday of our art.

But the next day, middle-class people, and if it were only them . . . I admit with pain: even progressive comrades revolutionaries, foaming at the mouth, hurled incredulous questions at us: "What kind of thing is this." Explain, explain, explain, is this proletarian art?

Pity, they undercut a mass assembly on art.[24] "I would have showed them, explained."

And finally, an Art College was established in the city. As soon as applications for admission were issued, some 125 persons registered. All of them poor and workers.

Let the petit bourgeois malice hiss all around us, we hope that new artists-proletarians will soon emerge from those working people.

At the Art College, a communal city workshop was organized to fill orders from the whole city. All the work for the production of theater decorations, posters for cinema houses, frescoes and signs, must be concentrated exclusively in the Subdivision of the Arts. The Subdivision sends the orders to the communal workshop and its sections, for planned distribution. The orders are filled exclusively by students and teachers of the school. All private cooperatives of artists in the city must first of all go to our school to study and liquidate their private "businesses." Enough. All of you must go study in the school, don't be ashamed of your age. There you will learn to work.

When the workshop opened, it received an order from the [City] Division of

Klever: Yury Yulyevich Klever, an "academic" landscape painter, widely popular in Russia in the late nineteenth and early twentieth centuries. The Klever family owned an estate in Vitebsk Province.

their miserable existence: Apparently a jibe at Yury Pen. At a later point, Chagall was less fanatical about "Leftist Art" and appointed Pen as a professor in the Art College, in the name of pluralism.

November 6: The eve of the anniversary of the October Revolution, according to the European calendar.

proletarian art: Chagall painted green cows and flying horses (Russian folktale figures), which were multiplied by his students and hung all over the city. Naturally, he got in trouble with the Communist authorities.

People's Enlightenment to produce 60 new artistic signs for individual workers' schools, workers' libraries, and the Proletarian University. For each order, a competition was announced. The best drawing was carried out.

The old street signs were taken off the main streets of the city to be repainted.

The Subdivision of Graphic Arts issued a decree demanding the registration of all art objects in the city and the province and their concentration in the newly organized Provincial Museum.

The teaching of art in the schools of the city and province is also to be reformed. Yet before the institution of a general reform, all the art teachers in all the current schools are to be reelected, then appointed and approved by the Subdivision of the Arts only after they submit their "personal" works, several samples of drawings by their students of every grade separately, as well as a short presentation of their ideas on the teaching of art in school. Those old teachers who do not fit the contemporary requirements of art lose their warmed-up seats, and new teachers are appointed in their place. Here no compromises are allowed.

Remember the "unforgettable" art classes, this artistic killing of the young. In every teaching institution in the city, a special class—a drawing workshop. The teacher of drawing no longer goes from class to class, but the students must go to him, to a special class-workshop of every teaching institution, each group of students in its time.

Let us end this note with a call: Give us people! Artists! Revolutionaries-painters! From the capitals to the provinces! To us! What will tempt you to come?

Marc Chagall

Inviting Important Faculty

In December 1918, Chagall traveled to Petrograd and Moscow and invited some of the best artists of the time to join his faculty. Among those who came to Vitebsk were Ivan Punyi (Pougny) and his wife K.L. Boguslavskaya, Chagall's former teacher Mstislav V. Dobuzhinsky, and his friend from Bakst's school and from Paris, the future art historian Aleksandr Romm. In the summer of 1919 he invited Yury Pen (though not a Leftist artist) and El Lissitzky, and in November came Kazimir Malevich. The conditions of starvation and cold in the capital cities, and the relative proximity of Vitebsk to both Moscow and Petrograd, encouraged the artists to join Chagall's famous school of Revolutionary art. Overnight it became one of the major centers of Russian avant-garde art, and remained so for several years.

Marc Chagall in Vitebsk to Mstislav V. Dobuzhinsky in Petrograd (1918)[25]

[Russian] Dear Msistlav Valeryanovich,

Forgive me for writing on a dirty postcard. I want to use the opportunity of Comrade [Golubinsky's?] travel to send you regards and an invitation. We will always find a place for you here. Please write how you are.

Zadunovskaya St. 9

I press your hand/   Your Chagall

Marc Chagall: Notes on Art (January 1919)[26]

[Russian] Finally we are back in our impoverished homeland [Vitebsk].

Well we, as "not attached," had no right to eat dinner anywhere [in the capitals] or under any circumstances, and tried in vain to alleviate our hunger in some public eatery, and in the evening returned to our "room" in total darkness . . .

not attached: Chagall was not attached to any institution, in order to get food rations while in the capitals.

But a half-starving official in the capital—why is it so hard to tempt him here [to Vitebsk] for cultural work?

—I do understand them . . .

But what are we to do? What will, nevertheless, entice those leftist activists, those innovators in art, who are so indispensable to us at this moment for the best local artistic and cultural life of the masses in [our] city and province.

This is the kind of society we paid attention to during our sojourn in the capitals [Moscow and Petrograd]. It was impossible to ignore the fact that forces of political agitation are generously being sent to the various military-political fronts, whereas the domain of culture, particularly the arts, is being overlooked. It is somewhere considered superfluous to send the most energetic and leftist activists in the field of art in all its forms—to provincial cities and villages.

Yet the creation of such revolutionary vanguards would have been entirely expedient.

Everybody agreed with me on this issue.

But . . . "The minority in art" [i.e., Leftist Art] is a most pitiful minority.

Still, I cannot sufficiently express my joy at the achievement—to entice such activists and artists as Dobuzhinsky, Radlov, Annenkov,[27] and others, and with pleasure to offer the directorship to Dobuzhinsky. Only now can we boldly open the doors of the Art College, a provincial school that is to be a model for schools of a new type for the needs of our province. Yet we shall open without the traditional pomp, without celebration and "speeches."

Will you come, workers and men of the people, to sharpen your artistic-cultural inclinations and tastes? Please come diligently and modestly to learn and work; much easier than this year, you will see and understand the decoration of the city toward the next anniversary of the October Revolution.

It will be enough for you to get slightly acquainted with the elementary work in the workshops of the school, and you'll understand that we did not joke in the recent October days when we introduced art to the people.

In spite of some depressing conditions—the life of art in the capitals does not die. One after the other, agitational monuments are erected, a grandiose exhibition is mounted, an exhibition in the Winter Palace,[28] revolutionary theater studios ("The Red Cock" and others) are diligently creative, and the tireless Narkom [= People's Commissar] Lunacharsky, all inspired, is running from his Commissariat to the Winter Palace, from the Winter Palace to the actors, from them to the musicians and artists, and from all of them to the Smolny [Institute].

Smolny Institute: Lenin's headquarters during the October uprising.

"They are at war": Maria Fedorovna, Narkom of Theater [People's Commissar of Theater], with Meyerhold, and Meyerhold with Kameneva.

> Maria Fedorovna Andreeva-Gorky, an actress and the wife of the Marxist writer Maxim Gorky, was a powerful party functionary, especially in the theater and cultural affairs. Vsevolod Meyerhold was a prominent avant-garde theater director. Olga Davidovna Kameneva, the sister of Lev Trotsky and the wife of the Soviet leader Lev Kamenev, was influential in matters of art.

Let us fight too. Whoever can, give us a hand or—what do I say—at least, do not disturb, we have to work, even if your sympathy is not with us.

We shall do something for our somber homeland [Vitebsk] . . .

Marc Chagall

Telegram from Marc Chagall in Vitebsk to Mstislav Dobuzhinsky in Petrograd (January 4, 1919)

[Russian] I beg you come immediately. Impatiently awaiting Radlov Lyubavina.[29] Please cable—Chagall.—We shall call right away.

On the Concentration of All Decorative and Artistic-Painterly Works in the Communal Workshop of the Vitebsk Art College (January 16, 1919)[30]

[Russian] 1. All institutions, establishments of trade and industry, theater enterprises and private persons are required to submit all commissions for decorative and artistic-painterly works, such as: the painting of signs, banners, posters, placards, theater decorations, murals and color painting of the interior and exterior of buildings—exclusively to the communal workshop at the Vitebsk Art College, via the Subdivision for Graphic Arts of the Province Department of People's Enlightenment (Bukharin St. 10).

2. The commission and execution of works outside of the communal workshop is forbidden.

Signed: Chairman of Gorispolkom [City Executive Council]   Margolin

Province Plenipotentiary for Matters of Art   Mark Chagall

G. Grilin: A Corner of Art in Vitebsk

On the Opening of the People's Art College in Vitebsk (January 28, 1919)[31]

[Russian] On Bukharin St. (Former Voskresenskaya [= Resurrection]), in the lavish mansion of the former local magnate, the banker Vishnyak, the young child of proletarian culture—the Vitebsk People's Art College—took shelter today.

It was born almost by accident. From noisy Paris, the World War drove our famous fellow-countryman Mark Chagall into our backwoods. At first, from his corner on Ilyin St., he observed the life of Vitebsk and transformed pieces of this gray, monotonous existence into striking, colorful pictures on canvas.

But then he decided that Vitebsk can no longer live just "to bear children, trade, and die." And with the support of the highest Soviet power, Mark Chagall presented Vitebsk with a People's Art College with a whole gallery of famous names in contemporary Russian graphic art, headed by the famous artist of our day Dobuzhinsky.

It turned out simply, without screaming, noise and bustle.

Hundreds of young people in Vitebsk dreamed for many years about canvas and palette. The crowded and stuffy studio of the artist Yu. M. Pen was their shelter. There, bright little fires ignited sometimes and were soon extinguished, unknown not just to the world of art, but also to our despondent and gray city.

And suddenly the doors of a new temple of art opened wide. About 300 persons already registered in the Art College. All lovers of graphic art find a shelter there. At the Art College, a communal workshop was opened, where many young Vitebsk artists work.

*

The other day, the official opening of the Art College took place. From a "corner" of Bukharin St., from the lavish mansion of the banker Vishnyak, built on the blood and sweat, the suffering and tears of hundreds and thousands of people impoverished by usury—the dawn of a new culture rose above Vitebsk.

At the opening, a small group of people gathered. There were no mass audience proclamations and speeches, there was even no "program" of the opening. Everyone said whatever he wanted, what he sincerely thought, all felt they were in a dense, intimate circle of close people, linked by the invisible threads of the most noble emotions of the human soul.

Chagall spoke first, briefly and simply, then the artist Boguslavskaya, the Director of the College Dobuzhinsky, the comrades Medvedev, Margolin, Krylov, and others. They spoke simple, sincere words, as living people.

Pustynin read his brilliant poem about the College and Chagall, Yak. Okunev told a tale, Bay played the piano, the actor Gotarsky made the audience laugh with his anecdotes, they drank tea which they took straight from the kitchen without "servants," they talked unconstrained, those who felt like it laughed and joked—with no compunctions.

A good beginning. Let us hope that in the future too, this new corner of culture in Vitebsk may live with this unmediated life, which people in general should live, and which was obstructed for us till now by various "conventions" and "traditions," made up by the satiated and dumb bourgeoisie.

Medvedev: Pavel Medvedev, head of the city Department of Culture ("Non-school Education") and later a well-known Bakhtin disciple and Marxist literary critic.

Margolin: Chairman of the City Executive Committee (Mayor) of Vitebsk.

On Sending all Works of a Painterly Nature to the Section of Artistic Works (January 31, 1919)[32]

[Russian] In view of the observed fact that people are evading the resolution of the Vitebsk Division of People's Enlightenment No. 2, of January 10, and for the sake of realizing artistic control, it is hereby ordered henceforth to send all commissioned works of artistic nature (posters, theater decorations, signs, etc.) exclusively to the Section of artistic works at the Subdivision of Graphic Arts of the Vitebsk Department of People's Enlightenment (Bukharin St. 10).

Failure to respect this resolution will be prosecuted by law, as open sabotage.[33]

Chairman of Gorispolkom [City Executive Committee]   Margolin

Province Plenipotentiary for Matters of Art   M. Chagall

For a Revolutionary People—Revolutionary Art (February 6, 1919)[34]

[Russian] Recently, Vitebsk was enriched by a new, valuable good: the Art College. What the Vitebsk proletariat didn't even dare dream of—became reality. The October Revolution has liberated the working class, brought it to life, and set it an urgent task: to create its own, proletarian way of life, its own art and spiritual world that will replace the exhausted bourgeois world.

"with the Left": Allusion to Mayakovsky's march "With the Left [foot] Forward!"

Art "with the Left" ["marching with the left foot forward"] gave all its forces to help us in this difficult work. The Vitebsk workers must not scorn this help, but in closed ranks must move forward on the road to the ideal.

"For a Revolutionary People—Revolutionary Art." Forward, comrades!

We call the attention of the comrade workers to what has already been achieved, what is being done now, and what is planned for fulfillment in this area in our Vitebsk:

Composition of the Collegium for Matters of Art

The Provincial Department of People's Enlightenment approved the following composition of the Collegium for Matters of Art and Art Industry of Vitebsk Province: Marc Chagall—Collegium Chairman, Dobuzhinsky—Director of the Provincial Art College, Boguslavskaya—Director of the Section for Art Industry, Ivan Punyi—Art Agitation and Propaganda, Lyubavina—Pedagogical Section, Tilberg—Director of the Sculpture Workshop, Romm—Instructor, Shpiro—Secretary of the Collegium. In addition, the following persons are invited: Director of the Provincial Department of People's Enlightenment—Comrade Shifres, Director of the City Department of People's Enlightenment—Comrade Sheydlina, a representative of the District Dept. of Edu., 2 representatives of the Central Soviet of the Trade Unions, one representative of the cultural-educational organization of the Red Army, one—of the students of Vitebsk Province, one of the Cooperation.

The Provincial People's Art Museum

The Collegium of the Division of Art approved the report about organizing a Provincial People's Museum in Vitebsk, consisting of a Historical-Archeological and an Art Department, and an Art Library.

Propaganda for Contemporary Art

Brik: Osip M. Brik, a theoretician of Russian Formalism, close to the Futurists.

Mayakovsky: V. Mayakovsky, a major Russian Futurist poet.

The Section for Art Agitation and Propaganda initiated a series of assemblies, lectures, brochures and leaflets on the most urgent themes, such as : "The Old and the New Art," "For a Revolutionary People—Revolutionary Art," etc. Among others, O.M. Brik and Vladimir Mayakovsky were invited to lecture. The Section has acquired photos of works of art by contemporary artists, both from the re-opened State exhibition in Petrograd and the whole collection of the former Shchukin gallery in Moscow.

Artistic Decoration, Wall-Paintings, and Signs

The Section of Artistic Work began filling various commissions via the Communal Workshop of the Art College. Of orders already completed, we should note the decorations of the City Theater made from drafts by the artist Dobuzhinsky on January 9 (Old Style [sic]) and in memory of Comrade Karl Liebknecht. The Section organized a competition of sketches for artistic signs for institutions. In the near future, a major work of wall painting and decoration of the Vitebsk Permanent Book Exhibition will be undertaken.

Liebknecht: Karl Liebknecht and Rosa Luxemburg were the leaders of Spartakus in Berlin (later, the Communist Party of Germany). Liebknecht was killed in the Spartakus uprising on January 15, 1919 and became one of the saints of the left.

Applied Art

The Section of Art Industry has finished its internal organizational work. At present, steps are being taken to open experimental exemplary workshops for applied art, there work will be conducted both to produce useful things as well as objects of demonstrative artistic culture in the sense of applied art. In addition, for those productions where art can be applied, their unification, merging with the Communal Workshop, and introduction of artistic control are planned.

In Moscow and in Peterburg, objects were bought for the Museum of Applied Art. At the Permanent Vitebsk Book Exhibition, to be opened in the near future, the Section is organizing an exhibition of artistic bookbinding.

In the newspaper of the same day, an address by Chagall and a debate (cancelled in December) were announced for the coming Sunday.

From Chagall's Art Workshop (March 6, 1919)[35]

[Russian] In view of the return of Mark Chagall, Director of the painting workshop, all students of the abovementioned workshop are requested to attend classes. Those who do not appear will be excluded from the workshop.

In the Painting Workshop (March 9, 1919)[36]

[Russian] We are informing all those who registered in the painting workshop, directed by Chagall, that, in order to conduct serious, systematic and regular studies, a re-registration of all registered students will be opened. The candidates are requested to submit individual applications directly to the director

Chagall (to the secretary, daily between 10–4 and 6–8) no later than March 16. All those not registered by that date will be excluded.

The First State Art Exhibition in Vitebsk (March 30, 1919)

Iskusstvo Kommuny [= Art of the Commune]

Organ of the Department of Graphic Arts at the
People's Commissariat of Enlightenment

No. 17, Peterburg, Sunday, March 30, 1919

We Are Beautiful In The Relentless Betrayal Of Our Past

From the Vitebsk Subdivision of Graphic Arts

[Russian] The Vitebsk Subdivision of Graphic Arts is preparing the first State Art Exhibition in the city of Vitebsk and Vitebsk Province and asks the comrade artists to send their applications concerning their wish to participate to: Vitebsk, Bukharin St. 10, Subdivision of Graphic Arts.

The application must list the number of works exhibited as well as the sizes of the proposed works in square *Arshins*.

The exhibition has no jury.

Expenses of transporting the paintings from other cities will be paid by the Vitebsk Subdivision of Graphic Arts.

The Opening is tentatively scheduled for the end of April this year.

Province Plenipotentiary for Matters of Art and Director of the Subdivision

Mark Chagall

The Management of Matters of Art in Vitebsk (April 16, 1919)[37]

[Russian] The artist Chagall appealed to the Center to release him from his duties as the Province Plenipotentiary on Matters of Art.

Until such time as a substitute is appointed, the management of matters of art will be placed in the hands of the Province Collegium on Matters of Art.

On Chagall's Departure (April 24, 1919)[38]

[Russian] In response to the Telegram of the Plenipotentiary for Matters of Art in Vitebsk Province M. Chagall concerning his release from his obligations, a Telegram was received from the Center that he must remain in his post.

In M. Chagall's Workshop (April 24, 1919)

[Russian] The artist M. Chagall is working at present on the stage design of N.V. Gogol's play "The Wedding." Chagall has already accomplished several paintings for this play. At the same time, M. Chagall is preparing a series of pictures for the Yiddish schools, representing scenes from Jewish life in a realistic tone.

Appointment of the Artist Romm (May 10, 1919)[39]

[Russian] Hearing the report by comrade Chagall, the Center accepted Chagall's proposal to appoint comrade Romm as Province Plenipotentiary on Matters of Art of Vitebsk Province. Comrade Chagall remains Director of the College.

The Future Proletarian Artists (Velizh, June 29, 1919)[40]

[Russian] The Vitebsk People's Art College, where only children of the workers and the poor are studying, opens the first exhibition of young artistic forces, who emerged from the depth of the Vitebsk working masses. At the head of the school stands our glorious Vitebskite—a son of the Jewish working people, the famous artist Marc Chagall.

Re-Registration and Admission of New Students in the Art College (July 31, 1919)[41]

[Russian] [. . .] Admission to the free workshop of Marc Chagall (in view of the limited space) is considered exclusively for those who present their works and who went through a successful course of studies in the College.

Marc Chagall: About the Vitebsk People's Art College (July 1919)[42]

On the First Annual Student Exhibition

[Russian] I shall try objectively, as a "disinterested" party, to say a few words about the white house on Bukharin Street.

Within its walls we never remember its former owner with "gratitude."

From the windows of his house, day and night you can see the whole poor city. But today, we don't feel that poverty.

You were poor, my city, when strolling in your streets, I would meet no one

white house on Bukharin Street: Israel Vishnyak's former mansion, now housing the People's Art College.

but a sleepy storekeeper. But today I encounter many of your sons, abandoning the poverty of their homes, on the way to the Art College.

There are willing ears.

I want to say briefly what has been done and what is planned for the future.

But who would be interested in the practical history of creating any phenomenon in the field of Art?

I myself would gladly have refrained from answering the question: "How did you, you such-and-such, paint this or that painting? How did it work out for you?—One answer to the "spectator": "Look at the final result," what business do you have and what interest may anyone have in the "*dirty work*" . . . Who would be interested to know how much you went through in your life before and after. Show your finished work!

For the history of these things, as the history of the emergence of the Vitebsk People's Art College—is normal, but the history of the emergence of so many dormant Vitebsk talents between its walls—is unusual.

The dream that children of urban poverty, somewhere in houses daubing on paper, would join Art—is being realized. But that is not enough; we had to make sure that the artistic education received would be useful without the loss of valuable time, and that, according to each person's studies, the work would really be a product of Art with a capital A, that from the start the methods and devices of artistic education would take the right direction, so that they won't result in artistic invalids and dead souls with no resurrection. But even that is not enough; we had to make sure that the institution, granting knowledge and access to Art, would radically turn away from the most "understandable" and dangerous path—the path of routine—and would March on the Revolutionary path in Art, the path of searching.

individual peculiarities: It was a principle of Bakst's education, as well as Chagall's own insistence, that the artist's individual originality would not succumb to the collective demands.

Above all, it was imperative, and will be in the future, to be careful not to erase the individual peculiarities of each person, *while working in a collective*, for the future collective creativity needs only an awareness of the spirit and values of earlier periods, but not a gathering of effaced monotonous persons.

And though, from the very beginning, in order to achieve the assigned, above-mentioned plan, we did conduct an appropriately monolithic artistic policy—now we are not afraid of a certain "retreat" and a seeming "softening" of our activities.

all trends: Now Chagall tries to assert pluralism against the domination of the avant-garde in art.

We can afford the luxury of "playing with fire," and within our walls, the leading artists and workshops of all trends—from left to "right" inclusively—are represented and function freely.

Those are our goals.

But the best proof for what I said could be the First Annual Student Exhibition which just closed.[43] I would have to mention the names of almost all its participants and single out the names of those students whose works were awarded prizes and placed in the school's museum.

It is hard to know how these young Vitebsk forces will crystallize in the future, but the artistic consciousness of these students is no doubt remarkable for Vitebsk.

No less remarkable is another fact: the same unfortunate workers you could see in the heat of summer on red rooftops or window sills—housepainters, painters, trapped from childhood in the workshop of an artisan-businessman without talent—today, in the same humble pose, they paint a still-life in the workshops of the Art College.

And you must give them their due: no less than the "intelligentsia," do they strive for the right of "the calling of an artist."

The future will reinforce even more the achievements of the College in the first half-year of its existence.

Neither repetition nor stagnation can be allowed.

The future should expand the goals of the College; graphic art and architecture workshops are being set up. Despite the industrial crisis, applied art workshops will try to move from projects and sketches to practical work. The question of courses about art will, no doubt, be raised on an appropriately high level, and at the same time, the school will take measures to expand the art library at the students' club. For that purpose, I hereby appeal to all individuals and institutions to give our College as many books as you can, art books that are so necessary for the artistic growth of the students.

In the economic-material domain, the College considers it necessary to take all measures to provide the poorest students (they are too many) with social welfare and to supply them with artistic work.

The city, the enterprises of the city and the province, in spite of all the current hardships, must consider the situation of the artistic elements in the city, the students, and the members of the State Decorative Workshop, and offer them work.

Where are our clubs, people's homes, dining halls, libraries, theaters, museums?

Give us walls! Give the local talents opportunities to expand, for their and your benefit.

Those are our goals.

Artist Marc Chagall

Enemies from the Left

Arguing with the party bosses, Chagall insisted that Revolutionary Art must be a revolution in art itself and not a reflection of the political revolution, or art painted by proletarians or about proletarians. Yet he wanted Art—as he understood it—to spill over into the life of the city. Hence, the call for walls to paint on, in order to achieve art on a large scale and to extend individual creativity into the public domain. This idea parallels and precedes the Mexican muralists of the 1930s, bridging the gap between a modern and individual style, on the one hand, and the artist's social idealism and political commitment, on the other. A year later, he made large murals for the walls of the Moscow Yiddish Theater, and ever since repeated the cry: "Give me walls!" The origin of this cry was not in the Yiddish theater, as is generally assumed, but in a Revolutionary manifesto.

Yet a new front opened on the artistic left. Chagall had claimed that a revolutionary society needed a revolutionary ("Leftist" and "searching") Art; but in time he modified that view, advocating pluralism. Indeed, the Suprematists Kazimir Malevich and El Lissitzky were more extreme revolutionaries in art and banned figurative representation altogether. This schism eventually contributed to Chagall's abandoning Vitebsk, in June 1920. It was a revolutionary atmosphere of increased radicalization and whoever had more radical slogans won the day.

Chagall devoted his soul and energy to his College, and often went to Moscow to secure money and tools from his high-placed supporters. Perhaps he also behaved as a capricious and high-handed commissar. He had the support of many students, for he was the local poor boy who had made it in the world and now opened art to many more local poor boys and girls—something that could not be said about the big names from outside. The second year of the Art College started on September 1, 1919, and shortly thereafter the general assembly of the students made the public appeal to keep Chagall in his place. We don't know what the causes of that disturbance were. Malevich, invited by Chagall to join the faculty, arrived only in October or November.

Yet as soon as Malevich came, he organized a "new party in art" and a school within a school: "The unique stage of art of the collective UNOVIS," where

Ermolaeva, Lissitzky and Nina Kogan were teaching under Malevich's supervision, and Chagall was excluded. UNOVIS is an acronym for "The Affirmers of the New Art."[44] The key idea was that art was not an individualist creation but a collective effort, and that there was only one right method in art—namely, Malevich's "Suprematism" with its abstract geometrical and monochrome shapes, devoid of any "accidental" objects. At first, Chagall was proud of UNOVIS and supported their publications in the name of the college. Yet neither the collective aspect nor the "Non-Objective"—that is, nonfigurative—art could appeal to Chagall. But the decisive factor was Malevich's charismatic, megalomanic, and autocratic manner, which won over the revolutionary student body. On May 25, 1920, when Chagall returned from a trip to Moscow where he got a subsidy, painting materials, and selected paintings for the Vitebsk Museum, he found the banner of UNOVIS on the entrance to his school. In June 1920, he went on a mission to Moscow and took his wife and daughter with him, never to return.

Members of TeRevSat, the Theater of Revolutionary Satire, for which Chagall made all the stage sets, left for Moscow in April 1920, and Chagall joined them there a month later. He prepared some decorations for a Soviet pastiche of Gogol's "Inspector General," but TeRevSat closed in the fall and did not stage that play. Instead, Chagall accepted an invitation to the new Yiddish theater.

The Departure of Comrade Chagall (September 19, 1919)[45]

Resolution of the General Assembly of Students of the People's Art College
    [Russian] Whereas we heard the report by Comrades Tsiperson and Kunin on the critical situation of the College in view of the desire of M.Z. Chagall to leave the College as well as the city of Vitebsk, and taking into consideration:
    1. that M. Chagall is not only one of the first pioneers of planting art in our city, who often experienced the thorns on the road to this great cause;
    2. that M. Chagall is the only moral support of the College, without which the latter cannot exist;
    3. that M. Chagall's departure under these circumstances can ruin the Art

College which has already proved its vitality by the success of the First Student Exhibition;

4. that the machinations of certain individuals who have recently created an impossible atmosphere detrimental to the activity of M. Chagall as director of the College are absolutely inadmissible and deserve a sharply negative treatment;

5. that the only guarantee for restoring the usually calm pace of life of the school would be a radical change of the conditions that would make work possible; the General Assembly of the students appeals directly to M.Z. Chagall, insistently asking him not to leave the school.

The General Assembly expresses complete and unconditional confidence in M. Chagall and promises its support in all activities and plans. The General Assembly also severely condemns the individuals whose acts have created the present situation.

present situation: At the time, this strong support helped keep Chagall in Vitebsk for almost another year. It was apparently directed not against Malevich (who arrived later) but against Aleksandr Rom.

Marc Chagall in Vitebsk to Pavel Davidovich Ettinger in Moscow (April 2, 1920)[46]

Pavel Davidovich Ettinger (1866–1948) was a collector of graphic works, a bibliophile and chronicler of the life of art. From 1920, he corresponded with Marc Chagall and continued when Chagall was in the West, the only person in Russia who did so in the 1930s. During the purges of 1937, the correspondence stopped, but it resumed after World War II. Chagall always supplied information about his exploits and achievements for Ettinger's records.

[Russian] Kind Pavel Davidovich,

Thank you very much for your letters and please forgive me for not answering right away. First, I am unbelievably absent-minded, and second, I am also busy. But mainly there is something that won't let me write altogether, and probably, has something to do with the fact that I barely touch . . . the brush.

Such is our time and the situation of the contemporary artist. I am very happy that you wrote to me; and you shall see that I shall write to you much more in my answer—as soon as I sit down to do it. First, you asked me for material about the Art College, about the artistic life here in the city and in the province. I don't think there is much interest in collecting all the local printed material, but as Director of the College and by destiny the "head" of the local artistic life of the province, I shall share with you some concrete information about the artistic life. The idea of organizing an Art College popped into my head after I returned from abroad, when I was working on the "Vitebsk series" of studies.[47] Vitebsk still abounded then with . . . poles, pigs, and fences [objects of Chagall's paintings], yet the artistic talents were sleeping somewhere. Breaking away from my palette, I ran to Petrograd, Moscow, and the College was established in late 1918. It includes about 500 boys and girls[48] of various classes, various talents and already . . . "trends." Aside from myself, the professors and directors were Dobuzhinsky, Punyi, Boguslavskaya, Lyubavina, Kozlinskaya, Tilberg. Now they include Malevich, Ermolaeva, [Nina Osipovna] Kogan, Lissitsky, Pen, Yakerson, and myself (along with special instructors). There have already been two student exhibitions.[49] Today the competing groups of "trends" have reached a cutting edge; they are: 1) the youth around Malevich and 2) the youth around me. Both of us are striving toward the leftist domain of art, nevertheless we see its means and goals differently. It would, of course, take too long now to discuss this issue. It would be better to talk personally or to write separately. Perhaps I shall allow myself to send you my thoughts separately. I shall tell you one thing: though born in Russia (and in the "Pale of Settlement" at that), but educated abroad, I am especially sensitive to all that happens here in the domain of art (especially fine art). I remember too *painfully* the luster of the *original* . . .

I continue: the College has an art library (though still a small one), a considerable carpenter workshop, a graphics shop, a printing shop, a decorative shop, and a casting workshop, in addition to normal painterly and sculptural studios, our own store of materials, our own . . . bath. We are oganizing a school museum of works by prize-winning students and significant study drawings. At the College, there is a student cooperative and a dramatic-theatrical circle which, by the way, has recently staged Kruchenykh's *Victory over the Sun*, with sets by the students themselves. Now they are preparing *The Crucified*.[50] A College Almanac is also being prepared. However, there is some snag about getting paper. This is more or less the life of the Vitebsk People's Art College. Outside of the College, the [City] Division of Fine Arts is preparing to put up two monuments in Vitebsk: one for Karl Liebknecht and one for Karl Marx (toward May Day); they're preparing to decorate the city on May Day, a *regional* art school is being organized,[51] a "showcase of the arts" is opening. On May 10, the Division begins acquiring the works of local artists to fill the Museum of Contemporary Art.[52]

Last year, a City Museum was begun, but so far, unfortunately, it is still dominated by archaeological artistic material rather than painting; in this respect, I asked both the Museum Division and the Division of Fine Arts of Narkompros [People's Commissariat for Enlightenment in Moscow] to send us paintings. Art schools are being opened in regional cities: Nevel, Velizh, Lepel. There are also State Decorative Workshops (to fill all orders, where all arts are united). A weak

myself: Chagall himself conducted a "Free workshop of painting."

special instructors: For carpentry, molding, etc.

the original: Implying that Russian art was derivative from the French "original."

Victory over the Sun: A Futurist "Opera," with music by M. Matyushin, "trans-logical" language by A. Kruchenykh, decorations and costumes by K. Malevich. It was first performed in St.-Petersburg in 1913.

showcase: A showcase of propaganda posters by the Vitebsk section of ROSTA (Russian Telegraphic Agency).

point are lectures about art. Lecturers from the capitals do not come and in the Art College there is no trained lecturer of art. Perhaps you could help. If you find one—let us know, send him to us. In the meantime, we organized several public meetings about art on our own.

All in all, our city is now "dominated by artists" . . . People argue fiercely about art, and I am overtired and . . . dream about "abroad" . . . After all, an artist (in any case, I) has no more decent place than at his easel and I dream of getting stuck exclusively with my paintings. Of course, I also draw a little, but that's not the same. As for your request for various reprints, I shall make an effort to bring you some things personally, as far as possible. As for my own drawing of you, I feel bad about sending it, I don't know if you'll like it. This has to be done somehow face to face, so you can select.

I hope to get to Moscow (and Petrograd). I was asked to organize my own show, but what is the point in arranging an exhibition of old works made before 1918 (and many are sold and scattered anyway).

What do you think? I would also like to travel on behalf of the College, etc., and bring from Petrograd some works for sale to the department, as they asked. This letter has grown enormous. Enough writing. Awaiting your answer. Regrettably, I don't see Lissitzky and cannot give him your regards, and I couldn't have[53] . . . You can find out about that from Abram Markovich [Efros]. Did you hear, by any chance, about the fate of my paintings in "Der Sturm" gallery in Berlin? I know that [Ludwig] Baer went there, and according to Lunacharsky's article, some information was brought back. By the way, Baer et al took the letter from the "International Bureau"[54] to Walden [the editor and owner of *Der Sturm*].

You may write either to the address of the Art College or to Zadugovskaya Street 9.

Regards, I shake your hand   Marc Chagall   2/IV 192[0]

Our publication (a little book by Malevich)[55] will be sent to you; I gave him your card.

Chagall's Paintings Bought by the Department of Art

A. From the list of works acquired by the Government Foundation of the Department of Art of the People's Commissariat for Enlightenment for the years 1918–1920:

Korovin, K.A.—12 paintings and one drawing—215,000 Rubles
Malevich—31 paintings—610,000 Rubles
Kandinsky—29 paintings, 6 graphic works, 9 drawings—922,000 Rubles
Chagall—10 paintings, 10 drawings—371,000 Rubles

B. Minutes Number 5 of the meeting of the Purchasing Committee of IZO [Department of Art of the People's Commissariat for Enlightenment] of July 7, 1920, the list of works approved for the museum of the city of Tula includes: "One painting ('Landscape with House') by Chagall for 20,000 Rubles and two drawings for 7,000 Rubles."

C. Minutes Number 17 of October 8, 1920, of the meeting of the Purchasing Committee for the Government Art Foundation of the Division of Art, it was decided to buy five watercolors by Chagall for 20,000 Rubles and six drawings for 10,000 Rubles. The drawings were given to the museum of Kostroma.

CHAPTER SEVEN   **Modern Yiddish Theater—Moscow: 1920–1922**

The Yiddish Chamber Theater in Moscow

The culmination of Chagall's second Russian period was his work for the new Yiddish Chamber Theater, directed by Aleksey Granovsky. Founded in Petrograd in June 1919 as a small, experimental theater studio, the theater moved to Moscow, where it opened on January 1, 1921. Within a few years it became one of the most original and acclaimed theaters in Europe, as evidenced by the exuberant critical praise it received on a tour of Germany and Western Europe in 1928.[1] In 1920, when the young theater moved to the new capital Moscow, Chagall (who was age thirty-three to Granovsky's thirty) lent it his international prestige. In 1928, Chagall could rely on the fame of this theater to highlight his own contribution, which he invoked ever after.

As Chagall argued correctly, the modern Jewish cultural "renaissance" was strongest in literature and ideology. Modern Jewish theater, music, and art were more marginal and came later, although they were often as innovative as their literary counterparts. In 1916, still before the Revolution, a society for the Promotion of Yiddish Theater was founded in Petrograd; in 1919, under the auspices of the new cultural power, a Yiddish theater studio was formed, headed by Aleksey Mikhaylovich Granovsky (in German: Alexander Granowsky, pseudonym of

Aleksey Granovsky, the Director of the Moscow Yiddish Theater, a drawing by Chagall probably made during the theater's visit to Chagall's home in Boulogne s/S, 1928.

Abraham Azarkh, 1890–1934). Granovsky was born in Moscow and was expelled in 1891 along with most of the city's Jews. Having grown up in Riga in Russian and German culture, he knew no Yiddish and spoke Russian to his actors. Granovsky studied in Germany, was an assistant to the prominent theater director Max Reinhardt,[2] and introduced Reinhardt's conception of mass performances to celebrate the anniversary of the October Revolution in Petrograd.

Granovsky had Jewish national sentiments and tried to express them through the creation of a new Jewish art theater. He strove to mold a young theater on the highest international standards, with no connection to the Yiddish popular melodrama and sentimental acting tradition. For that purpose, he first established a theater studio in Petrograd. He announced a competition for candidates who fulfilled two requirements: a) had never acted in a theater; and b) were not over the age of twenty-seven. Granovsky himself was twenty-eight. There was only one exception to the rule: Shloyme Mikhoels, his main actor and eventual successor, was also twenty-eight.

Granovsky conceived the new theater as a precisely choreographed multimedia event. He gave the actors the best training in all the arts that starving Petrograd could offer for a few government Rubles: the best teachers in music, dance, acrobatics, and literature. Granovsky held up to 250 rehearsals for one masterpiece performance. Mikhoels was his right hand. He coordinated the work of the actors and mediated between the aloof, Russian-speaking director and his Yiddish-speaking team. He also mediated Chagall's vision to the members of the ensemble.

In November 1920, the studio moved to Moscow and merged with a Yiddish theater group there, to establish the Yiddish Chamber Theater. In 1921, the title "State" was added to the name; the theater became GOSEKT, the State Yiddish Chamber Theater. Later, the theater moved to a larger space, dropped "Cham-

Chagall and the actor Shloyme Mikhoels as Reb Alter in *Mazel-tov*, a one-act play by Sholem-Aleichem, performed by the Yiddish Chamber Theater in Moscow, January 1921.

A scene from *Mazel-tov* by Sholem-Aleichem, setting by Chagall, including the long-lost curtain with an upside-down Chagallian goat and the diagonal board above the stove with decomposed letters: "Sholem Aleichem." Sitting: Shloyme Mikhoels as Reb Alter.

ber" from its name, and changed to GOSET, the State Yiddish Theater, as it became famous throughout the world.

The Moscow art critic Abram Efros, who had coauthored a book on Chagall in 1918, became literary director of the theater and prevailed on Granovsky to invite Chagall to do the stage sets for the opening performance. The Yiddish Chamber Theater was located in the nationalized private apartment of a Jewish merchant Gurevich, who fled after the Revolution. The kitchen was rebuilt as a stage and the living room could hold an audience of ninety.

During November—December 1920, Chagall worked furiously for forty days; instead of making a painting within a stage, he enclosed the entire theater space

A scene from *The Witch* by Goldfaden, 1922. Director: Granovsky. As Chagall said, "They Chagalized after Chagall." The Labor Zionist leader David Ben-Gurion, who came from Palestine on a visit to Moscow, wrote in his Hebrew diary (November 22, 1923): "The performance is 'Leftist,' they sit on roofs, banisters and stairs, they don't walk but toddle, don't climb but clamber, don't descend but leap and somersault—no trace of Sholem Aleichem." Chagall, of course, was right: This is Sholem-Aleichem's grotesque and topsy-turvy world.

in his paintings, the so-called "Chagall's Box." He also made the sets and costumes for the first evening of three short pieces by Sholem-Aleichem. His work combined some of the formal attributes of modern art with a grotesque, deformed, but powerful presentation of the bygone religious Jewish world. These murals were practically suppressed in Soviet Russia for seventy years, and were restored and have been shown around the world only since 1992. Yet just as important as the murals was Chagall's impact on the theater itself: The avant-garde style achieved in art was now transferred to another medium—the theater. It undermined both the realism and psychologism of the celebrated Stanislavsky tradition in theater, yet created a new, collective mythology of the vitality of the Jewish past.

A scene from *The Travels of Benjamin the Third* by Mendele, 1927. Director: Granovsky.

Various witnesses of the time observed Chagall's decisive impact on the Moscow Yiddish theater, which gave it its unique character and placed it at the top of the theater art of its time. Yet the disheveled, wild and associative, "crazy" Chagall found no common language with the "European," German-educated and restrained Granovsky, who defined silence as the normal state of human beings. The conduit between Chagall and the theater was Granovsky's right-hand man. Shloyme Mikhoels (pseudonym of Sh. Vofsi, 1890–1948), a university-educated intellectual (rare in the Yiddish sphere) who became one of the great actors of his time, inserting a tragic dimension into his comic roles and comedic undertones into his tragic roles (such as his legendary King Lear). Barely thirty years old at the time, Mikhoels admired Chagall and tried to translate his vision of art into theater. After the tour of the theater in Western Europe in 1928, Granovsky remained there; Mikhoels returned to Moscow and became director of GOSET. Granovsky had one major success in staging Arnold Zweig's *Sergeant*

Scenes from *It's a Lie*, a one-act dialogue by Sholem-Aleichem, 1921. Decorations and costumes by Chagall.

Mikhoels, the leading actor and director in *A Night in the Old Market* by Y.L. Peretz, 1925.

A scene from *A Night in the Old Market* by Y.L. Peretz, 1925. Director: Mikhoels.

Grisha in Berlin, then was unemployed and died in obscurity in Paris at the age of forty-four.

Simultaneously, HaBimah, a theater in the recently revived Hebrew language, a rival of Yiddish, was founded in Moscow in 1917. It was directed by Stanislavsky's disciple Vakhtangov and staged, among others, Ansky's mythopoeic *Dybbuk*, based on Yiddish folklore, in Bialik's Hebrew translation. Chagall believed the settings were influenced by him, even though they were done by Nathan Altman and others. HaBimah toured Western Europe in 1926; it had great success in Moscow and Berlin, visited America, and stayed in the West. HaBimah settled in Palestine and eventually became the Israel National Theater.

Abram Efros: Chagall in Granovsky's Theater[3]

[Russian] Granovsky had to understand that in the artistic revolution, as in the social revolution, you always have to steer the most extreme course; the resultant force of intentions and possibilities will sort itself out. The Yiddish stage needed the most "Jewy," the most contemporary, the most unusual, the most difficult of all artists. And so I mentioned Chagall's name to Granovsky. Granovsky's always-sleepy eyes opened with a start and rounded like the eyes of an owl at the sight of meat. Next morning, Chagall was summoned and invited to work on Sholem Aleichem's miniatures. This was the first production of the Moscow period. Chagall began a dynasty of artists-designers.

He had just returned from Vitebsk, where he had been Commissar of Art, but, fed up with power, had abdicated this lofty title. At least, that's his story. The truth was that he was deposed by the Suprematist Malevich, who took over Chagall's students and usurped the art school. He accused Chagall of being moderate, and of being just a neo-realist, still entangled in depicting some objects and figures, when truly revolutionary art is objectless. The students believed in revolution and found artistic moderation insufferable. Chagall tried to make some speeches in his own defense, but they were confused and almost inarticulate. Malevich answered with heavy, strong, and crushing words. Suprematism was pronounced the heresy of revolution. Chagall had to leave for (I almost wrote "flee to") Moscow. He didn't know what to do and spent the time telling stories about his experience as commissar in Vitebsk and about the intrigues of the Suprematists. He loved to recollect the time when, on revolutionary holidays, a banner waved above the school depicting a man on a green horse and the inscription, "Chagall—to Vitebsk." The students still admired him and covered all fences and street signs that had survived the Revolution with Chagallian cows and pigs, legs turned down and legs turned up. Malevich, after all, was just a dishonorable intrigant, whereas he, Chagall, was born in Vitebsk, and knew well what kind of art Vitebsk and the Russian Revolution needed.

Meanwhile, he quickly consoled himself with work in the Yiddish theater. He set no conditions, but also stubbornly refused to accept any instructions. We abandoned ourselves to God's will. Chagall never left the small auditorium on Chernyshevsky Lane. He locked all doors; Granovsky and I were the only ones allowed in, after a carping and suspicious interrogation from inside as from the guard of a gunpowder cellar; in addition, at fixed hours, he was served food through a crack in the half-open door. This was not simple intoxication with work; he was truly possessed. Joyfully and boundlessly, he bled paintings, images, and forms. Immediately he felt crowded on the few meters of our stage. He announced that, along with the decorations, he would paint "a Jewish panel" on the big wall of the auditorium; then he moved over to the small wall, then to the spaces between the windows, and finally to the ceiling. The whole hall was Chagallized. The audience came as much to be perplexed by this amazing cycle of Jewish frescoes as to see Sholem Aleichem's skits. They were truly shaken. I often had to appear prior to the performance with some introductory remarks, explaining what kind of thing it was and why it was needed.

I talked a lot about leftist art and Chagall, and little about the theater. That was natural. Today we can admit that Chagall forced us to buy the Jewish form of scenic imagery at a high price. He had no theatrical blood in him. He continued doing his own drawings and paintings, not drafts of decoration and costume designs. On the contrary, he turned the actors and the production into categories of plastic art. He did not do actual sets, but simply panels, processing them with various textures, meticulously and in detail, as if the spectator would stand before them at a distance of several feet, as he stands in an exhibition, and appreciate, almost touching, the beauty and subtlety of this colorful field plowed up by Chagall. He did not want to hear about a third dimension, about the depth of the stage. Instead, he positioned all his decorations in parallel planes, along the apron, as he was accustomed to placing his paintings on walls or easels. The objects were painted with Chagallian foreshortening, with his own perspective, which did not consider any perspective of the stage. The spectators saw many perspectives; painted objects were contrasted with real objects; Chagall hated real objects as illegitimate disturbers of his cosmos and furiously hurled them off the stage; with the same rage, he painted over—one might say plastered with color—that indispensable minimum of objects. With his own hands, he painted every costume, turning it into a complex combination of blots, stripes, dots, and scattering over them various muzzles, animals, and doodles. He obviously considered the spectator a fly, which would soar out of its chair, sit on Mikhoels's hat and observe with the thousand tiny crystals of its fly's eye what he, Chagall, had conjured up there. He did not look for types or images—he simply took them from his paintings.

Of course, under these conditions, the wholeness of the spectator's impression was complete. When the curtain rose, Chagall's wall panels and the decorations with the actors on the stage simply mirrored each other. But the nature of this ensemble was so untheatrical that one might have asked, why turn off the light in the auditorium, and why do these Chagallian beings move and speak on the stage rather than stand unmoving and silent as on his canvases?

Ultimately, the *Sholem Aleichem Evening* was conducted, as it were, in the form of Chagall paintings come to life. The best places were those in which Granovsky executed his system of "dots" and the actors froze in mid-movement and gesture, from one moment to the next. The narrative line was turned into an assembly of dots. One needed a marvelous finesse, with which Mikhoels was endowed, to unify in the role of Reb Alter Chagall's static costumes and images with the unfolding of speech and action. The spectacle was built on compromise

and tottered from side to side. The thick, invincible Chagallian Jewishness conquered the stage, but the stage was enslaved and not engaged in participation.

We had to break through to the spectacle over Chagall's dead body, as it were.
He was upset by everything that was done to make the theater a theater. He cried
real, hot, childish tears when rows of chairs were placed in the hall with his frescoes. He claimed, "These heathen Jews will obstruct my art, they will rub their
thick backs and greasy hair on it." To no avail did Granovsky and I, as friends,
curse him as an idiot; he continued wailing and whining. He attacked workers
who carried his handmade sets, claiming that they deliberately scratched them.
On the day of the premiere, just before Mikhoels's entrance on the stage, he
clutched the actor's shoulder and frenziedly thrust his brush at him as at a man-
nequin, daubing dots on his costume and painting tiny birds and pigs no opera
glass could observe on his vizored cap, despite repeated anxious summonses to
the stage and Mikhoels's curt pleas—and again Chagall cried and lamented when
we ripped the actor out of his hands by force and shoved him onto the stage.

Poor, dear Chagall! He, of course, considered us tyrants and himself a martyr. He was so deeply convinced of it that, ever since, for eight years, he never
touched the theater again. He never understood that he was the clear and indis-
putable victor, and that, in the end, the young Yiddish theater had struggled because of this victory.

May 1928

Marc Chagall: My Work in the Moscow Yiddish Theater[4]

[Yiddish] "Here are the walls," said Efros. "Do what you want with them."

It was an apartment, rundown, its tenants had fled.

"See, here we will have benches for the audience, and over there, the stage."

To tell the truth, "over there" I didn't see anything but vestiges of a kitchen,
and "here?"

I shouted: "Down with the old theater that smells of garlic and sweat! Long
live . . . "

And I dashed to the walls.

On the ground lay sheets,[5] workers and actors were crawling over them,
through the renovated halls and corridors, among slivers, chisels, paints,
sketches.

Torn tatters of the Civil War, ration cards, various "queue numbers" lay around.
I too wallowed on the ground. At moments, I enjoyed lying like this. At home they
lay the dead on the ground. Often, people lie at their heads and cry. I too love, finally, to lie on the ground, to whisper into it my sorrow, my prayer . . .

I recalled my great grandfather, who painted the synagogue in Mohilev, and I

garlic and sweat: An allusion to stereotypical Jewish lower-class manners.

wept: why didn't he take me a hundred years ago at least as an apprentice? Isn't it a pity for him to lie in the Mohilev earth and be an advocate for me [in the World to Come]? Let him tell with what miracles he daubed with his brush in the shtetl Lyozne. Blow into me, my bearded grandfather, a few drops of Jewish truth! . . .

> Chaim Segal was an eighteenth-century synagogue painter in Mohilev Province.
> The connection to Chagall is possible, for Lyozno was in Mohilev Province, but
> this is not supported by any additional evidence. On the other hand, "great-
> grandfather" (in Yiddish: *elter-zeyde*) may simply mean "forefather, ancestor,"
> with no hereditary basis. "Jewish truth" also connotes well-founded, reliable,
> warm, supported by the community.

To have a bite, I sent the janitor Ephraim for milk and bread. The milk is no milk, the bread is no bread. The milk has water and starch; the bread has oats and tobacco-colored straw. Maybe it is real milk, or maybe—fresh from a revolutionary cow. Maybe Ephraim poured water into the jar, the bastard, he mixed something in and served it to me. Maybe somebody's white blood . . . I ate, drank, came to life. Ephraim, the representative of the workers and peasants, inspired me. If not for him, what would have happened? His nose, his poverty, his stupidity, his lice crawled from him to me—and back. He stood like this, smiling feverishly. He didn't know what to observe first, me or the paintings. Both of us looked ridiculous. Ephraim, where are you? Who will ever remember me? Maybe you are no more than a janitor, but sometimes by chance you stood at the box office and checked the tickets. Often I thought: they should have put him on stage; didn't they take janitor Katz's wife. Her figure looked like a square yard of wet wood covered with snow. Carry the wood to the fifth floor and put it in your room. The water streams . . . She screamed, declaimed during rehearsals like a pregnant mare. I don't wish on my enemies a glance at her breasts. Scary!

Right behind the door—Granovsky's office. Before the theater is done, there is little work. The room is crowded. He lies in bed, under the bed wood shavings, he planes his body. Those days he was sick. "How is your health, Aleksey Mikhaylovich?"

So he lies in bed and smiles or scowls or curses. Often acrid words, of the male or female gender, fell on me or on the first comer. I don't know if Granovsky smiles now, but just like Ephraim's milk, his futile smiles console me. True, sometimes I felt like tickling him, but I never dared to ask: "Do you love me?"

I left Russia without it.

female gender: A reference to Russian pornographic curses (matershchina).

*

For a long time, I had dreamed of work in the theater. Back in 1911, Tugendhold wrote somewhere that my objects are alive. I could, he said, paint psychological sets. I thought about it. Indeed, in 1914, Tugendhold recommended to Tairov, the director of the Moscow Chamber Theater, to invite me to paint Shakespeare's *Merry Wives of Windsor*. We met and parted in peace. The goblet was overflowing. Sitting in Vitebsk, commissaring away, planting art all over the province, multiplying students-enemies—I was overjoyed to get Granovsky's and Efros's invitation in 1918[6] to work in the newly opened Yiddish theater. Shall I introduce Efros to you? All of him legs. Neither noisy nor quiet, he is alive. Moving from right to left, up and down, always beaming with his eyeglasses and his beard, he is here and he is there, Efros is everywhere. We are bosom buddies and we see each other once every five years. I heard about Granovsky for the first time in Petrograd during the war. From time to time, as a pupil of Reinhardt, he produced spectacles with mass scenes. After Reinhardt's visit with *Oedipus Rex* in Russia, those mass scenes created a certain impression. At the same time, Granovsky produced spectacles using Jews of all kinds of professions whom he assembled from everywhere. They were the ones who later created the studio of the Yiddish theater.

goblet: "The goblet of tears and suffering is overflowing," an old Jewish motif, memorably embodied in a Yiddish poem by Shimon Frug.

students-enemies: Chagall alludes to El Lissitzky, who was his "pupil" in Yiddish book illustrations, and "reneged," accepting Malevich's Suprematism; so did his own students.

Once I saw those plays, performed in Stanislavsky's realistic style. As I came to Moscow, I was internally agitated. I felt that, at least in the beginning, the love affair between me and Granovsky would not settle down so fast. I am a person who doubts everything under the sun, whereas Granovsky is sure of himself, and a bit ironic. But the main thing is that, so far, he is absolutely no Chagall.

They suggested I do the wall paintings and the first production for the opening of the theater. Wow, I thought, here is an opportunity to turn the old Yiddish theater upside down, the Realism, Naturalism, Psychologism, and the pasted-on beards. I set to work. I hoped that at least a few of the actors of the Yiddish Chamber Theater and of HaBimah, where I was invited to do *The Dybbuk*, would absorb the new art and would abandon the old ways. I made a sketch. On one wall, I intended to give a general direction, introducing the audience to the new Yiddish People's Theater. The other walls and the ceiling represented *Klezmers*, a wedding jester, women dancers, a Torah scribe, and a couple of lovers hovering over the scene, not far from various foods, bagels and fruit, set tables, all painted on friezes.[7] Facing them—the stage with the actors.

These Jewish types were described in the Russian invitation to his exhibition in cosmopolitan terms: "Music, Drama, Dance, Literature," "Love on the Stage," and "Wedding Feast," respectively. It is interesting that in the West in 1928, Chagall reverts to the names of the authentic Jewish professions.

Chagall's sketch for the mural "Introduction to the Jewish Theater."

The work was hard; my contact with the work was settling down. Granovsky apparently lived slowly through a process of transformation from Reinhardt and Stanislavsky to something else. In my presence, Granovsky seemed to hover in other worlds. Sometimes, it seemed to me that I was disturbing him. Was it true? I don't know why he did not confide in me. And I myself didn't dare to open serious discussions with him. The wall was breached by the actor Mikhoels, who was starving just like me. He would often come to me with bulging eyes and forehead, hair standing on end, a pug nose and thick lips—entirely majestic.

He follows my thought, he warns me, and with the sharp edges of his hands and body he tries to grasp. It is hard to forget him. He watched my work, he begged to let him take the sketches home, he wanted to get into them, to get used to them, to understand. Some time later, Mikhoels joyfully announced to me:

"You know, I studied your sketches, I understood. I changed my role entirely. Everybody looks at me and cannot understand what happened."

The Dybbuk: A classical Yiddish play by Sh. An-sky, based on Jewish folklore.

I smiled. He smiled. Other actors quietly and carefully snuck up to me, to my canvases, began observing, finding out what kind of thing this is. Couldn't they also change. There was little material for costumes and decorations. The last day before the opening of the theater, they collected heaps of truly old, worn-out clothes for me. In the pockets, I found cigarette butts, dry bread crumbs. I painted the costumes fast. I couldn't even get out into the hall that evening for the first performance. I was all smeared with paint. A few minutes before the curtain rose, I ran onto the stage to patch up the color of several costumes. For I couldn't stand the "Realism," and suddenly a clash: Granovsky hangs up a plain, real towel! I sigh and scream.

"A plain towel?!"

"Who is the director here, me or you?" he answered.

Oh, my poor heart, oh sweet father!

I was invited to do the stage for *The Dybbuk* in HaBimah. I didn't know what to

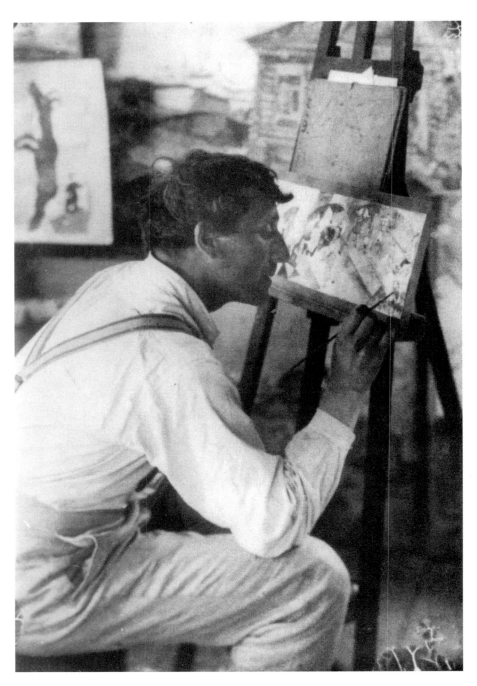

Chagall in the children's colony Malakhovka near Moscow, painting a detailed sketch of his mural "Introduction to the Jewish Theater," 1920.

Chagall teaching children in the Colony for Jewish Homeless Children at Malakhovka, surrounded by his paintings, 1921.

do. Those two theaters were at war with each other. But I couldn't go to HaBimah[8] where the actors didn't act but prayed, and pour souls, still idolized Stanislavsky's theater.

If between me and Granovsky—as he himself put it—the love affair didn't work out, Vakhtangov (who had then directed only *The Cricket on the Hearth*) was a stranger to me. It will be very hard, I thought, to find a common language between the two of us. To an open declaration of love, I respond with love; from hesitations or doubts, I walk away.

For example, in 1922, they invited me lovingly to Stanislavsky's second art theater to stage, together with the director Diky,[9] Synge's *Playboy of the Western World* . . . I plunged into it body and soul, but the whole troupe declared a strike: "Incomprehensible." Then they invited somebody else and the play was a flop.

At the first rehearsal of *The Dybbuk* in HaBimah, watching the troupe with Vakhtangov, I thought: "He is a Russian, a Georgian; we see each other for the first time.—Embarrassed, we observe one another. Perhaps he sees in my eyes the chaos and confusion of the Orient. A hasty people, its art is incomprehensible, strange . . . Why do I get upset, blush, and pierce him with my eyes?"

I will pour into him a drop of poison, later he will recall it with me or behind my back. Others will come after me, who will repeat my words and sighs in a more accessible, smoother, and clearer way.

At the end, I asked Vakhtangov how he intends to conceive of *The Dybbuk*. He answered slowly that the only correct line is Stanislavsky's. "I don't know," said I, "of such a direction for the reborn Jewish theater." Our ways parted.

And to Zemakh: "Even without me, you will stage my way. There is no other way." I went out into the street.

Back home in the children's colony in Malakhova, I remembered my last meeting with An-sky, at a soirée in 1915, at "Kalashnikov's Stock Market."[10] He shook his gray head, kissed me, and said: "I have a play, *The Dybbuk*, and you're the only one who can carry it out. I thought about you." Baal-Makhshoves, who stood nearby, blazed agreement with his eyeglasses and nodded his head.

"So what shall I do? . . . What shall I do?"

Anyway, I was told that a year later, Vakhtangov sat for many hours at my projects when he prepared *The Dybbuk*. And they invited someone else, as Zemakh told me, to make projects à la Chagall. And at Granovsky's, I hear, they over-Chagalled twentyfold.

Thank God for that.

Malakhovka 1921—Paris 1928

P.S. I just heard that the Muscovites are abroad. Regards to them!

In 1928, the Moscow State Yiddish Theater toured Western Europe.

didn't act but prayed: From a Yiddishist position, the Hebrew language was a language of prayer, which, in a Soviet context, was reactionary and "clerical."

Zemakh: Nakhum Zemakh (1887–1939), founder of the first modern Hebrew theater, HaBimah, in Moscow in 1917.

Marc Chagall, a teacher at the Colony for Jewish Homeless Children at Malakhovka 1920—1922, shown with a group of Yiddish writers and children. Front: Chagall; first row, left to right: literary dramaturgue of the Yiddish State Theater in Moscow Yikhezkel Dobrushin, composer Yoel Engel, poet David Hofshetyn; behind Dobrushin, novelist Der Nister.

Chagall in Moscow

Chagall's close friend in Moscow was the Yiddish literary critic Baal-Makhshoves (Dr.Isidore Zakharyevich Elyashev, 1873–1924), whom he knew from war-time Petrograd.[11] Born in Lithuania, Baal-Makhshoves had the right to opt for citizenship in the new, independent Lithuania. In the summer of 1922, he left and helped Chagall get out of Soviet Russia, via Lithuania, to Berlin, where Elyashev headed a Yiddish publishing house, and where he died in 1924.

According to Efros, Chagall won the war between artist and director over who was to dominate the theater performance and its impact, but that was the last time Granovsky invited Chagall. TeRevSat was closed, and Chagall had no job in a theater or any other source of income. He lived in the village of Malakhovka, to the east of Moscow, where he worked as a teacher of Yiddish literature and painting in a Colony for Jewish Homeless Children, primarily children who had survived the pogroms of 1919 in Ukraine. The children's colony was funded by the American "Joint" (the Jewish Joint Distribution Committee) but was named after the "Third International." The colony served as a meeting point for Yiddish writers and cultural activists. There Chagall did the illustrations and graphic designs for Dovid Hofshteyn's long poem *Troyer* (*Grief*), published in a large album format.

Marc Chagall to the Management of GOSEKT

[Russian] When I finished my work, I assumed, as was promised, that it would be exhibited publicly like many of my most recent works.

The management will agree that, as an artist, I cannot rest until the "masses" see it, etc.

Instead the works appear to have been placed in a cage and can be seen, crowded (though happily so), by at most a hundred Jews. I love Jews very much (there is plenty of evidence for this), but I also love Russians and various other peoples and am used to painting serious work for many nationalities.

Hence, my demand and appeal to the theater are natural and legitimate; I am asking you to put at my disposal twenty-eight hours in the course of two weeks— two hours a day—for the organization of an exhibition and survey of my works for all interested parties. The expenses for the organization of the exhibition, such as posters, etc., will be borne by IZO NKP[12] or by me. I cannot give up this demand.

Expecting an official answer,

Marc Chagall   12/2/21

Cubist Collage

The management of the Yiddish Chamber Theater did grant Chagall's request, and an exhibition of his murals was officially arranged, hosted by the Art Division at the Commissariat of Enlightenment. Chagall made a colorful Cubist "Collage" (1921), including a cutout from the Russian invitation to the exhibition, a slab of wallpaper, representing the gesture of Chagall marching forward, and on top, a brown triangle, as on a cemetery monument, with the Hebrew (and Yiddish) inscription: *Tsedek* (*Justice*).

Chagall invited the influential People's Commissar of Enlightenment Anatoly Lunacharsky to the opening.

Marc Chagall to Anatoly Lunacharsky [Summer 1921]

[Russian] Most esteemed Anatoly Vasilyevich!

On the 6, 7 [July 6] next week IZO of the NKP arranges an exhibition of my works of 1920 (in the aud of Yid S Cham Theater [= auditorium of the Yiddish State Chamber Theater], Chernyshevsky St. 12).

I am not saying that this work is my last word for the past year. But it was at least "the first word" for the Jewish street, as it were. Furthermore, to paint *like this* I could have done only in Russia. I have been thinking endlessly about the destiny of art (especially of my kind) in Russia. Does what I did (though it was somewhat buried in the inclining hall) have any meaning for anybody? Who needs it? Is my path altogether right? For it seems there is nothing in the world more "individualistic" (despicable word) than I vs. the "collective." But is it possible that I, the son of an eternally poor clerk = worker, don't have somewhere an intimate relationship to the masses . . . For, on top of all that, I suddenly found myself, by a whim of fate, an unwilling culprit and participant of that European "Expressionism," which you apparently cannot stand, and which only here in Russia I discovered I am related to. Think about those "smiles, grimaces, and animosity" which I was not the only one to encounter from either one or another camp of artists. You yourself recently noted all those charming things at the famous assembly of artists in the Bolshoi theater.

You don't like the West, Anatoly Vasilyevich. But I don't like it either. But *I love* those artists from whom I can learn, whom I can admire, who were in the West before 1914, whose "smiles and grimaces" I would lovingly tolerate. Such artists we didn't have even from 1914 to this day. But for that we just squabble with each other, quarrel, but in the name of what? What schools of art or traditions have we inherited from all the previous artistic quarrels, except for 2 or 3 historical names. That is why, in the dispute arranged at the opening of the exhibition (The Division will tell you day and time), I would like you to put your own dots on every *i*, even in relation to such an unbearable character as me.

Devoted   Mark Shagal

Marc Chagall in Moscow to the Russian Museum in Moscow

To the Committee of the Museum
Application
Artist Marc Chagall
Moscow, Bolshoy Chernishevsky 12 [Yiddish Theater]

I apply to the Committee of the Museum with a request as to whether you can possibly temporarily lend my work ("Outing," 1917) to be sent abroad for an exhibition in Berlin by the Division of Art.

As far as I know, this work has not yet been hung in the Russian Museum, hence no blank space will appear.

If, however, the Committee cannot find a way to satisfy my request, *I*, considering "Outing" one of my most essential works of the years 1917–1918, would be happy if it were not kept for a long time in the museum storage, but was hung along with other contemporary paintings.

Artist Marc Chagall
March 7, 1921

The Russian Museum in Moscow to Marc Chagall in Moscow

17 March 1921. No. 71   To the Artist Marc Chagall

The Committee of the Art Department, having discussed your application at its meeting of March 8, considered that sending your painting, "The Outing," to an exhibition in Berlin under the conditions of this time would entail certain risk and would deprive the Russian Museum of the possibility of presenting the creative work of the artist in an exhibition of the Russian Museum, since the museum has no other works by him. In addition, on artistic grounds, the Committee could not consider it possible to show the painting, "The Outing," before the repainting of the location dedicated to the works of contemporary artists which is planned for the near future.

I consider it my duty to inform you of the aforementioned decision of the Art Committee.

Director of the Art Department

Russian Museum

[No signature]

Marc Chagall: The Artist Y.M. Pen[13]

[Yiddish] The press devotes little space nowadays to questions of culture, especially to such an unpopular field as art. Nevertheless, I would like to say a few words about one Jewish worker, an artist.

Modestly and stubbornly, in the Jewish city of Vitebsk, a Jewish artist has worked now for 25 years.[14] On the one hand, he educates dozens of young future artists in his beginners workshop-school, and simultaneously educates the taste of the masses in the area. On the other hand, he himself creates, as far as he can, works, some of which must take their place in the historical division of the future Jewish Museum, if it is ultimately created.

Y.M. Pen is a realist artist of the old school, a pupil of the old Russian academia. But in his creation, there are a great deal of purely Jewish [elements]. Y.M. Pen was the first in Vitebsk to educate the young generation toward love and self-sacrifice for the sake of art. No young artist in Vitebsk could avoid him. He also was my first teacher. All this did not prevent many of his students to part roads with their teacher in their artistic directions, and still remain his good friends.

His art workshop, plastered from floor to ceiling with his works, he himself—at the easel, with his weakening eyesight—this picture is both moving and evokes great respect. We cannot overlook his merits. And I believe that the Jewish proletarian masses must know about such a cultural worker, such a unique proletarian.

In Vitebsk, an exhibit of all his works has recently opened. I greet my first teacher, the honest worker-artist Y.M. Pen on the 25th anniversary of his work in Vitebsk. I hope that I will not be alone in congratulating him,

Marc Chagall

From the Editors

The Editors of *Der Emes* congratulate the artist Y.M. Pen on the 25th anniversary of his cultural creative work in one of the great Jewish worker centers in R.S.F.S.R., in Vitebsk.

Marc Chagall in Moscow to Yury Pen in Vitebsk[15]

Yu. M. Pen's anniversary exhibition opened in Vitebsk in early September 1921.

It celebrated 25 years from the opening of Pen's school in Vitebsk.[16]

[Russian] Dear Yury Moyseevich!

So Vitebsk, for whom you did a lot, has arranged or will soon arrange an anniversary celebration, and on this occasion I cannot refrain from sending you these lines. I remember myself as a boy climbing the stairs of your workshop. With what awe did I wait for you—you were to decide my fate in the presence of my now-deceased mother. I know how many fates of young people in Vitebsk and the whole Province you have decided. It was your workshop that was the first one in the city to beckon for dozens of years. You were the first in Vitebsk. The city won't be able to forget you. You have raised a great generation of Jewish artists. Jewish society in Russia must know it and will know it. I am convinced that Vitebsk, to whom you gave 25 years of your life, will sooner or later immortalize your labor as it deserves. Your best works, characterizing a certain area in the life of Russia and the Jews, will be collected in a special place in the future museum of the city of Vitebsk, and some of them will go to the Central Jewish Museum, and we, some of your first pupils, will remember you especially. We are not blind. No matter what radical trend hurled us in the domain of art, far away from your own direction—your image of an honest laborer-artist and first teacher is still towering. I love you for that.

I kiss you, my dear first teacher, on the day of your 25th anniversary—25 years of your activity in Vitebsk. May you live long and continue your beloved activity in the new conditions of life . . .

Your devoted Marc Chagall

Moscow, September 14, 1921

Dovid Hofshteyn's Yiddish long poem *Troyer* (*Grief*), with illustrations by Chagall, Kiev 1922. The poem evokes the apocalyptic birth pangs of the world, giving birth to paradoxical twins: the utopian World Revolution and a wave of exterminating pogroms of Jews in Ukraine in 1919. (Hofshteyn was liquidated by Stalin in 1952.) Cover page: Hofshteyn's head above Chagall's; their names beside their heads. The Yiddish is in stylized "geometrical" (constructivist) letters, replete with whimsical variations. The title in diagonal: *Troyer*, mixing printed and cursive letters and using their surfaces as painterly spaces. In the second letter (from right), the fiksl (little fox); in the fifth, *troyer* in written letters; the last (on left) turned into a shofar, depicting horse and wagon going into exile.

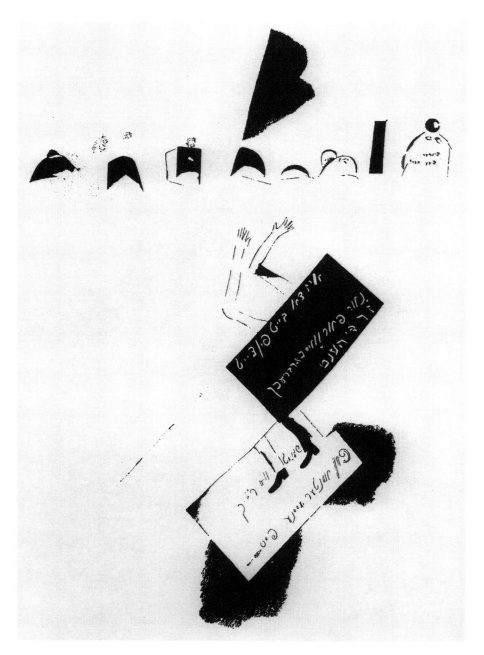

An illustration for Hofshteyn's *Troyer*. On top, a cemetery of slaughtered children. Covering the person, fragments of quotes from Hofshteyn's poem (Chagall's text in italic): "As sturdy as the world is the *change of epochs* . . . / *but why are the hands wringing in despair?* // The cold earth with all its rust / *floats like smoke under my feet* . . . "

Chagall's world: his (deceased) parents, his wife, and daughter arriving in Berlin in 1922. On his head the "House of the Head," part of the tefillin (black box) is pushed aside by his parental house in Vitebsk: he carries the memory of home with him.

Born in Lithuania, he was a Hebrew journalist, writer, and historian of Russian Jewry. Katz edited several newspapers and journals, including the Hebrew *HaAm* (*The People*), published in Moscow during 1916–1918. The journal was critical of the Bolshevik Revolution and was shut down in 1918. As a historian, Katz got an academic food ration, but, as he tells it, the ration was taken from him by the Yevsektsiya (the Jewish Section of the Communist Party) and given to Chagall. When independent Lithuania emerged in 1918, he served as a historian in the Russian-Lithuanian negotiations and had a Lithuanian Diplomatic Passport. Katz claimed that he persuaded Ambassador Baltrushaitis to take Chagall's art in the diplomatic pouch to Kaunas. In 1920, Katz left for Lithuania, then went on to Berlin, and immigrated to Palestine in 1931.

Chagall in Berlin

In May 1922, Chagall left Russia without his family. He stopped in Kovno (now Kaunas, the capital of Lithuania), where Dr. Elyashev organized an exhibition of Chagall's works of the Russian period. Shortly after, he left for Berlin, where he was joined several months later by Bella and Ida. He had visited Berlin briefly in the summer of 1914, for a one-man exhibit of 200 paintings and drawings in Herwarth Walden's gallery, Der Sturm. In his absence, Walden continued fostering the image of Chagall, made an exhibition of his work in 1917, and devoted the first *Sturm*-album to him in 1923.[2]

The German-Russian front, the Revolution, the isolation of Soviet Russia, and Chagall's own immersion in revolutionary activity—all contributed to the lack of correspondence. Chagall was a world apart from the avant-garde scene in Western Europe, and no letters from him arrived. Both in Paris and in Berlin, it was assumed that Chagall was dead. The young artist Baroness Hilla Rebay (who later played an important role in promoting Chagall's work in the Guggenheim Museum in New York) was close to the group of Der Sturm in Berlin during World War I. In a letter to her brother, she wrote: "Marc Chagall and Franz Marc, the two painters, are now immortal because they are dead yet a few years ago they were starving . . . " In Paris and Berlin, Chagall's friends sold his paintings. Walden sold some of Chagall's paintings to his rich wife Nell and other collectors.

Franz Marc: Marc was killed in 1916 near Verdun.

Now, suddenly resurrected eight years later, Chagall was unable to retrieve most of his paintings, and the money for the sold works, kept with a lawyer, was devalued in the inflation of the early 1920s. Chagall threatened to sue Walden, but by 1926 they reached an agreement; Nell, now divorced from Walden, gave Chagall three of his foundational paintings and ten gouaches. Paradoxically, the two major losses of his works, in Paris and Berlin in 1914, made Chagall's name: The lost paintings were sold to art collectors and raised the prices and fame of the amazing artist, who had disappeared in Russia. During the Nazi period, Chagall was an obvious example of "Jewish" and "Degenerate" art. Some of the paintings held by German collectors resurfaced after World War II, and Chagall saw them again only in 1951 in his exhibition in Bern. When Hitler came to power, Walden fled to the Soviet Union, where he was liquidated in Stalin's purges.

Chagall's friends in Berlin included the Yiddish literary critic Baal-Makhshoves (Dr. I.E. Elyashev), who spent long hours with Chagall in Petrograd and Moscow; the Hebrew poet Chaim-Nakhman Bialik (1873–1934), who left Russia in 1921 for Palestine but soon returned to Europe and established a Hebrew publishing house in Berlin; and Frieda Rubiner (widow of the German Expressionist poet Ludwig Rubiner), whom he had known in Paris and who had translated into German (1921) the first book about Chagall by A. Efros and Ya. Tugendhold (1918).

In Berlin, he was immediately recognized within the general art world. In January 1923, the Gallery Lutz, at Unter den Linden 21, exhibited 164 works. The dealer and publisher Paul Cassirer intended to publish Chagall's autobiography with his own illustrations, but before the text was ready, he published a small edition of the illustrations alone. Many Chagall exhibitions in Germany were held throughout the years (except for the Nazi period); the affinity to Expressionist rather than formal aspects of art endeared Chagall to German perception.

In Berlin, Chagall learned various techniques of multiple-copy graphics from the Jewish-German artist Hermann Struck: black-and-white lithography, etching, engraving in wood. Hermann Struck (1876–1944) was born in Berlin and served in the German army during World War I in Lithuania, where he was deeply impressed by the spirit of Eastern European Jewry. In 1923, he moved to Palestine and settled in Haifa. He was a specialist in copper etching and other graphic techniques, which he taught to such prominent artists as Liebermann, Corinth, Israels, and Chagall. Chagall excelled in those techniques and won First Prize for his engravings at the Venice Biennale in 1948.

Marc Chagall in Berlin to Yury Pen in Vitebsk[3]

[Russian] Berlin, July 8, 1922

I am writing to you from Berlin, where I have already been for a month and a half. How are you? I regret very much that I could not travel to Vitebsk. Nothing doing.

What shall I write about myself? In short: in the fall, my first exhibition of my Russian works (still unknown here) opens in a major gallery. Then it will travel to Paris and other cities. At the same time, my drawings and my memoirs (where I write a lot about you too) will be published by the Cassirer Gallery.

Some monographs [about me] are being prepared, and for that we would very much need photos of all the works located in the Vitebsk Museum, in particular, reproductions of your portrait (made by me)—this is important.[4] Of course, the photos must be good. I shall pay for it.

What are you doing? I have an idea for you: no matter how you see yourself—this should not prevent you from quietly starting to write about your life from the moment of your birth to the last days. You can transfer it to me, I shall undertake to submit it to a publisher later. The material side will be guaranteed for you. A man's life is interesting in general, especially when he is one of the first Jews-artists working in the field of enlightenment, etc.

In any case, I spontaneously called Europe's attention to you, never mind if I am partial, I am sincere in my feelings.

In short, my dear, work and devote yourself, honestly and seriously, to your autobiography—description of your life. Describe not necessarily what happened (both inside and outside of you), but the most characteristic, that which pulls in one direction or another, your life and the conditions around you.[5]

All the best! Write to me, I will be very happy. Write in detail, but not "joking."

Please send the photos and your own photos

M. Chagall

Marc Chagall About the Artist Y.M. Pen

Excerpts of Chagall's letter published in Vitebsk in January 1923[6]

[Yiddish] I would like to call the attention of my Vitebsk compatriots to the fact (I am writing separately about it to Moscow) that in their midst lives one of our oldest artists, Y.M. Pen, the only one who deserves to get the position of the Director of the Vitebsk Art College. We know him. We may differ in our opinions about art, but I must scream it aloud: if you cultural activists of Vitebsk will not turn your attention to the artist Pen and his colossal achievements for art, it will be done later anyway, but you will have to bear the shame for such coldness and neglect. This is my request as a native of Vitebsk. Though I now live outside the country, because of artistic enterprises, spiritually I am bonded to the city of my birth.

My request is supported by the famous sculptors of Paris: Meshchaninov and Zadkin (both born in Vitebsk) who were Y. Pen's students.

Oskar Meshchaninov (1886–1956), a successful sculptor, was a Russian Jew born in Vitebsk. He lived in Paris from 1907, and in the United States from 1944. Ossip Zadkine (1890–1967), a major modern sculptor, was Chagall's classmate in the Russian school in Vitebsk during 1900–1904 as well as in Pen's art school, and his friend in Paris in the 1920s.

Y. M. Pen must be appointed director of the art college and this will be a great favor for the school itself and will give satisfaction to the artist Y. M. Pen for his fruitful creative work for many years, and it will convince us that our request was accepted.

Berlin   Marc Chagall

Marc Chagall in Paris to *The Dial* in New York

> *The Dial* was an influential literary journal, edited by Scofield Thayer (1889–
> 1982) during 1920–1925. Thayer had his own collection of modern art, includ-
> ing works by Picasso, Matisse, Chagall, and others. He bought some paintings by
> Chagall in 1922–1923, when Chagall was in Berlin, and published the reproduc-
> tions in *The Dial*. Chagall's response was written soon after he arrived in Paris on
> September 1, 1923.

[French] Paris 23 Oct [1923]
3 Allée des Pins (Parc des Princes)
Paris Boulogne

Dear Sir,

I have received your magnificent album.

Thank you very much for your kind attention. It has given me a great deal of
pleasure.

With my best greetings,

Marc Chagall

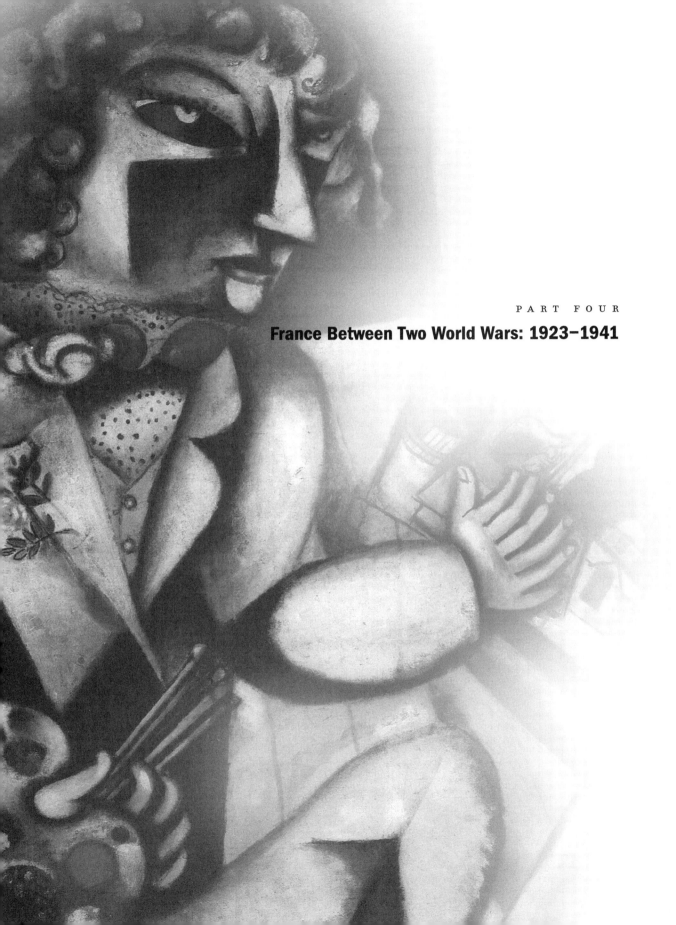

PART FOUR

France Between Two World Wars: 1923–1941

CHAPTER NINE

Paris—"My Second Vitebsk": 1923–1929

Invitation to Paris

Blaise Cendrars, the French poet who had been Chagall's friend during his first Paris period, wrote to him in Berlin that the art dealer and publisher Ambroise Vollard wanted to see him. Vollard (1865–1939) had organized the first important exhibition of Cézanne in 1895, and that exposure placed Cézanne in the center of attention of modern art. Vollard also promoted Rodin, Pissarro, Renoir, Degas, Derain, Picasso, and Matisse. He commissioned prominent artists to illustrate classical and contemporary works of literature and published the illustrated books.

On September 1, 1923, Marc and Bella Chagall and their seven-year-old daughter Ida arrived in Paris by train. In his second French period, Chagall became truly famous, acquired a network of friends among French intellectuals, traveled around France, and exhibited in many countries. He made hundreds of engravings, illustrating the works of Gogol, La Fontaine, and the Bible, all commissioned by Ambroise Vollard (but published only after World War II). He also illustrated books by several contemporary French and Yiddish writers. In an interview for the journal *l'Art vivant* (1927), Chagall said: "For me, Paris has been a living school, with its air, its light, its atmosphere. And it is in France that I have been reborn."

"Self-Portrait with a Smile," 1924–1925.

As an emigré artist, Chagall became an enemy or a nonperson in Stalin's Russia. His correspondence with his old friend Pavel Ettinger still continued, but it was abruptly stopped in 1937, the year of the great purges, to be renewed only after World War II. On the other hand, he maintained contacts with Yiddish writers in Paris and New York. Yiddish literature was still a creative and viable cultural movement around the globe at that time, centered in Poland, America, and the

Soviet Union. Chagall continued his personal and emotional ties with Yiddish writers and institutions, all the while lamenting the lower-class tastes prevalent in the internal Jewish sphere along with a lack of interest and money for art.

With Yiddish Avant-Garde Writers in Paris

In 1924, Chagall befriended two Yiddish expressionist writers: the poet Perets Markish (then age twenty-nine) and the novelist Oyzer Varshavsky (age twenty-seven). They translated Chagall's first autobiography from a Russian manuscript into Yiddish, and Chagall illustrated the Yiddish avant-garde journals they edited. He made an inspired and hilarious front page for *Khalyastre* (*The Happy Gang*), No. 2 (1924), edited by Markish and contributed illustrations to both *Khalyastre* and *Pariz revi* (Paris Review, 1926), edited by Varshavsky.

Chagall's closest friend in the Yiddish sphere and lifelong correspondent was the prominent Yiddish novelist and short-story writer, Yosef Opatoshu (pseudonym of Opatowski, 1886–1954)[1], Opatoshu was born in Poland (then Russia), immigrated to the United States in 1907, and worked as a journalist at the New York Yiddish daily *Der Tog* (*The Day*) from its inception in 1914. Most of Chagall's Yiddish-speaking correspondents were "Litvaks" like himself; yet the Polish Jew Opatoshu, with his different Yiddish dialect and Hasidic background, had a major impact on Chagall's Jewish consciousness. Opatoshu sent him the brilliant Yiddish translation of the Bible by the modern American Yiddish poet Yehoash, and it is from this translation that Chagall made his famous Bible illustrations throughout the years.

Between Two World Wars

World War I had prevented Chagall from returning to France in 1914. World War II again interrupted Chagall's stay in his adopted homeland. In 1937, with the aid of the writer Jean Paulhan, Chagall became a naturalized French citizen. Yet

The Jews conquer Paris! Cover of *Khalyastre* (*The Happy Gang*), No. 2, Paris, 1924, edited by Yiddish poet Perets Markish, illustrated by Marc Chagall. Editor Markish holds the number 2. A topsy-turvy Chagall on top of the Eiffel Tower holds a banner-cum-building: *Khalyastre*. On the right, poet and editor Oyzer Varshavsky raises a banner: "Paris."

he was stripped of that citizenship by the Vichy government in 1940 or 1941, and barely got out to the U.S. in May 1941.

This part of the book begins with Chagall's regained French identity and concludes with two poems he wrote about leaving Europe (near the end of Chapter 13). We precede the chronological order, however, with an interview of 1927, assessing Chagall's place in France.

Jacques Guenne: Interview with Marc Chagall for *L'Art vivant*[2]

[French] *Chagall told me:*

I was born in 1887, in Vitebsk, of poor parents, half peasants, half-workers. My father had blue eyes. But his hands were bumpy with calluses. He worked. He prayed. He was silent.

Chagall still uses the Soviet categories. His father was neither a peasant nor a worker according to any strict class definition, but rather a "petit-bourgeois." He only worked as hard as a worker, and was as uneducated as a peasant. (In Yiddish, "peasant" also means "ignoramus.") His "blue eyes" are code words: He was like a real, healthy Goy—a positive description. In his resumé of 1921 Chagall wrote about his father: "He had less in common with 'typical' Jews and looked like a Byelorussian peasant."

to turn away from the sky: As did his father, working in a herring cellar.

Like him, I remained silent. What was going to become of me? Would I stay like that, all my life, in front of a wall, or should I too lug barrels around. I looked at my hands, my hands were too fine . . . I had to find a delicate trade, an occupation that wouldn't force me to turn away from the sky and the stars and that would allow me to find my reason for living. Yes, that is really what I was looking for. But in my province, no one before me had ever uttered these words: "art, artist." It was completely by chance that a friend who had come from [the center of] the city saw the drawings I was making and exclaimed: "Why, you are a real artist!" "What's an artist?" I asked him.

Yet, I am gradually discovering myself . . .

At the age of nineteen, I flee to Petersburg without any money. I study. But I eat so rarely that I sometimes faint in the streets. I have, at least, the satisfaction of contemplating the menus in the windows of the restaurants.

I enter the Academy of Fine Arts, but take flight immediately. Academies are the same the world over, aren't they? Shortly afterward, I am introduced to Léon Bakst who was the first one to talk to me about Paris, and about Cézanne, Gauguin, Van Gogh. He even offers to take me to Paris as an assistant decorator for the Ballets Russes. But I refuse. In 1910, I go to Paris by myself, to Monparnasse, to La Ruche.

What was your first contact with the museums?

In the Louvre, I went through all the halls, all the galleries, without a guide, at random. I saw the painters from Italy, those from Flanders. But I was hoping for something else. Suddenly, leaving the big gallery, I entered the Hall of the States. I was really stunned by the revelation of Delacroix, Courbet, Manet, of French painting.

Was it the grandeur of expression that won you over for Delacroix?

No, I didn't even note the subject of his paintings. But it was the material I admired especially in Delacroix, as in Manet. My studio was soon full of canvases. Blaise Cendrars and Canudo sometimes brought me coffee or offered me lunch. A small circle of friends kept up my morale. Those I mentioned, plus Apollinaire, Max Jacob, André Salmon, Delaunay, André Lhote, Gleizes, Raynal, Roger Allard, Segonzac, André Warnod.

I exhibited in the [Salon des] Indépendants from 1911 to 1914. I also sent [works] to the Salon d'Automne, but I was rejected.

It is definitely fate that pushes all juries to error, even when they gather on behalf of independence and in the name of freedom of art. For we must not forget that the Salon d'Automne was created against official art.

So, as a result, I decided to refuse the assessment of juries.

In 1914, on the advice of Apollinaire, I sent two hundred paintings to Berlin, to that exhibit of [my work in] "Der Sturm." I took the train to go see that exhibit, and from Berlin, I went to Russia to see my fiancée, who has since become my wife, and without her inspiration I wouldn't do any painting or any engraving. I was caught in Russia by the mobilization, and then by the war. Thus, I had to say farewell to my Paris, to my studio in La Ruche, to leave my paintings in Paris, piled up under my bed, and in Berlin, hanging on the walls of a gallery.

Three years later, the Revolution erupted. I went back to Vitebsk. I was gradually swept up by the revolutionary fervor. I took the house painters off their scaffolds and put them into an academy I founded, a school born of my ecstasy and my torments. I invited teachers from all over Russia, leaders of all artistic movements. And I myself became teacher, principal, commissar, and anything you can imagine. It was impossible to remain indifferent to this current. I was caught up, carried away. I held meetings, I made speeches, I discussed proletarian art, I undertook [projects], I organized. In 1918,[3] I received from Moscow an offer to do the mural paintings and to paint the sets of a theater that had just been founded: the Chamber Theater.[4] In fact, I was weary of all the administrative services of my office, and of the eternal arguments which had made my task even more difficult for two years. It was especially keeping me from resuming my painting. Without waiting any longer, I and my family took the first freight train to Moscow. If I had been bolder, if I had turned my situation to good use, I could probably have travelled at least third class, but why not mix with the peasants, the speculators, that whole crowd loaded down with samovars, jugs of milk, infants! We piled up as best we could, one on top of the other, in a cattle car. The train progressed slowly with a concert of curses and insults. We lived in a stinking atmosphere. After many incidents, we reached Moscow. The station was occupied by an army of peasants flanked by countless bundles. When we succeeded in getting out of that horde, we went to find someplace to live. I was then lucky enough to find an empty room. I didn't realize that that room was extremely damp. Did I even know what dampness was! I thought the room would be heated and that the water coming out of the ceiling and the walls would gradually evaporate! But every morning, when dawn awoke us, we—my wife, my little Ida, and I—were all covered with dew. My paintings turned yellow. What to do? I didn't dare protest. Unfortunately for me, my voice has always lacked authority. Never mind! I threw myself on the walls and ceiling of the Chamber Theater and covered them with paintings in all directions. I was happy to destroy the old traditions the old Jewish theater was rotting in, and thus to give an impetus to the new movement. If I encountered great difficulties at the beginning, my task subsequently became easy. If you saw the productions of HaBimah in Paris last year,[5] or if you are lucky enough in Moscow to go to the *Kamerny* [Chamber], the theater of the Jews, you will perhaps judge that my years of anguish and hunger were not in vain.

But I was nostalgic for Paris. I understood that my art couldn't develop anywhere else but in France. And although it was extremely hard at that time to leave Russia, and I was hardly thinking of abandoning my country, I informed the People's Commissar of Enlightenment, Lunacharsky, of my intention to leave for France.

I passed through Berlin, hoping to recover my two hundred paintings from the exhibit of "Der Sturm." A hope soon dashed. I returned to Paris in 1923. There, on the other hand, I had the lovely surprise of finding most of the canvases I had left under my bed, carefully preserved and framed by Gustave Coquiot, who was my first collector and remained my most faithful friend up to his death.[6]

So it had been almost ten years since you left Western Europe. What changes in art did you find most striking when you returned?

It was pleasant for me to note the triumph of Expressionism in Germany, the birth of the Surrealist movement in France, and the appearance of Charlie Chaplin on the screen. Chaplin seeks to do in film what I am trying to do in my painting. He is perhaps the only artist today I could get along with without having to say a single word.

Did you then have the impression in the Paris School that you were cutting an isolated figure?

They made a lot of fun of my painting, especially of my paintings with the upside-down heads. Their criticism of me was not aimed at the way I translated the forms. All sorts of barbaric denominations have put deformation and plastic interpretation in fashion, haven't they? I didn't do anything to avoid those reproaches, you know. Quite the contrary. I smiled, sadly no doubt, at the meanness of my judges. But I had given meaning to my life all the same. Around me, moreover, from the Impressionists to the Cubists, all painters seemed to me to be too "realistic," if I dare use that term.

Unlike them, what has always tempted me most is the invisible aspect, the so-called illogical side of form and spirit, without which the exterior truth isn't complete for me. Which doesn't mean that I am appealing to the fantastic.

Consciously, voluntarily fantastic art is absolutely alien to me. From this point of view, I have nothing in common with such painters as Hieronymus Bosch, Breughel the Elder, or Odilon Redon. Their fantastic is imagined, desired, symbolic, often literary, but it isn't "real."

Sometimes, wandering in a museum, going from one masterpiece to another, from one master to another, haven't you felt dissatisfied after a while, noting the absence of something, of that thing I always find missing and which was missing even in my childhood? This is why, in the sense that some intend, I have preferred to lose my mind rather than obey all the rules of the schools, all their technical methods. I wanted to put a limit on the triumph of theories, not that we don't need any, on the contrary, but because I wanted to bring the human organism back to the point of departure, the human organism with all its instincts, even if they were abnormal, and not relying solely on the mind. An intellectual art can't move us completely.

Aren't you aware that, by appealing to that human emotion your art is so rich in, you are also fighting against the danger of certain decorative tendencies of painting in our day?

Certainly. I have stated, in sum, that pictorial art is going more and more toward decorative art, is losing itself in abstract ornamentalism, is tending toward the symbolic arabesque, toward hieroglyphic writing. Pictorial art is entering the service of the applied arts. Isn't it too bad that our very intelligent and ingenious century has been able to resurrect only that purely formal art in which the artist can easily hide.

Alas! For a long time, humanity has been content to admire the exterior, the garment of art, and has neglected to look at what is going on inside. Now, if we can't give our work the breadth of the vistas of nature, isn't it preferable to give

Marc Chagall, his dealer Ambroise Vollard, Ida, and Bella, Paris.

up our brushes and our colors? Isn't it enough that nature is already fragmented and divided among all the senses?

So, you seem to repudiate everything in art that is not inspired by an interior necessity?

From the time I began, I have broken on all issues with "professional" art. It is impossible to acquire the trade of painter as one acquires that of cobbler, doctor, or carpenter.

Can we talk of method when confronting the Egyptian pyramids, the Hindu, Chinese, or Negro graphics which were born, in fact, from the interior necessity of the artist or from religious sincerity?

Some people have reproached me for putting poetry in my paintings. It is true that there is something else to demand from pictorial art. But let them show me a single great work that doesn't have a share of poetry! Which doesn't mean that I believe in inspiration, in an explosion dictating a work. It is my whole life that is identified with my work and it seems to me that I am the same even when I am sleeping. Others, on the other hand, are amazed that, during my summer vacation, I take pleasure in painting flowers or landscapes. The need for classifica-

tion forces them to assume that I am a realist or a poet by turns! As a man, do I
no longer have the right to depict the place where I have lived for some time?

There is no way I can accept being imprisoned in a system in any order whatsoever. And I have often dreamed of that fine day when I would be able to isolate
myself completely, as the monks once did in their monasteries. If I could have
so much pleasure doing the etchings for Gogol's *Dead Souls*, it is because Mr.
Vollard gave me the possibility of expressing myself in the freest way. His confidence in me encouraged me very much and allowed me to finish the hundred
gouaches that will be engraved in color on the margin of La Fontaine's *Fables*. I
will then undertake a series on the Circus, and later on the Prophets. Yet I tremble with fear whenever I take my work to Mr. Vollard. Can I really forget that he
was the contemporary and friend of Cézanne and Renoir?

In general, I can't talk about art. I always run the risk of not being understood.
Don't force artists to talk. The art that consists of talking about art is not our art.

What I sometimes regret is noting that my confused psychology differs from
the Latin mind. If I regret it, it is because I love France and respect its masters.
For me, Paris has been a living school, with its air, its light, its atmosphere. And
it is in France that I have been reborn.

to depict the place:
Chagall refers to his
new paintings of
French scenes, nature,
flowers, buildings,
and churches that are
not thematically
"Chagallian."

Marc Chagall in Paris to Pavel Ettinger in Moscow

10/3 [March] [19]24

[Russian] Dear Pavel Davidovich,

As you see, I don't forget you; from time to time you hear my voice. Though I'm
afraid that my "image" is little by little . . . fading . . . It is no wonder. I have
been here for quite a while, in the homeland of painting. What shall I say about
myself. I could say a lot, but I have to be brief. Gradually, they are beginning to
notice me in France and my works are displayed in prominent Paris galleries.
Gradually, indigenous French publishers invite me to do engravings, too. Recently, I participated in the Paris exhibition of artists and engravers.[7] Right now
I am busy with work for Ambroise Vollard (friend of Cézanne, Renoir, Degas,
and others); I am doing Gogol's *Dead Souls* for him, with 75 big etchings.[8] The
book will be published with a new translation,[9] a deluxe edition printed in the
Imprimerie Nationale. I also made a large etching for his album, *30 Artists*, including Matisse, Maurice Denis, Bonnard, Rouault, Utrillo, Picasso, and others.[10] I have no time to do something for Cassirer, who will, nevertheless soon
publish my new lithographs, which I made while in Berlin. I am sorry that my
graphic works probably do not get to Russia. I assume that if ordered, or demanded by an institution, Cassirer would have sent a complete set of my etchings, the file *My Life*, and lithographs.[11] Let it be in Russia too.

*the homeland of
painting:* As opposed
to the homeland of
his birth, Russia.

How are you? And what is new in the field of art?

I am now exhibiting in a one-man show in Brussels.[12] Then in Vienna, and in the fall in Paris.

To Moscow, I am writing almost exclusively to you, for others have almost forgotten me and are hardly interested in me . . . And I cannot direct my "warmth" to the indifferent . . .

I will be very happy if you ever plan to travel [to the West].

Please accept my regards and best wishes.

Your devoted Marc Chagall

Marc Chagall in Paris to Sh. Nigger in New York

Shmuel Nigger (pseudonym of Shmuel Charny, 1883–1955) was the most prominent Yiddish literary critic of his time. Although Charny in Polish does mean "black," the choice of this name was a demonstration of solidarity with the oppressed American "Niggers." Nigger was born in Byelorussia (Jewish Lithuania) and was active in Vilna, where he wrote the pathbreaking brochure *Yiddish Literature and the Female Reader*. He emigrated to New York in 1919, where he played an influential role in Yiddish literature and was its most prolific critic. B. Vladek and Daniel Charny were his brothers, and all of them corresponded with Chagall.

5/IV 924 Paris Avenue d'Orléans 110 Marc Chagall

[Russian] Highly Esteemed Mr. Nigger,

Please forgive me for writing to you even though we don't know each other (and in Russian at that). Several mutual friends, Yiddish writers, including my late friend Baal-Makhshoves, told me about you. I assume you are the only person for me to write to in America.

I recently finished a work of an autobiographical nature, as it were. Before it appears here in several languages in a separate book with my drawings, I would like to publish it in America (I also have material concerns in mind). If you could submit it to one of the best [Yiddish] newspapers or journals in America with which you have relations—please make an effort to write me and I shall send you the manuscript. (The Yiddish translation is by Perets Markish from my Russian original.)

At this opportunity, please write a few words in general about Jewish cultural life in America.

With regards and deep esteem/   Marc Chagall

Marc Chagall in Paris to A. Lyesin in New York

A. Lyesin (pseudonym of Abraham Walt, 1872–1938), born in Minsk, Byelorussia, arrived in New York in 1897. He was a Russian revolutionary and a Yiddish poet and became long-time editor (1913–1938) of the prestigious Yiddish literary-cultural journal *Di Tsukunft (The Future): A Monthly for Science, Literature and Socialism*, published by the Forwards Association in New York from 1892 to the present. Lyesin changed the subtitle to *A Popular-Scientific, Literary-Socialist Monthly*; in a matter of eight months, he increased the circulation from 4,000 to 20,000—a large number even for English intellectual journals. In 1925, Chagall's autobiography was published in *Di Tsukunft* in five installments, and in 1937, his autobiographical long poem, *My Distant Home* appeared there. Chagall also illustrated the three volumes of Lyesin's collected poetry, published posthumously.[13] The former Socialist Lyesin's nostalgic and historical view of the traditional Jewish religious world, as well as his poems on persecutions and heroism throughout Jewish history, influenced Chagall's shift from grotesque or deformations of stereotypical Jewish figures to idealized, even sentimental representations of that world.

Paris, Avenue d'Orléans 110   22/V 924   Marc Chagall

[Russian] Highly Esteemed Mr. Lyesin

I know about you from stories of my deceased friend Baal-Makhshoves, as well as from Nomberg[14] and Sholem Asch.[15]

Recently, Leyzerovich[16] wrote to you in Yiddish, and now allow me to address you myself in Russian—all about the same thing.

In short, I have a written text. I don't know whether it is "professional literature." But it is I, and that is how it was desirable and necessary for me to write it. I assume that it will be interesting for everyone (the "bourgeois," the intellec-

the "bourgeois," etc.: Addressing the Socialist Lyesin, Chagall is still using Soviet categories, albeit ironically.

tual, and the worker) to read this piece of my life, especially since among Jews this kind of thing by a Jewish artist has not yet appeared. But I cannot talk about myself. In late autumn, it is supposed to appear in German along with my 25 engravings in copper,[17] specially made, and other reproductions of my work (at the publisher Paul Cassirer, Berlin); in French (publisher Ambroise Vollard, Paris), and in Russian. So far, it has not been published anywhere.

I hope, nevertheless, that you won't refuse me the highest royalty, and would be grateful to you if you could let me know how much I can count on.

It is about 80 pages, typewritten on one side (translated by Perets Markish). As soon as I get your answer, I shall send the manuscript. It would be good if you could simultaneously print several photos [of my paintings] in the *Tsukunft*.

Devoted, regards

Marc Chagall

Marc Chagall in France to Sh. Nigger in New York

[Stationery: "Hotel Central, Ile de Bréhat (Côtes-du-Nord)"] 23 August 1924

[Yiddish] Dear Mr. Nigger,

I am trying to write in Yiddish. Once I used to write Yiddish well, but since I became a Goy, I write with mistakes or in Russian-Jewish. I must ask you to forgive me for taking so long to answer your kind letter. My family was ill, my wife had an operation, my child is not quite well.

I became a Goy: Meaning he is working in a non-Jewish culture and environment.

For artists and for me, "time" has no value. You can even avoid writing for years, for you're writing inside yourself. About my "writings" [autobiography], I wrote to Mr. Lyesin. As soon as we go over it, I will send it to you, and you will see what a "crazy" Jew I am, "thank God." I will be very happy if you then write to tell me how I am wrong. What you write about [Yiddish] cultural life in America is painful. There are many intelligent Jews. They want good things. But our generation is unfortunate, it seems to me, and there are always only a few good persons. But I love Jews, just simple, common Jews, the people—what a pleasure it is to wander among them . . .

"thank God": He uses quotation marks because he doesn't believe in God. Yet he uses "God" all the time, as a higher power (his "destiny") or an abstract addressee, part of the Yiddish discourse he learned from his mother.

I beg you again to forgive me my delayed response. As soon as I get back to Paris, I shall send you several photos and articles about me. Please write some time.

Your devoted

With friendly regards

Marc Chagall

Paris, Av. D'Orléans 110

"Self-Portrait with Adorned Hat," 1928. Note all the things he carries on his head.

Marc Chagall in France to A. Lyesin in New York

[Stationery: "Hotel Central, Ile de Bréhat (Côtes-du-Nord)"] 24 August 1924

[Yiddish] Most Esteemed Mr. Lyesin,

Please forgive me for taking so long to answer. Things have been quite difficult lately. My wife had an operation and my child was ill at the same time. Only now, here, am I somewhat more free. In general I am a bad correspondent. It seems to me I write you every day, but . . .

My manuscript takes longer. Before I did not have the time, and now we [Chagall and his translators] must go over it again. This will take a few more weeks. I would like to send you the complete text. But if you wish, we can send it piecemeal. The thing has not been published in Yiddish anywhere yet. It will soon be published in German and French when the translations are ready.[18] When I get back to Paris from the country, I shall send you several photos of my works, and perhaps add several articles or a monograph about me.

Again please forgive me. Your devoted

With warm regards

Marc Chagall

Forgive me for my spelling mistakes [in Yiddish]

Marc Chagall in Paris to Pavel Ettinger in Moscow

Paris—Boulogne, 3, Allée des Pins, [December] 1924

[Russian] Dear Pavel Davidovich,

I send you regards along with the catalogue of my exhibition which opened a few days ago in the best and largest gallery of Paris.[19] It is my first, especially after an 11–12 year absence.[20] All French *contemp*[orary artists] residing now in Paris, beginning with Picasso, Matisse, Segonzac, and others, came, but I do not intend to talk about myself.

It is hard, as you know, to send something published, where so many contemporary Frenchmen write [about me]. And perhaps I am such a lazy person . . . I am glad that good people here remember you. For example, a few days ago the director of the publishing house Morancé visited me—they publish fantastic journals [with reproductions] of the most advanced artists—and he talked to me about you. I asked him to supply information to you (they prepared an issue with copies of my work, etc.).[21]

By the way, I gave your letter to Vollard a long time ago. He promised to write you. He is so slow . . . For example, I have no idea when *Dead Souls* will see the light of day. I have already made 60 engravings for it (in part, exhibited).

So how are you? How do you live? Work? You don't think of travelling here? What's new? And what do the artists do—still Rodchenko? Or Malevich? Or they are searching quietly? {*Ach* art} [crossed out.] Will there be a Russian pavilion here on the Intern. Decor.?[22]

Perhaps they could then bring my murals of the Yiddish Theater for the exhibition.[23] I think it won't harm.

Please write. I will be happy getting regards from you.

Your devoted Marc Chagall

it won't harm: A Yiddish expression of encouragement meaning: They should do it, high time.

Marc Chagall in Paris to A. Lyesin in New York

20/1 925 Paris—Boulogne s/s. 3, Allée des Pins (Parc des Princes)

[Russian] I am finally sending you the manuscript [of my autobiography]. Forgive me if I held you up. It is the fault of the writers [Markish and Varshavsky] who procrastinated. It has not been published anywhere to this day, though I was asked for it. But the translations into German and French are almost done, and I hope that before those books appear, there will be time to publish it with you. I hope you will be lenient with my "work"—I do not pretend to write literature. I am just a Jew in the style of our fathers, and that is enough for me. I think it would be better to print it all across the page and not in two columns.[24] If you need some photos—I could send them to you. Naturally, if you don't like some words, you can substitute more pertinent ones.

I also ask you to note in the journal that reprinting this thing or a part of it by anybody else is absolutely forbidden.

I bow to you all / And shake your hand / Marc Chagall

Marc Chagall in Paris to Pavel Ettinger in Moscow

Written on the back of an invitation to the Opening of the Third Exhibition of Independent Artists-Engravers, January 16–February 3, 1925, in the Barbazanges-Hodebert Gallery, Paris.[25]

Thank you for your answer. I went to Vollard and he gave me a letter for you with stamps and an envelope. You must not wonder why he didn't answer so far. But I talked to him about you. By the way, about his books. I don't think there is anything better than his personal books on Cézanne, Renoir, Degas, since he was their friend and first art-dealer. Of course, they should be translated into Russian. Could you think about it? He will be delighted if the translation is in good hands. Now you can write to him personally. Vollard is an unusually interesting and historical type. And my Gogol is moving ahead. There is already paper, and I am calm about it. Now, an exhibition of our Society of Independent Artists-

Engravers. This is the only movement in the domain of engraving (after the academic one). As to my theater murals[26] for the exhibit of Decorative Arts in Paris, I do not know [what is happening]. Please write. Regards, be cheerful, as far as possible. Next time, I shall write more.

Devoted to you, Marc Chagall

Marc Chagall in Paris to Gustave Coquiot in Lyon

In the summer of 1914, Chagall put his paintings under the bed in his room in La Ruche, went to Berlin, and disappeared for nine years. His friend Blaise Cendrars retrieved some of the paintings and sold them to Gustave Coquiot. Coquiot framed them and became the first French collector of Chagalls. Coquiot was an art critic and one of the first to write seriously about Chagall, notably in his books, *Cubistes—Futuristes—Passéistes*, (Paris: 1914) and *Les Indépendants, 1884–1920*, 4th ed. (Paris: 1921). Chagall illustrated Coquiot's books, and after his death, his widow sold fifty-eight works by Chagall at auction.[27]

3 Allée des pins / Boulougne   7 March

[French] Dear Monsieur Coquiot

Thank you very much for the invitation to exhibit at the Salon d'Automne of Lyon. I gladly accept, especially since it would not have been arranged without your sponsorship.
    I hope to see you and Madame Coquiot in my home someday. We would be very happy to receive you.

With my most devoted feelings
Marc Chagall

Marc Chagall and Yiddish Expressionist Writers in Paris to Adele Opatoshu in New York

The Yiddish writers Perets Markish and Oyzer Varshavsky worked with Chagall on the Yiddish version of his autobiography and apparently came to celebrate its publication. Yosef Opatoshu was on his way to Poland. His wife Adele was in New York.

{24/IV/1925}[28] [Postcard from Paris with view of "Notre-Dame—L'Ange du Jugement Dernier et Chimères." Written by several hands.]

[Yiddish] Adke, we drink liqueur in Chagall's atelier, Lechaim Adke, Your Oppen.[29]

Marc Chagall

Three times Lechaim, three times dear Adelya—forgive me for allowing myself such a familiarity. We dip our pens not in ink, but in liqueur! In friendship, Perets Markish.

Bella Chagall

The bandit, the thief [Markish], took away the whole territory [of the postcard]—so I'll tell you in New York *Le-Shono Ha Bo'o*—O[yzer] Varshavsky

Le-Shono Ha Bo'o: Hebrew Passover wish: "Next year in Jerusalem"—here, ironically, with New York instead.

Marc Chagall in France to A. Lyesin in New York

Chambon sur Lac (Puy-de-Dome)   [July 1925]

[Russian] Highly Esteemed Colleague Mr. Lyesin,

I received the last issue of *Tsukunft* with the end of my notes [= memoirs]. If they gave you a little satisfaction—I am glad, though I am changing and adding a lot. After the first two issues, I received 50 Dollars each—altogether $100. I assume they are from you. I gave 1/2 of this sum to my translator Perets Markish. For the last three issues I received nothing. I gave you the right to publish it first, and I remember your promise to pay me the highest fee—hence I ask you to arrange to send me what is due me for the last three issues. Thank you in advance.

With friendly regards/and sincere esteem/Marc Chagall

P.S. You can send the money to my account: Marc Chagall, National City Bank, 39–41 Boulevard Haussmann, Paris.

Marc Chagall in Paris to Leo Kenig in London

In France, Chagall was isolated from Jewish books. To illustrate the Bible for Vollard, he needed a Yiddish translation (he could not understand the Hebrew). He asked and received the Bible in Yiddish from both Leo Kenig in London and Opatoshu in Warsaw. Opatoshu continued to send him volumes of the modern

Yiddish translation of the Bible by the American Yiddish poet Yehoash (pseudo-nym of Solomon Bloomgarden, 1872–1927). Yehoash developed a rich, Biblical language in Yiddish, incorporating archaic words, going back to medieval Bible translations, along with a refined, modern poetic language and pseudo-archaic neologisms.

> [July 1925]
>
> [Yiddish] Dear Kenig, I don't want to pester you. Opatoshu writes to me from Warsaw that he got the Bible in Yiddish and he will probably send it to me. Thank you in the meantime for running around for the sake of the Bible. What do you say, is the Yiddish in my letter good? Or is it better in Russian? Write sometime how you are and be well.
>
> About myself? It seems to me there is no need to write. Sensitive people know anyway what everyone does. In addition to several paintings, I finished Gogol's *Dead Souls*—100 engravings; I start (may He help) the Prophets. Later I have to do Apollinaire's *Alcools* and a book by Cocteau—if I have health for it all.
>
> Regards,
>
> Your Marc Chagall

Western Yiddish Writers Visiting the Soviet Union

When the isolation of the Soviet Union eased for a while, the Soviet literary establishment flirted with some writers in the West who were sympathetic to them. Books by several "progressive" Western writers were published in the Soviet Union (albeit with hedging introductions), and the writers were invited to visit the Soviet Union, where they could spend their high royalties in Rubles. Needless to say, it was a great temptation, especially for Jewish writers; many had left families there and were curious to see what was happening to Socialism and to the Jewish masses remaining in Soviet Russia. The poet H. Leyvik, born in Byelorussia, had been arrested by the Tsarist police at the age of eighteen as a revolutionary Bundist and exiled to Siberia. In 1911, he fled from Siberia, reached the United States, and became a prominent Yiddish poet. In 1925, he went back to

Painting a portrait of Yosef Opatoshu.

see his parents in the small Byelorussian town of Yehumen, and wrote a book of poems about the Soviet reconstruction and his nostalgia. Chagall could not have done this because he was a renegade from the Soviet Union.

Marc Chagall in France to Yosef Opatoshu in Warsaw

[Postcard: L'Auverge —Lac Chambon] Chambon sur lac Puy-de-Dome, Stamped 25.7.25]

[Russian] Dear Opatoshu,

Heartfelt thanks for the *Tanakh* [= Hebrew Bible]. Regards to you from here, where I am with the family. Regards to Leyvik. Is he breathing the Jewish air? I shake your hand. Hope to meet

the Jewish air: Meaning in the former Jewish Pale of Settlement in the Soviet Union.

Your Chagall

Marc Chagall in Paris to Leo Kenig in London

Paris   21 September 1925

[Russian] I didn't forget that you would like to get the [Yiddish] Bible back as soon as I get another one from Opatoshu. But . . . unfortunately, yours also has a Hebrew side and his doesn't. While working, it is convenient to glance at it too. But as soon as there won't be a need for it, I'll send it to you, gratefully. Agree? I shall do the Prophets (for the publisher Vollard, Paris) in spite of the fact that the "mood" all around is not prophetic . . . on the contrary, it is evil . . . But we must oppose it. Strange as it many seem, in our time which, in spite of many achievements, I consider to be foul, one feels like escaping into other dimensions and not to forget that fashions lose the image of belief of any religion. For quite some time now, art stinks because the purity of the soul has been substituted by a cesspool . . . Forgive my sharpness. What do you think? You were always thinking and made the strongest impression on me.

Be well,

Your Marc Chagall

P.S. My exhibitions lately (outside of the earlier ones in Paris and Berlin) were recently in Dresden and Cologne, and now an American gallery drags it off—for January 1926 in America.

Marc Chagall in Paris to Yosef Opatoshu in New York

After Opatoshu's visit in Europe and return to New York. Written in the ironic,

mocking tone customary among Yiddish speakers.

spat on us: Russian idiom meaning "you don't give a damn."

Kultur-lige: The Yiddish culture organization founded in Kiev in 1919. Chagall mocks their Marxist terminology.

my yikhes: An allusion to Chagall's autobiography *My Own World*, published in installments in *Di Tsukunft*. Chagall perceives his biography as a clue to his paintings.

3, Allée des Pins, Boulogne s/s [late 1925]

[Russian] Dear Opatoshu

You left and spat on us Europeans! It serves us right. Otherwise, various *Kultur-lige* persons want us to be close to the people, the workers, and wherever else! So we have the honor to inform you, Your Highness, that we shipped you "bourgeois" art—please see to it over there[30] that your people and workers (Jewish) go to crowd around my paintings (on 5th Aven. 730 Reinhardt[31]). They may understand nothing, but they must not touch with their hands. I am sure you will explain to them . . . if you understand. But finally, I hope that after they've read (in the *Tsukunft*) where I came from (my *yikhes* [= pedigree]), etc.—they will understand.

Write a few lines. How do you live? Sholem Asch is already here, but not for

Marc Chagall, Paris, 1925. This photograph was sent by Chagall to the collector of Jewish autographs, Dr. Abraham Schwadron, in Jerusalem at the foundation of the Hebrew University.

sure—I suggest he buy an airplane and constantly fly the route of Poland, La Rotonde, America, and back.

La Rotonde: La Rotonde was a famous literary café in Paris.

Regards   Marc Chagall

Sholem Asch (1880–1957) was a prominent Yiddish novelist who used to travel around the world. Born in Poland under Russian rule, he lived in the United States from 1910. He returned to Poland after World War I, lived in France, moved back to the U.S. in 1938, moved to Israel in 1954, and died in New York. Yiddish writers loved to hate Asch, who appeared as arrogant, obnoxious, and successful with the "Goyim"; his novels were translated into many languages and he actually could make a living from writing. Chagall encountered him in various stages of his life. Thus, during World War II, Asch was President of the pro-Soviet Committee of Jewish Writers, Artists, and Scientist in New York, and Chagall was a member of the board. At the same time, Asch wrote a trilogy of novels based on the life of Jesus Christ (*The Nazarene*, 1939; *The Apostle*, 1943; *Mary*, 1949) and was attacked and ostracized by the Jewish establishment. Chagall was also attacked for his images of Jesus Christ, especially in his Holocaust paintings; yet he tried to dissociate himself from the analogy with Asch and continued to perceive Jesus as a suffering, crucified Jew.

Marc Chagall in Paris to A. Lyesin in New York

Allée des Pins   Paris-Boulogne s/s 925

[Russian] Esteemed Colleague Lyesin

Thank you for the journals I am reading with pleasure.[32] Since you published my life on your pages—I want to let you know that "part of my life" in pictures was sent to America, the American gallery Reingardt [sic][33] (Fifth Ave. 730) is arranging my exhibition (in early January it seems) in New York, Chicago, and Detroit—I would like to ask you to (somehow) convey to our dear Jewish masses my request that they go crowd around my works (. . . but don't touch with the hands . . .) and even if they don't understand (it is not necessary . . .) they could accept my love, as it is.

My sincere greetings / Marc Chagall

Marc Chagall in Paris.

Chagall's living room in Paris.

Marc Chagall in Paris to the Publisher Au Sans-Pareil in Paris

21/X 25

[French] Dear Sir,

I received your letter and the proposed contract.[34] Thank you very much.

I take the liberty of correcting it a little.

1. For example, I do not always make drawings for the engravings, often they are small sketches, a few lines I develop immediately on the surface.

2. I would like the copper plates to be destroyed after the first edition.

3. As for the deadline, I would ask you not to specify the date. I will not forget

that it is necessary to hurry. I may even do them before the deadline, but I would like to be free.

4. As for the payment, I would ask for 2000 francs on signing the contract and the rest on submission of the coppers.

To ease my work, I ask you to have the engravings done by my engraver, M. Fort (289 rue St. Jacques) because I am already used to working with him and he is very familiar with my way of working.

Thank you very much for your book, it is very interesting and raises a lot of emotion.

I would always be glad to see you.

My best memories,

Marc Chagall

Marc Chagall in Paris to the Same Publisher

26/XII [1925]

Dear Sir,

Please have Mac Orlan's[35] text sent to me as soon as possible.

The work has stopped. That bothers me enormously. I must tell you that it is almost impossible for me to do all the engravings by January 15. I still need to find ideas and the printer also needs days to do the printing. I cannot work in haste. Also, please send me as soon as possible the photos of all the authors, never mind which, so they will have a little resemblance, and that is all.

I need them. / I would be infinitely grateful.

Best wishes, / Marc Chagall

P.S. My printer, M. Fort, not having any commission from you, is not hurrying with the engravings. Please settle this matter with him so that I can work in peace.

Katherine S. Dreier in New York to Marc Chagall in Paris

Katherine S. Dreier (1877–1952) was the founder (with Marcel Duchamp and Man Ray) of the Société Anonyme, one of the prominent collections of avant-garde art, now at Yale University. She offered to exhibit Chagall's work in New York, in addition to his exhibition in the Reinhardt Gallery on 57th Street in January 1926.

Bella, Ida, and Marc in Paris.

[French] 18 February 1926

Dear Mr. Chagall:

Before her departure for Buffalo, Miss Dreier asked me to let you know that she had forgotten to mention in the letter she recently sent you that she would exhibit any of your paintings that Reinhardt was not brave enough to show; she would do it in New York not only through the Société Anonyme, but also through the Brooklyn Museum. The latter and the Metropolitan Museum of Art are the two most important museums of fine arts in New York.

The exhibition next season will be a major international event of modern art.

Perhaps it would be good to send Miss Dreier a separate cablegram saying: "Dreier, Warranted, New York City. Accepted, Chagall," or "not accepted" or "not in agreement, Chagall."

Please accept my sincere greetings. / For Katherine S. Dreier

Bella Chagall posing for her portrait, Paris, 1927. Ida is age eleven. In the background is the painting "Birthday."

Marc Chagall in Paris to Pavel Ettinger in Moscow

[September 1926]

[Russian] Received your letter. Thank you. I so rarely get a word from Russia, though I think about it. I consider the silence or even ignoring former friends and acquaintances as natural. [That's] life! But you are not of this kind, and your sympathies were established once and for all. Therefore, it was especially pleasing for me to send you several engravings (from the series, *Dead Souls*) via Margolin[36] from Vakhtangov's studio, who visited Paris. I hope you'll receive it and take it.[37] Naturally, I do not suppose that a few pages would give you a concept of the whole. This work is finished, and Vollard must now show his own art, making himself and Imprimerie Nationale publish it soon. But I wrote you that I am swamped with other work, in part from the same Vollard (the Bible, Prophets, and LaFontaine— in color, 50–60 large watercolors). I am also making the "Seven Deadly Sins" for Edition Kra[38] and Apollinaire's *Alcools* for Nouvel Revu Française [sic].[39]

visited Paris: The Moscow Hebrew Theater HaBimah (not to be confused with the Yiddish Theater) toured Western Europe in 1926 and came to Paris in September.

However, I am tired. When will I do it all. For I also have to do my own paintings. My exhibition opens now in America. How do you live? Please write. Don't forget [me].

Your devoted Marc Chagall

Marc Chagall in Paris to Pavel Ettinger in Moscow

Throughout the years, Chagall wrote several obsequious letters to Aleksandr Benois and Benois reviewed his work favorably, though he swore he could not survive one day in the "Yid's Hole" (the Pale of Settlement), which Chagall elevated in his paintings (see various letters in this volume). Still, the difference between the aristocrat, esthete, and high Soviet official, on the one hand, and the lower-class Jew, on the other, could not be obliterated. Moreover, the Russian emigration in Paris did not regard such conspicuous Jews as real Russians. In a letter to Benois in Paris of March 1935 (see p. 440), when Chagall was at his height of fame and wealth, he confronted the issue, telling Benois: "You and I cannot find a common ground" because he was "a man of different roots." "Though I was born in Russia and am bleeding with ('undivided') love for her," continues Chagall, "I remain a stranger to all its regimes—old Russia, Soviet Russia, and the emigration." Now he complains about Benois disregarding him entirely as a Russian artist.

[December 1926–January 1927]

[Russian] Dear Pavel Davidovich,

How are you? You know, I am almost cut off from Russia. No one writes to me and I have "no one" to write to. As if I were not born in Russia . . . You are the only one to whom I write a Russian word. Do I "have to" become a French artist (never thought about it). And it seems: I don't belong there. And I often remember my Vitebsk, my fields . . . and especially the sky. To show you how France treats me, I enclose at least a small clipping from the press. Impossible to send more, but at least something concerning my 2 latest exhibitions of engravings and paintings.[40] I heard that [Aleksandr] Benois, for example, traveled to Russia[41] and wrote about the Russians in Paris, not even mentioning me.[42] My paintings scattered all around the world, and in Russia they apparently don't even think and are not interested in an exhibition by me . . . I make books for French publishers, and the Russians don't need my work.

That's how the years are passing.

Even the *Dead Souls* will not reach Russia. Because all [copies] are by subscription.

So you see, I am complaining . . . But against whom, against myself? . . .

What am I doing now? Paintings that disappear as soon as my signature dries. And a book of Prophets for Vollard with 100 engravings. And over 100 large watercolors for LaFontaine and over 100 drawings for the *Circus*.[43] All for Vollard. And Apollinaire's *Alcools* for N.R.F. [Nouvelle Revue Française].

The head is spinning from so much work, more precisely, from what has to be done.

Recently I had a hall in Antwerp in the Salon of French painting. Well, enough talking about myself.

The book, *7 Deadly Sins* with my engravings has appeared, as well as *Motherhood*.[44] But how could I send books, which are already hard to get? With whom?

I would very much like to

Marc Chagall in Paris to Yosef Opatoshu in Warsaw

Boulogne 1 July 928

[Russian] Dear Opatoshu

I hope you will receive this [postcard] in Poland.[45] Not bad [to be there]. I hope you saw our small towns, landscapes, Jews. Look for me too . . . And when you get to Russia, look even more, and again for me too. How I envy you . . .

Well, all the best. Do not forget the loving

your

Marc Chagall

Marc Chagall in Paris to Yosef Opatoshu in New York

Paris 8 Nov. 928

[Russian] My dear Opatoshu

Just as soon as you left [for America], parted the water like Moses, walked on it like Christ (whichever you prefer . . .), I received from you a marvelous Bible by the marvelous poet Yehoash.[46] What thanks shall I send you—I don't know myself. Don't forget that I love you—which makes it even more difficult for me.

[Yiddish] You are a good person Opatoshe[47] and a great Yiddish writer to boot (a rare combination . . .) and it pains me that I don't see you here. My "2 women" [Bella and Ida] greet you from their heart

Your devoted/[French] Marc Chagall

Marc Chagall in Paris to A. Lyesin in New York

In response to Lyesin's wish that Chagall illustrates his collected Yiddish poetry.

France   Boulogne s/s 3, Allée des Pins   28/XII 928

[Russian] Dear Mr. Lyesin,

I gave your communication to Serouya.[48] As for your question about drawings for your book—I can answer you that, even though I am swamped with French editions and refuse many [requests] here—for you, I shall do it with pleasure. This is to show my respect for you and your Jewish activity, which our late friend Baal-Makhshoves often discussed with me. Please send me several of your best poems, your portrait-photo, and the size of a page of the book. How soon do you need the drawings?

Awaiting your answer—your devoted

Marc Chagall

P.S. Of course, the publisher's fee of $400 is not much—I get much more.

Marc Chagall in Paris to Yosef Opatoshu in New York

After Chagall's exhibition in New York, an important painting remained at the Reinhardt Gallery. Chagall accused Reinhardt of having "stolen" it. The gallery claimed, apparently, that Chagall had promised it to them, but they had no proof. Chagall tried to sue them through B. Vladeck in New York and asked Opatoshu to help encourage Vladeck. Eventually, Chagall retrieved his painting with the aid of a Paris lawyer.

The Moscow Yiddish State Theater on its triumphant tour of Western Europe in 1928, visiting Chagall in his home in Boulogne s/s, near Paris. Sitting at table, fifth from right: Marc and Bella Chagall; Director A. Granovsky. Back row: on the left, S. Mikhoels, on the right, actor Benjamin Zuskin. Published in the Yiddish journal *Di 7 teg ilustrirt (The 7 Days Illustrated)*, Paris-London, August 3, 1928, No 8. The caption says: "The house of the famous painter Marc Chagall in Boulogne near Paris has been a center of Yiddish artistic interests in France for quite some time now."

Borukh Vladek (or B. Vladeck, pseudonym of Borukh-Nakhman Charny, or Charney, 1886–1938) was the brother of the literary critic Sh. Nigger in New York and the Yiddish writer Daniel Charny in Paris. A native of Byelorussia, he participated in the Jewish revolutionary and cultural movement in Tsarist Russia, where he took the pseudonym Vladek, and was an admired Socialist orator, nicknamed "The Jewish Lassalle." He arrived in New York in 1907 and was active in city politics. Elected as a Socialist from the Williamsburg district, he became majority leader of the City Council and had many contacts with the American and international labor movement. Vladek initiated the first public housing for immigrants and the poor in New York City under Mayor Fiorello La Guardia, and built what is still called the Vladeck Housing Project in Lower Manhattan. He was managing director of the Forwards Foundation and published the Yiddish daily newspaper *Forverts*. Vladeck was also a fine, minor Yiddish poet and published Lyesin's three volumes of poetry with Chagall's illustrations.

porridge I cooked up:
Yiddish idiom:
farkokht a kashe,
"opened a can of
worms."

goy Reingard:
Meaning not a
Yiddish-speaking
Jew.

[Yiddish] Dear Opatoshu, no word from you. How are you in the great heat? I am melting like ice . . . And what is new about the porridge I cooked up about the painting in Gall.[ery] Reingard [sic]? Now, the question is why should I torment you with these questions . . . I don't know. You are a good man, good people are being tormented in the world . . . So please take a look, ask Vladek if it pays to start the whole business, because the goy Reingard spits on us . . . And I don't feel like being duped by him. Now, one more question (or an answer). I beg you (*just between us*), tell me your opinion of *Lyesin as a poet.* Does he, will he occupy a place in Yiddish poetry—your opinion.[49] Though I don't know him personally, I have heard about him from afar (from my friend Baal-Makhshoves). He asked me (indeed, as you wrote) to illustrate his poetry book. Please write your opinion as a friend.

When you see Leyvik, tell him for me that I was often excited about his long poem, "Letter to a Friend," in *Literarishe bleter.*[50]

How are you? What are you writing? My family send their *warm* regards.

Your friend Marc Chagall

Marc Chagall in France to Yosef Opatoshu in New York

[Postcard: Environs de PONTARLIER (Doubs)—Lac de St. Point—Port Titi]

[Yiddish] Dear Opatoshu, regards, almost summer regards. Thanks for the books. Now I will have to "do" the Bible . . . Little by little. So far, I have done Samson and Delilah. That's where I am.

How are you? My wife is here. She has to rest after all the operations. There is not a single Jew here, or even a Russian. So we feel our Jewishness even more, and what else. If you were here, we would have chatted about everything, especially Soviet Russia, which I feel in my guts.

Your Chagall. Wife greets.

Marc Chagall to Yosef Opatoshu in New York

Paris 9 [March?] 929

[Yiddish] Dear Opatoshu, here I am writing to you again. It is in part your own fault—your "advice." I sent Vladek the power of attorney for the trial against the gallery Reingard. Now I beg you to remind Vladek as a Jew and a friend not to let Chagall fall on his face, because Reingard has strong and rich shoulders and I . . . Let them now do whatever is necessary not to lose . . .

I seem to have become an expert on trials. Not bad enough that they steal from us.[51] In every country we have to conduct trials. A fine business . . . And some people say I am an angel. How are you? When will you be here? What are you writing?

Warm regards from us, dear Opatoshu (and forgive my Yiddish)

With warm regards, yours Chagall

Marc Chagall in France to A. Lyesin in New York

[Postcard with view: "La Roussillon / Port-Vendres (Pyr.-Or.)," stamped: 28–10 29]

292 Ceret

[Russian] Dear Lyesin. Within a few days I shall return to Paris from here (on the Spanish border) where I worked, to start the drawings for your poetry which I received and read. I think that we can make the plates in Paris afterward, to oversee it directly, and then send them to you. But we shall see about that. So long. Your dev. Chagall

Marc Chagall in France to Yosef Opatoshu in New York

{8/17} 1929 St. Georges du Didoine

[Yiddish] Dear Opatoshu, thank you for your letter. I am amazed at your heat wave (as you describe it). Here I was in the sun and became a pink hamburger, so I have to lie in bed.

I wonder about the friendliness of the Jews in Moscow who added a few words to your book. But you know the word "zavist'" [Russian: "envy"]. It exists in all republics. From a Vevyurka one could expect something.[52] I send you an issue of *Selection*[53] for the lawyer (I forgot his name); on p. 113, they printed the picture I underlined for him. Please give him the book with the reproduction of the painting. It may be useful for him at the trial. Furthermore, I have several letters by Brinton at my home in Paris, begging me to give him this painting, either to lend it to him, or to give it to him as a gift; and there is no word there that I gave the painting as a gift or am willing to give it, or promised it. I have not yet sent the letters, because I did not think the trial would start. Please also ask Vladek or the lawyer if he needs these letters. Then I'll send them.

We shall soon move into a big house in Paris. If you come to Paris you can stay with us. There is room for your whole family . . . Please come.

I beg you, dear Opatoshu, forgive me for pestering you with these things. But—

My family send their warm greetings. How are you? Your friend

Marc Chagall

friendliness: Ironically. It was common practice in the Soviet Union to publish a "bourgeois" writer with a "politically correct" introduction by a Soviet critic.

Brinton: Christian Brinton, of the Reinhardt Gallery in New York, organized the Chagall exhibition.

CHAPTER TEN   **Toward a Jewish Art Museum: 1929–1930**

For many years, Chagall cherished the idea of creating a Jewish art museum. One influence may have been his major collector in Russia, A.F. Kagan-Shabshay, who bought thirty Chagall works for that purpose. Another model was the scholar and writer Sh. An-sky from Vitebsk who collected folklore and folk art for a future Jewish ethnographic museum. An earlier influence was his Yiddish-speaking friends in La Ruche in Paris (1911–1914), who talked about "Jewish art" and published a Yiddish journal for art, *Mahmadim*. Chagall did not join them at the time; he cultivated French friends and tried to dissociate himself from the parochial proponents of "Jewish art," as he tells us in his manifesto "Leaves from My Notebook" (1922).[1] Nevertheless, in his proposal for a People's Art College of August 1918, he envisioned a section of Jewish Art in the future Art Museum in Vitebsk; he also mentioned a future Central Museum of Jewish Art in his praise for his teacher Yury Pen in 1921.

Now, living in Paris, far from the Jewish masses and from Jewish culture, Chagall suggested the idea to the two emerging centers of the secular Jewish renaissance, the YIVO in Vilna—in Yiddish; and the first Jewish city, Tel Aviv—in Hebrew. In 1925, the Yiddish (Jewish) Scientific Institute YIVO was founded in

Vilna. The term *scientific* indicates the serious, academic conception of the humanities as "sciences of the spirit" in the sense of the German *Geisteswissenschaften*. "Jewish" and "Yiddish"—the nation and the language—are the same word in Yiddish, thus making the language the vehicle of Jewish culture. The YIVO covered a wide field of research, from linguistics and literary studies to history, sociology, and economics. Chagall rightly claimed that the renaissance of Jewish culture was primarily verbal, based on literature (and ideology, one might add), while other fields of culture and art were neglected.

This letter was addressed to the first YIVO Conference in Vilna in 1929. His proposal of 1929 was eventually adopted, and Chagall came to the YIVO's Tenth Anniversary conference in 1935 to deliver the opening address of the newly founded, though modest, Central Jewish Art Museum.[2] At a collection of support for the YIVO, held in Paris in December 1929, in a rare gesture, Chagall donated a painting to the YIVO.

Marc Chagall: Letter to the YIVO (1929)[3]

[Yiddish] Allow me to say a few words about the Jewish Scientific Institute. We Jews, scattered around the whole world, badly need cultural institutions to unite us. You absolutely must not postpone the organization of a Section for Art. It is as necessary as the whole Institute.

I admit, for quite some time a bitterness has been building up in me since, even in the better Jewish circles, there is no discussion of the need to create a Jewish art museum. Few among us are aware of how important it is, and not just politically. The centers for collecting for the museum will be Vilna, Berlin, New York.

I know it would have been easy to establish in Paris, for example, a society of "Friends of a Jewish Museum Foundation" with branches in all other cities. But I also know the fate of such societies dealing with the issues of Jewish art. The Jewish Scientific Institute, since it stands on its own two feet, and wants to take care of it, must do so as soon as possible.

You will tell me: "Be our guest, come work, help." Thus far, I haven't refused. If I had two lives, I would have given one to the Jews. But our art is a terrible art, it demands all of your soul, your entire devotion.

You will say: and means? Means as always must be given by the Jewish government, that is, by the whole Jewish people. While we are wasting enormous sums on, I admit, important but temporary needs, we must especially find money for such a goal. We Jews have often been accused of not being capable of art. Now we could show the world what we really possess.

But we possess absolutely no art connoisseurs, while we do have many specialists in Yiddish literature. Hence, the Institute should set up courses to study the problems of art in general and Jewish art in particular.

This is more or less what I wanted to tell you. It may look like an illusion, but illusions are often important and vital. I greet the YIVO warmly and wish it success.

Your devoted, / Marc Chagall

Marc Chagall in Paris to Pavel Ettinger in Moscow

10/II [February] 1930 Boulogne S/S

[Russian] Dear Pavel Davidovich,

I was so pleased to get news from you. I am happy that you are well. How are you. I remember you as a philosopher in life[4]—this is good and useful. I use the opportunity to enclose in this letter a catalogue of the LaFontaine exhibition,[5] in which you will see the text written by Vollard himself and a listing of this terribly [hard] craft which I have mastered (successfully or not—others should judge). Believe me, it would please me very much if my few Russian friends could see them before the [engravings], alas, are scattered around the world for good. For Vollard sold the whole collections, 100 items [gouaches], and now they are exhibited in turn in Paris, Brussels, and Berlin. True, I also engraved them. Well, here you are. Today is the opening. And I, who cannot stand these days [openings] and ceremonies, I don't know whether I shall be able to stay. I hope we shall see each other someday. I shall, of course, be happy to see you. My general exhibition was supposed to be arranged after Paris also in Berlin, in the National Gallery, but I don't know when and how they will gather the things, and to tell you the truth . . .

fifth wheel: Yiddish idiom meaning "Superfluous, impractical, outsider."

I would really be delighted if they organized an exhibition for me in my homeland [Russia]; that's a different thing, and though I am the eternal fifth wheel to myself—all the same . . .

Don't forget to send us regards sometimes. You know very well that every word pleases me. I shall do the same.

All the best, regards from my wife

Regards, Devoted /   Marc Chagall

Marc Chagall in Paris to Yosef Opatoshu in New York

Paris 1930 {12/6} [June]

[Yiddish] Very dear Opatoshu I am so happy—

Got two more Bible books from you—is it all now? Indeed I need it immediately for my work . . . Many thanks to you—how are you? A few days ago I was in Berlin for a few days where I was called for my exhibition: LaFontaine.

Vladek seems to have thoroughly forgotten my case, and I gave him all the rights. Didn't you write that Jews especially promise a lot . . . And—I too thought this was so, but there are truths I am afraid to utter . . . for now at least . . .

promise a lot: An allusion to the Yiddish proverb: "Promising and loving costs no money," i.e., doesn't have to be fulfilled.

Please be the nice Jew and ask Vladek if he wants to conduct the case energetically; if not, I have to look for other ways. And what is the address and name of the lawyer?

be the nice Jew: Yiddish idiom meaning "be so kind."

In about a month and a half, we are moving [to Villa Montmorency], but the address remains the same. I hope to send you soon my [drawing of a] little Jew . . .

And what kind of Yiddish do I write?

Recently I have been somewhat sad . . . from a philosophical point of view . . . Are you coming to Europe? Come.

Regards

And from my family

Your Marc Chagall

Hilla Rebay in Paris to Rudolf Bauer in Berlin[6]

Hilla Rebay (1890–1967), moving spirit and first director of the Guggenheim Foundation and Museum in New York, was an early admirer of Chagall's work. She was born in Strassburg, Alsace, as Baroness Hildegard Anna Augusta Elisabeth Rebay von Ehrenswiesen. Her father was a Prussian officer and a general in World War I. An original artist, she joined the Dada circle in Zurich during World War I and the group around *Der Sturm* in Berlin in 1916. Here, the Chagall legend was still fresh from his 1914 exhibition.

Rebay was an ardent propagandist for "Non-Objective Art" (a term coined by Kandinsky to indicate not just "abstract" art, abstracted from objects, but art not deriving from any specific objects whatsoever); yet she valued the spiritual in art, admired Chagall, and bought his paintings for the Solomon R. Guggenheim collection beginning in 1929. In a private letter in 1936, she wrote: "I prefer Chagall to most of the non-objective painters." In 1927, Rebay moved to New York, where she acted as Solomon R. Guggenheim's art adviser during 1929–1937, then curator of the Solomon R. Guggenheim Foundation and first director (until 1952) of the "Museum of Non-Objective Art" in New York, predecessor of the Solomon R. Guggenheim Museum. Her connections with European artists of the avant-garde and her influence on Solomon Guggenheim gave this collection the first, decisive direction. During 1938–1967, her home was Franton Court, Greens Farms, Connecticut. Chagall first met her in Paris in the 1930s, and he dedicated to her a version of his painting "I and the Village" (Paris 1923–1924). As a result of her and Solomon Guggenheim's efforts, the museum acquired fourteen oils and many works on paper by Chagall, more than any other museum in New York. In 1941, Rebay and Guggenheim helped save Chagall and his family from Nazi Europe.

[Excerpt, translated from German]   25 June 1930

D.R. [Dear Rudi]

Meyerhold Theater: In Paris; Meyerhold's theater from Moscow traveled in 1930 to Western Europe.

[. . .] Yesterday, in the [. . .] Meyerhold Theater I noticed a man sitting off to one side. His glowing, changeable, devout, and ecstatic face so fascinated me that I no longer looked at anything else, and I suddenly realized that he *had to be* Chagall. [Othon] Friesz, who was sitting behind me, said it was, and introduced us. Chagall is the most adorable, dearest person, just like a child. Immediately he seemed like an old friend. I introduced him to the Guggies right away. Cha-

the Guggies: Solomon R. and his wife Irene Rothschild-Guggenheim.

gall had been in Berlin in search of his painting (*Paris Window*). He was quite delighted that G. owns it, and would like to borrow it for an exhibition in March. Walden stole the painting and sold it. He *never* received a penny for it. Later on I shall prevail upon Guggie to send him 1000 dollars if things are better. Today I am invited to the Chagalls.

Chagall is really such a dear fellow, and still poor. There is something special and beautiful about his art, and nobody else has it.

All the best, Hilla

My Meeting with Max Liebermann[7]

Max Liebermann (1847–1935), a leading artist of the German Impressionist
school, was the founder of the Berlin *Sezession* in 1899 and President of the
Berlin Academy of Art from 1920 to 1933, when the Nazis ousted him and removed his paintings from German museums. The son of a Jewish Berlin industrialist, Liebermann said he was "very much aware of belonging to the Jewish
people," yet his paintings had hardly anything Jewish about them, except for occasional themes such as "The Amsterdam Jewish Market." There was a small audience at his posthumous exhibition, because non-Jews could not attend an
event for a "Jewish" artist in Nazi Germany. His wife was sent to Theriesenstadt,
where she died.

When Liebermann was urged to visit a Chagall exhibition in 1923, he responded in his Berlin dialect:

"Nee, da jeh ick nich hin."

—Aber an dem Chagall ist wirklich etwas dran.

"Nee, ick will nich! Womöglich jefällt mir das Zeug!"

["No-o-o, I ain't goin' there."

—But there really is something to that Chagall.

—"No-o-o, I don' want to! I might like the thing!"][8]

But seven years later, in May 1930, when Chagall came to Berlin for an exhibition of his engravings to La Fontaine's *Fables*, he and Bella visited the eighty-
three-year-old Liebermann. Chagall's essay was written upon Liebermann's
death.

[Yiddish] "Today I showed your drawings to Max Liebermann, and you know
what he told me . . . ?"—That's what the famous Berlin art dealer Paul Cassirer
said to me [in 1923], as he sat comfortably in his red-draped gallery hung with
paintings by French Impressionists. I stopped looking at the paintings, looked
at him, and casually asked: "What did he say?" Thinking meanwhile: "What

could he have said? Surely, he didn't like it, he must have expressed himself sharply . . . I don't care. Our roads parted."

"He told me: 'This fellow has talent, but he is a little *meshuge* . . . '"

To tell the truth, in my eyes, he became more sympathetic, and I decided to get acquainted with him, to visit him. Let him see for himself that I was not *meshuge* (not *meshuge* enough). I had just arrived from Soviet Russia [in the summer of 1922] and wanted to walk into his palace, bring into his home the smell of the Malakhovka Colony, where I carried on my shoulders the burden of hundreds of tattered, homeless orphans—my students.[9] I wanted Pokrova Street in Vitebsk to be felt in Liebermann's palace, for Liebermann to finally learn about the new, emerging generation of artists, who came out of the ghetto, with no right of residence, unrecognized, mocked, starving, but with souls fluttering like banners!

But I visited him only seven years later, when I returned to Berlin. He was informed of the visit, and my wife and I were told he was expecting us. We were warned in advance that it was hard for him to stay with visitors for more than half an hour. On Brandenburg Square, beside [Kaiser] Wilhelm's palaces, stands his Jewish palace. Sadly, I watch this assimilated house, surrounded by the spirit of Wilhelm II. I remember the great Greco and Rembrandt, who lived in the Jewish quarters of Toledo and Amsterdam, and I don't feel like going there . . . I don't know how he will receive me, how he will look . . . And I am so sensitive. But I am already in the entrance hall. My wife at my side. Thank God, she is so brave, noble. She is pale as a bride, but she walks so simply, not tense like me . . . She walks ahead of me on the stairs, freely, easily, and I—as if I were slicing through a river . . . Hard to lift a leg . . . I think to myself—"I don't want to go to capricious old men, if they are not Cézanne, Renoir . . . "

No one seems to be home. Old wooden stairs, an old door. Somewhere, a screech is heard, and quiet again. The two of us stand alone in a large salon, the windows looking onto the Königsplatz. The distant walls are decorated with paintings of the masters. I'd love to walk over and observe them closely . . . Suddenly, a serious screeching. A man in black stood on the threshold with a face like Max Liebermann as we see him on his self-portraits and engravings. On his face, a pale yellow color, and under the nose two dark lines, as painted with a thin brush: a mustache with the tails down. His figure trembled subtly and stopped, and then elegantly walked over to us.

We walk over to him: I to his left hand, my wife to his right. I hear something rumbling in his eighty-year-old belly, but he immerses his gaze in my wife. He looks calmly into her eyes, observes her hairdo, her features, her clothing from bottom to top and from top to bottom, and all the time he is stammering joyfully "Is this really your wife? And you are both from the same city? How do you call your city—Vitebsk? You met there and got married there?"

I don't know what to do when he gazes at her like this. When will he look at me

---

meshuga:"Crazy," a code word for assimilated Jews, designating the Eastern European Jewish ethos and signaling that they too belong to the tribe.

*Pokrova Street:*The street in the railroad station area where Chagall grew up.

Chagall conflates several stages in his own biography: the emerging generation of artists who studied with Yury Pen in Vitebsk and broke the laws of the ghetto; the Right of Residence: Jews could not get in the capital St.-Petersburg, where Chagall went to study art; and the generation with revolutionary banners that attended Chagall's People's Art College in Vitebsk.

too? I cannot just walk away to the side—can I?—and leave my wife with him. Meanwhile, I observe the rooms. I wait. Finally, he looks at me too, but only to make a comparison between me and my wife. "As everyone knows, I am very good natured . . . My smile is also well known . . . "

"So, you live all the time in Paris? Please tell me, do you meet with the painter Pascin there? Listen, explain to me, they say this Pascin has a lot of success with women? A talented 'fellow,' a little, black-haired guy . . . And you personally, do the French treat you well? You don't suffer there as a Jew? Yes, well, they will be well rewarded for that."

Pascin: An unspoken Jewish link.

"You see, over there, the building of the French Embassy. Today I received an invitation to a celebration of a French writer who came here, whose name is, I think, wait a minute, I'll remember soon, yes, André Maurois. Is he any good? I won't go."

"You know," I tell him, "he is half a Jew."

"Then, I shall go."

"Please tell me, Mr. Liebermann, why don't you come for a visit or arrange an exhibition of your work in Paris?"

"Well, you must know that during the war [World War I], I signed the manifesto of the German scientists against . . . You understand what I mean."

"Come along, I'll show you my collection of engravings by Rembrandt, Goya, Daumier."

I see his back, leading us into another room. On the way, I observe a wall covered with paintings by Manet, Sisley . . .

"Please tell me, Mr. Liebermann, you personally knew Pissarro, could you tell me something about him? How did he look?"

"Pissarro," a sarcastic smile, and Liebermann's face and mustache become even more Liebermannian.

"He, you understand, this Pissarro, had such a long beard. He played the role of a patriarch." Liebermann laughs. I wait, amazed.

And Cézanne, did you know him too? What do you think of his painting? He stopped laughing. "You know, what Cézanne was seeking was very interesting, but what he created" . . . He gestured with his hand high and wide—and smiled nevertheless. "Better observe these engravings. They are by Rembrandt, Goya, Daumier. You know, I love above all only these three artists."

The selection is really beautiful . . . But Cézanne and Pissarro are his contemporaries, and the others died long ago.

Two hours passed. We had been warned not to stay longer than half an hour. But even at the threshold, he doesn't let us go, and keeps talking.

In the street, I say to my wife that painters too are divided between "*Misnagdim*" and "*Hasidim*." Liebermann and his generation were *Misnagdim* in art. But the new art among Jews began with *Hasidim*. You saw that I didn't ask him to

"Misnagdim" and "Hasidim": Something like an opposition between the rational and the emotional.

show me his own work nor did he ask me how I work. Nevertheless, I see his major role in German art. In Germany, there was no one greater than him in the nineteenth and twentieth centuries. But he made a mistake, rare for a Jew but natural for a German: he went to study art not in Paris but in Holland. Hence, both Paris and Art took vengeance on him, Liebermann's art assumed the specifically Dutch grayness of Israels and did not place him on the same level as the French Impressionists Monet, Renoir, Pissarro, Sisley.

We are going to Paris!

Marc Chagall in Paris to A. Lyesin in New York

[Yiddish] Dear Lyesin,

I am writing to let you know that I shall definitely make the drawings for you. I have not shown any signs of life so far because I have been terribly busy with all sorts of things. But I keep thinking about the drawings. *How many* drawings do you think we should make for the book? How large? I think that both the size of the page and the text should be on the smaller side. How much of this and of that? I think it is better to make the plates of the drawings here, so I can oversee the production, and then send them to you. Write me your opinion. This time I am going to be busy with you.

Regards, Devoted

Marc Chagall

[Russian] My new address:
[French] 15, Avenue des Sycomores, Villa Montmorency, Paris, XVI

Marc Chagall in Paris to Sh. Nigger in New York

[Yiddish] My new address: Paris XVI, 15 Avenue des Sycomores, Villa Montmorency 1930 16 July

Dear Nigger,

Bratslaver: Rabbi Nakhman of Bratslav (also Braslav, 1772–1811), the founder of the Bratslav Hasidic sect, told allegorical stories, published bilingually in Yiddish and Hebrew.

I was happy to receive your letter and read the name Bratslaver. I remembered that our exquisite friend Dr. Elyashev copied a story of his especially for me in the Asiatic Museum [in St.-Petersburg] . . . I was happy. I said to myself (with or without tears . . .) that I shall leave Gogol, LaFontaine, and everything else for a while—to do only this—and, indeed, with your introduction. And even in other languages as well. *But*—I received the manuscript and I saw *a different name*

attached to the holy stories of the Bratslaver.[10] Perhaps he has talent. I don't
know. But I love the original—too much. So my dream fell apart and I am quite,
quite sad. A pretty nation we are—we Jews. All my life I am surrounded by   *pretty nation*: Ironic.
goyim, and goyim have commissioned great books from me, and except for a few
tales a long time ago, Jews have not asked me to make [any illustrations for their
classical writers:] (Bratslaver, Peretz, Sholem Aleichem . . .)[11]

Forgive me for writing to you so sadly. It's pouring rain. Maybe it's that too.
But believe me, I wanted very much to do something to please you—

You will probably forgive me *all* my mistakes, in Yiddish [they are merely] external. I prefer to write Russian.—

Be well. Are you coming to Paris? Any time? I shall be glad to see you.

Your devoted   Marc Chagall

P.S. Is it possible to get the Bratslaver's stories anywhere?

Marc Chagall in Paris to A. Lyesin in New York

[Stationery: 15, Avenue des Sycomores (xvi-e)/Villa Montmorency] 1930 Paris

[Russian] Dear Lyesin,

I received your letter. As I wrote you, I often read your poems and make sketches.
In your poetry, I feel sincerity, authenticity, and many of them are close to me in
spirit, because we are from the same homeland (*Litah*).

By the way, you did not tell me how many drawings are necessary for your
book. Considering the honorarium your publisher suggested ($500), I could
give you 4 or 5 drawings, because each drawing demands a lot of my work and
time, and I generally get paid more. Please write to me about that.

Warm regards/Devoted/   Marc Chagall

Marc Chagall in Paris to Yosef Opatoshu in New York

Paris   Octob. 930 {11/3} [November]

[Yiddish] Dear Opatoshu

Thank you for your book *The Dancer*.[12] It exudes freshness, health, and when I
read it I am a little sad . . . that I am not in your city [New York]. I would like so
much to mingle with your characters. When will I be among authentic (Jewish)
people and see the Jewish nature. Paris is not it.

How are you doing? What do you think about the nice times mankind is going   *nice times*: Ironically.

through. Nice human beings, may the devil take them, all the trouble comes from them . . . I am asked to go [for a visit] to Palestine, but the vicinity of Vitebsk would be better. Maybe. We'll see. Be well.

Warm regards from my family, don't forget us

Your Marc Chagall

I am not talking about my [spelling] mistakes

Chagall

CHAPTER ELEVEN   **First Visit to Palestine: 1930–1933**

From March 1 to June 4, 1931, Marc and Bella Chagall and their fifteen-year-old daughter Ida went to Palestine, on the invitation of the founder and first Mayor of Tel Aviv, Meir Dizengoff, in conjunction with the plan to build a Jewish Museum in the new city.[1] They were invited to stay in Dizengoff's large house in Tel Aviv, but they also traveled to kibbutzim and to holy places.

For Chagall, it was an extremely emotional trip; he spent almost three months in the Land of Israel, longer than in any other place he ever visited. As Chagall remarked, his father would weep whenever he mentioned "Jerusalem." Chagall was not a Zionist in any ideological sense, but he was always emotionally involved with the destiny of the Jewish settlement in Palestine. Skeptical about the vitality of Jewish life in the Diaspora, he admired the new Jewish presence in Palestine, the "straightened back" of the new Jew, the building of a Jewish city, and the new class of Jewish workers in the communal settlements: kibbutzim and smaller kvutzot. "In a party-line sense," he said in an interview in Jerusalem, "I am not a Zionist. I was inclined to be interested in the building of the Land, but only my visit here convinced me that this is the right way. The opponents of Zionism should visit the Land—here they will become Zionists."[2] He also had a close rapport with many "Palestinians" (Zionist Jews)[3] who came from Eastern Europe, spoke Yiddish and Russian, and had a mentality Chagall could easily relate to. He went there several times after the establishment of the State of Israel.

Meir Dizengoff (1861–1937) was born in Akimovici, Bessarabia (then Russia). He was active in the Russian revolutionary movement, was arrested, then became a Zionist. In 1891, he graduated from the University of Paris as a chemical engineer, resided in Palestine from 1892 to 1897, returned to Russia, and went back to Palestine in 1905. In 1909, he was one of the founders of the Jewish quarter north of Jaffa that became Tel Aviv. First Mayor of "the first Jewish city after two thousand years of exile," with a vision for a great commercial and cultural center, he was also active in many private business enterprises and Zionist organizations. As he described it, after building a few dozen houses, they had to make a "movie-picture theater," then some public institutions, "a hospital, a synagogue, a slaughterhouse, bath houses, and so forth," and then "we began to feel the need to foster beauty"—which meant art and an art museum. In 1930, Tel Aviv had a population of 50,000 and three repertory theaters. Dizengoff donated his private mansion to the future Tel Aviv Museum.

The issue of a Jewish museum had interested Chagall for many years.[4] He proposed it in 1929 to the center of Yiddish culture, the YIVO (Yiddish Scientific Institute) in Vilna, which bore results in 1935. Now the new center of Hebrew culture initiated one too. On a visit to Paris, Dizengoff apparently improvised an artistic committee, chaired by Marc Chagall and including the French poet and essayest Edmond Fleg (1874–1963) and the sculptor Chana Orloff (1888–1968, a Palestinian who lived in Paris) to advise on the plans for a museum in the first Jewish city. Chagall described it in the same interview:

> As Herzl came to Baron Rothschild, asking for help to build the Land [of Israel]—so Mr. Dizengoff came to me in Paris, asking for help in building a museum. I couldn't believe that this man was seventy years old, his eyes sparkled,

and he was all excitement about his favorite idea. Though once (still in Russia) I had decided to stay away from any public position,[5] and though I intended several times to go to the Land of Israel, and every time I cancelled the trip—this time, Mr. Dizengoff's enthusiasm influenced me. I packed my things and decided to give him a hand.

> To this day, people assume that Chagall was sent to the Holy Land by Vollard, to nourish the artist's biblical imagination, but this has no foundation in fact. When asked if he had come on Vollard's initiative, Chagall responded:

For the last five years I have carried inside me the idea of painting the book of Prophets, which I was invited by Mr. Vollard to do [. . .] I could, of course, make those paintings while living in Paris. Thus I made the illustrations to Gogol's *Dead Souls* without knowing the life in that period [early nineteenth century]. And so I prepared the pictures to LaFontaine's *Fables* though I did not live in the eighteenth century.

> And elsewhere he said: "Is it a matter of some palm tree or mountain? The same palm tree and almost the same mountain, the same colorful Arabs and camels, you can find also a few hundred miles outside of Palestine. For that, it's enough to go to [French] Algiers or Morocco . . . "[6] "On the contrary, I thought my wish to visit the Land of Israel was quite natural, for every Jew must closely feel his past. But I think it unnecessary to copy the life of the Land on paper." Vollard did not pay for this trip. Chagall was invited by Dizengoff and apparently used the "Vollard excuse" when speaking to non-Jews, to cover up his emotional "Zionist" attraction.
>
> In early March 1931, the Chagall family sailed on the ship *Champollion* to the Near East. Other passengers included the Jewish French poet Edmond Fleg and the Hebrew national poet Chaim-Nachman Bialik (1873–1934), whom Chagall had met in Berlin in 1922. Bialik had written some Yiddish poetry and loved to speak Yiddish, and they had long conversations during the voyage. After visiting Cairo and Alexandria, they arrived in Beirut; from there, the Chagalls travelled by

Marc Chagall, Hebrew poet Chaim-Nachman Bialik, and Ida Chagall (age 15), on board the French ship *Champollion*, traveling to Palestine in 1931.

train to Haifa to visit Hermann Struck, the Berlin artist who had taught Chagall engraving techniques in Berlin in 1922 and had emigrated to Palestine in 1923.[7]

In Tel Aviv, the Mayor, who had no Jewish army, met the Chagalls at the railroad station at the head of his fire brigade. An exhibition of the Palestine artists, as well as horse races on the seashore, were organized to honor Chagall. At Chagall's suggestion, committees of "Friends of the Tel Aviv Museum" were established in several countries (as he had earlier proposed to the YIVO in Vilna).

Yet Chagall refused to compromise his high standards of art. Dizengoff's ideas of a museum were bewildering at best. He wanted "everything," especially art on Biblical themes, and didn't mind reproductions. In Italy, he bought cheap reproductions of Michelangelo's "Moses" and Bernini's "David," placed "Moses" in the center of the museum, and exclaimed: "*Nu*, praise the Lord, we finally have a museum. Could there be a Tel Aviv Museum without a Moshe Rabeynu?"[8] Just a few weeks before Chagall's visit, the German Jew and prestigious artist Hermann Struck wrote to Dizengoff: "The Committeee must first decide on a method . . . " But Dizengoff was a Russian Jew, his way was to do first, and plan later, as they built Tel Aviv: "Had we been absorbed too much in making plans when the city was founded, we would probably still be at the beginning."

A major public argument ensued. Chagall remembered his frustrating experience as a public official in Soviet Vitebsk, and withdrew from any involvement.

From Meir Dizengoff in Tel Aviv to Marc Chagall in Paris

17 October 1930

[French] Dear Master,

I have just asked you to accept the invitation delivered by Madame Chana Orloff to come spend some time in Tel Aviv.

We will arrange a bedroom and bathroom, living room and open terrace for you, and I would be happy to offer you hospitality in my home as long as you want to stay with us.

open terrace: Essential for getting the breeze from the sea (before the days of air conditioners).

I will be very grateful to you if you let me know when and how you plan to travel. Palestinian Lloyds in Paris will set the best route for you and will indicate the best ship to take.

As for the best time for a trip to Palestine, we should note that the period November–April is the best weather to visit the Holy Land. It is not too warm, it rains now and then, the air is very mild, for our winter is not severe. However, it is necessary to bring warm clothing.

I wait to hear from you and, meanwhile, offer you my best wishes, dear Master.

[Meir Dizengoff]

Marc Chagall in Paris to Pavel Ettinger in Moscow

1930–31. New address: Paris. 15, Avenue des Sycomores (XVIe) Villa Montmorancy,

[Russian] Dear Pavel Davidovich,

How are you? I haven't written to you in a long time. What are you doing? Please write some time, for me a word (alas, rare) from the homeland [Russia]—is a pleasure. I wished and still do wish to see you somehow; didn't you plan to travel on a mission.[9] I would have used the opportunity to give you then samples of my engravings of different periods. You are such an inveterate bibliophile. What a pity you cannot see now the exhibition of Vollard's publications in Paris, where, among others, Gogol and LaFontaine (my engravings) are exhibited, along with works by Cézanne, Renoir, Bonnard, Picasso, Rouault, and others. Now I want to ask you the following. Indeed, I asked Efros too, but he is unreliable in writing letters (and, perhaps in "love"). Palais des Beaux-Arts in Brussels asked to arrange a "retrospective" exhibition (in April 1931).[10] I agreed and they are busy gathering my works of all periods, from 1907 on. In my homeland, presumably in museums, there are several of my works of 1914–1917. Would it be possible for the abovementioned official institution to borrow, with all the guarantees (and all expenses paid) such works of mine as A Stroll, Above the City, The Wedding, Vision, Old Man with Red Beard, Mirror, Barbershop, Clock, and others.

The institution is very solid; it recently arranged similar exhibitions of Rodin, Maillol, Bourdelle, Ensor. But I feel that I don't "deserve" and am afraid they'll refuse . . . But I could give them in gratitude a gift of one of my recent works. Could you, Pavel Davidovich, ask in my name about it—I don't know whom, perhaps the Tretyakov Gallery and the Russian Museum. And to whom should Palais des Beaux-Arts appeal.

Awaiting your prompt answer. Be well and best wishes for the New Year. Regards from my family.

Your Chagall

Russian Museum: Chagall's many works preserved in Russian collections were not exhibited in the West until the demise of the Soviet Union.

Marc Chagall in Paris to Meir Dizengoff in Tel Aviv

[Stationery: 15. Av. Des Sycomores, Villa Montmorency, Paris 16e]

Paris, 1930 [Received: 14/1/1931]

[Russian] Dear Mr. Dizengoff,

I have not yet been in Palestine, but I saw you. In the local "Goyish" atmosphere—the acquaintance, the meeting with you excited me, us. I who, in recent years, have somehow moved away from Jewish "public activity," was stimulated when I saw you. And we are prepared to help you. I am happy that finally a Jew has emerged who wants to establish a Jewish museum, and who understands how indispensable it is (not only as a useful element of tourism). I admit that I have despaired in recent years when I saw the Jewish apathy toward the destiny of Jewish art and, worst of all, I was afraid of anti-artistic (and therefore harmful) attempts in the establishment of a museum. Jealous people deny our Jewish right to a state, but we must not forget that "up our sleeve" we still have other states: along with the spiritual culture of Jewry, there is also the renaissance of art among Jews. I think we will not be ashamed to show it to strangers and perhaps they will refresh somewhat their respect for us. The Jews have to finally begin to collect systematically and with rigorous selection the art of the Jews (the old and the new). Once upon a time, when I first entered the road of art, I was almost alone—now I am surrounded by a whole army of Jewish artists. I would be uncomfortable, about interfering technically in this matter, to avoid unleashing various passions. For I previously experienced something of this kind in Russia. But . . . for your sake and for the sake of the general ideal, I have decided to participate as far as I can.—Today, Fleg, Chana Orloff, and I discussed your Memorandum. It is very good as is, but some concrete points are somewhat changed and the list of artists should not be published for the time being. We decided that, in the major centers of Europe and America, societies of friends of the Jewish museum should be established, considering that the museum itself has already been established by you (though not yet opened), and that a (secret) jury exists already.[11] Hence, what is left for those friends and all of Jewry is to publicize, to collect *money* and artistic material fit for a museum; and to send the former [the money] to active accounts, either to you or to us here in Paris. The latter [the art] here, into a specially chosen site for judgment and selection (this can also be done from photos, if it comes from far away). I foresee an ideal museum if you trust in the *jury* and will not impose on our taste. I will be happy if you create not only the first Jewish city, but if you also build the first truly Jewish museum.

Let us get to work!

My wife sends warm greetings, my daughter Ida often thinks of you. We also think of the trip, of course. I will soon talk to *Efroykin* about it.

Best regards/Your devoted

Marc Chagall

Efroykin: Israel Yefroykin (1884–1954), a Yiddish cultural activist, lived in Paris from 1920.

Marc Chagall in Paris to Meir Dizengoff in Tel Aviv

Paris, 1931 [beginning of January]

[Russian] Dear Mr. Dizengoff,

We're thinking these days about our travel, but we learned that a [Zionist] Congress will convene [in Europe], they say in February. We assume that you and all the Palestinians will travel from Palestine to Europe. In this case, don't you think we should postpone our voyage? Or will the Congress be postponed? Your opinion?

In the meantime I learned that in London and Berlin certain circles collect the ancient, archeological part of a Jewish museum for Jerusalem. [??] Don't you think we should therefore preoccupy ourselves with collecting only plastic art created by Jews in the 19th and 20th centuries for the Tel Aviv museum? This is much easier and fits the spirit of the new city. For the New Jewish City—the New Jewish Art.[12]

Please accept our greetings for the new year, and regards from all my family.

Love/with anticipation/devoted

Marc Chagall

Meir Dizengoff in Tel Aviv to Marc Chagall in Paris

23 January 1931

[French] Dear Madame and Monsieur,

I have just received your kind letter and am eager to inform you that the Zionist Congress was adjourned for June and I do not plan to leave the Land before spring. Hence, I am impatiently awaiting you, as I wrote you in my last letter.

I have just received a letter from Mr. Fleg also talking about the committee which is being organized in Berlin for the Archeological Museum at the University of Jerusalem.

I agree with you that we should limit our Tel Aviv Museum to works of modern Jewish art of the nineteenth and twentieth centuries. I also wrote that in detail to Mr. Fleg and ask both of you to rewrite the Memorandum as a result.

We will speak of it again when you are here.

Mr. Bialik is now in London and plans to return in late January or early February, perhaps you will arrange with him to leave together.[13] You will be able to get his address from the Zionist Organization in London or from the Palestine Lloyds in Paris.

So, I shall wait to hear from you about the name of the ship and the date of your arrival in Tel Aviv.

Cordially, / [Meir Dizengoff]

Marc Chagall in Paris to Yosef Opatoshu in New York

[Stationery: 15, Avenue des Sycomores (xvi-e) / Villa Montmorency] 4/II 1931 Paris

[Yiddish] Dear Opatoshu,

Received your letter. You are going to Russia. I want to ask you to hide me in your pocket . . . and drop me off in Vitebsk. When you get to Paris you must stay with us. We will be happy. I am sure you feel our sympathy for you. I assume you will be here (as you wrote) in the beginning of May, because we are about to go to Palestine where we were invited by Dizengoff, the Mayor of Tel Aviv. This [trip] will be useful for me (I hope) for my future [paintings of the] Prophets . . . And we shall hopefully return toward the end of April or beginning of May. Now I can tell you that the painting the wiseguy [at the Reinhardt Gallery in New York] stole is here in Paris. The Paris lawyer pulled it off. Soon I expect to get it. But nevertheless, I am grateful to you and Vladek for your efforts.

How are you? Asch's anniversary was recently celebrated in Paris.[14] We are still at odds . . . What can I do. When you love too much in your life, reactions come back at you. You have to be cold-blooded—and everything will be smooth. That's why I love Russia . . . No matter what happens and no matter what you say, the blood is boiling over there . . . with no ceremonies, and it seems, for an ideal.

Be well. See you. / My family sends their love

Your devoted Marc Chagall

(and my spelling mistakes)

P.S. The "exhibition" you write about is small, I don't even know what there was, I didn't organize it.[15]

Marc Chagall in Paris to Meir Dizengoff in Tel Aviv

Paris 13/II 1931

[Russian] Dear Mr. Dizengoff

Thanks for your letter. On the third we are leaving Marseilles. We have already reserved three tickets for the first class. We hope that everything will go well.

Upon leaving or at sea I shall cable you. I will bring with me, just in case, a complete file of my engravings for the *Dead Souls* and the LaFontaine *Fables* and perhaps I shall exhibit them.—

I also have in mind to write a book about Palestine or about my "voyage to Palestine," which I was asked to do by a French and a German publisher. In addition, I would like to give a public reading of fragments from my forthcoming book *Ma Vie*. And afterwards if need be, some of my thoughts about modern art.[16]

Afterwards, I contemplate "secluding myself" and working—with the aim of at the end of April, beginning of May to Paris, where my exhibition is waiting for me in Brussels and in Paris, as well as the publication of my book *Ma Vie*. We also think that by that time we should be in Paris for the Jewish [Palestinian] section of the Colonial Exhibition. Where I hope that Jews in the field of art will show something.

My family greets you warmly and sends their love. We will be happy to see you and the new world. Entirely devoted to you,

Marc Chagall

Marc Chagall in Paris to A. Lyesin in New York

[Stationery: 15, Avenue des Sycomores (xvi-e)/Villa Montmorency] 16/II 1931 Paris

[Russian] Dear Mr. Lyesin

Aronson[17] came to me in your name to ask about the illustrations for your book. This showed me that you probably did not get my recent letter, where I wrote to you about it.

Therefore, I am writing to you again. Even though I am busy outside of paintings—with a book of the Prophets, LaFontaine's *Fables*—out of esteem for you as a man and a poet I agreed to do it. I plan to do a series of 25–30 drawings and make one of them exceptionally in color for the cover or the frontispiece.

I plan to do drawings that neither of us need be ashamed of . . .

Nevertheless, I would like my labor to be minimally paid, as other, younger artists are paid. Therefore, for the series of 25–30 drawings for your book, I want to get $1000; and after you use all these drawings, they will become your own property. You could add the originals as an appendix to a deluxe edition, and sell it for several times more, or whatever you like. I repeat that I am doing all this for you out of respect, and because we are from the same land [Jewish *Litah*] . . .

So, on this question I await your answer, also in order to calm poor Aronson,

Chagall in Palestine in 1931, on a visit to the old agricultural colony Petah Tikvah. From left: Israeli painter Reuven Rubin, Esther Rubin, Ida and Marc Chagall.

who is very upset about it . . . I am soon going to Palestine, invited by the Mayor of Tel Aviv, but we shall return in about 1 1/2 months.[18]

Your devoted

Marc Chagall

The address in Paris or for 1 1/2 months from March 2: Tel Aviv, Mr. Dizengoff— à Marc Chagall

Marc Chagall in Paris to Pavel Ettinger in Moscow

18/II 1931. Paris. 15, Avenue des Sycomores (xvi-e) / Villa Montmorency.

[Russian] Dear Pavel Davidovich,

I am very happy to give your man some of my samples. Just let him call earlier, and you will see that I remember those, alas few, who remember me. From March 1, I am going on a distant trip,[19] but I shall be back in May, when an exhibition will open on the publication of my book *Ma Vie*,[20] near my return, and will include several new paintings. That is a good time for him to visit me.

I am happy to get regards from my homeland [Russia] from time to time, for my longing is great, even more so since they think in your country that I am an "alien." To show you how they treat me here, I am sending you an article by a former authority concerning Vollard's exhibition, where I especially don't let him sleep.[21] You will see that neither in your country nor here can my countrymen stand me . . . It would be good if you brought this article and this situation to the attention of artistic circles in my homeland.

Be well. / Write, don't forget me. I am always happy [to hear from you].

P.S. About the Brussels exhibition. They are busy now. I would like them to postpone it till 1932, when it may be possible to move it to Paris, too, for from 1907[22] to 1932, it will have been . . . 25 years, that your humble servant has been busy with what is called "Art"—

Your devoted / Marc Chagall

Marc Chagall: Words at a Reception in Tel Aviv (April 5, 1931)[23]

The Hebrew "national poet" Chaim-Nakhman Bialik also wrote Yiddish poetry and spoke the language with all three Chagalls, but he would not do it in a public speech in Palestine. He greeted Chagall in Hebrew, even though the guest of honor did not understand that language. All the Hebrew writers at the assembly (with one possible exception) came from eastern Europe and Yiddish was their mother tongue. Yet in the time of the "war of languages," they would not betray their ideology in public.

[Hebrew] I am grateful to my friend the great poet Bialik for his warm words which I could not understand, and thank all of you for coming to welcome us. Without having seen my paintings, you must imagine that my face can fill their lack, my smiles are watercolors, and my longing is a sad picture. Yet the opposite is true . . .

You surely expect me to tell you about the impression the Land made on me? In the first days of my visit I could answer this question, but now it became impossible. Simply: I cannot, my words diminish daily. From all I saw, my tongue is numb, and perhaps I shall turn, happily, from a tourist to a simple Jew living in the Land? Or perhaps I lack words because I am not a writer . . . And if you ask: Why do I stand here and talk to you? Because a lot of Jewish feeling fills my throat . . . The new waves of Pioneers and the builders of new cities—on the one hand, and the stones of old Jerusalem and the mountains of Tsfat, on the other.

Tsfat or Safed: An ancient town in Galilee and center of the (Lurianic) Kabbalah.

You surely expect to hear a poignant word from me . . . But from all my eyes saw, I am so amazed, endlessly amazed . . . I only sigh and sigh . . . It would be preferable to express my feelings on a canvas. But to express even the slightest thing that my eyes saw I would need the power of a stone, the courage and purity of heart of our Prophets, yet we are in Exile for two thousand years . . .

in Exile: An allusion to the dictum: There are no Prophets in Exile.

Only two roads are open to me: to take the stones of this Land and crush my head with them, or return quietly as I came, as if nothing happened.

I am amazed how a handful of people, surrounded by hatred rather than love, builds and creates a new land. I am jealous of your idealism, and I wish you from the bottom of my heart—to continue what you started. And for me I wish to come and wallow among you, and maybe I shall be able as an artist to do something for your future Jewish museum as well, and you would be satisfied with me more than I am myself.

Marc Chagall in Paris to Yosef Opatoshu in New York

[Stationery: 15, Avenue des Sycomores (xvi-e)/Villa Montmorency]

4 June 1931 {6/9} [received June 9]

[Yiddish] Returned from Eretz Israel. Happy. Though not a Zionist and not a "nationalist," but as a Jew. You don't seem to be going to Russia yet. It may be hot in Eretz Israel, but I think you will be happy as an artist [to be there]. Just don't listen to that . . . Tunkeler . . . [24]

I shall be glad to see you. My family sends their love.

With thanks—for the *Bleter* for Ida

Your devoted   Marc Chagall

Bleter: The Yiddish literary magazine *Literarishe Bleter*, published in Warsaw. Opatoshu went on a trip to his native Poland and subscribed the journal for Ida.

Chagall on Palestine: An Interview in Paris with Ben-Tavriya[25] (June 1931)

[Russian]—*Your trip to Palestine was connected with the organization of an art museum in Tel Aviv?*

Yes, I was invited by M. Dizengoff to attend to this problem. For a long time, I wanted to visit Palestine. Dizengoff's visit [in Paris] and his invitation speeded it up . . . Do you know Dizengoff, this seventy-year-old young man? It was impossible not to respond to his call.

. . . Did Palestine attract me as an artist? You see, I went there as a Jew. I wanted to see it all with my own eyes—how they build a country. With me it is always like that—the man precedes the artist. On the other hand, all that exotics of the East, which people usually are after, all that ethnography, which some artists hasten to put on their canvas—seems to me inessential . . . Is it a matter of some palm tree or mountain? The same palm tree and almost the same mountain, the same colorful Arabs and camels, you can find also a few hundred miles outside of Palestine. For that, it's enough to go to [French] Algiers or Morocco . . . No, European standards will give you nothing. Quite a different thing is if you look at all this with your *inner* eye, do you understand? . . . Of course, Delacroix and Matisse, unlike Gauguin, saw something in Northern Africa—but they are not Jews—they don't have our past. No, I looked at it with the eyes of a Jew, nothing else.

. . . Yes, there is a lot of joy in Tel Aviv, the sun is shining, the youth smile in your face . . . Since the Jews settled in that sunny country, they acquired a new, healthy element, which is lacking in *Goles* [= Exile]—it is a special calm, self confidence. A Jew walks there assertively, and works—this small group of 170,000 people intends to continue what they started, in spite of the political and economic atmosphere; and this Jew reacts to any shock—even to the Yagur killing— much less than the Jews outside of Palestine . . . And all are like that—they all have this enthusiasm: the merchants and citizens in the city as well as those in the kibbutzim, where life is, of course, much harder . . . But there are still too few Jews there! . . . Material for generals there is plenty, but an "army" is lacking . . .

. . . Of course, not everything goes smoothly. There is, perhaps, some apathy to the political problems of Zionism . . . But what do you want—they all work very

170,000: The Jewish population of Palestine at the time.

Yagur: During Chagall's visit on Passover, April 5, 1931, three members of Kibbutz Yagur near Haifa were killed by Arab terrorists in an ambush 200 meters from the gate of the kibbutz.

hard—do you know how workers live and what they eat?—They invested there all
their strength, they built, created—and, naturally, they are now careful about
changes and any risk one may have to take . . . By the way, I felt especially good in
Emek Jezreel, in the kibbutzim . . . I even wanted to live among them . . .

My general impression? In Palestine I was impressed by the constant presence everywhere of the confrontation of two elements: on the one hand, enthusiasm for the future, struggle for the new—on the other hand, the glory of the
long ago fossilized past; both of those are equally strong and exciting.

This must be felt especially in Jerusalem?

Jerusalem? In this city you feel that from here there is no more road *further* . . . I felt that in these narrow streets, with their goats and Arabs, in the al-
leys where red, blue, and green Jews are going now to the Wailing Wall—Christ
walked not long ago . . . Here you can feel how Judaism and Christianity are one
family—for it was one whole—and then came some devils, tore it all apart and
divided . . . You feel what a powerful culture grew here in the past . . . If it is
destined to be resurrected, it will be one of the richest on earth—I am saying
that, though I am not at all a chauvinist . . . Yet all the rest in Jerusalem—the
Omar Mosque, where Edwin Samuel made me go, and the Holy places—in spite
of my great interest in Christ as a poet and prophetic figure—left me indifferent . . . After all, in two and a half months I traveled everywhere and lived in
Safed, in Haifa, in the settlements . . .

So how is the situation about the museum?

This is a difficult issue and—I shall say it openly—I have little hope that it will
be resolved in a satisfactory manner. At first, they assumed that the functions
will be strongly divided. In Tel Aviv there is a committee: Dizengoff, Bialik,
Shoshana Persitz—very well, but the artistic responsibility, i.e., the selection of
the material must be realized here in Paris.

red, blue, and green Jews: From Chagall's pictures, now in the garb of Ultra-Orthodox Jews.

Edwin Samuel: Son of the first British High Commissioner of Palestine, Lord Herbert Samuel. Edwin 2nd Viscount Samuel (1898–?) held high positions in the British administration in Palestine, yet became a Zionist and helped establish the future administration of Israel.

Shoshana Persitz (1893–1969), born in Kiev, was the daughter of the banker and
Zionist leader Hillel Zlatopolski. In Russia, she was a leading figure in the revival
of Hebrew and the *Tarbut* network of secular Hebrew schools. In 1917, she established the Hebrew *Omanut* (*Art*) publishing house in Moscow; in 1920, *Omanut*
moved to Frankfurt, Germany, then to Israel. In 1926–1935, she was Director of
the Tel Aviv City Education Department; in the 1950s, she headed the Knesset
Education Committee. Chagall would have met her in Moscow in 1920, in Tel
Aviv in 1931, in Paris and Jerusalem in 1951.

The artistic committee is composed of E. Fleg, Chana Orloff, and myself; and we could visit [Tel Aviv] from time to time. The whole question is how to approach such a beginning. I sketched a nonambitious artistic plan, indicated the halls: Israels, Liebermann, Pissarro, Modigliani, Pascin,—as a foundation, a basis, around which authentic artistic youth could gather and grow . . . For it is much easier, I emphasize, to realize a serious plan for collecting Jewish artistic values—I am talking about a real museum—with a pure, 100% consistent program, rather than something poor, full of compromises, where even the cultural tourist will not peep into . . . For that, for several years a real dictatorship is needed of people who are rigorously competent, whom one can trust, and to whom the artistic management is fully entrusted . . . But what do you want—Tel Aviv is not Paris and—I must say that we, Jews, in general do not yet understand art . . . Jewish society, like flypaper, first of all attracts all the petty, the transient . . . There is a danger that this museum may become a second Bezalel . . . They want portraits of famous Jews . . .

Blum: Leon Blum (1872–1950), French Socialist leader; later, Prime Minister of France.

Is it important for a museum that this is a portrait of L. Blum? What is important is how and by whom it was made, and the fact that it portrays specifically Blum is a secondary issue . . . They want to flood this museum with plaster casts, copies—who needs it? Why do you need this moldy junk? There is no place here to be kind—one has to know even how to reject a gift, if it contradicts the designed artistic plan. But if all this is not serious—I shake off any responsibility for the development of this business . . . Either-or, either the organizers trust us, or let them act according to their own taste, but in that case I cannot allow any committee to use my name as a cover—it must not even be mentioned! . . .

Marc Chagall in France to A.Z. Ben-Yishay in Tel Aviv

Aharon-Zev Ben-Yishay (1902–1977) was a polyglot intellectual and scholar of a wide-ranging erudition. Born in Russia, he came to Palestine in 1920. He was a prolific Hebrew writer, poet, translator, literary and cultural critic, and editor. He edited the annual and monthly periodicals of Tel Aviv City Hall and was Dizengoff's personal advisor on matters of culture. He may have met Chagall in Moscow in 1920 and certainly in Tel Aviv in 1931 and 1951.

[Yiddish] In a village near Grenoble   3/VIII 1931[26]

My Dear Ben-Yishay

Thank you for your regards from Vienna. Isn't it the Café Vienna in Tel Aviv? I remember everybody in the Land of Israel and you especially, with warmth and love. We are now in a village in the mountains, where I am working on my Prophets.

In Paris I saw Madame Persitz. As she told me, a big scandal arose from my interview in *Razsvet* and Dizengoff is even angry with me and doesn't write to me.

I didn't make the scandal, it was made without me. I don't know whether you read it. Naturally, the reporter translated my words into his language. And since *Doar Ha-Yom* also made an interview with me, and I have no idea what he wrote there, I would like to tell you the truth.

The truth is that I did indeed resign from responsibility for the museum in Tel Aviv. Many facts convinced me that as I imagined [the museum] and as I would like to create something in my country with all my love—for the time being, it certainly cannot happen.

Dizengoff is a dear Jew, I love him dearly, he has a good, warm heart and loves his city passionately and wants indeed to do the best. But he is too good, and regrettably, he lacks a specific program to create the museum. He cannot have it and one cannot demand it of him, but when he approached me, I assumed he also wanted to listen to me. But outside of me, there are in Paris a thousand Jewish artists, women and men, and they certainly have a stronger voice than me. That's how it is in the world—whoever screams louder succeeds.

For me, the Land of Israel is holy, I don't want to get anything out of it, I am pleased to contribute to it, and, as you know, I made many gifts at a time when all others only sold. But that is not the issue.

If only you had seen what a shame it is to see the painting exhibition in the Palestine pavilion, in the eyes of the whole world that observes the Colonial Exhibition [in Paris].

When I was in Tel Aviv, I participated in a meeting of the French Consul, [Mayor Meir] Dizengoff, [the painter Reuven] Rubin, and myself, and we decided that only artists living in Palestine will exhibit in the pavilion. And what came out?

Rubin: Reuven Rubin (1893–1974), a prominent Israeli artist.

Neither Palestinian artists nor Parisian ones, but a few women who hung around the committee. Can I with my name protect all the women who paint Jewish ships?

This is not what I dreamed about. And I wasn't even invited to the opening, neither did they ask my opinion. Three months after the opening I went to take a look at the pavilion and it pained me plenty. And if the Palestine artists are angry, they are right. What can I do about it?

Perhaps I demand too much, and perhaps it is enough for the Jews just to see Jewish ships, and whether it is art, they don't care.

I could have done something, and easily, as [Hermann] Struck thinks too, we would have helped create a small, selective, but valuable museum that the Jews would not have to be ashamed for the world. I wouldn't mind making an effort for a useful thing for the Land of Israel, but I have no interest in collecting the garbage of every woman or man who is a Jew.

They malign me with whatever a mouth can utter. I am used to it. One day, sooner or later, Jews will see that I am not looking here for any advantage or honor for myself.

But never mind. Let it be. I have no courage to quarrel with Jews. For I love them.

Be well, my dear, and write some time. When I get back to Paris, I'll send you something.

Your   Marc Chagall

M. Dizengoff: Remarks on the Birth Pangs of the Tel Aviv Museum (A reply to Chagall)[27]

[Hebrew] I read Chagall's letter to A.Z. Ben-Yishay concerning art in the Land of Israel (*Ktuvim* 38) and also his interview in *Razsvet*. In everything concerning art, no doubt, his opinion is preferable to mine, and not I will teach one of the great Jewish painters in our generation anything in the theory of art. But since he touched a matter very close to me, the issue of the Tel Aviv Museum, a matter I devoted to and, if God gives me life, will devote in the future a lot of time, energy, and work, I feel obliged to explain the matter in public.

I came to the idea of a museum in Tel Aviv from various impulses, and the major impulse—my wish to make our city, the city I love and want to see her greatness and splendor, also into a center of art (a center of literature it became anyway). Our young city, which has neither ancient buildings nor ancient graves, and has no burden of tradition and a past, should become a center of culture and art—and it has all the qualities for it. First of all, I dedicated my home to this goal. Thus, there is a vessel, and has to be filled with wine. And here the birth pangs began. True, all beginnings are hard, especially in an enterprise that needs elucidation and judgment and a great deal of discrimination and guidance and designing a plan, but it is apparently most difficult to create a Hebrew museum in the Land of Israel. There are many who question, pester, offer advice—each in his own direction. Who needs a museum altogether? Is everything already finished in our country and we lack just that? And someone asks: A museum in Tel Aviv? Don't we have a museum in Jerusalem, "Bezalel," and it too is hanging on a hair? The well-known argument: why do you need to get married and have children, etc.—here is a woman and five children, all ready—go ahead and feed them . . . My life's experience taught me that in such cases it is better not to talk much, not to argue, polemicize, explain away difficulties and problems, but to do, to work. "Talk little, do much." I paid no attention to anything and started working. The plan will clarify itself in the course of time. Even when we approached the building of Tel Aviv, we didn't know clearly what will happen in a few years from then. We built, worked, corrected, improved—and the plans came afterwards. Had we been absorbed too much in making plans when the city was founded, we would probably have stayed even today at the beginnings. For me, one thing is clear, that Tel Aviv needs a museum, that is: a center for art, for improving beauty, for the development of an aesthetic sensibility in the community, and for the advancement of creative art. I want our city to be not just a center for trade and industry, but also a permanent home for spiritual culture, through the development of literature and science, art in all its kinds and music. The Education of our future generations and preparing them for a full and complete national renaissance, requires the development of all aspects of physical and spiritual culture of the people. And we cannot imagine the functioning of the Jewish renaissance in the Land of Israel without art taking its due place in it.

But when I approached the work, I deemed it necessary first of all to ask the advice of artists. Yet as soon as I stepped into the temple of art and approached the high priests working there—I discovered a whole world, as well as little and big worlds in it, with questions without answers and requests that have no chance of being fulfilled. I learned that every artist is a world in his own right, with light and darkness and skies and earth of his own. Everyone is subjective, individual. And there is no wonder that two artists cannot merge into one opinion concerning the nature of art and the ways of organizing an art museum. Every blessed artist can give you an extensive explanation and complete view of the ways of artistic creation and the mode of organizing an art museum which he prefers, but his conclusions must be confined to his subjective thinking and his own school, because in his view there is no truth outside of his own. When I tried, for example, to invite two important artists in one place, one old and one young, to discuss the arrangement of the museum, both refused. The young one said he won't meet this senile person, whose art and school are passé; and the old one said he cannot meet a person who is not a painter but a photographer and caricaturist. Several artists refused to give their works to the museum when they heard that also artist x or y will participate, though XY is also considered one of the great artists. Every time I tried to create some committee or group of artists to aid the establishment of the museum, I failed, because the important ones refused to participate for various reasons or raised conditions impossible to fulfill.

All my negotiations with artists taught me, at least, one thing: as a person may be a great writer and not have any special talent for editing a monthly, in the same way, a person may be an excellent artist without knowing how to arrange an art museum. So I approached another kind of art connoisseurs, lovers and crit-

a whole world: Yiddish idiom: *A velt mit veltelekh,* literally: a world filled with little worlds, meaning "each is a world for himself," all with their own interests and quarreling with each other.

ics of art, such as Solomon Renac [?] in Paris; Dr. Eisler, Professor of art history in Vienna; museum directors in Paris and Brussels (Jews and non-Jews), etc. From them I gathered that the foundation of an art museum is a discipline in its own right, one has to learn it. There is a science of founding museums—Museology, and many books have been written on it. There are historical museums, professional museums, art museums, ethnographic, or specialized museums, etc. Sometimes a small country organizes a general museum, that contains many departments, such as the Land museum in Klagenfurt [Germany] that has ten different departments.

In the foundation of our Tel Aviv Museum I did not establish any principles, for whatever principles we establish now, we may have to cross their boundaries in the future. I think, however, that we should work along the following three main lines:

A. *Modern Art*: (1) Works by *Jewish artists* of the 18th, 19th, 20th centuries. Sculpture, painting, etching, architecture etc. on any theme whatsoever. The purpose is to collect chef-d'oeuvres created by the Jewish genius in the last three hundred years; (2) Works on *Jewish topics*, whether the artist is a Jew or not; (3) A gallery of famous Jews, represented in paintings and sculptures by famous artists.

B. *Biblical Reproductions*. This department will contain a collection of drawings, etchings, copies of pictures and various reproductions of works describing the legends, events, and heroes of the Bible, according to the works of the art geniuses of all generations and nations, that are in all the museums of the world.

C. *Department of Ethnography and Folklore*. In this department, all objects and documents will be collected—clothes, work tools, furniture, pictures, documents, etc., from which we can learn about the life, manners and behavior of the different ethnic groups of the Jewish settlements in various countries, and especially in the Orient.

This plan may perhaps change with time, get larger or smaller, according to circumstances. Naturally, we intend to collect in this museum *only chef-d'oeuvres*, for only the quality and not the quantity is important for us. If for the time being—while we cannot establish one jury committee in the whole country—we sometimes may have to accept works without preliminary examination, it does not mean that everything will be included in the museum. Before the official opening of the museum, a serious jury committee will be convened to decide what to accept and what to reject in an unbiased manner. We are determined not to include professional artists in the governing body, not to leave any shade of doubt about partiality or any conflict of interests. But the governing body will endeavour always to be in contact with the artists, the art critics, and art lovers, and will pay attention to all their suggestions and advice. We also intend to invite a professional director for the museum. If it will all advance properly and all the promises we received will be fulfilled, we hope to open the museum in the spring of 1932. We also hope to establish an art library at the museum, whose lack is felt in our city.

And now—about Chagall. His announcement, published in his letter in this issue, and in his earlier talk to journalists, that he resigns from responsibility for the museum, is superfluous. I have never intended to burden him with the responsibility in any form, I only asked for his help, as I asked for the help of other great artists. Chagall is a great artist and an individualist, but to organize a museum just on his wish—would be a bit difficult. I heard his advice on many matters, and even now I am prepared to get his advice and help, but that does not mean to close our ears to the advice of other great Jewish artists, from other trends in art. I wholeheartedly agree with Chagall about the Eretz-Israel pavilion in the Colonial Exhibition in Paris. The best proof is that I resigned from the Committee of the pavilion. This is a sad story and requires an investigation. But no need to connect this issue with the Tel Aviv Museum. There are many obstacles on the road to the Museum, yet I still hope that we can skip those obstacles. And I believe that in our dear city Tel Aviv one day a splendid temple of art will be erected, and I would like to urge the artists and the art lovers to bring this day as soon as possible.

M. Chagall's Response[28]

[Russian] I read M. Dizengoff's article and would like to say a few words to the point.

There is no argument between us. I respect and value Mr. Dizengoff too much, I am too enthusiastic about the sincerity and fruitfulness of his work in all other domains for me to quarrel with him. But my "nervousness" derives from the fact that I often saw that good people with good intentions is one thing, and the realization of those intentions—quite a different one.

No matter what the disagreements among artists, they agree more or less in evaluating the good and the bad. Therefore I think that the Jury, even when it has people highly representative of society, without artists—is nonsense. I think that only with the participation of artists with some dose of personal tolerance for others can the goal be achieved of a Jewish Museum fitting its purpose. Only artists can insist that the Jewish Museum be based first of all (as I stressed repeatedly) on rooms for Pissarro, Israels, Liebermann, Modigliani, Levitan, Pascin, Bakst, etc. The museum does not need any copies or plaster casts, no matter on what subject. The museum cannot rely only on gifts by "the artists of the whole world," not only because not all artists of the world should be in the museum but also because one must not always think that the artists should give and give gifts and forget that they too have to make a living, especially in this hard time.

I shall not dwell now on other departments of the museum. No need to be afraid of the so-called "leftist" or new art. Some thirty years ago, the Luxemburg museum was afraid to accept a gift by Guilebot, which included "leftist" artists: Cézanne, Monet, Pissaro, Rodin, etc. And what turned out? Those leftists were recently brought to the Louvre, whereas the works of those artists who protested remained in their places—and even that only because management is shy to take them right down into the cellar.

As to Mr. Dizengoff's statement that he placed no responsibility on me—I think it is important to note, in the name of the so-called "truth"—for, in addition to me, some other persons are involved in it—and in order to stop this polemics, depressing for me, that before my departure for Palestine, Mr. Dizengoff in Paris determined the composition of the Museum Committee, including Ch. Orlov, E. Fleg, and myself, and gave us all artistic authority. Now I am not surprised at all that Mr. Dizengoff, as it were, "retired" me personally, because it seems I do not fit the role of a "committee member." Other prominent artists of other trends will surely be more in their place here. I want to assure my dear and beloved Miron Yakovlevich [Dizengoff], that I am not offended at all. On the contrary, I am grateful for it, because now I can sit at my easel with more freedom and nonchalance.

I hope that this small "misunderstanding" will be somewhat useful and will contribute to the further development of the future museum, close to the heart of all of us.

Marc Chagall

Marc Chagall in Paris to Yosef Opatoshu in New York

[Stationery: 15, Avenue des Sycomores (xvi-e)]   26 Oct 1931

[Yiddish] Dear Opatoshu

Many thanks for your-my Bible. I am not worthy of it. After a small ceremony at the customs office, I got it. How shall I thank you? I don't know. I shall try soon to do the Jew for your book. I guess it is not late. I would like you to live here so we could see you more often . . .

How are you and how is your writing?

Warm regards from us and again many thanks. Your devoted and loving

Marc Chagall

Marc Chagall in Paris to Leo Kenig in London

5, Avenue des Sycomores (xvi-e)   [1931]

[Russian] Dear Kenig,

I had a brainstorm: wouldn't you agree to take on the directorship of the Jewish museum in Tel Aviv. You know, of course, about the perturbations around it and about my travel there and about my efforts with Dizengoff, etc. (I gave him your address so that he goes to see you.) In short, what do you think? If you are sympathetic, I myself would set it in motion and appeal to them to invite you. This time I hope that our talks, difficulties, even "quarrels" between us will lead to a real museum. But I think that once and for all, a new director is needed and I remembered you. I am impatient. I wait for your answer. Are you "blood-related" to London? I was in Palestine, it is "marvelous."

> *marvelous*: Chagall was often shy of grandiose words or trite epithets and puts them in quotation marks.

Write sooner/Devoted/Marc Chagall

P.S. I cannot now introduce you to our "controversies" concerning the museum. We have to "kill" Bezalel once and for all.

> The Bezalel art school and museum was founded in Jerusalem in 1906. Kenig was one of its early pupils. For Chagall, this was a symbol of ethnography and tourist kitsch. Yet his own exhibition in Jerusalem in 1951 was in the Bezalel Museum (before it merged into the Israel Museum).

[Addition on the margin:] Do you master Hebrew? Do you have an "administrative talent?"

Marc Chagall in Paris to Leo Kenig in London

[Yiddish] [1931] My Dear Kenig,

You will surely think that Chagall is not "clear"—that I attached myself to your person because of the museum. That is, it is clear only *for Jews* what is clear. It turns out that *they* [the Tel Aviv museum] need a "shnorer" and only "later" maybe a real person.

> "Shnorer" is a Yiddish derogatory label for a person begging for money in an undignified manner. It was a key stereotype for the presumably unproductive

existence of the Jews and used as a pejorative slogan of Jewish self-criticism. To-day, it would be a dignified job of "money raiser"—not such a bad idea for the president of a new institution in a poor country.

> You see, there's enough to get sad about. And not in vain am I in "conflict" with dear Mr. Dizengoff. I send you both letters. The one by Struck you will somehow return to me.
>
> How are you. You are, probably, like everyone else . . . In all fatherlands. Can you imagine: the "shnorers" say that it is not so bad in the beautiful Palestine . . . I believe them.
>
> You don't read French, do you? The book I wrote, *My Life*, was just published here and is to be published in German and in Russian. Would your Englishmen like to have the book in English?
>
> Now you will see [in London] the great French exhibition of ancient art. Do you still think that the French were and remain great men—artists?
>
> It seems to me that England, London museum, must have some beautiful paintings. I would love to use the opportunity when there will be an exhibition of my work in London (and I don't know when and where and how) to come over for a visit.
>
> Well, I greet you warmly. Please forgive my Yiddish mistakes. I write just as my mother taught me to write, and I cannot forget it . . . Let it be with mistakes, that's how my mama taught me—

> Your devoted
>
> Marc Chagall

Meir Dizengoff in Tel Aviv to Marc Chagall in Paris

11 November 1931

[French] Dear friends,

Are you still angry? I wrote to you and you didn't even deign to answer me. Fortunately, our mutual friend, Hermann Struck, intervened to make peace between us. But, my God, what unpardonable crimes did I commit that make us implacable enemies?

According to Mr. Hermann Struck, the indictment can be summed up in the following felonies:

1) That I said or wrote that you weren't a member of the Museum Committee or that they weren't planning to make you the only one in charge of the develop-

ment of the Museum. First of all, allow me to say that I would be prepared to beg your pardon a thousandfold if I had committed the slightest attack on your honor or your name. But I am sure that I did no such thing, for your name and your honor, as an artist, a writer, and a man, are very dear to me. Perhaps some misunderstanding slipped into a sentence which certainly was beyond my thought, and I am willing to clear up any misunderstanding in any form that will be required of me, even in the press.

2) That I promised to buy a certain number of paintings from painters; I had visited with Madame Orloff and did not keep that promise and did not give them any response. Now, here are the facts:

a) I bought two statues from Mrs. Orloff and paid for them in advance;

b) I bought a painting from Kissling which I paid for immediately.

The last part of the letter is missing.

Marc Chagall in Paris to Meir Dizengoff in Tel Aviv

Telegram of 10.3.1932 [March]

[French] Best wishes inauguration of museum.

Chagall

Marc Chagall in Paris to Leo Kenig in London

Paris (16th) [Stationery: 15, Avenue des Sycomores (xvi-e)]

[Yiddish] Dear Kenig,

How are you? Received your letter. I don't lose my hope (about the museum). And would like, at an opportune moment—to push you . . .

I asked the publisher for a book for you. I am sending it. The Jews certainly don't know about it. Tell them.

You probably saw the great French exhibit [in London]? It is strange: the French, who rarely make a good exhibit here, have apparently made a special effort for you . . .

You write whether I would like to exhibit in London? Why not? But I don't know why of all countries only England, which is not far from here, has never asked me. Either-or (*monevsekh*—as my mama used to say).[29] Try to find out . . . I am totally ignorant about the orientation in art of the English. Or if an important gallery wants to exhibit me (a small one—for it is hard to gather from the collectors for a big one)—let them propose and we'll see. And then it will be in order to visit London.

In the meantime, the paintings I own (from the years 1907–1932) have left for 3 exhibitions in Holland. They ask me to go there.

And the drawings and engravings went to Budapest, to Dr. Patai. (Do you know him?)

Be well, write sometime. Don't be lazy.

Regards, Your devoted

Marc Chagall

Dr. Patai: Jószef Patai (1882–1953), Hungarian and Hebrew poet and scholar, editor of a Hungarian Zionist monthly, 1912–1938; then immigrated to Palestine.

Marc Chagall in Paris to Pavel Ettinger in Moscow

2/IV 932, Paris, 5, Avenue des Sycomores (xvi-e)/Villa Montmorency

[Russian] Dear Pavel Davidovich,

Thank you for your letter. How are you?

Rarely, very rarely, do I get greetings from my homeland. So please don't forget [me]. I would like to give you my book, *Ma Vie*. It is not my fault that you don't have it yet—but it is always waiting for you.

How are you? What are you doing? Here, as before, I work as much as I can. Now my exhibitions are in Holland; in Amsterdam[30] (was before in the Hague,[31] and is scheduled for Rotterdam[32]) in the Salon of the Dutch Society for Art. The opening was so official (I was personally invited with my wife) that during their speeches, my heart, as always, was heavy and I thought about something else . . .

I finished the books, *Dead Souls* and La Fontaine long ago, but Vollard, of course, procrastinates; such is his nature.

I am doing something else for him, too; but now I am procrastinating.

Be well, regards from my family.

Your   M. Chagall

my heart . . . was heavy: In his letter to Opatoshu of April 12, 1932 (see below), Chagall explains why his heart was heavy: During the speeches of the Prince Consort, the Mayor of Amsterdam, and the curator, "they talked to all the Goyim about my Jewishness," and Chagall was afraid it might "end with a . . . pogrom . . . "

something else: An allusion to the Bible, which was considered a "clerical" book and could not be mentioned in a letter to the Soviet Union.

Marc Chagall in Paris to Yosef Opatoshu in New York[33]

[Stationery: 15, Avenue des Sycomores (xvi-e)/Villa Montmorency] 1932 12/IV Paris

[Yiddish] Dear Opatoshu—how beautiful is your Purim gift . . . When we held the little book in hand and all 3 of us read it, we thought about you . . . You know how much we love you. How is your life? How are you? What are you writing and when will you come?

all 3 of us: Evidence that, along with Russian, Yiddish was spoken at home and Ida could understand it.

We just returned from Holland where I was invited by the Netherlands Art Society which organized my large exhibition. At the opening, the Prince Consort (the Empress's husband) came, and the Mayor of Amsterdam [made] a speech, and there was a lecture, and they talked to all the Goyim about my Jewishness . . . I just didn't know whether it wouldn't all end with a . . . pogrom . . .

My book, *My Life*, just appeared in French.

I thought of asking you if you could ask a good American (Jewish) publisher about publishing the book (with drawings from my youth) in American-English, [or] Yiddish. If there is any interest. Here, the French liked the book very much. Do you read French?

Be well. Heartfelt regards from my family.

Your faithful

Marc Chagall

Kosher le-Pesakh[34]

How many mistakes?

pogrom: Typical Jewish worry: If we Jews are too conspicuous (the Yiddish idiom is "we are large in their eyes"), it might end in a pogrom.

Marc Chagall in Paris to A.Z. Ben-Yishay in Tel Aviv

[Stationery: 15, Avenue des Sycomores (xvi-e)/ Villa Montmorency/Auteuil 22–69]

April 1932

[Yiddish] My Dear Ben-Yishay,

What do you think about me? Whatever you please, but not that I forgot the dear beloved Palestine or you personally. When I think about Eretz Israel, my eyes grow dark: why should I not still be with you and be able to paint it quietly. Well, we shall see. And now, how are you, how is everybody. And how is our dear Dizengoff? We get so sad when we think about him, we are so used to him. I am again on good terms with him, I shall not make any more artistic demands. Hopefully, we shall have a museum as in other nations.

What you are writing about my book *My Life*, which just appeared in French in Paris (with the publisher "Stock")—to give it to Shlonsky to translate, [publish] a fragment in *Ktuvim* and publish a book—I would not oppose it in principle; but since I promised Bialik many years ago that he would translate and perhaps publish it, we must first know whether he can do it. Could you please ask him, if you don't mind, whether he intends to translate the book and publish it, and also about conditions . . . This is a delicate, but necessary matter . . .

Isn't it too much bother for you? Please write. The book should also appear in German and English. And it is indeed good to publish it in the holy Jewish [i.e., Hebrew].

The poet Abraham Shlonsky (1900–1973), editor of the literary journal *Ktuvim*, promoted modernist Hebrew poetry in the spoken language and revolted against the Romantic Diaspora poetry of Bialik, written in the elevated "Holy Tongue." Despite Bialik's high prestige, the modernists were in vogue in the avant-garde Hebrew society in Palestine.

Please write. Be more diligent than I am. I shall be too. My regards to you. It was so joyful [in your country] . . . When I think about it . . .

> With regards, your devoted
>
> Marc Chagall

Forgive my [spelling] mistakes—

Meir Dizengoff in Tel Aviv to Marc Chagall in Paris

2 May 1932

[French] Dear friends,

I have been unable to write all this time since I had an enormous amount to do during March and April, when celebrations and meetings took place in Tel Aviv, which you probably read about in the newspapers.

The Purim Carnival, the Olympics, the Maccabbee Games and the Exhibition were extraordinarily successful this year. Thousands of people came to Tel Aviv to admire our city, which is developing more and more, and to attend the big athletic, national, and economic demonstrations.

I am satisfied to state that our efforts have not been in vain and that we have succeeded in placing Palestine and Tel Aviv in the rank of economic entities that create and produce[35] and consequently have the right to a place in the sun, like any ethnic and national group.

Returning to our Museum, I have the pleasure to inform you that it was open to the public last April 2, and despite all the difficulties of the beginning, we have four halls well adorned with works of art, which can appear in any museum. Even you, dear Master, who are so strict and demanding, would certainly be happy to be able to see how we have been able to select our paintings. Following your advice, we became very strict and refused about thirty or fifty works and kept only the best, in exchange for replacing them later on with even better ones.

You will receive in the mail the first catalogue that we published and you will be able to judge by the names that you certainly know.

I am glad to inform you that during the official opening of the Museum which was attended by the governor and dignitaries, I mentioned your name with gratitude to you, your talent, your advice, and the creativity you contributed to us so generously, enthusiastically, and out of love for "culture."

You can see from the documents that we have established an official board which includes 100 "Curators," which is to determine the fate of the Museum.

We were all sorry that you were not here for the opening of the Museum and we hope that you will be able to come next spring to celebrate Passover with us,

includes 100: This is either a snide remark, meaning "too many," or one superfluous zero.

and I shall try to present to you a great and rich Museum with works of art that will give you genuine pleasure.

Please accept my friendly, loyal, deep greetings, dear friends,

Yours

[Meir Dizengoff]

Marc Chagall in Paris to Yosef Opatoshu in New York

Paris 1—1933

[Yiddish] Dear Opatoshu,

Your [woman] artist could call me—Auteuil 22-69

If you are still publishing Yehoash's Bible—that's very good. I read somewhere that it stopped.

You write that Jews are angry with Asch for the medal. What can you expect from Asch who thinks only of himself. Both Asch's work and Asch's person are a "problem" for the "Jewish people," but not for artists . . .

You want to travel to Eretz Israel. There you will see real Jewish workers and the *settlements* as you feel them in the Bible. This was my strongest impression of the new Palestine.

I wish you a good year. All of you. We shall be happy to see you.

Your devoted

Marc Chagall

Asch: In 1932, Sholem Asch was awarded the Polish Republic's prestigious medal of the new Polish independence, Polonia Restituta. Jewish public opinion felt that the Polish government was anti-semitic and one should not legitimize it.

Marc Chagall in Paris to Yosef Opatoshu in New York

12/V [May]—33

[Yiddish] Dear Opatoshu

The book is beautiful, as [in other cultures]—the drawing came out perfectly.[36] I am happy. And your text is as strong as your shoulders (Thank God). I wish you success in the present time. About the country called Germany, I (like all Jews) cannot think quietly. May they burn . . . When will you be here?

If you have extra prints of my drawing in black and white (or a photo), please send it to me so I can give it for printing, if asked. How are you? You and the rest of the Jews in America? Warm regards from my family. Your devoted Marc Chagall.

Don't forget to forgive my mistakes

Marc Chagall in Paris to Yosef Opatoshu in New York

Paris   27/VI 1933

[Yiddish] Dear Opatoshu,

Thank you for the repros.

So you are staying in America this summer. Hopefully, we shall soon go to the countryside. To rest from "world politics"[37] . . .

The last news for me personally—a painting of mine from a museum in Germany (Mangeym) was carried around the city in a wagon and then burned.

Be well, your devoted Marc Chagall

Mangeym: Chagall's painting "The Rabbi" was burned in a Nazi ceremony in Mannheim. Chagall spells the H as G, and pronounces the name as in Russian.

Marc and Bella Chagall in Paris to Mayor Dizengoff in Tel Aviv

[Stationery: 15, Avenue des Sycomores (xvi-e)/Villa Montmorency]

3/IX 33 [stamp: Received 24 Sep 1933]

[Russian, in Bella Chagall's handwriting, often interspersing Latin letters]

Dear Miron Yakovlevich,

We wrote to you some two months ago. Did you get our letter? We have trouble, a mouthful, and no heart for letter writing. We don't even know whether you are in Tel Aviv or Prague. We are writing to you in any case, in connection with the first-rate German musical artists that have been hurled into France and could have found an application of their talents in Palestine. Rakovsky writes us that he told you everything.

He writes that you are close to the Philharmonic society which is headed by a young conductor. We don't know him, perhaps he is a talented man, but surely, even for his youth, is not as experienced as Oscar Fried. The latter wants to go to Palestine anyway. We are trying hard to convince him [to do so]. Though he is 60 years old, he is in full possession of his strength, which he is eager to give to Palestine.

Indeed, it would be good if Palestine could use such a major talent, good both in the sense of organizing an orchestra and in the sense of the propaganda for his concerts which were very successful throughout the world. Sometimes, we have to do with what is at hand, but why not use—from the very beginning of the creation of a Philharmonic Society—such a major talent who wants to go to Palestine anyway. But of course, he would be encouraged if he knew he wasn't going there in vain. What will remain for him to do in Palestine if he finds a young conductor in his place. It is enough that the musicians are young, they

Prague: The Eighteenth Zionist Congress was held in Prague, August 21–September 4, 1933, under the impact of the Nazis' rise to absolute power.

must be organized by a more experienced hand. The success and achievements of your musical society, which is dear to us, even from afar, depends on the strength and talent of the conductor-director.

Please find a moment, dear Miron Yakovlevich, and write to us about this matter. We embrace you strongly strongly

Marc Chagall   Bella Chagall

On a Music Academy in Palestine

In response to the previous letter, Dizengoff sent Bella a letter expressing great interest in her proposal and attaching a detailed response in German, written by Wolfgang Friedlander and Dr. Joseph Weisgerber in Tel Aviv. The authors stated: "Now that the foundation of a Palestine Philharmonic Orchestra has become a reality, the foundation of a Music Academy with Professors Bruno Walter, Oscar Fried, Arnold Schonberg, Godowsky, and Ossip Gabrilowich would be a further and significant step forward to the cultural building of Palestine, received with great joy by all those interested in music." In the present situation, with only a quarter of a million Jews in Palestine, the authors could hardly see enough local students, yet with such a famous faculty, students from abroad would be attracted. If the initiators could get the financial support for this enterprise in Europe and America, the Mayor and the musical circles in Tel Aviv would joyfully offer their collaboration.

The Tel Aviv Museum in Israel to Marc Chagall in Paris

September 17, 1933

[French] Dear Maitre,

The members of our Museum Committee have learned with sorrow that your painting in Mannheim was destroyed by a rampaging mob of Nazis who destroyed and burned it.

Fortunately, that auto-da-fé will inflict no damage to the spirit of your works or to your genius: the canvas is burned, but we still have Chagall as one of the great masters of the present time who reflects so majestically the life, faith, and hope of our people.

We send you our condolences for what happened to your "Rabbi," but at the same time we congratulate you on that baptism by fire that places you among the great Jewish painters who have achieved immortality.

As we enlarge our museum, we are planning to establish a "Chagall Room" in it, where we will gradually collect all the works of the great master.

Here, in the Tel Aviv Museum, your works will be protected from all sacrilege and will continue to serve the ideal of Beauty and Truth as long as the nation of Israel and the city of Tel Aviv shall live.

Yours,   [M. Dizengoff]

Between the Open Sky and the Fires of Broadway

Chagall's Illustrations for A. Lyesin's Poetry

Chapters 9–12 include many letters between Chagall and his Yiddish editor in New York, A. Lyesin, concerning illustrations for Lyesin's collected poetry. A. Lyesin (pseudonym of Abraham Walt, 1888–1938) was editor of the prestigious Yiddish cultural journal *Di Tsukunft* (*The Future*) in New York, where Chagall's memoirs and poems were published in the 1920s and 1930s. In 1938, three volumes of Lyesin's Yiddish poetry were published posthumously by the Forwards Association in New York, with thirty-four drawings by Marc Chagall. The drawings were never published in another language in conjunction with the poems they illustrated. A selection of the drawings with summaries of or quotations from the poems is given here.

Abraham Lyesin, editor of the Yiddish monthly *Di Tsukunft* (*The Future*): *A Popular-Scientific, Literary-Socialist Monthly*, published in New York from 1892 to the present.

Illustration for Lyesin's poem "Shavuoth"

On the night of the holiday, the sky opens, the boy has a vision of Mount Sinai, he hears God's voice and sees Moses descending with the Tablets; the face of Moses is a Sun shining in Mama's smile and in Father's gaze.

Illustration for Lyesin's poem "The Tall Rabbi—Rabbi Leyb"

The boy's grandmother tells him of an ancestor, a famous Rabbi and scholar, and both see him appear in the door, the ceiling is rising, so the tall Rabbi doesn't have to bend. He wears tefillin and a shroud, like a ghost coming from a cemetery at night.

Illustration for Lyesin's poem "The Water Drawing Festival [*simkhat beyt ha-shoeva*]"

Written in Metuchen, New Jersey in 1905. The poem describes an exulted Hasidic dance in the synagogue. A few excerpts in a literal translation:

Shouts, screams, deafening noise,
But no danger here—
Those are Jews raising their voices loud,
Not Ivans, God forbid!
Bottles of brandy stand ready
But throats are dry.
Jews get drunk to death
Just on smells, just on sights.
And when Jews get drunk,
Everybody, move away,
For the circle is determined
With a tune and with a stress:
In the shadow of his hand will he hide me
Under the wings of the Shekhina!

Tapping their feet,
Shaking their forelocks,
The dance carouses on benches and tables,
In a Cossack way for all to see.
God's Cossacks, hot Jews,
They forget the Exile,
The great calamities,
Roll up their sleeves.

Free, ever freer, wild, ever wilder
[. . .]
Oh, these are not the same people,
Those crooked backs,
Those yellow faces,
The languished, mute lips.

Thousands of years of longing,
　yearning,
reverberate in this blaring;
Souls burst and break out,
Chains break, jails fall!
Desolate Jewish souls,
Sated with sorrows,
Suffered to the fill in wars
Against every evil passion,
Burst out in a storm,
Free of matter, free of fear,
Free of the earth, and free of pain,
They bombard the Creator:
In the shadow of his hand will he
　hide me
Under the wings of the Shekhina!

Illustration to Lyesin's poem "Weariness"

New York 1928. The poem describes the author's studies in the prestigious Yeshiva (Talmudic academy) of Volozhin.

An image from the past emerges in my mind:

I sit in the yeshiva and study,

Compressed, forehead to forehead;

Dozens youths study aloud around my table.

Dozens of tables stretch out,

Screams mixing with screams.

Each student roars his own Talmud,

Yet the scream is all merged together.

Each one reveals lights and wonders,

But such a woe blows from it, such a woe.

[And the poem ends with a wish to escape, anywhere!]

Illustration for Lyesin's poem "The Pioneers"

New York, 1922. The poem is dedicated to the memory of Arkady Kremer, founder of the Jewish Socialist party Bund in Vilna in 1897. Lyesin describes the revolutionary elation, straightened back and dignity of the revolutionaries in terms of Jewish "Redemption." The demonstration carries red banners with the beginning of a Russian slogan: "Long live [Freedom]."

Illustration for Lyesin's poem "The Storekeeper"

Minsk, 1896.

The little storekeeper sits in his little store,
The hundredth store on the street.
He sits and waits for a customer;
The street is dark and wet.

Customers show up so rarely,
he sits and trembles with cold,
He yawns and conjures up dreams,
And ponders the world.

Illustration for Lyesin's poem "The Fires of Broadway"

New York, 1924. The poem describes the dance of lights and "flaming" buildings on Broadway, evoking images of his distant home town. The moon is lonely and lost above the fluttering lights of Broadway, while in his old home, a full, big, golden moon looks sadly down at the old synagogue. Chagall divides the painting into two worlds: Broadway and the Wandering Jew leaving his old hut.

Illustration for Lyesin's poem "My Poems [My Songs]"

Illustration for Lyesin's poem "Don Quixote"

Illustration for Lyesin's cycle "Distant Echoes"

The echo here is Chagall's own cemetery, a corpse in a shroud leaving his grave at night.

Illustration for Lyesin's poems

A violinist-cum-beggar.

Illustration for Lyesin's cycle "Poems about Russia"

New York, 1928. A merry-go-round Russian peasant.

Illustration for Lyesin's poem *"Fear not, Oh Jacob, my servant"*

New York, 1920.

I see him on the road to Haran, wandering—
The first Jew walking on his Exile path

Of all his wisdoms, he is left with a wandering staff,
Yet he dreams of a ladder to the sky.
At his head, a hard stone, all around a world full of fears,
Yet he sees just angels, he hears in ecstasy:
Fear not, Oh Jacob, my servant.

Illustration for Lyesin's poem "Yet Another Page, My People"

Minsk, 1894. The poem begins:

I recognized yet another page, my people,
yet another horror image of your book of life.

In Chagall's drawing, a pogrom in a small town. Sign in Russian "Lavk[a]" (store),
with the familiar three steps of his mother's grocery store. The church and the
store are shrinking, taken out of their city context.

Illustration for Lyesin's poem "The Grave"

The funeral procession gathers in fear
And looks out, like sheep to their slaughterer.

Chagall's mother on the three steps of her store, giving alms to the Burial Society.

Illustration for Lyesin's poems

King David. This is foreshadowing the great colorful image of King David in the National Museum Marc Chagall Biblical Message in Nice.

Illustration for Lyesin's poems

A revolutionary studying books in a Tsarist prison. Outside, gendarmes are lining up people for expulsion.

Illustration for Lyesin's poem "The Exile"

This shape of the man was later used for an image of the prophet Jeremiah.

In Years of Crisis: 1933–1939

The Guggenheim Connection

Solomon R. Guggenheim (1861–1949) was the fourth son of Meir Guggenheim, founder of the American branch of a Swiss Jewish family that had a mining business in the United States. Solomon Guggenheim collected modern art and founded the Solomon R. Guggenheim Foundation for the advancement of art in 1937. On May 31, 1939, "Art of Tomorrow": the Museum of Non-Objective Painting opened in New York. It became the Solomon R. Guggenheim Museum after his death, and moved in 1959 to its present location on Fifth Avenue, in a building designed by Frank Lloyd Wright specifically for the museum. The moving spirit and first Director of the Guggenheim Museum was Hilla Rebay.

Chagall was among the first artists in the collection. The Guggenheims met Chagall in Paris in the 1930s, bought some of his important paintings, and were instrumental in saving the Chagalls from Nazi Europe in 1941. Chagall's exhibition in Basel, in German-speaking Switzerland and on the German border, during Hitler's first year in power, was a "very important demonstration" indeed.

Marc Chagall in Paris to S. Guggenheim in New York

23 Sept 1933 [Stationery: 15 Av. des Sycomores, Villa Montmorency, Paris 16th]

[French] Dear Sir,

I hope that you and Mrs. Guggenheim are well. And I hope that you have not completely forgotten me. We have a very good memory of our jolly and amusing dinner at the Cochon au Lait.

You told me the other evening that you bought my "Paris Through the Window" of 1912, which pleases me very much. I am writing you now to tell you that I have received an invitation from the (Swiss) Kunsthalle of Basel to do a big exhibition of my works for their museum. They are making a great effort to gather the largest number of my most important paintings from 1907–1933 from all over the world. Many collectors and various museums have already agreed to lend their canvases. It is to be a very important demonstration. This institute of modern art has done rare, but important exhibitions of various French masters. I think that you must be informed about their fine propaganda for modern art.

Since I find in your collection a painting I like very much, I am enormously eager for it to appear in this large ensemble. Wouldn't you be kind enough to lend it (if you have only that one) for the exhibition. It will take place in November.

Mr. W. Barth, the curator of the Kunsthalle, has probably written to you about this. I entrust him with the shipment and insurance, and on that point you can be absolutely calm. I hope that your obvious affection for modern art will indicate to you the importance for the artist of this great presentation and I think that you would certainly agree to lend your painting, which would please me very much.

Please give my regards to Madame Guggenheim and please accept my best wishes.

Marc Chagall

Marc Chagall in Paris to Hilla Rebay in New York

[Stationery: 15. Av. Des Sycomores, Villa Montmorency, Paris 16e]

Sept. 26, 1933[1]

[French] Dear Madame,

Where are you? We don't see you anymore and we no longer know where to look for you. Do you still remember us?

But perhaps this letter will find you in New York nevertheless. I wanted to tell you that I have received an invitation from the Kunsthalle in Basel (Switzerland) to do a big exhibition. This institute of modern art is well known. It is making great efforts to gather the largest number of my most important paintings of 1907–33, sending for them from all over the world. Many collectors and certain museums have already agreed to lend their paintings.

I wrote to Mr. Guggenheim and asked him to lend my "Paris Through the Window" of 1912 for this exhibition. It is an important painting of the prewar period and it has to be part of that large whole. As an artist, you must understand that.

Urge my request with Mr. Guggenheim who is probably very busy. Your intelligence and your charm have always had a great influence on him.

Give us a sign that you haven't completely forgotten us and that you intend or at least want to see us again some day. Don't you?

With friendly greetings,/   Marc Chagall

Marc Chagall in Paris to Yosef Opatoshu in New York

Paris 1934   24/1

[Yiddish] Dear Opatoshu,

Forgive me for not writing before. I was busy, caught up . . . Your little book[2]— not quite little . . . Thank you. Jews seem to be starting to appreciate illustrated books, bibliographical[3] [items]. And what did people say about my drawing for your book? I'm "afraid" my life will pass and I will not have done the old and the new Jewish classics . . . Where are the crazy Jewish publishers? . . . And as to my Bible, the following happens: I made about 40 (copper) engravings of *Genesis* for Vollard—my publisher—and . . . "for the time being" (?!) I stopped because as my [Polish] maid told me *yesterday*: "*Panie*, in the street they say there is a 'crisis.'" But perhaps the crisis will change a bit and we shall be able to continue the Bible. Recently I was in Switzerland. The Swiss made a beautiful exhibition for my 25 years of work: 1908–1933, in almost 10 halls of the Basel museum, about 200 works from all the years.[4] I walked around the halls among strangers, Goyim . . . Unfortunately, it had a huge success, I think.

But all this is far from my confused head now . . .

You plan to come here, and to Palestine. It is worth seeing the Jewish historical stones and the new life in the colonies of the pioneers. I believe it will have a great impact on your art.

Dear Opatoshu, be well and don't forget us. My wife, still in bed with a "grippe," sends her regards, and my big daughter[5] remembers you very well.

Best regards, your devoted/   Marc Chagall

---

crazy Jewish publishers: In Chagall's lexicon, "crazy" means creative (like himself) or willing to risk for a cause they believe in.

Unfortunately: A typical Chagallian expression of modesty, and also a Yiddish way of belittling success, to ward off the Evil Eye.

Marc Chagall in Paris to A. Lyesin in New York

Paris 1934   24./I

[Yiddish] Dear Lyesin,

I look at the cover and see: Your *Tsukunft* [= *The Future*] is 20 years old.[6] True, our Jewish future is still in the future . . . Nevertheless, I want to send you my best wishes on your—our birthday.

Your devoted /   Marc Chagall

P.S. What happened to your book of poetry for which I made many illustrations?

Marc Chagall in Paris to Yosef Opatoshu in New York

Paris 1934

[Yiddish] My Dear Opatoshu

I got your note from Palestine. Happy man that you are, you looked at our Jewish stones, which (it seems to me) our Yids won't be able to rebuild . . . Your heart grows bitter when you see their new tiny houses and the "palaces" and the taste . . . I read in the "newspapers" that they received you well—a good sign. Go in good health to Russia. And from time to time, please don't forget your somewhat sad Chagall. If you travel near my city, think about me. I hope we shall see each other before you return to America. Here with us.

Be well, my dear Opatoshu. / Your most devoted   Chagall

And my family greets you from their heart.

And please go to the Moscow Yiddish theater to see Mikhoels, and tell them that they all forgot me over there, and I don't know why.

Marc Chagall in Paris to A. Lyesin in New York

15/III 1934   15 Ave. des Sycomores, Paris 16e

[Yiddish] Dear and Esteemed Lyesin,

I was happy to get a letter from you. You are well again, thank God. This is, surely, the main thing. You want to publish your poems. You must really show what a true Jewish heart can accomplish.

You want me to illustrate them. With pleasure. I love to crawl with my brush

our Yids: "Unzere yidelekh," a pejorative epithet, conveying the negative self-image of the Jews.

they received you well: Opatoshu was a Yiddish writer, whereas Palestine was revived as a Hebrew-speaking society. By accepting Opatoshu, the Hebrew community seemed to signal good will toward Yiddish.

I don't know why: A typical and naïve Chagallian complaint. It was dangerous in Stalin's Russia to correspond with friends or relatives in "capitalist" countries, especially with a "traitor" who had left the Soviet Union for the capitalist West.

inside a warm Jewish soul. But now comes a small problem. It is a side issue, but unfortunately, important. The dollar has fallen almost in half. And life here is very expensive, except for Sofol. [?]

I propose to make you carefully conceived illustrations, with the best imaginative powers of my heart and my craft.

Every illustration will be your property. And I ask $100 for every illustration. I shall make as many as you want. I hear that every young Jewish artist in America gets much more. I don't have their *khutzpa* and I don't want it, but unfortunately, I make a living from art and to tell the truth, I am ashamed to diminish myself in comparison with the others. I believe you recognize that I am asking the minimum.

You will get the things 1) as your own property; 2) with the right to publish them in an edition; 3) in addition to a regular edition, you can make a certain number in a deluxe edition. And fourth, I suggest you publish the originals in a separate album. I hope that all this will cover your expenses.

I am sorry we have to talk in another language as well [the language of money]. But we both understand what forces us to do it.

Think about it. In any case, I shall be happy to read your other poems. They are sincere and come from the heart.

With warmest regards/   Marc Chagall

You write that you want to have one of my works. It touches me very much. Please write about how much you want to spend, and I shall send you a few photos to select.

Marc Chagall in Paris to Meir Dizengoff in Tel Aviv[7]

[Russian] Paris, Passover 1934

From the very moment when I got closer to the Land of Israel, while I am still permeated by memories of the ghetto—Tel Aviv became my incessant vision. As soon as I recall it, I am sad that I do not travel to it again and do not settle there for good.

Never mind, dear Mr. Dizengoff, if we had some differences concerning the understanding of art . . . you, however, created a city—and its surface is caressed by all the colors, lines and volumes, mixed with the aroma of orange blossoms.

One might think that in those twenty-five years, Tel Aviv was built haphazardly, in haste, as our forefathers baked matzos in the desert. Future generations will celebrate the birthday of Tel Aviv as we celebrate our eternal Passover.

The commotion of politics, the persecutions of the Hitlerites, could squeeze our body (we are used to it), but our spirit is fresh and impenetrable, as it was and always will be.

Yet we are still not understood. And it seems to me: the more they humiliate us, the more we possess the "only truth," that with time perhaps others too will touch. And who knows, at that time Tel Aviv may become the second Jerusalem. And I am jealous of my grandchildren and great-grandchildren who will stroll in the boulevards of the sprawling city and will feast their eyes on the sight of Dizengoff in bronze riding a bronze horse in the city square.

bronze horse: An allusion to Pushkin's poem "Bronze Horse-man," with the bronze sculpture of Peter the Great riding a bronze horse in the city he founded, St.-Petersburg.

Marc Chagall in Paris to A. Lyesin in New York

Paris 27/VII 1934

[Yiddish] Dear Friend Mr. Lyesin

I got your letter. So, I shall make illustrations for your book for $700, as you suggested. And my drawings, after being printed, come back to me. I shall make them as good as I can. I hope you will be satisfied with them.

you will be satisfied: Eventually, Chagall made thirty-four illustrations for Lyesin's three volumes of poetry, published posthumously. See the Lyesin section following Chapter 11.

If this is agreed, please send me an advance, as a token that I have to work on them right away. As soon as all illustrations are ready, I shall write to you.

Will all your poetry get into one book? Once you sent me one book, typewritten. Will other things get into the same book? I am asking so I can understand the structure of your book.

As to my painting for your collection which you want so warmly to bequeath to Eretz Israel after 120 years, I shall send you several photos as soon as I have them, and you'll tell me which you like best. Then we shall conclude an agreement.

after 120 years: Meaning after his death. The Jewish blessing for long life is: "May you live to be a hundred and twenty."

I hope you will be satisfied with me and that we shall remain good friends as before, as I esteem you always

With my best, friendliest regards/   Chagall

Marc Chagall in Paris to A. Lyesin in New York

Paris 15 nov. 1934

[Yiddish] Dear Lyesin,

I am back from Spain and see no answer from you to my letter of July 27, 1934. Did you receive it? I don't know what you decided about the book. Should I continue the work?

438 *France Between Two World Wars: 1923–1941*

At this opportunity, I ask you: would the *Tsukunft* like my [essay], "An Artist's Journey to Palestine, Holland, and Spain"?[8]

> With best regards/   Your devoted   Marc Chagall

Ida's Wedding

On November 22, 1934, at the age of eighteen, the Chagalls' only daughter Ida married Michel Rapaport. Ida was a child of wanderings: She was born in Vitebsk, raised in both Yiddish and Russian, lived through times of hunger in Moscow, then in Berlin and Paris. She never went to school and was educated by private teachers, especially for music and ballet (which she studied with Madam Kshesinskaya, the former official mistress of Tsar Nikolay II, then in exile in Paris). Ida was raised to admire her genius father, center of all family life. Indeed, she devoted much of her life to Chagall, promoted his interests, cultivated friendships, initiated exhibitions, and helped her second husband Franz Meyer write his monumental Chagall biography. According to her first husband, Ida was highly intelligent, smart, quick, and a fine painter in her own right. She was a well-regarded and well-connected figure in French society after World War II.

Michel Rapaport was born in Berlin in 1913 to Russian Jewish parents. His grandfather owned a bank in Mogilev-Podolsk and sent his son to study abroad. Michel's father earned a J.D. in Heidelberg, but as a Jew, he could not practice law in Russia. The Rapaports spent World War I in Russia, came to Berlin in 1920, and to Paris in 1926, where they joined the elder Rapaport's sister Leah and her husband Osip Bernstein, a world-class chess champion and business lawyer. Michel's father became a dry-goods salesman and later, a representative of movies in Strassburg. Michel received a law degree and worked in the office of the tax lawyer I. Shchupak, a Polish Jew, a sociologist and highly erudite man, who spoke Yiddish and was Chagall's lawyer and friend. Though Michel came to France as a child, he carried a Nansen Passport (for "passportless" ex-patriots), and only in 1937 did he become a naturalized French citizen.

Michel met Ida in a summer camp for Russian children in France, when she was thirteen and he was sixteen. At the age of eighteen, when she was pregnant, her parents forced her to marry Michel and terminate the pregnancy; revolutionary sentiments seem to have had little bearing on bourgeois habits. From Chagall's point of view, economically, it was "marrying down," yet Michel's upbringing was superior to Ida's in culture and literature. Apparently, the marriage was not ideal, but there was a communion of cultural understanding between Ida and Michel, which survived their divorce in 1948. In October 1937, Michel was drafted for two years into the French army as an infantry private. In November 1938, after the appeasement of Hitler at Munich, he became a translator from Russian and German for the Deuxième Bureau (French intelligence) and served in the army until the collapse of France. He was demobilized in July 1940.

Marc Chagall in Paris to Sh. Nigger in New York

Daniel Charny (Charney, 1888–1959), was a Yiddish writer and cultural activist, the brother of Sh. Nigger and B. Vladek; he lived in Paris in the 1930s and came to the U.S. in 1941.

Paris 1934, Nov.

[Yiddish] Dear Mr. Nigger

I was happy with your gift [the tales of Rabbi Nahman] Bratslaver, received via [your brother Daniel] Charny. Thank you! One look at the book is enough for me—to see my "former" city with my parents and all the Jews. But when will I be able to make drawings for such a book (and the other, authentic Jewish books) . . . When will a Jew, a publisher ask me to do it . . . [Continuation in Russian] I sit at the seashore and wait for the weather . . . In "hundreds" of years maybe the Jews will have a "renaissance" and our progeny—the artists will have great "mazl" [good luck]. Instead of us, it is they who will produce books (with prefaces by other Niggers) and painted murals.

In the meantime, be very healthy/And let us not forget each other

Your Marc Chagall

Marc Chagall in Paris to Yosef Opatoshu in New York

[early 1935]

Dear beloved Opatoshu, how are you? Warmest regards to you on your 25th anniversary of writing.[9] You've read my words—be well and write ever better and
better, as you wish for yourself. Thank you very much for your book, where I read
with pleasure about Soviet Russia. True, it is after your voyage there. But I believe that you are the only writer who will say the truth about what you saw there.
We regret very much that we didn't see you then. It is always so interesting to listen to you. When will you come now? I heard that you are travelling around
America? And what shall I write about myself? I am now "sad" because the work
for the Bible which I began to make for the Christian publisher—Vollard—was
stopped because of the crisis. I made 40 pages of engravings for the first volume
(as in Yehoash). He printed these pages in 375 copies, and like *Dead Souls* and
LaFontaine's *Fables*, he hid it all in the "cellar" and that's it. So now they are
looking for a crazy publisher who would continue the Bible . . . But Jews . . .
Have you ever in your life heard of a [Jewish] publisher who would "dare" to
make individual volumes of the Bible with Chagall's engravings (as Vollard did)?
That's how it is. They [the Jews] think about a committee, they think about who
knows what. If you were here, [we] would have heard an opinion.

What are you doing now? Write sometimes, don't be lazy. My family (they live
upstairs here) greets you warmly.

Be well/your devoted/   Marc Chagall

first volume: The first
volume of Yehoash's
Bible translation
included the books of
Genesis and Exodus.
Indeed, Chagall's
engravings of that
time illustrate these
two books only.

Marc Chagall in Paris to Aleksandr Benois in Paris

Paris 1935 March

[Russian] Esteemed Aleksandr Nikolaevich,

I am not in the habit of writing to critics. For criticism is "free." But you are also
a Russian—and for me this question immediately assumes a "sick" turn. Don't
think that I am complaining about anything, though over the years I have gotten
the image of a complainer. But believe me: I may have some internal reasons for
that, which are not familiar to you, a man of different roots. In essence, it seems
that you and I cannot find a common ground, as people and artists of different
generations and artistic world views. We might have said "our dialogues are
short" . . . if I had not remembered the excited lines you wrote once upon a
time—when both around us and inside us everything was exciting (I had lost
those reviews in Russia and was happy to reread them now). But a great deal of
water has flowed under the bridge since those days.

different roots: An
allusion to the Jewish
feeling of alienation
vis-à-vis Russians, in
Russia or in Paris.

But before that period (1914) I was unknown to you, because everything I did abroad from 1908 to 1914 got stuck abroad, and there and then I was an "other," whom you would not have "accepted." Only one thing is painful to me: that you may think I was not and am not "serious." I am sorry I don't have a copy of my book *Ma vie* with me—you would have seen: was I born in the world to be "not serious" and "indulge in whims," or "joke" . . . Especially since, in my childhood, I had a *chemistry* of seeing our Russian art beginning with the time of Stasov, and both before and after the Revolution. No, we shall apparently never be able to communicate with the Russian artists in our artistic language, though I was born in Russia and am bleeding with ("undivided") love for her, I remain a stranger to all its regimes—Old Russia, Soviet Russia, and the emigration. But I do not want to finish this letter in a "weeping" tone. On the contrary: I am grateful to you for many warm words in your article. And I would like to hope that sometime in the future the work of some Russians abroad will be taken seriously for the good of the homeland and its art.

emigration: In Old Russia, Chagall had no Right of Residence permit in the capitals; for the Soviets, he was a renegade; and the Russian emigration in Paris all but boycotted him and other Jewish artists born in Russia.

With deep respect to you/Greetings/Marc Chagall

Marc Chagall in Paris to Hilla Rebay in New York

March 25, 1935

[French] Dear Friend Hilla Rebay,

I am really not to be forgiven for answering your nice letter only now.

But if you knew how hard it is for me to sit down to write. I am extremely lazy, except perhaps for my work. But believe me, I think of my friends more often than it seems. And when I do think of you, it seems to me that I am talking to you. But you don't hear me.

Thank you for your nice thoughts about me. Right now I have a room at the Petit Palais where I exhibit with a group of artists: Dufy, Lhote, Laurens, etc. I have a great deal of moral success—but no one buys anything. It is quite discouraging. In January, the Kunsthalle of Zurich organized an exhibition of my gouaches of that summer, made in Spain where I spent my vacation. I had a very great success and I sold some things. I hope that it is already very good.

When will you return to Paris? You are, perhaps, the calmest voice here. How is the interest in art in your place at this moment? Difficult? And I have a crazy desire to paint murals, frescoes. And my Bible, which Vollard interrupted (the Depression has also struck him). I did Genesis and Exodus for him in 40 engravings. I think you saw them. I like that work so much and I penetrated it so deeply that I can't stop at that first book. I am seeking a means of continuing it. A book on the Prophets, Kings, The Song of Songs—so many interesting things. Perhaps you would think of finding me a big publisher in America. Would Mr. Guggenheim be interested in doing that book. It doesn't require a lot of money. I would be grateful to you if you interest Guggenheim or someone else in my Bible or in mural painting. Mr. Guggenheim is so nice and I think he likes what I do.

My hands are burning with the desire to work. If you write to me I will be very happy and don't be angry that I haven't answered you.

With friendly greetings,/Marc Chagall

Marc Chagall in Paris to Leo Kenig in London

April 1 [?] Paris 1935

[Yiddish] Dear Kenig. How are you?

I am writing to tell you that Leicester Gallery [in London] suddenly invited me to exhibit with them this month. I accepted their proposal, though apparently they don't have much space. This is regrettable because I shall be able to send only *some* of the last works, not many and not of all the years as it was recently in the museums of Basel and Zurich. But let it be a first greeting . . . to you—my first friend from our young years, and to the Jews. The exhibition (not large in numbers or perhaps in space) is sponsored by the [British] Ambassador [in Paris] Lady Clark, which I accepted—for she is a friend of ours (an artist herself) and offered it herself.

In the present time of anti-Semitism, we must value Gentile friends. I personally will probably not come (with my face, which I myself am fed up with . . .) My dear daughter is eager to go. I don't know whether she will stay with the daughter of [Sholem] Asch or with her [Ida's] uncle (for she is married). Please look her up. I'll give her your address.

Ida's uncle: Michel Rapaport's uncle lived in London.

And how are you? Don't be lazy, write!

Your devoted   Marc Chagall

Marc Chagall in Paris to André Dunoyer de Segonzac in Paris

[1935?]

[French] Dear friend,

Would you like to come on Sunday, April 7, at 5 o'clock to have tea with us and a few friends, including Lady Clark who will also be happy to see you. We hope to see you.

Segonzac: He taught at the art school La Palette, which Chagall attended for a while during his first stay in Paris. They met also on Friday evenings at Canudo's.

Lady Clark: Wife of the British Ambassador in Paris.

Best wishes/   Chagall

Bella and Marc Chagall in Paris to Meir Dizengoff in Tel Aviv[10]

May 1, 1935

[Russian] Our Dear Friend,

How are you? Are you entirely well? We have no time to write, yet we would like so much to know how you are, how is your health, are you in full bloom, how is Palestine now, and simply we would like to embrace and kiss you.

We are now for a few weeks in a village. We were sick and very tired. And here, in the expanses of fields and woods, we are resting. We travel by car on all the major and minor roads, as the Eternal Jews, and when we look at the old churches, rising to the sky, it seems to us that the true sky with the God that shines to us is with you [= in your country]. We often think and daydream about you [= your country]. We are here, "grandpa and grandma" alone, our daughter is in London, there we have an exhibition, just opened (April 27–May 18).

From the first impression, it seems to have a great success. The exhibition was opened and sponsored by our good friend, Lady Clark, l'Ambassadrice de la Grande-Bretagne à Paris. She came from her estate especially to open the exhibition. It seems that the English like it and even bought paintings, and all, of course, "Goyim," and I dream so much of being in "Jewish hands." But for that (not for the price) one needs to bring together *a por minyonim Yidn*[11] [= several dozen Jews[12]], as was done for Liebermann's paintings at his last exhibition, which was posthumous.

Max Liebermann (1847–1935), President of the Berlin Academy of Art 1920–1933, deposed by the Nazis. There was no audience for Liebermann's posthumous exhibition, for non-Jews could not attend an event for a "Jewish" artist. Chagall associates Jewish separateness with persecution.

Well, when will we see you again. Please come especially to see us, where we would hug you hard and kiss you,

Your friends,/   Bella and Marc Chagall

If you cannot come to us [= to Paris], we shall venture out to you, but this is a dream, as sweet as Palestine *mit mandlen un rozinkes*[13] [= with almonds and raisins].

Chagall in Vilna (then Poland) for the YIVO Tenth Anniversary Conference, 1935. Entrance to the forest colony for undernourished city children. Sign in Yiddish and Polish: "Colony for Weak Children in the name of Tsemakh Shabad, at the society TOZ, Vilna." TOZ—Polish initials (OZE in Russian) for Society for the Protection of Health among Jews. From left to right: Director of the Colony Dr. Abraham Hrushovski (father of Benjamin Harshav), Daniel and Mrs. Charny (Yiddish writer and cultural activist in Paris), Bella and Marc Chagall, distinguished Jewish historian Shimon Dubnov, TOZ officials dentist Nudelman and Grisha (Hersh) Matz.

At the Tenth Anniversary of the YIVO in Vilna

A conference on the occasion of the tenth anniversary of the founding of the YIVO (Yiddish Scientific Institute) was held in Vilna (called by the Jews "Jerusalem of Lithuania," to indicate its stature as a cultural capital of East European Jewry). The conference celebrated the scholarly achievements of the YIVO, and it was attended by Marc Chagall and the prominent Jewish historian Shimon Dubnov (Simon Dubnow, then age seventy-five). Chagall opened the new Museum for Jewish Art at the YIVO, which he had initiated in 1929.[14] He exhibited 116 engravings for the Pentateuch, La Fontaine's *Fables*, Gogol's *Dead Souls*, the Bible, and his own *My Life*. An exhibition of Jewish artists was also mounted.

Vilna belonged to Poland between 1920 and 1939, and it was close to the Byelorussian border. Chagall felt the proximity, in spirit and nature, to his mythological Vitebsk, which he could not reach.

Marc Chagall in Paris to Yosef Opatoshu in New York

16/7 1935   Paris

[Yiddish] Dear Dearest Opatoshu,

border of my city: A reference to Chagall's ostracism in Soviet Russia, including his city of Vitebsk.

without entering: An allusion to Moses, who was allowed to see the Promised Land but not enter it.

What are you doing in the heat? Finally, I move to travel to Poland, Vilna, *Litah*. To get up to the border of my city and tell her that she does not love me, but I love her . . . And shall return without entering her . . .

We shall probably be there several months. We use the invitation of the Vilna Institute [= YIVO]. And you? Where, what? Write.

Your devoted   Marc Chagall

Collective Postcard from Vilna to Yosef Opatoshu in New York

Wilno,[15] 12/VIII—1935

[Yiddish] Dear Opatoshu. Best greetings to you from here. And you will come here too. The city is like Vitebsk—even more beautiful. [Marc Chagall]
Warm regards to the dear friend—once in a long time—Sh. Dubnov
Great, warm regards almost from our homeland/Bella Chagall

At the Colony for Weak Children, Vilna 1935. From left: Daniel Charny, Shimon Dubnov, Mrs. Dubnov, Bella and Marc Chagall, Grisha Matz.

Marc Chagall in Vilna to the Tel Aviv Museum in Tel Aviv

Wilno, 6 September 1935

[German] To the Tel Aviv Museum

Dear Sir,

For some time I have been traveling and hence your letter[16] was delayed, as well as my reply. I am currently in Wilno, where I was invited by the Yiddish Scientific Institute [YIVO] to open the local museum.

Thank you for your offer to participate in the opening exhibition of the Tel Aviv Museum. Palestine, Tel Aviv, the Museum, Dizengoff—are all close to my heart.

I was once invited to Palestine by Mr. Dizengoff and we talked a great deal about that.

But unfortunately, for a long time I have not participated in group exhibitions. If there is to be a special exhibition of myself, as was organized in many other countries, that would lead to shipping costs which are always covered by the organizers.

Yet, you have so many of my things that I gave as gifts to the Museum, that you can easily fill a hall, especially since, as I am told, my things have almost never been presented.

At any rate, I thank you for your kind offer and hope that you will organize the exhibition beautifully.

I wish you great success. / Marc Chagall

Marc Chagall in Paris to Pavel Ettinger in Moscow

Paris. February/1936 Vezelay [Postmarked February 15, 1936]

[Russian] Dear Pavel Davidovich,

I was happy to get your greetings . . . though rarely. True, I too get "lazy," though often I start writing somewhere, and all those begun letters sleep their "eternal sleep." I got your regards in time for the exhibition at the Beaux Arts "Stages" of art history: "Expressionism."[17] I even thought of sending you an illustrated catalogue . . . By the way, in 1935, I had exhibitions at the Kunsthalle in Zurich, in Prague, in the Petit Palais in Paris, in galleries in London and Amsterdam. In its size, it is half of Europe.

I hope that some time, the second half of Europe, the closest to my heart [Russia], will want to see my exhibition . . . "sing, swallow, sing" . . .

Concerning my books, i.e., the engravings I did for the publisher Vollard, they sleep their sweet sleep without waking—in his storage . . . 100 engravings of Gogol's *Dead Souls* lie there (I gave a complete set as a gift to the Tretyakov Gallery [in Moscow]),[18] along with 100 engravings for La Fontaine's *Fables*, 40 engravings for the Bible and their continuation . . . I don't know how to shake him up to publish it . . .

My specialists saw it, remembering my early engravings, made for Cassirer in Berlin in 1923, *My Life*, and praise it. And more about my life, I think, you hear from L.O. My daughter married into their family. A good boy. Do you remember my wife, whom you met, I think, in Moscow?

Write [to me] sometime. It is pleasant to think that somebody remembers you in your homeland. What's new, how do you live?

Devoted to you / Marc Chagall

L.O.: Leah Osipovna Rapaport-Bernstein, the aunt of Michel Rapaport, Ida Chagall's husband.

Marc Chagall in Paris to Dr. Otto Schneid in Vilna[19]

[Yiddish] Dear Dr. Schneid!

. . . I am very happy that you were invited to [head] the Jewish Museum at the YIVO. I shall be happy when we Jews finally have a museum, where you can feel and see our history, the old and the new. You will have a lot of work, for unfortunately, our people are both poor and do not live in the spirit of art. We lack not only "leaders" in life, but young, new, modern men of art, who would show and explain. I thought about you.

I wish you success and please let me know once in a while how it goes.

With best regards, your devoted / Marc Chagall /   Paris 1936/III/23

Marc Chagall in Paris to Yosef Opatoshu in New York

III/31—Paris 1936—III/31

[Yiddish] Dear Opatoshu. Received your book. About the childhood years. I am very grateful that you often send me Yiddish books. This way I have more "contact" with Jews . . . True, I sit in "contact" with the Bible, which I am "dying" to finish . . . There are a hundred buts. This is how the time goes. You write that next year you will be 50 years old. So I looked especially in my passport and made calculations from "all sides," and the same story appears with me (after 30 years of daubing). *Gevald!* A man with a smile. They will not believe me. Neither will I myself. Perhaps my father daubed in a few years for me because of the *prizyv* [= army draft]? All the same, nothing doing. You are not just an American, but Polish, and a Jew. My fatherlands are perhaps only on my canvases,[20] but "Vitebsk" is "closed off" for me (for me as *such* an artist . . .), not France (a different spirit), and not Palestine or other Jew-countries (for Jews do not love and appreciate art . . .)

Where are the Jewish "Medicis" of the Renaissance and the walls where we could express our artistic feelings as I once did on the walls of the Moscow Yiddish theater.

But dear Opatoshu, in the meantime I kiss you.

As I love you from the depths of my heart.

My wife is now in a clinic. She had another operation. Well, it is better now. We send our warm regards. Please write sometime.

Your very devoted / Marc Chagall

Marc Chagall in Paris to Yosef Opatoshu in New York

Paris 22/IV 1936

[Yiddish] I hasten to send you a few reproductions of my Palestine things. Would it be useful to you? Thank you very much for your book of short stories. I'll read it in bed (the best way) and learn Yiddish. Well, Bella is better, though she is still in bed. And I work and sigh like all the Jews in the world, who are being beaten now even in the Holy Land . . . And because of all that, I become even more Jew. Pity on us . . .

Holy Land: A reference to the so-called "Events" (or, as the Arabs called it, the "Great Revolt"), Arab attacks on Jews in Palestine, 1936–1939.

In the meantime, be well/My wife greets you/Your very devoted

Marc Chagall

Marc Chagall in France to Yosef Opatoshu in New York

Chagall received the first volume of *Zamlbikher* (*Collections*), thick literary almanacs, edited by Y. Opatoshu and H. Leyvik in New York. Those were the most prestigious publications of worldwide Yiddish literature of their time. Volume 1 was published in May 1936, 447 pages. Subsequent volumes were published in 1937, 1938, 1939, 1943, 1945, 1948, and 1952.

[August] 1936

[Yiddish] Dear Opatoshu, I congratulate you. Received the *Zamlbikher*. Much success and long life. And may the literature not forget the poor Jewish art. We sit here among Goyim. A year ago this time we were in Vilna . . . I would be happy to be next year in . . . Vitebsk . . .

Fantasies—with best regards to you

from us, devoted   Marc Chagall

Marc Chagall in France to Pavel Ettinger in Moscow

1936. August 29.

[Russian] Dear Pavel Davidovich,

I sit in a "dacha" and remember you [=your country]: our tree is different, the sky is different, it is all not that, and with the years, these comparisons play on your

nerves . . . With the years, you feel more and more that you yourself are a "tree"
which needs its own soil, its own rain, its own air . . . And I begin to think that,
somehow, I hope soon, I shall pull myself together to travel to refresh myself in
my homeland and work in art [there]. I want first of all to finish with Vollard. For
my books, *Dead Souls* and LaFontaine's *Fables*, which I did a long time ago, are not
yet published by him, and the Bible, started long ago, is still in process . . .

Well, how are you? What's new? How is the field of art in the homeland? I
would like to get some art journal—to have some kind of contact, otherwise I am
too much forgotten and alienated. Write sometime. Nobody writes to me [from
Russia] except you.

I press your hand./Your devoted   Marc Chagall

Marc Chagall in Paris to Otto Schneid in Vilna[21]

[Yiddish] Dear Dr. Schneid:

On the publication of the first issue of the *Journal for Jewish Art* by the Museum at
the YIVO, I send you my best wishes.

I have thought a lot about it.

Humanity today is far from both art and humanity. And I have often thought
that my erstwhile talks and plans about a museum and about art are perhaps off
the mark.

And after my trip to Poland, when I saw the Jews almost dying of starvation, I
was even more upset.

But—no!

May everyone help build our real Jewish art, our Jewish museum foundation,
our science of art, our strength! May your journal serve those goals successfully.

Paris, October 1936/Marc Chagall

Marc Chagall in Paris to Pavel Ettinger in Moscow

Oct. 4, 1936. Paris

[Russian] Dear Pavel Davidovich,

I was so happy to get a brief letter from you and the books and journals about art,
which gave me an idea about what is happening in the field of art in my beloved
homeland. Thank you. How can I show my gratitude to you? This Vollard won't let
anything out of his hands that I could send you. Are you interested in any books or
journals published here? I would gladly send you. You are writing that soon (?)

you'll be 70. When? Let me know so that I could send you my warm greetings "on time" . . . I myself will be 50 next year and 30 years of work. And if anything warms my heart thinking about it, it is my passion for my homeland; for it bathed in its own way in my art, and I think about it all the time. Though in the world I am considered an "international" [artist] and the French take me into theirs, I think of myself as a Russian artist, and this is very pleasing to me. Be well. Thank you for not forgetting me. My voyage [to Russia] ripens in me gradually. It will, I hope, re-

because of the "Crisis":
Some people returned
to Russia for economic
reasons, because of
the Depression (the
"Crisis") of 1929.

fresh or renew my art. But I shall not go, like others, because of the "Crisis" . . .

Not bread, but my heart . . .

> Be well and don't forget me./Your devoted Marc Chagall

New address: 4, Villa Eugène Manuel, Paris XVI

Marc Chagall in Paris to Pavel Ettinger in Moscow

Paris [October] 1936

[Russian] Dear Pavel Davidovich,

It pleases me to send you these lines on your 70th birthday [October 27, 1936]. Though, true, we met each other, regrettably, very rarely; true, you almost never wrote about me; and I, alas, read so little of you; and nevertheless—you are so close to my heart—why?

I value the human being in you and the human being who loves art. I am grateful to you, moreover, because you are almost the only one who sends me from time to time a few words from my homeland. Without its air, it is difficult for me to live and work. I send you my warmest wishes and embrace you hard, hard.

> Sincerely devoted to you   Marc Chagall

P.S. I am sending you some books about art.

Marc Chagall in Paris to A. Lyesin in New York

Paris 10/IX 1936

[Yiddish] Dear Friend Lyesin

Received your letter with the advance. Thank you.

I was sorry to read that you think I did not send you my letter, for I make a "business." First of all, when I wrote you lately, I was in the country and didn't have the letter with me. Secondly, I didn't think you needed it back. I send it to you in this letter. And to finish this, I shall only tell you, dear friend Lyesin, that I have been working for 30 years and next year, God willing, I will be 50 years old, and I think I have nothing to be ashamed of before other artists—but not one of them lost so many paintings and was cheated as much as I in my life. That is how "practical" I am.

As I wrote to you, I read all of your poems all summer and made drawings to them. I tried to match their innermost sense to the various cycles and moods of your poetry.

Vladek visited me. He liked it. So I hope you will like it too and you will be content with me. Vladek was nice enough to take them with him. Thus it will reach you faster. I gave him the 26 drawings and discussed the technical side of printing it with him. I want each little dot, that also plays a role, to be noticeable and the whole thing should be delicate. I asked Vladek to make sure that they send me proof-sheets of each drawing before printing.

Be so good as to send me the remaining $400, as agreed in your letter. But please write my name on the check: Marc Chagall. This is more correct.

> *Vladek*: B. Vladek (or Vladeck) was director of the Forwards Association, the publisher of Lyesin's poetry in New York.

Regards. Your devoted /   Marc Chagall

Marc Chagall in Paris to A. Lyesin in New York

[Stationery: 4, Villa Eugène Manuel. XVIe]   1936   Paris

[Yiddish] Dear Friend Lyesin. I received your letter and the check. Thank you. I am glad that you like my drawings to your book. I hope they will be well and beautifully printed. As to the other drawings to other chapters—I did it, as you wrote—according to your old plan. Since the book is apparently now planned differently and we need to make a few more drawings—so what can I do—I shall have to make a few more. Though I spent my summer on them. But I think that either/or: either the drawings are all my property, or are all yours, for what is important is *the ensemble*. Not to divide them. And when I say yours, I mean that they will enter as originals in one original (best paper and something from your manuscript) special books which (I need not give you any advice) could be bought by a bibliophile or can be given as a gift to a national library, whatever . . .

If you need a few more drawings, I shall charge about $35 per drawing.

As to the front page—I think—it should not be in color but we can make a drawing in black-and-white in the *middle* of the page and the typesetter can print the letters (not all, just the title, or your name) in another color . . . And the rest in black-and-white. This, it seems to me, will be noble. This is how my Paris publisher makes his greatest books.

You are writing about the paintings. As I understood, you offer me for both paintings—"At the Wailing Wall" and "In the Gaon's Prayer House"—$200. I am very sorry, but I must tell you, though I would have liked my Jewish paintings to be in Jewish and friendly hands—still your proposal is very far from my prices. Those are large, elaborate oil paintings. The size of "The Wailing Wall" is 92 x 73 [cm] and the Vilna Synagogues are 81 x 65 (the old Vilna Synagogue with the green [?]) and 63 x 74 ("The Gaon's Prayer House") respectively.

Well, write me what you think. With best wishes

Your devoted   Marc Chagall

P.S. You know, I wrote a long poem in Yiddish ["My Distant Home"[22]]. If you give me a "respectable place" and pay a good "poetic" honorarium—I shall send it to you—if you want—

M.Ch.

Hilla Rebay in Paris to Rudolf Bauer in Berlin

[Excerpt, translated from German]   12 September 1936

Dear Rudi,

[. . .] We have bought four excellent Chagall oil paintings (unfortunately, he is very badly off) and it is the first time G. [Solomon Guggenheim] has bought anything from him himself, but he is such a dear, touching person. Actually, we bought a great deal: one very large Chagall of 1914, the *Violin Player*, almost two m. [meters] high, extremely important and more expressive than *Paris through the Window*, and the *Birthday*, also 1914, of which there exists another version (that I like less) in Germany. We also bought two newer works, all together for 10,000 marks—or 60,000 francs. He *gave* me a present of seven watercolors, that is, one is a drawing which I chose myself, another is even an oil. All of them are excellent, two of them are from 1914, one from 1917, and signed.

He was *overjoyed* when I told him that you love his paintings. A load fell from his shoulders, for he always thinks he is no good and ought to paint as all of you do—which is not at all his style. Still, I prefer Chagall to most of the non-objective painters.

Postcard from Marc Chagall to Yury Pen in Vitebsk

(January 1937)[23]

[Russian] City Vitebsk, to the artist Yu. M. Pen

Dear Yury Moyseevich, how are you? I have not heard from you for a long time. True, I didn't write myself. And you are responding in the same coin. I am so eager to know how you are, how is your health, how are you working, and how is my beloved city. I am sure I would not recognize it now. And perhaps even my Pokrovskaya Street has changed. And how are my little huts where I spent my childhood and which we both once painted together.

How happy I would be on my (alas!) 50th birthday, which is approaching—to sit with you on a porch at least for an hour, and paint a study. You must write [to me]. When I die—remember me. I am waiting for your letter. Then I shall write more. I promise.

Your devoted Marc Chagall

Yury Pen's Death

Chagall's first teacher, the artist Y.M. Pen, was a Professor in the Vitebsk Technical Art School, founded by Chagall. The new name of the school inadvertently returned to the ideas of Israel Vishnyak. On March 1, 1937, Pen was brutally murdered in his own apartment. His students assumed it was done by the NKVD, the People's Commissariat for Internal Affairs—that is, the political police. But a Soviet trial was staged with trumped-up charges against the artist's niece and nephew and a student of Pen.[24] During the years of Stalin's terror, anybody with relatives or connections abroad (often as much as a post card received from outside the USSR) was persecuted as an enemy of the people. That would be worse in the case of contacts with such a traitor as Marc Chagall, who left Russia after the Revolution, and whose "unrealistic" art became unmentionable, especially in Vitebsk. Even anti-Semitic motivations were not beyond the imagination of the NKVD. Soon after Chagall's letter arrived, Pen was murdered. Was it a coincidence? The letter (partly damaged) is now in the Vitebsk Museum of Local Lore. Did it get there from the censor or NKVD? Did Pen ever read it?

Marc Chagall from Paris to the Relatives of Yury Pen in Vitebsk

(March 1937)[25]

[Russian] I cannot calm down and I don't know how to express my deep sorrow concerning the unexpected, gruesome death of Yu. M. Pen. I envy all of you who *my body here, my soul there*: An allusion to the famous "Zionide," a poem by Yehuda HaLevi (or Judah Ha-Levi, 1075–1141), a major Hebrew poet in Spain, who lived at the far West of the known world, and was longing for Zion in the East. Its opening line: "My heart is in the East and I in the end of the West."

one of his early pupils: Pen started his school in 1896–1897. Chagall started perhaps in 1900, and thus could have been one of Pen's early students, but if so, he studied with Pen about seven years, between 1900 and 1907, not "for a short time."

could attend his funeral, walk on our earth behind his grave, and all around you was the air of the sky I have tried so often to recreate in my paintings. Why doesn't this air reach me here, in the airless space? Why did destiny divide me in two—my body here, my soul there?

And I keep hoping I shall see Pen again, be in my city, go with Pen again to make sketches, as before, and paint again and again our now resurrected city.

Understandably, the Revolution has created other, new, unknown, "relatives," but I would like to tell Pen a few words. Pen loved me. His love continued for thirty years, from the moment I became myself, regardless of the differences in our artistic directions. He was my first teacher, though for a short time. I was one of his early pupils, and he knew that though I have lived in Paris since 1910, with short interruptions, nevertheless, spiritually, I remained devoted to my homeland, which I showed as much as I could in my art.

There are not as many colors and gloomy shades in which I would like to turn my last greetings to Pen.

Marc Chagall

Repeated Invitations to Palestine

The first Director of the Tel Aviv Museum, Dr. Karl Schwarz, invited Chagall to arrange a special Chagall Hall at the opening of the museum in October 1935. A long correspondence ensued, and Schwarz renewed his proposal for an exhibition to celebrate Chagall's fiftieth birthday in 1937. However, Chagall found various difficulties, although he declared that "Palestine is very dear to me." In 1937, on his fiftieth birthday, Chagall had his paintings committed in important exhibitions in Europe—always his first priority. Moreover, the Arab attacks on Jews in Palestine during 1936–1939 made the proposal dangerous. In a letter of February 4, 1938, Chagall wrote to Dr. Schwarz: "Your situation is not calm enough now either to think about a big exhibition. But the time will come, and I hope to exhibit nicely in Eretz Israel as well." The invitation was renewed by a later Director of the Tel Aviv Museum, Dr. Haim Gamzu, during the tense days before the United Nations decision on Palestine in 1947. Yet only in 1951, with the backing of the Israeli government, did a major Chagall show in Israel materialize.

Dr. K. Schwarz in Tel Aviv to Marc Chagall in Paris

Tel Aviv, 31.3.37

[German] Dear Mr. Chagall,

Since the last time I wrote to you, a great deal has changed here. Mr. Dizengoff had the joy of opening the new Museum building which has become a genuinely monumental building and one of the sights of the city. From the small and modest beginning, an impressive museum has emerged. We now have at our disposal a truly good collection which is generally respected. Since Dizengoff's death last autumn, we have made considerable progress. Dizengoff's appeal in his will to increase and take care of his favorite child, the Museum, has guided the attention of the entire Jewish world to the Museum. We now have beautiful, big halls, and also arrange regular exhibitions which are extraordinarily well attended. The artistic life is growing considerably here.

You, who are one of the founders and first donors of the Museum, will certainly be pleased at this news. To our joy, we can increase our collection with three of your big paintings through a special legacy. I am sending you at the same time a small guide which came out at the opening last year and is meanwhile, however, long outdated.

Why do I write all this to you now? You will soon celebrate your 50th birthday. Everywhere you will be celebrated on July 7, but I believe that the Tel Aviv Museum, the first Museum in the first Jewish city, has very special reason to celebrate the fiftieth birthday of the first and most significant Jewish artist of our time. The name Chagall is important everywhere, but here it has a special ring. I also think I am not mistaken if I assume that your constant interest in Palestine and especially in the Tel Aviv Museum will move you to support our intentions to mark your fiftieth birthday with a generous exhibition of your works. A Chagall exibition, for which we gladly offer the halls of the Museum, would release a storm of enthusiasm here.

Since, however, the month of July is the most difficult month here, I would like to put on this exhibition on September 15, around Sukkoth, opening the autumn season with it. I would gladly accept your suggestions and ask you to answer this letter soon so that we can calmly prepare the exhibition. There is enough space to hold a large selection of your works, 7 halls, including 2 smaller ones appropriate for graphics and drawings.

I look forward to hearing from you soon before I take further steps, and meanwhile all the best.

Your devoted, / [Dr. K. Schwarz]

Marc Chagall in Paris to Dr. K. Schwarz in Tel Aviv

22 April 1937

[German] Dear Sir,

I received your letter. Thank you very much for the good news about the Museum. I would like to hear such news all the time. [?] I am very glad that the Tel Aviv Museum is growing constantly and apparently is in the process of becoming an impressive museum. I am just sorry that the main founder, my good and dear friend Dizengoff, is no longer here.

Thank you very much for your invitation to organize a big exhibition of my works for my fiftieth birthday (How do you know that?) You put your halls at my disposal. Thank you. I once wrote you that I never organized an exhibition by myself and never covered the costs of it. I was always invited to do small, big, and very big exhibitions (like the retrospective exhibition in the Museum of Basel in 1933) and shipping to there and from here, insurance, advertising, catalogues—everything was covered by the museums or the galleries that invited me. Sometimes a certain sum of sales was even guaranteed. Can I be sure that someone will buy my paintings in Palestine? I don't say that as a complaint,—by no means—but only as a test.

When I was in Palestine, I was received very warmly, which touched me very much, but it didn't occur to anyone to commission something from me or to buy my works.

Palestine is very dear to me, I myself don't hope to profit from anything there. On the contrary, I gave a great deal as a gift to the Tel Aviv Museum, even though many Jewish artists, even those in Palestine, were bought. Dizengoff always wanted, as he often wrote me, to organize a Chagall hall in the Museum. But if that doesn't exist, it doesn't matter—no one is a prophet in his own country. Where is my country? And I'm not a prophet either.

To come back to your letter, if you want to organize my exhibit, please, write me if you can meet all the expenses.

Best wishes, / Marc Chagall[26]

no one is a prophet: Hebrew proverb: "No one is a prophet in his own city."

I'm not a prophet: So said the prophet Amos. An expression of modesty.

Marc Chagall in Paris to A. Lyesin in New York

Kreplyak: Yakov Kreplyak (1885–1945), a Yiddish writer and journalist, Editorial Secretary of *Di Tsukunft* under A. Lyesin during 1917–1938.

[Stationery: 4, Villa Eugène Manuel. XVIe]   Paris [May–June] 1937

[Yiddish] Dear friend Lyesin. Received the letter from friend Kreplyak. I hope you are well again. Soon, in the country, I think I'll do the rest of the drawings.

In the meantime, you can make negatives of the ones you have. How is it going? Let them write to me about it and send me proofs, as I agreed with Vladek.

Here is my first long poem in Yiddish (in the past, I sometimes wrote [poems] in Russian, but I lost them). To tell you the truth, I am afraid of your opinion . . . Therefore, you can imagine what I mean about your art of poetry and the spirit of your poems, and their Jewishness. But you saw some of it in my drawings. Well, be well, your devoted

Marc Chagall

As to the title of the long poem—I don't know how to call it. Perhaps simply: a poem of myself——

P.S. Take a look at my [spelling] mistakes (Yiddish I was taught by my mama, not the rebbe in *Heder*). Perhaps send the proofs later/in case a word is not clear? It would be better—more air—to print only one column on the page. But, [do] as you understand.

Marc Chagall in Paris to Dr. K. Schwarz in Tel Aviv

4, Villa Eugène Manuel, Paris 16e.　　　30/7 1937

[German] Dear Dr. Schwarz,

First, thank you very much for your good wishes on my fiftieth birthday.

Then, please forgive me for taking so long to answer your letter.

I have been very busy lately. I have participated in various exhibitions and was too tired to consider your offer.

Of course, I would be very happy to exhibit in Eretz Israel, especially in the Tel Aviv Museum which I helped my dear deceased friend establish.

But unfortunately, there is always a "but."

1) During the general exhibition of 1937 [in Paris], I am participating in various exhibitions, that is, many representative pictures are out (for how long, one doesn't know yet).[27]

2) For next season, I have various invitations. They are organizing a personal exhibition of my works in Paris and afterward in America.

Of course, your exhibition can be arranged in 1938 (30 years of my work, since my first picture "Death" of 1908). But then too, there are the issues of shipping, insurance (without frames, especially oils, I wouldn't send, accidental frames sometimes don't fit), and most important, when the things go out for 4–5 months—I won't have them.

Perhaps you like an exhibition of only watercolors and etchings? Thus you would have fewer expenses.

Any organization that invites me for an exhibition is either buying several pictures from me (if that's a gallery) or guaranteeing a certain amount of sales (if it's a museum). Palestine is dear to me, I cannot haggle with her, but I cannot lose everything. I doubt if anyone will buy anything from me in Tel Aviv. Unfortunately, I must think about it—for I live from that.

Please consider all these issues and write me. I am always willing to accomodate you and our Land. / With best wishes, / Chagall

Dr. K. Schwarz in Tel Aviv to Marc Chagall in Paris

23 August 1937

[German] Dear Mr. Chagall,

You wrote me all your arrangements about a big exhibition in Tel Aviv and I understand, even if I regret that in the interest of our Land. Of course you will do better business in Paris and America. But I think that the moral success—especially in these times when Palestine is in the middle of world interest—carries a lot of weight and that it is obvious that a famous Jew must show the utmost support for Palestine, now of all times.

I recently wrote to you of the amazing development of the Museum. I think you would be impressed if you saw our Museum: it is a very dignified building, very modern, with big bright exhibition halls, 20 by 10 meters bit, 2 stories; it is the most impressive sight of Tel Aviv. And the whole thing came about out of pure idealism, without money. And if anything here is crucial, if we Jews are disliked throughout the world, yet they have to accept our validity, it is only because of our *achievements*! This also involves the gradual conquest of this country for art.

I don't want to persuade you, but rather to invite you to make an exhibition in our Museum. I wrote you that we cannot behave like rich hosts. I wrote you that we assume all costs, but we cannot make any guarantees about sales. But I think I can guarantee you one thing: neither in Paris nor in America will there be as much excitement about an exhibition as here. Here an entire people will be grateful to you! And is that nothing?

You have reservations about sending oil paintings 1) because you need them for other exhibitions, 2) because you don't want to send them without frames. And you propose an exhibition of watercolors, etc.

If a large enough number of watercolors, gouaches, and drawings is available to make a *truly representative* exhibition, that is fine. I gladly accept this suggestion. But I ask you to arrange the selection so that it is a truly unified exhibition.

How many watercolors, gouaches, drawings, and graphics can you send?

When can we get this material?

Sending this material won't involve any difficulties for everything can be packed in one box. The sheets can be without passepartouts, for we will take care of the entire mounting here. We have several hundred clip-on frames. I only have to know *very soon* when you can send us the exhibition, for I now have to arrange my time. We have already lost a great deal of time and we are now missing the best time of the year. So, I ask you for your answer *by return post*. I hope that everything is now clear and that I will hear from you very soon.

Best regards,/[K. Schwarz]

A box with the materials in question needs to be lined only with oil paper and is to be sent by freight to the following address (please be very precise!): Museum Tel Aviv, Tel Aviv, Port Tel Aviv. Marc Chagall

Marc Chagall: My Distant Home (Autobiographical Poem)

Completed between March and June 1937. The poem covered the same territory as his autobiographical prose writings, presenting a world through its key figures. It was published in different versions in New York and Moscow; later separate sections (but not the complete text) appeared as separate poems and were translated into other languages.[28] The poem contains a section on the death of Yury Pen, who was murdered on March 1, 1937, thus it could not have been finished in 1936, when he wrote to Lyesin, offering it for publication (see the letter to Lyesin above). Yet elsewhere he moves the date of the poem back to 1935, apparently marking his awakening to write poetry in Yiddish during his visit to the Yiddish cultural fortress of Vilna. It is plausible that the inception of the poem was in Vilna, where he was nostalgic about his unreachable home town across the Soviet border.

I

It rings in me—
The distant city,
The white churches,
The synagogues. The door
Is open. The sky blooms.
Life flies on and on.

It yearns in me—
The crooked street,
Gray tombstones on a mountain.
Deep lie the pious Jews.

In colors, in daubs,
In light, in shadow,
My picture stands at a distance.
I would cover my heart with it.

I walk flowing and flaming,
The years flash.
My world comes to me in a dream—
I am lost.

Don't look for me today, don't look for me tomorrow.
I have run away from myself.
I will make a grave for myself,
I will melt in tears.

II

I see my father
Lying far away in the earth.
All night long he prayed.
He cast off all earthly things,
A cold sword slew him.

In synagogue, you waited for miracles,
A bitter tear would fall on your beard.
To Abraham and Isaac from the depths of your heart
You cried a word for sweet Jacob.

In the sweat of your brow you toiled all your life,
The weeping was the weeping of your hands.
Pale and mute, you fed us all—
Your children in the poor four walls.

You left me a legacy—
Your old, evaporated smell.
Your smile flows in all my senses.
Your strength moved into me.

My dead mother hovers in the air,
Barely breathing, crying alone:
"Where is my son, what is he doing now?
Once I rocked him in his trough,
May his path be blessed and pure.

"In travail I carried him, nursed him,
He sucked my first strength.
I taught him to say the *She'ma* at bedtime,
I led him by the hand into the world.

"Where are you now, my son?
You're in my memory.
Deep inside me sleeps a starry night."
And quietly she closed my eyes.

Only bones remained of you.
The young beauty is no more.
You lie alone among stones,
You abandoned me here.

I would have kissed your sand and grass,
Like your stone I would have cried.
I would have left my soul to you
And crowned you as a queen.

My old Rabbi's head is flying
Toward me with regards:
"I gave you my Torah,
You will not set foot in my home again."

No more my teacher with his brush, his little beard.
A robber killed him for two cents.[29]
A black horse carried him away
To the other world, through the gate.

His lamp went out.
A cloud peeps into his home.
Facing it, like a dolt,
Stands the church, bolted shut.

Your Jewish painting in the mud
A pig's tail daubed it over—
My teacher, I'm sorry
I left you long ago.

Let your name be mentioned, David,
My young brother is gone.
Left life with no honor
And no one knows where he lies.

My sisters laugh and cry.
They stand together in the door,
Look for something in the window
Always seeking happiness.

An old house with no window,
Inside it is dark at night.
I came out first
And stretched out my hand.

I see the river, the cool water.
At dusk I walk to the bank.
It flows into me a prayer
Singing calmly in the abyss.

You walk with your long hair,
With love, trembling, toward me.
You bestow on me a pair of eyes.
And I always want to ask you:

Where are my white flowers
From our *khupa* on the roads?
For the first time I came to you,
The whole night I lay with you.

We put out the moon
And ignited white candles.
My love flowed to you
And opened your face.

You became a wife to me,
For long years, sweet as almonds,
Your belly gave me a gift—
A daughter pretty as the New Year.
Thank you, God from the Ark of the Covenant,
For that day and in that month.

III

Oh, descend, my white cloud
And raise me up to you!
I hear the bells ring down below
And smoke rises from the houses.

My mouth wants to say a word
To them, covered in snow.
As long as my breath carries me,
My soul will be with them.

Did you forget me, my city?
Your water flows in my body.
On your benches, I sat
And waited for my calling.

Where houses stand crooked,
And a road leads to the graveyard,
Where a river overflowed its banks—
I dreamed my days.

At night an angel flies in the sky,
Flashing the roofs with white.
He tells me from far away:
He will exalt my name.

I sang to you, my people.
Who knows if you like my song.
A voice rises from my lungs,
Makes me sad and weary.

I made my paintings from you,
The flowers, forests, houses, people.
Like a wild man, I paint your face
And day and night, I want to bless you.

I painted the bright walls,
The *klezmers*, dancers on the stage,
With colors blue, red, yellow,
I adorned them like the Holy Spirit.

You played, sang, and frolicked,
You played an old king,
You played with me and swallowed me.
It was a jolly caper.

The moon comes over
From that land to me, a guest.
A red flag waves to me.
I wake up on our street.

The world there is renewed.
Families, near and far,
Make a wedding without me.
Winds blow from there.

I hear the voices from afar
Of people crowding together in joy.
They possessed a life, liberated
With hot rifles and with words.

Oh, crawl out of deep graves,
Aunts, uncles, grandfathers.
You are free citizens, congratulations!
I am your witness from afar.

You are silent, my homeland.
Do you want my heart to break?
Shall I beg on bended knee for my days?
Should a fire boil inside me,
Should I leave you all I have?

I will send you my dreaming blood,
My breath will drip slowly like tears.
The air will sway blue
And I will lie quietly at the fence.

Are you, my homeland, angry at me?
I am open to you like water in a bottle.
Long ago, you hurled me into the distance,
I will come to you to sleep forever
And you will cover my grave with ash.

IV

My people, poor people, you have no more tears.
No cloud walks before us, no star.
Our Moses is dead. He has long been lying in sand.
He brought you to our land and exiled you from it.

Our last prophets are silent, mute,
They have shouted their throats hoarse for you.
You no longer hear the melody of those songs
Flowing from their mouth like a river.

Everyone wants to break the tablets in your heart,
Trample your truth and your God.
A guilty world wants to sap your strength
And leave you a place only in the earth.

They pursue, they beat my people from all sides.
Its crown is falling.
Its Star of David is falling.
Where is its light?
Where is its honor?

My people rends the scarlet sky,
Hurls its exile to the ground.
A lightning burns its old mold,
It runs at it with a sword.

And if you have to be destroyed
For old sins since the last Destruction,
In your place, perhaps another star will rise,
And doves will fly out of your eyes.

I want to immortalize your wish,
To engrave a new truth.
Of life, let art remain—
The sound of thunder and lightning.

1937

French Citizenship

It was hard for Eastern European Jews living in Paris between the World Wars to acquire French citizenship (indeed, many of them perished in the Holocaust). For Chagall, it may have been doubly difficult because he presumably had had the dreaded title "Commissar" in Bolshevik Russia. As the 1930s progressed, however, in view of the menacing atmosphere in Europe, the Nazi persecution of Jews and the Moscow trials, obtaining any citizenship was a matter of life or death for Chagall, and he did feel at home in France. Finally, through efforts of the writer Jean Paulhan and other French intellectuals, Chagall and his family became naturalized French citizens on June 4, 1937.[30] Less than four years later, the Vichy security police stripped them of this citizenship.

Marc Chagall in Avignon to Friends in Paris[31]

Le Prieuré / Villeneuve lès Avignon   9/V 37

[French] Dear Friends,

I hope that you received my card. Thank you very much for all your attention and forgive me for abusing your kindness. It's a matter of issuing my passport. It is an odyssey.

My real name (the only legacy from my father) is really Chagall.

In the Tsarist passport with which I lived in Paris before the war, an "off" was sometimes added to Chagall [= Chagalloff]. Apparently, that sounded more Russian to the ears of the policemen. The same with my first name. Ever since my return to Paris in 1923, my identification cards have been issued with the first name of Marc (called Moïse) Chagall.[32] But for 2–3 years, I don't know why, the police have omitted "Marc." That causes me a lot of trouble, for in life and as an artist, I am called Marc Chagall.

Couldn't a very proper passport be issued? Marc Chagall, or Marc (called Moïse) Chagall, the two first names if that is indispensable. Perhaps that would be easier before the naturalization decree appears. (I have already paid.) I will be especially grateful to you if you could intervene with the authorities to settle this little matter which has grown into a detective novel.

We will return next week and will be very happy to see both of you.

Cordially, /   Marc Chagall

Marc Chagall in Paris to Yosef Opatoshu in New York

[Postcard of Avignon, postmark: 12.5 [?] 1937]

[Yiddish] Avignon 1937

Dear Opatoshu, it was a city of the Pope and there is not half a Jew here. And in Carpentras where a very old synagogue survived, there are still 30 Jews. Received your beautiful bibliograph book. Thank you. I wish you and Leyvik many such collections (*Zamlbikher*), issued for Yiddish literature.[33] How are you? My wife here greets you. Be well.

bibliograph: He means bibliophile.

Your devoted   Marc Chagall

Marc Chagall in Paris to A. Lyesin in New York

{6/30/37}

Dear Friend Lyesin,

Received your letter. I am glad that you are well again. Thank you for liking my long poem. As to what you write: thoroughly to repair it,—but that would be Lyesin and not Chagall. I do not claim to be a professional poet. I would rather stay with my mistakes and weaknesses. Therefore—I beg you to send me back the poem. As to the drawings, I am quite busy now. As soon as I have time, I shall do it.

Lyesin and not Chagall: Lyesin gave in and published Chagall's poem as is.

Regards. Marc Chagall

Marc Chagall in Paris to Z.Y. Anokhi in Tel Aviv

Z.Y. Anokhi (in Ashkenazi Hebrew: Oneykhi, 1878–1947), born in Mohilev Province, Byelorussia, one of the young generation of Hebrew prose writers in Russia in the early twentieth century, switched to Yiddish. In 1923, he lived in Berlin when Chagall was there. In 1924, he immigrated to Palestine and worked in the Tel Aviv municipal administration. During Chagall's visit to Palestine in 1931, Anokhi took him on a tour of the country.

1937 Paris 4 Villa Eugène Manuel. XVIe

[Russian] Dear Oneykhi,

I learned about your 60th birthday. Oh! But you are so young . . . Do you remember how we traveled together in the colonies, how you guided me and we slept in a room in a "kvutsa" [small kibbutz] and awoke before cockcrow to a pink sky. You were eating tasty sandwiches. May God give you many years of eating such sandwiches—for the glory of Jewish literature.

You should be happy that you live in your own country, that you are being honored, and remembering your smile, I think: how you deserved it. I am happy for you. Regards from my wife

Devoted / Marc Chagall

[Yiddish] I greet you from my heart / Bella Chagall

Marc Chagall in Paris to Pavel Ettinger in Moscow

[Postmark: August 1937]

[Russian] Dear Pavel Davidovich,

Braun: The publisher Little Brown.

I have not heard from you in a long time. How are you? Recently I sent you 2 little art books by the publisher Braun. I hope you received them. As you know, there is now an international exhibition here;[34] to see it properly you have to wear out a pair of boots. My first visit, of course, was to the Soviet pavilion, and every time I want to smell my homeland, I go there . . . I did nothing in the way of decorative murals for the exhibition. For I am an "alien." The Spanish pavilion invited the Spaniards Picasso[35] and Miró, who [also] live permanently in Paris. Their pavilion is beautiful, with respect to art.

Related to the international exhibition, I exhibited a lot in various places. In October, I shall have a separate exhibition of water colors.[36]

And do you know, your "humble servant" was 50 years old this year, according to his passport, and next year 30 years of work, if we count from the painting "Death"-"Street" [= "The Dead Man"], 1908. In such (joyless) moments, I think about my beautiful homeland—for all my life I did one thing—I expressed it in my art, as well as I could.

Someday, the future Chagalls will be happy when the capital of art will be, perhaps, Moscow and not Paris. Their lives will not then be split into two. By the way, please tell, perhaps, those who may be interested: in Vitebsk, my old teacher died, the artist Pen; he kept several of my pieces (paintings, water colors, drawings, and among others, my portrait of Pen). Let a museum take it if they want.

Be well. Devoted, Marc Chagall

The YIKUF Congress

On September 17–21, 1937, the First World Yiddish Culture Congress was held in
Paris[37] with the participation of several hundred Yiddish writers, artists, musicians, lawyers, doctors, scientists, and cultural activists from around the world.[38]
It was a demonstration of unity by hundreds of Yiddish organizations and cultural figures in the face of Hitler; an impressive show of force of a waning culture,
hovering on the brink of an abyss. As Y. Opatoshu put it: "From a world stage, the
Yiddish Culture Congress posed to the World People [Hebrew: *am olam*] the
challenge of its existence as a cultural unity." The participants included liberals,
Communists, and so-called "progressive," Yiddish-oriented intellectuals.[39] Influenced by the "Popular Front" of left-to-center parties in France (who were
then in the government), the organizers called for a united Jewish [= Yiddish]
"cultural front" "for the defense of modern Yiddish [= Jewish] culture" in view of
the unprecedented "tragic situation" of European Jewry.

The World Yiddish Cultural Alliance (YIKUF) was founded, centered in Paris,
Warsaw, and New York, along with a journal, *Yidishe Kultur (Yiddish Culture)*, edited by Nakhman Mayzel in New York from November 1938. Chagall was elected
to the Central Board of YIKUF, as a member of the French delegation. But he was
outside of Paris and did not bother to return for the Congress.

Among several other initiatives, a Committee for the Exhibition of Modern
Jewish Culture was established, including Chagall. At the International Exhibition in Paris in 1937, they erected a Jewish Pavilion, which was supposed to move
on to the 1939 World's Fair in New York. The Jewish Pavilion had 350 square
meters of space; it exhibited Yiddish literature, the Yiddish press, publishing
houses, Yiddish schools, social organizations, art, and science. And it stood
across from a section of the German Pavilion. As Y. Opatoshu put it:

> What did the Jews exhibit in their pavilion? Manuscripts of the 13th and 14th cen-
> turies, books of the 16th and 17th centuries, old Yiddish literature, modern Yiddish

literature, Chagall's paintings, Soutine's paintings, student papers of the modern Yiddish school. And the Germans? The Germans exhibited the newest cannons, the newest rifles. So the rifles stood and competed with the Jewish alphabet. And the Jewish alphabet won. Even the Hitlerites were ashamed for promoting rifles against the Jewish alphabet, and the next week they took away the rifles.[40]

Just two years later, World War II began in Europe and the "Jewish alphabet" went up in fire. Following the Hitler-Stalin pact in August 1939, many prominent cultural figures, including Opatoshu, Leyvik, and Chagall, abandoned the YIKUF, which fell under the sway of the left. Nevertheless, Chagall published several pieces in the Paris Yiddish Communist paper *Di Naye Presse* and in *Yidishe Kultur* in New York. *Yidishe Kultur* never became a Communist party journal and fulfilled an important role in publishing Yiddish literature, criticism, and journalism. It was especially instrumental as an outlet for Soviet Yiddish writers and a link with them, as long as they were alive.

Marc Chagall in Italy to Yosef Opatoshu in New York

[Postcard from Venice] Venezia   1937   14/IX

[Yiddish] Dear Opatoshu, since I think that you are either on the way or in Paris, I send you my thanks—for your dear letter of congratulations [on Chagall's fiftieth birthday] and also my, our, best regards and wishes for the [Jewish] New Year. Will we see each other in Paris? As you see, I am apparently late for the Congress. The Tintorettos and Michaelangelos turned my head. But I greet you all. I press your hand. Devoted   Marc Chagall/My wife sends her love.

Marc Chagall: Greetings to the World Yiddish Culture Congress

[Yiddish] Unfortunately I have been caught up in my work—and am sending you my greetings.

a man screaming:
Hitler.
On the one hand, I hear a man screaming, a man who makes himself into a god, and wants to devour the Jews.

On the other hand, [in Italy] I see how real gods have once created art and culture for all people.

So why does my people appear today so poor, and yet rich in its poverty?

No one knows that a bone is stuck in our throat and they want to cut the throat as well.

It would be good: if from a corner of the city square, a prophet of ours would emerge and scold the world.

from a corner of the city square: An allusion to Peretz's expressionist play *At Night in the Old Market Place.*

All the great artists in the past dealt with Jewish types in their art. They brought out all aspects, but not our spirit. And now, they want to suffocate the spirit of our life, our culture, and our young art. Who, strangers want to stifle it? Even our own Jews, if they do nothing for Jewish culture and art, stifle it too.

I am one of the people, the workers, as my father was, and I want to belong to the workers. May the Congress—as it is, as it should be and as it will be in the future—do everything to bring the culture to the people, for it emerges from the popular man and must belong to the people, be beloved, enriched, and strengthened by them. Let it be, as in the past, our permanent banner, which we shall raise against our enemies.

Marc Chagall in Paris to Yosef Opatoshu in New York

[Stationery: 4 Villa Eugène Manuel. XVIe]   Paris {11.26/37}

[Yiddish] Dear Opatoshu,

Thank you for the book. It is beautiful, not too much and not too little. Books in your place are published well. How do the Jews appreciate it? The "Wall" came out not badly. Indeed, it is better on matte paper than on glossy. Though in the left corner half a dozen Jews are missing . . . Either or . . . We read your text aloud all together [with Bella and Ida]—beautiful!—in *Zamlbikher* No. 1, with great pleasure. I know well the places where it occurred . . . And perhaps I too slept in that "pretty" room in the colony [in Palestine] where you were.

the "Wall": Chagall's drawing "The Wailing Wall."

Listen, Opatoshu, I think I want to publish my little book of my life in Yiddish (it still needs some work) and perhaps with drawings (the negatives of the French [edition]). Please advise me how much it should cost, roughly, and where it is better to bake the book, here in Paris or where. Externally, the book should be similar to the style of your recent books. I wrote it some 14 years ago, it seems I am very lazy——[41]

Be well and fresh/Regards from my wife/Your Chagall

Marc Chagall in Paris to Yosef Opatoshu in New York

1937 Paris 15/XII

[Yiddish] Dear Friend Opatoshu, Many thanks for your gift—the Jewish History. I shall, indeed, read it now and not after my work on the Bible. For the work is gradually advancing, I have already made about 70 plates. Oh, how beautiful is our Bible! Thank you for the book. You are the only one who spoils me. Especially on my birthday. So you are almost the only one I love . . . Why are you so far?

All best wishes to your new apartment, health and happiness . . . And since a new year starts in a new apartment—may it be with good luck. I am working now on the painting "Revolution" (you saw the little study); the director of the Palais des Beaux Arts in Brussels saw it and asked for this painting too (when it is ready), along with the others for my exhibition they are organizing on 15/I in Brussels. And this is indeed a date for me: since my painting "The Death" (the dead man in the street) of 1908.

Dear Opatoshu, the more time runs out (and you know it as I do), something gets strange in your heart . . . You feel like working, you feel like crying, and often not just about yourself (why?), but about our people, too. Though it seems I am so far from them, alone in my apartment, in my heart I am still "too much" connected with our Jews.

Be well, regards from Bella and daughter. She, poor soul, is still alone for the time being. Her husband is in the service—a soldier. And not in Paris (for the time being). Greet Leyvik . . . I knew that Palestine would move him . . .

Your devoted

Marc Chagall in Paris to Dr. Schwarz in Tel Aviv

4 February 1938

[German] Dear Dr. Schwarz,

I have meanwhile been very busy. I have been working in the country. I have participated in various exhibitions in Paris, London, and now in Brussels.

Your situation is not calm enough now either to think about a big exhibition. But the time will come, and I hope to exhibit nicely in Eretz Israel as well.

Best wishes,/Marc Chagall

Exchange of Letters Between Marc Chagall and a Volunteer in the Spanish Civil War

The Spanish Civil War seemed to many liberals and leftists and to many Jews an apocalyptic effort to stop Fascism and prevent a second world war. In an article in the Paris Communist Yiddish newspaper *Naye Prese* of May 24, 1938, Chagall equated the struggle to save Jewish culture with the resistance to Fascism in Spain. On July 16, 1938, an exchange of letters appeared in the same paper between A. Lisner, a volunteer fighting in the Spanish Civil War, and Marc Chagall. (Lisner was a worker from Paris; during the Holocaust he was a resistance fighter in France, and after the war he became a trade union activist.) Typically Chagall was both excited about the militant response of the left and saw it as an act of dignity and renewal of the Jewish people. The memory of the expulsion from Spain in 1492 was still alive in Jewish popular mythology, and the 500-year rabbinical ban on going to Spain was still intact.

Excerpt from A. Lisner's letter

[Yiddish] In the *Naye Presse* of May 24 this year, I read with great interest your article: "Our Jewish Culture and Our Resistance." The thunder of the "non-intervention" cannons and the noise of the [German] aviation could not stop the Jewish volunteer from reading a Yiddish workers' [i.e., Communist] newspaper and thus learning about events around the world.

In the comfort provided by the trenches I noticed a sentence in your article: "And our contemporary culture? It is not only Spinoza, Freud, Einstein, Mendele, Peretz, Sholem-Aleichem, Bialik, Israels, Pissaro, today those are also our Jewish folk people and the workers of all countries who, with their sharp gaze and their fists, will resist our enemies who have offended us. And I want only one thing: to be among them during the action."

Allow me, distinguished artist, to ask you whether you haven't noticed that the Jewish masses and the workers of the whole world will not only "with their sharp gaze and their fist," as you write, resist our enemies who have offended us, but for the last two years the Jewish masses have not been content with a mere fist. They took up powerful weapons against the enemy and forced many a sup-

"non-intervention": A reference to the one-sided "embargo" on weapons to Spain, imposed by the Western states, which did not stop the arming of the Fascists in the Spanish Civil War.

porter of Hitler's *Mein Kampf*, who claims we are not capable of anything—to change his mind. No doubt, your age won't allow you to take a rifle in hand. But you, comrade Chagall, with your artistic rifle, your brush, you can also strike anti-Semitism, as we Jewish workers of the whole world do.

[Here Lisner tells episodes from the war, worthy of the artist's brush. E.g.:] During an attack I carried comrade Hefetz of Palestine to an ambulance, because he was hit by a bullet in his eye. On the way Hefetz told me: "I cannot see any longer. But I saw how I killed several Fascists with my own rifle."

I believe that those are images that Jewish artists can use to show the non-Jewish world that we are not cowards.

A. Lisner

Marc Chagall's answer

[Yiddish] I am moved by your letter of a fighter in Spain to me. It is a great honor for me, for I believe that your names will shine in our history.

I am grateful to you for the trembling fresh motifs you sent me. In my consciousness, the Jewish resistance against the enemy already looks Biblical.

No doubt, the new "Biblical" motifs are worthy of being immortalized, as was done for the old Biblical motifs. If not we—others will do it later.

Marc Chagall

in our history: For Chagall, the struggle in Spain is part of Jewish history.

Marc Chagall in Paris to Yosef Opatoshu in New York

Paris 26/Oct 1938

[Yiddish] Dear Opatoshu, you are still at sea and I am already writing a few words to you, because I read your interview in the *Literarishe bleter*[42] and am very happy with your words about everything: about the "word," about religion, about art, Jewishness. I feel that you are indeed right, for apart from everything else, you have a "historical perspective" and though in my art it also gets in intuitively—I think—I am missing it *in life* . . . And therefore I plunge into sadness especially in recent years when I see the terrible injustice [done to the Jews]. Therefore, possibly, in my speech on your evening such moods [voices?] crept in, which have infected the others. By the way, I would like to know what you actually think, concretely, about my doubting questions.

Be well, dear Opatoshu, and regards.

Also from my wife (I also read your interview to her . . .)/ Your devoted

Marc Chagall

Marc Chagall in Paris to Yosef Opatoshu in New York

Paris 1939

[Yiddish] Dear Opatoshu, How are you? I haven't heard about you for a long time. [You] forgot us; today—you must not. The "World Thief" [Yiddish: *velt ganev*—i.e., Hitler] thinks he is such a genius that my heart drops from him and his deeds. We place our hopes in you over there [i.e., America] . . .

Are you working? Not long ago, I made quite a big picture, which I would have loved to show you[43] . . . You must come here. It feels lonely here.

Listen, dear Opatoshu, in the meantime, the following [story]: you saw at my home several copies of the drawings I made for Lyesin's books.[44] According to the contract with Lyesin (I have all the letters), the originals belong to me. I gave him the rights to reproduce them for his books and he (as well as Vladek) promised me to send them back [after the printing]. In response to my letter, Kreplyak[45] fell silent. Where are they?

Could I ask you as a friend to "grope about" in the matter, ask around, and ask them to send me back the *34* original drawings as soon as possible. I assume they won't make any fuss about my drawings (and will know how to separate the copies from the originals . . .). they must send it to me immediately, I need them for an exhibition. Forgive me, dear Opatoshu, for bothering you with this. My wife and daughter greet you.

Your devoted   Marc Chagall

P.S. In a previous letter, Kreplyak wrote me that they sent me back the originals. He thinks that the few copies (you saw) are the originals. This is not true.

World War II and the Flight from Nazi Europe: 1939–1941

World War II

In the summer of 1939, Marc and Bella Chagall stayed in a farmhouse on the Loire. In late August, when war became imminent, Chagall imagined he was in danger from the farmer and barricaded himself into his own part of the house.[1] The Chagalls moved to Saint-Dyé-sur-Loire, where Chagall transferred his paintings from Paris (without the stretchers) and Bella began writing her memoirs in Yiddish, her childhood language.

World War II began with the German march into Poland on September 1, 1939. Two days later, France and England, observing their pact with Poland, declared war on Germany. But nothing changed in France; the Maginot Line of border fortifications separated it from the German army and seemed impenetrable, and the nominal "World War II" was dubbed "the phony war." In Paris, exhibitions went on as usual. Chagall sent invitations to Opatoshu—for his own exhibition and for Picasso's, held in the same gallery a few months apart.

Chagall Exhibition in Paris, Sent to Opatoshu in New York

[Addressed to: Mr. Opatoshu, 306 W. 100th Street, New York City, New York, USA]

[French] The honor of your presence is requested
at our exhibit of *recent works* by

MARC Chagall

to be held on Thursday 26 January to Saturday 24 February 1940.

Gallery Mai
12 rue Bonaparte
Paris—6th

Private viewing of the Exhibit
Thursday 26 January 1940
at 5 o'clock

Marc Chagall in Paris to Sh. Nigger in New York

Paris IV [April 1940]

[Yiddish] Dear Friend Nigger,

I did not yet thank you properly for your efforts to return the drawings for Lyesin's book to me. Indeed I did get back 26 drawings from *Tsukunft*, but I must get the *remaining* 8. So I would like to ask you to bring your efforts to a final conclusion. I would be most grateful to you. For I shall soon have an exhibition of "black and white" here and I shall soon need them. Let *Tsukunft-Forverts* finish the business with me. I only wanted good things for Lyesin and I beg them to close the matter properly.

   I recently read about you in the book, *Childhood Years* [by Nigger's brother Daniel Charny][2] and enjoyed it.

Regards, Devoted   Marc Chagall

Marc Chagall in Paris to Yosef Opatoshu in New York

Under the pressure of Nazi anti-Jewish policies and French anti-Semitism, Chagall developed some new iconography. "The White Crucifixion," 1938 (actually;

1939) features Jesus on the Cross wearing a Jewish prayer shawl on his loins, as in Uri-Zvi Grinberg's Yiddish poem "Uri-Zvi Before the Cross." Jesus here represents two-thousand years of Jewish suffering. In the background, there is a "burning *shtetl*," a key image of M. Gebirtig's popular Yiddish song by the same name, written in 1938 and immediately known and sung worldwide. Its ominous tone was perceived as a foreboding of the Holocaust. Chagall was proud of this achievement and needed to dissociate himself from the Christological novels of the ostracized Yiddish writer Scholem Asch.

actually; 1939: See Chagall's letter to Opatoshu, p. 476.

{4/18} 1940 Paris

[Yiddish] Dear Opatoshu, you wrote me a sad letter (received a while ago and still not answered). Was busy with my small-big exhibition where I exhibited Christ (but, I believe, not such as in Asch's work). I am despondent that you did not see it, because I consider you a *maven* (that's how I want it). I don't like it that you are, apparently, somewhat gloomy (my information comes often from Charny). True, we were "duped"—I'm talking about the "YIK . . ." [YIKUF], but the art remains with us, which is today the most important thing, along with love. But my God, how far we Jews are from all that. It's terrifying. Forgive me.

YIKUF: After the Hitler-Stalin Pact in August 1939, several non-Communists, including major figures such as Leyvik, Opatoshu, and Chagall, exited the YIKUF in protest; in Chagall's view, they were the real artists.

Now, listen, Opatoshu, I didn't yet thank you (and Nigger), because they finally sent me from *Tsukunft-Forverts*—the 29 [should be: 26] drawings I made for Lyesin, but 8 drawings are *still missing.* Indeed, I'd like to ask you to finish the business. Let there be an end to it, ask whoever is involved to send me the remaining 8 drawings, I shall need them for an exhibition of "black and white."

Isn't it too much trouble?

Please write, do not forget us. And what are you doing? How are you? Regards from my wife and daughter. Her husband is in the army, of course.

Your devoted

Marc Chagall

A few days ago, we read together the "Childhood of a Writer," which you sent me. About yourself, and enjoyed you, your father, grandfather . . .

Picasso Exhibition in Paris, Sent to Opatoshu in New York

[Addressed to: Mr. Opatoshu, 306 W. 100th Street, New York City, New York, USA]

la galerie MAI

Tél. Danton 49-47   12, rue Bonaparte, 6e

EXPOSERA du 19 AVRIL au 18 MAI 1940
des aquarelles, gouaches et dessins
de

PICASSO

Vernissage:
Vendredi 19 Avril 1940 à 15 heures

la galerie MAI: This is the same gallery that exhibited Chagall in January.

The Fall of France

On May 10, 1940, with the encouragement of his old friend, the painter and art historian André Lhote, Chagall bought a house in Gordes, a small town near Avignon in Provence. The same day, the German army invaded Belgium and the Netherlands, and on May 12 they marched into France. The Chagalls hired a truck and transferred the paintings to Gordes. On June 14, France surrendered, and on June 22, an armistice agreement was signed, leaving an "unoccupied" zone under French administration with the capital Vichy in the South of France, which included Gordes. Chagall's son-in-law Michel Rapaport, in the French army since October 1937, was demobilized in July 1940 and eventually joined Ida and her parents in Gordes.

It is usually assumed that Chagall hesitated for a whole year to leave France, but the following two letters make it clear that the Chagalls understood the situation and were desperate to leave. The letters are written in English—both for the censor and to be used as documents for visa purposes. Though impersonal toward the addressee, they scream in many ways: "We want to see you!"—Yiddish code for: "Get us out!"—using the traditional hints and euphemisms of Yiddish letters in such situations. Indeed, the letters triggered the actions of both writers in New

Gordes (Vaucluse), where the Chagalls bought a house in June 1940 (the house with two windows at lower left, circled).

York, who eventually managed to raise money for transatlantic tickets and U.S. entry visas for the Chagalls. The Fund for Jewish Refugee Writers contacted Alfred J. Barr, and Chagall got an invitation for an exhibition at the Museum of Modern Art (MOMA) and, on that basis, an American visa.

Marc Chagall in Gordes to Yosef Opatoshu in New York

[English; in Ida Chagall's handwriting. We left her language as is.] September 1st, 1940

Very dear friend,

It seems to me that we have not seen each other since a very long time, and that centuries have passed since our last meeting took place. How are you? I hope you can work as well as before, while I . . . Sure, now one must have more courage than usual to do pictures. We are living in the country, in the South, near Avignon, where the children succeeded finally to join us,—we were separated the ones from the others, during the last events. Our son-in-law has just been demobilized. Happily, he is safe and sound. Meanwhile, we are living. It is out of question, actually, to return in our Paris, in our homes, and we are asking ourselves how we will pass the winter. I miss you—your energy, your deep voice—very much, my dear friend. If I could expect to see you again one day, it would give me, perhaps, more courage for my work. I hope the same for my people, for my family. What I miss the more—are my friends, my close friends as you are. Be with you would certainly give me more strength. And I will hope that I will see you again one day and that this day will not be too remote, as we are not becoming younger . . . May I expect it? Perhaps it would be possible to have now a big exhibition of my work—and even to see it for once myself.

to see you again: A euphemism for "bring us to you."

more courage for my work: Chagall clutches to his value as an artist to save his life.

Let us hear very soon about you, about our friends, about all our world.

Waiting impatiently for your answer and your encouragement, we both embrace you with love

all our world: The Yiddish cultural establishment in New York.

Marc Chagall

I do write you in English, hoping it would be much easier to you to answer in the same language. And this letter is obviously only for you.

My address: M.C. [= Marc Chagall] Gordes (Vaucluse)

only for you: Meaning the exact opposite, i.e., try to use it to get a visa.

Marc Chagall in Gordes to Sh. Nigger in New York

Writing to the literary critic Sh. Nigger, he hoped that Nigger might be more influential than Opatoshu and closer to the Jewish Labor Committee, founded by his late brother B. Vladek. The committee was engaged in saving Jewish political activists and Yiddish writers and intellectuals from Europe. Chagall had never seen Nigger before and their limited, occasional correspondence was not on a personal level. This letter is written in the Yiddish language of *Sagi Nahor*, using the exact opposite of the intended meaning.

[English; in Ida Chagall's handwriting]　　1 Sept. 40

Dear friend,

I did not write to you since a very long time, but you know yourself that our times were not propitious for writing letters. How are you, you and your family? Did you have any news from Daniel? I did not hear from him since June 10th, date of

Daniel: Daniel Charny, Nigger's brother, who lived in Paris. He eventually got out to America in May 1941.

his last letter from Paris. If you had later news from him, please let me know about them as soon as possible.

All of us have been rather separated the ones from the others. The children too took a long time before they could join us. Happily—for the present time—we live altogether in the country. My son-in-law is just demobilized, actually he is resting here, as he do need it after 2 years military service and one year of war. What he will do afterwards is a question for us. In these terrible times we would like at least to remain together.

What I miss the more are my friends—close friends like you, to whom I would be so happy to talk personally. I have found again the impressions of my childhood (Cherta . . .), the same as yours were. One needs a lot of courage nowadays in order to work—and a lot more at my age. Please let me hear about you very soon. I would be so happy if I could see you again, and I hope it will come one day—a day which will be not too remote, as we are not becoming young again. Give my greetings to all our friends. Say them I would be happy to hear from them. Hoping to see you again in more favorable conditions, I embrace you very affectionately,

Marc Chagall

to remain together: Michel was unemployed and in danger of being shipped off to a concentration camp, either as a soldier or as a Jew.

to talk personally: Implying: Get me out!

Cherta: The Pale of Settlement (in Russian), where Jews had no civil rights. A transparent hint at the second-class status of the Jews in Vichy France.

I do write you in English, hoping it would be much easier to you to answer in the same language. And this letter is obviously only for you.

My address is: M.C./Gordes (Vaucluse)/Près Avignon

The Flight from Nazi Europe

It is generally assumed that the Chagalls were saved by Varian Fry, who headed a mission in Marseille on behalf of the American Rescue Committee in New York. Indeed, as we shall see below, Varian Fry had organized Chagall's actual departure from Vichy France via Spain and Portugal to America. But, without taking anything away from Fry's heroic mission, it must be emphasized that the story was much more complex than that.

It was an extremely hectic and confusing time. Members of many institutions and organizations in the United States tried to rescue their friends from the European countries that were rapidly being devoured by Hitler. The initiators explored all possible avenues of egress: through Vilnius in the tiny but still independent Lithuania via Siberia and Japan, or through southern France via Spain and Portugal, or French North Africa to America. Every witness recalls his or her own activities, which seemed the center of the world; yet such memoirs are never complete or fully reliable—and written evidence was kept to a minimum. Ida Chagall wrote later : "As you can imagine, I am very indebted to the Emergency Rescue Committee in its time. Unfortunately I have no photocopies or documents related to that time. It was a most difficult period when nobody could keep any copies whatsoever."[3] Especially neglected are the efforts made by Jewish organizations, recorded in the all-but-forgotten Yiddish language. From whatever written and oral accounts I could gather, I assume that the following story is as close as we can get to the facts.[4]

The American Rescue Committee was founded in New York on June 25, 1940, three days after the French government signed a humiliating armistice agreement with Germany. But for the Yiddish world the decisive event was earlier, on September 1, 1939, with the fall of Poland, the strongest center of worldwide Yiddish culture. About 1000–1500 Yiddish writers lived in Poland, as part of a full-fledged Jewish cultural network, including political parties, cultural institutions, schools, newspapers, publishing houses, etc. It all collapsed overnight and the writers were stranded in various countries or fell under German occupation.

In November 1939, the Y.L. Perets Yiddish Writers Union and the Jewish Labor Committee in New York agreed to create a Fund for Jewish Refugee Writers. The Yiddish Writers Union represented all Yiddish writers and journalists of the three major New York Yiddish daily newspapers: *Forverts*, *Morgen-Zhurnal*, and *Der Tog* (where Yosef Opatoshu and the poet A. Glanz-Leyeles worked). The Jewish Labor Committee was a powerful organization with connections to the American and international non-Communist labor movements. The Fund for Jewish Refugee Writers, actually established in January 1940, conducted "a one-time emergency appeal" among Yiddish writers in America and their supporters; those were usually not the rich Jews, but simple members of the immigrant masses, who contributed a dollar or five dollars, and often more.[5] The literary critic Sh. Nigger, to whom Chagall appealed in September 1940, was Co-Chairman of the Fund; young Dina Glanz (Glance), daughter of the Yiddish Introspectivist poet A. Leyeles, worked for two years as the Fund's operating secretary.

The activists and their supporters in the U.S. were not just philanthropists or humanists, shaken by an abstract sympathy for the fate of Jews in Nazi-occupied Europe, but were people who had deep personal ties there. Both organizations, the Writers Union and the Labor Committee, were intimately related to the Yiddish secular culture in Eastern Europe. Almost all their members came from that Jewish world, they had family, childhood friends, and former party comrades in Poland or Russia. Yiddish writers in Europe wrote for American publications and vice versa, in what was truly one "Yiddish World Literature." They were half of one cultural body, whose vital center was falling into an abyss. The Fund tried to save as many Yiddish writers and political and cultural activists as possible. In fact, the Fund did manage to bring several thousand of them to the U.S. and it sent financial support to many others who were stranded in various places around the globe. As a letter from the Fund pointed out:

> These people, who were respected writers in their home countries, are now facing their third winter of the war in many far places such as; Teheran, Iran; Bombay, India; Shanghai, China; Tashkent and Samarkand in Asiatic Soviet Russia; Algiers and Casablanca, Morocco; Toulouse, Nice and Marseilles in unoccupied France. They and their families are in great need of food, clothing and medicine, etc., with no one else to turn to but us."[6]

One of the two graphic artists included in the list of writers was Marc Chagall. It seems that Chagall's friends went to Alfred H. Barr, Jr., who invited Chagall to exhibit his work at the Museum of Modern Art (MOMA) in New York and included him in the list of artists to be saved from Europe. A fund-raising effort for Chagall was launched through the art dealer Curt Valentin of the Buchholz Gallery, 32 East 57th St., New York, who had known Chagall in Berlin during 1922–1923. Yosef Opatoshu, together with his son's father-in-law, the lawyer Aaron Weinberg, prepared a legal "Affidavit of Support" for the Chagalls, which involved guaranteeing a considerable amount of money.[7] A notarized statement of support for the Chagalls was signed by George Goren, a journalist for the Jewish daily *Forverts*. But a simple guarantee would not do: A bond of $3000 (a huge sum at the time) had to be posted as collateral. The Yiddish world was not rich in means and connections and needed outside support. In collaboration with Mrs. Alfred Barr, wife of the Director of MOMA, the Fund worked to obtain a Visa of Entry to the United States for the Chagalls. The Fund also approached Hilla Rebay and Solomon Guggenheim to help guarantee an Affidavit of Support for the Chagall family.

Fund for Jewish Refugee Writers to Baroness Hilla von Rebay in New York

February 6th, 1940

[English] Baroness Hilla von Rebay
Carnegie Studios
56th Street and 7th Avenue
New York City

Dear Mme. Rebay:

Mr. Kurt Valentin of the Buchholtz Galleries has told us that he spoke to you the other day about visas for Marc Chagall and his family. Mr. Valentin suggested that we get in touch with you about this matter personally.

    We have already made application for visas for M. Chagall and his wife, as well as his daughter and son-in-law. We have been informed that the visas will be granted upon the presentation of support which will guarantee that neither M. Chagall nor his family will become public charges. Unfortunately, our organization, besieged by thousands of requests for aid and visas, is incapable at the present moment of securing such financial affadavits. We have therefore been forced to turn to others who are interested in M. Chagall for help. We sincerely hope that you will be able to assist us in it.

We would like to ask you to use your good offices to enable us to procure these financial statements, either through intervening for us with the Guggenheim family or other art patrons concerned with the fate of one of the finest painters of our day. We assure you that we will be more than grateful for any assistance that you can render us.

We are certain that you are as anxious as we are to have M. Chagall here with us in America. We hope that you will see your way clear to helping us.

Please accept our sincere thanks for your cooperation and assistance.

Sincerely yours,

[Dina Glanz]

For the Fund

Hilla Rebay in New York to Dina Glanz in New York

November 12, 1940

The Solomon R. Guggenheim Foundation
Carnegie Hall
7th Avenue at 56th Street
New York

Miss Dona [sic] Glanz
Fund for Jewish Refugee Writers
144 Henry Street
New York

Dear Miss Glanz:

If you will please let me know what statement is needed for Mr. Chagall and his wife and how to go about it I shall see to it that Mr. Guggenheim will do this for him.

As we had quite some money sent for his account to England when last we bought some paintings I presume that he is quite well off and could care for himself over here.

Very truly yours,

Hilla Rebay

Dina Glanz in New York to Hilla von Rebay in New York

January 29th, 1941

Baroness Hilla von Rebay
Carnegie Studios
56th Street and 7th Avenue
New York City

Dear Mme. Rebay:

It was through your kind intervention and assistance last November that we received the affidavits from Mr. Guggenheim for the Chagall family. May we trouble you again to intercede for us in the same matter?

The latest reports we received indicate that Chagall and his wife have received American visas, although his daughter and son-in-law have not gotten theirs. Chagall and his wife are in need of passage money—about seven hundred dollars, if he is to bring over his paintings too—and we hope Mr. Guggenheim will be able to help. Like all other organizations, our limited funds are so taxed that we find it impossible to lay such a substantial sum of money on the table for one case, even though we think it more than worthy. We are certain that Mr. Chagall, once here, will do everything to repay Mr. Guggenheim for his generosity.

May we count on you again? We sincerely hope that you will not turn us down.

Please accept our thanks for all your kindness.

Sincerely yours,

Dina Glanz

For the Fund

Solomon R. Guggenheim in Charleston, S.C., to Dina Glanz in New York

9 East Battery
Charleston, S.C.

February 1, 1941

Miss Dina Glanz
Fund for Jewish Refugee Writers
144 Henry Street
New York, N.Y.

My dear Miss Glanz:

Baroness Rebay handed me your letter of January 29 with reference to Chagall, and requested that I reply to it. While I should like to be in a position to assist all the people who appeal to me, my list is already so extremely heavy that I do not feel I should care to take on anything more,—especially since, as you must realize, the enormous expenditures of our government have caused taxes to be extremely high, and therefore a very small proportion of income is left after taxes have been satisfied. Consequently, I regret that I must ask you kindly to excuse me from making the contribution suggested by you.

Very truly yours,

S. R. Guggenheim

Curt Valentin in New York to Walter C. Arensberg in Hollywood

February 15, 1941

Mr. Walter C. Arensberg
7065 Hillside Avenue
Hollywood, California

Dear Mr. Arensberg:

I realize that everybody in this country these days does his utmost to help people in need. Before writing this letter I thought things over very carefully, still I find it necessary to ask a great favor of you in behalf of the painter Marc Chagall and his wife who are both in Marseille, waiting to come over to this country. The Fund for Jewish Refugee Writers and Mrs. Alfred Barr, have been working for a long time on his case and finally succeeded in procuring the Visa of Entry to the United States. Furthermore a considerable amount of money was raised to pay for the expenses of the passage, but as things now stand we still need $500. We are informed by cable from a friend of ours who is in constant contact with the American Consul in Marseille, that this amount has to be raised within the next ten days.

I am trying to collect this money in small amounts from various people who, in my belief are interested in Chagall's work or, at least are willing to help him. Therefore I would like to ask you to participate with the amount of $50. It is my firm belief that this money can be repaid at some future date either in cash or in the form of one of his works, as soon as Chagall has arrived in this country and is able to work again.

It is needless to say how much I would appreciate your cooperation and since

the money has to be raised very quickly, I would be very grateful for your immediate answer.

Very sincerely yours

Curt Valentin

Among those who contributed $50 each were Bernard J. Reis and Edward G. Robinson in New York, Saidie May of North Carolina, Walter Arensberg in Hollywood, and Mrs. Inez Cunningham Stark of Chicago, and $100 came from Helena Rubinstein. On February 21, 1941, the secretary reported: "Received $500 for Chagall and wife's passage bought through HIAS, the American Hebrew Immigration Aid Society. Dina Glance, for Fund for Jewish Refugee Writers." However, a second appeal to help Chagall's daughter and husband, who actually carried all of Chagall's paintings, was not as easy.

Curt Valentin to Helena Rubinstein in New York

May 6, 1941[8]

Mrs. Helena Rubinstein
715 Fifth Avenue
New York, New York

Dear Mrs. Rubinstein:

A few months ago you had the great kindness to contribute the amount of money which was needed for the passage of Marc Chagall and his wife. They are now both on their way to this country and will arrive soon.

At the time you asked me through your secretary, whether the amount of $100, which you were so generous to give, was enough, and at that time it was enough. Unfortunately a new problem has presented itself as far as Chagall's daughter and her husband are concerned, who are still in Marseille. Everything is done for their visas, but we have to raise some money for their passage. I am glad that I was able to raise a little money for them but there are still $275 missing. I hardly dare to ask you, but I thought you might find it possible to give us some of the money we need. Of course the matter is rather urgent and I would be extremely grateful if you could give me your answer soon.

Needless to say how grateful I would be if you could help us again and I hope you do not mind my asking you.

Very sincerely yours,

Curt Valentin

Helena Rubinstein to Curt Valentin in New York

May 7, 1941

Mr. Curt Valentin
Buchholz Gallery
32 East 57 Street
New York City

Dear Mr. Valentin:

I was delighted to hear that Mr. and Mrs. Chagall are on their way to this country and will be very pleased to see them upon their arrival.

I would be more than pleased to help Mr. Chagall's daughter, but the demands on me are growing in such a proportion that I am afraid I have to refuse your appeal this time. I do hope you will understand.

Mr. Chagall has many friends in this country and I feel that as soon as he arrives, it should not be difficult for him to raise the necessary sum to bring over his daughter.

Sincerely yours

Helena Rubinstein

The Emergency Rescue Committee

In 1933, Albert Einstein founded the International Relief Association to save prominent cultural figures from Nazi Germany. In June 1940, after the fall of France, an Emergency Rescue Committee was organized in New York. By that time, the Nazis had occupied or subdued most of the European continent (except for the Soviet Union), yet the United States was still neutral and some lines of communication were open. Specifically, the U.S. maintained diplomatic relations with the Vichy regime of Marshal Pétain in the "unoccupied" zone of France.

The Emergency Rescue Committee worked under the patronage of First Lady Eleanor Roosevelt and was chaired by Dr. Frank Kingdon whose Executive Assistant was Dr. Ingrid Warburg. Postal service to Europe was erratic and slow, and the State Department was at best "a bottleneck" in issuing visas, actually hindering the rescue effort to prevent America from being flooded with leftist intellectuals. Nevertheless, many people were saved from certain annihilation.

In this context, Alfred Barr, Jr., Director of the Museum of Modern Art, drew up a list of artists to be contacted and rescued from Europe. The list focused on modernist masters of what the Nazis saw as "degenerate art"; it included Jean Arp, Max Ernst, his Jewish ex-wife Louise Strauss Ernst, André Masson, Jacques Lipchitz, Marc Chagall, Wilfredo Lam, Brauner, Matisse, Freundlich, Reder, Man Ray, Kandinsky, Klee, Maillol, Picasso. Not all of them accepted the offer or could benefit from it: Picasso, Matisse, and Kandinsky stayed in France; Louise Strauss Ernst and Otto Freundlich perished in concentration camps. The work was mainly carried out by Barr's wife, Margaret S. Barr, who had to secure at least $400 for the ocean passage and underwrite $3000 per person, to ensure that they would not become a "burden to the government." In 1944, the International Relief Association merged with the Emergency Rescue Committee to form the International Rescue Committee, which operates to this day. But that is beyond the scope of our story.

The real hero of this effort was Varian Fry (1908–1967), who arrived in Vichy France on August 15, 1940, where he launched a "private rescue operation." He was "an American Pimpernel in Marseille,"[9] who operated under the nose of the Gestapo, fabricated documents, provided financial support to thousands of refugees, and explored ways for shipping them out of Nazi Europe, mostly via Spain and Portugal. Although authorized to grant only 200 U.S. visas, he actually saved over 2000 writers, artists, German intellectuals, Socialist leaders, and other political activists from various countries, shipping them with their families (at least 4000 people, many of them Jews) to the United States, which was still neutral in the European war.[10] Among them were André Breton, Jacques Lipchitz, Max Ernst, Lion Feuchtwanger, Franz Werfel, Siegfried Kracauer, Victor Serge, Marc Chagall, Heinrich Mann, and Hannah Arendt.[11]

Varian Fry, a Harvard graduate, was a reporter in Berlin in the 1930s, where he had witnessed a horrifying Nazi pogrom of Jews in Berlin in 1935.[12] After 1935, he edited a journal for international affairs, *The Living Age*. He volunteered for this rescue mission and, in August 1940, left New York for the "unoccupied zone" in France, where he established the American Relief Center in Marseille and stayed for thirteen months. Various devious ways were used to transport refugees, but there were also failures. The underground roads through Spain were physically difficult and risky, and many hesitated to go. Many were also trapped—for example, Walter Benjamin, who committed suicide on the Spanish border.

On October 3, 1940, the Vichy government issued a "Statute on Jews," ousting French Jews from all public institutions and barring them from teaching on any level. Many Jews residing in France were foreign-born and either had no French citizenship or were stripped of it; they were forbidden to work and were subject to internment. Varian Fry brought Chagall an invitation by Alfred Barr for an exhibition at the Museum of Modern Art in New York, and in January 1941, he arranged a U.S. visa for Chagall.

As Varian Fry tells it, Chagall first hesitated, apparently out of fear of the journey and of losing his recently acquired French citizenship.[13] On March 8, 1941, Varian Fry and Harry Bingham, American Consul General in Marseille, visited Chagall in Gordes, where they spent a weekend and persuaded him to leave. Chagall, always hedging, asked Fry whether there were cows in America, and only when he was reassured that there were, did he agree to go. Serious Fry did not understand the joke: Chagall identified with the cow, saw himself as that stupid animal (*beheyme* in Yiddish), and wanted to use the image of a cow on his personal calling card. What he meant was: would they accept a *beheyme* [= an idiot] like me?

Margaret Barr in New York to Dina Glanz in New York

The Museum of Modern Art
11 West 53rd Street

February 12, 1941

Miss Dina Glanz
144 Henry St.
New York

My dear Miss Glanz,

It is rather hard for me to get you on the telephone so I am writing you this letter hoping that it will reach you the minute you get to your office.

I want to communicate to you the following cable that we received from the Secours Américain in Marseille:

CHAGALL MYSTERY SOLVED EVIDENTLY YOUVE BEEN TRYING VISITVISAS AND
THERES ABSOLUTELY NOTHING IN THEIR DOSSIERS HERE NEVERTHELESS
CONSULATE GRANTED CHAGALL AND WIFE IMMIGVISAS STOP REFUSES DO SAME
DAUGHTER SONINLAW UNTIL GUARANTEES ARRIVE STOP SUGGEST YOU EXPLAIN
SITUATION GUGGENHEIM PERSUADE HIM REPEAT BY CABLE TO CONSULATE
GUARANTEES HE GAVE STATEDEPT NOVEMBER STOP ESSENTIAL THIS BE DONE
BEFORE FEBRUARY 25 STOP ADVISE

    FRY

You know that I have done lots and lots of things about Chagall just for the principle and because Fry is a personal friend of ours. But Fry is an employee of the Emergency Rescue Committee and Chagall is not a case of his as I have long since informed him. Neither is Chagall a case of mine seeing that the Baroness von Rebay and Mr. Guggenheim had taken on the Chagalls since November. I simply cannot continue work on it because it is too complicated, I do not know the beginnings of the case, I cannot understand what Fry is alluding to at all. Also, while I have received wonderful cooperation from you the Baroness von Rebay could not quite see, I fear, why we were bothering her with the matter and took particular objection to there being a term of time given in Fry's first cable— the one in which Fry requested that Mr. Guggenheim repeat his assurances by cable before Jan. 10. She felt this to be incomprehensible and seemed to doubt the plausibility of such a deadline.

I communicate with Fry by cable addressing AMSECOURS MARSEILLE. I have kept you completely informed of what I have done on my side, could you carry on from here? Fry is deeply interested in Chagall, is doing all he can to help, he is most evidently trying to help Chagall in his dealings with the Consul. All details of passage should also be made clear to Fry so that Fry can help Chagall to get his exit permit and port visa.

Sincerely,

Margaret Barr

[in longhand:] Please forgive the awful typing—I have no secretary and I am writing this at midnight, hoping that it may reach you in the morning.

From Varian Fry's Diaries

March 3 Afternoon [1941]

[. . .] I have come to the conclusion that the American consulate at Marseille [meaning: the Consul Harry Bingham] is a good deal more generous and a good deal more liberal in its attitude toward refugees than the State Department. Chagall's experience proves it, I think. The Museum of Modern Art asked the State Department to grant him an "emergency" visa last November. Not knowing this, I took him to the Marseille Consulate in January and got him an immigration visa with no affadavits at all. In fact, all he had in his dossier was a letter from me guaranteeing him politically. It was not until February 10 that the Consulate received the Department's authorization to grant Chagall a visa. Meanwhile, he had already had his visa a full month.

In other words, it took the Department three months to grant him an "emergency" visa, whereas the Consulate only required a day or so to give him an ordinary immigration visa.

Monday, March 10, Morning [1941]

Spent the weekend with the Chagalls at Gordes. Drove out with Harry Bingham on Saturday morning. We passed two truckloads of German soldiers between Marseille and Aix, and not another car all the way. We arrived in time for lunch. Gordes is a charming, tumbled down old town on the edge of a vast and peaceful valley. It used to manufacture shoes, but when shoe-making machinery was introduced, its craftsmen moved away, and most of the town is now in ruins. The Chagalls' house is the only one in the immediate neighborhood which has not fallen in. I can see why they didn't want to leave; it is an enchanted place.

Chagall is a nice child, vain and simple. He likes to talk about his pictures and the world, and he slops around in folded old pants and dark blue shirt. His "studio" contains a big kitchen table, a few wicker chairs, a cheap screen, a coal stove, two easels and his pictures. No chic at all, as *chez* Matisse. Chagall kept asking me anxiously whether there are cows in America. But he is already beginning to pack. He says that when they have gone I can have his house to hide people in. A good, remote place.

In the spring of 1941 it became somewhat easier to transfer people; as Fry reported, "April and May were the high point of the Committee's work." In May, a French Committee of Patrons was formed, including such prominent figures as André Gide, Jean Giraudoux, Henri Matisse, Pablo Cassals, Blaise Cendrars, André Lhote, and others. But Fry felt the heat from all directions. The liberal U.S. Consul Harry Bingham was recalled. The U.S. State Department cabled its Consulate in Marseille: "The government cannot countenance the activities as reported of Dr. Bohn[14] and Mr. Fry and other persons in their efforts in evading the laws of countries with which the United States maintains friendly relations" (implied: the regime of Marshal Pétain, recognized by the U.S.). According to Fry, "the Embassy [in Vichy] cooperated with the French police in bringing pressure on me to go"[15] and eventually approved his expulsion ordered by the French Ministry of the Interior. The head of the Marseille police explained why: "because you have protected Jews and Anti-Nazis," which he certainly did. Even Eleonor Roosevelt wrote to Fry's wife in New York on May 13, 1941: "I think he will have to come home because he has done things which the government does not feel it can stand behind." In 1967, the French government awarded Fry the Cross of the Legion of Honor, and the Israeli government, posthumously, accorded him the title of "Righteous Gentile" in 1996.

In April 1941, under German pressure, a Department for Jewish Affairs was established in Vichy France. The Chagalls were stripped of their French citizenship. Marc and Bella moved to the Hôtel Moderne in Marseille, to prepare for the voyage. Early in April, all the Jews in Marseille hotels were arrested by the French security police, among them Marc Chagall. Fry immediately called a high police official and threatened him with an international scandal if Chagall was not free within half an hour. In fact, Fry had no power to do so, but he said he would call the *New York Times*—and Chagall was released.

Varian Fry: Memorandum to the French Government (Excerpts)

January 14, 1941

The American Rescue Center has been painfully impressed by the suspicions and prejudices which the French Administration seems to carry against it—according to certain recent incidents.

The regrettable judgement to which it is subjected, and which it realizes is not deserved, can only be explained with false knowledge—due to insufficient information—of the kind of work on which its efforts are concentrated.

In order to put right what it sincerely hopes is only a misunderstanding, the Center endeavors to provide the French Authorities with the most complete explanations and to specify in all details the role and the limits to which it restricts its activities.

Initiated and supported by a group of outstanding American personalities, collaborating with important associations such as The Museum of Modern Art, The New School for Social Research, The New World Resettlement Fund, the Unitarian Service, The Emergency Rescue Committee, The American Rescue Center has been built up in order to help, without any distinction of race, nationality or faith, those intellectuals, scholars, writers and artists, who are in distress, owing to present circumstances, and who therefore need moral as well as material support.

Thanks to funds granted by generous donors, the American Rescue Center is supporting those who are most in need. It sends parcels with food, clothing and blankets to the most unfortunate internees, and covers the expenses for medical help and medicaments. To those persons eager to find asylum in another country, the Center gives advises of the conditions and the formalities to be fulfilled in order to obtain either an Immigration—or a special Visa.

[. . .]

Contrary to rumours spread by different sources, the American Rescue Center is not at all a Jewish or a Pro-Jewish body. It is interested without difference in intellectuals of any nationality of any faith and of any race, and it helps, independently of the French, Austrian legitimists, Russian or German Monarchists,

Poles and Czechs, Republicans or members of left organizations, Catholics, Protestants as well as Jewish people. The Center realizes that as a result of the political events, the proportion of Jews among the refugees is very high. But this is a fact for which the Center cannot be held responsible. At any rate, the Jews are not at all privileged nor are they more favorably treated.

[. . .]

Apart from those cases assigned to it by the Central associations of New York to be helped according to nominative lists, the Center is interested in all other cases worth consideration. All those persons—and nobody else but them—are excluded who are affiliated to the Communist Party or suspected of Communist sympathies, who are members of Nazi or Fascist organizations, who belong to a subversive group, be it closely or not, of the right or the left. In all these cases any help is categorically refused, even if the distress is very great. [. . .]

Communist sympathies: At the time, the USSR was an ally of Nazi Germany.

The American Rescue Center

From Varian Fry's Diaries

Thursday, April 10, Evening

Herbert Katski of the JDC [the American Jewish Joint Distribution Committee] and Peggy Guggenheim have both had the same experience as Chagall. When the police came for Peggy and asked her if she were Jewish, she answered, "I'm American." She was held for several hours and closely questioned about her "race," but they couldn't get anything more out of her than that. Eventually they released her. Poor Katski spent a whole day in the jug.

May 1

Official anti-semitism is very strong here now and getting stronger every day. We are already in bad odor because we help so many Jews and have a number of Jewish employees. I have even been "accused" of being a Jew myself. Jews—even American citizens—are now treated with supreme contempt officially.

Monday, June 2nd

[. . .] Almost every day the *Journal Officiel* carries long lists of Frenchmen who have been deprived of their citizenship either because they have joined de Gaulle or because they were naturalized under the Republic. In Marseille they are telling the story of a young Frenchman who was recently deprived of his citizenship because he was Jewish. His father went to Vichy when he heard the news and pointed out that his son had been killed in the fighting around Sédan and had received the *Croix de Guerre* posthumously for extraordinary heroism under fire.

Vichy, they say, has now restored the boy's citizenship—also posthumously, of course.

Saturday, June 28

I saw the [U.S.] Consul this morning and got some unsolicited advice.

"Why do you have so many Jews on your staff?" he asked.

I told him I didn't have as many as the police accused me of having. Less than half the staff is Jewish.

By Nurenberg laws, making anybody with even one or two Jewish grandparents a Jew (or a half-Jew), he may have had a problem. Of his two close collaborators he writes: "Whereas Danny was a Protestant, or had been brought up as one, Jean was a Catholic—at least, he had been born a Catholic."[16] Fry knew very well of their Jewish origin.

"Well," the Consul said, "I think you make a mistake to have even that many. The Department withdrew all the Jews on the Embassy and Consular staffs shortly after Pétain came to power. I think there is only one left, a clerk down at Nice. If the Department thinks it necessary to play in with the French authorities on the race question, I think you make a serious mistake defying them yourself."

On May 7, 1941, Marc and Bella Chagall crossed the Spanish border by train. On May 11, they arrived in Lisbon, where they waited for Ida and Michel with all of Chagall's paintings, which were left behind in Spain.

Marc Chagall in Lisbon to Solomon R. Guggenheim in New York

[The letter is written on a small sheet of extra-thin paper.] 1-VI-41 [June 1, 1941]

[French] Dear Mr. Guggenheim

Allow me, first, to thank you for the care you took to ease my departure.

Your attention moved me deeply and I appreciated it even more in these sad and hard times. You know, perhaps, that Mr. Barr (Director of the Museum of Modern Art) has invited me to do an exhibition. I hesitated for quite some time to undertake this long trip. By nature I am lazy about the slightest move and have trouble traveling.

But now I am already waiting impatiently for the day when I will set foot in America. I would finally like to start working, working freely, as I am used to doing. I am already in Lisbon and I am waiting for my paintings which are still on the way.

As soon as they arrive, I will leave. When I arrive in New York, I will be very happy to see you again and to thank you in person. I am happy to count you—at least I allow myself to think so—among the friends of my art.

That moves me and gives me courage.

Please accept our warmest regards

Marc Chagall

Marc Chagall: In Lisbon Before Departure (Poem)

[Yiddish]

A wall grows up between us,
A mountain covered with grass and graves,
The hand that creates paintings and books
Has separated us.

Have you ever seen my face—
In the middle of the street, a face with no body?
There is no one who knows him,
And his call sinks into an abyss.

I sought my star among you,
I sought the far end of your world,
I wanted to grow stronger with you,
But you fled in fear.

How shall I tell you my last word,
You—when you are lost.
I have no place on earth
To go.

And let the tears dry out,
And let the name on my stone be wiped out,
And I, like you, will become a shadow,
Melt like smoke.

[June 1941]

Marc Chagall: On the Ship (Poem)

[Yiddish]

> I came to the ship,
> Told you farewell—
> You took over my earth,
> The graves on the river.
>
> But you wiped out my grief,
> Veiled my home from me,
> Opened a new page for me,
> Revealed a new land.
>
> Don't leave me adrift in mid-sea,
> Where hordes of weary brothers, pitiless,
> Remind me of my pedigree and my race.
>
> Let my road stretch without menace—
> How shall I bless you, my God,
> And on what day shall I fast?

Michel, Ida, and Chagall's Paintings

Meanwhile, Michel and Ida Rapaport were stranded separately from her parents. When Michel was demobilized and joined Ida in Gordes, his parents where living in Vichy, then moved to Nice in the Italian Zone of occupation, where they survived the war. Unemployed and penniless (and with no help from the Chagalls), Michel and Ida stayed with his parents in Nice for three months. In February or March 1941, a cousin of his father, Jacob Frumkin, gave Michel a job at ORT in Marseille. ORT is an organization for the professional training of young Jews, which then was preparing children for emigration to Palestine. A police raid in April closed the institution, some children were carried off, others joined the resistance. After three months in Marseille, Michel and Ida went to Gordes, where they stayed alone in June 1941.

"Laval's Law" stripped Jews who had received French citizenship after 1936—

that is, during the Popular Front government headed by "the Jew," the Socialist leader Leon Blum—of their citizenship, and pronounced them "foreign Jews." Michel Rapaport had come to France as a child and served three years in the French army; nevertheless, his name was listed in *Journal officiel* among those who were stripped of their French citizenship. In awe of Chagall's fame, he and Bella were erased from that list, but the Rapaports had a different name. Two gendarmes came to their home, to demand the return of all their documents. One of them was sympathetic and gave Michel twelve hours "to find the documents." Michel took the hint and fled to Marseille to see Varian Fry. Fry wrote in his report:

> Exit visas are now refused to Frenchmen of military age. Ida Chagall has gone to Vichy for the 17th time to try pull more wires but there is nothing we can do to help. We can intervene in cases of foreigners but we cannot very well intervene in a matter which concerns a Frenchman with his government. So unless Ida succeeds herself, I'm afraid that they are stuck here for the duration of the war.

From Varian Fry's Diary

Tuesday, June 17

Ida Rapaport, Chagall's daughter, told me that the whole Chagall family was on the list of people to be deprived of their French citizenship until someone pointed out that Chagall is such a great artist that it might look foolish for France to denaturalize him. So they crossed the names of Mr. and Mrs. Chagall off the list. But they forgot that Ida and Michel Rapaport, who were on the list only because of their relation to Chagall, are his daughter and son-in-law. They were deprived of their French citizenship by decree yesterday.

In spite of the searches on the train, Michel risked a trip to Vichy, where he found his former intelligence bosses, a Colonel and a Major, who were now in charge of internal intelligence. They made it clear that he must disappear immediately and, tongue in cheek, gave him a military "marching order" to Martinique (a French colony) via the U.S.!

Ida left for Spain a few days earlier, trying to save Chagall's art. According to her second husband Franz Meyer, "all his pictures, all his portfolios of drawings and studies, packed in trunks and cases totaling three thousand five hundred pounds" were shipped to Spain. This figure certainly came from Ida herself, yet it seems exaggerated.[17] The art had been delayed in customs in Spain for five weeks, apparently under Gestapo pressure.[18] But how did it get to Madrid? Michel Rapaport assumes that Chagall shipped his paintings to Madrid with the French Ambassador in Spain, François Pietri (a former right-wing member of the French parliament, government Minister, and friend of Chagall). Michel, stripped of any citizenship, was again arrested while crossing from France into Spain, but Ida found Pietri at a party and at night Michel was smuggled out of his cell and arrived in Madrid. Ida pulled all her connections through French, American, and Spanish friends, and succeeded in releasing the art. But now there were no ships to travel across the Atlantic.

In Marseille, Michel had bought two tickets, at $600 each[19] (which he got not from Chagall but from his own father), for a Spanish (or Portuguese) private ship, commissioned by HIAS, that would take them to America.[20] The ship *Navemar* was supposed to sail from Seville. To everybody's disappointment, it turned out to be a cargo ship, intended for mixed cargo and twelve passengers. But it was converted and equipped with bunks inside huge holds that absorbed 1200 people, mostly Jewish refugees, including old German Jews, over sixty-five, who were allowed to leave Germany with $5 a person, as well as some Germans freed from concentration camps.

The American consul in Seville did not find the conditions hygienic enough and refused permission for the ship to sail to the United States. The *Navemar* went to Cadiz on the Atlantic shore of Spain, where it took on some more passengers and got a sailing permit. All passengers had American immigration visas, but by the time they acquired French exit visas, Spanish transit visas, and means of transportation, the short-term United States visas had expired, and the American consul had orders not to renew them. An exception, however, was made for the *Navemar*. The ship docked for ten days in the sea facing Lisbon, and the passengers took turns going to the shore on little boats under guard to renew their visas in a slow process.

The first day, a riot over bottles of water erupted. Then there were quarrels over chairs on the deck. Cows lay on the deck and turned up in the daily goulash. Some people had cans of food or bought food during the trip. The holds were overcrowded and smelled. Whoever could got onto the crowded deck and slept there. According to rumors, there were orgies on the lifeboats. The fascist sailors abused the passengers; Michel and Ida and two other couples formed a group, bought food, and protected their women from rape. Food was distributed in a lower hold, a piece of bread was given on the way. Sea water was used for washing and the women washed superficially, intimidated by the sailor watchman. On the deck, young Claude Kirschen saw a red-haired woman with blue eyes distributing hot tea and imperiously watching to make sure that nobody tried to get into the tea line twice. She sat on a large crate (6' x 6' x 3'), protecting it against anyone who tried to kick it. Ms. Kirschen later worked in the Office of War Information in New York, along with Michel Rapaport, whose wife was this same woman, Ida Chagall. Michel also remembered only one crate. (When confronted with Franz Meyer's figures, he said perhaps there were two or three crates, certainly no more, but he doesn't remember those.) The art was apparently sent from Marseille to Spain in small boxes and packed in one large crate for the ship.

The ship was at sea for forty days or more; it had to zigzag to avoid German submarines that torpedoed the traffic across the Atlantic. On the open seas, there was a typhoid epidemic on ship; sixteen people died, and after the *Kaddish* prayer was recited, they were thrown into the sea. At last, they reached Havana, where representatives of Jewish organizations met them. Another stop was in

Bermuda, where everybody was carefully examined. Most of the luggage was on the lowest level, were it was soaked with sea water, and the customs officers in Brooklyn, where the ship docked, threw the rotten luggage into the sea. On its way back to Europe, the *Navemar* was torpedoed by German U-boats and sunk in the Atlantic.

Some of Chagall's work and furniture remained in his apartment in Paris. Some time in 1941, Michel's aunt Leah Bernstein, who was still in Paris and had Chagall's key, and her brother David Gourvich, saved the art. Because there was no gas, cars could not be used, but they hired a horse and wagon and, risking grave danger, as gendarmes roamed in the streets, they took the paintings out of Paris.[21] This was the art saved in André Lhote's house in Le Raincey.

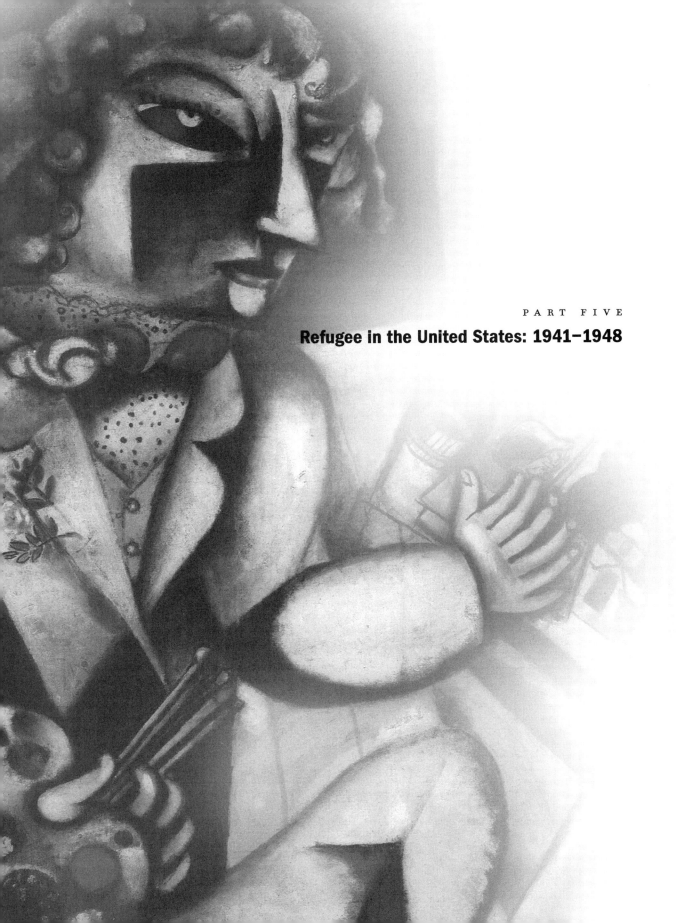

PART FIVE

Refugee in the United States: 1941–1948

CHAPTER FOURTEEN

With Bella in America: 1941–1945

Crossing the Atlantic

Marc and Bella Chagall crossed the Atlantic and arrived in New York in the evening of June 21, 1941, to hear that the German armies had attacked the Soviet Union.[1] In New York, Chagall had friends and collectors in the art world. Pierre Matisse, New York art dealer and the son of the painter Henri Matisse, met the Chagalls at the dock. Solomon R. Guggenheim and his wife Irene Rothschild-Guggenheim gave them a boat tour around Manhattan, entertained them, and helped bring Ida and Michel to the United States. Hilla Rebay, who lived in Connecticut, provided a car and driver for the Chagalls to find a home in the country.

Chagall also established contacts with many Yiddish writers and Yiddish-speaking intellectuals in New York, especially his old friend Yosef Opatoshu. Since Marc and Bella knew no English, they occasionally read Yiddish newspapers and learned of the destruction of the Jewish communities in Europe. They also participated in various Yiddish cultural enterprises, especially on the left, and Bella wrote her memoirs in Yiddish, which were published posthumously in two volumes. Chagall received commissions for major works. He coauthored the scenario, stage sets, and costumes for the ballet *Aleko*, to music by Tchaikovsky which, because of Union requirements, was first produced in Mexico City, then

Marc Chagall, New York 1943.

in New York in 1942[2]; and for Stravinsky's *Firebird*, produced at the Metropolitan Opera House in New York City in October 1945.

In mid-September, after a perilous six-week voyage across the Atlantic, Ida and Michel Rapaport finally arrived in New York with Chagall's paintings. Ida was exhausted and ill. Michel didn't know English and had a hard time adjusting, but he eventually found work at the Office of War Information (OWI), translating from English into French; in September 1942, he was invited by Pierre Lazareff to broadcast to France. In 1944, he became Editor-in-Chief of Voice of America French broadcasts in New York. Since Michel had a Russian accent, his texts were read by a native Frenchman, the Surrealist leader André Breton, who was a refugee in New York. To signal to his father in occupied France, Michel took the name "Gordey," from the village of Gordes, where Chagall had a house and Michel and Ida had spent their last days in France. After Bella's death in 1944, Michel, Ida, and Marc Chagall rented a spacious apartment on 42 Riverside Drive in New York, where Marc had his studio and paid two thirds of the rent. Michel Gordey went to France in April 1945 and became an international reporter for the influential newspaper *France-Soir* (edited by Pierre Lazareff from 1945 to 1972), as well as editor of the Russian, German, and American sections.

Marc Chagall in New York to Hilla Rebay in Greens Farms, Connecticut

[Stationery: Lakeview Inn on Lake Waramaug, New Preston, Connecticut]

[June–July 1941]

[French] Dear friend,

Thank you very much for offering the car. Mr. Penny Cent kindly drove us to the country.

Barely arrived, not even having had time to move in or even to write to friends, to you, to thank you, we have already received a heap of telegrams concerning our daughter.

That disturbed our vacation and we all hurried to return to New York to try to obtain the visas that our daughter and son-in-law lack.

We are leaving again for the country.

Are you well? Can you rest a bit?

When you come back, perhaps you will come to us?

We would be very happy to see you.

Meanwhile, our cordial regards,

Marc Chagall

Solomon Guggenheim in New York to Hilla Rebay in Connecticut

July 22, 1941

[English] Dear Hilla,

I have read your latest letters with great interest, and am returning them herewith. It is most gratifying to see the large number of art students that are being brought to the Museum, and this in itself shows the wonderful work that we are doing.

    With reference to Chagall, it would not do for us to become too much involved, otherwise he will depend on the Foundation [The Solomon R. Guggenheim Foundation for Non-Objective Art] rather than on the Modern Museum [MOMA], and they will claim all the credit, probably, when the time comes, for having brought him over here. I don't mean by this that you should not give him any assistance; on the contrary, help him as much as you can without committing the Foundation,—in other words, with discretion.

    I am perfectly willing to give Delaunay an affidavit, but I don't know what kind he wants, and of course provided it does not mean I would have to support him.

    With reference to the supplies allowance for John Sennhauser, as long as you don't become too deeply involved and have men like him dependent on you permanently, I feel that this man should be helped out, but only for a *very limited time*.

Delaunay: The painters Robert and Sonia Delaunay. Robert was a pacifist and fled to Portugal in World War I, to avoid the draft; Sonia was Jewish. Nevertheless, they stayed in Europe. Robert died in 1941, and Sonia survived the war.

Ever,

Sol.

Marc Chagall in New Preston, Connecticut, to Yosef Opatoshu in New York

[Stationery: Lakeview Inn/on Lake Waramaug/New Preston, Connecticut]

29/7 941

[Yiddish] Dear Opatoshu, here we are, settled in by our friends. There is not even half a Jew here. And who knows what they think about us (not very highly, I fear). We eat like real Americans. That is, a cucumber is not sour, but sweet . . . and so on.

    We are worried about my daughter and her husband, we still don't know where they are. We are ready to run to New York for them. How are you? And your fine wife and the young couple? What is new in the Jewish world? "God knows" (if he knows) what will happen to us. I am irked that I cannot read here on Sabbath, Sunday, the newspapers where you and others are published—to know what is

cucumber: Chagall is used to Jewish sour pickles rather than fresh cucumbers.

happening. But please, if you encounter interesting Yiddish articles about Jewish problems, cut it out for me later.

I would like to come back to N.-Y. and perhaps we shall soon come back, for it is, after all, quite gloomy here.

With warm regards from both of us

Marc Chagall

Bella Chagall to the Opatoshus

[Yiddish] How are you, dear friends? It surely must be hot. Here, there is a lake, a forest, a pine tree, a birch tree—a piece of Russia. (God knows what happens to Russia—our Vitebsk is burning.)

Warm regards to both of you   Bella Chagall

Vitebsk is burning: The German march on Moscow in the summer of 1941 swept through Vitebsk.

Marc Chagall in New York to Yosef Opatoshu in New York

[Stationery: Hampton House/28 East 70th Street/New York City]

[beginning of September 1941]

[Yiddish] Dear Opatoshu,

Goyish place: In the Chagalls' Jewish folk conception, nature is "goyish."

a Jewish word: A pun on a Yiddish idiom: "Give me a Jewish word" means "Warm me up with some good news, optimism." Here, also a request for Yiddish newspapers or books.

Came back from the Goyish place—summerhouse. For us it is an altogether new milieu which you probably know. I am longing for Jews—How are you and your wife? What are you writing? Give us a Jewish (your) word to read.

Call us.

The children, God knows, swim, with the Spanish boat "Navemare" via Cuba.

With best regards from both of us

Marc Chagall

Marc Chagall in New York to Hilla Rebay in New York

[Stationery: Hampton House, 28 East 70th Street, New York City]

12/IX/41 [September 12, 1941]

[French] Dear friend,

I hope that you have returned well rested and full of new strength.

We have returned long before we thought, having had many troubles and emotions concerning our daughter who has unfortunately sailed in a very bad boat, where she has fallen sick. Fortunately, she recovered and is arriving this Wednesday. And I decided finally to live in the country very close to N.Y. I think I could not work in the city.

She recovered: Actually, Ida arrived very sick; she had heart trouble and had to stay in bed.

I remember you were very nice to offer us the car to find a house around N.Y. For the moment, we are living here, where the noise, alas, pursues us.

We await the pleasure of seeing you. All our best,

Marc Chagall

Marc Chagall in New York to Sh. Nigger in New York

[Stationery: Hampton House/28 East 70th Street/New York City/BUtterfield 8-2700]

21.9.1941

[Yiddish] Dear Friend Nigger,

I greatly enjoyed reading your [Jewish] New Year article. I'll tell you the truth, I have been waiting a long time for such "simple" words in print, especially in America. You are saying what must be said without "literature," just don't let your voice be a *Slovo v pustyne*. I enjoyed the fact that you even think about "color" (alas, a rare thing among *Jewish* writers), you see how important "Art" can be. If Jews had it in mind, in their soul, we would not be lying torn apart, with no form and no color, deep in Exile.

Slovo v pustyne: Russian: "voice in the wilderness." In a Yiddish text, he writes the biblical Hebrew phrase in Russian!

I use the opportunity to wish you and your wife and yours—all the best from both of us for the New Year

Your Marc Chagall

Pierre Matisse

Pierre Matisse (1900–1989), the younger son of Henri Matisse, was born in France and moved to the United States in 1924.[3] He opened his own gallery in New York and became "the great American dealer of the European Surrealist generation" (William Rubin). Before he left Paris, Matisse worked at the Barbazanges-Hodebert Gallery, where he saw Chagall's exhibit of December 1924 and was attracted by the painter's "wild" side.[4] Shortly before the war, Matisse went to see

Chagall's first exhibition after arriving in the United States during World War II, at the Pierre Matisse Gallery, New York, February 1942. Pierre Matisse, Bella, and Marc Chagall.

Chagall in Paris and intended to make an exhibition for him in New York. Now the idea materialized. In September 1941 Chagall settled in New York, and in October he got an exclusive contract with Matisse with a regular income. In November, the first Chagall exhibition opened in the Pierre Matisse Gallery on 57th Street in Manhattan (featuring early works, from 1910 to 1914). The next year, Matisse showed Chagall's work of 1931–1941, including the ambitious "Revolution," now presented toward the 25th anniversary of October (October 13–November 7, 1942).

From October 1, 1941, Matisse guaranteed Chagall a monthly allowance of $350, raised to $500 in November 1943, and $700 in April 1947. When sales were good, the payments were higher.[5] Yet the beginning of the war was not the best time for selling art. In a letter to Chagall of April 2, 1943, Matisse wrote: "Let us hope that with the good news coming from Africa our collectors will relax and give us more of their attention."

When Chagall returned to France in 1948, he first hesitated, then settled on the dealer Aimé Maeght, who represented such artists as Picasso, Léger, Miró, and Braque. Thus, Matisse's role was diminished, and he even returned many of Chagall's paintings and gouaches.[6] Yet from January 1968 until after Chagall's death in 1985, Matisse was again "the official representative of Marc Chagall and his exclusive agent for the sale of his works in the United States" (contract of October 17, 1967). On Chagall's 100th birthday in 1987, Matisse went to Moscow to facilitate the first Chagall exhibition in Russia since 1922. In his New York gallery, he staged sixteen Chagall exhibitions over the years.

Marc Chagall in New York to Yosef Opatoshu in New York

{12/3} 1941 [December]

[Yiddish] Dear Opatoshu,

I hope that you are well and walking again. Be so kind and send me the names and addresses of the persons who have my drawings for Lyesin's books. I want to send my son-in-law M. Rapaport to them. I don't want to bother Nigger.

And meanwhile I am bothering you—

With best regards
Your devoted
Marc Chagall

Marc Chagall in Connecticut to Yosef Opatoshu in New York

[Postcard] New-Preston, Conn. 1942

[Yiddish] Dear Opatoshu,

We greet you and your dear wife from here, where I sit and try to work for the Ballet [*Aleko*]. How are you, my dear Opatoshu? Work, write, perhaps doing it we shall live through the sad times. Regards to your son from both of us. When you go to Leyvik, give him our love, too. We shall stay here quite a while. In June, when we arrive [in New York] and if everything is a bit "normal," I have to travel to Mexico. Be well, Your devoted

Marc Chagall

From Bella:

like pigs: Implied: We eat, get fat, and don't think about the world.

[Yiddish] Warm regards to all of you. We live here like pigs. Horror to think what happens in the world.

Your Bella

[Attached to previous letter]

Yiddish present and future: The permanent crisis of Yiddish; the Yiddishists were worried about whether their culture would survive. In New York, it got a boost with every wave of immigration from the Yiddish heartland in Eastern Europe.

My dear Opatoshu I would like to add something to our conversation today—about Bella. It is important—now when there is all kinds of talk about Yiddish present and future—here came a woman, who was Russian in her upbringing and education (she completed the Historic-Philosophical Faculty of Moscow University, as a student she was for a while a journalist in Moscow Russian newspapers and later successfully translated my book into French) and suddenly—spontaneously, with her inner soul—she fell to the wellspring—to Yiddish, and *she cannot in any other way*. This in itself is worth noticing and encouraging. True, she is so shy that for "dozens" of years I begged her to write her "Life"—

Warm regards to both of you. She does not know that I am writing to you. She would have "scolded" me for it—

Your devoted Marc Chagall

P.S. I was indeed very sad before you called. *Not for myself*. Alas and woe. I need nothing for myself. But woe for our Jews. Because I am apparently a terrible Don Quixote. I dream: they are as pure as angels . . . And great. Otherwise, it makes no sense to be an artist, a writer and everything—

Your Ch.

From the FBI files

On October 27, 1941, Chagall applied for a reentry visa to the United States in order to travel to Mexico "to fulfil theatrical engagements under contract with Ballet Theatre"—that is, to do the sets and costumes for *Aleko*, first staged in Mexico City. The U.S. Immigration and Naturalization Service (INS) noted: "Since there is nothing in the files of this service which would preclude the issuance of a permit to the alien, it is the opinion of this office that a permit may be granted."[7] Yet the FBI was more cautious.

Almost from the beginning of Chagall's seven-year sojourn in the U.S., the FBI kept an eye on him, as can be seen from the following declassified letter, signed by J. Edgar Hoover. The reason could have been a category recognition: Chagall was a Russian Jew and he left the Soviet Union not before, but after the Revolution—ironically it was the same reason he was barred from visiting Russia for fifty years (1922–1973). Furthermore, there was the rumor that Chagall had been a "Commissar" in Vitebsk. But that was a misunderstanding: Chagall was never a Communist and would not have been granted the title "Commissar" in the Soviet Union, except as a nickname. He was "Plenipotentiary on Matters of Art in Vitebsk Province" and had a budget and a great deal of power in matters of public art in his city for a year and half. Indeed, he was one of many non-Communist intellectuals and cultural figures (the poet A. Blok, the painter V. Kandinsky, the theater director V. Meyerhold, and many others) who helped rebuild Russian culture in the first years after the Revolution, without being Communists.

FBI in Washington, D.C., to the U.S. Department of State

JBM: JLK 40-35810-1, RECORDED

To: VISA DIVISION, DEPARTMENT OF STATE   July 18, 1942

In connection with the below entitled reentry permit applicant case, the files of the Federal Bureau of Investigation reflect the following information.

Very truly yours,

CONFIDENTIAL

[signature]

John Edgar Hoover

Director

Enclosure

ATTENTION: [XXXXXXXX][8]   TITLE: MARC CHAGALL,
Reentry Permit Applicant;
PASSPORTS AND VISAS

FREEDMAN & SLATER, INC
8 Bridge Street
New York City

Derogatory information concerning the above organization[9] was furnished the Visa Division in connection with the reentry permit application of Antal Dorati[10] under date of February 10, 1942.

Your original request for information is returned herewith.

[Stamp:] Communications Section/ Mailed 12/ JUL 18 1942/ Federal Bureau of Investigation/ US Department of Justice

Marc Chagall in Mexico to Yosef Opatoshu in New York

[Stationery: Hotel Monejo, Mexico, D.F.]

10/9 1942 [September][11]

[Yiddish] Dear Opatoshu, How are you? [I am] freer from the ballet "Aleko," i.e., yesterday was the premiere and it was so successful that they "searched" for me in the "cellar" of the theater, where I was hiding, and dragged me out to the stage. During the search, the Mexican audience applauded, waited, and screamed "Chagall," but from the "cellar" below where I was hiding (why, I don't know), I only heard: . . . AL . . .

about us Jews: The ballet was based on the Russians Pushkin and Tchaikovsky, and in Chagall's mind the Gypsies are analogous to the Jews.

I hope that my dear friends and all other friends in America will see this ballet, which I made thinking not only about the great Russia, but also about us Jews . . .

I wish you a good year and thank you from the bottom of my heart for seeing Bella's chapter into print with your love and art.[12]

I kiss both of you,

Your devoted   Marc Chagall

Regards to everybody

Bella Chagall to the Opatoshus

Dear friends

Finally I sit at the desk to write a Jewish word. You see, for over three weeks we have been in a commotion, turning our brains, and about what? About dresses, not even for me [= the actors' costumes].

We painted dresses like dolls. Chagall's decorations are burning like the sun in heaven. And the whole ballet Chagall's spurts with light and joy. We hope you will enjoy it. May the costumes only arrive fresh and clean.

Thank you for your letter. A sad letter, your dear son is leaving [for the army]. But surely he will return soon fresh and healthy. It just cannot be otherwise. I don't know how to thank you for going over my article. I am sure you feel my deep, warm, great thanks. I shall not be able to express it with words. So many mistakes—as only a woman can make. If I could ask you also to make an effort and go over the printed proofs! Here in the Yiddish papers, they made mistakes—even more horrible than mine, whole lines dropped out, it makes no sense.

Happy New Year to you, dear friends. Let us see each other in health. Happy New Year to all our friends,

Bella Chagall

only a woman: In traditional Jewish society, most women did not study Hebrew, and Bella could not spell Hebrew words in Yiddish, but neither could Marc.

Marc Chagall in Mexico to Pierre Matisse in New York

17/9/42   Hotel Montejo

[French] Dear Matisse,

How are you and yours?

We have just received your telegram. Thank you!

It has only been a few days since I finished the ballet (I still need to work a little more). "Aleko" has had a great success here. God knows what will be in NY?

I worked very hard. Bella helped me a great deal. But the atmosphere of the theater was not very favorable. I had to struggle with the old routine, with the lack of artistic consciousness, lack of polish—I suffered from that. It exhausted me. Is it the general fatigue, the climate, the food—but I feel numb in this pretty country.

To this day, I haven't been able to work for myself. And you're making an exhibition! And on the 13th (!) of October. I would very much like to give you something new. Perhaps when I get back, I will work. Here, right now, I am not sure of anything. I want to get out as soon as possible. I hope to get back at the end of the month.

Couldn't you postpone the exhibition a little? I am sure that you will do it very well, but I don't know if I'll have any new things. But you understand much better than I what you have to do.

Hurok: Sol Hurok (1888–1974), a famous New York impresario who specialized in bringing Russian ballet and cultural performances to the U.S.

Hurok would like to exhibit the sketches of "Aleko" in his place or somewhere else—I don't know exactly. He has already returned to NY. Do you want to talk to him? (Plaza 3-0820, 711 Fifth Ave.) He opens the season with "Aleko" on October 6. I am afraid of how Aleko will be received in NY. As long as the costumes don't arrive too worn out. They (the administration) are not very careful and are quite negligent.

See you very soon. And good wishes from both of us,

Marc Chagall

Marc Chagall and the Morgn Frayhayt

Morgn Frayhayt (= Morning Freedom) was the Yiddish Communist newspaper in New York, edited by Pesach Novik (1891–1989). Although its distribution was far lower than that of the major three Yiddish newspapers, it had a small but faithful readership and at various periods attracted important Yiddish writers. It was anticapitalist and often brought information from "the world of tomorrow" that seemed reliable to its adherents. The Special Committee on Un-American Activities (Report, March 24, 1944) described the "Morning Freiheit"—even during World War II!—as "one of the rankest organs of Communist propaganda in this country."[13]

Chagall's ambitious painting "Revolution," created in France in 1937 on the 20th anniversary of the October Revolution, was prominently featured in the Matisse Gallery Chagall exhibition near the 25th anniversary of the Revolution[14] and favorably reviewed in the *Frayhayt*. Politically, the painting is not as pro-Communist as the name might suggest: Lenin stands upside-down on one hand, performing an impossible acrobatic trick, but the real revolution is of the Jewish masses who appear both with their religious iconography and Torah scrolls and with red banners. This positive review apparently started a relationship between Marc and Bella Chagall and the New York Yiddish-language Communists and sympathizers. In his letters and speeches of the time, addressed to leftist audiences, naïve Chagall thinks he is talking directly to the Soviet Union and displays his allegiance to the "homeland."

Marc Chagall in New York to the *Morgn Frayhayt* in New York

N.Y. 7 nov. 1942

[Yiddish] Dear Friends,

7 nov. 1942: The 25th anniversary of the October Revolution.

Thank you for your response to my picture, "The Revolution," which I made almost for the 25th anniversary of the Soviet Revolution.

I have never been cut off from the land of my birth. For my art cannot live without her and cannot assimilate in any other country. And now that Paris—the capital of plastic art, where all artists of the world used to go—is dead, I often ask myself: where am I?

I send my sincere greetings and wishes to my great Soviet friends and colleagues—writers and artists, and the even greater artists—the heroes of the Red Army on all fronts. I hope, and I am sure, they will paint with their blood the best and most beautiful "picture" of life's revolution, which we, simple artists and people, will have to observe and admire and live in its light.

Marc Chagall

The New York Communists and Yiddish Culture

Ever since the 1930s, American Communists had toed the Stalinist Party line in literature and art, but relaxed their orthodoxy whenever the party line encouraged it. Several Yiddish writers, alienated by the blatant aspects of American capitalism, shocked by the trial of Sacco and Vanzetti, and by the Great Depression, sympathized with the Communists and enjoyed their audiences. Yet at various times, many prominent so-called fellow-travelers resigned from the cultural institutions of the left and became their bitter and relentless enemies. The protests were aimed especially at Soviet policies concerning Jewish issues, such as the Communist support for the Arab pogroms in Palestine of 1929, for the Hitler-Stalin Pact of 1939, for the liquidation of Soviet Yiddish culture of 1948–1952, and the Slansky Trials in Prague of 1952.

Nevertheless, the Yiddish Communists had a "warm Jewish heart" and attracted considerable audiences in Yiddish, primarily through their cultural front organizations, their support for literary standards, and their multifaceted cultural activities. Marc Chagall often conflated the Communist concept of the "people"—the "working class," whom the Communists claimed to represent in the class struggle—with his own image of "the people," those uneducated, simple Jews, imbued with Jewish folklore and intense feelings of Jewish identity he had known in his parents' home.

Bella Chagall submitted her Yiddish memoirs to a leftist publishing house, the Book League of the Jewish People's Fraternal Order, IWO, where they were edited and published posthumously in two volumes.[15] Yet there was nothing politically Communist about her memoirs; on the contrary, those were lyrical and nostalgic descriptions of Jewish religious life and holidays in her parents' wealthy home in Vitebsk.

World War II and the Soviet Ally

The utopian ideals of a just society propagated by Communism appealed to many in the West. During World War II, as Nazi armies overran most of Europe, the Herculean Soviet effort to stop Hitler overshadowed many misgivings about the Soviet system. Moreover, for many Jewish immigrants, this was not just an abstract, ideological matter; it also concerned their personal lives and memories.

Hence the fierce and acrimonious fights between pro- and anti-Soviet trends in American Yiddish culture.

In Yiddish cultural circles in America, most writers, activists, and audiences were immigrants from Eastern Europe for whom Poland and Russia were "the old home" and the authentic centers of Jewish life, education, and literature. Furthermore, many still had close family ties there and were both worried and nostalgic about their "old homeland." After the Warsaw Ghetto Uprising in April 1943, the annihilation of Polish Jewry loomed as a terrible fact. Yet in Soviet Russia, over two million Jews were evacuated deep into the hinterland and survived, and it was the Red Army that could still save the remnants of European Jewry.

At the same time, many German Jewish refugees still remembered Communism as the only force that had stood up to fascism. For such German intellectuals, the fate of European Jewry was relevant to their own trauma of Jewish identity.

The Committee of Jewish Writers, Artists, and Scientists

On April 7, 1942, a Jewish Antifascist Committee was formed in Moscow, led by the celebrated actor and director of the State Yiddish Theater Shloyme (Solomon) Mikhoels (1890–1948). It was one of a series of such "antifascist" committees established in the USSR during the war. Since Jews in the USSR had no territory of their own, they were not considered a nation and could have no separate Jewish organization (except for some cultural institutions). Now the Jewish Antifascist Committee became the only legitimate representative of Soviet Jewry. Moreover, for the first time in Stalin's Soviet Union, it acknowledged a worldwide Jewish nation and stretched out its hand to unite with the "brethren" abroad. "Unity" was their irresistible slogan.

In response, a Committee of Jewish Writers, Artists, and Scientists was established in New York in 1942 (with bilingual stationery, in Yiddish and En-

A delegation of Soviet Jewry visiting American Jewry at the height of the Holocaust, September 1943. From left to right: Soviet Yiddish poet Itzik Fefer; Albert Einstein, Honorary President of the Committee of Jewish Writers, Artists, and Scientists; Joseph Brainin, organizer of the committee; actor and Director of the Moscow State Yiddish Theater Solomon Mikhoels, Chairman of the Jewish Antifascist Committee in Moscow. Chagall was a member of the Board of the American Committee and a friend of Mikhoels and Fefer from his Russian years.

glish). It included several German-Jewish intellectuals and a wide range of liberal Yiddish writers and scholars who lent their names and prestige to the lofty humanistic and Jewish national goals of the organization. Its Honorary President was Albert Einstein, its President was Sholem Asch, its Chairman was the Yiddish journalist B.Z. Goldberg, and the Vice-Chairman was the Labor-Zionist Jewish historian Dr. Rafael Mahler. The several dozen members of the board included Yiddish writers, the American painter Max Weber, the German writer Lion Feuchtwanger, the American writer Waldo Frank, the Yiddish theater director Morris Schwartz, and Marc Chagall—all of them hardly Communists (except for the organizer Goldberg, who apparently tried to please the Soviets). The committee issued a journal in Yiddish, called *Eynikeyt* (*Unity*), echoing the name of the parallel Yiddish newspaper, launched in Moscow. A few years later, this

A reunion with Solomon Mikhoels, actor and Chairman of the Jewish Antifascist Committee in Moscow, New York 1943.

cultural committee was pronounced in the United States: "among the Communist front organizations for racial [sic] agitation."[16]

Messengers from Soviet Jewry

In the summer of 1943, Shloyme Mikhoels was sent to New York along with the Soviet Yiddish poet Itzik Fefer (1900–1952) to mobilize American Jewish public opinion to aid the Soviet war effort. Fefer was a charming, dashing man, a soldier in the Red Army during the Civil War, and a Yiddish poet of Soviet optimism. Chagall knew Mikhoels personally from their work together in the Moscow Yiddish Chamber Theater in 1920.

Yet Stalin's strings stretched as far as New York. From the outside it seemed that Mikhoels could not talk freely because Fefer was assumed to be a NKVD agent watching over him (as we learn from the FBI report, Mikhoels was actually the

Chagall with Soviet Yiddish poet Itzik Fefer, during Mikhoels' and Fefer's visit to America in the middle of World War II, New York 1943.

more important spy). The Jewish cultural establishment was critical and wary of their visit. Chagall, on the other hand, correctly felt that they were not simply Stalin's agents, but in their hearts they were "our kind of Jews" and that it was "not necessary to criticize them."

A later summary of Chagall's activities in such "front organizations" prepared for the Visa Division, U.S. Department of State, reflects both his pursuits and the suspicions of the FBI.

FBI Report on Marc Chagall

Security Information (Confidential) SECRET[17]

January 3, 1952

Marc Chagall

No investigation has been conducted by the FBI concerning the subject of your inquiry. However, a check of the Bureau files reveals considerable information regarding Marc Chagall.

ACTIVITIES IN CONNECTION WITH CITED ORGANIZATIONS

Summary

The January 24, 1944, issue of the "Daily Worker" stated that Marc Chagall, prominent Jewish painter, was a speaker at the Unity Conference of the American Committee of Jewish Writers, Artists and Scientists, Inc., held in New York City on January 22 and 23, 1944, at Carnegie Hall and the Hotel Commodore. (100-127710-2, p. 12).[18]

The American Committee of Jewish Writers, Artists and Scientists, Inc., has been cited as "among the Communist front organizations for racial agitation" by the California Committee on Un-American Activities, Report, 1947, page 45.

A confidential informant, of known reliability, advised that Marc Chagall was one of the sponsors of a dinner given on December 4, 1944, in honor of William Gropper for the benefit of the Joint Anti-Fascist Refugee Committee. (100-127710-2)

The Joint Anti-Fascist Refugee Committee has been cited by the Attorney General as coming within the purview of Executive Order 9835.

In September, 1945, the name of Marc Chagall, artist, was included on the list of sponsors in an undated mailing circular "Announcing a New School of Jewish Studies, 13 Astor Place, 5th floor, New York 3, New York." Chagall was also listed

Gropper: William Gropper (1897–1977), a Jewish American painter and graphic artist known for his sharp political caricatures, published in Communist periodicals in English and Yiddish. His themes included anticapitalist and anti-Nazi satire, as well as the plight of the American Negro, the Jewish exile, and the Holocaust.

as a sponsor of this school in the 1946 and 1948 catalogues of the School of Jewish Studies for the Winter Terms, January through April. (105-6781-2, 4, p. 7, 13, enc. p. 4.)

The School of Jewish Studies, New York City, has been cited by the Attorney General as coming within the purview of Executive Order 9835.

Marc Chagall was listed as one of those sending messages of greetings to the World Youth Festival held in Prague from July 25, to August 17, 1948, according to a statement issued by the American Delegation upon their return from the Festival. The Festival was sponsored by the World Federation of Democratic \ (100-185087-246X, p. 60)

The World Federation of Democratic Youth has been cited as one of the "long established Soviet-controlled international organizations" which "speak identical lines of propaganda and stand together on all phases of Soviet foreign policy" by the Congressional Committee on Un-American Activities, Report Number 271, April 17, 1947, pages 12 and 13.

On June 30, 1950, a confidential informant, of known reliability, furnished a mimeographed document, prepared and mimeographed at Communist Party headquarters, San Francisco. This document, which was entitled, "Every Party Member a Fighter for Peace," listed the name of Marc Chagall, artist, as one of the initial national sponsors in the United States of the World Peace Appeal. (100-3-81-1253, encl.)

World Peace Appeal: If every member of the Communist party must support the Peace Movement, it hardly follows that every supporter of the Peace Movement is a Communist.

Marc Chagall, artist, was listed as one of the "Americans Who Have Signed the World Peace Appeal" in the program issued by the Crusaders for Peace, at Philadelphia, Pennsylvania, on July 13, 1950, in connection with a rally held at the Adelphia Hotel, under the auspices of the Civil Rights Congress. (61-10149-1305, encl. p. 3) The World Peace Appeal has been cited as having "received the enthusiastic approval of every section of the international Communist hierarchy" by the Congressional Committee on Un-American Activities, House Report Number 378, on the Communist "Peace" offensive, April 25, 1951, original date, April 1, 1951, page 34.

Committee for the Negro in the Arts: Chagall was not in the U.S. at the time. His name was probably used without his knowledge.

The January 19, 1951, issue of the "Daily Worker" in an article on page 10, entitled "Committee for Negro in Arts Sponsors Art Exhibit" listed Marc Chagall as one of the contributing artists to an exhibit to be held on January 19 through 21 at Riverside Museum, 103 Street and Riverside Drive, New York City, under the auspices of the Committee for the Negro in the Arts. Confidential informants, of known reliability, have advised that with the merger of the National Negro Congress and the Civil Rights Congress, the Cultural Division of the National Negro Congress was discontinued and in its place the members of that Division organized the committee for the Negro in the Arts. (Dr. Max Yergan, and XXXXX Staff correspondent, New York World Telegram and Sun; 100-373195-A). The National Negro Congress and the Civil Rights Congress have been cited by the Attorney General as coming within the purview of Executive Order 9835.

The May 28, 1945, issue of "Morning Freiheit," New York Jewish Communist newspaper, carried a report of an open meeting at Madison Square Garden on May 26, 1945, celebrating the 50th Jubilee Liberation of the Jewish People's Fraternal Order.

This is the sort of information the FBI received. The 50th anniversary would mean from 1895, while Communism did not start before 1917. IWO, the International Workers Order, was founded in 1930 and later renamed the Jewish People's Fraternal Order (JPFO). Thus, the celebration was on the 15th anniversary of IWO. An informer calling on the telephone with a Yiddish accent would blur 15 and 50. And in Yiddish, "Jubilee" means any anniversary with a round number (5, 10, 15, etc.). But the JPFO needed no "liberation"; the celebration obviously was for the victory over the Nazis in Europe on May 8, 1945, and the "Liberation of the Jewish People," not the "Liberation of the Jewish People's Fraternal Order." Furthermore, the "Order" was, indeed, a pro-Communist front organization, but all they did was conduct intensive activity in Yiddish schools, at cultural events, and in publications. They were a cultural organization, intensely and sentimentally Jewish, as was Bella Chagall in her memoirs, which were published by the Fraternal Order. Indeed, the leader of IWO was expelled from the American Communist Party in 1949 for "factionalism" (i.e., separate Jewish activity).

Marc Chagall was listed as one of the speakers. According to the article, this meeting contained an appeal to suppress anti-Soviet propaganda from spreading in the United States and at the same time drew the conclusion that anti-Soviet feeling and anti-Semitism went hand in hand. (40-62732-4, p. 10)

The Jewish People's Fraternal Order has been cited by the Attorney General as coming within the purview of Executive Order 9835.

CONTACTS WITH SOVIET NATIONALS:

A confidential informant of known reliability advised that Marc Chagall and his daughter, Ida Chagall Rapaport, also known as Mrs. Michel Rapaport, 4 East 74th Street, New York City, were frequently in the company of Professor Solomon Michoels and Lieutenant Colonel Itzik Feffer, members of a Jewish delegation from the USSR who made a tour of the United States from June 17, 1943, to

frequently in the company: Apparently, Ida Chagall had an affair with Fefer in New York. Since, according to the FBI, she visited him often, it is hard to know whether the affair was a cover for information (what could she have known?) or vice versa.

October 20, 1943, for the alleged purpose of straightening relations between the Jewish people of the USSR and the United States. Michoels was the head of the Moscow Jewish State Theatre and helper [holder?] of the Order of Lenin. Investigation reflected that Michoels was interested in a scientific report in Russian prepared by a Russian physicist concerning the theory of the atom structure. The informant further advised that Feffer was a poet and a Lieutenant Colonel in the Red Army. (NYT-117; XXXXXXXXX *Sun; 100-373195-A)

A reliable confidential informant reported that Marc Chagall and his daughter Ida had exchanged New Year's Greetings with Mr. and Mrs. Eugene Kisselev, Vice Consul of the Russian Consulate at New York City, on January 1, 1945, at which time they advised the Kisselivs [sic] that they had received greetings from Michoels and Feffer from Moscow. (NYT-117; XXXXXXXXX)

In August, 1945, a confidential informant, of known reliability, advised that Mark [sic] Chagall, Russian born artist, had addressed a letter to Joseph Stalin in which he appealed to Stalin for permission to go to the Soviet Union for the purpose of a "live contact with the Soviet soil, skies, and the people." Chagall also mentioned that he had not broken his ties with the motherland and that his love for her, his artistic contact with her was being emphasized in his art. He also stated that he considered it his duty to give his accumulated experience and share it with the young artists of the Soviet Union. (Anonymous; 100-138350-111, Page 30)

In regard to the above letter, a reliable confidential informant reported that on September 20, 1945, Bruslov of the Soviet Embassy, Washington, D.C. had advised Mikhailov, of the Soviet Consulate in New York City, that Marc Chagall had written a letter to Joseph Stalin, wherein he indicated indirectly a desire to be invited to Moscow, Russia. Bruslov was of the opinion that Chagall would like to be invited officially. According to the informant, Mikhailov indicated that Marc Chagall, although a progressive man and entirely a Soviet man, was *not well enough known* as a painter in his own right and therefore did not deserve the honor of being invited to Moscow as a guest of the Russian government. The informant advised that Mikhailov promised to put his views regarding Chagall in a letter and send them to the Soviet Embassy at Washington, D.C. (NYT-117; XXXXXXXXXXXXX)

The January 15, 1948, issue of "Morning Freiheit" contained an article reporting the death of Solomon Mikhoels, Director of the *Jewish Government Theater* in Moscow and head of the Jewish Anti-Fascist Committee of Russia. According to the article, expressions of condolence were sent to the Jewish Anti-Fascist Committee in Moscow by the "Morning Freiheit" Association and by the Artist, Marc Chagall. (100-46808-239, page 45)

The "Morning Freiheit," published by the Morning Freiheit Association, Inc., has been described by the Special Committee on Un-American Activities, Report, March 24, 1944, Page 75, as "one of the rankest organs of Communist propaganda in this country for almost a quarter of a century."

not well enough known: Of course, because Chagall's work was banned in the Soviet Union.

Jewish Government Theater: The exact name is Yiddish State Theater. Most theaters in the USSR were state institutions; the translation "Government" makes it a direct organ of the Soviet government, which it was not.

The above information is furnished to you as a result of your request for an FBI file check only, and is not to be construed as a clearance or nonclearance of the individual involved. This information is furnished for your confidential use only and should not be disseminated outside your department.

    The FBI summary has to be read with caution, both as to the retroactive interpretation of some activities and the facts themselves. Thus, from other sources we know about Chagall's (and Albert Einstein's) prominent affiliation with the Committee of Jewish Writers, Artists, and Scientists, founded in New York in 1942. The events in Europe, the destiny of the war, and the unfolding Holocaust were of special interest to American Jews. But in all the publications there is no trace of "racial agitation," which, according to this document, was the purpose of this organization (unless the word "Jewish" or the opposition to anti-Semitism imply that). Neither Chagall nor Einstein could be described as racists.

    The Committee did support (morally) the Soviet war effort, but the Soviet Union was America's major ally in Europe in the war against Nazi Germany, and the stakes of that war were crucial for the survival of the Jews as a nation. Indeed, in the tradition of the Popular Front of the late 1930s, collaboration with the Communists against fascism was not a taboo at the time. Chagall participated in a "unity conference" "in support of post-war global cooperation as laid down in the decisions [by Churchill, Roosevelt, and Stalin] at Tehran," called by the American Committee of Jewish Writers, Artists, and Scientists. The conference was held on January 22–23, 1944, at Carnegie Hall and the Hotel Commodore in New York. It greeted all allied armies, protested the British discrimination of Jews in Palestine (in the British "White Paper" of 1939)—which at the time was an anti-Soviet position, endorsed the publication of a "Black Book" of Nazi atrocities against Jews, and called for actions against anti-Semitism in the U.S.

    A tragic irony lies in the accusation that Chagall sent condolences upon the death of Mikhoels, Chairman of the Jewish Antifascist Committee in Moscow. Mikhoels had been Chagall's close friend during their work together in the Mos-

cow Yiddish theater in 1920. They met again in New York in 1943. In 1948, Mikhoels was murdered by the NKVD. Chagall's message of condolence and protest
on Mikhoels's murder was suppressed by the committee and never published
(see Chagall's February 1948 letter of protest to the Committee of Writers, Artists, and Scientists, p. 631). However, it found its way to the FBI.

An interesting story is Chagall's letter to Stalin, for which there is no corroboration elsewhere. After Chagall left the Soviet Union in 1922, in letters to his
friends in Russia, he repeatedly expressed his longing for his "homeland," its
skies, its people, and his own sisters. Thus, in a letter to Pavel Ettinger of July 12,
1948, he writes: "I am happy that, as far as I can, and though from afar, I am useful to my homeland, to which I have been and am devoted in my art for the last
forty years." But how was he "devoted"? The sentence continues: "for it seems to
me, a Russian artist never was given an exhibition in the museums of America and
Europe, and a living artist at that." And in 1943, in a "Statement on Russia" for the
New York Russian emigré newspaper *Novoe Russkoe Slovo*, Chagall wrote: "for
thirty-five years, as an artist in his art, I ran around like a possessed man with my
love for my homeland." Yet he mentioned this identity as a "Russian painter" only
in letters to Russia, hoping for an invitation (which came only in 1973, i.e., 51 years
after he left the Soviet Union!). Chagall may have written to Stalin as the highest
authority that could grant him permission to visit. But, of course, he was "unmentionable" in the USSR and therefore rebuffed as an unknown painter. In any case,
a wish for "live contact with the Soviet soil, skies, and the people"—of the land he
was born in and reflected in his painting—or teaching the Soviets some modern
art (that was anathema to them) is not exactly serving their purposes, even if he
did write a letter to Stalin, as suggested by the Soviet Consul in New York.

The FBI summary is cautious and points out that it did not conduct an investigation; the "considerable information" found in the files was apparently just
informants' material and may or may not have been correct, hence it was "not to

be construed as a clearance or nonclearance" of Chagall. During 1952–1958, however, it was sufficient to refuse him a U.S. visa.

Marc Chagall in New York to Sh. Nigger in New York

[Stationery: 4 East 74th Street / New York City / Rhinelander 4-5826]

1943 5/7 [July]

Dear Friend Nigger,

I didn't want to send you the poem, but since you asked—never mind. If you really like it—publish it.

I am not so afraid of printing poems as of an exhibition of my paintings. If they curse me for the poems—I still have a hope left . . .

And what about the frontispiece plate for my "Martyr"? You see that I am jittery even over a reproduction of a painting.

—I hope it won't be so hot and you all will be able to see it.

With best regards / Devoted /   Marc Chagall

Marc Chagall in Upstate New York to the Opatoshus in New York

Cranberry Lake [NY, Adirondacks]   {7/24} 1943

[Yiddish] Dear Opatoshu, Finally we left [the city]. Someplace at the end of the world. But, unfortunately, we shall not remain here for long. We shall spend a few days in New York and go somewhere else.

How are you? Several times I saw my "pupil"—Mikhoels (and Fefer). From up close, they are very good Jews. When we meet, we shall discuss it all. In any case, I think it is not necessary to "criticize" them—they are our kind of Jews. True, the "Committee" (what a Committee!) stands in the middle . . . Be well. How is the Frigidaire? I hope you live like an emperor. Love to Adelya. If you see Leyvik and others, give them our love.

Devoted   Marc Chagall

From Bella Chagall:

[Yiddish] My dearest,

We sweated enough in NY. One day (a few days ago), we got in the car and rode so far that we wondered why they didn't ask us for a visa. In a few more hours, we'd be in Montreal!

what a committee: The welcoming committee was in the hands of Communist operators. It is hard to imagine to what extent every step of such a visit, even in New York, was controlled by the Soviet apparatus and its yea-sayers in the U.S.

like an emperor: The first refrigerator!

Here, the only Jews are God Himself and . . . us. The food is American, the talk is American, nature—American-Russian, French-Swiss . . . A lake—as large as the sky and the air—strong, clean. This is the place to gather strength. But . . . in a week we are dragging ourselves again.

How are you? Is it cold or hot?

Be well! From my heart, your   Bella

Marc Chagall in New York to Andrey Sedykh in New York

Chagall was also in contact with some Russian emigré circles in New York, notably with the Jewish editors of the major newspaper of the Russian emigration, *Novoe Russkoe Slovo* (*The New Russian Word*), published in New York. Andrey Sedykh (1902–), pseudonym of Yakov Moyseevich Tsvibak, or Jacques Zwibak in French, was born in Russia and emigrated to the West in 1920. Sedykh was a prominent writer in the "first wave" of the Russian emigration in France and the United States. He arrived in New York in 1942 and became city editor and eventually Editor-in-Chief (after the long-time editor Mark E. Veynbaum's death in 1973).

New York 1943

[Russian] My Dear Sedykh and editors,

If you absolutely must have a few silly words of mine for your questionnaire—here they are. If you find them "not to the point," throw it in the wastebasket . . .

I regret that I couldn't be at your wife's concert—(some other time).

Regards,

Marc Chagall

Marc Chagall:
Statement on Russia

Everybody now sings the praises of Russia. But should I shout along with everybody else? For they are praising my own relatives. But to my shame, I have not helped them in the critical moment—it was not I who took Rostov, Kharkov . . . along with them.

Rostov, Kharkov: Russian cities occupied by the Germans, now liberated by the Soviet army.

Unless you consider that for thirty-five years, as an artist in his art, I ran

Chagall reads a lecture at a meeting in New York, June 3o, 1944, dedicated to the publication by ICOR of Itzik Fefer's book of Yiddish poetry *Heymland* with Chagall's illustrations. Seated: Editor I.A. Ronch and Bella Chagall.

around like a possessed man with my love for my homeland, like a person in love chasing the moon.

Marc Chagall

1943. NY

Marc Chagall in Cranberry Lake to Yosef Opatoshu in New York

[Stationery: Cranberry Lake, N.Y., Adirondacks]

{8/3} [August] 1944

Thank you for the clipping about the general from Vitebsk—Beskin. I think it is a boy—a student and especially an overseer in the Academy of Art I once founded in Vitebsk—he was a fine young man of 16 or 17, wearing khaki jodhpurs and a gun on his hip, because the youth—I don't know why—used to come to school with their weapons. Maybe it is he, but never mind, there are many Jewish generals and the liberator of all the Vitebsks, General Chernyakhovsky, is worth a treasure.

Chernyakhovsky: General I.D. Chernyakhovsky (1906–1945), commander of the army that liberated Vitebsk, Vilna, and Koenigsberg; he fell on the battlefield in East Prussia.

Marc and Bella Chagall with art historian Lionello Venturi. A refugee from Europe during World War II, Venturi invited Chagall to deliver a lecture on modern art at Mount Holyoke College. He also wrote a book about Chagall, published in 1945.

Listen, I don't have the Bible handy—tell me, how is it written on each of Moses's two tablets? [Give me the words] in Hebrew?

I got a nice letter from your son. One can see that he is a fine, intelligent young man. You may be (and you are) very proud of him.

Regards from both of us/To both of you/   Marc Chagall

From Bella Chagall:

peasant trees: Jewish folk imagery still operates: Nature is non-Jewish, healthy, and strong, like a peasant.

[Yiddish] Warm regards from me too. All around us—a lake, a forest with peasant trees—we want to draw strength from them.

Your Bella

Marc Chagall: Introduction to an Evening of Yiddish Poetry Reading

And now, in conclusion—since I am among poets—allow me to become a bit of a poet for a moment and read you a few of my poems, which I stray into from time to time.

You must not be amazed that an artist writes poems, for, in the past, some artists, though very great ones like Michaelangelo, Leonardo da Vinci, Delacroix, wrote poems and prose. Recently, too, Gauguin and Van Gogh, and in our own time, Picasso and others.

The first poems I shall read you were written in the years [around] 1935,[19] the last on the way to America.[20]

Marc Chagall

Marc Chagall: The Vilna Synagogue[21]

[Yiddish]

> The old *shul*, the old street,
> I painted them just yesteryear.
> Now smoke rises there, and ash
> And the *parokhet* is lost.
>
> Where are your Torah scrolls?
> The lamps, *menorahs*, chandeliers?
> The air, generations filled with their breath?
> It evaporated in the sky.
>
> Trembling, I put the color,
> The green color of the Ark of the Covenant.
> I bowed in tears,
> Alone in the *shul*—a last witness.

Marc Chagall: Jacob's Ladder

[Yiddish]

> I walk in the world as in a forest.
> On my hands and feet do I crawl.
> Every tree shed its leaves,
> They wake me. I am scared.
>
> I paint my world as sleeping in a dream;
> And when the woods are filled with snow,
> My painting is from another world,
> But for a long time, I alone stand on it and stand.

Alone in the shul: An allusion to Ch.-N. Bialik's Hebrew poem "Alone" ("Levant"), depicting the last man in the prayer house, when the whole generation was swept away by "Light" (Enlightenment).

I stand and wait for a miracle to embrace me from afar,
To warm my heart and drive out my tremor,
I wait for you to come to me from all sides.
And I shall stand no more, but fly—
And rise with you on Jacob's Ladder.

Marc Chagall in Upstate New York to Sh. Bickel in New York

Shloyme Bickel (Bikel, 1896–1969), a Yiddish writer and literary critic, was born in Kolomeya, a Jewish town in the Carpathian Mountains in Galicia in the Austro-Hungarian Empire; after 1918, it was incorporated into Poland on the Romanian border; today in Ukraine. It was the home town of the BeShT, founder of Hasidism. Bickel lived in Romania, arrived in the U.S. in 1939, and was literary critic of the Yiddish daily newspaper *Der Tog*, where Opatoshu worked. His son, Alexander Bickel, was a famous law professor at Yale University.

[Yiddish] Dear Dr. Bickel

Thank you for your book. You erected a gravestone on Kolomeya. I hope that your gravestone will endure and survive the scattered stones of our homes . . .
    We are here for a few days.

Regards from both of us

To both of you   Marc Chagall

Marc Chagall in Upstate New York to the Opatoshus in New York

distant sons: Opatoshu's son David, who served in the Pacific theater of the war.

until the elections: A reference to the U.S. elections of November 1944 and rumors about a possible deal between the West and Germany. In the pro-Soviet propaganda, after such a deal, a Third World War may be unavoidable in the future.

[postcard] 1944

[Yiddish] Dearest, we are here where you find no dog,[22] only mosquitos. You must probably enjoy nature. May the distant sons come back soon from the other nature. It's only regrettable that the bastards "want" to wait with their "Kaput" [Capitulation] until the elections here . . . So that our grandchildren will go 3 times to fight the thieves.
    What's up?

Love from both of us to both of you

Marc Chagall

Chagall longing for Paris. "The Eiffel Tower," New York, 1943, hand-colored etching. Published in *VVV*, a portfolio of eleven original works: etchings, frottage, objects. Special edition of the Surrealist magazine *VVV*, with André Breton, Alexander Calder, Leonora Carrington, Max Ernst, David Hare, André Masson, Matta, Robert Motherwell, Kurt Seligman, and Yves Tanguy.

Marc Chagall to Pierre Matisse

Harbor Hills, Cold Spring-on-Hudson, NY   [Late August, 1944]

[French] Dear Pierre,

Not being able to see those paintings, we admire your catalogue—it is a master-piece. Such a warm black, contrasted with a mild ivory, every short line has a rhythmic interval—almost like music. If only the paintings were beautiful . . .

Just imagine, that to top it all, we will meet the Genauers here (for the week-end). That's the last straw, one doesn't get away from painting. But she (let's hope temporarily) already has her eye on the black. So it goes, you are in style this year. Here one sighs and works.

What's new with you *at shop and at home*? Best wishes to all of you.

Chagall

the Genauers: Emily Genauer, art critic for the *Herald Tribune* in New York, wrote favorable reviews on Chagall.

From Bella Chagall:

I (Bella), like an idiot, I fell ill as soon as we arrived. That is called being lucky.

This must have been one of the last days of Bella's life.

Bella's Death

Paris was liberated on August 26, 1944. The Chagalls stayed in a summer house at Cranberry Lake in the Adirondacks, upstate New York, and planned to return to New York City, but Bella fell ill and suddenly died on September 2, 1944. Chagall's inspiration, a central theme and symbol of love in his paintings, the woman who devoted her whole existence to him and knew the world he came from, his languages and gestures, died with no warning at age fifty-five or fifty-six (officially: forty-nine).

Pierre Matisse in New York to James Johnson Sweeney[23] in New York

[Telegram; identical telegrams to a list of other people]

Madame Chagall died (last Saturday) after short illness. Funeral will be held Wednesday morning at 11.30 at Riverside Chapel (76th and Amsterdam)

[Michel Rapaport—erased]   Pierre Matisse

Bella Chagall's tombstone in New Jersey. The date of her birth makes her younger by six or seven years.

There are several versions of this event. The closest to the source is a direct quotation of Chagall's account of it, as recorded in Virginia Haggard's book:

> We were having a holiday in the Adirondacks, and she suddenly got a bad sore
> throat. She kept calling me to give her boiling hot tea. The next day she was so
> feverish that I took her to the hospital, and when she saw a lot of nuns in the corri-
> dor, she became upset. I must explain that in another place where we had been
> staying, in Beaver Lake, she had seen a sign saying that only white Christians were
> welcome, and she had been brooding on that. [. . .] Well, when she got to the hos-
> pital, they naturally asked for particulars—name, age—but when they asked 'reli-
> gion' she wouldn't answer. She said 'I don't like it here, take me back to the hotel.'[24]

A similar version was retold by Meyer Shapiro, who heard it from Chagall: "As a
Jew she was refused admission and died soon after."[25] Yet Lilyan Opatoshu, who
was then staying in her in-laws' summer house in Croton Falls near New York
City, does not believe the story. She remembers a frantic call from Chagall to
Opatoshu. Apparently, even though Bella had a sore throat, she continued taking care of Marc and tried not to be a burden. Finally, Marc realized that the situation was severe. He knew no English and called Opatoshu, who advised him to
find a doctor. She died the next morning in Mercy General Hospital, Tupper
Lake, New York.

On the other hand, Ida's account, written half a year later in a private letter to
her cousin in Europe,[26] mentions no anti-Semitism. Bella had a streptococcus
infection in her throat, there was no penicillin, and the whole thing was over in
forty-eight hours. It took Ida twelve hours by train to get from New York to Cranberry Lake, and she was too late. If that was so, Chagall, in what Virginia describes
as "his tortured sense of responsibility," covered his guilt feelings with a story
about an enemy: anti-Semitism.

In fact, Bella was often ill and had undergone several mysterious operations
during the 1920s and 1930s in Paris. In her last years she withdrew into herself,

"grew weaker every month" (Ida), and was preoccupied with writing her memoirs in her childhood language, Yiddish. According to Chagall, a few weeks before her death, she sorted out the manuscripts of her memoirs. "I asked her with a hidden fear: 'Why all of a sudden such order?' and she answered with a pale smile: 'so you will know where everything is . . . ' Everything inside her was a quiet and deep premonition."[27] The official death certificate indicates "Diabetes Milletus" as the cause of death. After her death, Chagall published her memoirs in Yiddish in two volumes, edited by I.A. Ronch.[28]

Marc Chagall : On Bella Chagall[29]

Bella Chagall (Bellochka) was born on December 15, 1895,[30] in Vitebsk, to a well-to-do family of Lubavich Hasidim. Her father—Reb Shmuel Noah Rosenfeld, her mother—Alte (*née* Levyant).

Bella was the youngest of the seven Rosenfeld children. As a child, she was almost always alone at home, which was connected with the store. Bellochka would hide in the niche under the window and always read and dreamed. She was an extremely exalted soul, permeated with Hasidism, which weaved inside her a subtle lyricism and a plastic quality.

In 1909, as a young girl, she met Marc Chagall . . .

B. graduated from the Vitebsk Women's Gymnasium. In 1911 she was admitted to Moscow University, to the Historic-Literary-Philosophical Faculty. Upon completion, she wrote two dissertations[31]: "The Liberation of the Russian Peasants" and "Dostoevsky."

In her student years, she collaborated on the Moscow newspaper, *Utro Rossii* [*The Morning of Russia*] and studied at the studio of the Moscow Art Theater. She made several public appearances.

In 1914, Marc Chagall returns home from Paris to Vitebsk. Marc and Bella, friends from their youth, married in Vitebsk on July 25, 1915. She immediately became his inspiration and content.

In 1922,[32] the Chagall family settled in Paris. Bella translated into French and edited Chagall's autobiography, *My Life*.

Bella's journey to Eretz Israel in 1931, her trip to Vilna in 1935—Jewish life influences her so much that she begins to write in Yiddish.

Bella died on September 2, 1944, in the summer resort of Cranberry Lake, New York.

Pesakh Novik in New York to Marc Chagall in New York

[Yiddish typescript] Wednesday [?] evening, September 6, 1944

Dear, Warm Man Marc Chagall!

Dear Friends Ida and Michel!

All the time I have wanted to say something to you—and I cannot say anything. The words have gone bankrupt. Now I feel like writing something to you—something that would express the innermost feeling, and especially something that would strengthen you, console, lift your courage and your heads, and again I have no words.

On the velvet grass we just left the mortal remains of the deceased Bella. If she could speak, she would have spoken,—*indeed, she is speaking*: Marc Chagall must be strong! He belongs to the Jewish people, he belongs to the most beautiful in the human race. He must create! The people needs it! And Ida must create. And Michel must be strong.

I don't know what else to say, but be strong!

And be consoled!

Body and soul,   [place for signature]

P.S. Here is Sholem Asch's cable. Also a column I wrote Monday, which was printed on Tuesday.

most beautiful: The left intellectuals.

Ida must create: Ida Chagall was a painter.

BenZion Goldberg in New York to Yosef Opatoshu in New York

[Stationary: Committee of Jewish Writers, Artists and Scientists]

Sept. 15, 1944

[Yiddish] Distinguished Colleague Y. Opatoshu,

On the thirtieth day of the death of Bella Chagall, we organize an intimate evening of mourning for about two hundred persons in Carnegie Chamber of Carnegie Hall, where her closest friends will say a few words.

The evening will be held on October 6.

As a friend of the deceased and of the Chagall family, you are invited to participate in the evening with a speech of some ten to fifteen minutes. Please let me know if you will come.

Respectfully,

B.Z. Goldberg

Marc Chagall in New York to Pesakh Novik in New York

[Stationery: 4 East 74th Street/New York City] 1944

[Yiddish] P. Novik—*Morgn Frayhayt*

Distinguished Friend,

You asked me to write something for you on the anniversary of M.F. [*Morgn Frayhayt*]. But you fell into my current "dry"— sad state, when I am waiting for "miracles" . . .

   —What does it mean: especially for the anniversary issue? I send both an anniversary and a mundane wish: that you may always seek the truth in life. Seek the saving of the Jewish remnants and help develop the true human culture and art.

Greetings,

Marc Chagall

Exhibitions in the United States

In March 1941, Varian Fry and Harry Bingham, the American Consul General in Marseille, drove out to Chagall's house in Gordes and brought him an invitation from Alfred J. Barr for an exhibition in the Museum of Modern Art in New York (MOMA). Only three and a half years later, after D-Day and the liberation of Paris, did the thought of a major exhibition of this Jewish artist come to fruition. Even by then, it was not without apprehension: "All of us feel that there is danger of arousing a certain anti-Semitic feeling towards Chagall's art"—if Meyer Shapiro were to write an introduction (Daniel Catton Rich of the Art Institute of Chicago, November 27, 1944; see p. 550). The Art Institute of Chicago and the MOMA began contemplating a major retrospective of Chagall's work—the first ever in the United States. It finally materialized in April 1946. Daniel Rich was Director of Fine Arts at the Art Institute of Chicago, 1938–1958; Monroe Wheeler was Director of Exhibitions and Publications at MOMA; Carl Schniewind was Curator of the Department of Prints and Drawings at the Art Institute of Chicago, 1940–1957.

Daniel Catton Rich in Chicago to Monroe Wheeler in New York

November 13, 1944

Dear Monroe:

Carl Schniewind and I have been talking over the possibility of an extensive, retrospective exhibition of Chagall's work to be held at the Art Institute of Chicago for about a month, beginning February 1, 1946. We would include not only oils and water colors but drawings and prints. Carl has secured a loan of the artist's unique illustrations for the Vollard publications, most of which have never been shown or published.

I am wondering whether the Museum of Modern Art might be interested in a cooperative exhibition, details to be worked out along the lines of our double venture in Picasso and Rousseau. You discuss the matter with Jim Soby and let me know if it interests you.

Kindest regards, always

Very sincerely yours,

Daniel Catton Rich

Director of Fine Arts

Monroe Wheeler in New York to Daniel Catton Rich in Chicago

The Museum of Modern Art
New York
Monroe Wheeler
Director of Exhibitions and Publications

November 18, 1944

Dear Dan:

Your letter proposing collaboration on a Chagall exhibition was very opportune. At the last meeting of our Exhibitions Committee a Chagall exhibition was approved and we have tentatively scheduled it for the early autumn of next year. What we would like to know now is whether, since you are planning to show it in February, you would be willing to have it shown here first, or whether there is a possibility of your showing it this summer. In any case, I want to say that we shall be delighted to make it a cooperative venture.

I have been talking with Alfred [Barr] and Jim [Sweeney] about a text for the catalogue and we should like you to write a survey of his work and perhaps Carl Schniewind could do a separate appraisal of his prints. We all feel, and I think you will agree, that it would be desirable to have a contribution from someone who would write with understanding and sympathy about the background of Russian-Jewish culture and mysticism. Two people who might do this occurred to us; Meyer Shapiro, for one, and Raisa Maritain, the Jewish wife of Jacques Maritain, who is a very close friend of Chagall's, and could, we think, interpret the emotional qualities of his work very well. I think that under war conditions a book of 64 to 80 pages would be as large as we could undertake. That is about the size of the Rousseau. Please let me have your views on these points as soon as convenient. [. . .]

With kindest regards, I am

Faithfully yours,

Monroe

Marc Chagall in New York to Louis Stern in New York

> Louis E. Stern (1886–1962), was born in Balta, Bessarabia, which was then in Russia (today, Moldova). He joined his father in America in about 1900, and received a law degree from the University of Pennsylvania in 1909. Stern was an attorney who represented foreign companies, and an avid art collector. He collected paintings by modern masters, illustrated artists' books, and prints, and arranged a special Chagall room in his Manhattan apartment. Chagall had been in touch with him since 1942. Since Chagall could not communicate in English, and Stern was more practical and spoke both Russian and Yiddish, he accompanied Chagall to Chicago in March 1946 and to Paris in May 1946. He became a close friend of Ida Chagall and they corresponded on acquiring and exhibiting works by Chagall, as well as on intimate family matters. Stern left his art collection to the Philadelphia Museum of Art.[33]

42 Riverside Drive   November 19th, 1944

[English] Dear Louis Stern:

I understand that Mr. André Seligmann[34] has asked you to lend pictures of mine for the Exhibition of French Art, which he is organizing. I send you a copy of a registered letter addressed by me to Mr. Seligmann. I cannot have my name in an Exhibition in the same time as some collaborationist artists, who have been

excluded, for their Pro-German activities, from the Paris "Salon de la Liberation." I am sure that you will agree and cooperate with me in this matter.

With friendly greetings,

Marc Chagall

Marc Chagall in New York to André Seligmann in New York

19 Novembre 1944

[French] Sir,

I have learned that you intend to exhibit some of my works at an Exhibition of
French Art. I would have been very happy about it, as about each of my partici-
pations in French cultural events. However, I have heard that the exhibitors
would also include painters who collaborated with the enemy under the German
occupation, and who were excluded from the Salon de la Libération in Paris because of that.

For the prestige of French art abroad, I hope that you can give me a full and
complete guarantee to the contrary, otherwise please withdraw my name from
the catalogue and my works from the exhibit.

Awaiting your reply, please accept, sir, my very polite greetings.

Louis Stern in New York to Marc Chagall in New York

New York 22 Nov 44

[English] Dear Marc Chagall

Since receiving the copy of the letter which you addressed to André Seligmann,
I have talked to him on the telephone.

This is the situation as he tells it to me. Both Hopinaut, the French Ambassador at Washington, and the De Gaulle government in Paris are fully posted on
the forthcoming exhibition and have approved the catalogues. I take it, therefore, that they have no objection to the French artists who are included in this
exhibit. Seligmann denies that any of the so-called "collaborator" artists have
been arrested or are in jail. Under these circumstances, it seems to me "your
skirts" are clear and so are mine.

At any rate, my letter is written to you so that you may have a record of the
whole transaction.

Sincerely yours

Louis E. Stern

Daniel Catton Rich in Chicago to Monroe Wheeler in New York

November 27, 1944

Dear Monroe:

I was very interested to receive your letter of November 18 and find that the Museum of Modern Art was also planning a Chagall Exhibition and that you are willing to make it a cooperative venture. As to the Chicago period of the exhibition, I am afraid with our very tight schedule we would not be able to show it before February 1, 1946. We agree that you may show it first and hope that it might be shown in New York perhaps in December so that lenders would not rebel against too long an exhibition period.

You are all most complimentary in suggesting that I write a survey of Chagall's work, but I am afraid I cannot take this on, as I am more and more compelled to pull out of the curatorial side of the museum. I think Carl Schniewind's remarks on the prints would be excellent. He and I are very doubtful about stressing the "Russian-Jewish culture and mysticism." All of us feel that there is danger of arousing a certain anti-Semitic feeling towards Chagall's art. At any rate I would certainly be against Meyer Shapiro's contributing. Perhaps Madame Maritain could develop the mysticism without the propagandizing element which might be destructive to the situation.

We like the idea of the format.

> With kindest regards. Always
> Very sincerely yours,
> Daniel Catton Rich
> Director of Fine Arts

Marc Chagall at the Evening Honoring the Literary Prize of the Lewis Lamed Foundation to Yosef Opatoshu

Lewis Lamed Foundation: The most prestigious prize for Yiddish literature in America.

N.Y. 1944 24/XII

[Yiddish] Warm greetings to my personal friend and the friend of my Bella—the great writer Opatoshu, whom I would love to greet with a "Nobel" Prize, if we Jews had one.

Every opportunity is good for honoring our writer-masters, who must help lift up our neglected Yiddish literature—our culture to a high place and help bring together the torn Jewish people.

I greet all Yiddish writers and builders [of the culture]

Marc Chagall

Daniel Catton Rich in Chicago to Monroe Wheeler in New York

February 6, 1945

Dear Monroe:

I had a few minutes to talk over the proposed Chagall show with James Sweeney and am pleased to find he is greatly interested in the project and ready to take on the selection of paintings and do the catalogue. This strikes me as excellent. I believe we all agree that Carl Schniewind should do the section on the prints.

I am writing James Sweeney to find out whether the Museum of Modern Art is planning to go ahead with the exhibition.

Very sincerely yours,

Daniel Catton Rich

Director of Fine Arts

Grenier: Jean Grenier, a French art critic, who wrote about Chagall.

Marc Chagall in New York to Jean Grenier in Paris

7 February 45

[French] Dear Mr. Grenier,

Of course—I remember you and your visit to Gordes very well.

Your letter touched me very much and I thank you for it sincerely. I also hasten to tell you that I am happy and grateful for your good intentions and for the publishers' plan to put out a book about me.

I am trying to get you some reproductions of recent works. Pierre Blanchar has taken a package of 35–40 reproductions. He will be back in Paris at the end of February or the beginning of March. Call him or have him call you about this, if possible.

You probably know that, if need be, older reproductions can be found with Marc Vaux, Rep, Gaughier (rue Buffault), Illustration. Perhaps with Zervos at Cahiers d'Art, too.

I am very miserable at this time. I have lost the one who was everything to me— my eyes and my soul. If I continue to create and to live, it is because I hope to see France and the people of France again soon. My happiness, now, is the rebirth of France, which I had never doubted. How could one live without that certainty?

Write to me, dear Mr. Grenier, and accept my regards—

Marc Chagall

I have been advised to write
on the typewriter because of the
censorship. Forgive me.

Monroe Wheeler in New York to Daniel Catton Rich in Chicago

The Museum of Modern Art
New York
Monroe Wheeler
Director of Exhibitions and Publications

February 15, 1945

Dear Dan:

I have been in the south for a little rest and hasten now to reply to your letter of
February 6 regarding Chagall. I am delighted that Jim Sweeney is willing to undertake the direction of the show and do the text as well, with Carl Schniewind
doing the print section and, if we find it desirable, a personal impression from
Jacques Maritain, and perhaps a note on the Russian background by Boris Mir-
ski (this last is a suggestion of Alfred [Barr]'s).

The only problem now is one of dates. Jim feels that he will need more time
than an early autumn opening could give him and we should like to have the exhibition run at least two months here. We should, therefore, like to open the
show here about December 1 and have it run to February 1. Would it be possible
for you to open the exhibition between the 20th of February and the 1st of March
to run as long as you desire? This would make it fit perfectly into our schedule
and I hope it can be done without inconvenience to you.

Inasmuch as this is to be a joint undertaking may I suggest that the costs be
divided as follows:

> The Museum of Modern Art would pay costs of assembling the exhibition, arrange-
> ment of loans, photographs, express and insurance charges on all out of town ship-
> ments. We suggest that the assembly charges on our part be balanced by your paying
> for the packing and shipping to Chicago and the return of loans to lenders. All New
> York loans may be returned in one lot to us and we will assume the responsibility of
> delivering them here.

Does this seem to you an equitable arrangement?

As to the book, we shall provide you at cost with as many copies as you wish to
take. We should like to do a paper covered edition with several color plates to sell
in the two museums only at $1.25 or $1.50, and a cloth bound edition for the
trade to sell at $2.50 or $2.75. The exact number of pages depends upon our paper quota but we envisage a publication about the size of the Rousseau book or
larger. In view of the importance of the print section we ought to have at least
sixteen more pages than in the Rousseau, if we can manage it.

paper quota: During the
wartime allocation of
paper.

Won't you let me know what you think of these suggestions at your convenience?

With best wishes, I am

Sincerely yours,

Monroe Wheeler

In spite of all the odds, the organizers of the Chagall exhibit were excited about it. Daniel Rich, Director of Fine Arts at the Art Institute of Chicago wrote to James Johnson Sweeney, Curator of the exhibition, at MOMA in New York: "I believe the show will be a most fascinating one and should do a great deal to clarify Chagall's place in the development of modern painting." Attempts were made to bring certain pictures from Russia, France, and Switzerland, and indeed, some works from France and six paintings from Chagall's early collector Regnault in Belgium arrived. "Many of the paintings are flaked, rubbed, poorly stretched, etc."[35] Shortage of paper for the catalogue, labor difficulties, tight conditions for color reproductions, and matters of logistics, all combined to postpone the original dates of the exhibition.

Ida Chagall in New York to the Rosenfelds in Paris

Bella Chagall's brother Isaac Rosenfeld, his wife Hinda, and their daughter Bella Rosenfeld (today, Zelter) were hiding in Paris and miraculously escaped the roundup of Jews in July 1942. Their apartment was ransacked by the Gestapo, yet they escaped to the "free zone" and survived. In Vitebsk, Bella Chagall's father Shmuel Noah Rosenfeld had been robbed to the last stitch by the Bolsheviks (as a jewelry store owner, he was considered a bourgeois and his house was ransacked to find jewelry); he died in Russia in 1924 or 1925. His daughter Bella Chagall and her brother Isaac lived in Paris and tried to bring out their mother, but the Soviet authorities would not agree, claiming that Chagall cheated them and did not return to the Soviet Union. Bella's mother died in Moscow in 1943, during the war. This letter was the first message from the Chagalls written half a year after the liberation of Paris and Bella's death, but before the end of the war.

NY/USA/27 March 1945

[French] My very dear dear ones,

I cabled you a long time ago, more than six months ago, six months which were dark and terrible for us. And from your letter, which arrived a few days ago, I see alas, or fortunately for you, that you did not receive our cable . . .

I am so happy and I must say that we are so happy to know that you are alive, safe and sound. From Bellochka's letter, we see what a big and sensible girl she is. How I would like to have a photo of her. How is Isaac? Where is he? What do you plan to do or where to live? We are happy that you, Hinda, along with Bellochka, are with your family. Thank God, they are also alive.

This letter will be taken to Paris by Michel who is going there for a short time on assignment from the radio. He has been working for the radio all those years for the Voice of America, where he is the editor-in-chief of French broadcasts and very very often you can also hear his comments under the name of Michel Gordey.

Papa is working, he has resumed his work after a break that was very hard to overcome. You know how he could always work only with Mama, with her devoted help. Mama, our Bellochka, has been very weak and tired since her arrival in this country. She grew weaker every month and I was frantic to see her growing weaker. But she worked hard on her book which is going to appear in a month.

My dears, I don't know how to tell you. Perhaps it was Fate that spared you all these months by not letting you hear about the resounding tragedy that broke us. We have remained alone, without our guardian angel, without Bella, without Mama. It is over. It is over. She was struck down by an illness, a streptococcus infection in her throat. It was in the country, six months ago. It lasted forty-eight hours. When I arrived at the hospital, which took twelve hours by train from New York, it was too late. Mama was in a coma for fourteen hours, and on September 2, 1944, at six in the evening, she died.

Papa cannot write. He isn't strong enough to write. You understand. He has suffered so much that I would like to spare him that torture of telling you.

Mama was very tortured by your fate, by the fact that you remained in Europe. You know, Isaac, everything she always desired and wished for you.

Bellochka, don't forget, darling, that now you are Bellochka and that nothing was ever so perfect, so high for her. Hinda, she loved you, she loved you tenderly. Do convey her affection for your family that she respected so much, Hinda, and may God help you all.

We are living with Papa, we have been with him ever since and we live in the same apartment. No doubt next year, if we can still make plans, we will return to Paris. Before that we cannot. Papa has been *very very* sick and it is a struggle every day to help him recover his strength. We know that Jacob, Mama's brother, and Isaac's, is safe and sound. Abraham was in Moscow, no news from Grandmother, and that also tormented Mama.

I must end. Goodbye. Write about your situation and we hope to help you as much as possible. Kisses and blessings,

Ida

Marc Chagall: On the New Dawn in Poland (April 1945)[36]

Poland was the major center of Jewish life between the sixteenth and twentieth centuries. The liberation of Poland by the Soviet Army, the establishment of a pro-Soviet Polish Government and a Jewish Central Committee associated with it in the temporary capital of Lublin, the return of many Holocaust survivors and the eventual repatriation of three hundred thousand Polish Jewish refugees from Russia, the establishment of Jewish institutions, pre-war parties and news-papers—all these may have looked like the resurrection of a culture. This delu-sion of a "miracle" of rebuilding Jewish life in Poland after the Holocaust (the slogan was: *"Oyfsnay"*[37]—a new beginning) was especially emphasized by the Communist and pro-Soviet press around the world. The same was claimed for the two million Jews that survived in the Soviet Union.

Chagall, an inveterate optimist, wanted to believe in it and was influenced by their propaganda. His triptych of paintings: "Resistance," "Resurrection," "Lib-eration" reflects this perception (see discussion in the Introduction, p.5). The facts of the Holocaust were not yet brought home in their full horror; the Jewish resistance to the Nazis was aggrandized, assimilated to the general ideals of re-sistance, and thus provided some dignity to Jewish self-esteem. And yet, Cha-gall kept telling the left what was anathema to them: the equally important dig-nity of the revival of a Jewish nation in Eretz-Israel.

[Yiddish] For two thousand years, the Jewish people cried and gave rise to a Jeremiah, a Yehudah HaLevi, a Bialik . . . Others looked at us, listened. But now we are shedding tears every one of us separately over lost individuals that were close to our hearts. Millions of individuals. Not the whole Jewish nation.

Could it be that tears do not help any longer? Do not touch—

Did the old, sentimental mechanism of the "soul" break down?

A time comes of new means, new actions, a different content. Just as once, the old, overhauled art changed and the new art was different.

From afar, I see the first, new, tragic steps: millions of Jewish victims gave us the Jewish resistance in the ghettos. Their flaming light and shadow falls upon us. Such a light that we can see more clearly, in an enlarged focus, our external and internal behavior—our doubts and our silence.

We see—a legitimate, liberated Jewish nation comes to life in one country— the Soviet Union—to live equally with others. Not in vain did two great Jews come to us recently to bring us tidings and call us to happy unity.

two great Jews: The Soviet Yiddish leaders Shloyme Mikhoels and Itzik Fefer visited New York in September 1943. Ironically, both were murdered by Stalin a few years later.

New people emerged in Eretz-Israel and they will continue fighting in their place. And from Polish ghettos and forests Jews emerge, new Jewish Committees and new governments are established—let us hope that their new light will be so big it will devour the shadow, in which we, better-off Jews, are still dwelling in darkness.

Happy are our brothers who will feel the tremor of joy, as an artist rejoices when he finds overnight a new path in art—a new trend.

Marc Chagall in New York to Pavel Ettinger in Moscow

Chagall's correspondence with Ettinger was interrupted during Stalin's terror in 1937. Some correspondance was renewed after World War II, mainly through "friendly occasions," somebody going to the Soviet Union. Ettinger was now almost eighty years old.

30/IV 1945   42 Riverside Dr., New York

[Russian] Dear Pavel Davidovich,

I was so happy to receive your letter. Here it is so hard to recover yourself, to take pen in hand. I use a friendly occasion and write these lines. I am sure you have heard of my personal tragedy—on September 2, 1944, I lost her, who was the meaning of my life, my inspiration. Now—as "easy" and [un]clouded as my life was, so it is now full of tragedies. I am lost. Though I still stand on my feet and continue working, and as they say, am "successful." For the time being, I am here in America—I was "saved" [from the Holocaust]. I exhibited in the Gallery Pierre Matisse every year. My books, illustrated with hundreds of engravings: Gogol's *Dead Souls*, *Fables* by LaFontaine, and the Bible. Though the edition of the engravings was made, in Vollard's lifetime they were not published. He left no will. I don't know yet what is happening to them now in Paris. The Museum of Modern Art in New York, and in November, the museum of Chicago are preparing a big retrospective show of my work for the next season.[38] Outside of several smaller books, a large book is being published in English—a monograph, published by Pierre Matisse, with a text by Lionello Venturi and 100 reproductions.[39] I illustrated several books, including my wife's book, which appears first in Yiddish, with 25 of my drawings. I live now with my daughter Ida Gordey, who is herself a very fine painter, and fortunately for her, quite unlike her father . . . Her splendid husband Michel Rapaport-Gordey has been gone for several months on a business trip to Paris. His parents, thank God, survived [in France], as did his sweet aunt Leah Bernstein and his Uncle Osip. But their son is a prisoner of war . . . How are you? I am happy about the news from you and will be happy if you don't forget me in the future.

I press your hand warmly and wish you and the whole homeland happiness.

Devoted   Marc Chagall

P.S. Previously, I did a ballet here (decorations, costumes, and scenario of Pushkin's *Aleko* with Tchaikovsky's music). It was staged here at the Opera.

Leah Bernstein: Michel Rapaport-Gordey's paternal aunt and her husband, the chess master Osip Bernstein.

prisoner of war: Michel Rapaport-Gordey's cousin spent World War II as a French POW in a German camp and was liberated after the war.

Marc Chagall in Upstate New York to Yosef Opatoshu in New York

[Stationery: Beaver Lake House, Krumville, Ulster County, N.Y.]

1945 14 May

[Yiddish] Dear Opatoshu, for a long time I have wanted to write to you from here, but couldn't. Despite all my thoughts about work, exhibition—I am still steeped in thoughts about [Bella]——[her] attitude toward Yiddish—toward art in all aspects. It seems to me—I am falling into pits on my roads, wherever I stroll or travel. I must cure myself of myself.

If she could she would have said to me: let me rest in peace . . .

How are you? Warm regards for Adelya.

We will probably see each other soon.

Be well, devoted
Marc Chagall
[English] Love to you both, Your Ida

Marc Chagall in Sag Harbor to the Opatoshus in New York

> Ida rented a house for her father in Sag Harbor, Long Island, where he could work on the scenery and costumes for Stravinsky's ballet *Firebird*.

Sag Harbor, L. Island N.Y.   [Yiddish] July–August 1945

Dear Friends, though I am here, where it is truly beautiful, the house is big and lies on the seashore, I would very much like to be at your home for a day. But this is apparently very hard to do from here. On the contrary, I would like to ask you to come here—Why not? Opatoshu sits and writes . . . And I too have to work. Of course I work. I just don't know what comes out of the working. Since Chagall is still as on his paintings—head upside down . . .

So don't think that I have forgotten you. I cannot write (that is, I can—), but I could talk with you till dawn. Now the night is so hard that I crawl into bed to forget myself—

Be well and write to me some time about something good

Devoted   Chagall

Regards from Idochka

[English] and love greetings

best wishes from Ida

Marc Chagall in New York to Pesakh Novik in New York

1945 N.Y. [October]

[Yiddish] Dear Novik,

I am sending you, with my best regards, the few words. And though I am involved with the "Bird" that should fly on the 24th in the Metropolitan Opera, as a greeting (if only I could), or maybe a kiss or a lament [?]

Your Chagall

the "Bird" that should fly: The performance of Stravinsky's *Firebird* with Chagall's sets at the Metropolitan Opera, New York.

May my "Firebird" which I make now—be my flying greeting—

Statement on the 28th anniversary of the October Revolution

I would like to live not one time 28 years, but two times, three times as long, to see even more the miracle and greatness of the Soviet Revolution . . .

Through the window, looking at me—at me, the sad one—the great sun setting across the river.

28 years: Written on the 28th anniversary of the October Revolution

But there [in the Soviet Union], a sun looks at everyone, a sun striving to turn our life into a Garden of Eden here on earth—

Marc Chagall

1945 N.Y.

Marc Chagall: My Tears

[Yiddish]

My tears fall like stones,
Melt and flow into a river,
Float like flowers on the water,
Thus I live, my God. Why?

I live and breathe.
I seek you, I seek.
For you are with me
And far from me, my God. Why?

I hear no word around me.
Roads and forests crisscross.
I begin my day with a smile
And wait for you, God. Why?

I bear the cross every day,
Pushed and led by the hand,
Night grows dark around me,
Have you forsaken me, my God? Why?

Marc Chagall: [I am your son]

[Yiddish]

I am your son,
Born on the earth to crawl,
You put paint and brush in my hand—
I don't know how to paint You.

Should I paint the earth, the sky, my heart?
The cities burning, my brothers fleeing?
My eyes in tears,
Where should I run and fly, to whom?

There is someone who gives us life,
There is someone who gives us death—
He could have helped me
Make my paintings bright with joy.

Marc Chagall: [My hour, my day, my last year]

[Yiddish]

My hour, my day, my last year.
How sweet is my hot tear.
My heart is silent, waiting.
I see the sun flowing above—
Covering my face with red beams.

It promises me consolation:
I shall not shed more tears,
I shall go alone with my luck,
My hope hidden deep inside me,
And hear your distant call.

CHAPTER FIFTEEN ## "My New-Found Love" and Liberated Europe: 1945–1946

Love

Aleksandr Blok was the admired Russian Symbolist poet during the time of Chagall's youth. At least in his poetry, Blok idealized his wife *Lyubov'* (Love) and wrote poems to a feminine "You," which could be his beloved, Love itself with a capital L, Mother Russia—or all those combined. Chagall's first wife Berta (at home: Basha), renamed Bella, was idolized in his writings and paintings: She was his angelic, divine muse, his intelligent authority, art critic, and social guide, as well as the embodiment of beauty and Love. In his youthful "Cendrars Notebook," he wrote an abstract quasi-Symbolist prose poem "Love" (1909–1910). He took up this theme again in his series of murals for the Moscow Yiddish Theater (1920); the murals represented the past Jewish world yet culminated in an almost transparent, cosmopolitan image, "Love on the Stage." Later in his life, "Love" became an all-embracing, unifying, yet diffuse concept, the salvation of humanity and art, a mantra in his lectures and a recurrent image in his work:

> For me life divides itself into two parts—Life and death—and for me whatever is not an inner truth is death. But maybe—to be a little more concrete—or, if you prefer, more truthful, one must use the word 'love,' because there is the true color, not only in art, but in life.

Without love an art is not art, and a life is not life. Without love we see all the chaos into which art and life periodically descend, in which I fear they find themselves at this moment.

The great crisis of art and of life is a crisis of Love.[1]

Bella was not only the embodiment of that ideal Love; she was totally devoted to Chagall's genius, and assumed the role of both his mother and his business manager. She knew literally where he came from—the languages, the traditions, the gestures—and she understood him with a wink.

When Bella died suddenly on September 2, 1944, Chagall was devastated. The poem "Your Call," addressed to a "You" who may be God, or Bella, or both, expresses his mood at the time.

Marc Chagall: Your Call (Poem)

[Yiddish]

I do not know if I lived. I don't know
If I am alive. I watch the sky,
I don't recognize the world.

My body sets toward night.
Love, the flowers in paintings—
They call me back and forth.

Don't leave my hand without light
When my house is dark.
How will I see your glow in the whiteness?

How will I hear your call
When I remain alone in my bed
And cold and calm is my body.

New-Found Love: Virginia Haggard

Yet there was also earthly love in his life. After Bella's death, Chagall rented a large apartment in New York overlooking the Hudson, at 42 Riverside Drive,

Marc and Ida Chagall at Riverside Drive, New York.

together with his daughter Ida and her husband Michel Rapaport-Gordey. Devoted daughter Ida, who took her mother's place as Chagall's caretaker, and
whose own marriage was in trouble, wanted to go on a badly-needed vacation.
She found a woman who could mend Chagall's socks, and who soon became his
housekeeper: Virginia Haggard. Virginia was British; she had married a Scottish
painter and set designer, John McNeil, in London. In 1939, they moved to New
York, where her father was British Consul General at the time. John McNeil had
been suffering from serious depression and was unemployed; Virginia was poor,
the mother of a five-year-old daughter, and needed work. Born in Paris in 1915
of English parents, she was thoroughly bilingual and hence could easily com-

Chagall at Riverside Drive, New York, 1945.

municate with Chagall in French. Moreover, in her youth, she had studied art herself in Chicago and Paris and could understand Marc's artistic concerns.

Virginia's father, a nephew of the famous writer Rider Haggard, was British Consul General in France in the 1930s, and after 1939, Consul General in New York. In 1944 he was called back to England, became head of the Department of Anglo-American Relations in the British Foreign Office, and was knighted Sir Godfrey. Virginia's brother was a successful young actor in London; he wrote three books (one published posthumously) and also worked in British intelligence in the Middle East during World War II, where he died, presumably in an accident, at the age of thirty-two. The gap between Virginia's social status and her background was striking. She had an impulse of independence, striving, as she puts it, "to break with a life that was too privileged and secure."[2]

Marc and Virginia fell passionately in love (Virginia was twenty-eight years younger than Marc). Both of them were "starved," as Virginia put it later. They were together first in the New York apartment on Riverside Drive, then in Sag Harbor, Long Island, where Chagall rented a house to prepare the sets and costumes for Stravinsky's *Firebird*. Subsequently, Chagall bought a house in the country, in High Falls, New York, which Virginia renovated in Marc's absence. When Virginia got pregnant, she stayed there with her five-year-old daughter Jean McNeil. What began as an affair became a common-law marriage, blessed with a son, David, born June 22, 1946.

Virginia's husband refused to grant her a divorce (David's name remains Mc-Neil), and when he finally did, seven years later, she left Chagall to marry the Belgian photographer Charles Leirens. Virginia Haggard recounted those seven years in her book, *My Life with Chagall: Seven Years of Plenty with the Master as Told by the Woman Who Shared Them*, based on notes taken throughout the years. Much of it is vividly described in her letters from that time, especially to Adele Opatoshu, the wife of Chagall's old friend, the Yiddish writer Yosef Opatoshu,

"Flowers to Pregnant Virginia," December 1945.

and to Chagall's friends and collectors Louis Stern and Bernard Reis, as well as to various business relations. Indeed, during those seven years, Virginia was the main correspondent in all of Chagall's affairs, and only his Yiddish correspondence (and some Russian letters) were written by Marc himself. Virginia did not see her letters for almost half a century, until they were recovered for this book. For reasons of space, only part of the letters have been reproduced here.

In his imagination, Chagall conflated the two images of Virginia and Bella, the sensual and the spiritual. In his poem, "The Painting," he writes:

My departed love,

My new-found love,

Listen to me.

I move over your soul,

Over your belly—

I drink the calm of your [young] years.

And in the paintings of those years we can see both figures: the angelic Bella and the elongated, pure, and feminine image of mother-and-child (a Christian icon), inspired by the tall, young Virginia.[3]

When he reverts to his early fears and emotions, Chagall sees the world in the stereotypical categories codified by life in the Pale of Settlement: Individuals carry the imprint of their origins; people are divided into Jews and Goyim (Gentiles); the world is full of our enemies; the Jews are ignorant about art, lack unity, and are in decline. For Chagall, those are categories of perception rather than valuation. Contrary to the beliefs of his parents (though using the same stereotypes), the Gentile world may be more positive and attractive. Thus, Chagall loves Virginia as a healthy, loving, wholesome person, without Jewish complexes; "simple," young, and close to nature, like the woman offering love to the peasant in his early painting, "I and the Village" (1911). Virginia is also a representative of England. He feels apologetic toward his friends, because at that time

loving, wholesome person: The "love of the shikse" (= Christian young woman) is a widespread topos in modern Jewish literature, up to its parodic hyperbole in Philip Roth's *Portnoy's Complaint.*

England was oppressing the Jewish national liberation movement in Palestine; and on the other hand, he expresses love for England because it reminds him of Virginia. No doubt, seeing each other in terms of ethnic stereotypes enhanced both their mutual attraction and eventual their alienation.

"Getting out of the Ghetto" also meant getting close to nature. Ever since his first marriage, Chagall yearned for the quiet of nature, and with Virginia's help, he first moved to Wallkill, New York, then bought a house in High Falls, New York.

Monroe Wheeler in New York to Daniel Catton Rich in Chicago

The Museum of Modern Art
New York
Monroe Wheeler
Director of Exhibitions and Publications

January 3, 1946

Dear Dan:

I was delighted to receive your letter of December 27 saying that the Art Institute finds it possible to contribute $250 toward the cost of making the color plates for the Institute's Chagall painting *The Rabbi of Vitebsk* for use in the Chagall book. It will be entirely agreeable to us to permit you to borrow this plate whenever you need it.

In regard to the paper for your edition of the Chagall book, we shall need 3,300 sheets of #1 or #2, 70 pound glossy coated stock, grain long, 30 1/2 x 40", for each 1,000 copies. We have already calculated in our own estimates 1,000 copies for you. If the paper is available in Chicago we would like to have you get the paper for all the copies you will want because the situation here is desperate and we are having to reduce the size of the editions of the books we are printing because of the inability to get what we need.

I am glad you are coming to New York so soon. Will you let me give a little cocktail party for you on Monday, the 14th? If you would like this, it might provide an opportunity for you to see some friends you might not otherwise have time for.

With best regards, I am

Faithfully yours,

Monroe

James J. Sweeney in New York to Daniel Catton Rich in Chicago

The Museum of Modern Art
New York
Department of Painting and Sculpture
James Johnson Sweeney, Director   March 2, 1946

Dear Dan,

In Chagall's autobiography, *Ma Vie*, he recounts the manner in which he painted what apparently is the Art Institute Chagall, or at least the original version of this subject. I don't know how close together the three different versions were as all are apparently dated 1914. But Chagall has told me that the first was that at present in the possession of Charles in Obersteg, Switzerland. He writes:

> Another old man passes by our house. Gray hair, sullen expression. A sack on his back . . .
>
> I wonder: is it possible for him to open his mouth, even to beg for charity?
>
> Indeed, he says nothing. He enters and stays discreetly near the door. There he stands for a long time. And if you give him anything, he goes out, as he came in, without a word.
>
> "Listen," I say to him, "don't you want to rest a while. Sit down. Like this. You don't mind, do you? You'll have a rest. I'll give you twenty kopeks. Just put on my father's prayer clothes and sit down."
>
> You've seen my painting of that old man at prayer? That's the one.

Apparently the tallith and phylacteries are not peculiar to a rabbi. From this I find that the painting was not an actual portrait of a rabbi of Vitebsk, and with your permission we will return to the older title, *The Praying Jew*. Under the reproduction we will describe it as: "The Praying Jew" (or also known as "The Rabbi of Vitebsk"). Please let me know if this is acceptable.

I forget to mention the above to you this morning about the forward and the Regnault and Arensberg problems.

With all best,

JS

Lecture at Chicago University

The newly established Committee on Social Thought at the University of Chicago invited Marc Chagall to deliver their third lecture entitled "The Works of the Mind" on March 5, 1946. His host was Professor John U. Nef, Chairman of the

Executive Committee. Chagall wrote and read the lecture in French, and it was translated into English by Robert B. Heywood as "The Artist."[4] On the first trip to Chicago, Chagall's son-in-law, Michel Rapaport-Gordey, was supposed to accompany the artist (who knew no English), but eventually, it was Chagall's friend and collector Louis Stern who went with him to Chicago.

Marc Chagall in Chicago to Virginia Haggard in Wallkill, New York

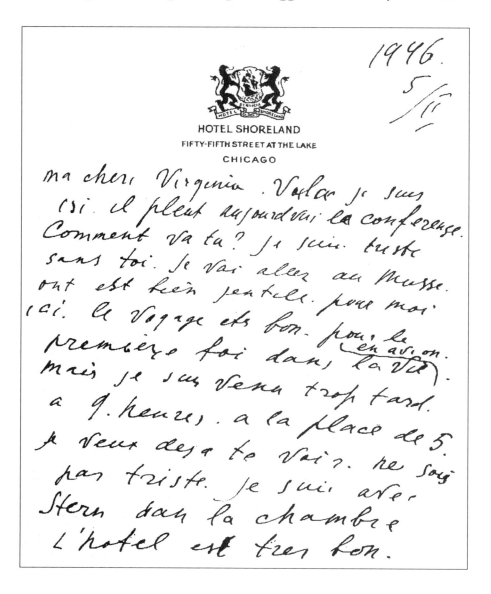

tu vois comme je ecrit
Mal fransais?
Mais tu peux sentdze
comme je t'aime —
et je te ~~st~~ souhait
tant de bonne chose
dans la vie.
Je t'embrasse.
ton.
Marc

5.III 1946

[French] My Dear Virginia,

how badly I write French: This observation, however true, became a formula with Chagall, which he repeated in many of his Yiddish and French letters.

Here I am. It is raining. Today is my lecture. How are you? I am sad without you. I am going to the museum. They are very nice to me here. This trip is good. For the first time in my life on an airplane. But I arrived too late, at 9 o'clock instead of 5. I already want to see you. Don't be sad. I am with Stern in the room. The hotel is very good. You see how badly I write French? But you can feel how I love you—and I wish you so much good in life.

Kisses,/   Your Marc

Marc Chagall in Chicago to Yosef Opatoshu in New York

[Postcard with image, described as "Portrait of a Rabbi, Marc Chagall, French, 1887–"][5]

5.III [March] Chicago 1946

[Yiddish] Dear friend, After my lecture at the University, I sit down to send you my brief regards. It seems all went well—to hold an American Goyish audience in French—they say, is difficult, but they sat through it and listened to the English translation when I was done.

Be well! I flew! On the earth, it is calmer.

Your Marc Chagall

I flew: Flying figures were a central image in Chagall's self-perception as an artist, a move transcending reality. For him, flying in an airplane for the first time was like realizing one of his pictures.

Daniel Catton Rich in Chicago to Marc Chagall in New York

March 13, 1946

[English] Dear Mr. Chagall:

I did not find the opportunity to tell you on your recent brief visit to Chicago of our plan for the opening of your exhibition next October. The President and the Trustees [of the Art Institute of Chicago] are most anxious to have you and your daughter, Mrs. Ida Chagall Rappaport, present for the opening on Wednesday, October 23. Undoubtedly either the President or I will arrange a dinner for that occasion to precede the formal preview for Members. It will add greatly to our pleasure if you and Mrs. Rappaport can be with us and see your work on the walls of the Art Institute.

May I tell you how much I enjoyed your conference [= lecture] at the University? It was one of the most enlightening and human expressions on art that it has been my privilege to hear, and all of us were much touched by your words. I am, too, happy that our museum is to hold for several months so many of your great works, for I have long been an admirer of your art, and hope that many more Americans will come to appreciate it as I do.

With kindest regards, I remain / Very sincerely yours,

Daniel Catton Rich

Director

Virginia Haggard in Walkill to Adele Opatoshu in New York

Dixie Farm, Walkill N.Y.   March 14 [1946]

[English] My Dear Adele,

I haven't seen you for such a long time, and I do so want to see you when next I come to New York. I've been quite preoccupied looking for somewhere to live in the country, and now at last I've found a nice farm house where it's quiet and they give us very good food.

   I wrote to two theatre friends about David, and I hope to hear from them soon. One is an actress and the other is a scene designer. I hope David is successful, I was very much impressed by his acting. I think he acted with a great deal of feeling.

Opatoshus' son David (1914–1996) was an actor on stage and in films, as well as a short story writer in Yiddish and English. At this time he was beginning his career in the theater. Virginia calls on the connections of her brother in London. The actress is Peggy Ashcroft, who acted with Stephen Haggard in London in a play written by him. The "scene designer" was Elizabeth Montgomery, a member of the "Motleys," a collective of English theater designers, then in New York. In Sag Harbor, Long Island, in the summer of 1945, Virginia helped them make costumes for Chagall's production of Stravinsky's *Firebird*, choreographed by George Balanchine at the New York City Ballet.

   I am looking for a house somewhere near here, but it takes a long time to find. If we ever get settled I hope you can both come and stay with us, it would be lovely to spend a few days with you. I feel so completely happy with you and Opatoshu, as if I had known you all my life, and Marc loves you both so much too.

   I don't know when I shall be able to come and see you. Marc will be going to New York fairly often, but I shall not be able to unfortunately. And since you are such a dear friend I must tell you why. I am expecting a baby in June, and for Marc's sake I don't want people to know.[6] It is a most unfortunate time to have a child, but there was nothing I could do about it. My doctor absolutely forbade me to have an operation, he said it would be very dangerous in my case because I have anemia. But I hope everything will turn out all right. Marc is worried about how Ida will take it, but I don't think there is anything to be scared about, although it won't be easy to tell her. If I can find a nice house with a garage or a

Ida: Chagall's daugher Ida, who took over caring for Marc and played an important role in organizing exhibitions and promoting Chagall's art, was a year younger than Virginia.

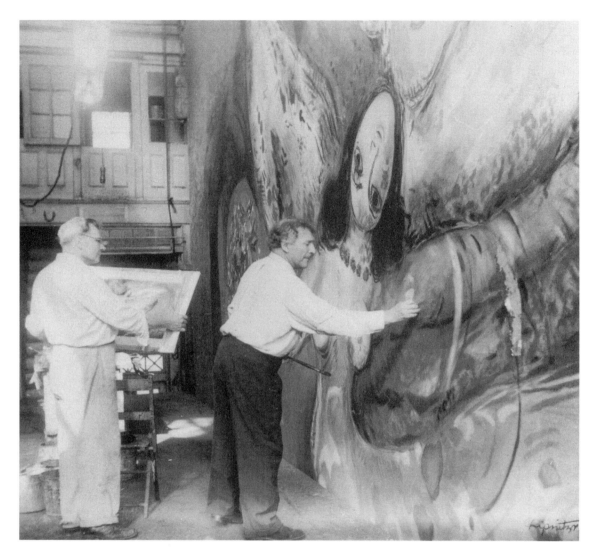

Chagall working on stage sets for Stravinsky's ballet *Firebird*, New York, 1945.

barn which can be made into a studio for Marc, then he will be able to work in peace, and if I can find someone to help me, I'm sure he won't feel upset. I'm going to stay in the country all the time and no one will know about the baby yet.

Please tell Opatoshu that I am reading his book and enjoying it enormously,[7] and please write to me soon, dear Adele, I would like to hear from you so much.

Love to you both from

Virginia

Marc Chagall in Wallkill to the Opatoshus in New York

% Dixie Farm, Wallkill, N.Y.   {3/25}[8] 1946

[Yiddish] Dear Opatoshus

Thank you for the story you sent me. It is alive, as always. It has your charm, your breath, as always. How *well* you know the local, American landscapes, and more-over—you *love* them. Indeed, when one gets to know it closer (though I don't know the language), you sense something that evokes emotions. And you must realize, I am not like your "Big Willie"[9] but like the "fantastic" Marc who crawled into some God-forsaken place and "bought" some other [place], even without [his friends'] "advice" because the "authenticity" just sprang to our eyes, and I hope when you come you'll say so yourself. There will be a *separate* atelier in a hut outside the house. It is near Rosendale. What shall I do if things happen without me and "for me"—

Thank you for your very dear letter. I am moved and feel your deep friendship—I attach a letter for Mr. Small—for David [Opatoshu]—*let him go to him* in a week and tell me.

for her faster: Apparently, her pregnancy.

And V. [Virginia] writes separately about another move and for her faster [= soon]. I hope to come over [to New York] about April 1 for a day. Maybe.

Warm regards for Adelye

Your devoted

Chagall

Virginia describes the house Chagall bought in High Falls:

It was a simple wooden house with screened porches, near a superb catalpa tree. It had been fondly built by a contented carpenter who had enjoyed it to the end of his days. A grassy valley lay before it; behind, the ground rose to a jagged ridge of rocks, crowning a wooden ravine. Next to the house was a small wooden cottage that immediately enchanted Marc—it reminded him of an isba [Russian peasant hut][10]

Chagall's concept of "authenticity" still stems from Russian populist admiration of the life of the peasants.

Virginia Haggard in Wallkill to Adele Opatoshu in New York

Dixie Farm, Wallkill NY, April 5th, 1946

[English] My Dear Adele,

I'm so sorry I couldn't come and have supper with you, it was sweet of you to get the chicken. There were hundreds of things to do for Marc at the last moment,[11] and I had to get the apartment [at 42 Riverside Drive] straightened out for Ida.

Will you be busy on the 9th or 10th? I'd like to phone you when I get to New York on the 8th. I have to see the doctor and dentist on the 8th.

Marc told me some time ago you offered to take me to a Rabbi and help me in any way I need in order to become converted. Thankyou dear Adele, I want your help so much. You know that I love Jews and I want to be like them; I shall not be a religious Jew, but like Marc I believe the way they do, and their idea of God is the very same as mine, in spite of my upbringing. Strangely enough I always had that conception of God, quite independently and privately, although I knew nothing about what Jews believed, and I was being incessantly schooled in Christianity. I never liked the idea of the trinity and I used to scandalize my schoolmates by my disbelief. But I always believed in God, and God only, and I used to like going into the church when no one else was there. Would you tell me dear Adele what things I should know, I am very ignorant. I am reading Opatoshu's bible. Marc says he would like me to keep it as a souvenir of you both, would you mind? Sometimes I read it to Marc in English, although he doesn't understand, he likes to hear it.

Looking forward to seeing you/ Yours affectionately

Virginia

First Return to "the Abysses of Europe"

The first great American retrospective exhibition of Chagall's work, curated by James Johnson Sweeney, opened at the Museum of Modern Art in New York on April 4, 1946.[12] Right after the opening, Chagall's daughter Ida went back to Paris to prepare a major exhibition there. Chagall himself had many misgivings about going back to "the abysses of Europe" after the Holocaust. And, at the time, his apprehension was enhanced by the fear of a Soviet invasion and a Communist takeover of Western Europe. Yet the memory of the eighteen years spent in France between the wars, the lingering sense of Paris as the center of art and culture, the promised large retrospective exhibitions in Paris, Amsterdam, and London, the fact that he could communicate in French and was a French citizen, and several prominent French intellectuals and poets enjoyed the company of Chagall and accepted him as a major modern painter—all those influenced his decision.

Chagall went to Paris for the first time after the war during May–September 1946 and, typically, missed the birth of his son. In several early paintings, called "Birth," birth appears as a mysterious event, awesome and fantastic. Birth obviously frightened Chagall, as he himself indicates in his memoirs. Even when Ida was born to his idolized Bella, he disappeared (with the excuse that he wanted a son), and returned only four days later. It is also part of a broader pattern of evasion before making political or social decisions.

Marc Chagall on Board Ship to Virginia Haggard in High Falls

3 days voyage on the ship [Stationery: S.S. Brazil] 1946, Monday [May 26], toward Paris

[French] My dear, I am on board the ship. It is long, but calm, a lot of people—some military. Six (6) persons in the cabin. I am with Martin Chauffier[13]—he is good. Another 6 or 7 days to travel. How are you? I think? And I am sad when I think. But I think that you are brave and your friends love you and will protect you. The time is long here. The days pass monotonously. I would already like to get a letter from you. Surely there is a letter from you in Paris. How is your health? You know that I am thinking of you—and I can't not think of you because you are goodness and charm. I wish you happiness and send you my love. I caress you and kiss you hard.

Your M.

May 30

Another 3, 4 days and I will arrive. It really is hard to bear, but there is nothing to do. You can imagine how I feel. The ship is strong but not very comfortable. But when I think of you—it is clearer.

I kiss you for today.

Your M.

Saturday evening, June 1

How are you? Have already seen your land. Your land—England from a distance. Tomorrow we reach port in England, then to [Le] Havre and Paris. Monday. I think of you. And you? What are you doing? There is surely a letter in Paris from you.

All the best

M

Sunday, 2

One sees England. I am looking for you here. I love England because of you. It is pretty from afar. It is long. Tomorrow—Paris.

Yours

June 4

I am in Paris

Kisses

Marc

47. Ave d'Iéna Paris

Ave d'Iéna: Ida rented three rooms for Chagall in the house of the art critic Jacques Lassaigne. He had separated from his wife Assia, and she was living alone in the house. Assia was of Russian origin and apparently tried to flirt with Chagall.

Marc Chagall in Paris to Virginia Haggard in High Falls

Marc and Virginia went for advice to Quest Brown, an English woman living in New York. "She had studied psychology and used palmistry and graphology as a means of scrutinizing the unconscious" (V. Haggard). (See illustration of Chagall's inked hand.). She was a mother-figure to Virginia, had an emotional influence on her, visited her in High Falls, and corresponded with her for several years. Chagall was impressed with her prediction that they would have a son and be happy together.

Paris, June 8, 1946

[French] My dear,

I don't have any letters from you. What's wrong? Write me more often. Otherwise I am not calm. I see many people but I think of you always and I would al-

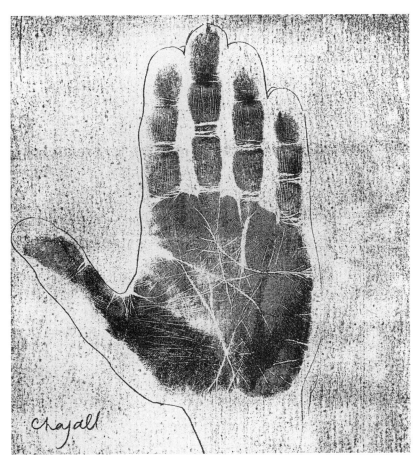

Inked imprint of Chagall's hand, made by Quest Brown, New York, 1946. On front side, a printed form: "Handprint Record Sheet for Character Analysis, Vocational Guidance and Positive Identification / Make your hand print on reverse side / . . . Scientific Publications — New York, N.Y. / Patents Pending."

ready like to return. I received your 3 letters. Thank you. Write like that, at length. How is your health? Where are you? At Mrs. Braun's? She is very nice. She told you good things. True.

Did you get a letter from Ida? I haven't yet gotten a letter from her. Write to me about everything. You see that I can't write very well. But I want to know about your health? Work. I can't forget—for the moment I have dinner and lunch with people—am invited. But I also want to work a little. I am worried about your health.

Kisses, M.

Marc Chagall in Paris to Virginia Haggard in High Falls

Paris, June 10, 1946

[French] I am quite sad and I don't know where you are right now. In the hospital or at Mrs. Braun's. God knows if everything is well with you?

Since June 1, I haven't gotten any letters from you (3 in all). But I hope I will have a letter from you. Or if you can't write yourself dictate it to someone else. Has your aunt arrived?

Did Ida answer your letter?

I can't be calm or "work" or anything else.

Yours

M

Marc Chagall in Paris to Sonia Delaunay in Paris

> Sonia Delaunay (1885–1979) was born Sonia Terk, a Russian Jew. She went to Paris as a child, married Robert Delauney, and became a prominent artist and designer in France.

47. Av. D' Iéna   Paris 1946 [June]

[Russian] Hallo my dear Sonia.

How are you? I am in Paris and would be happy to see you.

You have no telephone. Could you please call me. Pas. 52-20

With warm regards

Chagall

Marc Chagall in Paris to Virginia Haggard in New York

> The date was approaching and a name had to be found for the boy. Stephen was the name of Virginia's brother, who was killed in service in the Middle East in 1943. The name David was highly meaningful for Chagall: King David was the model artist-violinist of Chagall's childhood and loomed large in his later biblical images; his admired, learned grandfather (quite unlike his coarse father)

was David Chagall; and his beloved and only brother David died of consumption

in the Crimea around the age of thirty.

Paris, June 12, 946

[French] Darling,

I finally got a letter from you (June 8, 10). I am calmer and am happy that your aunt has come. But am sad for Genia. Remember, I find that impossible, I don't understand—is it the food at school or something in her. Well, she must be in the country. The story with Dr. Turel is bad, but it's good that you are arranging something else. I hope it will be all right. If you need money, ask Oppen [Yosef Opatoshu]. Write how you are. It's true, you came to the city a bit too soon because of Turel. But don't get too tired in the city. As for the name (if it's a boy), do what you wrote (David, Stephen—is that your brother?).

Genia: Virginia's daughter Jean McNeil (born in 1940) was nicknamed Genia by Chagall (a Russian name, which reads *Zhenya*); her name Jean was restored when they went to France. She is now an artist and lives in London.

Oppen will help you with the rest, I hope—I hope.

But naturally I am worried, you understand. Have you gotten an answer (from Ida) to your letter or any other news from her? I am happy that you are working, that you are writing and drawing (do you have to do a lot of manual work? Isn't that monotonous?) But Mrs. Braun is so nice and you, we owe a lot to her. What she told you about him and Genia (in your letter before) is quite true. It's funny that I thought the same thing before. You remember how I spoke to you of all that? It's not the head, but the instinct or intuition that dictates all that to me.

I think that Mrs. Braun is a great woman.

In truth, it's hard for me to be alone here. But if you write to me often about everything, that will be better for me.

Lhote: André Lhôte (1885–1962), a French painter and theoretician of art. During World War II, Chagall's furniture and probably some paintings were hidden in his home in Le Raincy, Seine St.-Denis, near Paris.

Mr. Stern is here. He often takes me to lunch and dinner. He is a friend.

Ida's attitude makes me sad. My regards to your aunt. All the people who will take care of you—I love them in advance.

You see how badly I write [French]. Nothing to be done.

Gordes: Gordes in Provence, where the Chagalls bought a house before the collapse of France in June 1940, and where they lived until their departure for the U.S. in May 1941. After the war, Chagall gave the house to Ida.

Here there are three rooms that Ida rented from the Lassaignes. On Saturday I want to see Ransy [= Le Raincy] with Lhote. I don't know when I am going to Gorde[s] to see where one can live. Perhaps in the Hotel de Gorde[s] if not in the house. Alone. I haven't told you anything about Paris. It is pretty as always, but the people, life, character, art, etc., have changed. It is for the moment not the same as before. There is more dynamism in America even though it's primitive. In art it's always the same names. I have a general idea of all that.

The Carré Gallery (the main one) and Maegh [sic] do want me, but P. Matisse doesn't like Carré—("competition"). We'll see.

Kisses/Your Marc

47 Avenue d'Iéna/Paris

Finding a Gallery

While longing for his young bride in High Falls and expecting the birth of a child in America, Chagall had to reestablish his ties in Paris. One of the first concerns was to open a market for his paintings and secure a new gallery without antagonizing his dealer in New York, Pierre Matisse. Louis Carré and Aimé Maeght competed for the rights to represent Chagall in France. This required the consent of Pierre Matisse. Eventually, Maeght won exclusive rights and Chagall lived near the new Maeght Foundation in St.-Paul de Vence.

Monroe Wheeler in New York to Daniel Catton Rich in Chicago

The Museum of Modern Art
New York
Monroe Wheeler
Director of Exhibitions and Publications   June 12, 1946

Dear Dan:

At long last our Comptroller's Office has furnished me with detailed information on the costs of the Chagall shipments. You will notice that we have not yet got all the bills covering the Paris shipment but this will give you all costs to date.

We have informed San Francisco that you will be opening your show later and we are still hoping to get them to take the exhibition in the late summer and early autumn. Meanwhile we should like to know what adjustment you are prepared to make regarding these excessive ocean freight costs which it was impossible for us to estimate in advance.

We were unable to get paper to provide you with more than one thousand paper bound copies of the Chagall book, which we shall be glad to let you have at cost. We have not yet received the binder's costs on these but we shall retail them here at $1.75 or $2.00. The bound copies will retail at $3.00 and we can let you have fifty at a discount of 40%. We have ordered the one thousand over runs of *The Praying Jew* and these, unmounted and uncaptioned, will cost you about $15.00, considerably less than our original quotation because we were able to run the plates four up.

With best wishes, I am

Faithfully yours,

Monroe

Marc Chagall in Paris to the Opatoshus in New York

Paris 1946   15/6

Opatoshele: An affectionate Yiddish diminutive of "Opatoshu."

[Yiddish] Opatoshele and Adelye how are you?

Believe me I am longing to travel to the woods [High Falls] and work for myself. I am staying in rooms which Ida had earlier rented for herself and I don't know whether I am "chez nous" ["at home"]. But one must immerse in "work." It is not easy with Vollard (his brother) to finish the business with my books. And even Idochka who is a master at conquering worlds and people [cannot pull it off] . . .

shoulders: In his youth, Chagall worried that he didn't have "shoulders" like his father (who carried heavy herring barrels), and would have no livelihood. Here, the meaning is metaphorical: the ability to shoulder a burden.

How are you two. Are you working? Do you remember me? And how is V. [Virginia]? She is probably "ready" by now [to give birth]—take care of her, though she has a head on her shoulders herself, I think. It is, perhaps "too much" for me, for my so-called shoulders. But what can one do, that's how it is.

Leyvik: H. Leyvik (1888–1962), a major Yiddish American poet and cultural figure.

Leyvik was here but he did not phone me and I didn't know where he was. If it were *you*, I would have gotten "sick" [= offended].

I kiss you both—please write

Devoted   Marc Ch.

Ronch: I.A. Ronch, Yiddish poet and critic, editor of Bella Chagall's memoirs.

P.S. How is Bellochka's book advancing—did Ronch call you?

47, Avenue d'Iéna   Paris France

Marc Chagall: My Land (Poem)

Coming from the affluent United States, Chagall's first confrontation with postwar Paris once again posed the dilemma of finding a homeland for himself. Its sharpest expression was given in the famous poem "My Land," which is usually read as a general statement about the fictional world of his art, yet it was actually based on a very concrete historical and personal situation. Now he had to decide whether to stay in the U.S. or return to France, to attach himself to the Jewish world or to keep away from it. His audience, consisting mainly of Eastern European Jews saved or stranded in France, was as homeless as he.

The poem was written on the occasion of Chagall's renewed contacts with the Yiddish-speaking left in Paris. Just two days after his arrival in Paris, on June 6,

1946, Chagall visited the Yiddish Communist newspaper *Di Naye Prese*. At the emotional reception, speeches were made, hailing Chagall as "a progressive Jew" (i.e., sympathetic to their cause) and as the great artist who is himself of the simple people and expresses their spirit. A Chagall issue of the paper was published on June 18, including Chagall's statement "To the Jewish People in Paris."[14] His poem "My Land" was written in Yiddish some time between the reception of June 18 and the speech he delivered at a public event held for him on July 8, 1946.

The event occurred in the same Hotel Lutetia in Paris where German refugee intellectuals congregated during the 1930s, where the Gestapo had its headquarters during the Nazi occupation, and where returnees from concentration camps now resided. His audience included remnants of Yiddish-speaking Parisian Jews, surviving resistance fighters, and recent refugees from Eastern Europe, survivors of the Holocaust. Echoing the prophet Isaiah's "Comfort ye, comfort ye my people" (Isa. 40.1), Chagall called his speech "Let Us Find Consolation . . ."[15]

In private letters throughout the years, Chagall wrote about his homelessness: "My fatherlands are perhaps only on my canvases" (see Chapter 12, letter to Opatoshu of March 31, 1936). But now the dilemma was acute: whether to stay in the U.S. or return to France in the current political situation. And it was intensified by his audience, the Jewish remnants of East European origin. The Jewish world was annihilated, and there was no place for them on the map. Could they become French citizens? Or emigrate to Canada or Australia? Or go fight for independence in Palestine? (Returning to Communist Poland was out of the question, even for Communists.) Chagall's poem resonated with this audience.

Emotionally, this was his audience, but the world of art was elsewhere. In 1947, Chagall translated the poem into Russian, and from that variant other translations were made.[16]

[Yiddish]

Only that land is mine
That lies in my soul.
As a native, with no documents,
I enter that land.
It sees my sorrow and loneliness,
Puts me to sleep
And covers me with a fragrance-stone.

Gardens are blooming inside me, flowers I invented,
My own streets,[17]
But there are no houses.

They have been destroyed since my childhood.
Their inhabitants stray in my air,
Seek a dwelling. They live in my soul.

That's why I smile sometimes
When my sun barely glimmers,
Or I cry
Like a soft rain at night.

There was a time
When I had two heads,
There was a time
When both faces
Were covered with a veil of love—
And evaporated like the scent of roses.[19]

Night and space . . . [20]

Now I imagine
That even when I walk back
I walk forward—
Toward high gates—
Beyond them, wide steppes spread out,
Where wornout thunders sleep,
And broken lightning——

Only that land is mine
That lives in my soul——[21]

two heads[18]: An allusion to two paintings of 1911–1913. In "Self-Portrait with Seven Fingers" two images hover in nebulae above his head, with Yiddish titles, "Russia" and "Paris," representing his double cultural orientation. "A Window on Paris" presents a Janus head looking through a window in two directions.

wide steppes: This may be an allusion to forbidden Russia after the devastating war. In the later versions, the line is substituted by: "Beyond them, walls are shattered,"—the cliché symbolism of the walls of the ghetto.

Chagall with a painting of the Holocaust (the burning *shtetl* and Jesus Christ in a tallis).

Recovering the Prewar Etchings

One of the important issues preoccupying Chagall on his first trip to Paris was the destiny of his prewar etchings. Commissioned during the 1920s and 1930s by Ambroise Vollard, the legendary dealer of some of the major modern artists in Paris in the early twentieth century, Chagall created about 300 engravings for the Bible, Gogol's *Dead Souls*, and La Fontaine's *Fables*. Chagall saw this work as one of his great achievements and mentioned it in his letters throughout the years, as did others. The New York art critic and prophet of Abstract Expressionism, Clement Greenberg, who did not particularly like the "Chagallian" Chagall (too Jewish, too Eastern European, too figurative), wrote: "In any case, as an etcher and lithographer, as distinct from painter, Chagall belongs alto-gether in the first rank, unrivaled except by Picasso in this century; and his book illustrations together with that master's, make a last glorious burst in what seems to be an expiring art."[22]

Because of the worsening economic situation in the 1930s, the engravings were not published and the plates were hidden in a cellar. When Michel Gordey first went to Paris in April 1945, Chagall asked him to find out about it. After the death of Ambroise Vollard, Chagall had difficult negotiations with Vollard's brother, and was aided by his lawyer Shmuel-Alexander Shchupak. Eventually, the plates were bought by Tériade, editor of the journal *Verve*, and published in several volumes. At the International Biennale in Venice in 1948, Chagall was awarded First Prize for his etchings.

Marc Chagall in Paris to Virginia Haggard in High Falls

Paris, June 19, 946

[French] My darling Virginia,

I am so happy to get your letters and to know that you are well. But it is surely hard to be alone and even work. But I see people. Haven't yet settled with Vollard about the publication of my books: Gogol, LaFontaine, the Bible. He's very difficult, Vol-lard. But nevertheless I hope. I eat lunch and dinner with people, am invited.

You ask me if it is nice in Paris. Of course it is pretty as always, but life here isn't the same and you understand why. Art especially, after the great masters, isn't the same, nor is the rest. Of course I have to look again. I am very sure that as an artist I have to live here and in America too—not to cut ourselves off from America completely. In any case, I will live in America next autumn and winter and we'll see later. I already want to work in my little house with you beside me. You ask me if I love you. Of course! My darling—what do you think? You are good and you are the only one and I don't know how to kiss you and maybe the child

All the best,

Marc

maybe the child: As long as the child is not yet born, a Yiddish speaker would use a hedging expression, to ward off the Evil Eye.

I'm sending a card to Genia/And your health?

The Birth of David

Virginia gave birth to David in Brooklyn Hospital on Saturday, June 22, 1946. The doctor was a friend of the Opatoshus. The circumcision was performed on the eighth day, June 29, and was presided over by the Yiddish novelist Yosef Opatoshu.

Marc Chagall in Paris to Virginia Haggard in New York

June 25, 1946

[French] I got your telegram. I answered by telegram as soon as I returned from Ransy [Le Raincy] (at Lhote's) (Monday). I am so happy for the two of us. You don't know yet how I love you? You know very well that I don't say those words too easily, but you feel. For me, you are—my life. I can't live anymore without you. Fate wanted me to meet you after dear Bella (whom you love too).

Thank you for the child—a boy. I hope he will be good and strong. We will love him with all our might (like Genia). Watch your health. And I hope that you are going to return soon to our country house.

Many kisses as always and even more. Believe me that I really want to come back already. I will write you again soon, but I want to send these words right away for you with other news.

All the best to you / My little Virginia / Kiss the child for me

Your Marc

Regards to Mrs. Braun and thank her.

Marc Chagall in Paris to the Opatoshus in New York

Paris 1946 25/6

[Yiddish] My dear loving friends,

Thank you for your dear letters, their warmth gives me joy. Do I deserve it? Thank you Opatoshu for the article from *Tsukunft* and Adelye for the letter [describing] everything about her.

And now congratulations to you. For you are the first to know [about the birth of Chagall's son]. I am writing only to you: the first (and the only ones). Well, what do you say about me! About her it is clear. It is *Nature itself* in its simplicity, and why does God do it to me and where does he lead me, that I, so weak and sad, must smile because somewhere there a little boy came into the world . . .

Dear friends, I thank you and I hope that you will make an effort to help her with everything necessary at my expense, and to do all that needs to be done, as Opatoshu once said, in a Jewish manner.

I hasten to send you these few words.

I hope you are in good health and working. And I shall be happy to meet you

And kiss you, your

Chagall

Please give her a flower in my name—thank you.

47 Av. d. Iéna, Paris

P.S. Just received your happy letter about the child. Congratulations to you! It is breathtaking, all that is happening over there! And all without me. But you are so good and she loves you as her own father and mother, she wrote. I kiss you both from my heart.

Love to David [Opatoshu] and his wife.

Marc Chagall in Paris to Virginia Haggard in High Falls

June 29, 946

[French] My dear, Now I am calmer about you and the baby. I got your letter and you don't know how I would already like to be at home with you, to see you, to know that you are happy and I am too. I think that you may be in the country? I can write there. I hope that you will make a photo of yourself but don't get tired with that stove there. You will unfortunately have work with the little study house but not too much. The exhibition is in principle *officially* decided. I don't yet know where in what museum. But with Vollard—the book—he has unfortunately given it to another publisher, as Ida thought, so that it is I who buys the editions (3). Perhaps it is better like that so as not to have any worries. I want to hope that they won't do the books too badly.

It is quite a tale with that Vollard brother. It is very hard to talk to him. With Stern's help, I am now in contact with Carré for [representation] in Paris on condition of agreement with [Pierre] Matisse. We'll see. But I would so much like to know a lot about you and the baby and other things. Write to me about you. You don't doubt me? My little big girl. You are brave and it is you I love. The happiness of being with you, feeling you together. And you know that, even though I can't write how I adore you.

Kiss the baby and Genia and kisses for you

Your Marc

Regards to your aunt.

Marc

I shall write to the address in the country.

    Do you have enough money?

Marc Chagall in Paris to the Opatoshus in New York

> On June 29, on what came to be known as "Black Saturday," the British army in Palestine cracked down on the Jewish underground army, Haganah (= "self-defense"). A large cache of Haganah arms was dug up in Kibbutz Yagur and confiscated; the Zionist leadership was arrested and interned in camps. It was also the day of David's *Brith*.

1/7 [July 1] 1946, Paris

[Yiddish] Dear friends, I know that you left for your country home. But I hope you'll get this letter there. I keep thinking how good you are in my situation, and so warm, that I should not feel such "guilt," I don't know myself toward whom. And I thought (and still think) that life is simple, just as she (Vir.) sees it, and that in art, all the art is to be natural, simple. How are you? You are probably agitated by the Jewish (and world) news. And this is not a simple matter. I pity her (V.) who thinks it is the fault of her people. I shall try to work something [= to paint here]. But with Vollard (my 3 books) the matter is bad. He sold them to someone else, not to us, and who knows what people will make of them.

    Adelye, thank you for your warm letter. Don't forget to write me more, if you have time. And you, Opatoshu, about everything you're thinking, for I rely on you.

    Thank you for giving her [Virginia] the watch, and what do you think of the little one, you probably made him into a Jew . . .

    I received Foshko's article from you.[23] Thank you. It is not bad, and written by an artist himself. I shall send you a Yiddish page from the local Yiddish newspaper, so you'll have some impression about life here among the Jews.

made him into a Jew: Ritually circumcised; Opatoshu had indeed presided over the *Brith*.

4/7 [July]

Just received your letter of 30/6. I am so happy and thank you for it and for the love you give me. I shall never forget it. I am so lucky. I don't know what world I am in, but apparently God . . . protects me (so I think, I must not sin [by complaining]). And you know how she loves you from the depth of her heart. Is it too much to ask that my "sins" [of having an affair] should be recognized by my dear ones—you are my dear ones——

Rest in the country, Opatoshu, and work. The nervous atmosphere around the "worries" with Vollard, [Pierre] Matisse (here), exhibition "projected" (here) and the ersatz "eating"—all make my *stomach* nervous, I would love so much . . . to go back. I kiss you   Chagall

Virginia Haggard in High Falls to the Opatoshus in New York

Box 108 High Falls   July 3 [1946]

[English] Dear Adele and Oppen

I wanted to write sooner but David kept me busy and Jean wanted to talk to me such a lot! She is in paradise. She adores her little brother and wants us all to stay here for the rest of our lives.

How are you two dear people? I hope you are having a lovely rest and a very well-earned one. What wonderful things you did for me! It has been such a joy to be near you and I shall miss you a lot. I have never had friends like you, each time I see you I long for the next time. You give me such a feeling of security, you're so *good*! You make me feel that everything is fine! Without you I should have been quite unhappy and quite uncertain at times.

Our house is so lovely. There are some big thick catalpa trees with white blossoms that smell very sweet and great big leaves. There are big white lilies and poppies and roses. I wish you could come sooner. I'm afraid most of the flowers will be gone, and Marc will miss them too.

I have a wonderful room for the baby, with a sleeping porch. I put him out there in his carriage and everything is very convenient. But we have had some rather serious plumbing difficulties. We have a rainwater cistern and it has run practically dry. Our hot water boiler sprung a leak and flooded the cellar so the cistern became empty. Anyway the cistern is most impractical, and I'm afraid that for a family that likes to bathe (I don't think the owners were great washers) we may run short of water. So I have decided there is nothing to do but drill a well. I have to find out the cost, but even if it is rather expensive it is absolutely essential. Of course the owners didn't warn us that the water supply wasn't very abundant, they told us it was, but I have just found out what their idea of abundance is!

I shall write again at length when things get a little more settled. My aunt is wonderful, she helps me such a lot. Unfortunately she has to go home on the 1st of August, because her daughter is expecting a baby then. I shall have to try and find someone to help me. My aunt was reading [Opatoshu's novel, *In*] *Polish Woods*

My aunt: Virginia's Canadian aunt, "Tante Phine" (Josephine Jenkins), lived in Springvale, Maine, and stayed with Virginia to help with the baby during Chagall's absence.

while I was away. She didn't know it was by my friend Oppen, and she's sorry she couldn't tell you herself how much she enjoyed it, she said it was wonderful.

Jean sends you her love and a picture of some little creatures worrying a jester's legs. Jean decorates our house with flowers and we have a gouache of Marc's on the mantelpiece which he left for us, it looks very lovely.

David is well and happy.

I must try and catch the mailman or you will think I have forgotten to write to you.

Much love to you both and thankyou from the bottom of my heart. I wish I could tell you how grateful I am, dear Adele and Oppen, but I can't, so I'll just tell you that I love you very much

Virginia

Virginia Haggard in High Falls to the Opatoshus in New York

July 4th [1946]

[English] Dearest Adele and Oppen,

I'm so sorry I was out when you phoned. I'm afraid you were worried and it was very bad of me not to write before but the first few days were so busy. I had to get David some bottles because my milk dried up. Now we are quite settled down and David is very well. He is such a sweet boy and I'm very happy. I'm glad you think he's nice. He's going to love you so much too.

You made me very happy on Sunday when you came to see me off. You do so much for me! You sacrificed such a lot of things and took so much trouble. Our journey home was very nice and we enjoyed the chicken and lovely fruits. When we got home we had the neighbours in to drink sherry.

to see me off: After the birth and circumcision the following Saturday, June 29, the Opatoshus came to see Virginia off on her trip back to High Falls.

I'm sorry I wrote my first letter so hurriedly and filled it with so many domestic problems!

A big rain storm filled our cistern so we have more water now. We also have water in the little house, so we're not badly off.

My aunt is leaving the week after next. Her daughter is expecting her baby earlier than she thought and my aunt wants to be there a little while before. But I can manage by myself until Marc comes home [from Paris]. I shall try and find someone to help me later.

I haven't had a letter from Marc since I came home but maybe I shall have one tomorrow.

It's so beautiful here, we sit on the verandah and look at the mountains. Jean and I were sun bathing today and picking blackberries. We have so many and I'm going to make jam for you and Marc.

Jean is a wonderful help. She runs errands for me and saves me a lot of trouble. She tidies David's things and makes her bed and keeps her room in order. She's wonderfully happy and getting much healthier.

How are you both? If you have any time I'd love to hear from you. How are Rose and Mrs. Leivic? Take care of yourselves and have a good rest.

Rose: Adele Opatoshu's sister.

Mrs. Leivic: Wife of the Yiddish poet H. Leyvik (Leivick).

Much love from

Virginia

P.S. David can really see now, he looks at me all the time with such curiosity. He's growing more good looking every day.

P.S. I'm afraid I have to ask you to lend me some more money if you can. Lots of unexpected expenses have cropped up. Firstly there's the doctor for the children. My aunt got him for Jean while I was away because she was unable to sleep, something has to be done about her tonsils and I want the doctor to look at David from time to time.

The taxi from New York cost me $5 more than the driver had originally asked for because I took him out of his way to pick up baggage etc. And I have to take another taxi for things from the Railway Express. I have to buy a bed (the friend who was going to give me one finally gave it to her brother!) and a chest of drawers and a table for Marc, each costs $15, someone has just offered them to me and I'd like to take advantage of the offer right away. Also I had to pay a phone bill of $7 and $10 to Mr and Mrs Sheely who did work for me in the garden and the house.[24]

Could you lend me $100 more? Forgive me. I'll try and save on the weeks allowance, but I don't think I'll save very much because food is very high here and I have to pay for laundry, phone and electric bills. Sorry to worry you.

Love from Virginia

Marc Chagall in Paris to Virginia Haggard in High Falls

Paris, July 8, 946

[French] Dear Virginia, thank you, my dear, for the telegram and the letters from you. But before I had no letters from you and I was very sad. The food here in general doesn't do me much good for the moment and I am often sick to my stomach. Now it is better. And all these business matters (Vollard, Matisse-Carré, exhibition, etc.) aren't easy on the nerves. I want so much to come and work at home with you beside me. How are you? And the baby? And Genia? Write often and about everyone. Have you received letters from England yet as before? I want to know—write. I hope you are listening to Mrs. Braun: not to complicate life.

letters from England: From Virginia's parents.

Michel came here on a plane and will stay for two or three weeks. In her letter to me, Ida asked about you. I answered. Don't write to her yet until she gives news. She is still sick with nerves, I think—an imaginary illness. But what can you do? She must be calm and only in art be "nervous." But you know her. Don't torture yourself too much with the studio, just what's necessary—light, walls, tables. Are you tired with the stove—is there hot water? I am happy that you write that Genia is nice. Are you happy, my dear? And our David? I know that our house is a paradise with its flower garden and its vegetable garden. Don't tire yourself out. Do you have enough milk? Write to me a little every day about everything, like a diary. Do you have time to write or draw? Do you have a lot of work in the house? My regards to your aunt. Have you gotten letters from your parents?

From time to time, I see some English people from the Embassy here. They invited me to listen to English music. I enjoyed listening very much and seeing them. I always seek you in them. And I love them with you. I don't confuse politics with people and I love the English more because of you. I also believe that when the big exhibition is made here in Paris, the English of [British Council] will transfer it to London and I think, my dear, that I will be with you there. Now . . . I certainly hope so.

I would also like them to make an exhibition in the London museum just as they will make, I hope, in Paris (May 1947). I expect details of the principles of the exhibition in Paris. It is very delicate. They have never yet made an exhibition in the museum of a living painter. The exhibition in London depends on the British Council. I am thinking of going to the country for a little while. I don't yet know where. But I hope to come back in August in any case. I will tell you my impressions here and my feelings about life and art in France. You know how badly I write, but I adore reading you. I am sad that I don't read English to understand your stories. But send them nevertheless. When I get to New York, we will have to think about a publisher for you. Is it possible to make photos of you? Do you have enough money?

I believe rather in your order and your calm for all those things and for our life.

I think: how is the food for the baby? I hope that you make sure he gets the best things that can be found in America. Maybe ask a doctor for his opinion about food? How is he [?]

My dear, many kisses. Don't torture yourself about me, I am calm. I haven't yet worked on painting but have made a few sketches for pictures. I don't eat much—diet. But don't send anything for me to eat.

Love to all,

Your Marc

Michel: Michel Rapaport-Gordey, Ida's husband, was working as a journalist in Europe.

"nervous": Meaning "neurotic" in the creative sense. Ida Chagall was an artist in her own right.

I love the English: Chagall is referring to the bitter feeling among Jews after the Holocaust toward the British policy barring Jewish immigration to Palestine.

I certainly hope so: Chagall never did go to London with Virginia and did not attend his first postwar exhibition at the Tate Gallery.

don't send anything: Food packages were sent from America to starving Europe after the war.

July 16

I read in the newspapers about the expensive life. How is it in the country with you? No letters from you today.

> Many kisses
>
> Your Marc

Marc Chagall in Paris to Virginia Haggard in High Falls

Paris, July 15, 1946

Mr. Schin: "Schin" (Shin) is the Hebrew name of the letter *Sh*; Chagall refers to his Paris friend and lawyer Shmuel-Alexander Shchupak, who later moved to Israel.

Mr. Cassou: Jean Cassou, Director of the Musée national d'Art moderne, Centre Georges Pompidou, in Paris, organized Chagall's first major exhibition in postwar Europe, October 24– December 22, 1947.

Nyla's address: Nyla Magidoff, a Soviet friend of Ida's, who stayed with them in Sag Harbor, Long Island, and apparently flirted with Chagall.

[French] My dear, the days pass and it is harder to live without you. And how are you? You are alone there. Unfortunately your aunt has left. Have you found a maid? Someone to help you? You have too much work. I am sad about that. When I finally come. Right now I have a friend, Mr. Schin, my former lawyer, and he is going to help me in the deal with Vollard and with other things, and I pushed him to write and ask for everything. I have just come from the country where he lives (with his married daughter and her children), L'Etang-La Ville, near Marly-le-Roi. It is so pretty there that I was sad not to live there . . . And who knows, maybe we will be there. We'll see later on about the question of the exhibition. Tomorrow, I shall see Mr. Cassou. We'll see what he tells me. I think of you. This is your birthday. I am very sad that I cannot kiss you in person and wish you, both of us, happiness, and the children too. But you feel my heart. Often, too often, I wake up thinking of you. I am afraid that you are alone. But you must find the charm of life when you can in drawing and writing and believe that I am certainly thinking of you with all my heart. Because you are good and worthy and you have begun another life. When I don't get a letter from you, I am sad. Write to me as a diary, little by little, of your charming life, your days, your thoughts. How is our baby? I am arranging for Open one of his books in translation with the same publisher that did Bella's life. I wrote to Ida for Nyla's address. I will send it when I get it. But don't worry. They are leaving soon for Russia. In any case, we will have friends here when we need to find a house in the country, when we want to. I am happy. For the moment I want so much to return to America, to work, to finish some paintings—at home and to feel you near me.

> Kisses, Your Marc

Love to the children. / Regards to your aunt.

Virginia Haggard in High Falls to Adele Opatoshu in New York

High Falls July 17th [1946]

[English] Adele dear,

I was so happy to get your letter and Jean was pleased with her part of the letter too. She wants to send you some more drawings. When I told her I was trying to find someone to look after her and David she said "I want Adele to look after me."

Thankyou for telling me I should write to Ida. I want to, and I shall, but I find it hard. I feel that everything I say will hurt her, without my wanting it to. I feel as if the mere thought of me hurts her and I wish it wasn't so. I love her, everything that is Marc's is dear to me and I don't feel any bitterness towards her, nor have I reason to feel any. Mrs. Brown thinks I have, and that's something I can't agree with her about and I don't like her personal bitterness towards Ida. But unfortunately Ida can't feel my friendliness to her because she mistrusts me and I understand that so perfectly well, but it makes me sad all the same. But I shall write to her if you think I should.

David is getting so beautiful and strong he can move himself about on all fours! He laughs a lot and is such a contented baby. The milk agrees with him wonderfully. I'll soon send you some photos of us all.

Marc's studio is being built now, it may be ready in a week. And I got my cistern cleaned and tomorrow it will be filled and the new boiler installed.

How is that dear Oppen? And how is Doodle. And your poor arm, is it better?

I wish your house was right next to ours. What shall we do without you if we go and live in France—I don't like to think of it!

Give Oppen a kiss from me and lots of love to you both [from] all of us

Virginia

My aunt send[s] her best regards to you.

Marc Chagall in Paris to Virginia Haggard in High Falls

Paris, July 22, 1946

[French] My dear, I am so happy to get your letters and even with a drawing of David [by Virginia]. Oh! Go on. I will also draw you when I am free. There are always meetings here, etc. It is exhausting and I would especially like to work at home. I don't know if you got the telegram I sent you for your birthday [July 19]? They aren't precise here—but you know how much I love you and how much I *matters of inheritance:* Marc and Ida had a serious argument about Bella's inheritance: Ida demanded her mother's share, but Chagall refused. The case had to be settled in France, where they were all citizens. The dispute was not legally resolved until 1948, and Ida got a collection of early Chagall paintings.

think of you and of the children and wish them happiness. I am very sad not to be with you on your birthday. But I hope to be there soon. You know there are matters of inheritance here with Bella, complications with the lawyer. Michel is here for personal matters—I don't think that I will have much fun with him. You know his character. And then there is the matter with Vollard, Carré, the retrospective exhibition, Bella's book (contract).[25] You see. But don't be sad. I hope nevertheless to resolve it little by little, and also thinking of you. Don't doubt my love. Don't be unhappy about the expenses. If it is necessary, do what has to be done. You know well yourself. Take a woman as you think and understand. But I don't know how you are doing with money. Do you have debts? I don't think I can send any money from here.[26] I think after returning or perhaps ask Miss Mathieu of the bank? Write me how much you need and I will perhaps write to her. I don't know if Oppen has any money to lend you. As for Ida, I wrote to her in answer to her question about you and that you are now living in High Falls. I didn't get a letter from her after that. Of course she is putting on an act, maybe under the influence of Buche (they are in Sag Harbor, Long Island, NY POB 696).

Buche, Chagall's French spelling for "Busch," Anne-Marie Meier-Graefe, widow of the German art historian Julius Meier-Graefe, author of *Entwicklungsgeschichte der modernen Malerei* (*History of the Evolution of Modern Art*) both were Jews. When Busch arrived in the U.S. as a refugee, she sold her family's paintings at an auction and had independent means, moving between New York and Paris. Busch was a friend of Ida and Marc Chagall, and after Bella's death, Chagall invited her to live with him, which she apparently refused unless he married her. Later she lived with the major Austrian writer Hermann Broch (1886–1951), who was also a Jewish refugee in the U.S. and taught at Yale University. They married secretly a week before Broch died.

The more time goes by, the angrier I get. You can write her if you like (as Adele advises), nicely, very short. You, my dear, have tact and you love truth. I don't know what address is better to write to her, 42 Riverside Drive or Sag Harbor. I'm sorry your aunt is leaving. I don't understand how you will be alone without help.

Virginia Haggard in High Falls to Adele Opatoshu in New York

July 26th 1946

[English] Adele dear,

I was so happy to hear your voice today, thankyou for phoning me it was sweet of you. I was just writing you a letter, having received yours. Your letters are very charming, just like yourself, and I enjoy reading them so much. Adele, I must ask you to reconsider coming to see me. I couldn't consent to it unless you stay at least three days, and if Rose [Adele's sister] is still not well, you shouldn't. Please darling don't tire yourself. I'm worried about your shoulder. I think you should rest. When Marc comes home you and Oppen could come and stay with us. But you have no idea how I'd love to see your dear face again! You spoil me too much, and Oppen spoils me and so does Marc. I have too many good things and everybody is too kind to me. Why not think of yourself for a change? You need rest while you can. Now I'm lecturing you! I'm so sorry Rose is not quite well yet, please give her my love and tell her that Adele's sister is dear to me, and I hope she gets strong soon. You must enjoy having little Daniel [Adele's grandson] with you. I have been so fortunate finding a girl to help me. A friend from Rosendale recommended her, she also lives in Rosendale. She is not quite seventeen, inexperienced but I can teach her, she is very gentle and intelligent. She will get on beautifully with Jean, they have already taken to each other and she is very fond of babies. She is starting on Monday and only wants $15 a week! I'm so pleased.

Marc's studio is almost complete, the carpenter is finished and now I shall paint and plaster up the cracks and put putty on the window panes!

It really looks splendid. There are five large windows and it is very bright. I got him a big work table, very strong, and he has walls to work on covered with sheet rock a sort of cardboard filled with plaster, which is soft enough for thumb tacks. The little house looks lovely, it has purple petunias growing all round it and more in window boxes, and catalpa greens and hollihocks at the side.

Marc will be pleased with his studio I think.

I must go to bed now, it's getting very late. Please take care of yourself and Oppen and don't go journeying yet. Love to Oppen and Rose and Daniel, and much to yourself from

Virginia

Marc Chagall in Paris to Virginia Haggard in High Falls

Paris, July 29, 946

[French] My dear, I got your letter and am so happy. But I am sad that you don't have a maid, servant, nurse. You are wearing yourself out with so much work. I am happy that you went bicycle riding—don't fall down. I am sorry that your aunt has left. But we will certainly sleep in the big house and that will please me. In the day I will work in the studio. Finally I am leaving, I hope, on August 20, by ship. I already want to work and even rest with you. I haven't finished this buisness, but am beginning. When Ida is here she will continue. Well, I hope. But it is a lot already. The retrospective exhibition, in principle, will be next season, April–May, at Cassou—Museum of Modern Art.

leaving for Canada: Ida went to Canada to pursue anthropological research.

I got a letter from Ida who asks about you. I wrote her. She is leaving for Canada for some time. She is thinking of coming here for November. As for Riverside Dr., I am thinking of whether to keep it or not, but we will talk about it. How is the baby? How is Genia? Is she eating well?

If you like, your papa can ask the British Council to bring the exhibition to London in the Tate Gallery after Paris at the Museum of Modern Art. The director of the Tate Gallery is Mr. Rotstein and in Paris, it is Mr. MacOwen who takes care of exhibitions. An agreement is necessary with J. Cassou of the Museum of Modern Art and perhaps also with Georges Salles, director of the Museums of France. The transportation and insurance of the paintings from America can be less expensive before the pictures are dispersed after the exhibition at the museum in Chicago at the end of the year.

My dear, I just got your letter with the 2 photos. You understand my emotion. Thank you for the photo and for the baby. I think he is good. But I am afraid: is he eating enough? Not too thin? Shouldn't he be eating some additional things? I don't know. Vegetable extract, for example? How did you feed Genia? How is his body? The head, bigger? The body thin? Eat well. Also give him sun if necessary—what does the doctor say? And you, how do you feel?

The Firebird: Apparently, Stravinsky's *Firebird* with Chagall's splendid sets did not go to London.

You know, in London, there is the ballet [Balanchine's New York City Ballet], I think only *Aleko*, Lucy [Lucia] Chase and Smith (at Covent Garden), without [Sol] Hurok who keeps *The Firebird* for himself.

Love to you my dear

And also the baby and Genia

Your Marc

Marc Chagall in Paris to Virginia Haggard in High Falls

Paris, August 3, 946

[French] Dear Virginia, I am so happy to get the album from you with your story, *written* by you—so happy but you will read it to me yourself, and I will keep it. And I hope that you will want to write more, for the English are a race of writers and drawers too. But I finally hope to leave soon. We are thinking of August 20 on the (French) ship "Athos" from Marseille. I have a lot of work sending my old pictures to me; work that I want to get done and finish at home. Yesterday I got a nice letter from you, but in which I learn of Genia's illness. That's why she was so pale before. I'll ask Miss Mathieu of the 5 Av. Bank [where Chagall had a bank account] to send Oppen and you what you wrote. We will see if she sends it, but maybe I will already be home. Of course, my dear, stay at High Falls, don't move. When I come I will phone you (and what is our phone number?)

August 7, 946

My dear, I haven't written in a few days. There have been so many things to do and talk about these last days. But I want to send you a few words and you will feel how I think of you. I will certainly write to the bank. But I am leaving soon.

Much love, Marc

Virginia Haggard in High Falls to the Opatoshus in Croton Falls

Croton Falls: The summer place of the Opatoshus.

August 4th [1946]

[English] Dearest Adele and Oppen

I just got your letter, very welcome and sweet, and it always makes me happy to get one. I'm glad you are all well. What a pity you have to go to New York again, Adele.

Everything is fine here, except that I still haven't found anyone to help me. Do you think it's any good writing an ad in Oppen's paper, in Yiddish? It would be so nice to have someone Jewish. If you think it's a good idea, would you be very sweet and write it for me and tell me how much it costs? This is what I want to write: *Wanted*—Nursemaid-Houseworker, pleasant country home, artists' family, infant and small girl, own room, good salary. Or something to that effect. I'm really despairing of finding anyone. I have scoured the countryside and written ads and answers to ads. I would love to have a Jewish woman. Do you think it is possible? Even the woman who was going to work in the house for me from time to time, now finds she is too tired. I do hope I can find someone before Marc comes, or he will find our home rather upset! But maybe I shall have luck.

Oppen's paper: Yosef Opatoshu worked on the New York Yiddish daily *Der Tog (The Day)*.

I'm so glad Oppen is writing a lot and Adele is typing, that's splendid. Love and many kisses to you and good luck in your work.

Yours

Virginia.

BBB

Virginia Haggard in High Falls to the Opatoshus in Croton Falls

August 8th {1946}

[English] Dearest Adele and Oppen,

I missed the mail man on Saturday. I wrote you a hurried letter to tell you that I had found a nursemaid. I'm so happy! Adele thankyou for your lovely letter and Oppen thankyou for phoning this morning, it was very, very sweet of you and nice to hear your voice again. I got a letter from Rose too, I was so pleased, I'm writing to her.

I found a very nice woman who has experience with children and two years training to be a nurse. She is very pleasant and her voice and face are nice. I am quite sure we shall get on very well. I was so lucky to find her. But of course there is a catch! She has a baby of 14 months and her husband has left her. She has to leave the baby with her mother, and I don't know how long she can stand being away from him. I can imagine how I would feel, separated from my darling David!

This is only a short note. I have to prepare the house and get her room ready.

Goodbye dears. Open write lots of beautiful things about love and Adele read them but don't type them!

I am very, very sorry about your arm getting worse. If you could rest a lot it would get well quick but I know you! One might as well ask a child to rest. You can't, you are too full of energy!

Excuse the hurried writing.

All my love and kisses

Virginia

Marc Chagall in Paris to the Opatoshus in New York

Paris 11 August 1946

[Yiddish] My dear friends. I have not written to you in a while. I am so busy here with so much work (not art), you cannot imagine—just a torrent of worries and discussions about worries, which can only besiege a person an "artist."

What I want is to sit somewhere in a hole and work. But still, everything is gradually marked and let others bring it to a conclusion.

Thanks, dear Opatoshu, for your letter. You are right, as always. And as you say, she would also think so. Obvious. I must not forget myself . . .

I would love to see how you live and how you both are.

I got tired here. I went to a doctor and have to heal myself—and institute a regiment. My doctor [Camille] Dreyfus (the friend) didn't tell me, I have "something" which is related to "prostate"—what exactly it is I don't really know. I have to cure myself and take pills several times a day . . . What do I know?

So I don't know if I am old, or crazy, or tired.

My ship will be late. She doesn't sail on August 20 but on the 25th, perhaps from Marseille.

Do you hear news from Vi [Virginia]. Poor soul, she is alone and has no maid. Don't tell her I am not very well.

I kiss you.

I am afraid I won't arrive for September 2 in New York [anniversary of Bella's death], because of the ship.

I kiss you both/Your/ Chagall

she would also think so: Bella would have approved of his new liaison.

Marc Chagall in Paris to Virginia Haggard in High Falls

Paris, August 13, 946

[French] Dear Virginia, how are you. Unfortunately I am leaving a little later. The ship leaves on 25-8 [= August 25]. I am sad that you don't find a maid. Pay a little more. It's hard—it's an area of hotel-boarding houses. I don't want you to tire yourself out too much. I don't know how you get along all alone. Don't think that that will influence our happiness, as you write. You know I love you. I was at the doctor's—I take care of myself with a diet. I would like to leave already. To be with you at home. To rest and work at last. I don't like the atmosphere here— 47 Av. d'Iena—and above all alone. How is David? And Genia?

I am leaving on the 25th, so I will come after September 2, unfortunately (Bella's memorial day). I got your letter of the 6th. I love your letters and your reasoning, my dear: you feel the "price" of all those words, printed in articles. But I sent them to you so that you can get a sense of the atmosphere here in the intellectual and artistic milieu. There are too many newspapers and journals, and everyone writes, publishes. From my point of view it is especially a kind of chattering, an artistic and intellectual inflation. Even of the soul [in spiritual or poetic works], one is content with almost everything I detest. But there are a few poets like Paul Eluard (who has become my friend), or R. Char—very serious.

Paul Eluard: Paul Eluard (1895–1952), a major French Surrealist poet, who became a Communist. Eluard wrote a poem about Chagall, and Chagall made the frontispiece design and twenty-five drawings for Eluard's book, *Le dur désir de durer*, Paris: Editions Bordas, 1946.

R. Char: René Char (1907–1988), a major French poet.

You know that I don't feel "famous," I am still the same. I love solitude, the simple life, and you—because you are simple, very honest and charming, in my style. And I want you to criticize me if you find faults in me. You know—I have many, like a child.

But here in France there are simple people, workers. I believe in them despite the war and other things during Vichy. I hope to rest a little on the ship (departure from Marseille). You can then write me here until the 18th or 20th, and then I will be yours without letters. But your thoughts will follow me along with the baby's smile. I think of you and I think I will be happy with you. And it is you as a person who will "take care" of me with my love and our work.

Love,/Yours

Marc

I send you my lecture, which was printed in "Art."

Can't Mrs. Sheely help you? Unfortunately one cannot speak openly about David because one never knows who (J. of London) can make a scandal. And that would be unpleasant, you understand. Because he can have bad advisors there. I am not making it up, but that does happen with other people. Do you think we need the little window on the big wall of the studio?

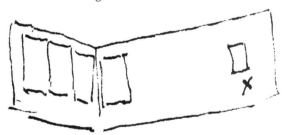

I think that if you could make hot water with a gas boiler that lights instantly (for bath and even kitchen use) except perhaps in winter when there is heating[?], because otherwise you have too much care and work to go up and down to the cellar. I enjoy looking at your charming drawing of David . . . The first time —and a drawing. I cannot look calmly—I think it is magnificent, good and as Oppen wrote, a little Chagall?

I would like to be home already and see all of you.

Love to Genia. Regards to your aunt. I'm sorry I won't see her.

And much love to you.

I won't go on a plane but on a ship. I'm sending you some articles about me. I think the French press is more intelligent about me than the American.

Love, my dear

Your Marc

workers: The discourse of the Communist Party, familiar to Chagall from the days of Revolution in Russia and renewed now. His friend Paul Eluard influenced Picasso to join the Party, but Chagall never joined.

Vichy: Collaboration with the Germans and the anti-Jewish policies of the Vichy government, which Chagall had experienced personally.

J. of London: John McNeil, Virginia Haggard's legal husband.

Virginia Haggard in High Falls to Adele Opatoshu in Croton Falls

September 7th {1946}

[English] Dearest Adele,

Thankyou for your sweet letter. You *must not* say that you have been neglecting me. I too, have not written for such a long time. I know that your time is all being used up in a most unprofitable manner and there is nothing quite so distressing as that for a diligent, constructive person like yourself. Dearest Adele I'm so sorry you have all this trouble, and I can only think that perhaps it may lead to some good thing eventually, as I believe almost all bad luck does. Be patient and sweet and soon it will be over. I wish you could come here and *really rest* for a while. You know we have an extra little room in the little house which is not furnished. Maybe Marc will want to furnish it for our friends. It would be quiet there, away from the children. The bedroom I had intended for you in the big house, I have made into a playroom for the children.

But by the way, I must tell you what you may not know already. Marc's boat arrived yesterday Friday but he can't disembark because of the seamen's strike. I spoke to Ida [in New York] three times on the telephone. She did her utmost to get permission for Marc to leave the ship, but they would not allow it. The ship is way out, not even in sight. Isn't it annoying? I am getting terribly impatient and I am sure he is, poor darling. Ida, I am afraid has not been at all well. But she was very sweet to me on the phone, and so kindly gave me all the news so that I should not worry. She is hating this climate and this country she says and longs to get back to France. Michel is still there trying to get a job which will enable them both to return (I think). But perhaps you know all this better than I do, if you have been in New York. Perhaps you saw Ida?

How is that dear Oppen? When is he leaving for Mexico? Is he preparing to go? I suppose the time draws near. Would you like to come here for a rest until he comes back? I shall try and cheer you up! And then maybe he can join you here after.

I have moved into the little house and I sleep here every night. The studio is all ready for Marc. I have been expecting him for so long. I even have bouquets of flowers, and a big bowl of beautiful fruits.

Anyway, it's a comfort to know that he really has arrived safely in the port of New York.

Genia (or Jean) was so pleased with your letter and the little leaf, she sends another one back. Take care of yourself darling. Love to Rose and Oppen and David [Opatoshu] if he is there. And kisses for all of you from

Virginia

P.S. My David is beautiful and healthy and all goes well.

Virginia Haggard in High Falls to Adele Opatoshu in New York

[English] Dearest Adele,

We are so happy to have Marc home.

He is such a darling man. He loves his little David and his house, and everything is beautiful. I'm busy getting things in order and shopping in Kingston. I'll write more later when I have more time.

Lots of love to you both from

Virginia

Virginia Haggard in High Falls to the Opatoshus in New York

High Falls Sept 30th [1946]

[English] Adele and Oppen dear,

I've been thinking about you a lot since my lovely visit. I was so happy. I feel so much at home in your house, more than ever I did in my parents' house. You make me feel that I am wanted and that is a very rare feeling. Your company is very exhilarating and at the same time soothing.

Everything is very well with us here. We had an aerial put on our radio and now we can get all the most beautiful music so clearly. Marc listens all day long without tiring and it helps him to work. David is very well and sweet and so is Genia.

Goodbye you two dear people, take care of yourselves.

Love from us both

Virginia

CHAPTER SIXTEEN

Exhibitions: Chicago and Paris: 1946–1948

Carl O. Schniewind in Chicago to Marc Chagall in High Falls

Schniewind: Curator
of the Prints and
Drawings Department
of the Chicago Art
Institute, 1940–1957.

October 4, 1946

[English] Dear Mr. Chagall:

We are working ahead now on your exhibition and since I have heard you have
returned to this country again, I will have a number of questions coming up from
time to time.

First of all, Mr. Sweeney tells me that you have an album of you and your family. I am wondering whether you would consider lending it to us. We thought that
we might rephoto some of your photographs and possibly relate them to certain
works in your exhibit if they seem to answer the purpose. If you would consider
lending us the album therefore, of which we would take the greatest of care, I
would appreciate your sending it immediately.

2. I am hoping that we would be able to acquire a number of your prints from
the exhibition and though I know that Pierre Matisse is your dealer, I think
many of your prints had never been priced and possibly you never even discussed the sale. Would you consider dealing with us directly or should we negotiate through Pierre Matisse? I am particularly interested in one of the etchings
entitled "Acrobate au Violon" in which the entire background has been touched
in and gone over with water color. This particular etching is reproduced in the
Museum of Modern Art's catalogue on page 73, right.

3. We would like very much to have some kind of a poster for your exhibition
and we have wondered whether you would consider making some outline drawing for us which could be printed in various sizes, possibly on a colored paper,
and then attractively lettered. The lettering part could probably be done right
here in the school. Of course, it would have been very tempting to ask you to

make a color poster, but the cost of printing would be so prohibitive in this country that much to our regret we felt that we had to give up the idea. If the idea of doing a line drawing appeals to you, we would appreciate hearing from you about this as soon as possible. I suppose printing takes a great deal of time nowadays. I am sending you this idea only now because I have only just been told that you returned to the United States and that you are now living in High Falls. I am sorry that this suggestion comes so late therefore.

Your exhibition in Chicago opens on November 14th as you probably know, and we consider ourselves very fortunate indeed that the Museum of Modern Art catalogue is at last out and that at least we will have it for your exhibition. I have been told that we may count on your coming to Chicago for the opening, and then I shall look forward very much to seeing you again here and discussing many things with you of mutual interest.

Hoping that you and Mrs. Rapaport are well, and with all good wishes,

Yours very sincerely, /   Carl O. Schniewind

Marc Chagall in New York to Carl O. Schniewind in Chicago

[English; typed by Virginia Haggard, signed by Marc Chagall]

42 Riverside Drive / New York City   October 14th [1946]

Mr. Carl O. Schniewind / Art Institute of Chicago / Chicago, Ill.

Dear Mr. Schinewind

Thankyou very much for your letter and for all your efforts in connection with my exhibition.

I read with pleasure your article on my engravings in the museum catalogue and I would like to thankyou again very much for your appreciation.

Concerning the drawing which you asked me to make for your poster: I tried some drawings and gave two to the Museum of Modern Art to send for me, hoping that one of them will answer your purpose. I also asked the museum to send you some photographs from my personal album.

And lastly, concerning the engraving "Acrobat au Violon" which the Museum wishes to acquire, you can negotiate with me directly, and I shall leave the matter entirely with you as regards the conditions.

As I wrote Mr. Rich, I hope very much that I and my daugher Ida Gordey will be able to attend the diner [sic] and opening to which the museum has so kindly invited us.

Looking forward to seeing you, and with all good wishes, / Yours very sincerely,

Marc Chagall

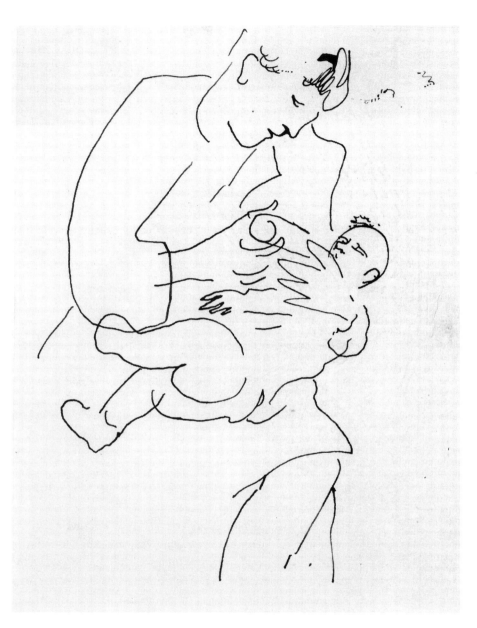

Virginia feeding David, High Falls, New York, 1946. Drawing by Chagall.

Marc Chagall in High Falls to Yosef Opatoshu in New York

High Falls 1946 16/X

[Yiddish] Dear Opatoshu, well done! You got up and went to Mexico. Once in a lifetime, one has to be there. I don't know if it is enough for three times.

I was there in my happy years in the Palacio de Bellas Artes. I worked there and "played" with her the "Aleko"—Zemphira looks on. Perhaps not so much at the . . . Jews as at the black-yellow Goyim. Something sings out of their souls, what—is hard to tell. The sky sings with them.

—Be well and return refreshed. / Your devoted /   Chagall

three times: The Yiddish saying goes "I was there twice: for the first and the last time," implying "I was there once and had enough." Thus, a "third" (i.e., second) time is redundant.

Carl O. Schniewind in Chicago to Marc Chagall in High Falls

January 12, 1947

Mr. Marc Chagall

[English] Dear Mr. Chagall:

It is indeed very bad of me that I have not written sooner. I intended to write you again and again shortly after you left and then, as I mentioned, I had a very disagreeable accident which thoroughly interfered with my work for a number of weeks. Then, before I knew it, the year was at an end and with it came a tremendous pile of work and as is usual in such cases, one puts off any sort of personal correspondence. So, though it is very late, I wish you and your daughter the very best for the new year as does also my wife and we hope very much that when we come to New York next week we shall have the great pleasure of seeing you again, even though it may be only for a short time.

Today is the last day of your exhibition in Chicago and so before the exhibition comes down I must repeat to you how grateful I was to have the experience and the thrill of working with the wonderful prints, paintings and drawings which we owe you, and which your magnificent talent has produced so abundantly. I can remember working on no other exhibition which gave me so much true artistic inspiration and which proved to be such a wholly satisfying experience. The exhibition will be dismantled tomorrow to my great regret. There are many of us who shall miss it more than I can tell you. However, we shall have a permanent reminder of the exhibition since I have been able to raise some money for purchases of the exquisite colored prints which were hung in the exhibition. I am attaching a list of the selections which I have made now and in the future, from time to time, I hope to be able to add to this small but important group, so that some day we will have a really representative collection of your work at the Art

Institute. Your magnificent and generous gift of etchings has set the corner stone for this collection and I am very happy that some of the friends of my department have made a number of purchases possible.

When I come to New York I shall get in touch with you immediately and reach a mutual understanding in the matter. I sincerely hope I will be lucky enough to find you in New York.

My wife and I will be in the San Carlos Hotel, 150 East 50th Street, from Sunday, January 19 until Monday, January 27. There will also be a number of questions to discuss about the catalogue raisonné where we still seem to lack a few plates and états and I hope that things develop more favorably in France, the missing items can be found and the publication of the catalog materialize in the not too distant future. There will be numerous details to discuss and plan and so I hope that you will have a little time for me.

The public response to your exhibition was extremely warm and the enthusiasm for your art as unanimous as I ever heard it on any exhibition. The importance of the graphic section surprised most people who knew you as a painter but did not realize your great importance as a contemporary print maker. This discovery had a tremendously stimulating influence on everyone and I was deluged with inquiries about the date of publication of your three great books. Now we have an exhibition of modern illustrated books and in my own mind I felt that this exhibition was not complete until a copy of each one of your books could be included in it. Espérons! [= Let us hope]

Looking forward tremendously to seeing you and your daughter in New York and hoping that you are well,

With kindest regards, / Carl O. Schniewind

Benjamin K. Smith in Chicago to Carl Schniewind in Chicago

Benjamin K. Smith, Appraiser of Works of Art: Antiques: Art Property
Room 1219 Chicago Temple Building
77 West Washington Street, Chicago

February 6, 1947

My dear Mr. Schniewind:

I have lately examined in the Print Department the following material:

> Woodcut by Paul Gauguin, title-page for Le Sourire, Guerin 73 $400.00
> (one of 4 impressions, Collection of Dr. Victor Segalen)
> The gift of Mr. *Cornelius Crane*, 240 Central Park South,
> New York City 19, New York

PRINTS BY MARC CHAGALL

1. Promenade, large plate, 1922 Drypoint $300.00
2. Portrait of the Wife of the Artist, 1925
   Etching and drypoint $250.00
3. Les Amoreux pres de la Rieviere, 1922
   Drypoint $200.00
4. La Fete, 1923, Drypoint $300.00
5. Acrobat with Violin, Paris 1924
   Etching and Drypoint, 1st state $400.00
6. Auto-portrait a la Grimace, 1st state
   Etching $500.00

                                                 $1,950.00

In my opinion, the foregoing prints should be carried on your inventory at the prices indicated. I hope the same will be satisfactory for your purposes, I am

Very truly yours,/   Benjamin K. Smith

Ida Chagall in Paris to Louis Stern in New York

17 juin 1947

[English] Dear friend Louis

Days are flying. Weeks and nothing is accomplished. Thank you for your letter. Thank you for all your thoughts. My trip was beautiful, interesting and quite difficult. [. . .] because out of a "Liberty" I saw the birth of a beautiful little French ship.

The captain coming one morning to us: "Madame, come, see if it is quite the red of the French line on the chimney and with these grand conceptions of a big nation—arrived in a desolated Cherbourg. [?]

Paris—well it is beautiful. More than I thought. Conditions are so much better than a year ago, that I can not tell. *Food is more plentiful.* Stores—expensive stores—are marvelous, but how people live is quite a mystery.

My arrival here was not such a happy one, because of Assia Lassaigne. I must find an apartment quickly. But how? Since this morning I started to work on Chagall show at the Museum. It is scheduled for October. Maybe you will come there?

I would love to have you now here but my summer plans are still uncertain on account of this show. And of Tériade. Hotels and everything for tourists are taken, overtaken. I could not arrange yet a maid for Gordes.

Assia Lassaigne: The estranged, Russian-born wife of Jacques Lassaigne still lived in the house and flirted with Chagall.

And still so many things to share, to talk about.

The vernissage [= opening of the] Braque [exhibit]. His show extraordinary. The Flemish [. . .] The Impressionists. A wonderful day with Eluard and so many other things. I bought for you the Eluard-Chagall but learned that you have it already. I will send you as quickly as possible the "Du Chene" Chagall.

Lucien Vollard promised to ask Fabiani for a Buffon. I said it was for father. So have a little patience and write for whatever you want.

Write often. I am very busy now. But I feel better. Younger. As if my skies was clearer!

Do you know? Eluard, Paulhan are enthusiastic about mother's book! [In Ida's translation.] What else? Michel is getting quite prominent with his articles. I did not even realize it was so much.

Write about your plans. If you are going to California, what about coming with father for his opening. It sounds difficult to me for him not being present.

> *Buffon*: In his letter of May 26, 1947, Stern asked Ida to get for him an expensive book by Picasso, *Buffon: Histoire naturelle*, published by Fabiani in Paris in 1942, under German occupation.

A big smile, a very big kiss/ Ida

Marc Chagall in High Falls to the Opatoshus in Croton Falls

> The lawyer Dvorkin, son-in-law of the poet Yehoash, bought a piece of land in Croton Falls near New York and built six summer houses for Yiddish writers-friends, including H. Leyvik and S. Bickel. Eventually, only Y. Opatoshu and A. Glanz-Leyeles bought houses there.

High-Falls, N.Y. 947 9/7 [July]

[Yiddish] Dear,

Received your letter. Thank you. Here in our place it is now so beautiful it isn't Jewish at all—berries, worms, chicken, wild grass—everything whispers to me: become an American, don't go . . . That doesn't mean I sleep calmly all night and don't think about this and that. In your place it is, probably, also beautiful and green. I must see it someday.

Dovid is as beautiful as his mother, who always laughs and is happy, I get ashamed of my Jewish sadness . . . You have to hear her, how she "whispers" about living-so——

I kiss you both

Marc Chagall

P.S./Here are the lines for you

Jean Cassou in Paris to Louis E. Stern in New York

Musée National d'Art Moderne/Paris-XVIe, 2 Rue de la Manutention

10 July 1947

[French] Sir,

I have reserved a gallery for temporary exhibitions in the Museum of Modern Art, which has just opened. The first of these exhibitions will be a large Chagall exhibition which will be next October and November, and is to welcome this great artist back to France and to follow the magnificent exhibitions of his work that have just taken place in the United States. You have two works by Chagall:
  "The Lamp"
  "A Gouache"
  Would it be possible to lend them to France for this show, in which I want very much to add the great American collectors. What I am asking from you now is an acceptance in principle. I will then inform you of the practical conditions of the transfer of the works to Europe. If you would do me the honor and pleasure of giving me a favorable answer, I would indicate the costs of your insurance.
  I hope that you can help us with a great painter whom you love and who is so well-known and appreciated in America. Thank you in advance.

Please accept my best regards,

Jean Cassou

Virginia Haggard in High Falls to Yosef Opatoshu in Croton Falls

High Falls July 17 [1947]

[English] Oppen darling,

Thankyou for your charming little note. You are being a very brave grandfather. Keep it up and you shall have your reward. Already I think that baby is beginning to inspire you. We shall soon be reading stories of babies and grandfathers.
  Marc's Paris exhibition is still in the hands of fate. It looks very unlikely now that it will take place in October. The most important of all the collectors, [P.A.] Regnault, refuses to lend his pictures, because of the danger of a revolution in France.

P. A. Regnault was a major early collector of Chagall in Belgium. He hesitated to

send his Chagalls in the precarious political situation in Europe. The strength of

the French and Italian Communist Parties, combined with the menace of Stalin's victorious army sitting in the center of Europe, made people fear a Communist takeover of Western Europe.

All the other answers from collectors are doubtful, and the time is far too short. I'm relieved, because it would have upset this ideal life to go rushing off suddenly. Marc works so freely here, he is so happy in his little house and what should we do without our dear friends Oppen and Adele? Even if we go in the spring I'm sure we shall come back. We love it here now, Marc feels more and more reluctant to go.

Get a nice sunburn on that wide brow of yours and keep well. Kisses from us both

Love/Virginia

Marc Chagall: The Painting (Poem)

[Yiddish]

If only my sun had shone at night.
I sleep—steeped in colors,
In a bed of paintings,
Your foot in my mouth
Presses me, tortures me.

I awake in pain
Of a new day, with hopes
Not yet painted,
Not yet daubed with paint.

I run up
To my dry brushes,
And I'm crucified like Jesus,
With nails pounded in the easel.

Am I finished?
Is my picture done?
Everything shines, flows, runs.

Stop, one more daub,
Over there—black paint,
Here—red, blue, spread out,
Calmed me.

"For Virginia/Marc/1947. High Falls."

Can you hear me—my dead bed,
My dry grass?
My departed love,
My new found love,
Listen to me.

My departed love:
Bella Chagall.

My new found love:
Virginia Haggard.

I move over your soul,
Over your belly—
I drink the calm of your years.

I swallowed your moon,
The dream of your innocence,
To become your angel,
To watch you as before.

Louis E. Stern in New York to Jean Cassou in Paris

[Stationery: Thirty Broad Street, New York]

July 18, 1947

[English] Dear Mr. Cassou:

I am acknowledging and responding to your letter of July 10th.

In principle you may depend on me to cooperate with you in the proposed exhibition of the works of Marc Chagall and I will be glad to lend my pictures "La Lampe" and one of my "Gouaches". I happen to have two. You do not indicate which one you desire. Chagall's daughter, Ida, will know which one you should have.

I assume also that she has or will tell you that I have a number of other Chagalls: two of the period of 1914 and the others of various dates in between up to the present. All you have to do is to advise me when and where to deliver the pictures. I will then indicate the amount of insurance for the two pictures mentioned in your letter. I would say that the insurance should be between $4,000 and $5,000.

I might add that by the time you receive this letter I will be out of New York and in California, not to return until after the first of September.

Awaiting your further instructions in the matter, I am/Sincerely yours,

Louis E. Stern

Marc Chagall in High Falls to the Opatoshus in Croton Falls

12/8 [August] 947   High Falls, N.Y.

[Yiddish] Dear friends

How are you? I am better, I can already walk, lie straight in the bath-tub and turn around. I am working little by little and everything in me functions little by little——

The English girl-wife "laughs" at the world, the boy too. But I don't laugh—especially at the Englishmen, her Englishmen——

I hope to come to the city and see the doctor. Would you be free for a while on September 2 [the anniversary of Bella's death]? I plan to take a car and perhaps go to her with you and the Frumkins——

the Englishmen: A reference to British anti-Zionist policies in Palestine.

go to her: To Bella's grave in New Jersey.

Be well your devoted

Marc Ch.

P.S./ I am glad that you liked Dovid's [Opatoshu] choice of his friend [Chagall's David]. Tell him that I give Dovid a drawing for him *personally*.

Marc Chagall in High Falls to Hilla Rebay in New York

On June 25, 1947, Chagall had asked Hilla Rebay for a loan of four of his works from the Guggenheim Museum for his first major exhibition in Paris in October. Those were "Paris Through the Window," "Green Violinist," "The Birthday," and "Street with Flowers." Baroness Rebay sent "Paris Through the Window" without asking for the approval of the trustees or Mr. Guggenheim, but nothing else.

August 26th, 1947

[French] Dear Baroness,

I wrote you some time ago about my retrospective exhibitions in Paris and London. I have not received an answer and I am upset because I do not know why, unless you did not receive my letter.

I will always remember how much attention you paid to my art, like Mr. Guggenheim you know my good feelings and my sympathy for you.

If I have not been seen for a long time it is because I have suffered and I am still suffering from a personal tragedy.

personal tragedy: Bella's death in September 1944.

But you cannot doubt that I am grateful to those who paid attention and were sympathetic to my art, like you and Mr. Guggenheim.

Now the national museums of Paris and London are organizing exhibitions and would like your most important paintings to be part of those exhibitions: "Paris Through the Window," "The Green Violinist," and "The Birthday."

I hope you will understand the importance of these exhibitions and that you would want to cooperate with the museums. The exhibition in Paris may be delayed until November or December, but the catalogue has to be prepared now.

Hoping soon to hear how you are and to receive the assurance of your collaboration. My most sincere wishes. / Yours,

Marc Chagall

Hilla Rebay in New York to Marc Chagall in High Falls

22/September 1947

[German] Dear Marc Chagall,

Sincere thanks for the lovely note, which pleased me very much and which I appreciate because it shows me that you, too, understand what a good and helpful friend I have been to you; and especially in times when you urgently needed one and no one else appeared so useful. For I certainly know that, without me, you and your family would not have been saved from the Nazi mobs.

Fortunately, Mr. Guggenheim has not minded that I have sent the painting off so quickly myself and, hopefully, it was well packed and isn't squashed. For a lot of shipping doesn't exactly help paintings.

With best wishes, / Hilla Rebay

Marc Chagall in High Falls to Sh. Nigger in New York

High Falls N.Y., Box 108

24/9 1947

[Yiddish] Dear friend Nigger,

I was told you sent a letter about Bella's books and that you will write about them.

I am very happy about it.

I intend to publish (by myself, or with a French publisher—) a memorial, an art book that will include paintings (she in my art), her remaining pieces of diaries-and-letters, and especially the best, the selected things written about her 2 books

Paulhan; *Spire*: Jean
Paulhan (1884–1968),
a French writer and
critic, helped Chagall
obtain French citizen-
ship in 1937; André
Spire (1868–1966),
a French poet and
Zionist spent World
War II in the U.S.

(perhaps printed in the languages they were written in). Among them J. Maritain, J.Paulhan, André Spire, Paul Eluard and a few other selected writer-critics.—

I hope you will agree to appear in that book.

I am leaving for Paris for my exhibitions in the museums of Paris, Amsterdam and London and this fact does not contribute more calm or even health.

Have a good year and regards to yours/   Marc Chagall

Aboard ship: Chagall left
for his first postwar
exhibition in Paris.

Marc Chagall Aboard Ship to Virginia Haggard in High Falls

[Stationery: Cunard White Star, RMS Mauretania]

October 3, 1947

[French] My dear,

Here I am. I slept in my trousers, shirt, sweater, etc., because I am a little crazy . . . But I am gradually calming down. Next to me in the cabin, Mr. Lopez speaks French, and I will eat at the same table with him. Naturally, I am sorry that you aren't in the same cabin. But that will come! I am missing you here. All the English people here, the staff are flexible, nice. As in Gainsborough's paintings. I am sad when I think of what you are doing right now. But your sun gives me life. Take care of everyone and kiss your son David for me and I hope that Genia is perfect and becomes proper. Kisses until tomorrow.

M

October 4

My dear. It's monotonous, this swaying a bit, but there is nothing to do about it. I always think of you—how you walk fast over the ground. And David? You are already in High Falls?

October 5, Sunday

They are singing mass next to me and I am writing you a few words. I am counting the days until I arrive. I don't think I will travel alone afterward—especially not on a ship. How I would like to see you. It is so far. I see how you run here and there. Don't tire yourself out and write to me about everything, everything.

October 6

I am counting the days and nights, the lunches and dinners that are all alike. On October 9 we arrive all the same. I am taking a ticket for [the train] Cherbourg-Paris. I don't know if Ida will come to Cherbourg. And you, my dear? How are you? I hope that you aren't too sad. You will forget, you have so much to do. Don't tire yourself out. How are the children. Does David say "peipe" and how is Dorothy [the domestic] working? I would so much like to see you.

Kisses, my dear.

October 7

I have to give this letter to the post. We arrive at 9 in the morning and I think of sending a telegram. It's terribly sad to be alone and I would already like to return. I am happy that I will have letters from you in Paris. On the boat I am a bit too well known. Every guy can approach me and say: Are you, etc. . . . I would like to say no, but these things are tedious. I think that the cabin class is more simple.

A thousand kisses to you and all of you. / All the best

Your Marc

Marc Chagall in Paris to Virginia Haggard in High Falls

Paris, Thursday 12 [October]

[French] . . . the exposition is postponed because of the strike for the 24th of October. Except for Belgium, all the paintings have arrived and are placed. There was a slight misunderstanding with the 2 directors about the hanging which they wanted [to do] themselves (badly hung, but I came with Tériade and changed it). I think it will be all right. They are going to photograph the walls, I hope, and you will see. Yesterday I ate here at . . .

Marc Chagall in Paris to Virginia Haggard in High Falls

Paris, October 13, 1947

[French] My dear, only today did I get the first letter from you of Oct. 7. I don't know how things are with you. You wrote to Ida that Dorothy left. Basically she was useless to you of course—and so what are you doing alone? Here with me, preparations are being made, the paintings from Holland and Switzerland should arrive. I hope they get here in time. Here in France it is always, as they say, at the last minute. I of course don't like that. We will see. The paintings have not yet been hung. Yesterday, Eluard telephoned that he received the package, but . . . "As if a tank had driven over it." That is, the package was too badly done. Aside from the boxes of linen, everything was crushed. Don't send him any more packages or else pack them specially. Wait . . . For example, the electric lamps that you gave me were also crushed. It is an art in its own right to make a

received the package: People in America would send packages to starving postwar Europe.

package and send it abroad. But I adore you all the same and I think of you and of your son. You see that I write [French] like a pig—even worse—write to me more and send photos. You know: Ida and Michel are getting divorced. I am sad. I don't know who she loves, she is very close to Robert, but definitely doesn't want him. There is Tériade (of "Verve") who is surely over fifty, who loves Ida, I think, but she is colder than he is. It's a real cinema. But I would like it to end. Mrs. Braun's opinion on it is interesting. Ida is in doubt. I pity her, she is still sick with her stomach and the years are passing. You are right about Robert. I don't know why Ida doesn't want him (as a husband). Robert doesn't leave her alone and is crazy about her.

Of course, I don't think he has had a brilliant career. I don't know—but he is young.

[Crossed out paragraph about travel arrangements] I shall write to you later about it.

Did Matisse come? Don't talk yet about the "prices" [for the paintings]. What did he say? As for the contract, did he give the rest of the guarantee for the year?

This has turned into a business letter.

But I would like to see you. But maybe you are having a "rest from me?" A little . . . That's good.

> Kiss the children and I kiss you hard and am yours forever, Marc

Robert: Robert Villers, a friend of Ida's.

Tériade: Eugene Tériade, editor and publisher of the Paris art journal *Verve* and publisher of Chagall's illustrations to Gogol, La Fontaine, and the Bible.

Marc Chagall in Paris to Virginia Haggard in High Falls

Paris [October 1947]

[French] My personal address: Hotel Alsina/39 Avenue Junot/Paris, 18th

Dear, I send you my address. How are things? I got your letter. I will send you the newspaper with the article before the opening. It is postponed until the 24th because of the strike. So much the better. The pictures from Belgium haven't yet come but I don't think the hanging will be bad. The catalogue is thin. The state doesn't have any money.

I say here that I am thinking of returning in the spring. I really am thinking of returning to France and living retired, perhaps on the Côte d'Azure [sic]. You see how J. [Jean] Cassou writes. Everyone asks me the same question. So is it definite? I am thinking of reserving a return ticket soon. France looks different than before. Despite the "strike," the exterior has changed. A lot of movement, variety of life, despite the deprivation, but less than before. There are a lot of things in the stores. Of course it is very expensive. But less expensive, I think, than in America. For the moment, I stay far away from Montparnasse—every day I am at the museum to watch the hanging because the director No. 2, the little

the same question: "Are you coming back to France?"

one, is an idiot. Ida is really working a lot for the exhibit. She has helped a lot. You didn't write anything to me about the "theft" in the studio. Is it true? And how are the children? David, health, food, outings, rest, and Genia, is she capricious? Does she help? Does she go to school? You are working a lot at home and I am sad when I think of that—

My dear, I kiss you and tell you soon. I will see how much time I will still be here.

Yours   Marc

Marc Chagall in Paris to the Opatoshus in New York

[On the back of an invitation to the exposition opening—in Chagall's handwriting]

[Yiddish] The exhibition is larger and, they say, more beautiful than the one in New York. It's "regrettable" that such a "maven" as Adelye isn't here—

Announcement of Exhibition

[French] The Ministry of Youth, Arts and Letters

Requests your presence at the opening of the exposition

Marc Chagall

Which will take place on Thursday, October 24, 1947, at 14:30[1]

Museum of Modern Art
Ave. Du President Wilson   Valid for 2 persons

Marc Chagall in Paris to Virginia Haggard in High Falls

Thursday, Friday 24 [October 1947] Paris

[French] Dear Virginia,

Happy with your letters and the photos. The little serious man is good. Tomorrow is the opening [of my exhibit]. It is postponed.

In two hours we are going to the opening. How I wish it were over. Of course I am sorry that you cannot see the exhibit. I'll try to make photos. I'm happy to get your letter.

Sunday, October 26, 1947, Paris

Darling. Disturbances all the time, visits, one can't write. No ink here in the hotel. Well. Don't think that I don't think about you always. I am sending you a *telegram*: Apparently instructions for money to pay for Chagall's return ticket. Virginia bought the ticket in New York.[2]

telegram and Ida another one. This is for the ship ticket. And then the opening which went very well. The papers wrote nicely, you will see it later. It's beginning to be cold here. Not much coal here or at Ida's. I would like to be gone already and to work quietly and be with you my darling. My health is all right, not bad. I don't eat too much, don't drink, and don't go out much to people. I am sending you the check for Dolson. I hope that Jean-Paul also paid you. You did well with Pierre M[atisse] concerning the paintings—their price. For the other price—the contract, don't talk about it. And what does he think of the rest of the guarantee? About another year? And how are things with you? I am impatient to be with you, see David and all of you. And we will talk of our plans for the future. I will soon write more to you.

For the moment, much love, my darling/Your Marc

Marc Chagall in Paris to Virginia Haggard in High Falls

Paris, October 27, 1947

[French] Darling, Thank you for the letters. I am happy to receive them. It is beginning to be cold here and there's not much coal. The exhibit is a huge success. For 2 or 3 days I didn't go there.

I didn't go there: As always, "shy" Marc disappears at a moment of success.

"antisemite": Chagall often puts unpleasant things, or things to be said only *entre nous*, in quotation marks or in parentheses. In spite of his concerns, Maeght became Chagall's major dealer.

Valentin: Curt Valentin was associated with one of the Berlin galleries that represented Chagall in 1922–1923. Now at the Buchholz Gallery in New York, he collected the money for the Chagalls' transatlantic passage in 1941.

My dear, as for the Maegh[t] engravings, don't give anything. Those are almost the last engravings of "Ma Vie." Besides, Ida said that Mr. Maegh[t] is a very unpleasant character and even (an "antisemite"). We will give the representative engravings to Valentin Buchholz who is very nice and has done me a great deal of good. He sent me telegrams here and on board the ship. (Answer that those are the last engravings and one cannot give them away. But that my books with engravings will soon appear—say which—with Tériade, and they can have them if he wants.)

In general, I want Pierre to have my paintings and Valentin my engravings and perhaps drawings if Pierre will allow. I hope he will make an exhibit of my engravings afterward.

Darling, how are you? Your health? Take good care of yourself. Sleep too. I am happy that you write good things about David and Genia. I will be happy with you if the children are good. I hope to God it will be calm in France. We will move to France (perhaps to the Côte d'Azur) next year. I am happy that they won't disturb us at 42 Riverside Drive and we will be able to live there again. Don't tell Pierre that we definitely want to leave since we will keep High Falls as an address nevertheless and other things. Much love, I think about you always, my darling—Marc

In Paris I don't want to have any art dealers or contracts. But we will talk about [it].

Marc Chagall in Paris to the Opatoshus in New York

29/Oct. Paris, 1947

[Yiddish] My dear Opatoshu. A long time since I have seen you or written. Such a commotion. "Bizy"—with what? You go around in circles. What? One exhibition after another, and the last is the best arranged, and beautifully, nicely prepared, though the French government is poor . . . And alas, poor me—what's my value . . . Yet the whole press responded too positively about it—what do I know . . . But don't let me talk about myself. Since you know nothing about all those things, so how are you? I would like to come "back" [to America], though here I was asked even on the radio to "stay." You were in High Falls—so? How is Adelye?

I am with Ida, she sends regards. She says the publisher of your book wants to keep it *in principle*, though for the time being, he is in dire straits. We'll talk about it. France is beautiful, though it lacks food, coal, and other things—but of course, one can (*those who can*) get everything. I am not talking about the politics here. I hope to be [back] around the 18, 20 [November]. I don't want to travel to Amsterdam, or to London, where the exhibitions will go.

I kiss you, Your Chagall

"Bizy": A Yiddish mock-expression, ironizing the stereotypical American ideal of keeping "busy," or running around.

what's my value: Yiddish formulaic words of modesty—to guard against any impression of boasting. It usually means the opposite.

in dire straits: In July 1946, Chagall tried to arrange a French publisher for Opatoshu's novel *In Polish Woods*, but nothing came of it.

Marc Chagall in Paris to Virginia Haggard in High Falls

Paris, October 31, 1947

[French] Dear Virginia,

No letter from you for a few days. I don't understand what's going on with you. I am counting the days here although the exhibit has been successful. It is hard not to work regularly. Here the cold is beginning. Often there is no light. A pretty country but it lacks a lot of things. Especially calm. But the air is so good here after that climate in America and I think how and when we will be able to come here. How is David. It is sad not to see [him].

November 1

Got a letter from you where you write about Pierre Mat[isse] at our house. Happy he liked it. Now I would like only one thing: to come back to you. And I can't write——

Paris, November 3, 1947

[French] Dear, thank you for the ticket, I am sending you the check here and the receipt for the ticket. I am happy that you have a maid. I have almost decided to come here for 1948, April [?], to the Côte d'Azur if everyone will be a bit calm (near Grasse). I think that, after I leave here, Ida will go look for a house there. She is a little tired, she is going to rest there a bit at the same time. It proves that she doesn't have any luck with those things [= relationships]. I don't understand. I am a little sad because of her. She is divorcing Michel.

Kiss David and Genia./Many kisses from me. You know that you are *in my heart*.

Your Marc

Marc Chagall in Paris to Virginia Haggard in High Falls

Paris, October ? [actually November], 1947

[French] Dear Virginia, the more time passes the more worried I am about you, thinking of you and the family. How are things? But soon I am leaving (Nov 18) and I will see for myself and we will talk. It is very hard to be alone even though I am surrounded by people here. I am still thinking of our move to France and the possibilities here. And when I will finally be able to work quietly and be isolated. I think that Ida will be able to take care of pictures in Paris if necessary.

13 Nov. 1947

Lifar: Serge Lifar (1905–1986), a French dancer and choreographer of Russian origin.

I had a visit from the artistic director of the comic opera and the opera concerning a ballet, but I refused because the choreographer is S. Lifar. I don't have much time—I'm leaving on Tuesday. How I would like to settle down somewhere —the exhibit here is extended to December 7. The museum wants to do some engravings after the exhibit. Write to Ida's address.

Visits here are fatiguing and there's always something.

I will talk with you. That will give me the greatest pleasure and happiness

All yours, Marc

Marc Chagall in Paris to Virginia Haggard in High Falls

Paris, Wednesday, November 4, 1947

[French] Darling, I am so happy to get your letters and yet I don't write much but you know that I am thinking of you all the time. I leave my hotel at 9 o'clock in the morning. At Ida's the day goes by and the mail from Montmartre is far— down below. Don't be *sad*. [*Inserted*: I received your letter. Thanks.] I will come soon and you don't know how happy I will be to be in our delicious house with you and the children and to work. It's true that we have to think about moving. We'll talk. Here in France, as I wrote you, it's delightful, but so many things are lacking. You can read that in the newspapers. It is sad for *the people*: God willing

Virginia's sketches of Marc.

it will be a bit better and in the world in general. My exhibit goes well. A lot of people and the press is also good . . . Ida just left with a photographer to make photos of the walls of the exhibit and some paintings separately. However, if you can ask at Colten's (through Caterine [at the Pierre Matisse Gallery]) for the other photos only of important paintings—like those too. Tériade comes today for the books (Gogol, LaFontaine, to sign the letter-contract). He is soon going to print the text of Gogol's *Dead Souls*, the rest is done. I hope that Reis talked on the phone with Schifrin about the *1001 Nights*[3] so that he would know—if not, remind him of that. My darling, my health isn't bad. But when I am with you I am happier. The more time passes, the more I feel how I can't live without you.

I just received an invitation from Venice. A hall was given for me. 20 paintings (May 1948, international exhibit, the Venice Biennale). I hope we will be able to go there together.

Kisses, my dear, Your Marc

Marc Chagall on Board Ship to Pavel Ettinger in Moscow

22/November 1947　　　on the ship

[Russian] Dear Pavel Davidovich,

How are you? I am writing on the boat that takes me back to America, where I am going to "liquidate" everything, in order to return for good to France in a few months.

In Paris, my big retrospective exhibition is mounted in the Musée d'Art Moderne, covering almost 40 years of work, 1908–1947.

As the press reports, the success is enormous. This is the first time an exhibition has been made in the official museum of a living artist in general and a Russian in particular. And though I have been forced to live and work far from the homeland [Russia], in spirit I have remained faithful to it. I am happy that I could thus be somewhat useful to it. And I hope in my homeland they don't see me as an alien. Isn't it true?

This exhibition will move to Amsterdam at the end of December. And from February 1948 will be in the museum in London (Tate Gallery). Earlier it was in America. Show this letter in my homeland. There they will surely be glad about it. I don't need to tell you that for me it would be a great joy if such an exhibition were mounted in my homeland. True, 3/4 of the paintings belong to various museums of various countries and collections.

42 Riverside Drive, New York C., USA

P.S. Did you get in the homeland a big color album with 17 of my paintings, Edition du Chêne, Paris, with a poem by Paul Eluard? Published in 1947?

Ries: Bernard J. Reis, Chagall's lawyer in New York.

Schifrin: Jacques Schifrin, publisher of Pantheon Books in New York. He fled Europe in 1941 with Varian Fry's help.

a hall was given for me: Chagall received a hall in the French pavilion in Venice.

in my homeland: Naïve Chagall writes as if Ettinger could influence the actions of his "homeland."

belong to various museums: They are hard to get on loan to Russia.

"To Virginia, 948/Happy New Year/Marc."

By the way

My illustrated books:

1) Gogol and *Fables de LaFontaine* (former publisher Vollard) will appear in the next few years with Paris publisher Verve.

I have to make a whole series of other books, including one Russian one. Write to me somehow. Be well. Your devoted   Marc Chagall

Louis E. Stern in New York to Marc Chagall in High Falls

January 30, 1948

[English] My dear Maestro:

I am writing to acknowledge with grateful appreciation the receipt of the stunning drawing for my copy of [Paul Eluard's] *Le Dur Desir de Durer*.[5] I am delighted to know that the original drawing will go to Ida and that I have one drawn especially for and dedicated to me. Thanks again.

Verve: The books were published by Tériade in 1948 and 1952, respectively.

one Russian: Iliazd (Ilya Zdanevich)[4] was one of the most radical Russian Futurists, constructing constellations of letters and crossing the boundaries between language and art. He lived in France.

You will be interested to know that at a recent book sale I acquired a copy of a little booklet of Clair Goll entitled *Journal D'Un Cheval*, in which you made the drawing for the frontispiece.[6] Did I tell you that sometime ago I acquired from the Sickles collection a copy of Gustave Coquiot's *En Suivant La Seine*, where you have a drawing of a nude?[7] Some day when you are in my home, which I hope will be soon, I will want you to sign the reproduction.

I am enclosing a letter received from Reverend McLane, together with a reproduction of a tremendously important Chagall which he has acquired. It sounds very exciting. Please return the letter together with the photograph as soon as you have read it and examined the photograph. I am frank to say that I envy Reverend McLane for having this particular Chagall.

A few days ago I was at the Matisse Gallery and saw a new gouache which I liked very much. It apparently belongs to the Mexican period.

It was a great pleasure to have you and Virginia at the house the other night, and I hope you will put me on the list for your next trip to New York. [. . .]

Marc Chagall in High Falls to Leo Kenig in London

February 12 1948   High Falls, N.Y.

[Yiddish] Dear Kenig, How are you? I thought you would write to me, that you'd be so excited at least to see my daughter in London—and would write. So I am writing myself. For in London there are several pictures which were "done" when you lived in a room downstairs in La Ruche, dreaming nicely, and I would come "ask" for your opinion: will I be an "artist" or not (not an artist like "Brazer"[8] or "Nalewa"[9] or Leger, or Altman[10] . . . and others, others . . .)

in London: The Chagall exhibition at the Tate Gallery.

So you would smile, and it seems to me that you believed in me a little . . . But I don't know why. Perhaps it was, as I often think, because of my "smile."

"Hundreds" of years have passed. Someday I shall be, or was, or already am, 60 (I corrected my years, according to J.J. Sweeney)[11] and as you see, I am still a "child." I slip into childhood in old age. And I am writing to ask you to describe for me precisely how the exhibit is. And as a specialist, perhaps you might inform the poor (rich and stuffed) Jews here, who are fonder of "delicatessen" than of delicacy in art. How is your life? Why don't you ever write to me? I hope to come to you in London for a while. I intend to "liquidate" here and move to the land where people still create [France]. By the way, Paris (like Amsterdam) was very nice to me lately and made the same exhibit in their museum. But as I see from the catalogue, the London exhibit is larger. What do they say about it? And are the Jews coming?

Be well. Your devoted

Marc Chagall

I am sending you an offprint, perhaps it may interest you.

What is your address? Do you have my Bella's second book—"Di ershte bage-genish" [*First Encounter*]?

The Death of Mikhoels

On January 16, 1948, the distinguished Yiddish actor and theater director, Shloyme Mikhoels, Chairman of the Soviet Jewish Antifascist Committee—and thus the highest official authority of Soviet Jewry, was lured by the NKVD from Moscow to Minsk, where he was brutally murdered. The act was immediately perceived for what it was, and the next day in Moscow, Perets Markish published a poem on Mikhoels (apparently without the censor's interference), seeing his murder as a new stage of the Holocaust: "The six million will rise in your honor, the murdered, tortured martyrs, as you honored them by falling for them at midnight, alone, in immense pain, on the ruins of [Jewish] Minsk." Indeed, the murder was a harbinger of the Stalinist pogrom, first against Yiddish literature and culture in the Soviet Union and then against assimilated intellectuals of Jewish origin (dubbed "Cosmopolitans" and "Passportless nomads").

Chagall had been an old friend of Mikhoels, from the time of their collabora-tion in the Moscow Yiddish Theater in 1920. Yet it took the *Morgn Frayhayt* in New York a whole month to break the news of his death, accompanied by Mark-ish's poem but without the Holocaust stanza (quoted above). On February 17, a large memorial assembly was convened in Manhattan Center, to which Chagall sent a long telegram; yet the Communist party hacks in New York suppressed the artist's "non-kosher" voice, thus betraying the principles of the ostensibly non-partisan "Committee" and showing who really pulled the strings behind the scene. Nevertheless, Chagall's condolences were leaked to the FBI and cited in the FBI report on Chagall under the heading "Contacts with Soviet Nationals" (apparently including dead "nationals").

Chagall working on his painting "Liberation," High Falls, 1948. Photo by Charles Leirens.

Marc Chagall to the Committee of Writers, Artists, and Scientists

Goldberg: Chairman of the American Committee of Jewish Writers, Artists, and Scientists.[12]

Marusya: Daughter of Sholem-Aleichem and wife of Ben-Zion Goldberg.

Braynin: Joseph Brainin (Braynin, 1895–1970) was the organizer of the Committee of Jewish Writers, Artists, and Scientists. Here he was toeing the party line.[13]

[February 1948]

[Yiddish] Committee of Writers, Artists——
NY

Dear Friend Goldberg,

As I learned both from you (and Marusya) and from the report in the newspaper *Morgn Frayhayt*, at the memorial evening for Mikhoels there was no mention of one long telegram-message of 170 words sent to you on 15/II. That is, not only did Braynin not read it, he did not mention it.

He only sent me a private note the next day after the evening, that the message was received. But I sent my message for Mikhoels and for the hundreds of his friends both here and over there—to the evening and not to Braynin.

I don't know how this can be explained.

Cordially./[Marc Chagall]

Chagall, High Falls, 1948. Photo by Charles Leirens.

Virginia Haggard in High Falls to the Opatoshus in New York

March 11th {1948}

[English] Dearest Oppen and Adele,

We are looking forward to seeing you next week. We are sorry Doovid's party is postponed. We shall be staying until Wednesday. Perhaps we shall go and see his play and film. We read the criticism of the play in the N.Y. Sunday Times but unfortunately he was not mentioned.

Thankyou Adele darling for your nice letter.

It does not look at all as if we shall be going to France in the spring or even perhaps in the summer. Ida has found a wonderful furnished house, very cheap, near Paris and it sounds lovely, but Marc does not want to go right away. The truth is, things look very bad [in Europe] and it would be wiser to wait and see what will happen.

We are looking forward so much to seeing you.

Love from us both / Virginia

Love to little Dan and his parents

Marc Chagall in High Falls to Mark Veynbaum in New York

Mark Efimovich Veynbaum (Weinbaum, 1890–1973) was born in Proskurov, Ukraine, and arrived in New York in 1913. He worked on the Russian émigré newspaper *Novoe Russkoe Slovo* (The New Russian Word) in New York, from 1920 on, and was editor-in-chief from 1925 to his death. After World War II, it became the major newspaper of the Russian Diaspora. Chagall corresponded with him throughout the years.

8/4 1948 [April]

[Russian] Dear Mark Efimovich

if you want, you could send somebody to get acquainted with this—I don't know how to call it—material, related to the exhibition [of my work] in London: an outpouring of "protests," caricatures, etc. The "enemies" will be happy.

"enemies": In Yiddish, the enemies of the Jews, i.e., the anti-Semites.

I shall be at the Chaliapin performance. I shall get to the city on April 12, for 3 or 4 days. I am liquidating the apartment from May 1.

Warm regards /   Marc Chagall / High Falls, N.Y.

This summer I travel to France and Italy, where my exhibition will be at the International Biennale in Venice, next to the Pavilion . . . of my fatherland [Russia] and other countries—(invited by the Italian government)

Bella Chagall's book "Burning Lights" is about to appear in French in my daughter's translation—in Switzerland and France, with my illustrations.

Chagall and Virginia, High Falls, 1948. Photo by Charles Leirens.

Marc Chagall in High Falls to Leo Kenig in London

April 27 1948   High Falls, New York

[Yiddish] Dear friend Leo Kenig. Thank you for your letter of April 22 with the
enclosed lecture. Your idea is good. I often said to myself that our fathers were
the best professors, and all that surrounded them. It is too great an honor for me
that you compare me with Sholem Aleichem. True, my art is Jewish, i.e., emotionally, and even "technically," hence it is neither literary nor "formalistic"—
and still technical. The poor Jewish artists "of the past" were poor because they
accepted the schools and academies from outside, which is not good for Jews,
who are just starting their work in art (this is your opinion as well as mine).
Please do not emphasize that I was especially "inspired" by the "Lubok" [Rus-
sian narrative folk paintings] or, as [Professor Lionello] Venturi thinks, by
"icons." I was inspired by everything, even the pig who scratched his back on the
fence in Vitebsk. There are no "academic" school rules in art in general (but
neither is there anarchy) which an artist once "invented" or discovered for himself (like Cézanne, Seurat, Manet, Pissaro . . .)—those are good only for them.

You must try to recover your article that you sent to the *Tsukunft* because there
are Jews there [among the editors] who, I think, probably don't "like" me (they
love me from a distance), for I am ostensibly a "leftist," i.e., a member of the
"Writers, Artists, [Scientists] Committee," and published Bella Chagall's two
books [memoirs] in the "Order." For the Yiddishist circles here are torn apart——

torn apart: Split into
fiercely opposed
camps; pro-
Communists and
anti-Communists.

Chagall and Virginia, High Falls, 1948. Photo by Charles Leirens.

I could send your lecture in your name, if you want, to the English-Jewish journal, *Commentary*. The editor is Elliot E. Cohen, 425 Fourth Ave., New York 16. It is a very serious journal, published by the American Jewish Committee. I think you could compress it, the first part especially, if you wish. Why don't you take a look at the journal somewhere.

Here in America, neither Christians nor Jews know anything about the exhibit at the Tate Gallery or in other cities. Soon I'll send you Bella's second book (which includes chapters on the first love and other figures and landscapes of the city). It is painting in words, perhaps even deeper and holier than mine—(perhaps because she was a Cohen and I am a mere Levi) (forgive my mistakes). I am sending you the lecture I delivered at the University of Chicago. Don't be upset about the 60 years. It is impossible that we are getting older. I myself corrected my age a bit.

> If only we stay healthy. Your devoted   Marc Chagall

Tate Gallery: There were no reviews in either the Jewish or the general press.

a mere Levi: Chagall cannot even spell such a simple Hebrew word as "Levi," and he knows it. If Chagall's name did come from "Segal," it is an acronym: SGL ("SeGan Levi"), meaning a "deputy Levi." Whereas a "Cohen" is a priest, a "Levi" (or Levite) is an assistant priest; both "Levi" and "Cohen" are hereditary titles.

Marc Chagall: The Good, Simple Person[14]

[Yiddish] Y. Levin came to America on the same boat as my daughter. And this made him one of us in our house. He walked in with words he heard from Bialik about me in his city—I don't know why, or how. He tried to convey them with Bialik's mimicry. He, the simple Jew, trembled before my art and kept claiming that he understands and feels everything. I believed him more than myself—

"Are there cows in America?" asked Chagall when Varian Fry persuaded him to flee Nazi Europe in May 1941. Marc Chagall in High Falls, 1948. Photo by Charles Leirens.

He loved my family. He loved the books of my Bella, he loved (may she live long) the paintings of my daughter.

I want to tell the truth. I grew very fond of the Jew, for he was not just a plain Jew and at the same time—was just a plain Jew. But he sighed too much, he mourned so much, that I wanted right there and then to revive somehow, at least on a canvas—his lost past in the old home, to show him "miracles," to cry along with him . . .

He was a poetic-simple Jew of the people, whose goodness and lyrical nature touched me often to tears. He was such a Jew, like a clock ticking away from some painting, all alone running from his wall and his city. He ran through distant countries, trudged along up to here. Where to?

His friends felt the comrade in him, his faithfulness. Such a type is close to my heart, I seek him and will always paint him. Such a type of Jew was taken away by our enemies in the ghettos and are being taken daily.

But the light of his life merges with the great, burning light of our people and our holy victims, for his dream was the happiness of our people in its own land.

our people: This was written during the bloody War of Independence, shortly before the establishment of the State of Israel.

Virginia and David with a cow in High Falls, 1948. Photo by Charles Leirens.

Levin is no more. I cannot believe that I won't see him here or there. He was not an artist, a writer, and precisely the death of such a Jew makes me unsettled, for his human beauty and goodness was more valuable than many paintings and books.

Hundreds of his friends will remember him—the young, loving and dreaming Levin, whose heart always trembled with love for his friends, his people and his Land.

Virginia Haggard in High Falls to Adele Opatoshu in New York

High Falls May 12 {1948}

[English] Dearest Adele,

a *friend*: Charles Leirens, Belgian photographer and artist, the future husband of Virginia Haggard.

You were sweet to phone us. *How* do you manage to think of everyone all the time? You have so many sisters, nephews, nieces, old friends and so on. We are really moved by your attention and affection. Please thank Oppen for his note. Don't think we forgot you before leaving New York or since. There were many things to attend to but you two are always in our hearts. We had a friend to stay

Marc Chagall strolling with his son in High Falls, 1948. Photo by Charles Leirens.

for 3 days. Everything is so beautiful here, the smell is exquisite. Our friend took over 75 photos of all of us with his very special cameras.

Dearest I have thought over and over about our conversation, about all the little problems and interesting things that happen in a half Jewish family and you gave me much food for thought. In fact I have digested it well and I feel stronger. I shall tell you all about this when we talk together. Meanwhile all my love to you both.

Yours / Virginia

We shall be in town on May 17th.

Marc Chagall [postscript to Virginia's letter]

[Yiddish] Thank you, dear Oppen, for the clippings. I congratulate you on our future government—with good luck!

Yours, with greetings to us both /   Chagall

with good luck!: The first government of the new Jewish State in Palestine, named Israel, was proclaimed on May 14 and Independence was declared on May 15, 1948. Typically, Chagall refers to it as "our" government.

Marc Chagall with David in High Falls, 1948. Photo by Charles Leirens.

Virginia Haggard in High Falls to Adele Opatoshu in New York

High Falls   May 31st {1948}

[English] Dearest Adele,

Isn't it terrible the way we rush around and don't even have time for a nice conversation on the phone? This is how it will be for another couple of months until our departure. We have been seeing a lot of people. Marc wants to get a comission to do mural paintings before he leaves, so that he will have something to come back here for and some sort of assurance for the future. We have had three lots of guests down here. Now it is a *little* quieter and we hope to be in town about the 10th or 11th. How are you both? We long to see you again. And how are the Doovid Opatoshus?

    Our friend Bush Maier Graefe and her possible future husband Hermann Broch are going to live in our house while we are away and keep it warm for us

Jean, Virginia, David, and Marc in High Falls, 1948. Photo by Charles Leirens.

which is quite a weight off our minds. She was down here getting acquainted with the neighbours and the house.[15]

Soon we shall have the joy of seeing you here again. Jean talks about you all the time. What do you think of the photos? I think they are very sweet of you.

Give Oppen a big hug.

All our love to you both / Virginia

Marc Chagall [postscript to Virginia's letter]

How are you? It is not yet joyful with us Jews. We have a strong God and maybe he'll show his strength; because human beings don't want to lift the embargo and it is easy to squash us (not so easy!)

Be well /   Your Chagall

not yet joyful: After the Israeli Declaration of Independence, five Arab states sent their regular armies to wipe out the new state. Jerusalem was besieged, the Jewish part of the Old City fell, and the fledgling Jewish army had a shortage of arms.

The West, including the U.S., declared an embargo on weapons shipments to the Middle East, although Israel was at a serious disadvantage, since she had had no regular army before May 15, as did the neighboring Arab states. For Chagall, the word "embargo" had a special ring, for an embargo was used by the Western Powers in the Spanish Civil War, which, indeed, helped to "squash" the Republic.

Ida Rapaport-Gordey in Paris to David, Virginia, and Marc in High Falls

[June 1948]

[English] David, Virginia, Papa

I think it must soon be David's birthday. At base I was never there either for that birth or last year and I am ashamed that I am not sure if it was June 28 or earlier.

Forgive me, but it [is] with all my heart that I ask for David all the best in the world. That his blue eyes will grow up and always see goodness and light around him and that he will bring you happiness, always more and more.

Your, Ida

Marc Chagall in High Falls to Leo Kenig in London

High Falls, N.Y. June 4, 1948

[Yiddish] Naturally I was upset that *Tsukunft* rejected your article about my exhibit in the London museum without even a word. I should "deserve it" as an artist or a "person." It seems you are lucky you live in Europe, for here in America people are divided into 2 "camps" (not ideologically, but artistically . . .). I plan to come to France in August. I regret that personally I have no strength to send your lecture about my exhibit to the Jews [i.e., to Yiddish publications], which is, by the way, more suitable for a Yiddish newspaper or journal, I think; for in the English-Jewish one they are extremely "anti-Jewish," international, placing more value on general "religious" ideas (the group around Rosenwald . . . "[American] Jewish Committee" . . .). I'm sorry I give you "worries." Did you get Bella's second book? (The book was also *silenced*, because it was published by the "Order.") Some day you may write a humoristic-satirical article about a group founded by an old man from "Forverts" and a dozen Bundists around him, who in their youth were so new, Jewish (I remember when I was a child in *shul* when they prevented the fathers from praying and interrupted the prayer . . .)—

And don't be amazed that I know about "everything." Art—my art (this too is an artifact) cannot be otherwise. Picasso may spit on Spain, even on Paris; but my colors come from Pokrova Street in Vitebsk. And are indeed Jewish, as you

---

2 "camps": The pro-Communists and the anti-Commmunists, who ostracized each other.

[American] Jewish Committee: At the time, an anti-Zionist and anti-Yiddish group.

old man from "Forverts": Abe Cahan (1860–1951), veteran editor of the Jewish Daily *Forverts* (*Forward*) and former Socialist, together with a group of former Bundists, conducted a sharp anti-Communist campaign in New York.

interrupted the prayers: As an underground Socialist party in Russia, the Bund was antireligious; still, they saw the center of Jewish activity in the synagogue, which they tried to disrupt.

artifact: In the original, a pun: *kunst* = art vs. *kunts* = trick.

Picasso may spit on Spain: Meaning, he doesn't give a damn. In Chagall's view, Picasso's art was abstract and not founded in any national culture, or "language-and-life," as he calls it.

say. I don't recognize art in general, as a matter of a *school*, but as a matter of language-and-life. I feel that I am "talking" to you in La Ruche. Regards   Your Marc Chagall

Marc Chagall in High Falls to Mark Veynbaum in New York

High Falls, N.Y. 1948 [Summer]

[Russian] Dear Mark Efimovich,

I am sending you the contents of the cable from the committee in Venice of the international exhibition (where there is apparently a Soviet pavilion too).
    Salle Chagall exaltée
    "unanimemente triomphe" (in Italian: . . .)
    I am going to Paris on Aug. 17. Perhaps I shall see you. I don't know how long I shall stay there and where I shall stay in general.
    I sent Araonson the book (Bella's 2nd): "God" knows whether he likes it. But he is great,
    I consider him a Vitebskite.
    As you see, I am a villager but sometimes I get to N.Y.

Regards,/   Marc Chagall

Marc Chagall in High Falls to Pavel Ettinger in Moscow

The XXIV Biennale was held in Venice, June–September 1948. Chagall had a separate hall in the French pavilion, including thirty-seven paintings and drawings, thirty etchings, and illustrations for Gogol, La Fontaine, and the Bible. He was awarded the First Prize for graphic art. Chagall wrote to Leo Kenig that he received the prize especially for the Bible; but he would not mention the "clerical" Bible in a letter to the Soviet Union, and emphasizes the Russian Gogol.

1948, July 12[16]

[Russian] Dear Pavel Davidovich, How are you? I was so happy to receive a letter from you several months ago and to know that you are in good health. You are the only one who writes to me from the homeland, and I am glad every time. Recently I was in Paris. You have surely received the catalogue of my retrospective exhibition, arranged in the National Museum of Modern Art. They exhibited

Chagall and his old friend, the Yiddish novelist Yosef Opatoshu (left), at the
Opatoshu summer place, Croton Falls, New York, July 11, 1948.

paintings, engravings, and theater sketches from 1908 to 1947. The same exhibition was transferred and later arranged in the museum of Amsterdam and recently in the Tate Gallery in London. They made decent catalogues. Now I am invited to exhibit at the Venice Beinnale, where I was offered a large hall. I was
informed that I received an international prize there for engraving (for *Dead
Souls* and other books). In August I move to France.

I am happy that, as far as I can, and though from afar, I am useful to my homeland, to which I have been and am devoted in my art over the last forty years, for,
it seems to me, a Russian artist never was given an exhibition in the museums of
America and Europe, and a living artist at that. Do not think that this gives me

Adele and Yosef Opatoshu, Virginia Haggard, Ray Elkins (Adele's sister), Marc Chagall.

more confidence in my art. No—I am like a beginner every time I approach my work,—though, alas, I am apparently, 60 years old.

Dear Pavel Davidovich. Write somehow about yourself, after you get this letter. I wish you all the best

Your devoted/   Marc Chagall

(P.S.) In Paris, in the National Typography, publisher "Verve," the *Dead Souls* will appear with 100 engravings. I hope at least one copy will reach my homeland. In New York, in the fall, the publisher "Pantheon" will issue an album-book of *1001 Nights* with color lithographs.

Marc Chagall in High Falls to Yosef Opatoshu in New York

28/7 1948

[Yiddish] How are you, dear Opatoshu. Our voyage to the abysses-perhaps of Europe approaches. I want to go as much as you want to dance. You are toiling now, and I am toiling on the packages [*peklakh*] together with the thin, young

as much as you want to dance: Yiddish idiom, meaning "I don't want it at all."

Virg. [Virginia], who must also taste a bit of what it means to be a Jew with the sack on your back.

But the very young David spits on the world, and demands attention and food for himself, no matter where we take him.

Love to Adelye. Of course we shall be sad not to see you frequently——But you will pray [for us] to our God. Your   Marc Chagall

Report of Pierre Matisse Gallery in New York to Marc Chagall in High Falls

[English] August 1, 1948

The following is our report at August 1948:

Credit due Pierre Matisse Gallery at June 1, 1948		$4,473
*Payments for contract guarantee:		
June 1948	$700	
July 1948	$700	
August 1948	$700	$2,100
		$6,573
Sales made in June:		
C-1604-280 Cheval volant	$2,352	
C-1858-306 The Clock	1,568	3,920
Credit due Pierre Matisse Gallery at August, 1948		$2,633

* Note: We are deducting from this payment of $2,100 our bill to you of May 29, 1948 amounting to $296.39. This leaves a balance due you of $1,803,61 for which we are enclosing our check.

Virginia Haggard in New York to Louis Stern in New York

Commander Hotel N.Y.C.   August 12th 1948

[English] My dear Louis,

It was a joy to see you looking so happy and so well. We enjoyed our evening and Alice's supper enormously.

At Stern's request, Chagall prepared an *Ex Libris* (a bookplate) for Stern's library. They corresponded about it for a while and, at first, Stern seemed to like the latest version, but soon enough disliked the price tag.[17]

The bookplate Chagall made for his friend and collector Louis Stern (rejected by Stern).

I'm sorry we weren't able to look at the proofs of the etching with you, but if you are satisfied then there is nothing more to discuss—except one thing and you can probably guess what it is! As you can imagine the bank balance is in need of replenishing on the eve of our departure and Marc wants to ask you if you would like to settle with him for the etching now. Firstly he wants to be sure that you are perfectly satisfied and more—that you are *pleased*. And if you are, he wants to ask you for $1,000 and hopes you will not think that too much.

We hope to see you at the boat—perhaps Mike too.

Love from us both/   Virginia

We shall arrive here on Monday afternoon at the same hotel/SU 7,1260

Marc Chagall: Bella (Poem)

On the Fourth Anniversary of Her Death

The poem was actually written on the last day of the Chagalls' life in High Falls, one day before he departed for Europe, as a farewell to Bella, left behind in a cemetery in America.

[Yiddish]

Your white dress swims over you,
My flowers untouched,
Your stone glimmers, gets wet,
I get gray as ash . . .

Today, like yesterday, I ask you:
Are you staying here, are you following behind me?
See—my steps swathed in tears.
What are you saying to me? I want to listen.

" . . . As red as our *Khupa*,
So is our love for our people and our homeland,
Go and wake them with our dream——

How green the fields lie on my body,
Every night the stars wink at me.
So you will someday return to me."

August 16, 1948

Louis Stern in New York to Virginia Haggard in New York

Monday, August 16, 1948, 11 A.M.

[English] Dear Virginia:

Upon returning from a week-end trip this morning, I found your special delivery. I must tell you that its contents were a shock to me, and having to question the amount asked is embarrassing to the nth degree. I would a great deal rather have gone without a book-plate than to have to write this letter. When I asked Marc whether he would be interested in making an "ex libris" for me, it never occurred to me that it would cost me more than $200 or $300. Without in any way attempting to evaluate an artist's labors, I must say frankly that this plate is not worth a thousand dollars to me.

With respect to the the plate itself, while it was agreeable to me, I was not excited about it. Nor is the question of its practicability solved. People who know this particular business tell me that the plate, as it is, cannot be put to practical use, but I am not raising that issue. I am only concerned with the amount involved. I would like to adjust this matter before you leave and to deposit the amount to Marc's account in whatever bank you tell me to. I frankly do not know what to do about it. I had heretofore made it an invariable rule not to conduct business with artists but always through their dealers or representatives. I guess I should have stuck to it.

I am leaving this note at the hotel so that you will have it on arrival, and I wish you would give me a ring as soon as you have read it. I would like to save Marc the embarrassment of having to discuss it, but I suppose it cannot be helped. I will, of course, abide by any decision that you make, for in my entire career I have never permitted myself to have anyone claim that I did not pay what I owed. I expect to be in the house all day, and this evening also.

Sincerely,   [Louis Stern]

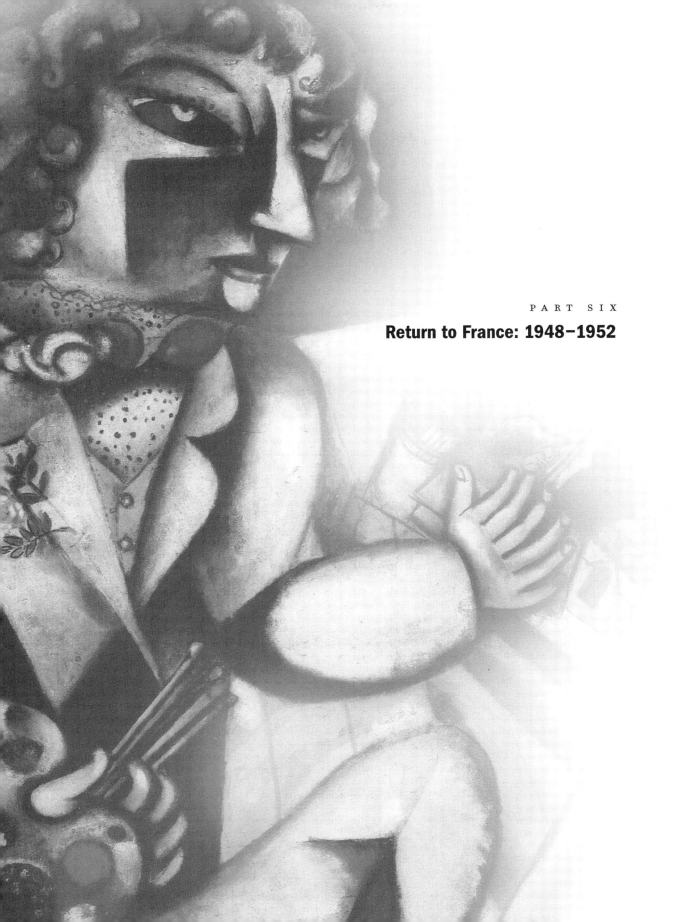

PART SIX

Return to France: 1948–1952

CHAPTER SEVENTEEN

Orgeval: 1948–1949

Why Did Chagall Return to France?

Many refugees of World War II (Hannah Arendt, Albert Einstein, René Wellek, and many others) stayed in the United States and contributed to American culture, science and academic life, but some of them did return to Europe. Several prominent French artists went back to France after the liberation: It was their country and culture, and their war was won. Theodor Adorno returned to defeated Germany; although he was half-Jewish, he felt part of German culture. Bertolt Brecht was a Communist and fled to eastern Germany, fearing persecution by the House Un-American Activities Committee. But most refugees from Germany and Eastern Europe, especially persons of Jewish origin, who could hardly return to their original countries, adopted the U.S. as their new homeland. Typically, Chagall hesitated between the two options and, finally, chose the "non-Jewish" one. Yet he was deeply disturbed about returning to Europe; paradoxically, he felt he was again taking up the stick of the "Wandering Jew."

Marc Chagall, whose Russian "homeland" was closed to him; who said himself that he felt at home only in his own few streets of Vitebsk, in America, and in Israel; who found a Jewish milieu in New York that reminded him of the world of his youth; and who prospered financially—why did he leave?

One reason was that he never learned any English, which meant that he would be reduced to living primarily in an immigrant sphere and would be considered a "Jewish" artist, a ghetto he always tried to avoid. Another reason was the relentless urging of his daughter Ida, who returned to France and prepared the ground for several major Chagall exhibitions in Paris, London, and Amsterdam. Ida and her husband Michel Gordey were typical left-leaning French intellectuals and preferred to return to Europe as soon as it was feasible.

Chagall may also have feared persecution in America because of his proximity to several Communist-inspired front organizations. Though never a Communist, he was a member of the board of the Committee of Jewish Writers, Artists, and Scientists, founded during World War II with "progressive" and pro-Soviet sympathies; he lectured at pro-Communist assemblies, and published two volumes of Bella's memoirs posthumously with the Communist cultural organization, the Jewish People's Fraternal Order, IWO.[1]

Paradoxically—or perhaps not—when Chagall arrived in France, he was worried about an imminent revolution or war or a Communist takeover of Western Europe (which, as he imagined, would send him straight to Siberia . . .).

Chagall always felt that there was a high regard for "Art" in France. He had been part of the modern art scene in its heroic period, before World War I. Moreover, he actually liked "living in somebody else's country" and being part of general rather than "Jewish" art. Indeed, after an exuberant period of formal and stylistic innovations, swept away twice, by World War I and World War II, Chagall's poetic or mysterious fictional world in art was refreshing and welcome. No doubt, the guilt feelings and sympathy of Christian Europe vis-à-vis the exterminated Jewish world that Chagall represented also played a role.

Four years after the liberation of Paris, and after two earlier visits, Chagall overcame his hesitations and went back to France. On August 17, 1948, Marc

Return to Europe: Marc and Virginia during the Venice Biennale, 1948, where Chagall got first prize for engraving.

Chagall, Virginia Haggard, and their two children finally sailed from New York to Europe. They arrived in time for the Venice Biennale, where Chagall was given a special hall in the French pavilion and received First Prize for his engravings. Ida rented a house for the family, "L'Aulnette," owned by a Mr. Goldsmith, in Orgeval near Paris.

Marc Chagall to the Opatoshus

Aug. 22, 1948

[Yiddish] Dear, beloved, regards from the *sea* which is so big that we grow even smaller . . . Smaller than a pin, but strange: of all people, David looks bigger and Vir[ginia] remains as tall as ever—how are you? Soon in 3 or 4 days we arrive, with God's help. And what will happen then—we'll see. I greet you both from my heart. Your devoted

Marc Ch.

[English] Love. Virginia

Virginia Haggard in Orgeval to Pierre Matisse in New York

Sept 3 [1948]   "L'Aulnette" Orgeval Seine et Oise

[English] My dear Pierre and Teeney,

How are you both? We were so happy to see you at the boat, if only for a minute, and it really was a great sacrifice on your part to come so far. Marc was particularly touched by Pierre's smiling face and waving hand as the boat left and he said "Cela, c'est un vrai ami!" [That is a real friend!] Thank you for the delicious chocolates, they lasted us just as long as the journey and the children enjoyed them almost too much—also the lollipops.

We got the photographs safely and we were very glad as you can well imagine after such a long time! Thank you for bringing them to the hotel, it was very sweet of you, Pierre.

We have almost established ourselves in a splendid house Ida found and arranged for us. She did wonders with this old abandoned house, once occupied by the Germans and ruined by looters. It is perfect from Marc's point of view and there is every reason for him to be happy here. He has two beautiful studios,

occupied by the Germans: Because it had a Jewish owner.

Chagall and Virginia at Villa d'Aulnette in Orgeval, their first house after returning to Europe, 1949.

one with two balconies and one hideout at the top of the house. There is a vast wild forest and there are fields and a cow, and as Marc says, he does not need to go outside his own grounds to search for subjects to paint.

Ida is looking well in spite of a terrific year's work—three exhibitions and then Venice and the house. How she did it I don't know. She has been incredibly sweet to me and altogether everything is very natural and happy. She is very fond of David and he of her.

Do let us know how you all are and what you are doing.

Marc and I send our love to you both.

Yours, / Virginia.

Chagall in Orgeval, 1949.

Marc Chagall in Orgeval to Pierre Matisse in New York

Orgeval 1948 [Apparently attached to previous letter]

[French] Dear Pierre,

Virginia wrote to you. I write badly, but nevertheless, I must send you a few words because I feel that you are going to do my exhibition and I am worried as always. I know how magnificently you organize exhibitions and I know your love. I am thinking of that big painting, the Crucifixion (in red) of the series of the three big paintings. I feel that I must rework it—I am not happy with it. But the other two (the sun and the white crucifixion) are better.

    I still think of High Falls where I was so wildly free, but I have to get acclimated here a bit. We will see how it will be later. One cannot move from one

three big paintings:
"Resistance,"
"Resurrection,"
"Liberation."

place to another all the time. And what to do when my art demands (extreme) solitude and forgetting oneself.

Perhaps the contract between us can remain as it is until we come back.

I saw your father [Henri Matisse] and I was so happy to talk with him. He is marvellous. How is your family? I will be happy to hear from you. Write me if you have time.

Best regards, / Yours, / Marc Chagall

Virginia Haggard from Orgeval to Louis Stern in New York

"L'Aulnette" Orgeval Seine et Oise   Sept. 3, 1948

[English] My dear Louis,

Your letter came here just after we arrived. Thankyou so much. We are extremely sorry to have missed you at the boat, we looked for you everywhere and never gave up hope until the ship actually left. It was sweet of you to bring that box of chocolates for the children.

The etching arrived safely. I do hope you have got over your peeve against Marc and that there is no ill feeling. Remember that artists are always unpredictable and I might say that it is more probably my fault than his because I didn't succeed in convincing him that it was far too much.

We are quite settled in a lovely old house Ida found and arranged for us. Nothing could be more suitable and it was really a stroke of genius on Ida's part. The house was completely abandoned and decrepit and Ida brought it back to life. It has several acres of very fine forest around it and nearby a charming village with a Norman church steeple and red roofs.

Ida is looking better and happier than I have seen her for a long time. Moreover she has become a very dear friend of mine and I am getting to love her more the more I know her. Gradually her father's guilt feeling towards her is vanishing and everybody is much happier. I think after all that it was a good idea to live near Paris, there is so much to be done there and it is nice to be near to Ida.

We have a small Peugeot which makes life pleasant and convenient and Ilsa has a miniature Renault.

When do you expect to come to France? When you come you will be more than welcome here. Now at last we have a real guest room. Marc has two studios, one of them is strictly private right at the top of the house and no admittance except by special permission. It is a good idea for him to be quite alone sometimes. The other studio has two fine balconies.

Needless to say the atmosphere here is most sympathetic and it seems almost incredible that he stayed and worked so long in the States without it. I hope he will be happy here and that no major catastrophe will happen in Europe.

Marc sends his love and Ida I'm sure would join me if she were here. She is in Paris. She comes every weekend and her room is here waiting for her.

Do let us know how you are and what you are doing.

Love from

Virginia

Virginia Haggard in Orgeval to Catherine at the Matisse Gallery

September 9 [1948]   "L'Aulnette" Orgeval Seine et Oise

[English] My dear Catherine,

How are you? We are extremely sorry that we weren't able to see you before we left. I did so want to spend a little time with you and have a long talk. Our last month or two was such a rush.

America seems so far away now, so undesirable, the thought of that panic-stricken life still makes my back ache and I would dread to return were it not for all you dear people, our friends in New York. Life is so worth living and worth enjoying here, there seems to be a reason for everything, nothing is outrageous and overwhelming, one isn't crushed by the tremendous futility of American life—I mean the way it is lived by the multitude. I can imagine you in this setting far better than in America. Your quiet tolerance and kindness, your patience and docility and your courage would be better appreciated here. I hope some day you can come and I hope you can spend some time with us in this lovely house near to a most beautiful little village.

Do write to us please, we would both like to hear from you so much. Marc is very happy here and I think he is going to want to stay.

Could you, dear Catherine, whenever it is possible, send us a receipt of the last pictures we gave Pierre and also Marc would very much like to have a complete list of all the pictures remaining at the gallery—with all the corrections made after the last list—additions and subtractions.

We send our love and hope to hear from you soon.

Yours, / Virginia and Marc

Marc Chagall in Venice to the Opatoshus in New York

On September 16–21, 1948, the founding conference of the World Yiddish Culture Congress was held in New York, with a grand opening in Carnegie Hall, attended by thousands of people. After the Hitler-Stalin pact in August 1939, most prominent writers and artists had left the pro-Soviet YIKUF (Yiddish Cultural Alliance), and here was an impressive alternative, free from Communist manipulations, thus fitting the atmosphere of the Cold War. The Holocaust wiped out the traditional centers of Jewish culture in Europe. As a result, the readership of Yiddish literature in New York was strengthened for a time by a wave of Holocaust survivors. A show of force, similar to the Paris Congress of YIKUF in 1937, was now launched in New York, supported by dozens of Jewish cultural and professional organizations. Chagall's friend Opatoshu was again active in the new "Culture Congress."

[Postcard from Venice] Chagall X/3 - 1948 [October]

[Yiddish] Dear, beloved, Happy [Jewish] New Year to you and to us all. I am here [in Venice] because I saw my hall in the "Biennale." A pretty city. Looked for Jews too—didn't find any. Tomorrow we go to Florence and from there back to Paris. Please write. Thanks for the letter (typewritten). Perhaps you can send me something about how the Culture Congress went. I kiss you both from us— Marc

Virginia Haggard in Venice to the Opatoshus in New York

[Postcard from Venice]

[English] Dearest Opatoshus,

Thankyou for your welcome letter. We think of you often in this beautiful city and soon it will be Roshasana [sic] [the Jewish New Year]. We wish you a very happy new year. We wish you could be ravished by all this beauty with us. Our hotel is on the Grand Canal and we have breakfast on the edge of the water in the sun. Marc's exhibition was a great success and drew the greatest crowds along with Picasso and the Impressionists. Nothing else seemed to interest anyone. We have been received royally. The Italians are the most enthusiastic.

I'm sorry that letter from the boat was sent by ordinary mail. It was not my fault, somebody made a mistake. I always send mine airmail.

Lots of love from us both, Virginia

Virginia Haggard in Orgeval to the Opatoshus in New York

Villa L'Aulnette, Orgeval, Seine et Oise   14th of October 1948

[English] Dear Opatoshus,

Thankyou for all your charming and kind letters and your wishes for Rosh Hashana. I also wish you every good thing and I love you both very dearly. I am beginning to be a little bit homesick for you, for I consider you my foster parents and it isn't right for you to be living there, and us here. But who knows maybe sooner than we think we shall be with you again, although on the other hand I hope it won't be so because only a serious international crisis will bring us back in a hurry. The news from Israel these days is sad, even sadder than when the heavy fighting was going on because one feels the beginnings of Jewish disunity after the first battle is won and one wonders if it is possible for all these people from different parts of the world to be united when the world is divided into two.

back in a hurry: Chagall was thinking of a possible flight to the U.S., for a second time, in case of a Soviet menace.

Jewish disunity: An allusion to Ben-Gurion dissolving the left-of-center Palmach brigades after the Israeli War of Independence.

Our holiday in Italy was very wonderful. Marc renewed his acquaintance with Tintoretto for whom he has almost unbounded admiration and Masacchio whose wonderful frescos are in Florence. I fell deeply in love with Giotto and Fra Angelico whose works I hardly knew and that lovely picture of Leonardo's the Annunciation took my breath away. I also had never seen all Raphael's fine portraits and Titian's. What splendid things there are to see!

I don't think I like modern Italy particularly. All its greatness is passed. It is rather a sad and wretched country. There are many rich people, many beggars and many tourists. It isn't nice to be a tourist in such a country. One feels the natural resentment of the poorer people who at the same time depend on tourists for their livelihood, and are forced to treat them with respect.

Marc is beginning, or rather continuing, to feel restless in France and he is quite unnecessarily preoccupied by the activities of the other artists which never bothered him at all in America. Naturally if we were to live here for long we would have to live in the south of France. But he still misses something America gave him, that complete independence.

The children are very well. Ida took wonderful care of them while we were away with the help of the maid and the guardian's wife. This is quite an establishment! There is a farmhouse where the guardian and his wife and son live and they keep a cow and rabbits and chickens plus several cats and a huge watch dog. The wife works for us occasionally, she is wonderful with the children.

Jean goes to school in the village and is very happy there. I am going to send David too because he will get too spoilt at home. He is quite a tyrant! They have children from 2 years on at the school and David is very anxious to go.

Our love to David & Lilly [Opatoshu] and the little one and also to Raye and her husband, and Rose. How are they all?

Raye and Rose: Adele Opatoshu's sisters.

Many kisses from us all.

Marc Chagall to the Opatoshus

[Yiddish] Dear Opatoshu, thank you for the letter and your speech. I always like to learn from you. What you're saying about the idea and mission of Jewish literature is clear—let there only be a *real* Jewish people. All those Congresses are meant to "awaken" it a bit. I am afraid that from all this remains only our creative work, if we have it in us.

I am quite cold here. Instead of coal—they sell "stones." You have to start the heating almost twice a day. I have a house—a "palace" to show people. Inside—in myself—I recall "High-Falls," my "wild freedom." Write to me (on a typewriter—is fine) what—about everything, and your health and Adelye. Dovid'l [Chagall's son] is gorgeous. She [Virginia] (as you can read her [in her letters]) is free of "Jewish" doubts—higher and even deeper. Soon you will have a "new" President. Let him, without hesitations, save us all—I was sorry about poor Hirshbeyn——

Your devoted, with regards to both of you. Chagall——

"new" President: A reference to the up-coming presidential elections in the U.S. in November 1948.

Hirshbeyn: Peretz Hirshbeyn (Hirshbein, 1880–1948), a major Yiddish playwright, who had died in New York on August 16.

Louis Stern in New York to Ida Chagall in Paris

444 East 52nd Street   October 21, 1948

[English] Dear Ida:

Even though you did not even as much as acknowledge receipt of my letter of June 23rd, I am not "broiges" with you. I have seen Busch [Meier-Graefe] since her return from Europe, and she has given me an account of how busy you are, which perhaps helps to explain your silence.

The primary reason for writing you now is with respect [to] Les ames mortes de Gogol. I am informed that the Gogol book is definitely scheduled to appear during 1948. Of course, I want a copy—one of the deluxe on Japanese paper, with the extra set of etchings. You may not recall, but before you left for Europe, after you made your arrangements, you and I discussed the matter. I see no reason for my buying my copy through the book stores, considering my relations with you and your father. You will, no doubt, hear from Bernard Reis, as well as from Busch, with respect to the same matter. Bernard and I discussed the business angle, and I see no reason why you cannot dispose of most of them directly, and when you place the Gogol books, it will undoubtedly apply to the La Fontaine, as well as the Bible. At least, it is so in my case. I want all three of them in deluxe copies.

I got conflicting information with respect to your possible visit here. Bernard tells me that you are definitely coming; Busch tells me that it is not certain. Please drop me a line and tell me about the books and also if and when you are

"broiges": "Broygez" in Yiddish means to be angry or cross with someone; not to be on speaking terms.

Gogol: Gogol's *Dead Souls*, which Chagall illustrated for Vollard in the 1920s, but which was published only after World War II.

coming to the U.S.A. If you do plan to come, I promise to stage a party for you so that you can meet as many of your friends as it is possible to get together.

With affectionate regards, I am/Sincerely yours,

[Louis Stern]

Bernard J. Reis (1895–1978), born and lived in New York City, was a lawyer, accountant, and art collector. He represented Chagall in various business affairs and managed his account with the Pierre Matisse Gallery. Later he became well known for his involvement in the Mark Rothko estate. Bernard and his wife Rebecca (Becky, author of a cookbook) were friends of Marc Chagall and the Chagall family, as well as of other artists. They corresponded with Mark Rothko, Peggy Guggenheim, Edward Albee, Jacques Lipchitz, and many others.

Virginia Haggard in Orgeval to Catherine in New York

November 15th, 1948   Villa L'Aulnette Orgeval Seine et Oise

[English] My dear Catherine,

Thank you so much for your letter and for all your work on our behalf. It was kind of you to make me such a nice list and I am very grateful to you for it. Everything is very clear now. The missing pictures must have been returned as you say, we shall forget about them.

The catalogues are very fine and the exhibitions must have been interesting. Marc hates to miss seeing his.

He has been working a lot and has finished a very fine series of gouaches. He is happy here and I really think that some day we might settle down in France. Naturally he is always full of doubts and misgivings, but actually things are so much simpler tha[n] he thinks and the proof is that he always manages to work his very best.

You will soon be seeing Ida who might come to the States in January. We think of going to the south near Nice in January to look around for some permanent place to live, or rather to decide whether Marc wants to live there for a part of the year. This house is rented. It is a very lovely place for the summer but rather too big and difficult to heat in winter. It is surrounded by wild wood and has a great deal of charm. We are becoming very attached to this village.

How are you and how is everything going with you? We do hope to hear from you again but we know how terribl[y] busy you are.

With love from us both/Virginia

Marc Chagall in Paris to Abraham Sutzkever in Tel Aviv

Abraham Sutzkever, a major Yiddish poet, was born in Smorgon, near Vilna, in 1913. During World War I, when the Jews were expelled from the front areas by the Russian army, his family fled to Siberia, where his father died. He returned with his mother to Vilna, where he became one of the leading poets of the Yiddish literary group "Young Vilna" in the 1930s. A master of poetic form, rhythm, and modernist, mythopoeic imagery, Sutzkever won a prize for his poetry in the Vilna Ghetto, during the German occupation. He then went with the Jewish partisans to the forests. The Russians sent a small airplane to take him and his wife from the German-occupied territory, over the front, to Moscow.

In 1947, Sutzkever came to Palestine, and after the State of Israel was established, he founded the Yiddish literary-social quarterly, *Di Goldene Keyt* (*The Golden Chain* [of tradition]), the major, prestigious organ of international Yiddish literature after the Holocaust. Published by the Histadrut (the powerful Israeli Trade Unions), it was the first official Yiddish publication in the Hebrew state. Its 141 volumes were edited by Sutzkever from 1948 to 1996. Chagall admired Sutzkever as a "partisan," thus a symbol of Jewish resistance and the new dignity that would supplant the old image of the "Wandering Jew," and corresponded with the poet almost to the end of Chagall's life. *Di Goldene Keyt* published most of Chagall's Yiddish poems and essays, as well as drawings and interviews; several special issues were devoted to him. Chagall also illustrated Sutzkever's book-length poems, *Siberia*[2] and *Fiddle-Rose*. After Opatoshu's death, Sutzkever was Chagall's main contact with Yiddish culture.

1948, Orgeval, S. et O., France

[Yiddish] Dear friend Sutzkever,

With great pleasure received your letter—from you, whose poems I love so much and value, and the person, of course, too. We often spoke about them with friends in America.

I am glad that a Yiddish journal will be published in Israel. Thank you for inviting me to participate. Very happily. Sometimes I "sin" and write something [in Yiddish], either a speech, or a piece of *My Own World* [*Eygns*], or even a "poem." If I am not "lazy" or bashful, I'll send it to you. In the meantime, I send you a poem (written by chance in Russian on my first visit to Paris after the war—1946. I cannot find my Yiddish translation of the poem, but I hope you will do it better.) I also send you a picture from the series 1948, dedicated to Israel: 1) "Ghetto"; 2) "Resistance"; 3) "HaTikva"—I send you the *third*.

I think you should print the picture as a frontispiece, i.e., the whole page preceding the text of the journal—as was once done in the *Zamlbikher* collections, edited by Opatoshu and Leyvik, or in another one of his [Opatoshu's] books.

I shall enjoy reading your journal and wish you all the best happiness.

With warm regards

Marc Chagall

"sin": Creative writing is a sign of arrogance, hence a "sin." In Yiddish, it is a normal expression when admitting that one writes poetry: "I sin and write poems."

I cannot find: The poem "My Land" (see Chapter 15) was written in Yiddish, read at a meeting of survivors in Paris on July 8, 1946, and published in September 1946. A Russian translation followed in 1947. Chagall had misplaced the original and suppressed the Yiddish origins.

the third: *HaTikva*, Hebrew: "The Hope," and the name of the Zionist national anthem.

Marc Chagall in Paris to Abraham Sutzkever in Tel Aviv

January 6, 1949, Orgeval

[Yiddish] Dear Abraham Sutzkever,

With great pleasure I got your translation of my poem ["My Land," translated by Sutzkever from Russian into Yiddish], your wonderful book of poetry *Geheymshtot* [*Clandestine City*], and finally the first issue of the journal *Di Goldene Keyt*. About your book of poetry, I am not one of those specialist critics. I, as an artist and a Jew, think that you are our brightest, young, colorful, fiery, true poet of our tragic time. You are close to my heart. Your poems are pictures, and though you write that you are fed up with "beauty," I understand you. You stand at the boundary of verbal art, but you are in such a Jewish atmosphere, and your (our) calamities gave you the most profound passport which other poets have painfully to extract from themselves—I wish you progress from the depth of my heart, for I shall be so happy.

Your translation of my poor poem is *an honor for me*. I don't have such a treasure of words at all (for I learned Yiddish from my mama . . .) In *heder* they

from my mama: Chagall perceives the considerable gap between literary and spoken Yiddish (his own).

studied more important things [i.e., the Hebrew Bible]. In the meantime I cannot find my own Yiddish translation.

One really has to read *Di Goldene Keyt*, and I shall read it to learn about the Jewish creative center, with such a rich content, vivid and not academic, but solidly edited.

I may recommend to you Dr. Isaac Kloomok from New York, a rare Yiddish art critic and a gentle Jewish person.

Dr. Isaac Kloomok (1888–?), an American Yiddish writer and art critic, published articles about Chagall, and a book in English, discussed in these letters: *Marc Chagall, His Life and Work*, New York: Philosophical Library, 1951. In spite of Stern's disparaging remarks, Chagall supported Kloomok and wrote a strong letter to the Guggenheim Museum on April 17, 1950, asking to help Dr. Kloomok in any way possible. On November 10, 1950, he wrote a similar letter to the Philosophical Library in New York. (Both letters are in the archives of the Guggenheim Museum.)

I don't know yet, I may possibly come to you (to us) [i.e., Israel], for the museum and the Jewish government want to arrange my great exhibition and asks me to come. But I think that today, hitting the enemy is more important, and my ear is happy to hear about it. What can we do if nations understand that better than art and poetry (ours).

With best regards/Your devoted   Marc Chagall

Louis Stern in New York to Marc Chagall in Orgeval

February 11, 1949

[English] Cher Maitre:

While I have not heard from you since my last letter, I have promised a friend of mine—Merle Armitage—to write to you, so I am doing it now.

I am enclosing a letter from Mr. Armitage to me concerning a proposed book, which tells the story. Perhaps I had better add that Mr. Armitage is a most unusual American. In appearance he is a breezy Westerner. His career is a most amazing mixture of artist, impressario, gourmet, bon vivant, and many other

things. He is now the art director of the magazine LOOK. At one time he managed
Chaliapin, Pavlowa, as well as Stravinsky and many other stars of first rank. He is
a great friend of Stravinsky, and either got your name from Stravinsky or by association of your doing the decor for L'oiseau de Feu. And knowing that I was a
friend of yours, he asked me whether you would be willing to cooperate as suggested in his letter. I then told him to write me a letter so that I could forward it
to you. Here it is. Do as you like; I have no interest one way or another. I call your
attention to the fact that the drawing or portrait or whatever you may send along
would be only for reproduction in the book and the original would be returned to
you. Please let me hear from you so that I can give Mr. Armitage an answer.

L'oiseau de feu: Firebird,
Stravinsky's ballet,
choreographed by
George Balanchine,
sets by Chagall.

Ida is in town. I talked to her on the telephone yesterday. She is coming to my
house on Monday night when I am having some friends in. I am impatient to see
her and also to receive my copy of Mort de Gogol. On my part I will show her one
of the ten copies of the Arabian Nights.

Since writing you last I have seen Pierre Matisse and was very much surprised
to learn from him that he did not see you while he was in Paris. I still feel that
there is something wrong.

With affectionate regards to you and Virginia,

I am   [Louis Stern]

Merle Armitage in New York to Louis Stern in New York

[Stationery: LOOK, 511 Fifth Avenue, New York 17, New York]

January 27, 1949

[English] Dear Louis:

You'll recall that about twelve years ago I did a symposium-type book on Stravinsky, which has long been out of print.

I now am doing a similar book on Stravinsky, but with contemporary articles
written by such men as Sir Osbert Sitwell, W.H. Auden, Samuel Dushkin, Ernest
Ansermet, Edwin Corle, and other distinguished men. In addition, I will repeat
a few of the articles from the first book which are timeless, such as those by Jean
Cocteau, Eric Satie, Eugene Goosens, etc.

Included will be two remarkable portraits of Stravinsky in photography by
Edward Weston, and it would be wonderful if we had a portrait of Stravinsky by
one of the great modern painters. I know that you are a friend of Chagall, and I
am wondering if he would like to join in this enterprise. It is not a commercial
venture, and no money will be made because the budget will include the best paper, printing and binding, and we want to use color in the book. Therefore, all of
the contributors, literary and artistic, are participating on a complimentary ba-

sis, and if Mr. Chagall did want to participate, we would only want the reproduction rights for the portrait, which he would continue to own.

If you wouldn't mind approaching Chagall about this matter, all of us concerned with this project would be very grateful. We want to make it a really distinguished book on Stravinsky, and it will be limited to 2000 copies.

Sincerely,   Merle Armitage

Tériade

Eugene Tériade, born in Greece as Efstriatos Eleftheriades (1897–1983), became the new publisher of Chagall's prewar engravings. From the heirs of Vollard, he bought the plates of Chagall's etchings for Gogol's *Dead Souls*, La Fontaine's *Fables*, and the Bible—all done in the 1930s—and published them over the course of several years. He also initiated and published numerous bibliophile editions, illustrated by Chagall, from *Le cirque* to *Daphnis et Chloe*. Tériade had a house in St.-Jean Cap Ferrat on the Mediterranean and invited Chagall to come out to live near him and illustrate Bocaccio's *Decameron*. The house in Orgeval was cold that first winter in Europe, and Marc, Virginia, and the children gladly went south and rented a *pension de famille* in Le Rocfleuri, near St.-Jean Cap Ferrat. A.M. (Alpes Maritimes). Chagall did some fresh work, especially gouaches from nature and considered buying a house there. As Charles Sorlier described it,

> Tériade was the worthy heir of Ambroise Vollard. Like the latter, he had a rare, even exceptional gift for discovering talent half a century before most collectors of his age. The person was especially attractive since he seemed enigmatic. It was his erudition that seduced Chagall.[3]

Somehow there was a blow-up between capricious and suspicious Chagall and enigmatic and goal-oriented Tériade. Chagall lost the down payment on a house, which he decided not to buy, and left for Paris at the end of April. Virginia tried to appease Tériade (see her letter of May 1, 1949, p. 674) and they had a fruitful relationship for many years after.

Virginia Haggard in St.-Jean Cap Ferrat to the Opatoshus in New York

Le Rocfleuri, A.M.   Feb. 28, 1949 [Note on side: It's now March 10th!]

[English] Dearest Opatoshus,

Thankyou for your letters and your kind messages, for your news about Ida and about yourselves. Sad news from Boraisha, I'm so sorry for your loss, and Mrs. Boraisha, poor soul.

Marc is beginning to fret for his Jewish friends. He misses them all, most especially you, and that is one thing that makes him homesick for America.

But the climate, that's so important for him. I want him to live for a hundred and twenty years at least.

Here there is warmth and there's the sea for a stimulant and the pine trees for a tonic. Above all, the sun. There are giant cacti growing on crags that bear red flowers, called "red-hot pokers." Marc walks around with his sketch book. There are solitary walks, little paths that lead in and out of the great boulders and grass covered with pine needles.

But we haven't found a permanent abode yet, because we aren't sure of this home. David and Jean are wonderfully happy. Yesterday I took them to the Carnival in Nice to see the procession of monsters and chariots. They threw confetti and had tea in a terrace café by the sea.

Marc has done at least three magnificent pictures inspired by St. Jean. Something quite new, except that they rather resemble the Arabian Nights.

Adele, write to me. How is your little one, and your big one—Dan and Doovid. And how is your sweet self?

Love to you both from all of us and many kisses

Virginia

Boraisha: Menakhem Boreysho (Boraisha, 1888–1949), a Yiddish poet who lived in New York, author of the major epic of ideas in the modern Jewish renaissance, *Der Geyer* (*The Wayfarer*).

Marc Chagall in St.-Jean Cap Ferrat to Yosef Opatoshu in New York

St. Jean Cap Ferrat, A.M.   10/3 1949 [March]

[Yiddish] Dear friend Opatoshu. I haven't written to you in a long time, and the more time passes the more I would like to be with you for a while, to talk. *Ach*, why is life like this. We leave on March 15 *back* to Orgeval. Here, I shall not have a house. It is too "beautiful" here and impossible for me. I was very sad—to hear about the death of young Boreisho and Segalovich.

My dear Opatoshu, how can I console you, who can. We are mute human be-

Segalovich: Z. Segalovich (1884–1949), a prolific Yiddish narrative poet in Poland between the two world wars. During the war, he fled to Palestine; in 1947, he was in Paris and reached New York in 1948, where he died on February 19, 1949.

ings, asking only for some health for our work. Please give my warm feelings to the Boreisho family, his dear wife. And I kiss you both from my heart.

How are you? Write to me. I know so little of what is happening in Jewish America. Thank you for the clipping. About Asch—and my painting: I pity him. He is a blind man, though with some talent. But I don't know whether he is a *mentsh*? In any case, not a friend. His "human" speculations are foreign to me, and I am indifferent to all his "human" and "artistic" gestures.

I am happy you saw my crown: Ida. May she only be healthy. Dovid'l grows and moves around. Every day something new with him. I sit and work [= paint]: something from this landscape. And how many times do I think of finally [having] a home for my hands, head and legs. Mainly for my work. I am too much the Jew from the ghetto . . . And I am always haunted by the "sense" that I live in somebody else's country. True, I did not have that feeling in (my own few streets) in Vitebsk, in America, and in Israel, it seems to me. In all other countries I feel "at home" only in my apartment (and in my paintings, perhaps). So, of all my homes, dearly paid, I don't have even one.

But enough for today. Even here it rains and pours. We are preparing to travel. All in the car, with all packs and sacks.

How is Adelye? Do you think about us? How is your Dovid and his family? How is he doing? The son grows?

I kiss you, your devoted/   Marc Chagall

Merle Armitage in New York to Marc Chagall in Orgeval

March 14, 1949

[English] Dear Marc Chagall:

For a great many reasons, I was delighted to have your letter of March 9th, informing me that you were very interested in doing the Stravinsky portrait.

For years I have been a modest collector of etchings, lithographs and drawings, and one of the earliest things I purchased was an etching by Marc Chagall which I still value among my treasures. In fact, it has grown esthetically in importance to me during the years I have owned it.

It also seems completely fitting and appropriate that Marc Chagall is to do the Stravinsky portrait, because of the way you completely realized the spirit and profundities of the Firebird in the decor which you did for that great ballet. For once, a synthesis was created where the decor and the music were in proper balance.

As I explained in the letter which I wrote to Mr. Louis Stern, this book is a labor of love on the part of all of us who are contributing. The book will be limited to 2,000 copies, will be on fine paper, high quality printing and using considerable color. We want to make it a real homage to Stravinsky in every particular and department. That is why the Chagall portrait is so important. One line in your letter, relating to conditions, is not quite clear. We will try to meet any conditions as to proper credit, acknowledgements, etc., that you would want, and of course you would own the portrait.

We expect to go to press with this book early in June, and would therefore like to have the portrait as early in May as possible.

Looking forward enthusiastically,/Sincerely,

Merle Armitage

Louis Stern in New York to Marc Chagall in Orgeval

March 14, 1949

[English] Dear Marc:

I am addressing this letter to you to Seine et Oise for I learned from Ida that you changed your plans with respect to the house in the south. I confess I am disappointed and somewhat mystified. I suppose when I see you I will hear the details. At all events, I hope this letter will reach you without delay.

My friend, Merle Armitage, has just called me on the phone with respect to a letter received from you which is somewhat puzzling. In his letter to me which I forwarded to you, and in my letter dated February 11th, I thought I explained all there is to the project of the book on Stravinsky and the raison d'être for wanting your portrait of Stravinsky to be in the book. From both of those communications it is clear that this is not a commercial enterprise; also, that all Armitage wants is to reproduce the portrait and that the original would be returned to you. What did you have in mind when you asked about "conditions"? I will be very glad to act as intermediary if there is anything that has to be explained. I want to repeat that I have no personal interest in the matter other than my friendship for Armitage, and if there is any doubt in your mind, do not hesitate to reject the whole proposition. I will appreciate it, however, if you will let me know what you decide to do one way or another.

Ida delivered to me my copy No. 6 of Les Ames Mortes [= Gogol's *Dead Souls*]. It is a stupendous achievement and I congratulate you heartily. It should also give you some satisfaction to know that this is the highest price—almost twice as high—as I have ever paid for any book. Ida will bring the front sheet with her for an inscription. I will have it properly boxed so that the next time you are in the United States you will see how carefully your "offsprings" are preserved. I have seen Ida on several occasions and report to you that she looks especially well and appears to be in very good spirits. From what I can gather she apparently is hav-

Knoedlers: A prominent
art gallery in New York.
Chagall's 118 etchings
to Gogol's *Dead Souls*,
published by Tériade
in Paris, 1948, were
exhibited at Knoedler's
on March 22–April 9,
1949.

Sondberg: Willem
Sandberg, the influen-
tial director of the
Stedelijk Museum
for Modern Art in
Amsterdam. Later, he
was Director of the
Israel Museum in
Jerusalem.

Katia G(r)oniff: Katya
Granoff, the owner of a
gallery in Paris, was of
Jewish-Russian origin.
For several years, she
represented Chagall.
By deleting the r, we
get her Chagallian
nickname "Gonif"
(=*ganev*, colloquial
Yiddish for "thief"),
which may connote
somebody shrewd
in business.

ing considerable success with Les Ames Mortes. I understand that there is to be an exhibition of the book at Knoedlers. I am expecting her here for cocktails on Wednesday, the 16th. She will have with her the director of the Museum in Amsterdam, whose name I believe is Sondberg, or some such name. I also expect to entertain them and others for dinner on Friday if arrangements can be made convenient to everyone.

At last, that which apparently was an open secret for sometime is official. Pierre and Tini Matisse are being divorced. I had heard that sometime ago but could not believe it. In my opinion it is a great pity and a tragedy for the three children. While of course no one knows or can know the compelling reasons for such calamities between husband and wife, still one would think that civilized people could adjust themselves. I for one am very sorry to hear such bad news. I feel like patting myself on the back for I began to suspect something long, long ago.

You will probably be interested and a bit surprised to learn that I have declined to sell the 1925 Chagall picture which I bought from Katia G(r)oniff. You will recall my discussing the picture with you that I was never completely happy with it although the color was tremendously appealing and the design exciting, but sometime ago I decided to dispose of such of my pictures which were not up in quality to the rest of the collection, the object being three-fold; first, the ambition to have nothing but the best of each artist; secondly, to have funds with which to acquire good pictures; and thirdly, to make room for them when I do get them. I discussed the matter with Ida and she was in accord that this Chagall was not the equal in interest to the others which I have; and I recall distinctly your saying to me "Why not dispose of it?". Incidentally, I have never known its title nor anything about its history. The picture will be sold on March 30th at the Parke-Bernet and it would be very helpful to me if I could receive a letter telling me something about it. I would appreciate it if Virginia would write me a good story about it, if it has one,—or you could make one up!

I do not know of anything especially worthy of mention at this time so I will close with the warmest greetings to you Marc and to Virginia.

Sincerely,/   [Louis Stern]

Virginia Haggard in Orgeval to the Opatoshus in New York

Congress of Peace:
Soviet-sponsored
international con-
gresses for peace
drew many highly
visible left-oriented
Western intellectuals
into the orbit of Soviet
propaganda. This first
Congress of Peace was
held in Paris.

Villa l'Aulnette, Orgeval   April 23 1949

[English] Dearest Opatoshu,

I can't think how I can keep from writing to you for so long when I always have so much to tell you about. We are back in Orgeval and into the thick of it again. The Congress of Peace is the latest "divertissment" and quite a lark it is too. We went

Ilya Ehrenburg, a prominent Soviet writer, journalist, and peace activist, with an early Chagall self-portrait in his Moscow apartment.

twice. Everybody said what they ought to say and the audience dutifully applauded. Only one man went off the track, Rodgers from America, formerly undersecretary of state for Roosevelt, and there were uneasy coughs in the audience, murmurs and finally hisses. He simply said that capitalists have to learn to live with Communists and Communists with capitalists (boo!) and each had its merits and demerits (hiss!) They asked Marc to sit on the stage where all the speakers were seated, including Picasso, who passed him by with never a word. (Is it jealousy or is he afraid to mix with impure elements?) When we were in St-Jean Cap Ferrat we met Picasso at Tériade's home (that's the editor [= publisher] of the "Dead Souls") Marc and he had a very good heart to heart talk about politics and maybe since then Picasso prefers to remain aloof for fear of becoming defiled by acquaintance with undesirable people. He was on his best behaviour today because Ehrenburg was there. Marc wondered how Ehrenburg would receive him because once about two years ago when he was in Paris Marc wrote him a letter in which he complained bitterly about the way Russia completely neglected every contact he tried to make, his gifts, his letters and his telegrammes. He expected Ehrenburg to receive him very coldly but on the contrary he greeted him effusively and they embraced.

impure elements: Chagall was not a Communist, while Picasso was a party member and designer of the "Dove of Peace."

Ilya Ehrenburg (1891–1967), a Soviet writer and prominent wartime journalist, had spent many years in Paris in the 1920s and 1930s and frequented the literary café La Rotonde, where he had met Chagall. In 1940, after the Germans occupied Paris, he went back to the Soviet Union and became Stalin's chief journalist during the war. After World War II, he was a major force in the organization and respectability of such cultural events and Peace Congresses. He had close contacts with French intellectuals and Stalin's protection gave him some freedom of conversation while in the West.

Thank you for your letters and all your news about Ida. She also brought us news of you. She told you no doubt that she completely moved all our possessions [in High Falls]—forty-six cases full and everything is now assembled under one roof. That looks like burning our bridges [in the US] but no one knows what may happen and for the time being the house in High Falls is not to be sold but rented. If you know of anyone who would like it do please let us know.

Tomorrow Jean will be nine years old. I have decided to take her to England to see her father and her two sets of grandparents. My mother might come and stay here for a couple of weeks. David is just as fine as ever as you'll see by the photo. *Please* send us a photo of little Dan. Do you think you will come over to Israel and visit us in France? We do miss you so much.

Kisses from all of us / And love from Virginia

Marc Chagall in Orgeval to the Opatoshus in New York

26/4 [April] 1949   Orgeval

[Yiddish] Dear friends, I haven't written to you in a long time. Returned from St.-Jean Cap Ferrat, where the house I wanted came to nothing. In the process, I lost the serious "advance," because I acted first and thought later. Of all my houses and homes, I have no "permanent" home and *here* (Orgeval) is "beautiful" but cold in the winter and even now it is cool—but how are you? And Adelye?

Little David grows and "spits" on the world. He doesn't hear the speeches at the conferences, he doesn't see how grownups are often smaller than he . . .

Are you writing? I did some [new work] in the village near St.-Jean and now here [near Paris] it is different. One is running—people—telephones—no calm.

But since I don't want to "pester" you anymore, I stop and kiss you

from my heart / devoted
Marc Chagall

Virginia Haggard in Orgeval to Tériade

Orgeval, Seine et Oise   May 1 1949

Dear Tériade,

Marguerite came to lunch at our house today and we spoke a lot about you, your friendship, and your great kindness to us. I am sorry that our departure from St. Jean was not very happy for you because of an embarrassing situation. You made our stay one of the nicest and most profitable in terms of work. It is thanks to you that Chagall did his new gouaches, which he wouldn't have done elsewhere and his contact with you was one of the most precious. He asks me to tell you how grateful he is to you for your friendship and your encouragement and he will always remember the marvelous hours spent in conversation with you. I also await with pleasure to resume those conversations for it seems to me that we will never run out of topics.

Chagall does not know if you are disappointed by the choice of gouaches and drawings that you made for your house, but if you aren't, he would like to give you a gift of the gouache that you prefer and two little sketches. But perhaps you would prefer to see all the gouaches once more to assure yourself of your choice. You know that Chagall loves you very much and you understand better than anyone the idiosyncrasies of artists, so you will surely forgive him for "putting" you in a delicate situation with regard to him.

Ida left for Gordes a few days ago to rest. She is in good health but is nevertheless tired. All our forty-six boxes arrived safely thanks to her and now all our possessions are under the same roof—for how long I don' know!

Chagall did something beautiful in your book (*Dead Souls*).

We await your return and that of Madame Lang with pleasure—our best regards to her.

Affectionately, / Virginia

Hello and see you soon, / Chagall

Marc Chagall in Orgeval to A. Sutzkever in Tel Aviv

1949 Orgeval

[Yiddish] Dear Sutzkever,

Forgive me for answering so late. I am so busy here with a variety of things and especially with the three big books with my engravings which I started for Ambroise Vollard and will now appear one after the other. But, regardless of that, I would very much like to make illustrations for your poems which I love and esteem very much. Do you want to tell me how many illustrations you need? I shall gladly make a book with you, for I admire you both as a poet and a person.

Thank you for [No.] 2 of the journal *Goldene Keyt*, rich in content as the first one. Thank you for the book from America. Your long poem *Siberia*, which I read, is "colorful," "Russian," and like everything you write—artistic. I am so happy to read you. Not everyone succeeds in modelling (the language material) and being fresh and, of course, truly Jewish in tone. Your whole life (young as it is) nourishes you. May God bless you—in the future.

Recently, a poet of your group ["Young Vilna"] visited me, Vogler, with whom we talked a lot about you. We also spoke about the two Yiddish books with my illustrations, written by my wife Bella before her death, which he loves.[5] If you didn't yet read them, I can send them to you. Perhaps you could advise me about translating them [into Hebrew] and publishing them in Israel in Hebrew (perhaps both volumes in one, or separately. For those are short stories, not a novel—).

With my warm regards,/Devoted

Marc Chagall

P.S. About my poem you are right. Better to wait, I shall somehow send you [more] for a series.

Vogler: Elkhonen Vogler (1907–1969), an original Yiddish poet and member of the group of poets "Young Vilna" in the 1930s. He settled in Paris after World War II, a lonely poet. Chagall wrote an essay about him and a eulogy on his death.[4]

The Liquidation of Yiddish Culture in the Soviet Union

After the Russian Revolution, Hebrew culture in Russia was liquidated, and only a Communist literature in Yiddish was promoted, almost without a historical memory or ties to Jews in other countries. The Jewish Antifascist Committee, established during the war with Hitler, proclaimed "unity" of the Jews around the world in the fight against fascism. But in January 1948, its chairman, the famous actor and theater director (and Chagall's old friend) Solomon (Shloyme) Mikhoels was brutally murdered by the NKVD. Soon after, the Soviet Jewish cultural establishment was demolished; Yiddish newspapers were stopped; theaters and publishing houses were closed, the Jewish Antifascist Committee dissolved; the most prominent writers and actors were tried, forced to confess, and shot, and others were arrested, tortured, or sent to their death in camps.

After the Holocaust, this was a terrible blow to all Jews who were sympathetic to Soviet Russia. For a long time, however, Soviet representatives and the Yiddish Communist press kept denying the "slanderous" rumours. Ilya Ehrenburg in Paris and the Secretary of the Soviet Writers' Union Alexander Fadeev in New York lied through their teeth and claimed they "saw" the Yiddish writers in Moscow. In the atmosphere of the Cold War, it was easier for Western Communists to assume that the whole story was vicious anti-Soviet propaganda, for who could believe that the Communist state would imitate Hitler?[6] From the beginning, Chagall was extremely worried, yet he claimed he was afraid to protest publicly for fear of hurting his sisters and their families, who had remained in the Soviet Union. And perhaps he was reluctant to cut off his ties with the pro-Communist circles in France, to which he was loosely connected. Among leftist intellectuals in France—including Picasso, Chagall's friend the poet Paul Eluard, and the philosopher Jean-Paul Sartre—Communism was seen as the savior from fascism and protector from American imperialism; thus, "objectively," attacking it would mean joining the enemy.

In the spring of 1949, Chagall agreed to become Honorary President of the newly organized MRAP, Le Mouvement Contre le Racisme, l'Antisemitisme et pour la Paix (the Movement Against Racism, Antisemitism and for Peace). The MRAP included several prominent intellectuals, professors, former resistance leaders, peace activists, and such figures as Chief Rabbi of France Jacob Kaplan, the Communist poet from Martinique Aimé Césaire, and other black intellectuals from French colonies. It was also supported by non-Communist Jewish organizations and survivor groups, *Landsmanshaftn*.

A short time later, in his letter to Opatoshu, Chagall is alarmed again. He singles out three of the liquidated Soviet writers: Fefer, Markish, and Bergelson. Itzik Fefer (1900–1952) fought in the Red Army during the Civil War and became a leading Yiddish Communist poet. Chagall met him in the Jewish children's colony in Malakhovka near Moscow in 1922 and in New York in 1943, when Fefer came with Mikhoels to mobilize Jewish public opinion for the Soviet cause in the war against Hitler. Chagall also illustrated two books of Fefer's poetry, published in New York in 1944.

Perets Markish (1895–1952), a major Expressionist poet, met Chagall in Paris in 1924 and translated Chagall's autobiography from Russian into Yiddish. Markish returned to the Soviet Union and received high awards for his prolific and imaginative poetry, including a long narrative "Poem About Stalin." Dovid Bergelson (1884–1952) was a major Yiddish novelist, who lived in Germany in the 1920s and returned to the Soviet Union as a Fellow-Traveller. All three were arrested in 1948, tortured, confessed, tried in a mock trial and shot on August 12, 1952.

Marc Chagall in Orgeval to Yosef Opatoshu in New York

Orgeval S. et O.   16/5 [May] 1949

[Yiddish] Dear friend, received your letter from [?]. I would like to imagine how you live. I see you working hard, I see your beloved Adelye "circling" so lovely around you, and to tell you the truth: we miss you here. So, you think we have no time. Our head is spinning from the visits, the meetings, the speeches I have to make sometimes, again about us Jews and our troubles. In the meantime, this issue: you must know and probably do know very well that I cannot "rest" if it is true what they wrote in your country, I don't know where.

what they wrote: About the arrest of the Soviet Yiddish writers.

Korneychuk: Aleksandr Korneychuk (1905–?), the Ukrainian playwright and political figure, member of the Board of the World Council of Peace since 1949; served the Soviet machine of disorientation (blaming "anti-Soviet propaganda"), as did Ehrenburg.

A friend: Michel Gordey, Chagall's former son-in-law.

That is, about Fefer, Markish, Bergelson, and others. I immediately inquired about it in high places here. [Ilya] Ehrenburg came here [to Paris], along with Korneychuk, a friend of Fefer, and he said it is *not true*. A friend, the editor of a French newspaper, asked Fefer to send articles here, to which Korneychuk answered that for the time being it is difficult. But in two months he will be able to send them. In any case, the "rumor" is wrong. I personally of course can "guarantee" nothing for the future. I am glad that in the meantime it is not true. And if, God forbid, it does become true later, you understand that, like you, I shall not fill my mouth with water. But why prattle about "later." For us, the present is enough.

I am again in Orgeval, came from around Nice, but I intend to go back there near the beginning of the winter. Because here, though beautiful, it will be cold.

What is new in the Jewish circles? Are Jews still fighting each other? Maybe some unity and love could start among the Jews? You know, it seems to me that we Jews are not such a bad people. Maybe we have a few "dead souls" somewhere, but not "sold" yet, we must just look a bit deep into the eyes.

Listen, my Dovid'l is growing, no evil eye [should see it]. Soon, with good luck, he'll be 3 years old, and I'm sorry the two of you will not come to his birthday. It is poetry, a poem, a painting that cannot get onto the canvas. His mother is not bad either. The same innocent soul, you can do nothing about it. We shall see what kind of person her mother is. Soon she is coming to visit us. Then Vi. [Virginia] will send her young daughter (9 years old) for a while, or more, to see her father in London, and attend school there.

I kiss you, your devoted Marc Chagall

I want to publish Bella's 2 books in *one* volume here, and a separate memorial book on the 5th anniversary [of her death]. I shall write more to you.

Virginia Haggard in Orgeval to Adele Opatoshu in New York

Orgeval, Seine et Oise   May 18 1949

[English] Dearest Adele,

Three days late to wish you many happy returns of your birthday but none the less I thought of you and sent my love to you along with my thoughts. Many happy years more, darling!

We have both become bad letter writers—I should say we have always been so. Forgive us. We talk of you and think of you often. How is that old dear Oppen?

Today is Ida's birthday and she came here with Michel and a very nice man whom she is fond of. She is not well but as gay and active as ever. She has to have a very rigorous treatment because her condition is a little worse. And yet morally she is better than she has been for years. The man she has found gives her gaiety and optimism and a philosophical view of life.

These little photos I am sending you are not very good but they are rather amusing. You sound a little sad. I know that painful things have been happening but you are so brave and cheerful.

I have been working and enjoying it no end. I don't expect anything to come of it for years. The dramatist Granville Barker said that one must write for the waste paper basket for the first five years. And I'm quite prepared to do so.

We went to a wonderful Jewish marionette show. It was moving and beautiful—all in Yiddish with lovely old music played and sung, very comic and at the same time tragic and touching. The name of the company is Hakl Bakl, director Simche Schwartz. They did Bontshe Shvayg [Y.L. Peretz's story "Silent Bontshe"] and a

working: Virginia was writing stories and taking notes on her life with Chagall.

Schwartz: Simkha Shvarts (1900–1974), a sculptor and theater director, came to Paris in 1936 and created a successful marionette theater, *Hakl-Bakl* (Yiddish, from *ha-kol ba-kol*, the Hebrew equivalent of *Varieté*); in 1952, he moved to Buenos Aires.

play about David and Goliath. [King] David (whom his mother called Dovidl) looked *exactly* like your Dovid! He was a modern David with black hair growing a little thin. Please give my warmest affection to Dovid and Lilly [Opatoshu] and the little one.

Love to Oppen and yourself.

And don't forget "Next year in Jerusalem!"

Yours with love / Virginia

[Yiddish] I kiss you Adelye on your birthday / Marc

Marc Chagall in Orgeval to Abraham Sutzkever in Tel Aviv

Orgeval, June 14, 1949

[Yiddish] Dear Sutzkever,

Thank you for your letter. As you can imagine, though I am up to my neck in the Gogols, LaFontaines and Bible, and now also Bocaccio—it will be a pleasure for me to devote some time to you—which means also to myself, though I have never (not yet) been in Siberia—I hope your publisher is not in too great a hurry. But when I start, (I hope) it will go.

(not yet) been in Siberia: An allusion to Chagall's fear of exile in case of a Russian takeover of Western Europe.

your publisher: Chagall illustrated Sutzkever's long poem, *Siberia* which was published as a separate book in Yiddish, Hebrew, and English.

I sent you the two books by Bella. I am glad that, with your great sensibility and talent, you will take care of the text. She was my Muse. The embodiment of Jewish art, beauty and love. If not for her, my pictures would not be as they are. Read her quiet words, simple, ostensibly realistic, but pearls like the pearls in her father's store.—I think that it may be possible to make one book from the two, with the four love chapters ("The First Love") at the back of the book. The "staging" can go according to the Jewish "calendar" (holidays) and the four seasons of the year, with landscapes, uncles, aunts, and dachas.

titles: The book was divided into chapters by the editor, I.A. Ronch.

She passed away early and did not divide the chapters herself, did not give the titles of the books herself. By the way, I think that in the second volume, the chapters are not divided so well and the title (of book 2) is not especially good.

But I'm sure you will find something better. The books belong to my daughter, and it would be good if the publisher wrote a few words to her, or to me, I shall transmit it to her. This September it is 5 years [since Bella's death].

Warm regards, / Your devoted, with thanks,

Marc Chagall

P.S. Do you have any concrete information about the writers in Moscow? I cannot find out anything here.

Pesakh Novik to Sholem Asch in New York

Pesakh Novik (1891–1989) was a long-time editor of the Communist Yiddish newspaper in New York, *Morgn Frayhayt*. A member of the Communist Party and a prolific journalist, he defended the party line on every issue, including the "rumors" about the arrest of the Soviet Yiddish writers. Sholem Asch, apparently, wrote a sharp letter to the YIKUF (the Yiddish Cultural Alliance, a left-liberal organization, never Communist but not openly anti-Soviet either) which evoked Novik's wrath. Eventually, after Khrushchev's speech at the Twentieth Party Congress in Moscow in 1956, denouncing Stalin, and after the "official" disclosure of the crime against the Yiddish writers in the Warsaw Yiddish newspaper, the *Morgn Frayhayt* admitted the facts, took a pro-Israeli stand, and dissociated itself from the American Communist Party. In 1973, Novik was expelled from the Party.

But here we are still in 1949, at the height of the Cold War. In his letter to Chagall's nemesis, Novik invokes Chagall's name, surely without asking him, as Communists did on other occasions. The letter is reproduced here to show the kind of pressures exerted by the Communists even in the West.

[Stationery: "morning freiheit/Jewish daily"]

July 5, 1949

[Yiddish] Distinguished friend Sholem Asch,

I am writing to you as a member of the Board of YIKUF, but also—and perhaps mainly—as one to whom, on various occasions, even the last time we met, you expressed friendly sentiments.

Your letter, today received by the YIKUF, was an unpleasant surprise for me. I know that the time in America is difficult, the hysteria great, reaction rampant. But I also know that the reaction on the Jewish street was rampant *against you* for many years. Everything that was opposed to progress in America, opposed to the Soviet Union, took up its arms against *you*, to kill and destroy you. The same people who today—and always—invent libels against the Soviet Union, invented libels against *you* too. And just as they lied about the Soviet Union, and are lying today, so they lied about you too.

So I was astonished: That *you* should succumb to their pressure? That *you* should join the hysteria against the Soviet Union?

Your recent words about the role of the Soviet Union still resound in my ears. Those were words of poetic pathos, words of truth and justice. You rightly stressed what the enemies of the Soviet Union (and *your* enemies) tried to stifle: that millions of Jews were saved by the Red Army. You pointed out one fact that no Jews must overlook: *living* Jews! If only there are living Jews, you argued, there will be everything. *With* that, there will also be a Jewish culture, and there will be people to go to Eretz-Israel.

Indeed, what about the role of the Soviet Union in the emergence of Israel, a role the Jewish masses everywhere, and especially in Israel itself, will never forget? Let us remember that that role is not yet finished, because the enemies of Israel have not yet relinquished their plan to destroy Israel.

So how could you have written such a letter? On what grounds? On the ground of reports not yet verified? It would make no sense to ask the inciters to think about the *problems* related to some changes in the Soviet Union. But honest people must think. And honest people, when they hear the current reports about the Yiddish writers, and the incitement on this score, must say to themselves: in over thirty years there were many incitements, and every time it turned out that the inciters—were inciters. You surely remember the incitement after the Soviet-German pact [in August 1939]. The Leyviks, Mukdoynis, etc., left us. But you yourself were convinced during the war—and you expressed it in your speeches—that the Soviet government was right and helped to save America, to save Jews, because it gained time to prepare [for the war]. So now, on the basis of incitements of long-standing enemies, including those who fled to the Soviet-haters in 1939, you take a step that plays into the hands of the war-mongers?

I know how energetically they work. I have no doubt that they would have loved to get such a letter from *Marc Chagall*. But instead of joining the Soviet-haters, Marc Chagall stood at the head of the Jewish masses in France, that fight for peace, against anti-Semitism, as the Honorary President of the movement that conducts this struggle. *André Blumel* also belongs to that movement. You may have seen in today's *Morgn-Frayhayt* that *Yakov Fichman* joined the Peace Front in Israel. In that front you find *Yitskhak Grinboym* and Dr. *Moshe Sne*, and *Zerubavel*, and *Shlomo Kaplansky*, and the ghetto-fighter *Tsivya Lubetkin*, and the poet *Avraham Shlonsky*, and many others. And you surely know about the most beautiful spirits of mankind, who attended the Paris Peace Congress Picasso, Martin Andersen Nexo, Pablo Neruda, Fadeev, Ehrenburg, Wanda Wasilewska, Professor Joliot-Curie, and many others. You also know the role Professor *Einstein* plays in the movement for cooperation with the Soviet Union. So now you come out with a letter that will give joy to all war-mongers and will be met with

Mukdoynis: Dr. Mukdoyni, a prominent Yiddish journalist in New York.

Blumel: Former secretary to the government of Leon Blum, now a Communist sympathizer.

Fichman . . . Shlonsky: Israeli non-Communists, liberal and left-leaning writers and intellectuals

David imagining Virginia on her voyage with Jean to England. The French reads: "For Virginia/David./ 1949" and "bon voyage/Marc."

wrath by all fighters for peace, by the Jewish masses in America, the Soviet Union, Poland, Romania, France, Belgium, England, by the masses in Israel!

I remember *Ruven Braynin's* words in the time of the hysteria of 1939. He cautioned against *overhasty steps*. He built on trust of the land that had abolished antisemitism. And he was right. The war against Nazism showed that the trust was justified. The struggle for Israel showed it too (and, again, that struggle is far from over!).

That's all I felt necessary to tell you, as a member of the Board of YIKUF, to whom you sent your letter, and again, as one whom you considered a friend. As *such* a person I felt it to be my duty to write to you this letter.

Sincerely, / P.Novik

Marc Chagall in Orgeval to Virginia Haggard in England

Orgeval, July 25, 1949

[French] Dear Virginia, I haven't had any letters, but I hope I'll have some to-morrow. How are things? David is nice, but I am sad that he is alone without you: he is still good. You are busy with your problems. Write me often how things are and forgive me that I don't write much—my French is worse than bad. If I offend you, you know very well that I can't live without you, my dear, I need you—to live and to work.

Kisses, Marc

Tuesday, July 26

My dear, I don't know your exact address. This is why I didn't write sooner. How long it is without you. Your son is admirable.

Kisses

M

Kisses to Jean
    Thanks
    I got your letter of July 23.
    David drew this "picture" which he wanted to send for you
    He is adorable (like you).

Marc Chagall in Orgeval to the Opatoshus in New York

Orgeval 28/7 1949

[Yiddish] Dear friends, I haven't written to you in a long time. So busy, or confused, as often happens with me. As you know, I am poorly "organized" or disciplined. I work—though the results, it seems, are small—and I am especially confused about family matters. Idotshka was seriously ill. Had a major opera-tion. It went well. For the time being, she is convalescing here. She is gradually getting better. She sends her love and thanks you for the regards.

Virginia is in London with her parents and her daughter Jean. Looking for a school for her for later. She wrote that she'll come back with the daughter for two months, and from September back in London (for her daughter's school). Thus the wheel is turning. Her mother was here. She looks like a Canadian farmer woman of old, a "Goya" [i.e., a peasant woman] who later became a "lady" through her husband, who was attracted to her past youthfulness (Virginia says she was beautiful). But if you saw Virginia with her mother you wouldn't believe it: like a palm tree and a head of cabbage. But I have other "worries." There was a small exhibition of Raïsa Maritain's book about me, with several [of my] drawings from all periods (that's the custom here with newly published books) but the text about me could have been more important.[7] You have the book, but it is filled with photos . . .

You can imagine that, like all Jewish intellectuals, I am very sad, if it is true, about the Yiddish writers in Moscow. Here, some keep arguing (not the Jews) that it is not true. But it is terribly sad: the very fact that we cannot know the truth. That's the fine world we live in. Nothing attracts me to such a world, and you know well that as long as I live and work somehow, my soul will be opposed to all the "mannerisms" of such a life. Well, but we are patient, if it is possible to learn the truth. I think that somehow—it shouldn't be too difficult, because we are beginning to make contacts even with the moon.

As to what you are writing about Sh. Asch, I don't know how you feel over there—I was not at all impressed by his announcement. Because for many weeks we got used to assuming that all public appearances of Sholem Asch were, unfortunately, dictated by material and personal considerations. How that combines with his considerable talent—I don't know.

> Sholem Asch wrote a sharp letter to the YIKUF in New York, protesting against the persecution of the Yiddish writers in Moscow. Chagall, who disliked Asch, ascribes it to Asch's greed and his wish to please the "capitalists." As an example of the defiance of New York Communists, see Novik's letter of July 5, 1949, p. 680.

How are you both? And how is your Dovid, the very fine man?

How is your work going. I would so much like to see you. I am sad that we are so *far*. But you are surrounded by Jews and friends. America is Jewish. Where I am is "goyish." Though I myself cannot get out of Vitebsk. Sutzkever wrote me that he drove through Vitebsk. What remained of Vitebsk is a small, bowed head of a little church . . .

So the question is: what am I doing? And how long can it go on?

Be well. Your devoted / Chagall

---

wheel is turning: A Yiddish popular folk song, "The Miller's Song": *"Di reder dreyen zikh / Di yorn geyen zikh vu / un ikh ver alt un grayz un gro"* ("The wheels are turning, / The years are churning / And I get old and frail and gray"), often quoted by Chagall. The first line or two lines can be used as a proverb, indicating a resigned sense of aging.

peasant woman: Virginia writes: "She is the thirteenth and youngest child of a Quebec farmer, and the odds were very much against her marrying a man like my father" (Haggard, *My Life with Chagall*, p. 21).

"worries": Meaning the opposite: "pleasures." Again, a Yiddish reversal of tone, to cover up his boasting.

the fine world: Meaning the opposite: the ugly world.

Vitebsk: As soon as his native Vilna (Vilnius) was liberated by the Red Army in July 1944, Sutzkever traveled from Moscow to Vilnius, passing thousands of dead bodies on the road, and the ruins of Vitebsk.

Virginia Haggard in Orgeval to the Opatoshus in New York

Orgeval August 8th 1949

[English] My dearest friends,

At last a moment of calm! So many things have been happening. To begin with Ida's operation turned out to be very serious and we were all extremely anxious. The operation took three hours. The whole of her stomach had to be removed because there were two ulcers. The surgeon says that in a couple of months there would have been a perforation and if she had been in the country at that time, that would have been the end of her. However, the operation went extremely well and a new stomach is forming in the intestine which took the place of the stomach. She eats everything and is regaining her strength. She left for Gordes in the south of France a few days ago. She spent her first days of convalescence in Orgeval. Marc's niece Bella was here too. I went to England for a week. I have just come back. I went in a hurry because I wanted to get the only vacancy obtainable in a small school near my parents' home for Jean. The school is very nice and vacancies are much sought-after so I was glad to get Jean into the school. I brought her back for her vacation but I am going to take her over to England again in September and deposit her. I was glad to see my parents again and I find they have grown much more human since they are in more human surroundings. They work in the house and plant vegetables in their garden as if they had done it all their lives and my father goes off on his bicycle every now and then to bring in a supply of beer. Jean got on most wonderfully well with them both. She has a way of not taking them seriously which tickles their sense of humor. She calls my father Godfrey and pulls his red hair and he adores it. I should never have dared to do such a thing, nor would he have permitted it. I think it often happens that when one skips a generation there is a much closer contact. Or perhaps it's because people become warmer as they grow older and so many harmful and unnecessary things are discarded in their natures such as conventional ideas about education and etiquette and all the snobbery that goes with them. Naturally at their age they can see children from the right perspective, with the right detachment whereas mothers and fathers are often too involved in their children (but not my parents!) But the mistakes I made in that way with Jean won't be repeated with David. However much I love him I have to control my demonstrations of love because only in this way will he become himself instead of being a slave to my possessive affection. He's turning out to be very much himself—quite a character!—very attached to me but perfectly free at the same time. He is so completely free that his acts of generosity are delightfully spontaneous and not motivated by any sense of obligation. Jean was never so free. She was tied to me by a feeling of obligation because I never spared any pains or hid any emotion, I

Bella: Bella Rosenfeld-Ziter, a niece of Bella Chagall, lives in Paris.

chagall 1949   Pour Virginia Love Marc

Anniversary flowers for Virginia, Vence, 1949. Notice that the word "love" is in English.

shared everything with her. I unburdened myself to her. To this day she takes my attention so much for granted as well as everyone else's that she is very much involved in herself. Of course there are the inevitable jealousies, especially after the way I attached her to myself. But the outward signs are very rare and she has such a good heart and such a pleasant nature that I'm sure she will get over that. The trip to England (without David) had an excellent effect on her. We had a lot of fun together.

Thank you, dearest friends, for your letters and try to forgive me for not writing before. I drove up to town every day for about two weeks when Ida was ill. We are about an hour's distance from Paris. And apart from that the same kind of crazy life goes on as usual. In September we are going with David to the south again. This time we really hope to find a good house for *rent*. We have decided not to buy. Probably we shall be able to go to America next summer or autumn. We *must*, it's too long since we saw you. Once we are really *settled* then we can go off on another wild-goose chase all over the world. The only real advantage of settling down is that one is free to gad about!

Marc sends his love, the children send theirs, and so do I. / Yours as ever

Virginia

Marc Chagall to the Opatoshus

[Yiddish] My dear ones, how are you? I wrote to you recently. So busy with things, paintings that go hard. In September, we shall again travel to look for a house, though I recall High Falls with love.

Received your little book dedicated to your parents, with a story by Opatoshu. A splendid idea. How sweet it is to print such rare things, just for friends. Be well and write about everything. Your devoted Chagall

Marc Chagall in Orgeval to Abraham Sutzkever in Tel Aviv

Orgeval, August 18, 1949

[Yiddish] Received your letter. Thanks. Thank you also for the clipping from [the Israeli newspaper] *HaArets*. Now see—I began drawing for your book *Siberia*. I hope it won't be too bad. Please send me a *page*, what is the size of your book?

And what will be printed on the first title page? I think fine printed letters with a small drawing by me on the title page is not bad (as in Bella's books)? What do you think?

I am happy and thank you for taking care of Bella's books in Israel. True, I am somewhat worried about the "selection." I would like to ask the opinion of a few friends and my daughter about the selection. In this respect I would like to have unanimity between you, me, and the publisher. Her first book (*Burning Lights*) was well done. Personally I think it must remain untouched. Perhaps the second book (*First Encounter*) had mistakes in the order of the chapters. Or should we combine the two into one book and preserve all the drawings as far as possible. In France they are preparing a deluxe album with a selection of chapters from the two books. Only the first book was published separately, and they are preparing the second. I am afraid that if they make a selection of the two books in Israel, the rest of the chapters will never see the light of day. I would like to know which chapters (and which drawings) you have in mind for the book—your plan. Later I shall send you my opinion. I apologize for so much work.

September 5: The date was September 2.

Indeed, September 5 is the anniversary of her [Bella's] death.

Marc Chagall in Paris to Abraham Sutzkever in Tel Aviv

Orgeval, Sept. 7, 1949

[Yiddish] Dear Sutzkever,

This is *the paper* (and the format), on which I made drawings for your book *Siberia*, I hope they are not too bad. It is a kind of new manner for me: black and white with nuances. (All previous Yiddish books—by Bella, Lyesin, Fefer, Hof-shteyn, Peretz and others were only in black-and-white lines). In the drawings, I wanted to leave freshness, spontaneity, if possible.

Perhaps it is more difficult to reproduce them with subtle nuances. I don't know whether there is a printer and plate-maker for this kind in Israel—as in Paris. So if you wish I could ask the Paris specialists (who worked and are work-ing for me). Perhaps we should make the plates and even print on this paper (by the way, I think that here, though good, it is probably cheaper) and later print the text in your country. Here, there is also beautiful paper. I think it should be a book "deluxe." That is, not a book for the "bourgeois," but a beautiful book production (later, it can be printed more cheaply for the broader audience too). I think, in the *size* of *this* page (of the drawings). Recently, I made a book for the French poet Paul Eluard. It was even larger.

There is a good Jew here, a former publisher I think, who now works at a newspaper press. He could make some effort to find out and oversee (with my help).

As to Bella's books, it is good that you agree they have to include almost everything in a certain "scenario," as well as my drawings. Thick books are be-ing made. They will send it to me in advance. And it is a kind of monument "for Vitebsk." I hope the Hebrew will be like the Yidddish. You will supervise the translation.

I send you my speech in English ["The Artist"] for the journal. I hope the Yid-dish will be simple, as I like it. And perhaps send it to me *before printing*.

Nu, be well. Thank you for sending me the issue of *Di Goldene Keyt*, full of content, poetry. While sending it by post, it would be better not to "confuse" the issue number.

I wish you all a good [new] year. Be well, with my best regards,

Devoted /   Marc Chagall

Louis Stern in New York to Marc Chagall in Orgeval

October 14, 1949

[English] Dear Maestro:

Ever since my return here I have been meaning and wanting to write to you. I have of course been very busy, but added to that, I have delayed from day to day in order to be able to give you the information contained in this letter.

Barr: Alfred H. Barr, Jr. (1902–1981), Director of the Museum of Modern Art in New York, founded in 1929. He was instrumental in rescuing Chagall and his family from Nazi Europe in 1941.

About a week ago I visited the Museum of Modern Art, and Mr. Barr was good enough to show me the three Chagalls formerly in the Feldhaeusser collection, and acquired through the Weyhe Gallery. The pictures have been cleaned and restored and put on new stretchers. They are titled as follows:

1. *The Crucifixion Scene* or *Calvary* or perhaps *Golgotha*

2. *Anniversaire* or *Birthday Celebration*

3. *Over Vitebsk*, or perhaps *The Eternal Jew*

All these pictures are extraordinary in colour, in design, and are full of invention. I think it is a great compliment to you that the Museum, which is always "hard up" for money, should be willing to buy three of your pictures at one time. These three pictures together with those they already have will make their Chagall collection a notable one.

And now get ready for a surprise—I purchased two pictures from the same collection.

1. *The Purim Feast*

2. *The Trough* or *Die Tränke*

The Purim Feast is full of fire and flame, and appeals to me tremendously. At the moment I am prepared to say it is the greatest of all Chagalls. And I simply could not let *The Trough* go. Although I may have more difficulty in placing that picture on my walls. Your use of the black in *The Purim Feast* and the white in *The Trough* is fantastic and amazing. Only Chagall could have done that! I am having both of them put in good shape before picking out frames for them.

There are three Chagalls left of the Feldhaeusser collection as follows:

1. *Menschen am Tisch*, 1909 ["People at the Table"]

2. *Geburt* or *Accouchement*, 1911 ["The Birth"]

3. *Fundenfall, Fall of Man*, 1912

I have been so occupied since my return that I don't pretend to know all that is going on in the art world in New York. I can report to you however that the outstanding event is the Van Gogh show which opens at the Metropolitan Museum of Art on October the 20th. The majority of the pictures and drawings to be exhibited have never been shown in the United States before. Curiously enough, I saw them all in Holland just a few days before I spent that pleasant Sunday with you.

I dropped in at the Matisse Gallery but Pierre was not there, and in accordance with his most recent behavior, he has not called me, so I have not seen him.

I don't know of anything which warrants prolonging this letter, hence I will close with affectionate regards to you, Virginia, and the Children.

Louis E. Stern

Virginia Haggard and Marc Chagall in France to Louis Stern in New York

Chagall was invited by Père Couturier to contribute a work of art to the Church of Notre Dame de Toute Grace on the Plateau d'Assy, in Haute Savoie, decorated by Léger, Matisse, Bonnard, Lipchitz, and Chagall. Lipchitz, a religious Jew, made a bronze virgin with the inscription: "Jacob Lipschitz, a Jew faithful to the religion of his ancestors, made this virgin for the good understanding of mankind upon the earth, as long as the Spirit reigns." Chagall was tempted, yet characteristically hesitated until 1957, when he made a ceramic mural for the baptistery in Assy, representing the crossing of the Red Sea, as well as stained glass windows and bas-reliefs in marble. Above the door he placed an inscription: "In the name of freedom for all religions."

[Postcard; English] 22.X.49

Dear Louis, we visited the church, the baptistry of which Marc is going to decorate with mural paintings. Facade by Leger, windows by Rouault and others, sacristy by Bonnard, etc. Behind us is the Mont Blanc. We got your letter. Marc is thrilled and thanks you for the good news about your pictures. He will write later. Have you had photos made of your pictures? We were glad to hear all your news. Now we are bound for the south to search for a house. We shall be there perhaps when you next come to Europe. We both send our love, also David who is with us.

Virginia   Marc C.

Marc Chagall in Orgeval to Leo Kenig in London

Orgeval   October 1949

your book: Dos bukh fun lesterungen (The Book of Sacrilege), 1948.

[Yiddish] Dear Leo Kenig, thank you for your book. You are a very "courageous" Jew to write like this in our times. I read and am reading. Not yet finished and *underlined* so much. And you know, in many cases I agree with you, though not always. I personally have no strength, let us say, "entirely" to assimilate with *those* who slaughtered everyone, 6 million Jews, and it seems that, under "those," you include the Jews a little too. Nevertheless—you have so many subtle observations, which must come apparently especially at 60 years and because you are an artist (from La Ruche). Eh, not much hope that our (miserable) world of artists-and-writers will catch on to our "discoveries." Strangely, I believe (perhaps like you) that after Bialik, the deepest "pulse" died among us Jews. All the rest are "daubers," flatterers, roll their eyes and pound their chest: "We have sinned."

Chaim-Nakhman Bialik (1873–1934) was considered the major Hebrew poet-cum-prophet at the beginning of the twentieth century. In his poem "The City of Slaughter," written in a prophetic tone after the Kishinev pogrom of 1903, he chastized the Jews for their passivity in facing a pogrom.

Nevertheless, you should be able to go to Israel to see something fresh [alive]. I believe that you are too much of a skeptic (I observed it long ago). I know, it may not be possible otherwise, but this is our salvation. For you love Bach, Beethoven, Mozart, Shakespeare, the Bible (Oh the Bible!), and our innocent children and women. You are too gloomy, not just skeptical. I am sorry that you are far away, that I did not have time and could not chat with you, and indeed show you paintings and read what you know, you may say what you like. Perhaps I am (as some think) a "child," but I keep postponing *(that) truth* . . . Perhaps I escape from it into other worlds? But somewhere deep inside me I feel that I do not fool myself or others. And you know that I am your age (maybe older). Your book is an important and tragic book, even more so for a Jew. It is an abstract book. I think that your "abstract," highly developed power can be even more fruitful when applied to a reality. Here and there, I did see here and there good, nice Jews, men, you know? And don't forget that we recently produced several good artists and a few writers, though not Shakespeare or Michaelangelo.

Again I regret that I cannot see you and I do believe that I would evoke more smiles than skepticism on your face (forgive my chutzpah). Send me more of your writing, if you have any. I am going to the Côte d'Azur but the address is the same for the time being.

Sh. Asch wrote another nasty book about "God's Mother." Opatoshu sent me some clippings about it. It is a rare thing among us—to rush to describe the Goyish Gods *for money*, and furthermore, in the *evangelical line*. Where are our erstwhile Mendele, Peretz, Sholem Aleichem—kosher Jews.

> The three great Yiddish writers of the turn of the century, were pronounced "classics" of Yiddish literature. Chagall wrote their names on his mural "Introduction to the Yiddish Theater." All three were secular. By "kosher Jews," Chagall means that they were loyal to the Jewish people and Jewish cultural identity.

Why won't he convert to Christianity? It won't bring him money, only those books will.

Better look at the children. Your daughter had a pretty smile [on her visit] in Orgeval—

Simkha Shvarts, the *good intelligent* Jew, leader and founder of the Yiddish Marionette Theater (I think he is from Romania, a friend of Itzik Manger) will soon perform in Paris a play based on Bella Chagall's two books with costumes and decorations *inspired* by my illustrations to the books. If I am not mistaken, you did not express your opinion about them. Regretfully, many Jews (writers) did not grasp her innocent beauty, though perhaps the "subject matter," the tradition, is alien to you?

Manger: Itzik Manger (1901–1969), a major Yiddish poet, lived in Czernowitz (then Romania), Warsaw, London, and Israel.

Be well, with best wishes

Marc Chagall

Virginia Haggard in Vence to Louis Stern in New York

Le Studio / Ponte de St Paul / Vence A.M.   November 20th, 1949

[English] Dear Louis,

Thankyou for your long and exciting letter. Marc is thrilled to hear that two more of his pictures have found a safe haven in an art-lover's home and he is more than happy that they are with you. It is like a mother leaving her children with an old and trusted friend. She is sure that they will be loved and well treated with you.

Marc thanks you for all the information about the other pictures and he wishes he could see them all. It is forty years since he saw them, nearly half a century!

We just received our second extension of our re-entry permits to the U.S. That gives us until May to come back unless we try for a third extension, which is not usually given. There is talk of Marc doing mural paintings in a new synagogue in Woodmere, New York and they're now trying to raise the money. The rabbi is Irving Miller and he is most enthusiastic. If they are successful in raising the money, Marc will make a trip over to see the site and make sketches. That will give him a reason to go over to the U.S., also the possibility financially to make the trip. Otherwise he will probably not go. If we go we should like to sell our house in High Falls. Do you know of anyone, either buyer or real estate agent who might be interested? We want around 9 to 10 thousand for it. It cost 7,500 plus 1,500 for a well and septic tank and roof repairs. We hear there is to be an immense parkway through New Paltz to Buffalo and New Paltz is the next town to ours. Anyone can see the house by applying to *Victor Purcell, Box 106 High Falls*, he is our caretaker and lives next door. At present the house is rented furnished and I have warned the tenants they might have to leave after a year, that is, in June.

to sell our house: Yet in a letter of May 26, 1950, Virginia writes that they decided *not* to sell the house, in case they had to flee Europe again because of a Soviet invasion.

Chagall's letter to Virginia in England, December 16, 1949.

Forgive me for boring you with all these details. Don't bother unless you happen to know of someone interested.

We have settled in a comfortable house for six months here and we have our eye on a house belonging to a friend (Claude Bourdet, editor of "Combat") which is for sale. We are negotiating the price. So perhaps when you next come over we shall be there. It will be good to see you here. It is a lovely country, ever changing and always beautiful, much more beautiful than the coast where the vegetation never varies all the year round. From here we see the mountains and the sea without being too near either of them. But of course you know Vence. I expect you have been here often. The Matisse chapel is now being built. Marc is having a large exhibition of all the recent paintings at Galerie Maeght in May. Will you be there? You must try and come over. If we can get another extension to our re-entry permits we shall leave for U.S.A. in the fall, perhaps with you! Marc and I send our love, also David. Jean is in England. She took along the Schmoog to amuse her grandparents.

Yours ever/   Virginia

P.S. Marc would love some photos of your two new pictures.

[Russian] How are you? I kiss you, your Marc

Marc Chagall in Vence to Virginia Haggard in England

Vence, December 16, 1949

[French] Darling, how did you arrive. We miss you at home. It's sad without you. David is charming. He sleeps well, eats well, and I am waiting for you.

Monday

I am waiting for you
   Everyone is waiting for you

Kisses

Marc

Louis Stern in New York to Marc Chagall and Virginia Haggard in Vence

Louis E. Stern/30 Broad Street/New York, N.Y.   December 16, 1949

[English] Dear Maestro & Virginia

I have delayed acknowledging receipt of your letter of November 20th hoping to be able to give you some concrete information and advice with respect to the disposition of your property in High Falls.

This is not as easy as it would seem. Through a friend I located someone who was looking for a country home, and was interested enough to drive out to see your property, but apparently he was not interested in purchasing.

The best method to dispose of real estate is to place it in the hands of a local real estate dealer whom you know to be reliable and trustworthy. I don't suppose that High Falls boasts of a real estate agent, and perhaps a dealer in the nearest large city whether it be New Paltz or Poughkeepsie, or some such place, would be best. I have succeeded in getting the names of three real estate agents in Poughkeepsie. They are as follows:

Charles Boof, 2 Canon Street, Poughkeepsie, New York

Charles Corlin, 19 Canon Street, Poughkeepsie

E.I. Hatfield, 46 Canon Street, Poughkeepsie

I do not know anything about them other than that a friend of mine who is reliable gave me the names.

There is an Agency known as *Previews* who handle country property all over the United States. They do considerable business advertising both in the newspapers and through catalogues. Generally they deal with large estates, and the difficulty is that they ask an initial minimum payment of $350 which has to be paid to them before they will handle a property. That would seem to be impractical, even though they give assurance that by their methods they obtain a price sufficiently large to cover any expense entailed.

Unfortunately, in your letter you did not give me sufficient information touching your property. The first question usually asked is how much land there is, the number of rooms, etc. etc. If, when you write again, you would give me this information, and such other as you have, such as the amount of taxes, insurance, and all other carrying charges, it would be helpful. I would of course be very happy to assist you in any way possible, and if necessary, would drive out there to look at the place, and to locate the right sort of person to handle it. Incidentally, from and through whom did you buy it? Perhaps that person could dispose of it for you. Let me hear from you about this.

*

I assume that you have heard from and through Busch Meier-Graefe and Dr. Isaac Kloomok (of whom more later) about my Chagall room, which presents an exciting scene, and has aroused a lot of comment and admiration from all friends and visitors to my home. It is of course, not complete as yet, for the *Dans La Nuit* has been at the Carnegie Show in Pittsburgh, and while the exhibition has just closed, the painting has not yet been returned to me as yet. When it gets back here it will have a prominent place.

Incidentally, I have agreed to loan the *Purim Feast* to Klaus Perls, who is staging an exhibition during the month of January, 1950, of important Twentieth Century Pictures.

I assume that you have received some word from the Museum of Modern Art of the Exhibition of Chagall Prints from *Ma Vie* and *Les Sept Peches Capitaux* and a group of the illustrations from *Les Ames Mortes*. It was very well arranged by Lieberman, who is the Curator of Prints of the Museum. These prints are exhibited downstairs. Immediately adjoining is the New Acquisition Room where the three Chagalls recently acquired by the Museum of Modern Art are exhibited.—So you see that Chagall's name and Chagall's work is not neglected.

As you probably know, I had a long talk with Dr. Kloomok with respect to his proposed book on Chagall. He read to me your letter to him containing the generous offer of assistance. He left with me the English Translation of his manuscript, and I have read it with sympathetic interest. I hesitate to pass judgement upon it, but frankly speaking, it does not seem to me to add anything new to the literature on Chagall. It quotes and re-quotes from *Ma Vie*, or *Mein Leben*, and from Bella's *Burning Lights*. I think that Sweeney's book, and even Venturi's cover the ground.

Dr. Kloomok "accentuates the positive" by crying from the housetops that Chagall has a Jewish soul. To my way of thinking it is stretching it entirely too far to refer to a "Jewish landscape", "Jewish love", "Jewish flowers", etc. etc. Nor do I think it helpful to pigeonhole Chagall merely as a Jewish artist—or an artist concerned with Jewish lore. I do not believe that to be true, and as almost everybody knows, I have lived with my Chagalls, and loved them beyond almost any other pictures. I think that I am as capable of understanding, even though I may not be articulate.

I seriously question whether such a book, if and when published, would have any particular value in perpetuating the Chagall name. I of course don't want to set myself up as an authority. The fact that the Philosophical Library wants to be guaranteed against loss exhibits a lack of confidence in the salability of the book. I have not reported to Dr. Kloomok that I feel quite certain that Weyhes [gallery], with whom I have discussed the matter, would handle the De Luxe edition, if there be any.

I feel somewhat guilty in this matter, for it was I who, about a year ago, suggested to Dr. Kloomok that his manuscript be translated into English. I now feel that the original text in Yiddish might have a raison d'être.

I am writing at length and so very frankly to you, volunteering the benefit of my opinion, which you may use for what it is worth, without any intention on my part to influence you.

*

Having volunteered unsought for advice on one subject, I will venture into perhaps forbidden territory: I note with some concern the project of a mural in a Synagogue in Woodmere, Long Island. I seriously question the advisability of this project. To begin with, it is not in my opinion, in an important enough place. From my knowledge of the territory, I would guess that the congregation consists of a bourgeois group of people, who more than likely have little or no idea of art, and it is a safe prediction that there would be interference, dissension, criticism, etc. etc. Chagall must be free to paint as he feels, without dis-

"Jewish landscape": The image of "Jewifying nature," however, was a standard topos in Yiddish literary criticism, especially on the work of Mendele Moykher Sforim who described trees as standing in prayer, and so on. Chagall himself wrote that Peretz's art evoked "Jewish images and figures": "beyond a fence, a Jewish moon with a dark horizon behind it suddenly leaps at your feet from the sky."[1]

traction, and without the advice and interference of others. I don't believe that painting a mural under such auspices (assuming they could put such a project through) would bring happiness to Chagall.

*

I have of course been in Vence and know the territory quite well, having just recently been through there. I congratulate you on having found such an attractive spot, and I hope that you will stay there long enough to give me an opportunity to visit. When that will be I, at this writing, do not know.

Right now I am getting ready to go down to New Orleans to spend the holidays with my sister and her family, and also perhaps, to attend to some business matters in which my brother-in-law and I are interested.

It doesn't take much to stir me into thinking of traveling to Europe, and it is always a reasonable possibility that I will be with you soon again.

I had a few minutes chat with Teeny Matisse who brought news and greetings from you two and Ida. I was glad to see her looking so well. She has gone to Colorado to be with her son who is at school there, and promised to get in touch with me upon her return here, several weeks hence.

I have seen Pierre and have met the new bride who is an attractive young thing, notwithstanding all that, I cannot understand it all.

I think this letter is probably long enough, so I will conclude by sending you, Maestro, and Virginia, my love, and best wishes for the New Year.

Affectionately yours

[Louis Stern]

Virginia Haggard in Vence to Louis Stern in New York

Le Studio/Vence, A.M.   December 29th [1949]

[English] Dear Louis,

We thank you for your long, informative, and interesting letter.

First of all thank you for all the advice about the High Falls house. I have noted the addresses of agents in Poughkeepsie and I quite realize that it is most difficult for you to do anything other than suggest the house to any of your friends who might be interested. I have local agents and a caretaker trying to sell it. We want to try and get the money it cost Marc, namely $10,000. There is not quite an acre of land. The big house has 6 rooms, bath & kitchen, large porch, cellar with hot-air heating system & oil immersion water heater. The little house has a big studio, kitchen, two bedrooms. One mile from High Falls. 3 hours from New York. Soon there will be a parkway all the way to New Paltz (one mile and a half away) which will cut the journey to New York down to 2 hours. Tradesmen call at the house regularly and all shopping can be done at the door. There are fruit trees, lawns, flowers, and a chicken house. A fine view of the mountains. There is a mortgage on the house of about $4,000. Taxes are $25 a year (land) and $16 for the school. The house is insured against fire.

The agent we bought the home from is going to try and sell it for us. I only troubled you with all this because I thought you might know of someone interested, but beyond that, don't bother about it please.

Your Chagall room sounds *wonderful*. Marc is thrilled and wants me to tell you that he is longing to see it and that he is very happy about it.

He thanks you also for your advice regarding Kloomok's book and is seriously thinking over your comments. Unfortunately I never read any of the English script but his English letters are very haltingly written and I don't get the impression from them that he has a command of the language.

Marc is thinking over your advice regarding the murals in Woodmere. So far there is no definite news. You are right to put him on his guard against interference. There is a very energetic and sympathetic woman behind the plan and she is a collector of Chagall. Perhaps she will have enough influence on the others to make the whole plan possible for Chagall.

We are very happy here and Marc is just about to buy a house belonging to old friends. It is a beautiful place and has two studios. Our address will be the above until the end of April.

> We send our love and wish you a very happy New Year
>
> Virginia

Marc Chagall in Vence to Lionello Venturi in New York

Venturi: Lionello Venturi was an Italian art historian living in the U.S. during World War II; he wrote a book about Chagall.

[French; typed, signed by Chagall]

Vence/Alpes Maritimes   17 February 1950

My dear friend,

I was so happy to get your letter. I too always like to hear your voice and talk with you a bit, at least by letter.

Kimball: Director of the Philadelphia Museum of Art, 1925–1954.

As for that picture offered by Fiske Kimball to the Philadelphia Museum, I am a bit surprised because I don't remember doing a variation or a sketch of "To My Bride" of 1911 (that is, a picture of a red jackass in a bed with a woman on its shoulders and a lamp at the bottom). That picture is in the Roland Penrose collection in London and was formerly in the Hess collection in Berlin. I never sent Bella a present in Odessa, where she never went, and at that time I would never have dared to give anyone a gift of my paintings for lack of self-confidence. I would like to see a photo of that painting which I suspect is a forgery, as some-times happens. If these self-styled Chagalls at least had a more supple texture, it wouldn't be such a tragedy!

I hope you will be in Paris when the Galerie Maeght does my exhibit in April or May. You will calm me a bit and I would be so happy to see you again. How are the two of you?

I hope to move into a new house soon, "Les Collines," in Vence and Ida into a house in Paris. God help us all! Not the atomic God, but the God of health and art.

Virginia joins me in sending both of you warm thoughts.

> Your devoted,
>
> Marc Chagall

I suspect is a forgery: But it was Chagall's painting; see his letter to Kimball of April 1, 1950, p. 705.

Fiske Kimball in Philadelphia to Marc Chagall in Vence[2]

3/6/50 [March]

[French] Dear Chagall,

My friend Venturi sent me your kind letter about the painting "A ma Fiancée, 1911," telling me to contact you directly. I have fond memories of meeting you and Mlle. Ida at the formal dinner for Venturi when he left New York.

Enclosed is a photo of my painting, gouache, I think, 62 x 44 cm., which be-longed until 1937 to my friend Bernard Davis, who said that he knew you some-what in Paris in about 1928. At that time he acquired it there, he thinks, at the Hotel Drouet. I hope that it gives full satisfaction of your work.

The painting from the Roland Penrose collection in London (previously Hess), in oil, 215 x 133 cm, according to the listing in the book of Umbrio Appolo-nio, 1949, where it is reproduced on Plate V. It is also reprinted in Venturi's book, Pl. VI, as being in the "Hess Collection, Paris," without any dimensions given.

I am somewhat confused to find reproduced in the introduction to the cata-logue of your exhibition at the Museum of Modern Art, New York, 1946, page 21, a photo absolutely identical to the Hess-Penrose painting, with the listing "Owned by the artist," which measures 77 x 45 1/2 inclusive (as 196 x 116 cm!) The painting itself was not shown in the New York Exhibition. Hence, I think that these last details are wrong.

I cannot tell now where I got the mistaken idea that any of these paintings was sent to Odessa(!), or even sent at that time to Bella—perhaps it was derived only from the dedication.

You may be happy to know that the gouache sketch of "Me and My Village" is also in the collection of the museum.

After all these boring details, allow me to express my wife and my warm admiration of your art.

Hoping to read you on the different version of "A Ma fiancée" / Your devoted

Fiske Kimball

A House in the Riviera

In the spring of 1950, the Chagalls moved all their belongings from Orgeval to the new house they bought in Vence, named Les Collines. The house belonged to Claude and Ida Bourdet. Ida was a close friend of Ida Chagall ("the two Idas"). Under the Nazis, Claude Bourdet (1909–1996), along with Albert Camus, founded the Resistance journal *Combat*. He had been captured by the Gestapo, interned in camps, liberated in Buchenwald in 1945, and became a leader of the French non-Communist left. It was the house of Claude's mother, Catherine Pozzi, who had lived there with her lover, the poet Paul Valéry. During the Resistance, Claude Bourdet had a room there in a separate building, with an escape door. That room was called by the Chagalls "Claude's room," and Ida Chagall stayed there.

The Problem of Working for a Christian Church

The following letters discuss Chagall's temptation to do work in a Christian church. As "commissar" of art in Vitebsk after the Russian Revolution, Chagall strove to create public art, emanating from his own idiosyncratic expressions. One of his manifesto-type slogans was: "Give me a wall!" Soon after, he was commissioned to paint the murals for the Moscow Yiddish Chamber Theater (1920). All his life, he longed for large-scale projects, especially in temples or theaters, which came to fruition only after World War II. Yet no Jewish institutions were forthcoming, and he turned to stained-glass windows in Christian churches. At first he moved with great compunction and hesitation.

From left: Catholic philosopher Jacques Maritain, Ida Chagall, Father Pere RP Couturier (who invited Chagall to create art for a Christian church), and Marc Chagall, Orgeval, 1950.

Marc Chagall in Vence to the Opatoshus in New York

Vence (A.M.) 22/III 1950

[Yiddish] Dear friends Opatoshu how are you? Time flows and it is hard to believe I cannot drop in on you as in the past, see you, and even get a bite in Adele's kitchen.

Thank you for the clipping you sent me of your speech (YIVO) I am always happy to read you. It is wise and warm. But the more we live in the world the more our voice appears like a voice in the wilderness. I am not a pessimist. You know it. I am here in Vence, not far from Nice. I bought a house here (some time ago) with a garden (otherwise it is not easy to get an apartment). I want to try working here. May God help.

In the meantime in Paris in the Museum, as you see, my hall was officialy opened. (An honor too great in one's own lifetime, especially for a Jew.)

And now I feel like proposing you and with you—your friends (and mine too) —Jews with heads on their shoulders—for example, Rabbi Finkelstein, Chaim Greenberg, Glants [-Leyeles], Leyvik and others—a question I have never discussed before. I asked [President] Chaim Weitzmann in Israel about it. As well as here in Paris. And now what remains is to hear the opinion of several Jews in America. Chaim Weitzmann seemed to want to avoid the issue and answered

Finkelstein; Greenberg: Louis Finkelstein (1895–?), chancellor of the Jewish Theological Seminary in New York; historian, scholar, and talmudic authority. Chaim Greenberg (1889–1953), an American Zionist leader, essayist, editor of the Yiddish weekly *Yidisher Kemfer*, and a moral authority in Jewish New York.

more or less as follows: It is more a religious than a political question. He leaves the choice to my *bon sens* which so far (as he thinks) has served me well and he believes it won't ever abandon me—

The answer of (Judge) Leon Meiss, head of the Jewish Consistoire in Paris and several others here—was positive.

It would be good if there were answers to my question—on your side—let it be done on the typewriter—each person's opinion separately.

Well, I have filled your head with too much noise. Be well with my hearty regards for both of you. Your devoted Marc Chagall

Summary Translation of Chagall's Letter to President Weitzmann

This English summary of the letter to President Weitzmann (including the title) was probably made by Ida Chagall. It is typewritten, part of the Opatoshu file at the YIVO archive. We reprint it as is, with only minor spelling corrections. The original did not turn up in President Weitzmann's archives in Rehovot, Israel.

[English] . . . I write to you as our fathers in Russia used to write to their Rabbis for help in solving problems of conscience.

I have been asked to execute mural paintings in a 16th century chapel in Vence, which is a historical, cultural, and religious center on the Riviera. I have not yet accepted.

. . . Of course I shall be left entirely free to paint whatever I wish and if I accept I intend to do Biblical scenes such as appear in some of my paintings, strictly in my own manner and from my own point of view, symbolizing the suffering of the martyred Jewish people.

To decorate a chapel might give me the chance to do work that is only possible on large walls, instead of having to limit myself to relatively small canvases, destined to hang in private houses. To decorate walls in public buildings has long been my dream. If it were possible to decorate a synagogue my dream would be completely fulfilled.

If I decide to decorate this chapel I would not want the people of Israel to think that in my heart or mind—not to speak of my art—I have anything in common with non-Judaism. With my ancestors I shall always be bound to my people.

On a more temporal basis I do not know whether I should decorate a Catholic church at a time when the Vatican is not favorably disposed to Israel. At the same time, I wonder if the presence of a Jewish painting in a church might be good propaganda for our people.

In other cases I have solved similar cases myself. Thus I refused my friend Jacques Maritain's request to donate a picture to the Vatican's museum of modern art. I refused to exhibit in German museums after the war, in spite of the official invitation of the French Cultural Services. An exhibition that has recently taken place in Dusseldorf was organized without my consent and consisted of pictures from German and Dutch collections. I refused to be present at the opening of my exhibition in London at a time when British policy was unfavorable to our interests.

But today I have neither the strength nor the capacity to reply, and all the more because I have been asked to do work in other churches and in other towns.

But with the renaissance after 2000 years of the spiritual and political center of the Jewish people I can't help turning with all my doubts towards its most eminent representative.

Virginia Haggard in Vence to the Opatoshus in New York

> Early in his career, Chagall moved to widen the scope of the media in which he worked. During 1922–1923 in Berlin, he learned the techniques of etching and lithography. After his return to Europe, at the height of his fame, he applied his fictional world to stained-glass windows, tapestries, ceramics, and sculpture. Chagall's first ceramic plate is dated 1949, and in 1950 he produced several pieces at a ceramicist in Vence. Later he moved to the Madoura factory in Vallauris, operated by Suzanne and Georges Ramié (where Picasso had been working since 1946).[3]

"Les Collines," Vence, Alpes Maritimes   [March 1950]

[English] Dearest friends,

Since I last wrote many things have happened. One: we have bought a house in Vence. Two: we have been to Paris to pack up our belongings and within those two events there are dozens of others so you can well understand why we haven't written for so long. How are you? First of all thank you Oppen for Lysistrata. It is a lovely play. What do you think of the illustrations? Marc has been hesitating to write to you about our house, partly because he is superstitious and doesn't quite believe it is his until he is actually living in it and secondly because he is a little conscience-stricken about leaving his friends in America. He is afraid you might be sad about it. But I expect you are quite resigned to that by now and of course you understand how much better off he is here than in America except that he misses the Opatoshus. So do I. I wish it were possible to come over soon and visit you, but I don't know when that will be. Now we are busy trying to arrange the house. There have been many repairs to do and alterations which have taken a long time and are not finished yet.

Next month we shall go back to Paris for Marc's exhibition (recent work [in the gallery at the Maeght Foundation]) I shall probably bring Jean back with me. David is happy here and never looked so well. He is growing tall and slim like your David. How is your David? & your Dan and Lilly? And how is Oppen's book going?

Marc has been doing ceramics. He has done a series of biblical subjects. They are most powerful and unusual. He has painted them on large dishes. There is talk about him doing mural paintings in a theatre in London. And then there is the chapel in Vence that he has told you about. He awaits your opinion anxiously. I think I know what it will be! Everybody he speaks to about it is unreservedly approving and I seem to be the only one who has any reservations! We have had several interesting talks with Jews & non-Jews about this chapel scheme. Some of them succeeded in convincing me (especially the Jews) that an artist need not necessarily be in agreement 100% with the church in order to paint decorations on it. Perhaps they are right. In any case it doesn't look as if the Jews are ready to offer him walls to decorate and he has waited so long for the fulfillment of his great desire.

Our house is called "Les Collines" (The Hills). It is a handsome well-built house of some forty years old with a lovely garden. It was in a terrible condition but we have made a lot of improvements. We are longing for you to come and stay with us here.

Please write soon and let us know all your news./Love from us all & kisses

Virginia

Marc Chagall in Vence to Fiske Kimball in Philadelphia[4]

Vence   Alpes Maritimes   1 April 1950

[French] Dear Sir,

Thank you very much for your letter and for the photo of your gouache "To My Bride."

I did it in 1922 or '23 because I wanted to make a reminder of that painting of 1910 which had gone to Germany and because at that time a big retrospective exhibit of my work was organized and I wanted that painting to appear, at least in a variant form. I painted it from a reproduction. As there is no sketch for the big painting, your gouache is the only other extant version.

The details in the catalogue of the Museum of Modern Art in New York are not exact.

Thank you again for the photo and for your sympathy.

Very cordially,

Marc Chagall

Virginia Haggard in Vence to the Opatoshus in New York

"Les Collines", Vence (A.-M.)   Mai 26th 1950

[English] Dearest Adele and Oppen,

My silence means nothing more than that I have been busier than ever before, so please forgive me for not writing. These last few months have been the busiest of my life. First there was the packing up in Orgeval and only seeing is believing what an immense quantity of possessions we have. And then they all had to be sorted out amidst the disorder of workmen with pick-axes, bricklayers, plumbers with blow torches and fresh paint. A few masons are still here and the painters are still painting. But out of a dilapidated bourgeois villa—"Côte d'Azur" style painted yellow with a horrible roof like the brim of a hat and rusty iron railings around the top with black chimney pots that reminded me of New York, has arisen a beautiful simple square building with a red-tile roof ("provençal" style) and square chimney stacks. The tiles are more pink than red, like the very old ones that are everywhere to be seen in Provence and they are curved.

Now the house is going to be painted off-white with emerald green windows. The inside is all fresh & new. Marc's studios are a dream. There is a separate house containing three studios! There are two upstairs with old yellow-ochre tiled floors & big windows which we had put in and white walls and downstairs there is a big studio with "garage" doors that is going to be used for sculpture, pottery & various messy works. The children will be allowed to work there. I am going to teach them sculpture and pottery and puppet making and the gardener is going to teach them carpentry. Did you know that Marc has done some wonderful pottery? It was exhibited at his big exhibition in Paris in April to which we went and which was a great success. And now he is starting to think of sculpture.

I also went over to England to see Jean for her birthday. Her father has arrived in England from Scotland and the sparks are beginning to fly between him and my parents. I am going to bring her back in the summer for good. David is perfectly fine.

It was good to hear from you both & you are sweet to write and tell us about your part of the world. We have decided *not* to sell the house at High Falls! It might come in very useful someday. Nobody knows. So we still haven't burnt our bridges [to the U.S.] and there is [a] link between us still. Lots of love to you

Your Virginia

Hilla Rebay in New York to Marc Chagall in Vence

Baroness Hilla Rebay was Director of the Museum for Non-Objective Art, which later became the Solomon R. Guggenheim Museum in New York. The museum promoted "Non-Objective Art"—nonfigurative art without depicted objects. Nevertheless, Ms. Rebay admired and collected Chagall and had to build a special room for "objective painting" to accomodate Chagall's work.

12 July 1950

[French] Dear Marc Chagall,

I am sending you a drawing that has faded, and as it is certainly too bad, I wonder if it wouldn't be possible for you to add a bit of color to freshen it. It is a very pretty drawing and it would be really too bad to leave it in such a sad condition.

How are you? All is well here. Our museum is going to be built soon and they are going to add a wing for objective paintings, and they are going to make a section for each painter, including you. It will be very interesting, I think.

I think that you heard that Mr. Guggenheim died eight months ago. Fortunately, he did not have to suffer. He reached the age of 88 and, until the last moment, he rejoiced in the collection and in the art he did so much for.

I will be at the [Hotel] Georges V [in Paris] for two nights, the 25th to the 27th of July. Could you give me an answer there.

Meanwhile, my best wishes.

Hilla Rebay

Marc Chagall in Vence to Virginia Haggard in England

Chagall was persuaded to paint murals for "Watergate," a London repertory theater, by two Englishwomen, Elisabeth Sprigge and Velona Harris, who visited Les Collines and befriended Virginia. He made two large mural paintings, "The Blue Circus" and the "Dance," and sent them with Virginia to London. For the first time he accepted a commissioned work with no pay, on condition that it be returned in a year. The issue is mentioned in several letters, though Chagall keeps distorting the women's names.

"Les Collines" Vence (A.-M.)   July 13 or 14, 1950

[French] Dear Virginia, now you're gone and everything has become sad at home. And I think of how many days you will still be there. You are surely keeping very busy. David is nice and good, he eats, sleeps and says: when the tomatoes in our garden are red, you will come back. But you haven't yet sent a telegram. I am worried. How did it go? With the paintings? Write soon and I will write like a pig—badly. I love to read you, your writing and more. There is no news here. Except in the papers. And Rosa says that the public in Vence is already buying the food in the shops—with that news. I am trying to work a little. Write to me in detail.

Many kisses   Your Marc

[addition in red ink:] Thanks for the telegram   Kisses

Marc Chagall in Vence to Virginia Haggard in England

[No date; red ink, showing through to the other side, often illegible]

Mary Legg, Braemar/The Hot near Fainflam, Surrey

[French] I am so happy with your two letters of the 26 and 27. Finally the paintings are hung and Ida is calm and so are you and the public doesn't "grumble" too much! For I myself criticize too much—without doing anything [about it]. Have you seen the damn ballet? Rotten? How much did he change? Did he change much? If you like, say hello to Balanchine for me backstage. Is he thinking of coming to Paris with the ballet? Perhaps better not if he changed much for the worst. How are things? Don't get too tired. I am happy that you write very detailed letters to me and don't lose your head. Spend all the time you need in London to arrange everything. David is well—he is admirable, darling, and the whole house and garden, workers (ours and all) are waiting for you. You will have time. I see here in Vence the nice Rosa and Alexander, I dined at their house. I drank tea at Zazi's and the Countess's. And I am trying to work a little bit too.

But after the big ones [exhibitions], I am relaxed and that is what I need to really work on the "orders" for the "big ones" [murals]. I received letter from N.Y. from Mr. Steinmann and Polok, in Chicago, at the same time, that they are not

Rosa: According to Virginia, "a merry Italian housekeeper" who worked for them.

that news: On June 25, 1950, the North Korean army, backed by Communist China, unleashed an attack across the 38th parallel, which had separated it from South Korea. In France, there were serious fears of World War III.

Mary Legg: A friend of Virginia's, with whom she stayed during her visit in England.

"grumble": A Yiddish reversal, meaning the opposite; i.e., the public praised it.

damn ballet: Balanchine's New York City Ballet performed in England. Chagall had made the sets and costumes for Stravinsky's *Firebird*, but this ballet did not get to London; he probably refers to *Aleko*.

Alexander: The Chagalls' gardener, driver, and handyman. He lived in the basement of the house with his wife and child.

Zazi and the Countess: Zazi, the wife of Jean Darquet, was a clandestine artist, friend, and neighbor of Matisse when Matisse lived in Vence. Jean's mother, Edmé Casalis, was a good friend of Catherine Pozzi (Claude Bourdet's mother, who lived in Les Collines before Chagall); Jean nicknamed her "La Comtesse."

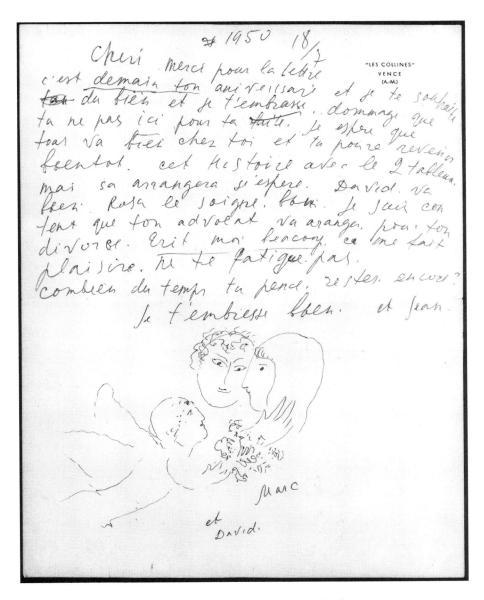

Marc and David longing for Virginia in England; letter from Vence, July 18, 1950.

compromised: Chagall is worried that he might not be able to get an American visa because of his participation in leftist cultural organizations.

abandoning the idea of a mural. Provided they see a bit of calm on the earth. On the other hand, I did not get any "news" from Marseille—the [American] Consul. Surely I am already compromised! With the painting of Abrahams . . . It's a pity. One makes fakes and sells them (without taking the trouble to go to Ida and Maeght). We have to get done with this scandal so that they'll pay attention. How did you settle the formalities with the theater pictures? I hope that everything is going to be settled for the best.

Kisses, my darling, it's been a long time since I've seen you. God knows how you are. Regards to your friends Vallone and Pilcher. All yours, Marc

write a short note to Opatoshu and Kloomok from London.

Now I may have a bit of courage to come.[5]

It is warm and there is a lot of noise next door. The house next to my atelier with a lot of children, maybe a dozen, and the radio. It's true that I have to ask for Joan of Arc who knows the boss to turn down the radio.

Alexandre's child is also noisy. He doesn't cry but he shouts loudly. That keeps me from working and as I told you I am not happy with Alexandre's arrangement. In any case, we need one worker (Josef is still working and he doesn't work badly. And I find Alexandre nice, but a bit nonchalant or he doesn't have time. Tériade— he was with me—tells me that he has a couple who are 50 years old, without any children.) We shall have to study this problem carefully, in general. I know that you get angry when I talk of it. But I need peace for my studio and the garden is unfortunately long and not wide, as at Orgeval.

The problem of the noise next door and the problem of Alexandre will be important for me. Don't get angry when I approach you. Rose is nice. Ida has not yet come. Perhaps she is waiting for you to be here. Rosa prepared (Claude's) room very nicely with the bed and rug and night table.

Well I have written a long letter (not too pleasant) with a thousand mistakes [in French].

Much love,

Marc

Vallone and Pilcher: Velona Harris and Elisabeth Sprigge. "Chagall improvised many versions of their names." (Virginia Haggard in a letter to Benjamin Harshav.)

Marc Chagall in Vence to Virginia Haggard in England

"Les Collines" / Vence / (A.-M.)   21/7 950

[French] Dear Virginia, Thanks for the letters. Don't worry if I don't write often. But you, please write. Stay there as long as you need to. I think that Ida already sent the pictures (Gea helped). How many cares you have. *Don't be upset.* Maybe the pictures won't *be damaged.* I hope that you will settle the material side with the people, as you told Ida. Do what you need to do in England—and then come back. Poor Jean! I hope she isn't too sick. Kiss her for me. David is well, the garden boy, he sleeps, and eats, and is nice. Rosa is also with him. Don't worry. Forgive me for writing little and badly. I can *speak* better to you. But my God you know that I love you. I would really like to write whole books in French to you, but I can't. But you write. I love that.

Gea: Gea Augsburg, a Swiss painter, was Ida's boyfriend for two years.

I am so happy / Kisses

Your Marc

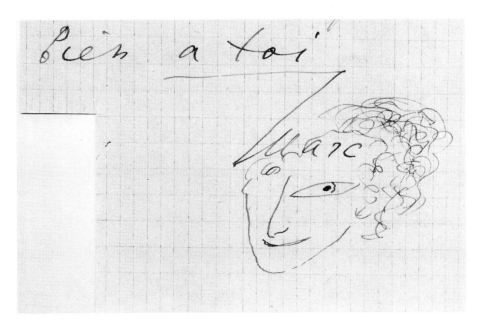

Marc's signature in a letter to Virginia.

When you come back to Paris you will talk in detail of business with Ida so that she will send me something by letter here. Today [. . .]

Valone and Pilser:
Chagall's distorted
names.

Regards to Valone and Pilser

Marc Chagall in Vence to Abraham Sutzkever in Tel Aviv

July 25, 1950

Dear friend Sutzkever,

the news: Apparently,
the news about the
liquidation of the
Soviet Yiddish writers;
"especially mine"
because he knew
them personally.

invitation: An
invitation from
President Zalman
Shazar to visit Israel.

the "sea": The sea is the
way to Israel. Here
he may also mean
the community,
the people.

I got your letter a long time ago. I apologize for not having answered till now. Virginia is in London, and the news is such that it chills you to the bone, especially mine, but I make an effort to work. If I could at least talk to you here—I would feel easier. By the way, Vence is a Gentile city, and in these nasty, murderous (non-Jewish) times, I am longing for Jews. So the only thing left for me to do is to take the Bible in hand, or paint Biblical images for myself, to calm myself.

And as to your letter announcing an [imminent] invitation. I am moved. I did not get it from any official source, and I believe, and know full well, that our government has and must have *many other worries*. What do they need me as a "guest," me, the weak, pale, too quiet Jew. Sometime, read again in *My Life*. But how happy I would have been to "circle" among the people—a "quiet," unknown person (the older I get, the more I am drawn to the "sea"). I am jealous of you,

you are so busy in the Land. Do you write new poems? I would like to read some. Soon, a new issue of G.K. [*Goldene Keyt*] will appear, and in it your new poems. How is the *Siberia* book advancing?

My dear friend, write to me. It consoles me, as you know.

Your devoted/   Marc Chagall

P.S. I cannot quite read your personal address.

Marc Chagall in Paris to the Opatoshus in New York

[Stationery: Quai de l'Horloge, 22, Place Dauphine, Paris Ie]

10/Sept 1950 Vence (A.M.) France

[Yiddish] Dear friends, I want to wish you from the depth of my heart all the best for our [= Jewish] New Year. *Health* and work. To both of you and your children. I cannot calm down in order to write to you more. The world is as always berserk and we, the "clairvoyant," watch it . . . Do not assume that I am "blind" and accept even 1/100 of the actions of the country of my birth. I would be not an artist but a cobbler, but on top of all the "troubles," I am a brother . . . In principle, I have 5 sisters, so? It is my heartache. Write to me. Virginia is confused and we are going to the country so she can rest.

[Drawing with Bella inside the clock of time, about a village scene. Underneath, in Yiddish:] Ay, bless God, it is already six years [since Bella's death]——

country of my birth: The leading Yiddish writers in Soviet Russia were arrested in 1948.

5 sisters: Whether Chagall ever corresponded with his sisters after he left Russia in 1923 is not known. Yet he was always careful and never criticized the Soviet Union publicly, for fear of hurting them.

Marc Chagall in Vence to Abraham Sutzkever in Tel Aviv

Sutzkever toured all around Africa, when Israel had good relations with the African countries. He wrote a beautiful book of poetry based on this voyage. See the section "Elephants at Night" in A. Sutzkever, *Selected Poetry and Prose* (Berkeley: University of California Press, 1991).

Sept. 13, 1950

Dear friend Sutzkever,

Received your cable, is it from Africa? For the [Jewish] New Year. I also want to wish you happiness and health, as well as our whole nation, may they let us go on to live and create. Unfortunately, there are many uncircumcised people who want to drown each other. And though I paint Moses a lot, he can do nothing concrete. You just have to read it [the Bible] . . . But apparently the people don't read it and God knows what mischief they will do in the world.

But I do believe in the "trick" of our Land, and may its star be eternally strong. Amen.

I received the very warm letter and invitation from Minister [of Culture] Shazar. I gave it to be translated, so I , the "Goy," can understand it. And I answered him I hope I shall be well and come [to Israel] in the spring and, of course, with my daughter, without whom I am as without hands. She has to take care of the exhibition that the museum plans and other things. It would be good if the trip could combine "pleasure" and work. If they are talking about "walls," I must see it and measure beforehand and see not to waste many years before the work starts. And I would like you, my dear, to be in the Land when (if) we arrive.

In the meantime, I was happy to receive your G.K. [*Goldene Keyt*], the last issue, that gets richer and richer in content and *your* poems, after I saw and heard you personally, are even closer to me. They are distinguished in the issue, as I wrote to you once, as *painting in literature*, but in true painting there is also literary content, and rarely the opposite.

Thank you for Dr. Kloomok's article with the illustrations, which, I think, should have been deeper. It is my fault. I am worried about Bella's two books. If they are published, I am worried, *how will the text look in translation?* It must be in *her girlish, Vitebsk style and not otherwise*. Who could *oversee* it? *If Yiddish, there are her two books*, if Hebrew—who? One must be careful before the printing. Six years past since her death and I am restless. Though she still lies alone in America, I would have liked her books in Israel to be her gravestone.

Gamzu wrote to me (he still has his project of a Hagadah [illustrated by Chagall]) that somebody in Tel Aviv is publishing an album of me. Though Jews are a people of genius, I still think it would be better to ask me or Ida what about and how to print. Please, sniff it out. And how is your *Siberia* book advancing? Ida told me that the paper for you was sent out. Please send me the trial mockup of the drawings. I think, it should appear as a fine deluxe edition, and if you need, I could sign several copies together with you (as is customary abroad among the Gentiles), and as for Bella's books: "measure seven times, before you cut the cloth."

Well, I pestered you too much. I am staying now in a little village near Grasse, in a room. Seeking rest (for Virginia) and quiet, but here you can hear anyway: roosters, children, distant honking of cars and various "zvuki" [Russian: sounds], which is typical for the earth we live on. Soon we go back to Vence.

Be well,

Your devoted/   Marc Chagall

Margin notes:

I, the "Goy": The invitation was, obviously, in Hebrew, which Shazar assumed Chagall knew; but Chagall was ignorant, hence a "goy."

"walls": Sutzkever assumes those are the walls of the Knesset; was it contemplated so early?

Marc and Ida Chagall.

Hilla Rebay in Green Farms, Connecticut, to Marc Chagall in Vence

30 September 1950

[French] Dear Marc Chagall,

A thousand thanks for the drawing with such pretty colors that you gave me. I am always happy to receive a work from you, which is going to adorn the Chagall section which we will have in the modern museum that we will build when conditions are favorable.

We have two million at our disposal to build. Unfortunately, Mr. Guggenheim's death on November 3, 1949, has delayed the project, but not for long, I am sure.

Thanks also for your kind invitation to the south of France. I was in Paris for only one day and two nights, and it is extraordinary what I could do in that little bit of time. I have so many responsibilities and so much work which doesn't allow me to pay more extensive visits to another country nor do I have time to spend coming to see you.

Do you stay in the south of France all the time and never come to Paris, and what is happening to your house in Montmorency? If I recall, I heard that you remarried and that you even have a little boy. Tell me if this is true because I will believe it only if you tell me so yourself.

If you could see nature around me with the trees in such a yellow and red color, I know that you would be thrilled. I love the mountains very much because the clouds and the mist always offer eternal changes and I very much like to see the clouds on the mountains in contrast with all the colors of the trees. So, I direct the museum by telephone and letters, even though I work from 2 o'clock in the morning until afternoon on correspondence and articles and other tedious things. At least in the afternoon I find a little time for my painting.

Have you seen my work on paper [?] in Paris? I will send you a drawing in green watercolors, which might give you a bit of pleasure.

My best wishes for your health and your art.

Sincerely,

Hilla Rebay

Ida Chagall in Paris to Louis Stern in New York

a house: In December 1949, Ida bought a house on the Quai de l'Horloge, with an entrance on Place Dauphine, in the Ile de la Cité in Paris.

September 30, 1950

[English] Dear Louis,

I feel so ashamed for my silence. To arrange a house, to move in, to expect you in this new home, is not an excuse. I dreamed about you the other night: You were saying: What for coming to Europe when Europe is filled with frightfull people. Come and I will tell you so many news that you will dream also.

How are you? How is your health? What made you not to come? I put you aside a plate of ceramic. Father in general is not[6] eager to disperse them, as he wants to gather as large a collection as possible, but I think yours is very beautifull. What to do about it?

My portrait reproduced in Katja Ganeff? Matisse donated this drawing to a Palestine fond [sic]. He did put my name on it: "May be it will bring more money like that" did he say. So Katja Ganeff bought it. But I do not know if she payed more . . .

I was very anxious to speak with you about a movie being prepared on father and probably in colour. A movie on his life but only through his pictures. Done by the same people that made the Van Gogh, Guernica, Toulouse-Lautrec. Do you think it would be possible for you to send photographs black and white of your Chagall-Collection? You have pictures which I have never seen and they probably must be as important as "La Lampe".

Of course, after one year silence, to ask you this is not done in good society, but the movie is going to be done.

I think it is enough for to-day, especially that I wonder if you will ever answer me.

Palestine: At that time, Palestine meant the Jewish community in Palestine and, after 1948, the State of Israel. The word "fond" (fund) is in the original.

With love and souvenirs

Ida

My new address: 22 Rue Dauphine/Paris Ie

Marc Chagall in Vence to Abraham Sutzkever in South Africa

Vence. Oct. 1950

[Yiddish] Dear Sutzkever,

You got yourself entangled in such a far away thicket. It is your university of life. Mainly observe the animals and the landscape. Is there a different sky and clouds there? and is there a "different" type of Jews, though all the types are already gathered in Israel.

I think I shall come for a while to Israel. But I hope you'll be there? It was a real pleasure to hold the No. 6 of G.K. [*Goldene Keyt*] with ever richer material (I wrote you about it in Israel).

Tomorrow I am going for a week to Italy—invited to Bergamo, where I have an exhibition. But with each trip I tremble a bit, though Virginia is driving the car. Is it old age, or the windy air, is it psychological, doubts about [my] art—

I want just to work. How many years will it take me to make something big? Meanwhile I am waiting until our Jews get together and agree as soon as possible on the "Walls" that finally have to be made, either in our parliament or somewhere else. Meantime, the Goyim won't let go and pressure me to make walls for them.

How is your *Siberia* book? It must be beautiful. But you'll see it when you return. And Bella's books? Poor Ida, who travels with me to Italy, toils over my things. She has to prepare my exhibition in Israel with somebody (I don't know who), she works with the director who is making a film about me (my art), she toils with the books. Oh, my daughter, she is the most beautiful wave that washes everything of [my table] (and the little Dovidl supports . . .)

Be well for the New Year (and later). I embrace you, regards from my family,

Your/   Marc Chagall

Marc Chagall in Vence to the Opatoshus in New York

"Les Collines"/Vence/(A.-M.)   24 Oct 1950

(prostate . . .): In parentheses and three dots, for he would not mention an unmentionable disease aloud. Chagall underwent two prostate operations with a two-month interval in a clinic in Nice, and he could not attend the exhibit of his work in Zurich in November 1950.

[Yiddish] Dear friends, forgive me for not writing in a long while. You know very well it doesn't mean we don't often think about you. Busy with various works, paintings, exhibitions, and so on, and now I think of going to Paris to a doctor, and I think I may allow them (with Ida's and Virginia's agreement) to operate on me (prostate . . .) I hope that my eternal guardians in heaven will, as always, protect me.

How are you. You are [?] because you sent me a journal from YIVO with an article by [Rachel] Vishnitzer. It reads more "serieux" than she looks. Who knows—maybe she does understand art, or better—feels.

Rachel Vishnitser-Bernstein (Wischnitzer, 1892–?) was an historian of Jewish art and the wife of Jewish historian Mark Vishnitser. With her husband, she edited an illustrated journal for art criticism in two parallel series: *Rimon* (in Hebrew) and *Milgroym* (in Yiddish), in Berlin, 1922–1924. During 1934–1938, she was Director of the Jewish Museum in Berlin, and lived in America from 1940. Rachel Vishnitser published books on Jewish art and synagogue architecture. She wrote a review in Yiddish of L. Venturi's book *Marc Chagall* (New York: Pierre Matisse, 1945).[7]

Touching up a lithograph.

I was more than moved by the poetic (for he is a poet!) about the situation of the Moscow [Yiddish] poets. But I got here from Michel [Rapaport-Gordey] who recently came from Moscow as the correspondent for a [French] newspaper. He told me that Fefer is alive, and was seen (by a man from our State) a few weeks ago. Michel saw Mrs. Fefer who lives in their apartment. Of course it is bad, the fact [of the arrest] itself. It is bitter even if they are still alive and there is no justification for those actions.

And unfortunately my tongue is blocked when I think about my living (who knows) sisters . . . over there. My hands are tied when I think about my poor friends and my sisters—even more unfortunate.

—Recently (Kloomok) sent me a clipping by Aharon Zeitlin from the *Morgen Zhurnal* of 6 Oct 1950, titled "Marc Chagall, Church-Painter." I did not think a Jewish poet-man could stoop so low and cover his heart which is not trembling much with a foot. You know yourself how many doubts and how many motivations I told you.

It is bitter that someone wants to teach me Jewishness and confuses me with Sh. Asch.

I don't know, if I have the strength I may write a few lines. But the barking of Mayzel[8] and Zeitlin and others is chilling.

We were in Italy. Bergamo, Venezia, where I exhibit (Bergamo) and tomorrow we go to Paris and see what the doctor says.

> I kiss you both from my heart. How are you? / Your devoted
>
> Chagall

from our State: Apparently, an Israeli Communist (Meir Vilner?) who certified he saw Fefer.

Zeitlin: Aharon Zeitlin, a major Yiddish and Hebrew poet in Poland; he lived in the U.S. from 1940. Zeitlin wrote a weekly column in the Yiddish orthodox paper *Morgen-Zhurnal* in New York, where he attacked Chagall for painting images of Jesus Christ.

Marc Chagall: For the Slaughtered Artists!

This poem was published as an introduction to an album-almanac, *Undzere Farpaynikte Kinstler (Our Martyred Artists)*, edited by Hersh Fenster (Paris, 1951). A memorial book for eighty-four Jewish artists who lived in France and were killed by the Nazis, it includes a short biography of each artist and sample reproductions of their work. An additional list of 138 Jewish artists from Poland, Hungary, and Czechoslovakia, who lived in Paris and perished, is appended.

[Yiddish]

Did I know them all? Did I visit
their atelier? Did I see their art
close up or from afar?
Now I walk out of myself, out of my years,
I go to their unknown grave.
They call me. They pull me into their grave—
me—the innocent—the guilty.
They ask me: Where were you?
—I fled . . .

They were led to the baths of death
where they knew the taste of their sweat.
Then they saw the light
of their unfinished paintings.
They counted the years unlived,
which they cherished and waited for
to make their dreams come true—
not slept through, overslept.
In their head, they sought and found
the nursery where the moon, ringed
with stars, promised a bright future.
They young love in the dark room, in the grass,
on mountains and in valleys, the chiseled fruit
doused in milk, covered with flowers,
promised them paradise.
The hands of their mother, her eyes
accompanied them to the train, to the distant
fame.

I see them: trudging alone in rags,
barefoot on mute roads.
The brothers of Israels, Pissarro and
Modigliani, our brothers—pulled with ropes
by the sons of Dürer, Cranach,
and Holbein—to death in the crematoria.
How can I, how should I, shed tears?
They have been steeped in brine—
the salt of my tears.
They have been dried out with mockery, and I
lose my last hope.

How should I weep,
when every day I heard:
the last board is torn off my roof,
when I am too tired to make war
for the piece of earth
where I rested,
where I will later be laid to sleep.
I see the fire, the smoke and the gas
rising to the blue cloud,
turning it black.
I see the torn-out hair, the pulled-out teeth.
They overwhelm me with my rabid
palette.
I stand in the desert before heaps of boots,
clothing, ash and dung, and mumble my
Kaddish.

And as I stand—from my paintings
the painted David descends to me,
harp in hand. He wants to help me
weep and recite chapters
of Psalms.
After him, our Moses descends.
He says: Don't fear anyone.
He tells you to lie quietly
until he again engraves
new tablets for a new world.

The last spark dies out,
the last body vanishes.
Calm, as before a new deluge.
I stand up and say farewell to you,
I take the road to the new Temple
and light a candle there
before your image.

Paris 1950

Louis Stern in New York to Marc Chagall and Virginia Haggard in Vence

444 East 52nd Street, NYC   November 30, 1950

[English] Dear Maître & Virginia:

I should have written you long before this, certainly as soon as it became apparent that I would not be in Europe this past summer. I didn't do so during the summer for I was vacationing—traveling around in my car. When the vacation season was over, I delayed from time to time, and then suffered from lethargy and inertia, always, however, thinking of you, and wondering whether your plans to come to the United States, as mentioned in your letter of May the 26th, would materialize. I hope that you will let me know if they do, so that I will not be too far away when you get here.

I have had reports from Bernard and Becky Reis and Minna Harkavy, and several others, whose names I don't at present remember, who had seen you and been with you in Vence. I envy them, and I hope that someday soon I will have the pleasure of visiting you in your beautiful situation.

Recently a lady who was entirely unknown to me, and apparently to any of you, was good enough to bring me the Chagall Céramique—I am thrilled and delighted with it. It is beautiful and exciting, and above all, typically Chagall, which is most important to me. Thank you very much. I wish you could see it hanging in a very prominent spot at the entrance to the Chagall room, attracting the curiosity and attention of everyone who comes here.

You will be interested to know that I have acquired a perfect set of *Mein Leben* which has with it a fascinating history.[9] It came here from Japan, where it had been since 1920 or thereabouts, when it was purchased in Berlin by a Japanese, who was probably in the diplomatic service of his country. He sent it to the United States to realize some dollars to help a son or relative who is at school here. The set is in a vellum case, and fills a niche in my collection.

I have, of course, bought all the books that have the name Chagall attached, including *Toward Daybreak*.[10] Quatre Chemins has written me that you made a drawing and inscribed the recent publication, *Visages de Chopin*.[11] I, of course, appreciate this very much. It has not yet reached here, but I thank you in advance.

Mr. Kerr of Knoedler's showed me a number of recent Chagalls which are beautiful and striking in design and colour. They tell me that they plan to have an exhibition in April, to which I am looking forward.

Mr. and Mrs. Philip James of the Arts Council of Great Britain were here the other evening. When they came here [added in handwriting: they do not know] whom, or where, they were visiting and both were astonished when they found *Dans la Nuit* and *La Tourterelle*. It then developed that James corresponded with

Philip James: Director of Art, the Arts Council of Great Britain, curated Chagall's exhibition in the Tate Gallery, London, February 4–29, 1948.

me when the Chagall Exhibition was staged at the Tate, and he was kind enough to send me two or three copies of the catalogue. We both enjoyed the experience of meeting each other. Another guest that same evening was a Mme. Marcell Berr de Turique, who told me she was an art critic, she told me that she knew you and your work, and is a great admirer of yours. Her name is a difficult one, and I asked her to write it for me; as soon as I saw it in black and white, I asked her if she was not the author of a book on Raoul Dufy—she was delighted when I showed her my copy of her book, which is now out of print, and of which she herself no longer has a copy.

The Museum of Modern Art is having an exhibition of [Chaim] Soutine. It is said to be the first one man show that Soutine has had in the United States. Unfortunately it does not correctly represent Soutine. There are, of course, some good examples; but of those who know Soutine's Oeuvre, all are of the opinion that it is a crying shame that he is so poorly represented. To show you how carelessly it was done—I have three Soutines, and the Museum didn't even look at them.

Knoedler's had a Lautrec show of the collection from the Musée d'Albi. I didn't think that collection contains many examples of the best of Lautrec. So far as I am personally concerned, the outstanding thing in the exhibition was a small portrait of Lautrec by Vuillard. It is an amazingly good picture, and in scale it is so fitting for Lautrec, for the picture is very small, almost dwarfed, as he was, but gay in colour. I wish I could acquire that little picture.

Wildenstein's is currently having a Goya exhibit for the benefit of the Art Department of New York University. There too, there are some fine examples of Goya, but in the main I would not call it a first class exhibit of Goya.

I suppose the Reiss told you that they are in some interested in the Louis Carré Gallery. Becky is running the Gallery, for Carré seems to be in Paris. It so happens that most of the painters they handle touch me not at all.

Rosengart: Gallery owner and Chagall collector.

I recently saw a watercolour, a small version of *Au dessus de Vitebsk*. I am very suspicious of the picture, and so told the dealer, Albert Duveen. I know that there are two versions of the picture, one which is now in the Museum of Modern Art, and the earlier one, painted in Vitebsk, which is in the hands of your friend Siegfried Rosengart of Lucerne. But did you ever do a small version of it in watercolour or gouache? If you did, please let me know—it is claimed to be owned by someone who lives in the West. I was given his name, but cannot remember it now. He has a letter from you written in Yiddish, which has been photostated, and is being hawked around in order to help the sale of the picture. Do you recall any such instance? If you do, it is important that you write to me and tell me about it, so that if it is a fake, I can stop the sale. If it is authentic, I might want to buy it. To make it more suspicious, the dealer was supposed to come here to compare signatures. After making an appointment, he failed to show up, and I haven't heard from him since. Sometime ago I understand that

Working on lithographs at the Atelier Mourlot.

Pierre Matisse had seen it and declared it a fraud. At any rate, let me hear about it, if you can possibly place writing a letter to someone who lives out west in the United States.

I have often wondered whether you finally decided to do the baptistry in that church in the South of France. I should like to hear about it.

I am writing this letter without any special order, dictating as the subject matter comes to mind, so I hope you will forgive me if the letter seems somewhat disorganized.

We here are very much concerned with the world situation, especially with the war in Asia. It is a dangerous state of affairs, and may lead to great catastrophe. It is only the strong desire that is in all of us to avoid such a tragedy that makes me feel that a way out will be found; but I fear that with the tactics employed by

Soviet Russia, that even if the current crisis is solved, something else will happen which will keep us on the anxious bench for a long long time.

At this moment I don't know of anything else that should go into this letter. Perhaps it is long enough—I do hope that you, Virginia, will find time to drop me a line and tell me about the news on your side, and especially as to whether or not you are coming to the U.S.A.

I send affectionate regards to both of you, / Sincerely yours

Louis E. Stern

Ida Chagall in Nice to Louis Stern in New York

Nice 7/XII 1950

[English] Dear Louis

operated: On December 7, 1951, Chagall was operated on in Nice for his prostate. He had to wait two months between the first and second operation.

I am writing you from father's room. He has been operated this morning. He was quite sick all these last months and the operation had to be done quickly. All is well so far. I pray God that father will feel better soon and relieved (prostate).

He was glad to receive your letter and happy that you like his ceramic. He waited to learn if you do like it or not, as he wants to offer it to you. Consider it as a too early Christmas gift. If father will feel better improving, I will fly to Zurich and come back here.

Zurich: Chagall's exhibition in the Zurich Kunsthaus, December 9, 1950– January 28, 1951.

I saved you a poster for Zurich as it is a masterpiece done by Mourlot. I forget what you wrote me lately, I am so tired and nervous in this room of a clinic.

Mourlot: Fernand Mourlot, the owner of a prominent lithography workshop in postwar France, produced all of Chagall's lithographs.

Virginia sends you her best regards and will write soon.

But I wanted you to know that father was happy to get your letter.

Love   Ida

Marc Chagall in a hospital in Nice to Virginia Haggard in Vence

[undated] Friday

[French] My dear,

I want to kiss you so much.
    Till Sunday morning
    Nice

Yours

Marc

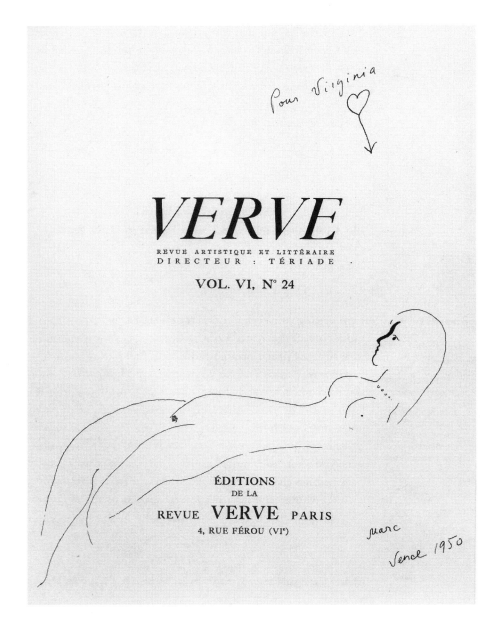

Pour Virginia

VERVE

REVUE ARTISTIQUE ET LITTÉRAIRE
DIRECTEUR : TÉRIADE .

VOL. VI, N° 24

ÉDITIONS
DE LA
REVUE **VERVE** PARIS
4, RUE FÉROU (VIᵉ)

Marc
Vence 1950

"For Virginia," Vence 1950: Chagall's drawing on an issue of Verve, edited by Tériade.

Virginia Haggard in Vence to Louis Stern in New York

"Les Collines"/Vence/(A.M.)   Dec 11th [1950]

[English] My dear Louis,

Marc was most happy to get your long letter. It arrived just in time to cheer him up before his operation. That was last Thursday. Now he is making very good progress & the doctor is very pleased with him. He is courageous, now that the worst is over, and he only thinks of getting back to work. He was so pleased to hear that you liked his ceramic because he wanted to make a present of it to you.

Marc is happy to hear everything you have to say about events in the art world in New York, about the Soutine exhibition, the Lautrec & the Goya. Also about your new purchase, the Mein Leben portfolio. About the watercolour, "Audessus de Vitebsk," he thinks it would be best to send a photo of this before committing himself as to whether it is a fake or not. Do you know if it was painted on cardboard. Is it in gouache or watercolour? And how large is it? Marc can't remember who the person living in the West could be, nor can he remember having written anyone there in Yiddish, but it is possible that he did. What do you think of the picture yourself? Is it good?

Dr. Kloomok has had one heart[ache] after another about his book. You know that it was accepted by the Philosophical Library (editor Runes) and that Dr. Kloomok was required to pay up out of his own pocket all the money needed for its publication. This he did, and most foolishly made no contract at all. It seems that Runes has cheated him and the book seems to have fallen through. But we do not know all the details. Meanwhile Marc made an etching especially for Dr. Kloomok's book, so that he could sell it as a "de luxe" volume & get his money back. He sent Kloomok over 50 prints (I have forgotten the exact number) and coloured many of them by hand. It was a present he made to Kloomok because Kloomok has to get some of that money back (he is penniless). So he is selling the prints. He has sold three to the Museum of Modern Art & is trying to arrange an exhibition. Marc suggested he go & see you & ask your advice. Would you mind? There may be some legal way out of the muddle. Marc would be so grateful if you could give him a word of advice, if it's not too late.

How is your health and what are your latest plans for coming to Europe? I suppose conditions in the world today hardly permit the making of plans far ahead.

Marc has neither accepted nor refused to do the paintings in the church at Assy. He hasn't quite made up his mind, but I have a feeling it will be "no."

We both send our love, also Ida who is in Switzerland for the opening of Marc's exhibition. She's flying back here tomorrow.

Yours, as ever, Virginia

Louis Stern in New York to Virginia Haggard in Vence

444 East 52nd Street   December 15, 1950

[English] Dear Virginia:

It was very kind of you, especially under the circumstances, to take time to write to me. The day before receiving your letter I had a short note from Ida, so that I knew of the operation. I am, of course, relieved and happy to hear of Marc's good progress. In the summer of 1946, when he and I were in Paris at the same time, about the time David was being born, I strongly advised Marc to have this operation, but he apparently preferred to suffer, rather than submit. Here in the United States this sort of an operation is an everyday affair, and quite a number of my friends have undergone it with successful results, the sole difference being that some have been discharged from the hospital in two weeks, and others take longer. I hope you will insist on Marc staying in the hospital as long as necessary—until he is completely recovered.

Dr. Kloomok was here a week or ten days ago, and showed me the coloured etching, which is stunning. He also told me of having received $200 from the Museum of Modern Art. When he came here, he didn't ask advice, and perhaps, at this point, advice would be of no value. Unless there has been a complete change, the book is coming out, although there is going to be no de luxe copy, as he is selling the etchings separately. I don't approve of the method, for it is imposing on the good will of Marc's friends, and in my opinion, selling that good will for petty sums. I find Dr. Kloomok rather difficult to deal with, for more than a year ago I had advised him that I had taken the matter up with Weyhe, and he had told me he was interested in a de luxe edition. I spent a great deal of time reading the manuscript, suggesting corrections in some of the stilted Yiddish English. When he came here, he never made mention of that, and treated me as another possible client to buy one of Marc's prints. It is my feeling, based on years of dealing with people, that he is crying poverty, and soliciting Marc's sympathy. At any rate, it is now too late to be of service to him, and what interests me more, to the proper publication and distribution of the book—but he is difficult, and life is too short. Moreover, he probably doesn't like me too much, for I was quite frank with him in some of my comments.

In accordance with your suggestion, I am enclosing a photograph of the version of *Audessus de Vitebsk* which is now in my possession. The picture is printed on cardboard. As far as I am able to judge, it has oil as well as other mediums—I may be wrong in this.

The suspicion which I expressed in my first letter rested largely on the unusual regularity of the signature—the *Marc* especially, the *M* being different from almost any one I have seen. Also the foreground of the snow aroused some doubts, but upon re-examination and reflection I feel differently about this, and no longer doubt the picture's genuineness.

I will appreciate it very much if you will return the photograph to me as well as the photostatic copy of the letter in Yiddish, by airmail, for they don't belong to me. I will be responsible for the postage.

Apparently the man to whom the letter was addressed was named Fenster, and he lived in Tulsa, Oklahoma.

Gershon Fenster (1895–1947), born in Kovno, Lithuania, went with his wife to Tulsa, Oklahoma after World War I, joined the family business, and did very well indeed. He had a *yeshiva* education from Lithuania, was a secular Zionist and was interested in intellectual matters. He corresponded with Chagall in Paris in the 1920s or 1930s and built a collection of contemporary American paintings and modern Jewish artists. After his death, his widow sold the Chagall painting to Louis Stern. Part of his collection is in the Fenster Museum of Jewish Art in Tulsa.[12]

With the return of the photograph and the copy of the letter—assuming the picture to be genuine—I should like you to ask Marc to give me the answers to the following questions:

1. When was it painted? The first version, which is in Switzerland, was painted in 1914, and has the word *Vitebsk* in Russian in the left hand corner. The second version, in the Museum of Modern Art, is dated 1915–1920. I assume that the 1915 is a mistake, as Marc must have forgotten that he painted the other in 1914. Query: When was this one painted, before, after, in the middle, or what?

2. The exact medium used, if he can remember it.

3. Has it ever been in anyone's possession, other than Marc's, and then Fenster's?

4. From the correspondence I take it that Fenster bought it direct from Marc, if so can he remember how much Fenster paid for it? The picture now belongs either to an estate, or to one of the heirs, and the cost has some bearing on the price that they will want for it, for if everything is satisfactory, I intend to negotiate for its acquisition.

5. It has a label on the back which is not in Marc's handwriting. It may be Bella's or Ida's. It reads as well as I can make out "des environs de la ville". Was this Marc's title for the picture?

The tablets of Moses, "For Virginia on our fifth anniversary—Marc/Vence 1950." Drawing on an old English Bible that Marc and Virginia bought in a flea market in Nice.

Will you please tell Marc that I deeply appreciate the gift of the ceramique. Dr. Kloomok told me of having received some photographs of other ceramiques on biblical subjects. If any of them are for sale, I would be very much interested in *buying* one.

You didn't say anything about traveling to the United States. If and when Marc gets here I want to discuss with him a project for my Chagall room—but that can wait until you all get here, or until I get to Europe.

For Ida: I appreciate your saving a poster of the Zurich Chagall Exhibition for me. I should also like to have a copy of the catalogue. One of these days, soon, I will write you a separate letter.

I am sure that Marc's progress will continue to be good, but please don't bother him with all these questions if you think it will tire him.

With best wishes to all of you for the New Year, and with affectionate regards, I am

Sincerely yours

[Louis Stern]

Virginia Haggard in Nice to Louis Stern in New York

Clinique St. Antoine, Nice   December 21st 1950

[English] Dear Louis,

We were very pleased to get your long letter. Marc is getting on very well and will be back home for the new year when Ida will come also. He has been working quite a lot in bed, making sketches for ceramics. They promise to be very fine. He has made sketches for sculptures too. I am sure he could do wonderful things in sculpture and he intends to start soon. On some of his latest plates the designs are in relief and they have great strength. There are some beautiful biblical ones and I shall send you photos of them as soon as I can. At present all the biblical ones are in an exhibition of Religious Art in the Modern Museum in Paris and I don't know if Marc will want to part with any of them unless he makes more.

He will have a new incentive to work at ceramics in the shape of a new kiln that is going to be installed in Vence and operated by Marc's own potter who worked with him in Antibes.

Today I sent you the photo of Fenster's picture and the photostat copies of Marc's letter. Marc remembers Fenster very well now. He never met him personally but carried on a correspondence with him. By the way the letters are written in Bella's handwriting and signed by Marc. Fenster was quite a touching character, very cultivated and idealistic. He felt so completely isolated in Tulsa and wanted more than anything a picture by Chagall which would console him a little. He wanted a Jewish subject. He had a certain sum of money at his disposition (Marc can't remember how much) and Bella and Marc chose this picture which one of two or three variations done in gouache or wash in about *1925*. The two paintings of which you spoke are much bigger and their treatment is quite different.

The medium is gouache with perhaps a little oil paint added. But Marc is not sure of this. The picture never belonged to anyone other than Fenster. The title was no doubt written in Bella's hand. It was "Aux Environs de la Ville". This is a Vitebsk suburb. The church with blue cupolas occurs in many of Marc's pictures. Perhaps it would interest you to have Fenster's letters. I don't know at all if they still exist but there is a whole trunk full of old letters waiting to be sorted out and it will be some time before we can find them. If only I could read Yiddish! I really believe I shall have to learn.

We are sorry to have troubled you with the Kloomok case and we quite realize that it is very difficult to do anything.

We wish you all the best for 1951 and hope to see you on either side of the Atlantic.

Affectionately yours   Virginia

Virginia Haggard in Nice to the Opatoshus in New York

Clinique St. Antoine Ave. Durante, Nice A.M.   Dec 22nd [1950]

[English] Dearest Adele and Oppen,

Your letter came yesterday and Marc was in tears while he read it. Your dream about Bella made him sob. He said "you see, she thinks of me always and I haven't done a thing for her. I have left her in America without any proper tombstone." And I comforted him as best I could and told him that perhaps fate had willed it so, because we can't be sure that we shall not go back to America again some day and anyway our little house is still there. You must have dreamed your dream at about the time he was operated—on the 7th. By now he is quite past all danger and really on the way to complete recovery. If you saw him all your worries would vanish. He has such a young, rosy face. He works incessantly in bed, making sketches for ceramics and sculptures which he hopes soon to execute. They promise to be exceptionally fine. I wish you could see his biblical ceramics. Lately he made a very large plate with a design in relief of Moses at the spring. It is wonderful. I long for you to see them all.

I am so glad he is rid of his prostate condition which caused him much apprehension and made him irritated and nervous. Now he feels young again and not afraid to travel. I am glad to see him so hopeful and enterprising again, as if

I have left her in America: A combination of Chagall's poor-boy stinginess and his fear of death. He expressed a similar compunction about not erecting a proper grave for his parents in Vitebsk. A rather simple stone was placed on Bella's grave, with her name in Yiddish and English, the dates, and two hands in a gesture of blessing.

he were a new man. And he is not yet out of bed! Before, each time he read the papers he became depressed and hopeless. Of course there is reason to be depressed, and even more so now. Heaven knows what's in store for us. But before, when he thought of a possible occupation of France by the Soviets he was fatalistic and defeatist. He used to say, "I don't care if they take me to Siberia." Now he says "maybe we could go to America." That gives me hope that he will want to save himself so that he can go on working. Of course nobody knows where the safe place in the world will be but at any rate America could not possibly be occupied by the Soviets and it would be better to perish in a war than be deprived of one's liberty.

Recently Marc had an invitation from the Art Center of Louisville, Kentucky, to go and live there and work for one year. The idea is not displeasing at all to Marc. He still has a certain nostalgic feeling for America.

Dearest Oppen, this is a birthday letter to you and we send all our love with it and wish you many more happy birthdays. Love to you too, dear Adele.

Yours

Virginia

Virginia Haggard in Nice to Bernard Reis in New York

Clinique St. Antoine, Nice   December 26th 1950

[English] My dear Bernard,

Your letter just arrived. Thankyou for all your kindness and trouble. Tell Becky that she is very *sweet* to send us packages and we feel that she is much too good to us and that we don't deserve it. As for telling you what to send us, that I cannot do! We seem to have all we need and you have already been so kind.

I have just written to Kloomok. Marc is very much surprised to hear that the book *will* be published and he is hurt and rather angry with Kloomok for selling the prints. Firstly he didn't ask Marc's permission and, after all, Marc gave him the engravings especially for inclusion in the books that Kloomok would receive as his share of the edition. This edition was not originally intended to be a limited edition as far as Marc understood, but an ordinary, well printed & fairly handsome book with a cover in colour (which Marc also gave Kloomok for nothing) and the addition of an engraving coloured by hand would make it a "de luxe" book which would sell for a good price. Marc is upset by the whole thing and I have written Kloomok telling him so. Marc asks him not to sell any more & to explain why the engravings cannot be included in the edition. If they are, there should be a notice printed in the books to the effect that the *frontispiece is an original engraving by Chagall* etc. There should be some sort of a contract and I have asked Kloomok to ask your advice on this subject. The selling of so many coloured engravings is bad for Marc's pictures and Knoedler, who is soon to have an exhibition would resent this, no doubt. Also Kloomok talked of trying to exhibit the engravings. This is ridiculous. No one ever heard of an exhibition of one single engraving and it would certainly not be a good thing for Marc. I cannot understand why Kloomok didn't ask Marc's permission before peddling them round the town.

Thankyou so much for talking to a future tenant of High Falls. I suppose he is the same as the one who asked for a year's lease. By now you will have got my letter saying that a year is too long. In this case naturally we cannot ask the tenant to take care of the repairs. Probably the best thing to do is to get the repairs done, put the house in good shape and then rent it for a few months at a time. Marc and I both feel that it would be wise to keep that house and make it easy to come and live there, if necessary, in a few months time. No one knows what may happen. Marc is suddenly filled with a great desire to go on working and being rid of his prostate trouble feels safer travelling. If ever France became a dangerous place to live in because of war or occupation Marc thinks he would like to go back to High Falls.

Victor tells me that he cannot do the repair jobs himself and I would like a contractor to give us an estimate on the job to be done. Do you know of a good one? Maybe Victor had better find me one on the spot. I want the house painted inside (all the paper taken off) and asbestos shingles put on the outside, they last longer than paint, in fact they last forever. And of course the roofs, water heater, cellar, garden and road all have to be taken care of. Then we could rent for a fairly good price.

Marc is getting on well but it takes a long time and he longs to be home.

All our love to you both and many good wishes for a happy New Year.

Yours,/   Virginia

Virginia Haggard in Vence to Bernard Reis in New York

Les Collines   Vence A.M.   January 3rd 1951

[English] My dear Bernard,

I expect you will by now have got my letter saying that we think it would not be wise to rent the house for more than a few months at a time. We would be willing to rent on a month-to-month basis as a furnished house, only to have someone live there and keep the house warm in winter, but Purcell could light a fire there from time to time. We now think that the best plan is to have *all* the repairs done and not bother about renting for as long as the repairs last. Also we have decided to pay the mortgage. There is a sum of $4,000 to pay to the Kingston Savings Bank and I suppose there is no reason why we shouldn't pay it all right away and save needless expense ($200 a year for interest) and if Marc's money were blocked (frozen) in the U.S., he would not be able to pay mortgage, that is in case of war, etc. Don't you think it would be much better to pay it all up? I am going to write to the Kingston Savings Bank. Should the payment be made from Marc's bank direct to Kingston?

The international situation certainly is very serious, & Marc now thinks that it would be foolish not to go to USA if there was a chance of Russian occupation of France. We could live in High Falls. Even if he earned nothing we could live modestly on his savings there. Now, as you know, we neither of us have any re-entry permits, they have both expired. We are thinking of asking for visitors' visas and then if necessary getting an immigration visa later by crossing the frontier into Canada or Mexico. I don't know if there's any possibility of Marc's getting an immigration visa since he is on the Russian (Soviet) quota. I hope there won't be any difficulty in getting a visitor's visa. Now we want to ask you a great favour. May we use your name as a *guarantor*? Can you advise us of the best way to go about getting this visa? Of course I shall make an application at the American Embassy but if there should be any difficulty, perhaps you know of a way out.

First I must tell you of another application Marc made at this embassy just after the expiration of his re-entry permit. (He had asked for two extensions, staying away for two years altogether. He didn't ask for a third extension because it would have brought us up to November of last year and Marc knew very well that he would not be able to go to America before that, and he had been told at the American Embassy in Paris that third extensions were only given in very rare circumstances, such as serious illness etc.) So after the expiration of his re-entry permit he made an application at the Embassy in Nice for a "returning alien's permit." The embassy [= Consulate] in Marseille requested proof of his property in America and I sent him a tax receipt on the property. But all we got as a reply was a quota number for Marc as a Soviet citizen which was hardly hopeful.

I really think that something serious should be done *now* about going back to USA because later it might no longer be possible. What do you think about this?

Without being unnecessarily pessimistic, it is well to be on one's guard.

Again, we wish you and Becky a very happy new year.

Love from

Virginia

P.S. We are still in the clinic but only for one or two more days. That will make it nearly a month. Marc is well now.

Virginia Haggard in Vence to Bernard Reis in New York

"Les Collines"/Vence/(A.M.)   January 14th [1951]

[English] My dear Bernard,

Thankyou for your letter of January 8th, and all the trouble you are taking about the house in High Falls. I got a letter from Victor [Purcell] today enclosing the tax bill which seems inordinately high. I can't understand it at all, as last year, if I remember rightly, it was about $35. Do you think anything can be done about this? I am sending you the tax bill hoping you can do something about having it reduced, as Victor says he thinks it might be possible & it would be a pity to pay it and thus create a precedent so that each year the taxes will be higher. They're supposed to be paid by January 31st.

Victor tells me that he has got his son on to the job of painting etc. inside the house and that the rest will have to wait until the spring, also that the cost of putting asbestos shingles all over the two houses would be $550.00, an enormous price and not worth it, so it is best to have it painted.

Please could you pay the mortgage out of Marc's savings bank? Also the taxes, repairs, etc? I suppose all that is needed is for Marc to sign a slip so that you can draw the money for him.

Thankyou so much for saying that you will stand as guarantor for Marc & me. You are right in saying that it might not be wise and in that case M. De Rochemont or Louis Stern or Adolph Juwiler (a collector of Chagall and President of Olympic Radios) could stand instead and it is kind of you to suggest Mr. De Rochemont. It may not be necessary to have a guarantor. We are still trying to get "returning aliens" permits, which are given very often to one-time immigrants. It should be possible to get them, but these things are often slow & get stuck if one doesn't give them a push. So Ida suggested, on the advice of our friend, Doctor Dreyfus, to get in touch with a lawyer in America whom he knows, who is specialized in such cases. Marc made an application for the permit and sent tax receipts from High Falls to the consul in Marseille but nothing happened. You are quite right in saying that in Paris it might have had more effect. But perhaps if I send all particulars to the said lawyer he can hunt up the papers, which are probably now in Washington. Ida thinks it would be most unwise to ask Barr for letters or anyone else from the museum, unless it is for the purpose of immigrating to America for *good*. Barr was not very favorably disposed towards Marc until quite recently and it would be better to do without his help if possible or save it for an emergency. Tomorrow I am going to make my own application for a "returning alien's permit." If we can get those then a visitor's visa won't be necessary.

Ida is staying with us and Gea too. They send you their love.

Barr: Alfred H. Barr, Jr., Director of the Museum of Modern Art, New York.

All the "Boccacio" books have been confiscated in America by the censors because they are "pornographic." Tériade is quite worried. They will probably all be destroyed.

The film on Marc will be in black & white because of the difficulty of obtaining pictures. The scope will then be greatly enlarged, as only photographs will now be necessary.

Marc and I send you & Becky our love

Yours   Virginia

Louis Stern in New York to Virginia Haggard in Vence

February 2, 1951

[English] Dear Virginia:

Thanks for your letter of January 27th.

First with respect to the signature—I hope I didn't cause any trouble by my inquiry. The fact of the matter is that I must have close to a hundred of Marc's signatures on paintings, prints, and books, and the one on *Aux Environs de la Ville* is, with one exception, unlike any of the others. Curiously, your statement—"Marc's signature on pictures is often a little bit awkward, as if it had been signed by someone else" is the very reason why my curiosity with respect to this signature has been aroused, for there is nothing awkward about it. The Marc and the Chagall are on one line, the letters are even, and there is a straight line underneath, as distinguished from the usual curled line. However, since Marc says it is his signature, I am entirely satisfied. Even if it were Bella's signature, it would not be a "forgery". "Forgery" implies something fraudulent; in other words, signing done with intent to defraud someone, whereas, in this case, the signature, even if made by Bella, would have been done with Marc's knowledge and consent. There are undoubtedly many instances where artists have permitted others to sign their names. Offhand, I know that Zbrowski, Soutine's dealer, often signed Soutine's name to his pictures. One of my three Soutines is, I believe, signed not by Soutine, but probably by Zbrowski.—When I was in Highschool, in my early teens, I was in the habit of signing my father's name to checks and notes, not only with my father's knowledge and consent, but I believe with the Bank's knowledge, also.

I am glad to know that the *Fables de la Fontaine* is soon to be published. This is to advise you that I want one of the special editions—

"with a double set of prints, one coloured, one black and white"

Most, if not all, of the Chagall books in my library are early numbers of special de luxe editions. I have Copy #6 of the special edition of *Les Ames Mortes*, Copy #10 of the *Arabian Nights*, Copy #6 on Japan, of *Les Sept Peches Capitaux*, Copy #39 of *Maternite*, Copy #61 of *Ma Vie*, Copy #1 of *Rose des Vents*, Copy #II of *L'Orage Enchante*, and Copy #XXII of the Venturi book. Will you please ask Marc to have me and Chagall library in mind when picking out a set of coloured, as well as the black and white plates. It is my present intention to keep my Chagall collection of paintings and books together, and when I become an angel, it will pass on to some museum or other public institution.

In my Chagall room, the wall where the *Purim Feast* now hangs is approximately 5 1/2 by 3 1/2 feet, which I have reserved for a Chagall "mural" on canvas, which could be moved. I want Marc to think about it, and when we next see one another, I will have the details, and we can talk about it, and perhaps he will have some ideas on the subject.

I don't know of anything special that requires extending this letter other than to tell you that many of Marc's friends continually ask me about him.

With warm regards to you and to Marc, I am/Sincerely yours

Louis E. Stern

Virginia Haggard in Vence to Adele Opatoshu in New York

"Les Collines"/Vence/(A.M.)   February 11th, 1951

[English] Dearest Adele,

Don't be cross with me for not writing sooner. It's always the same story—thousands of varied occupations crowding the days and weeks and months besides a host of unprofitable but necessary duties.

How are my dear Opatoshus? What is Oppen working at? And how is your work, Adele—not too strenuous and still interesting? I hope so.

I have been having a lot of worries about my divorce. I started a divorce-suit—on the grounds of moral cruelty. In the USA that's easy but not so in England. I really never cared very much if I got a divorce or not and I had reason to suppose that one day my husband would give me his consent to David's adoption by Marc. But my father nagged me about it so much & then started the ball rolling by having his solicitor go & see my husband, finally I put in a petition. Now everything has turned out as badly as possible. First my husband got a lawyer to defend him then he retaliated by countersuing me asking for a divorce on grounds of adultery, damages from Marc for the sum of $1,500 *and* the custody of Jean. My instinct was the best and I wish I had stuck to it from the beginning. I would have let things slide for a while and tried to get around him somehow and catch him in a good mood. He is a double personality & he has real goodness, as well as real badness in him. The divorce suit has brought out all the blackest side of his nature. Now it is an all-out fight. My lawyer says I have good chances of winning, & so has Marc, but it will be a revolting business and I am most unhappy about it. Somehow I have a presentiment that even if I win it will not be an advantage.

But I'm not going to bother you any more with that.

Marc is in splendid health now, completely cured. I am so happy that all went well. The children are well too except that David has to have his tonsils out. Ida spent a couple of weeks with us at the beginning of January. She is still working like a demon & the more she works the more there is to do because she is building up her father's reputation and fame brings with it increased activity. Personally I think fame is greatly overrated. I don't see what it brings to Marc. As for Ida, she is spoiling her health. I often think of our little home in High Falls and remember our simple lives and how happy we were without people or noise. I miss it.

Dearest Adele give my love to the David [Opatoshu] family & if it is soon little Don's birthday give him a special kiss from us. What date is his birthday? Jean keeps meaning to write to you & thank you for her wonderful butterfly book, but she works so hard in school that she has very little time. She was top of her class last term & this term they have put her into the equivalent of high school & she is already second of her class. She will be eleven in April. I am going to take her away from school because she works too hard & is getting skinnier and skinnier. Besides I don't believe more than a quarter of what she learns is really useful information.

We send kisses to you both /All our love

Virginia

Virginia Haggard in Vence to Louis Stern in New York

"Les Collines"/Vence/(A.M.)   February 21st 1951

[English] Dear Louis,

Thankyou so much for your letter.

Marc is enthusiastic about your plan to have him do a mural for a corner of the Chagall room and he wonders if it might be a good idea to design a panel consisting of ceramic tiles. This is only a suggestion of course. His idea would be to make one large design which would be divided into several tiles about one or one and a half feet square, set into the wall. He has done a few of these tiles and they are really beautiful. He has made one tile (about 18" x 12") with brilliant glazes on a rough reddish brick. The colour does not cover the whole surface of the tile but allows the rough mat texture to show in places, making a very pleasing contrast. I know you would love the tile. It is very rich and exciting. Tiles are extremely durable and can be removed if necessary providing they are set into the wall with a special kind of plaster or mounted onto a board which itself is set into the wall. Of course tiles are difficult and costly to transport whereas a canvas can be rolled. Marc asks what subject is particularly near to your heart—Circus, Lovers, Flowers, Animals, Dancers, Musicians, . . . or what have you?

The exhibition in Zurich seems to have been a success but the one in Berne, according to Ida, is the best Chagall show ever held anywhere. As soon as we get extra copies of the two catalogues we shall send you some. I believe Robert is bringing you some posters.

Now the next event is the exhibition in Israel. This will probably take place in April or May. Ida wants to go to America before that because her re-entry permit expires in March, so you will be seeing her most probably. Marc says he believes that you offered at one time to send some of your pictures to the Israel exhibition. Now is the time to make definite plans and perhaps you are already in correspondence with Ida about the matter. Marc wonders if you ever thought of going to Israel yourself. He would be most happy to meet you there! Only his own pictures are going to the exhibition and of course pictures that belong to collectors in Israel. It would be wonderful, says Marc, to have some of your pictures, particularly the ones with Jewish subjects.

Marc has just received an Israel edition of the English Faber album on Chagall. It is done with considerably more taste and care than the Faber one and Marc thinks you might like to have it. It is published by MIKRA—STUDIO EDITIONS, TEL AVIV.

We send our love and hope to hear from you again soon.

With affectionate regards,

Virginia

[Russian] How are you? / Be well.

Your Marc / Sh.

Marc Chagall in Vence to the Opatoshus in New York

Vence 1951 28 Fevral [sic; Russian for February]

[Yiddish] Dear friends Opatoshu. Forgive me for not writing. Maybe if my life was more "organized," I would find time to write more and do many things. But that's how it is. I shall try to improve. I left the clinic long ago and feel much bet-

another operation:
A Yiddish joke to
describe strenuous
work: If you exert
yourself too much,
you'll get a *killah*
(hernia).

ter, thank God. I become a person, and paintings, thank God, are standing and waiting for me. But working on them, I can again get ready for another operation, they exhaust me. Now, today I go to Switzerland, back to Bern, where there is my large exhibition (it is coming to a close). Ida goes too, though she was there maybe five times. We have to show Virginia the very old pictures that were borrowed, and also see how they look in their old age. Then comes April and I have to (I hope to) go to Israel, where I am invited by the government and where my exhibition should be but only with my own pictures, without the borrowed ones (it's expensive), so I am more "afraid" of the Jews there than anywhere else.[13] But I have to overcome it. I think I shall not get exhausted (mainly from myself). Virginia will not go, only Ida.

[French] 15 March

[Yiddish] You see. Came back from Switzerland, caught the flu. Lying in bed. I am trying to postpone the exhibition in Israel and especially my voyage (it is hard after an operation). Idotchka hopes to get to New York to my (small) exhibition at "Knoedler's" and God knows where she will get the strength for it, because everything is on her shoulders.

Vitebsk book: Two
collective volumes,
in Hebrew and
Yiddish, of studies
and reminiscences
about the Jews in
Vitebsk appeared.[14]

About the project of the Vitebsk book, it is nice. Why can't they write to me like human beings. I am interested in it. What and how. Give them my address. From the project in Israel by a man from Vitebsk (I knew him, a close friend of Bella's father), I see that they want to turn the city into 3/4 activists of Judaism, while socially the city was 3/4 mystical, poetic, and artistic.

Ida Chagall in Paris to Louis Stern in New York

[Stationery: 22, Place Dauphine - Paris, 1er/Odéon 40-68]

22/3/51

[English] Dear Louis,

Thank you so much for your letter and copies included. I received your letter when I was about boarding a train to Bern, where I met father.

I am deeply sorry that you could not see the last exhibition. It was certainly the greatest exhibit of father, the best blended, the best proof of yesterday and tomorrow. You should have seen father looking for the first time since 40 years at pictures which, he thought, were lost! It was a great event!

As father was too tired after Bern and the doctors are forbidding him the trip to Israel; the government over there has decided to postpone his exhibition to next autumn. The decision came when I nearly gave the pictures over for shipping.

I plan to be in New-York on April second or 3rd by plane, and I hope sincerely that you will be in town. I am looking to it, I will stay in New-York for about 2 weeks I guess, and I will call you from my hotel right away.

With love,/   Ida

Virginia Haggard in Vence to the Opatoshus in New York

"Les Collines"/Vence/(A.-M.)   April 12th 1951

[English] My dearest friends,

Thank you a thousand times for the Kafka book! Oppen, you are a dear to think of me always. But why do you write "To Virginia, with admiration"? "Admiration" for what? I feel so utterly unworthy of you both. I write so seldom. Yes, I am a thoroughly bad girl. But oh! You can't imagine what an impossible life we lead. Sometimes I wish we were back in High Falls. We were quiet there and hardly anyone came to see us. Here, they come all day long, phone, write, pester us, accost us in the street. It isn't possible to get away from them.

But in spite of it all we are thriving. Marc is working on one of the most superb of his recent paintings, a huge "King David" red, yellow & black. It is beautiful. David and Jean are fine & happy. They go to school together. They have private lessons. David is learning how to read & write. How is little Don? Has he got around to letters yet? Tell me please when his birthday is. Jean got a present of a little birthday book and we want to write all our friends' names in it. I know that Adele's is in May, at least I think so, but no, maybe it's in April. Tell me when, please, and if it has already passed then many happy returns, darling Adele! I know that David [Opatoshu] always brings you a branch of lilac for your birthday and there are lilacs just beginning to bloom now. The garden is full of apple and cherry blossoms and long green grass. I have had a lawn planted in front of the house. Lawns are very rare in this part of the world but I do so love them.

I have also planted daffodils, hyacynths & tulips in clumps on the grass like wild flowers. It reminds me of an English garden.

Have you seen Ida yet? I expect you will be seeing her in a few days' time. She writes saying that you were in Canada for three days. How was the journey? Did you do something interesting there? Is there any chance at all of your coming over here? How lovely it would be if only you could!

We went to Switzerland for Marc's exhibition [in Bern]. I don't remember if I wrote to you since our return. We saw all Marc's old paintings that had been in Germany ever since 1914. They were sold by Walden of "Der Sturm" Gallery & Marc never got a penny for any of them or saw them again until the other day. It was quite a thrill for him to see them again and I was completely bowled over by them.

They are stupendous! There was a whole enormous room of them and I have never seen anything so impressive.

We are still talking of coming back to America, some time, for a visit. We can't get "returning alien's permits" but we can come back again on the quota as immigrants. The world is in such a horrid mess that I think it is wise to get busy and think about the possibility of returning to the U.S., although Marc is loath to think of moving again.

Write soon, dearest Oppen & Adele. Tell us how everything goes with you.

Many kisses from us all. / Your

Virginia

such a horrid mess: The war in Korea, the ideological tensions of the Cold War, and the rise of Communism in Europe were felt as a possible prelude to World War III.

CHAPTER NINETEEN

Second Trip to Israel: 1951

Second Trip to the Land of Israel

In 1931, Marc, Bella, and Ida Chagall traveled to Palestine, traversed the whole country, and were enchanted by the pioneering Jewish settlement of the land. During the 1930s and 1940s, several attempts were made to organize a Chagall exhibition at the new Tel Aviv Museum, yet Chagall had more "prestigious" offers and was worried about sending his valuable paintings to such a dangerous region. After the war, those plans were renewed. The idea became more concrete with the foundation of the State of Israel on May 15, 1948, and the armistice agreements of 1949.

A special institution was formed for this event: the Association of Israeli Museums, including the Bezalel Museum in Jerusalem (founded in 1906), the City Museum of Tel Aviv, the City Museum of Haifa, and the Mishkan Ha-Omanut (Tabernacle of Art) in Kibbutz Eyn-Harod, which specialized in Jewish art. The exhibition was scheduled for May 5, 1951, in Jerusalem and May 12 in Tel Aviv; but at the last moment, Chagall got cold feet and asked to postpone it until autumn. One reason may have been Ida's urgent trip to New York in April (necessary to keep her American entry visa valid). However, the exhibition opened in

Chagall in the left-leaning Artists and Writers Club MILO in Tel Aviv, 1951. Front row, left to right: Marc Chagall, the Israeli painter Reuven Rubin, cofounder of Dada-Zurich Marcel Janco. Second row, left to right: Miriam Tamuz, Esther Rubin, the artist Arie Navon, the painter Nahum Gutman, the writer Binyamin Tamuz. Photo by Boris Carmi. Courtesy The Rubin House, Tel Aviv.

Jerusalem on May 30, 1951, and in Tel Aviv on July 7, Chagall's birthday. Then it went to Eyn-Harod and Haifa and lasted until late autumn.

As usual, Chagall's exhibition was first prepared by Ida, who went to Israel on May 6, 1951; Chagall and Virginia followed in June. As Chagall recalled, his own father had wept when he heard the name Jerusalem, and he himself went there with great trepidation. In the new Hebrew society, Chagall was not a simple problem: Israeli culture emerged as a revolt against the *shtetl*, its ugly, parochial and parasitic existence; and here was an artist who gave a sentimental and nostalgic view of "the lost Jewish world." It was also "too Jewish" and too thematic for the adherents of modernism and abstraction in Israeli art. Nevertheless, the exhibition was an enormous public success, and his reception in Israel was extremely warm. If not all of the artistic establishment, at least many of the Zionist leaders who were themselves born in a *shtetl*, succumbed to the charm of Chagall's pictures, as did the masses who visited the four museums where the exhibition traveled. Here they could show their nostalgia openly.

A few years later, when the Bezalel Museum was turned into the Israel Museum and inaugurated a new building complex, the artist invited for the first exhibition was Picasso, Chagall's nemesis. Chagall was offended by this, but the Israelis could not understand why; the Chagall exhibition of 1951 was the first major artistic event of the young state and could not be repeated so soon. Inviting Picasso was a signal that this was not going to be a parochial, or exclusively Jewish, museum, but one that was open to the best of modern, international art, as the young state itself was open to the most advanced modern science and technology.

Nevertheless, Chagall came back to Israel several times, made the twelve stained glass windows in the Hadassah Hospital synagogue, created mosaics and tapestries in the Knesset, and was invited to the Weizmann Institute on his 90th birthday—always in a quandary of ambivalence, somehow stemming from his excitement mixed with guilt for not joining the Jewish State. He actually came to the Weizmann Institute in October 1977.

Chagall had strong feelings about Israel. During the Holocaust, he compared the pioneers in Eretz Israel to the partisans fighting the Nazis (the highest praise in Communist discourse). Even in a speech for a Communist assembly in New York during the war, he called for the settlement of "millions of Jews in the Land of Israel"—when Zionism was still their enemy and the "Land of Israel" (rather than Palestine) was unmentionable. He was pessimistic about the continuation of Yiddish culture and saw the only possible survival of the Jews as a nation in the young Hebrew state. But he knew no Hebrew and corresponded with Israeli officials and friends in Yiddish or Russian.

Telegram from Marc Chagall in Vence to Moshe Mokady in Jerusalem

The Israeli painter Moshe Mokady (1902–1975) visited New York in 1948 and talked to Louis Stern about a Chagall Hall in the Tel Aviv Museum. When the State of Israel was established, he became Director of the Art Division of the Ministry of Culture and was instrumental in organizing Chagall's major exhibition in Israel in 1951.

> 3.4.1951 [April]
>
> [French] Very uneasy situation Israel fear danger send all my paintings now stop would like to postpone exhibition for autumn request this very sincerely with regrets greetings
>
> Chagall

Narkiss: Mordechai Narkiss was Director of the National Museum Bezalel in Jerusalem.

Marc Chagall in Vence to M. Narkiss in Jerusalem

"Les Collines"/Vence/(A.-M.)   7 April 1951

[French] Dear friend,

As you see from this copy of a letter to Mr. Mokady, which I am sending you, I ask that my exhibition be postponed until the autumn.

I am terribly sorry for all the bother this exhibition is causing you and I know how much trouble you have all taken.

I hope with all my heart that you will understand my motives.

Very cordially,
Marc Chagall

[Yiddish] I hope you're doing fine and please write me how you are. My daughter is in America until the end of the month.

Marc Chagall in Vence to M. Narkiss in Jerusalem

"Les Collines"/Vence/(A.-M.)   12 April 1951

[French] Dear friend,

Thank you for your telegram and I am really sorry to disappoint you so much. I am well aware of the trouble you have had so far and that you will still have because of this change of plan, but I cannot stop worrying about my paintings which represent all that I own as paintings. First, there is the situation in Israel, which is nevertheless worrisome, then there is the fact that I could not accompany my paintings. My daughter, who is currently in America, has a great many concerns now and I don't know if she will be able to return for the hanging and the opening. All these worries made me feel increasingly sure that it is better to postpone the exhibition until the autumn.

Forgive me, please, for causing you so much trouble, and do believe in my friendliest feelings.

Marc Chagall

Marc Chagall in Vence to Anonymous in Chicago

[on top: "Communicated by Ralph Seward—a letter written to his brother-in-law, I think."—JUN (=John Ulric Nef)]

"Les Collines"/Vence, A.M.

May 1, 1951

Dear Sir,

Thank you for your letter of March 30; I shall try to answer your questions about my two paintings, "Entre Chien et Loup" and "L'Obsession."

I am not surprised that sick people feel certain examples of modern art more deeply and more subtly. We artists and scientists know that art is the product of the highest human essence. The achievement of authentic perfection is an act of creation, an act of nature itself. The act of creation can lend itself to scientific study as the secrets of nature have been penetrated by scientists, but sick people can also sense something of those mysteries, perhaps more deeply than "normal" people.

I am personally very curious to know what such sick people may say about my art. I myself am unable to talk about my art, which is the result of my life, the life of my forefathers, and all the mental and material influences and who knows what else. Everything is so intermingled. I can only ask that you believe in my sincerity.

My best wishes./   Marc Chagall

Marc Chagall in Paris to Virginia Haggard in Vence

Chagall came to Paris on May 3 and stayed in Ida's house. Virginia and the children stayed in Vence. Ida left for Israel on May 6 and Marc worked throughout May doing lithographs at Mourlot's workshop.[1]

Paris, Sunday, May 1951

[French] Darling, here I am. Ida has to leave and everything revolves around her. Like the sun—and you? And the children. I want to see how I will be able to "work" afterward. I only just got here, and how long will I be able to stay? I want to send you these words and kisses. But you write.

Yours,/   Marc

A Letter by Marc Chagall on His Exhibition in Israel[2]

[Russian] At this moment, my pictures are floating on the high seas. My daughter is flying to Israel; I too would like to go right away. But I must wait until I am restored to health.

Strange! This exhibition excites me more than all my exhibitions in the world. It is the most significant for me. Moreover, I am permeated by an unusual excitement about a kind of responsibility towards those young people of Israel who on their own shoulders and with their own soul, opened a new page in our Jewish life, sacrificed their lives to cut the chains of the ghetto and lead us to new biblical horizons, to a new land, and new heroism.

To be exposed to the critical eyes of this youth is too great a responsibility and a great honor. And how could I, a son of the ghetto, not be excited?

Perhaps they will forgive my weaknesses. I am moved when I think that twenty years ago my friends Dizengoff and Bialik called me to them. And now, I stand here trembling with excitement, before the new Jews of the new country. For I would like to come, to try to get strength and inspiration, if I am still capable to absorb it at my age. On the third anniversary of the State's freedom and existence, I wish to send you my feelings of love and warm greetings—until the day when my feet walk on the holy soil and I will be delighted to look into your eyes against that background of the biblical mountains and creativity, and see how heroically you are fighting for the ideals of justice.

Marc Chagall

Vence, May 1951

Marc Chagall in Paris to Virginia Haggard in Vence

Paris, 1951   12/5 [May]

[French] Dear,

Happy to get your letters and to talk with you. I think I will be happy if you come here all the same afterward in a car. (I don't know when they close the exhibit in Arles and St. Remy.) I don't know when Ida will come here. I send you the letter from London. Nothing to do—we have to do what we can. That is a disagreeable Russian "kasha." Don't worry. We have to get through this moment which is more than disagreeable and commercial.

Russian "kasha": Pot of porridge, confusion, mess; a reference to Virginia's divorce from John McNeil in England.

Kisses / My very dear / Yours always

Marc

Later

I got a letter from Ida. Everybody and Ida thinks that we should go to Palestine *in June* for the end of the exhibit in Jerusalem and the opening in Tel Aviv. So I also think that to go with you in June—or later, is useless and too hot. Bouche [Busch Meier-Graefe] proposes asking Mrs. Schikele to take care of the children at our house. She (Mrs. Schickele) is very nice—Bouche will talk with her. So I will come to Vence before the end of this month. I will telephone her and then I think that you needn't come here—too tiring.

Kisses / Your

Marc

Marc Chagall in Paris to the Opatoshus in New York

Paris 1951   22/5

[Yiddish] Dear friends. So much time has passed and I still couldn't write to you. Something twitches in my ass and I can hardly be myself. I am here in Paris in Ida's house. I came from America [sic] to see her and now she went to Israel and in the meanwhile I do lithographs, in a special typography, and want to go back to Vence this Saturday. And I have to go again to Israel—I think so—though I'm afraid it will make me tired. The exhibition there, in Jerusalem, opens on May 30 and it is hard not to go there (in June).

from America: He came from Vence, of course. Chagall conflates this visit to Ida with his first arrival from America at her call, when she had not much time for him either.

When I go (with Virginia) I shall travel there for several weeks, because I have so much work to do here and it will be hot. How are you? I have not seen you—for an eternity. How is your health? I thank you very much for often sending me both books and journals (a fine book about you). There is plenty to read in it. May there only be enough time (and health). Indeed, I would like to use your help and ask you to buy me the 3 volumes of *Lyesin* with my drawings. My 3rd volume was stolen and they want it for the exhibition in Israel—I bought it once in America, I don't remember where, on the *East Side*. Since the Jews did not fully "appreciate" them, maybe one can still buy a "set" of books.

I shall be happy to see your Dovid. And I promise to sit down one day and write you more.

In the meantime I kiss you both heartily. Your faithful

Marc Chagall

Esther Rubin and Ida Chagall in Tel Aviv to Louis Stern in New York

June Third/Tel Aviv

[English] Dear Lou,

Ida is here for lunch and we have been talking about the Chagall show, his forthcoming visit, and other plans. She just said, and rightly too "Why doesn't Lou Stern also come in July?" So I have decided to write & ask you immediately! Will you? You will have a hearty warm welcome by all three of us & especially by your

ever devoted,/   Esther

From Ida Chagall:

[English] Dear Louis,

I lived the *greatest*, most tremendous event in all my life. The opening in Jerusalem by Sharrett. Do come. Father is arriving with Virginia *on June 19th*. I am
sailing (by plane tomorrow for Paris) and quite probably returning to Tel Aviv on
July 1st.

Sharrett: Moshe Sharet
(1894–1965), the first
Foreign Minister of
Israel.

The exhibition looks beautiful and I feel very happy to have brought it. I have
the poster and catalogue for you. You will get it through Michel on June 15th.

Come! You will see things which will refresh you in spite of the heat. And such
a warm welcome at the Rubin's that it is worth the trip.

Love   Ida

I have nothing to add/   Rubin
  Enclosed a clipping from today's Post

P.S. Whenever your package arrives I shall let you know. Meantime, thanks a
million! E. [Esther]

Marc Chagall in Vence to the Opatoshus in New York

Vence 1951   6/6

[Yiddish] Dear friends, happy to get your letter, thank you. Every time I seem
to see you, I sit in your home and eat tasty things that are "forbidden" me. I
thank you from the bottom of my heart for running around to find Lyesin's
books with my drawings, which your Dovid brings. I think he's arriving today.
Ida will see him in Paris and I (and Virginia) will see him, God willing, in Israel. And perhaps he could come here to Vence. We leave in a few days, around
the 10th and believe me I am "afraid" both of the little (big) Jewish ship and of
the Jews. I got very important cables from there. But what can I do, I must see
it, see and not get overtired, especially since I judge—or it really is so—that my
liver is in pain. Perhaps it'll calm down. With a strict diet. Virginia can do it
when she wants. The children, Jean and David, are in a boarding school nearby
and Virginia travels [to Israel with me] because I cannot be alone, otherwise it
is hard for her without the children. Ida came back from Israel very happy and
I am happy that she received Jewish joy in a Jewish state. The day after tomorrow she is supposed to come here for a short while. I kiss you warmly. And if
you write, my address for the time being is: Bezalel Museum—Jerusalem; or Tel
Aviv—Museum.

They are very nice—they open my exhibition in the Tel Aviv Museum on the

7th [of July], my birthday. And as I am told by cable, the Jewish ministers and diplomats and [President Chaim] Weizman opened the exhibition in Jerusalem.

I kiss you both warmly, yours as ever

Marc Chagall

Virginia Haggard in Vence to the Opatoshus in New York

[June 10, 1951]

[English] My dearest Adele and Oppen,

Thank you for your letters. We are just off to Israel and we are both thrilled at the idea of seeing that wonderful country at last. Marc has received the most overwhelmingly enthusiastic and affectionate telegrammes and the whole country seems to be awaiting his coming like the Messiah. Ida came back overflowing with excitement and pleasure. The pictures seem to have answered some long awaited need and touched off explosive emotions everywhere. I am rather scared and not at all sure that I should go but Marc begs me to go with him.

We hope to see David and Lily [Opatoshu] there because I don't suppose we shall be able to see them before we leave in four days time. Where is little Don?

My love to you both, dear ones,

Virginia

P.S. I am sending you back the photo of Oppen's father which Marc has had for a long time. It will come in a separate letter.

Marc Chagall: To Israel

[Yiddish]

> Should I pray to God, Who led my people into the fire,
> Or should I paint Him in image of flame?
> Shall I rise up a new Jew
> And go fight along with my race?
>
> Should my eyes lament without a halt,
> So the tears drown in a river?
> I won't let my grief approach
> When I swim to your shore.

Marc and Virginia in Israel, 1951, visiting the excavated Nabatean city of Avdat in the Negev.

And when my weary foot gropes the sand—
I shall lead my bride by the hand.
the holy bride in   For you to see her—the holy bride in the sky,
the sky: Bella.   As I will dream with her our last dream.

[1950]

Marc Chagall: The Ship

[Yiddish]

Two thousand years: Two thousand years—my Exile,
The stereotypical   My land is just a few years old.
figure for the length   Young as my son David.
of the Jewish exile   I crawl on my knees with hands spread out,
from Israel.   Seek the stars and the Star of David.

The Prophets swim past me,
Moses shines to me from afar.
I have long been enraptured by his beams
the wind: The biblical   And by the wind blowing from him.
idiom *Be-zaam appo*
(literally "with the
rage of his nose")   All those years I counted the tears,
is represented in   Sought you in the sky, on the earth,
Christian painting as   Two thousand years have I waited
rays of wind blowing   For my heart to calm down and see you.
from God's nostrils.
See also: "Out of his   Like Jacob, I lay sound asleep,
nostrils goeth smoke"   I dreamed a dream:
(Job 41:20).   An angel raises me onto a ladder,
Extinguished souls sing around me.

About the new land Israel,
About two thousand years of our Exile,
And about David—my son,
They sang sweeter than Mozart and Bach.

Marc Chagall: To Tel Aviv [3]

[Hebrew] We are too close to it, we still see ourselves in this historical picture, to
be able to see the range of colors and the significance of the whole picture. But we
already feel the greatness, the momentum of Dizengoff's fantasy. I am happy that

I met him in my lifetime, though only for a short time. Such a fantasist! May Dizengoff's city, its inhabitants and leaders, live and shine even more fantastically.

We have to have gigantic strength, as incessant as the waves of the sea, to live, to create. But in this difficulty lies the greatest art, while ease leads to decadence. Difficulty, like our Bible, leads to eternity. And when I see our youth—let us put our hand on our heart and say: "Thank God." It is a beginning. With their shining eyes, where love sparkles, and with our distant past—our ancient culture—we shall conflate our new cultural forces to give meaning to life for ourselves and for all of humanity.

                                                                    Marc Chagall

Virginia Haggard in Tel Aviv to Louis Stern in New York

Tel Aviv, Israel   July 11th 1951

[English] Dear Louis,

We feel very guilty, or rather *I* do, since I am the "scribe," for not having written to you long ago. We had all your news from Ida and you also had ours. First of all, thankyou for your letter received such a long time ago. I am happy to say the exhibition is a great success, thanks to Ida and to Mokady who did the hanging and the arrangements. I personally think the Tel Aviv exhibition is the best Chagall show I have ever seen, even though the pictures are only from his own & Ida's collections. It is a very representative and beautiful exhibition. Marc has just finished two very large paintings "Moses" & "King David" which are fine. All together there are 119 items including etchings, drawings & ceramics. It all looks very fine in the Tel Aviv Museum and has been well received by people of all kinds & conditions. I have never seen such a varied public and all of them so enthusiastic, about 1500 of them every day! Ben Gurion visited the exhibition, also Mr. Weitzman, & Mr. Sharett opened the first one in Jerusalem with Ida.

Weitzman: Chaim Weizmann (1874–1952), the first President of Israel.

> David Ben-Gurion (1886–1973), founder and first Prime Minister of Israel, was
> a pragmatist, quite distant from art and literature. As the story goes, Ben-Gurion
> said to Chagall: "Who ever saw a horse-and-wagon flying?" Chagall retorted:
> "Who ever saw Jews make a state?"

Are you planning to come over here? It's a pity we could not have met in Israel. But perhaps we shall meet in France. We have seen a lot of your friends the Rubins. They are charming.

We look forward to getting your news and we hope to see you soon.

Love   Virginia

[Russian] Dear, how I would like to chat with you, I wish you happiness—Marc Chagall

Marc Chagall in Jerusalem to Yosef Opatoshu in New York

Jerusalem 13/7 1951

[Yiddish] I snatched a moment to take pen in hand and write a word. You have no idea how we are being torn apart here—some work hard, some sweat a lot (these are the hottest months—how many) and then comes my first crowning, the "receptions" where you actually see the same faces. But you don't hear the "same" speeches, because, thank God, you don't understand——and therefore I could only see your Dovid for a short time (but soon, Sunday, for more) and your grandchild. About my impressions (remember, I was here twenty years ago), I am confused in various ways. They work very very hard here on the stubborn piece of land. Thousand-year-old stones have to be crushed, along with the "enemies," especially the big ones, "the clever, rich nations would just love to choke the little country." And it is little indeed—perhaps as big as the Vitebsk *Gubernia*, but in everybody's head, the country is big and getting bigger.

Vitebsk Gubernia: Chagall's childhood province in Tsarist Russia.

But just think that we Jews, in the course of 2000 years, have adapted to climates other than when our grandfathers were like the Bedouins. But children and youth grow up here, it's a pleasure to look at them. And their strength is great. It is a great holy deed that our people everywhere should help. It was only devotion to the Bible that drove the Jews to rebuild the country. But, as the saying goes, "God" himself lives in France. I myself think about planting my foot here. They all beg me and I have no strength to restrain myself, though my God does not live in France. Art here—is simply lacking and God knows how the poetry of color can radiate here—it seems that my exhibitions here make an impression. They cry here with tears from Vitebsk, my parents' tears and even Bella's, and strangely, they adapt to the Jews here. The people come [to the exhibition] and I melt like wax [with joy]—

"God" himself lives in France: A Yiddish saying: "He lives [as comfortably] as God in France," which may be ironic, a reversal of a view of French Enlightenment as the source of atheism.

28/7 1951   Vence

Came back. Sweated a lot, and on the [Israeli] ship "Kedma" there were 5 days of shaking. Now I need to work a bit. For over a month I didn't work. And Israel from afar is so far. I would like to help, but to come there—where do I get the strength. I should have been twenty years younger, and art lives in France——[?] I kiss you both, your Chagall

Virginia Haggard in Haifa to the Opatoshus in New York

Haifa, Israel   July 19th 1951

[English] Dearest Adele and Oppen,

Tomorrow we take the boat home after a month's visit in this wonderful country. You *must* come as soon as you can. Since I have seen this place I can't imagine you living anywhere else, nor us, for that matter. It was a joy to have seen David and family. The little one is charming and lively and both David and Lily seem happy and well. They are also most impressed by the country. I do hope they will decide to come & live here, because then *you* will too, maybe!

Did David tell you that Anne's sculpture of Marc is in a place of honor right in the entrance of Marc's exhibition? Marc has given it to the museum. It looks very fine. The exhibition itself is beautifully arranged and I think the one in Tel Aviv (it started in Jerusalem) is the finest Chagall retrospective I have ever seen.

We have visited the country from top to bottom and I think we have seen a fairly representative cross section. We have seen kibbutzim, schools, army camps, archaeological sites, museums, paintings, as well as all the towns of importance and the wonderful lake of Galilee. The scenery is too beautiful for words. I can imagine how much Oppen would be inspired by all this and what wonders he could produce here. Everyone thinks so highly of him here, he would be received like a visiting monarch is received in other countries, and that's the way Marc has been received too. We have heard that maybe Glans, Lewic & Bickel will come too. Is that true?

Do write soon, to "Les Collines" and tell us what your plans are and how Oppen's new book progresses.

Lots of love to you both.

Your/   Virginia

From Marc Chagall:

19/7 Israel 1951

[Yiddish] My dear ones, should have written to you more. But time flies and I shall write from Vence. I think that, whichever way you look at it, it is our country and from Vence I shall write to you more.

I kiss you. Your

Marc Chagall

Tomorrow back.

Anne's sculpture: Ann Wolf, Adele Opatoshu's sister, made a sculpture of Chagall's head, which he donated to the Tel Aviv Museum.

Glans, Lewic, & Bickel: Major Yiddish American writers and friends of Opatoshu: the poets A. Leyeles (Glanz) and H. Leyvik, and the literary critic and essayist Sh. Bickel. Though they were received with respect, there was no enthusiasm for Yiddish writers in the Hebrew State.

Marc Chagall in Vence to Moshe Mokady in Tel Aviv

27/7 1951 [after the Chagalls' return from Israel]

[Yiddish] Dear friend (I assume you can read well Yiddish . . . my Yiddish.)

Just returned from the journey and my head is spinning like the beautiful Jewish ship "Kedmah." We sort out all the impressions in our head, something of us (and not just something) was left in Israel and we recall all our friends and you dear Mokady (may God bless you).

I didn't see Ida yet. But I hope to visit her soon in Gordes. In the meantime I thought how it would be better in the future to arrange my coming to work in Israel. And I think that since I as an artist must have a base here in France, which is good for Israel as well. From another perspective (art) I think one need not build or buy a special house for the hard-earned Jewish money. Simply, when I come, rent a few rooms, even in Beit Daniel (in Zikhron Ya'akov). We shall write in advance. For one cannot have two houses, here and there, in our times. Better be modest. I must be here in France and I want to come from time to time to Israel, with God's help, to you—to myself—to work, see, and by the way, I can also work on these and those murals both here and there. I shall gladly help you when I am in Israel and am ready to help you from afar too, from here, if you need.

My sojourn in the Land made me happy and I am so glad that I met you. Both as an artist and a human being. And you know well that I don't like to exaggerate. You may write to me even in French if you don't know Yiddish, or in English (Virginia reads to me).

I kiss you both warmly. Regards to everyone, everyone. Especially to those who were at Avrekh's, and to him himself, on that evening, when we read poetry and sang the Rebbe's tune. Your Marc Chagall.

Marc Chagall in Vence to Sir Godfrey Haggard in England

[English; typed by Virginia Haggard]

"Les Collines"/Vence/(A.-M.)   July 28, 1951

Dear Sir Godfrey,

Thankyou very much for your letter. I haven't answered sooner because I didn't know how the trial would turn out. Now that we have the good news that John McNeil won't countersue and won't defend himself, the whole issue is changed. I am so happy that everything will work out more simply than we had hoped and you must also be happy after so many worries.

Virginia is awaiting her trip to England with pleasure instead of fearing it as before, and I myself hope soon to have the pleasure of coming and finally meeting you.

Do you want us to divide the costs of this trial? As soon as I can arrange to have money in England, I will make the next payment on account to Baylis Pearce. Thankyou for beginning to settle the account demanded by Mr. Kidd.

Best regards to you and your wife.

Yours,

Marc Chagall

Virginia Haggard in Vence to the Mokadys in Tel Aviv

July 30th 1951

[English] Dear Hedy and Mokady,

Israel seems a long way off because life there is so utterly different from life here. It couldn't possibly be more different, that is why a part of us, the part that needs Israel, will always remain there with our good friends and wait for our return. There is something very magical about Israel and it certainly cast a spell over us. Thinking back over our experiences they all seem most unlikely and yet they are true! Looking at it all from this comfortable, easy-going country it is difficult to believe there is such a thing as Israel.

You were so full of kindness towards us and we have very warm spots in our hearts for you both. Come soon to Vence so that we can give you back a little of that kindness and attention!

Marc and I have thought a great deal about living and working in Israel and being here makes it easier to see the whole question more objectively. He now feels very strongly that he must keep his base in France and not *establish* himself in Israel, even on a half and half basis. He feels that he would like to come for a month or two at a time and work on murals and other paintings. Since he saw the little apartment you lived in in Beit Daniel he thinks that sort of place would be ideal. The worry of moving our belongings again and looking after a house would take away all the feeling of freedom which he needs in Israel. All through his life his holidays have been the times when he worked most, the times when he got away from the habitual home life with all its distractions and concentrated on the one aspect of life that his new surroundings afforded him. I think Israel should be a "holiday" place for him because he is not young enough to be a pioneer or to make the fundamental change in his life that he would have to make if he came to life in Israel. His art needs stimulus, not upheaval. His heart needs the warmth of Israel's friendliness, but this he feels even at a distance. The contact will always be a strong one and he will always do what he can to help, so that even if he has not got a permanent domicile in Israel he will be in close touch with you and when he comes to Israel he will enter readily into its life just as he did in that short month he spent there. I begin to understand that he rather fears the heavy responsibility of a house in Israel and would like to feel free to come and go as he likes. I agree with him now and I realise that one cant live in two places, especially not two places so different as Israel and France and especially not at his age and after all the upheavals in his life.

I do hope you wont be disillusioned and I'm sure you will understand when you come here and see the way he lives and works. It would be a pity to upset all that and it might be dangerous to his art. In Israel neither he nor I realised the possible danger of another great change in his life (dont forget that he only came back from America three years ago) we were so carried away by Israel's heroism and enthusiasm, and rightly so, but we have to try and look at things cooly and logically, alas!

Many thanks for you nice letter and the photos. It was good to hear from you. Please give our love to all our friends and tell them that we think of them all and talk incessantly to our French friends about all the wonders of you wonderful land.

Love from us both,/   Virginia

"Chagall: 'My Heart Remains in France,' He Will Not Settle in Israel"

Article in the daily *Ma'ariv* in Tel Aviv, August 4, 1951

[Hebrew] In Paris, there is a "worrisome" rumor that Marc Chagall is about to settle in Israel. The French newspaper, *Artes*, asked the artist if it were true. Chagall replied:

> At last I am back in that land where even the space itself recalls the marvellous tradition of French painting; I returned weary of travelling and of all the other emotions, and the first person I come across asks me: 'So you're really going to settle in Israel. You're leaving France. That's what's written here'. It would have been nicer if they had said: 'How thin and pale you've become.'
>
> I have lived for a while in Vence, where my garden is waiting for me to be an 'Impressionist' or simply a painter.
>
> I have good friends here who were worried. I want to calm them as well as myself. Everybody knows: art lives in France.
>
> Here is the truth. I saw Israel—its heroism and its toil. I am grateful to her gov-

ernment for the invitation, for the lovely reception, and for the wonderful organization of my exhibition there.

As far as my physical strength allows, I will be happy to spend a month or two there from time to time in order to paint the murals they offer me, for in my heart lives an echo of the Bible. But my whole being lives in France, where I came in my youth to live and work.

Marc Chagall in Le Drammont to the Opatoshus in New York

> After returning from Israel, the Chagalls went to Ida's house in Gordes, where Chagall signed 9000 prints of the La Fontaine etchings and colored 4000. Then they went for two weeks to Le Drammont on the sea.

[Small envelope, return address Vence; 11/9 (September) 1951]

[Yiddish] Dear Opatoshus, we came here from Gordes because we visited Ida (where the American attack in Hitler's war in 1944, August 15, started from the sea). Thank you, my dear, for sending me something in print from time to time. The article by the historian Katz or Catz is a discovery for me. I remember less than he [does]. Something did happen in those times but whether it is precise— only God knows. True, of "his" saved paintings there was nothing in the exhibition in Tel Aviv, but he approached me, a beaming little old man. I think he is honest, but tends somewhat toward the sensational; he suffered quite a bit in those days [the early years after the Russian Revolution], and which of us did not suffer. But for that—each one in his own manner—was young, and we believed— we still believed [in Communism].

Katz: On Katz's involvement in getting Chagall out of the Soviet Union, see Chapter 8, p. 308.

Now, as for your collection, *Zamlbikher*, to write something about Fefer—Markish and others—whom I certainly knew very well!—I feel very sad to write about them. Just sad, meanwhile I hope. Maybe it is too bitter and too "early" to write about them, because what can we write now about them, that we are "dealing" with a whole tragic world. It may be better to print their creative works. And someone should draw a front page—an "eternal light." Well, this reminds me of my small and great dear friend, who lies over there, poor thing, in N.Y., and now she is 7.

very sad: At that moment the Soviet Yiddish writers were still alive, although they had disappeared into Stalin's prisons.

How long she will lie there alone—who knows.

In Israel I often recalled her for myself, and here—but I don't know in these times where we live—we stay alive.

she is 7: Seven years since Bella's death on September 2, 1944.

How is it going with your book? You work hard. But this is a work that must be lasting. I would like so much to talk to you personally about Israel and other things.

Recently Sholem Asch visited me, left a card, I was not in Vence, I am not in a hurry to see him. For me, he was lost long ago as a man and as a writer (except for his early Yiddish writings). Why Sutzkever publishes his long panoramic pieces [in *Di Goldene Keyt* in Tel Aviv]—I don't understand. Sutzkever walks around in Israel almost a "lost [soul]" and basically it is hard to understand the reason. He is complicated, not very free, though a good and fine man. But Markish was more *imaginative* . . . And how he was!—Perhaps he misses . . . Vilna—as Bialik missed his home town to write poetry.

It seems hard to create poems (and paintings) in the same place where they have to produce chickens, factories, gardens, soldiers. But there is a hunger for creative works, which the country will perhaps create later, years later, later. They are sweating a lot there, to create conditions for life, to defend the country from its enemies all around and even inside the country.

How are you and how is Adele? Now I am returning to Vence and one has to toil hard to do something—to try to be an artist. Did you see poor Dr. Kloomok? If I am not mistaken, his book in English is about to appear. Perhaps you could help him publish his book in Yiddish, as he wants. Perhaps in Canada where your beautiful little book was published—a fine printer.

I kiss you heartily/And love to Adele

Virginia sends her love—she is now busy, we are about to get in the car and go to Vence

Your/   Chagall

Virginia Haggard in Vence to the Mokadys in Tel Aviv

Chez Madame Boccart, Le Drammont (Var)   September 11th [1951]

[English] Very dear friends,

We got your nice letter, also the telegram, and we were very glad to hear from you.

Yes, we can understand how you must feel about our letters and the feelings they expressed. We await your arrival here with impatience as we would like to talk to you at length about these feelings which are difficult to convey in a letter. When do you expect to come here?

Marc is a little worried about the delay in opening the exhibition in Ein Harod because he was expecting the pictures back sooner. Some are needed for a film which is being made on Chagall and others are needed for exhibitions. When do you think the pictures will leave Israel? Marc asks that they be exhibited not more than two weeks each in Ein Harod and Haifa, so as to speed their return. Is this possible?

Marc thanks you for the copies of his articles and the other things you sent and also for having got in touch with the people at Beit Daniel who have so kindly

---

imaginative: The Yiddish expression Chagall uses here is *foygldik*, literally: "birdlike," meaning shrewd, exquisite, flexible, and soaring like a bird—all in one.

said they will put the apartment at our disposal. The thought of Zichron Yakob makes us want to come back so much, and also the thought of all our friends in Israel and you in particular.

Since we came back from Israel we have been on the move most of the time. We have been staying with Ida in Gordes (She is well and sends you her warmest greetings. She *will* write soon.) In Gordes Marc coloured 9,000 engravings for La Fontaine. It was a terrible job, very monotonous. He was tired after that so we came here to the sea-side. Next week we return to Vence. Then in November I shall probably go to England and Marc to Paris. So do try and come in October as you had planned. By the way did you manage to get away for a holiday on the [ship] Kedmah? We had a perfectly *dreadful* crossing home with two successive storms and a strong "mistral" in Marseille at the end of it. We were sea-sick all the way! I do hope you will have a calm sea. The captain said that our crossing was quite exceptional.

Marc asks you if you would be so kind as to send him the original of the letter from Bialik if you managed to get it. He would be most grateful for it.

Give our love to Ruth, the Avrechs, Sutzkever, and the Epsteins and tell them that we shall write to them soon.

To you we send our love most especially, Hedy and Mokady and to the two sweet children.

Avrechs: Yeshayahu Avrekh, an Israeli intellectual and journalist close to the Labor Party, was born in Brisk, *Litah*.

Yours Virginia

Virginia Haggard in Vence to Louis Stern in New York

"Les Collines"/Vence/(A.-M.)   27 Septembre 1951

[English] Dear Louis,

I am ashamed to have taken so long to answer your two long letters which we were very glad to receive.

Firstly thankyou for the article by Katz which you kindly sent us. Marc had received it in Yiddish from Opatoshu but I was interested to read it too. Marc says that so many years have passed since the Revolution that he cannot possibly say how much of what Katz says is true. Some of it, perhaps, he says. At any rate, says Marc, he is a specialist in historical matters and ought to know better than Marc does who has no memory at all for historical details! He may have exaggerated some things, Marc does not remember. At any rate he certainly puts the accent on himself!

Marc saw him at the Tel Aviv Museum and he seemed thoroughly pleased with himself, as if it was entirely thanks to him that the exhibition took place at all.

Israel was wonderful and you must go there when you come over. We got completely carried away. Marc felt very much like a fish in water and it was only when he came back here that he could judge all his impressions dispassionately and realise that he belongs here. We look forward to your next visit here so that we can talk to you all about Israel.

After Israel we went to Gordes and stayed in Ida's house for a month. While he was there Marc colored by hand each one of the 9,000 plates of the Fables de La Fontaine, it was a long and tedious job and he is glad it is over. Now he is working full steam ahead on ceramics and paintings.

Let us know your plans for coming over here. We hope it will be soon.

Affectionate regards from us both

Virginia

Virginia Haggard in Vence to Moshe Mokady in Tel Aviv

10 October 1951

[English] My dear Mokady,

How are you all? We are getting very homesick for you all and we are longing to know when you are coming to France.

Thankyou so much for replying so promptly to our telegramme. It is a great pity so many engagements had already been made over here for the pictures. Marc and I were not aware of these when we were in Israel, that is why he said he accepted on principle leaving the pictures for six more weeks in Israel. But I suspected there might be engagements that is why I said that we must telegraph Ida and ask her if it is allright. Unfortunately Ida did not answer right away but as soon as we got back we sent you a telegramme to the effect that the pictures would be needed urgently and that they could not remain in Israel for six more weeks. Now it appears that Kanyuk kept them in Tel Aviv for two or three extra weeks and that has put their departure back until the middle of November. We gather than Ein Harod and Haifa have each taken a week or two extra also. Marc is quite anxious as some serious promises have been made since we sent you the first telegramme in addition to the engagements already made before. There are two films being made on Chagall. One of them is in colour therefore the photos are made from the pictures themselves. The director is losing a lot of money waiting for the pictures to come back. Then there are exhibitions for which pictures have been promised. Do you think it is possible to send the pictures sooner? They will have been away for six months. Or course Marc knows the enormous expense and trouble that you have all gone to for this exhibition and that is why he was so loath to refuse your request to prolong the exhibition. But the different people with whom the engagements have been made dont understand that. However we know that you will do everything possible and that you will understand why we want the pictures back. Marc wishes it wasn't necessary.

We are longing to have news of you. We know how busy you are and we hope you are painting a lot besides your official work. How are Hedy and the children? Do ask Hedy to write me a little letter, I would love to hear from her. We hope you got our parcel of food safely.

We want to ask you a very great favor for a friend of ours in Vence who is in a very difficult situation. She is the great grand-daughter of Mendelsohn, the composer. Her children are in Israel, two sons and a daughter. She is extremely hard up for money and now a tragic thing has happened to her. She has to undergo a very serious operation (She has cancer, although neither she nor her children know it.) She had an operation only two years ago. This one is more serious. She has been trying to get money from her children but they are not allowed to send it. Also her daughter would like to be allowed to come to France to visit her mother, it may be for the last time.

Do you think that in a case like this a special permission could be obtained? Would you be a dear and ask Avrech and other highly placed people if such a permit could be issued? It might save the life of this woman who is a wonderful person. We would be profoundly grateful if something could be done.

Here is the daughter's address:

Mrs. Elizabeth Vandsburger/14 Jesreel Street/Bat Galim/HAIFA

Her husband is part owner of a bus company in Haifa.

I am sending you two certificates from the doctor who is operating on her. The operation is an urgent one, so I would be most grateful if you would reply as soon as possible.

Our friend's name is Mrs. Doernberg. She was told to send the certificates to the Israeli Consulate but it would take an awful long time and I dont believe anything would be done, that is why I am bothering you with this and I hope you will forgive me. I'm sorry that you should [be given] another worry, as if you hadn't already enough!

Marc and I send our love to you all. *Do* come here soon!

Yours,/   Virginia

Virginia Haggard in Vence to Moshe Mokady in Tel Aviv

October 15th 1951

[English] Dearest Mokady,

Our letters must have crossed. Thankyou so much for yours and thank you for all the news concerning the exhibition. Of course Marc understands all the trouble and expense it has cost Ein Harod and Haifa to arrange the exhibition and all the tremendous difficulties they have had to face. Naturally, in that case, he has nothing more to say. As you say, to refuse their request to keep the pictures a little longer would be cruel and we shall just have to do without them. Marc is happy that the exhibition has been such a success.

It is a pity that Ida is not able to go to Israel as she had expected because we thought she might be able to arrange many things before the pictures come back. But we hope that we shall soon be in Israel ourselves and it will not be too late to discuss the possibility of leaving some pictures in Israel. In any case Marc wants to come and do some work there soon. It is a pity that you dont know whether you can come to Vence or not. It would have been a good thing to have talked to you about everything again and perhaps make some decisions. But there is still a chance, we hope, that you can come here before the middle of November when we may have to go to Paris, or else we might see you in Paris at Ida's house.

Love to you all,   Yours,/   Virginia

Marc Chagall in Vence to Moshe Mokady in Tel Aviv

[Stationery: "Les Collines," Vence (A.M.)]

23 October 1951

[French] Dear friend,

How are you? Thank you for your letter which Virginia answered at length, telling you that, even though that represents a great effort on my part and even though the pictures are becoming increasingly necessary here, I was willing to leave them in Haifa for a month. Since I planned on getting the pictures at the beginning of October, I made several arrangements for them. I promised to lend them to exhibitions in Nice and in Italy, and they have been waiting for them in Sweden and in Geneva for more than a year. The two films made about me cannot progress because of the delay of the pictures. Because of the several difficulties created by this delay, I have decided to refuse the extension of the exhibition in Tel Aviv. In spite of that, the museum has kept them longer, and so has Ein Harod. Now Haifa also demands a month. Since you wrote me that the new halls in Haifa have just been arranged at enormous expense of effort and money, I couldn't refuse to grant them this month and Virginia told you that in her letter.

But now I have received a telegram from the mayor of Haifa demanding that the exhibition be extended to the end of November. I immediately sent a refusal. I am amazed that the mayor had the slightest hope of obtaining my consent for that, given my great hesitation to grant him a month. I learned that the exhibition in Haifa opened on October 7, so it will be able to end on November 7, and the pictures can be sent right after that date.

I ask you as a very great favor to send them to me as soon as possible at the beginning of November. I am planning absolutely on getting them in the middle of November.

If I was worried about them before, I have been even more concerned since the disturbances in Egypt. I hope that you will understand my concern and that you will do everything to get the pictures back as soon as possible. Be nice, write and reassure me on this point. Tell me, please, the date of the ship, the first one that leaves after November 7, on which the paintings can leave.

Egypt: In October 1951, Egypt abrogated its agreements with Great Britain, and unrest was rampant.

Answer me as soon as possible, please, to calm my anxiety.

Don't consider me selfish. You know that the paintings are like our children. No insurance company, with the best will in the world, could replace them.

Have you been able to work yourself on your own painting? I would very much like to hear how you, Hedy, and the children are.

I am waiting impatiently for your answer to set the *definitive* date for the departure of the paintings.

With affectionate thoughts from Virginia and me for all of you.

Your devoted,

Marc Chagall

Marc Chagall in Vence to the Opatoshus in New York

"Les Collines"/Vence/(A.-M.)   8 Nov. 1951

[Yiddish] Dear friends. It is strange—the "older" I get the more confused I am and can rarely put myself together—to write or anything else outside of "art." That's why I hardly write letters and write nothing else. But you know, friends get closer—no matter what you do. Now it's swirling in my head: I have to make pictures old and new (finish some still from America). Then, I am fascinated by ceramics and people praise my works—so I have to continue. I have to finish a "maquette" for a tapestry, i.e., a gobelin for a wall, and I hold talks and maintain contacts with our Israel because my exhibitions (now in Haifa) are continuing, and when and how the paintings will come back—God only knows. It seems to me that the whole nation went to my exhibitions. For such a difficult people to endure—from this alone you can get an "operation"—thank God I had the operation beforehand . . .

"older": The quotes indicate an unmentionable word (not to attract attention of the Evil Eye).

"operation": Yiddish expression: You can get a hernia (from overexertion).

How are you? I would so much love to be with you. How are you and your friends? When will your second novel, *Akiva*, be ready? You're working hard.

Thank you for sending me the *Tsukunft* with my introduction for the martyred artists.[4]

And Virginia thanks you for the books you sent.

You probably know—I gave Anna Wolf's head of me to the [Tel Aviv] museum in Israel. It was exhibited during my exhibition.

But my greatest news is that Idotshka is, I think, about to remarry and wants to do it in Vence at my home. With God's help. And Bella's too. You will know more precisely later, I hope.

My best greetings to both of you, your devoted

Chagall

P.S. Did you see Dr. Kloomok's book. I didn't get it yet. What do you think of it? In Israel I learned that the art publisher "Gazit," Editor Talpir, who published some time ago a little book written by a Belgian, a Christian—so the publisher gave Nakhman Maisel when he was in Palestine/Israel a package with books for me—apparently a dozen books, and Maisel gave me nothing. And now there is not a single copy. And I don't have it. Talpir himself told me about it in Israel.

Talpir: Gabriel Talpir, an avant-garde Hebrew poet in the 1920s, was the founder and editor and publisher of the Hebrew art journal *Gazit* in Tel Aviv.

Maisel: Nakhman Mayzel, editor of *Yidishe Kultur* (*Jewish Culture*), a left-leaning Yiddish literary journal in New York.

Marc Chagall in Vence to Moshe Mokady in Tel Aviv

[Stationery: "Les Collines," Vence (A.M.)]　　　10 December 1951

[French] Dear Mokady,

We are now in Paris at Ida's. Unfortunately, she hasn't left for Israel as she had hoped, but the doctor strongly advised against it. She has been very tired since her illness and her resistance is not strong.

As for the paintings, Ida is aware that there would be great difficulties getting the paintings to remain in Israel, except for those that Chagall gave as a gift, for the Central Customs demands the return of the paintings before the end of the year.

This is why I telegraphed you to ask you to send the paintings as soon as possible and I am absolutely counting on getting them before the end of the year. I will be infinitely grateful to you if you could take care of that as soon as possible and I am sure that everything will be in good condition.

I am waiting for your visit here to be able to choose with you all the paintings that might then return to Israel. I hope that you will be here soon.

How are you and how are Hedy and the children? We would very much like to hear from all of you.

Ida and Virginia join me in sending you our affectionate thoughts.

Yours,/　Chagall

Frustrations: 1952

Ida's Second Wedding: Ida Chagall and Franz Meyer

Ida's wedding to the Swiss museum curator and art historian Franz Meyer was celebrated at Chagall's home in Vence in January 1952, in the presence of distinguished guests and friends.

Ida Chagall in Ajaceio Corsica to Becky and Bernard Reis in New York

25/1/52

[English] Dearest Becky and Bernard,

Thank you from all my heart for your wonderful letter and your cable which arrived just in time. What a pity that you were not with us on that day in Vence.

It was a warm sunny happy joyful day in my life. After the "Mairie" [wedding ceremony at City Hall], we had a sitting lunch, which I asked to be in Papa's studio—it was beautiful. For fun and for Bernard's archives, I am mailing you a village clipping.

I brought my Paris maid to Vence and she danced with Prévert and Tériade until collapse.

Father looked very happy.

Virginia is getting her divorce probably on Feb. 11. So you see what a family we are going to be.

I believe father got his approval for the U.S. visa.

Dearest, now we are to expect you. To wait for you and it counts double.

U.S. visa: Ida was prematurely optimistic: Chagall's visa to the U.S. was declined, based on the FBI Report of January 3, 1952.

Ida

Marc Chagall and French poet Jacques Prévert dancing at Ida's wedding.

Marc Chagall in Vence to the Opatoshus in New York

[February 1952]

[Yiddish] Dear friends, I did not write to you in a long time, but I am in a state where I don't find a moment to sit down and write. Running around, and for what—exhibitions, work, ceramics, paintings, visits, travelling back and forth, family, children, marriage, book illustrations, and money, and paintings to give away. And in the meanwhile, letters from friends are lying around. [We] made Idochka's wedding, her husband is a very nice man. May she be happy, and I will be content. Thank you for sending me the *Zamlbikher* for the [persecuted] Yiddish Russian writers. Printed with tact and Jewish tremor. It is a tragic document how Jewish life (there [in Soviet Russia]) is . . . I lack the words to think, to talk about our calamity, for we live in a world where the ground is missing. It is indeed for the [. . .]

It was a pleasure to see the small (and great) Jewish land—Israel, such as it is, with all the faults, still it's ours. Thank you (for the Yiddish Encyclopedia) for sending me the 3 volumes with my colored painting (printed somewhat in reverse).[1] Poor Rokhl (?) Vishnitser[2] works herself to a frazzle. I shall be glad to read your book (not received yet), [I am] starving for a Yiddish (artistic) word.

From left to right: art critic Charles Estienne, Virginia's daughter Jean McNeil, art historian Arnold Rudinger, Marc Chagall, Ida Chagall, Ida's husband, art historian Franz Meyer, Busch Meyer-Graefe, Virginia Haggard. Vence, 1952.

And even more so for all of you. How are you? Your health? How is Adelye, the good, dear woman? I was so happy to see your Dovid in Israel (in the terrible heat), but he is such a good Jew. We miss you all. After tomorrow I go to Paris for 1 1/2 weeks. There is now my exhibition in the museum in Nice.[3] And in Paris at Maeghts again.

How can I thank you for the photos of Bella's grave. How sad, how gray . . .[4] True, the photos were made on such a day. But you, my dear, do me a favor. It seems to me I had no strength to cry, see [?] Idochka in these days (she asked [Louis] Stern to put flowers in her name). You see, my dear, how I am still cut up and cannot heal my wound [of Bella's death]. One image follows the other. Thank you for going to her. I kiss you warmly and please write more often. And send me anything about Jewish life. Love to your friends the writers.

Your devoted as ever

Chagall

[English] Dearest Oppen and Adele,

Thank you for your letters. You will have got mine by now. / All my love,

Virginia

The French poet Paul Eluard visiting Vence, with Marc Chagall and Dominique Eluard.

Marc Chagall in Vence to Leo Kenig in London

February 20, 1952   Vence

going to Israel: Leo Kenig was given an apartment in Haifa and moved to Israel in 1952. He knew Hebrew and published in Israeli newspapers.

[Yiddish] Dear Kenig, I got your letter some time ago but you don't know how difficult it is for me to take up my pen. So letters are lying and lying. But you must think that I am a "bad" man. Now—as to your going to Israel. You don't need any advice from me. A man like you can see, especially on the spot. But either-or: Israel is not a bride to choose or not to choose. If you want her, you need her, or are even in love with her—I was "morally" invited to [my] exhibition there, but I paid from my own pocket for the tickets of my voyage (as well as my wife and daughter) and even the *return trip* of my paintings to Paris. Though I know that there are many Jews and Jewesses traveling at government expense. Now you understand that I personally cannot ask for you, that they invite you "materially," because in principle, the government (I don't say the country) is poor.

But if you need "recommendations" from me over there, I am prepared [to give you].

If you come to France and perhaps here, near Nice—Vence, I shall tell you [about it]. In the meantime,

Be well and best wishes

Your Marc Chagall

Sir Godfrey Haggard on a visit to Vence, with Virginia Haggard and Marc Chagall.

Marc Chagall in Vence to Virginia Haggard in England

[French] My dear

he is a crook: John McNeil, Virginia's first husband. Apparently he sent a registered letter requiring some reparation, which Chagall signed by mistake.

your name: He means the similarity in writing between *cHAGAll and HAGGArd*.

You see, he is a crook that guy. Call him so he will be quiet and [tell him] that you don't have any money yourself now. Why did he send a registered [letter] with a return receipt? Unfortunately I signed for you and your name has a bit of mine. It isn't nice of him. Maybe he wants to have a "trial." I don't like those people.

You have gone and I would also like to be gone.

Kisses, M

Marc Chagall in Vence to Virginia Haggard in England

Vence 1952 12/II

I am happy: He is happy that Virginia got her divorce from John McNeil.

Ida: Ida came for the exhibition in Nice.

Ramié: Suzanne and Georges Ramié, owners of the Madoura ceramics factory in Vallauris, where Chagall produced ceramic sculptures and tiles.

[French] Dear, all is well and I love you even more. No doubts. The exhibit—opening—very good. But many people there missed you. I am happy that that is over. How are things. Write. I think of you always and I need you. Ida is leaving this morning. I am leaving Ramié-Vallauris. Many kisses. How is it there? Regards to your parents.

Yours,

Marc

Virginia Haggard in Vence to the Opatoshus in New York

"Les Collines"/Vence/(A.-M.)   February 23rd 1952

[English] Dearest Opatoshus,

Don't be cross with me! I have good news for you! I have just come back from England where I won my divorce and custody of Jean. Marc and I are so pleased and relieved. I wanted to write long ago but it has been practically impossible. Ida's wedding was a very joyous affair and we had the house full of people for several days. Two people stayed on for two weeks more and then Ida and Franz came back after the honeymoon so there hasn't really been time to breathe. Then I had to hurry off to London. The divorce hearing went through without any trouble at all since my husband dropped his defense. I had a couple of witnesses—friends who knew us when we were living together. I had a good time in England, it was a bit of a change for me and I saw a lot of old friends. I also went to a few theatres and spent some time with my parents who have very much changed in their attitude towards me. I am now the white sheep instead of the black!

Picasso and Chagall working at the Madoura ceramics factory in Vallauris, 1951.

Dearest Oppen, many thanks for the most interesting and attractive little book you sent me—Chesterfield's letters to his son. I expect I shall give just the *opposite* advice to my children, however! It's interesting to think how much parental advice has changed since that day and how out-of-date is that sort of moral teaching plus the snobbery, which, thank God, no longer is tolerated in England. I think England is a better place than it was, however hard and depressing life is now, at times. The socialist government *did* do a lot of good even though it never managed to change England's damned foreign policy which has remained the same for so long that there is absolutely no hope of changing it now. All the same there is a healthier atmosphere, more equality and a *much* better life for the working people.

no hope of changing: A reference to England's position on Israel.

Marc is terribly busy as usual getting ready for an exhibition in Paris. He is making large panels of ceramic tiles, something he has never done before, and they are to be exhibited with the Fables of La Fontaine which will be published at last by Tériade of "Verve" editions [publisher]. Marc is also doing sculpture for the first time. It is really fine, I think. We have a friend here who is a photographer and who is making a little film on Chagall. The sculptures are in the film and the ceramics and many pictures, besides Marc himself and occasionally a bit of the family and the house and garden—Ida's wedding also. You will probably see it one of these days in America.

photographer: Charles Leirens, who came for three weeks to stay at Chagall's and fell in love with Virginia.

What about your plans to come over to Israel. Will you be able to come to France? We so long to see you. The children too, remember you well, even David. He knows who gave him the Hannuka lamp and so many lovely books.

Give our love to David Lilly and Dan, and write to us soon, dearest friends.

Your loving/Virginia

Virginia Haggard in Vence to Bernard Reis in New York

"Les Collines"/Vence/(A.-M.)   [February 23, 1952]

[English] My dear Bernard,

I feel very guilty for not having written for such a long time. I owe you at least two letters and there is quite a lot to tell you about.

First of all I have just come home from a trip to England where I won my divorce without any difficulty. I am still to be given my decree absolute, but I have won the custody of Jean and I am most relieved it is all over.

We have been back and forth to Paris. Marc has a lot of work to do at the moment preparing for an exhibition at the Maeght Gallery in March. It is to be an exhibition of the Fables of La Fontaine together with some very large panels of ceramic tiles, something he has never done before. They are very fine.

Chagall working at the Madoura ceramics factory in Vallauris, 1952.

In Nice now there is a big retrospective exhibition of Marc's work, beautifully hung by Ida, a very attractive show and much too good for the people of Nice, unfortunately, who do not turn up in very large numbers because they are too busy with their roulette and their bouillabaisse.

We were so delighted to hear of the arrival of your new grandchild. Congratulations to Barbara [Reis's daughter]. Is all well with her and her family? How are you both and when do you think of coming over here? It is such a long time since you were here. Perhaps you will be over this summer.

We were profoundly shocked to hear of the dreadful catastrophe that happened to Lipschitz. Poor man, what a fearful blow it must have been. We hope he is recovering and getting courageous enough to start his big jobs all over again.

Lipschitz: The sculptor Jacques Lipchitz (1891–1973), born in Lithuania, was a French citizen from 1925 and settled in the U. S. in 1941. In 1952, a fire destroyed his studio, including a large model figure for the church at Assy, to which he devoted many years of work.

Marc wonders if you had any further news from Grace Borgenicht about the synagogue murals. Perhaps you could give her a fair idea of the price Marc would ask for them, according to the size she desires?

Balanchine is coming over to Paris for the festival that is being held there this summer. He is bringing over the Firebird and Marc and Ida have written to him for about the third time asking him to replace the scene which he cut out in the London production and to re-do the costumes according to the designs. I saw the ballet in London. It was a shocking production as far as the lighting and costumes were concerned. Balanchine had taken the liberty to cut out a whole scene and change a number of the costumes. The monster scene was flooded in a red light, the result being that none of the monsters were visible and that all Marc's colours might as well not have existed. Balanchine sent a telegramme saying he would phone us in Vence around the 16th of February. But we have no word from him yet. Have you got the contract that Marc made with the Ballet Theatre? It would be very useful to have and we would be grateful if you would send it to us.

Ida's wedding was a very joyous affair here in Vence. We had a big lunch in the Studio (upstairs) for 25 people and then about 40 more afterwards. We were all very gay for about a week. Ida and Franz are very happy. You will like Franz very much, he is a charming person.

Now about the house in High Falls: We have decided once and for all to get rid of it. Would you help us, Bernard? I know how busy you are and what a worry it will be but it would be lovely if we could sell it for a good price and be free of all the worries it entails. It is still empty. It seems that Victor Purcell, the caretaker, simply sends away all would-be tenants because he doesn't like the look of their faces. The would-be buyers are treated in the same way. Purcell is so well known in the neighbourhood and so disliked that no one will have anything to do with him. They literally don't want to buy a house that is so near to his. As for people who come from far away he always manages to choke them off. I wouldn't be surprised if he was sabotageing our chances of selling just from sheer cussedness. So the only solution is to get a New York Real Estate man to come and give it the look over and give it an estimate. But he would have to be warned about Victor

Virginia and Marc in Vence, 1951.

Purcell. I am sending you an extra pair of keys that I have so that Victor will not have to be troubled! He is quite likely to tell all kinds of stories to put people off the place. The trouble is that I can't get rid of Victor because if I do he will probably do even worse harm and I shall never get anyone to take his place because no one would take a place that belonged to Victor. Everyone fears him. He is a very queer person. He is absolutely honest as far as money goes. He is a Quaker and prides himself on his morals which he tries to teach to all the sinful population of High Falls. And he is a born policeman, always nosing into other people's business, trying to catch them out, get them into trouble and wield any bit of authority he possesses to make their lives utterly miserable. I enclose a cutting about the new parkway which is to be made. That should send up the value of real estate in High Falls. We paid 7,500 for the house and put in about 2,000 (roughly) in the shape of a well (excellent deep water) and a new sewerage system, a new roof on the garage, water in the little house (it used to have none) and dozens of little repair jobs. Maybe we could get something like 12,000 for it, what do you think? Of course it is in a very poor state now. The paint is all peeling off and the garden is a mess. I asked Purcell to re-paint the house but he hasn't got around to it. But it would be wonderful if you could spare an afternoon to drive out there with a real estate man and get his opinion on it. Perhaps it would be worth while re-painting it to make it look more attractive.

Dear Bernard, forgive me making you to do this. I wanted to avoid bothering you for such a long time but I see now that there is no way out of it.

Do let us hear from you soon. Marc and I send you and Becky all our love.

Yours, / Virginia

[Added in Virginia's handwriting]

My dear Bernard,

This letter should have gone off ages ago. Forgive my delay. We just received your last letter. Many thanks. I am writing to Forster asking for particulars about the textile designs. He has already left France & is back in America. He didn't phone us here. Thankyou so much for taking care of the matter. It is a good idea to ask to see the Picasso and Braque contracts before agreeing to anything.

Forster: A man named Forster got Chagall's permission to use images from his paintings in commercial enterprises.

Marc Chagall in Paris to Virginia Haggard in Vence

in Mentone: Virginia told Marc that she had stayed overnight with her friends Elisabeth Sprigge and Velona Harris in Mentone, but in fact she spent the night with her new lover Charles Leirens.[5]

Thursday 4 [March] 1952   Paris

[French] Dear, I wrote you. I telephoned you, but you are surely in Mentone. Here we work for the exhibit, I am working on the cover. Here are the number of

Marc Chagall with Charles Sorlier in the Mourlot offices.

ceramics that will have to be shown and they have to be brought here with the sculptures. This is the number chosen, that is almost all the best ones except for the ceramics that are already at Idas. The photo of the ascetic Chamote is missing, which is on the cabinet in the dining room: *The Goat on the Background of the Village* in width. So take *it all* and *pack it well* and all the sculptures that are *on the pedestals*. So I suggest that you come, with Alexandre, in the car with the ceramics (according to the numbers) and the sculptures inside. I hope that they are going to pack them safely. Alexandre will then leave for Vence by train. For the moment, the *big photos* of sculptures must be sent here. I think 29 x 30 [cm] (not small), for Maeght for the catalogue.

Chamote: According to Virginia, "Chamotte" was "a clay used for pottery into which a coarse, granulated substance is introduced to give it a rough texture."

How are the ceramic plaques at Vallauris? If they're good they should be sent quickly (3?)

How are things? You? The children? The house?

So, see you soon, kisses.

The exhibit is March 21, but the ceramics and sculptures have to be here sooner all the same.

I think that won't be too heavy for the car. But the *back seat has to be taken off* and maybe there are things that have to be sent by baggage on the train.

Kisses, my dear / Write me more / Kiss the children

Marc

Marc Chagall in Paris to Virginia Haggard in Vence

7/III Paris 1952

[French] Dear, it seems to me that an eternity has passed. Time passes. And I want to work, but I have to be here. I have to arrange the tapestry and Ida is nice—she is setting up a studio here so I can work on the tapestry and other things. When will you come? We are going to rent a room in a nearby hotel. How are things? And the trip here in the car with the ceramics and sculpture? You don't want to be accompanied by Alexandre?

I hope that everything will be wrapped well (taking out the second seat of the car). Did you send the photos (some of the sculptures and some of the ceramics—the best)? How are the children? And David? Jean? And you, my child. Do you go to bed late? And do you think of me? Ida got the oranges and is happy. How are the ceramic panels at Ramié? Bad? They have to be sent by express shipment. Three pieces (the matte and the two new ones—"Clock" and "Nude Woman"). Telephone me when you can in general from Vence. I love to talk with you and kiss my angel, and I kiss you—you know with so much love that I can't write or express. (Except in a Russian poem and in paintings—and again!)

Promise you won't stay in the studio too late.

Your

Marc

Perhaps have a little herb tea.

Marc, Virginia, and the children with art critic Jacques Lassaigne in Vence.

To: Department of State, WASHINGTON[6]

From: Amembassy, Paris

Subject: MRAP—The Movement against Racism, Anti-Semitism and for Peace

[English] March 12, 1952

DESPATCH CONFIDENTIAL

The information below is furnished in answer to the reference despatch inquiring about the subject organization.

Background

Immediately following World War II, the French Communist Party resumed its anti-racist propaganda, particularly among former deportees and internees. Its chief vehicle was a front organization, Le Mouvement National Contre le Racism (MNCR), the Secretary-General of which at that time was Charles FELD. This organization made unsuccessful attempts to capture others working in the same sphere, including the Ligue Internationale contre l'Antisemitisme (LICA), which carries on an independent existence today. When these attempts failed, the MNCR's activities diminished, and a successor group, the Alliance Antiraciste, took the field. Leaders of the Alliance Antiraciste were recruited mainly from the MNCR and from a left-wing splinter group of the LICA. Among the militants of the Alliance Antiraciste was Charles PALANT, present Secretary General of the Mouvement Contre le Racisme, l'Antisemitisme et Pour le Paix (MRAP). The Alliance Antiraciste ceased to function sometime during 1948, but with the launching of the MRAP in the spring of 1949 the CPF injected new life into its languishing anti-racist activity.

Aims, Activity and Strength

The MRAP proclaims that it fights racial prejudice and defends minority groups and peace. These good words thinly disguise its true nature. While combatting racial prejudice, it has extracted from such episodes as the Willie MacGee affair every possible opportunity for anti-American propaganda. Under the guise of opposing anti-Semitism, it publicizes the happy lot of the Jews in iron-curtain countries. It likewise carries on vigorous anti-colonial propaganda, paying particular attention to the plight of the Arabs in France and of the Jews in North Africa, and generally supports the various campaigns of the Soviet-inspired World Peace Movement, such as the Stockholm Appeal, the Five Power Pact and opposition to Western rearmament. Such activity readily identifies the MRAP as a para-Communist front organization, faithfully echoing the Communist line and furthering the aims of Soviet foreign policy.

As was true of its forerunners, the MNCR and the Alliance Antiraciste, the MRAP is predominantly a Jewish organization.

It may be true that many members were Jews, but the framework of the organization was intended to include persons of all backgrounds. Thus, the Committee of Honor included Gabriel D'Arboussier, Secretary-General of the Ressem-
blement Democratique Africain; the black poet from Martinique Aimé Césaire;
Yves Farge, head of the French National Peace Council; Maurice de Barral, President of l'Union Française des Anciens Combattants; and many others.

Its strength in metropolitan France is centered mainly in Paris, although it
has sections in other areas. Marseille, with its polyglot population has a particularly active group. The membership of the MRAP is unknown, but it is esti-
mated to be not very large as compared with that of leading Jewish groups in
France. Its influence, however, reaches way beyond its nominal membership,
through its close connections with a number of other prominent fronts, such as
the Union des Femmes Francaises. The MRAP is known to comprise at least
twenty-eight affiliated organizations and societies (See Enclosure 1).

Leadership

MRAP was dominated by Communists and fellow-travelers at its inception and
remains so today. Marc CHAGALL, painter and political crackpot, who has been
its honorary president since 1949, is little more than a figurehead. President
Andre BLUMEL is its driving force. A lawyer and former assistant to Leon
BLUM, he has been active in the World Peace Movement here. Another lawyer,
Maurice GRINSPAN, was Secretary-General between June 1949 and September
1951. Palant, Vice-President of the Youth Section of the Alliance Antiraciste in
1946 and previously a member of the MRAP Secretariat, who supplanted Grinspan in the recent re-organization, has proved to be more active than his predecessor. [. . .] It will be noted that among the thirty-three members of the
Committee of Honor, there are four known Communists, the remainder being
with few exceptions para-Communists or active fellow-travelers. [. . .]

Philip W. Bonsal
Charge d'Affairs, a.i.

Department: Please pouch copies to:
Amembassies MOSCOW, LONDON, ROME, BRUSSELS, OSLO, THE HAGUE,
COPENHAGEN, STOCKHOLM, PRAGUE, WARSAW, BELGRADE, BUCHAREST,
ATHENS, ANKARA, BERN, VIENNA,
Amlegation LUXEMBOURG

Enclosure 1—*Organizations and Societies*
Affiliated with the MRAP

Organizations

Anciens Combattants Juifs; Artisans; Cadets; Yasc; Hach. Hatz [Hachalutz Hat-zayir, Labor Zionist youth movement]; Intersyndicaliste Juive; Juifs Polonais; Unions des Juifs pour la Resistance et l'Entr'aide

Societies: Most of these societies were *Lands-manshaftn*, basically nonpolitical, philan-tropic organizations of Jews born in a certain town or area in Eastern Europe.

Societies

Amis Israelites de France; Les Amis de Paris; Amicale Russe; Brest-Litowsk; Chmielnik; Czenstochow; Fraternite des Tailleurs; Kielce; Lubartow; Nowy Dwor; Ochotow; Ozarow; Pietrokow; Praga; Radom; Sections Mutuels des Israelites, Paris; Siedlec; Vilnois; Wolomin; Yidische Briderliche Hilfe.

Marc Chagall left MRAP quietly in the summer or fall of 1952, shortly after the execution of the major Soviet Yiddish writers in Moscow, on August 12, 1952.

Virginia Haggard in Paris to the Opatoshus in New York

22 Place Dauphine Paris 1   March 26th 1952

[English] My dearest Opatoshus,

Thankyou for your letters and for the cutting from the newspaper showing David [Opatoshu] in the part of a policeman. It looks like him.

We are staying for a few days in Paris. Marc has loads of work to do. It's wonderful to hear that you will soon be in France! You must be looking forward so eagerly to your journey to Israel.

The reason why I didn't cash those checks for David & Jean is because I didn't quite know how to do it. I suppose I should send them to the bank in New York.

As soon as I get back to Vence I shall send you a copy of Boccacio [with Chagall's illustrations], I promise.

Love to you all. / Yours devotedly

Virginia

Catastrophe

Catastrophe came overnight.

Marc Chagall in Vence to the Opatoshus in New York

"Les Collines" / Vence / (A.-M.)   10 avril 1952

[Yiddish] Dear Opatoshu and Adelye. I haven't written to you in a long time, but I always wanted to. But how do I recover? Now I must tell you, my dearest friend, what is happening in my heart. After 7 years of living with Virginia I am almost crushed, as upset as you can imagine. Some character (old), came, some photographer, a sick man, to make (ostensibly) a film about me at my home and she "fell in love" with him. Of course, for her, there is no "interest" in it, the base man is a salon creature, who appears to be speaking mildly and is in general a skirtchaser [*curer*]. For 62 years he chased after women, and now he won her heart (or vice versa) in my house where he lived for three weeks as my "guest."

I think that in her craziness she fell in love with him more than he did with her, because she didn't understand my mission in life and art. She was looking for some "naturist" philosophy in a strange English way. Apparently, she complained about me *to strangers*, and that alone made her my "enemy" in my own house. She accused me of being a "materialist," an "egoist," that my paintings are "too expensive," that my house is too big . . . too famous. She is not interested in the people [who visit us], i.e., collectors, writers, museum directors, she cannot serve them . . . tea, she cannot be the wife of a famous man . . . and so on . . . that I am nervous and this is not proper for the children. Now you see the story of my life after Bellochka's death, when she came as a "poor maid" to Riverside Dr. from her even poorer and unfortunate husband, who drove her to others, and I dreamed of making her into a princess, though you once said of her that she had one fault, she *didn't read much*. But if she had the genius *to feel* art—and my art, she would have understood what kind of person I am—the creator of this art. But she began from the other end—from the man and did not (could not) get to the wellspring of the art. It means she did not have in herself even 1/10 of the genius of Bella, and in general of our Jewish wives of artists who stand at their posts, holy and devoted . . . This is my tragedy and my mistake. But still, I worked with her for 7 years. I was blind to believe that I had my son David with her.

This doubt in Chagall's mind was overruled in the same letter: "my rage over my son whom she takes away"—and in subsequent letters where he expresses his fear that "Dovidl" won't grow up as a Jew and wants to adopt him, which Virginia refuses. In any case, after Chagall's death, David McNeil was pronounced Chagall's illegitimate son and shared in his inheritance, according to French law.

And now, dark life has opened for me a grave more bitter than Bella's grave, because with her death I *lamented naturally* and our love stayed whole for eternity. But here, there are *2 tragedies*. The second one is the insult. But what can one demand of her, if her father and mother had no heart. My daughter laments [the situation] (after her wedding), but she begs God that she [Virginia] won't come back and will regret from afar, for presumably she goes on Wednesday to her father *with the children* and with the *whole pack of clothes* and everything I gave her, ostensibly "to think over" the situation (and the Belgian meanwhile sits in Brussels where he lived and will perhaps go on living; his name is Charles Leirens), and she will presumably make a definitive decision. But I ask God that if [she regrets], I have the strength to answer that she can remain wherever she is. In spite of my terrible love for her and my rage over my son whom she takes away with her own daughter, recorded in her passport. Just recently, she finally received her divorce [from John McNeil], so maybe she will use it with the other one. So it is, my dear, with the cold beauty, such characters are to be found, perhaps, only in England. And I had to go through this calamity too. Had she, at least, fallen in love with a young man—that is understandable, but he is a simple man (not a simple skirtchaser to catch Chagall's woman in his own house where he was invited for 3 weeks to do his "work"). Among millions of people [to find] a sick man, a "cardiac" case with asthma, 62 years old. This is the human, "philosophical" offense, which I as an artist, supposedly valued by the world, did not deserve . . .

One great calamity is that I cannot live alone. And not work. And why did God punish me—I don't know. Whom did I harm?

How are you? I was glad to receive your book and saw your picture in it. It is enough to look and leaf through your book to see and feel your high art. I'd like, perhaps, to have some heart and calm to enjoy you and your rhythm—your art, which is similar to mine.

I kiss you both warmly and give my warm regards to your Dovid.

Your devoted as ever

Chagall

The address: M. Chagall, Vence [A.M.], France

Virginia Haggard and Charles Leirens

Charles Leirens, a Belgian photographer, had visited the Chagalls in High Falls, New York, and taken pictures of the family. In February 1952 he came to Vence to make a film and stayed at Les Collines for three weeks. He was a year older than Chagall, suffered from a heart condition, but he and Virginia fell in love; she tells the story in detail in her book.[7] On March 4, while Marc was in Paris, they spent the night together. Then, Alexander drove Virginia to Paris to bring Chagall a collection of ceramics and sculptures for an exhibition on March 21. Virginia and Marc stayed in a hotel for several weeks, and on March 26, Virginia still wrote a letter to Opatoshu signing both her and Marc's names. But the secret leaked out, all hell broke loose, and in the first days of April, Marc and Virginia went back to Vence for two weeks. "During the eternity of those two weeks," wrote Virginia, "Marc tried to persuade me that Charles was too old for me [. . .], was in a precarious state of health and had no right to ask a young woman to share his life."[8] Virginia was thirty-seven. Among those who tried to persuade her to stay were Tériade—"He told me that I had a sacred duty toward Marc the artist, and that nothing in the world counted more than that"—Matisse, and the Maeghts. Virginia packed her bags, took the two children, and left for good on April 16. Marc missed her long into his marriage to Vava.

Ida Chagall in Paris to Bernard Reis in New York

22 Place Dauphine Paris 1   Thursday 2 May 1952

[English] Dear Bernard,

Thank you so much for your nice letter which I have just received. Thank you for sending my reentry permit.

When are you planning to come? There is no chance of us coming to the States this year, I believe. Franz is anxious to meet you as he knows you through me and so other people.

Unfortunately, I do not see what could be left to be done about a reconciliation between Virginia and Father, especially as they never quarrel. This all thing fell as a thunder the beginning of March when Virginia brought the ceramics and sculptures from Vence to Paris. Father was here preparing the posters and catalogs. From the extracts of a letter which was adressed to her from these friends of hers in Roquefort-les Pins where she wanted father to go on fasting in order to cure his prostate instead of operation. From this letter you will see how she felt about exhibitions and the rest. When she brought the sculptures and ceramics, her first words were: "Vous êtes le jouet des éditeurs et des marchands de tableaux" (You are being played by etc. . . .) ["You are being manipulated by publishers and art dealers"], and the same evening she told father that she fell in love with this Mr. Charles Leirens, that she discovered love finally and she was leaving.

They stayed for a couple of weeks in an hotel in Paris and it was hell. They leaved [sic] afterwards for Vence together. I was hoping and Father was hoping of course much more that the sight of the house, the children, will change her mind and she will come back to earth. For two weeks absolutely dreary, she packed in front of father's nose, doing it so calmly, so cold-bloodedly, without forgetting anything, araising [sic] even in their mutual address-book, the names and adresses that were more of her friends than of his.

I learned this morning that she lives in a flat in Paris, already with this person, the children are in a school in England. She had her divorce a month ago and father suffers hell that he could not declare his son before.

What will happen now, I do not know. Father, after dreadful weeks of frenzy is in such sadness and so despaired now that it is worse to see him than before.

I brought him back with me to Paris, but I am trying very hard to make him work again in his own house. On the other hand, I can not keep the house in Vence and I found a very nice friend of mine who consented to come and keep the house, keep company and make things run for father. It is a temporary solution that will be probably be none [sic], but I wanted to gain time for his own sake and health.

His cardiogramms are not good and it adds to my anxiety. May be [sic] he will be able to keep himself up with this solution for a little while. This lady friend is a Russian by origin; she speaks perfect English so you can write freely to father and she will translate.

I will speak to Tériade about the price of the "Fables de La Fontaine". The whole thing is not yet quite finished. The first copies showed already are exceptionally beautiful. You have not seen yet also the two covers done with two original etchings. I will let you know immediately. I am not going to do anything about the books in the United States as they are too few books. I will have something around five copies in all of the de-luxe ones.

Excuse this long letter, but I wanted you to know the details.

My love to you both,

Your Ida   (Chagall)

P.S. Included is a homage of a letter addressed to Virginia by friends of her, mediums and so on.

temporary solution: Ida is at it again! The housekeeper very soon became Marc's third wife, Vava Chagall.

On the tense day of Virginia's final departure from Vence on April 16, 1952, Chagall gave her a gift of two drawings, signed: "For Virginia/My love/Marc" and "My life, my art, my love—my Virginia/Marc." To no avail.

Virginia left Vence with her children on April 16, 1952, ostensibly to think it all over in London. On the same day, Chagall gave her a gift: a drawing of him and Virginia leaning sadly on his body, and another image of the abandoned, fallen Chagall with a dedication: "my life, my art, my love—my Virginia/Marc/16-4-

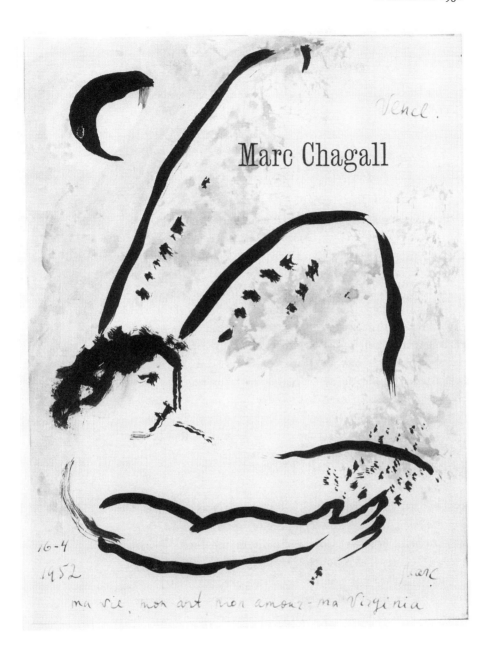

1952." Purposeful and practical Ida couldn't leave him alone in Vence, and found a housekeeper who arrived the same day, April 16. "It is a temporary solution," wrote Ida, "that will probably be none, but I wanted to gain time." Soon enough, the housekeeper, Valentina Brodsky, became Chagall's third wife.

Marc Chagall in Vence to the Opatoshus in New York

"Les Collines"/Vence/(A.-M.)   Paris 30/6 1952

[Yiddish] My dear friends Opatoshu. I got your letters long ago, they were forwarded here. It is so hard to take up my pen. I came here first to spread about
and I have to make lithographs for a book and then I wanted a lawyer friend to
find out something about what will happen to poor David. You can imagine how
low I feel, if [I don't write] even to you and your letter is also lying here. If she
wrote to you that she *did* know him . . . for ten years (that he came in 1942 or
later to America, possibly, and for the *first* time [they] met then. He came to take
photos in High Falls when David was about 2 years old, and now David is just 6
years old. And she wrote to you on June 15 that 3 months [passed] since she married him, while she left on *April 16* for London and only on *May 14* did she marry
him. But let us put an end to it. He is there. It has to be. There is no greater crime
than a lie. And no natural death and no other, "natural" calamity has upset me so
much as this pretty, false catastrophe. It is enough to read her "love" letters to
me when she got her divorce in February 1952 and before that, and how she said
after Ida's wedding in our garden that "now" was our turn to get married. It may
be enough just to read her old words in her letters to you. So I am at a loss of
breath to live, not just to understand. And now one may think of her whatever
you want, how she behaved . . . both in America and here.

May 14: Yes, but the love affair began early in March.

our turn: According to Virginia, Marc did not respond to her wish.[9]

Now this, my dear: it may be useful to have a document from the clinic where
she gave birth to the boy 6 years ago. You were there. A note certifying that I paid
the money (or you did for me?), in general, how I was the father of the child,
supported him from the beginning (not her first husband, McNeil), and maybe
such a paper from the doctor, too.

Dear Opatoshu, you can imagine how happy I will be to see you both at my
place in Vence. If you get to Nice, let me know when the train arrives, and I will
send someone with a car to bring you here. I am not alone in the house. It was
terrible. Ida and her friend brought me a housekeeper, a Jewish woman,and I
am not alone. I am waiting to cool off more and more. Pray God for me, to erase
from my heart the last bit of feeling, even "pity" for her [Virginia]. That she
should let me breathe free of lies and of all my dark and bitter feelings, that are
not nice even for a man like me (as they say).

How is your son Dovid? And their little boy? I want so much for her to . . .
"sell" me my son? That he should remain a Jew. Not in vain did I worry so and
wait for her divorce, so I could finally adopt him after our wedding. But she
thought about something else, not her children. But I shall pay her a monthly
pension (through the lawyer and bank) for the child. But unfortunately I cannot

yet see Dovid personally, even if she lets me. I am still too sensitive and upset to see him this year. At my home. For a while.

I kiss you both warmly, your devoted

Chagall

Virginia Haggard in Paris to the Opatoshus in New York

54 Ave Simon Bolivar   Paris 19e   July 14th [1952]

[English] Dearest Adele and Open,

I am hoping very much to have a letter from you soon saying that you still love me and that my leaving Marc has not altered our friendship at all. I hope you got my letter, written about a month ago. It is difficult to explain everything that happened but I dearly hope that I shall be able to see you when you come over here. Do please write to me.

It was very sweet of you Open to get a little ring for your god-son David. The children are still in England until the end of July and then they will spend the summer with Charles and me. David will go and stay with his papa whenever his papa wants him. It is very sad when families split up but if the parents are kind to each other there is no need for the children to suffer. Marc has said things about me that I don't believe real friends will take seriously. Just the same it hurts.

Dearest friends, write to me.

Love from Virginia

P.S. Did you have a good trip to South America, Open?

Adele I would love to have news of you all. Did I tell you that Charles & I are going to America on the 7th of October for about 2 months?

Marc Chagall in Vence to the Opatoshus in New York

"Les Collines"/Vence/(A.-M.)   23/7 1952

[Yiddish] Dear friends, I got your letter and thank you for the gifts you sent me from Brazil. I shall be happy to see you in Vence with good luck. Write me precisely when you come. And now the following. There must be an end to my life with the English woman. It is a fact that he came. She wanted it with her inexplicable craziness. She was in a big hurry to marry the Goy. And now, you see, the Jewish woman who came the same day, April 16, to rescue me from the sadness alone in the house, became my wife on *July 12*. That's it. I hope that somehow the other one will gradually let me have David, though it seems that, formally, he cannot be adopted. I shall pay her a pension for him (through the bank). It makes no sense to talk about her. No one understands it, maybe not even she herself.

For me she is dead. Sometimes I'd like to pity her. But she didn't have pity for me. Or for her children.

How are you, my dear friends. I shall be happy to spend time with you here. Though my soul is not the same. And you can understand because you can understand.

I kiss you warmly. / Your devoted

Chagall

P.S. I want to sell my house in High Falls. I am asking Bernard Reis.

Virginia Haggard in Paris to Bernard and Becky Reis in New York

54 Ave Simon Bolivar / Paris 19e   September 21st [1952]

[English] My dear Bernard & Becky,

The news of my separation from Marc will have been somewhat of a shock to you and your first reaction will have been one of protest and condemnation of my decision. But one day I hope to tell you in a way that you will understand all the circumstances that led to my decision, and meanwhile I shall not try to justify myself because I hope you still have the same warm feelings towards me that I have towards you and I hope you don't think me capable of taking this very serious step in a hasty or light hearted manner or of forgetting everything that Marc did for me. I am still fond of him, as fond as ever, and deeply attached to Chagall the artist but his life is no longer his, he is caught up and carried away by an immense machine which is his fame and he likes it. Gone are those rare moments when we could get away from money talk, "prestige," publicity and art extras, when Marc just *worked* like the devil in some quiet place and had no thought for the money value of his paintings. Those were blissfully happy moments and we loved each other then. But at other times he treated me very much as a favorite piece of furniture, I was useful and a little bit ornamental too, but I hadn't any soul. I was there to fetch and carry, administer to his needs and help the "machine" to turn round smoothly. I wouldn't have minded so much if the high powered mechanism hadn't interfered with his work. Alas! He was receiving orders for certain types of productions which would fetch high prices. Instead of being his own savage self and painting all the wild and beautiful things he is capable of, he consciously turned his hand to certain works which he was encouraged to make and convinced himself that it was what he wanted to do. His greatest desire was to paint from nature. This was firmly and severely discouraged. Crucifixes were frowned on. He was urged to produce more "fantaisies Chagallien," nothing gloomy, nothing approaching the realistic. And so he repeats himself. Fortunately Tériade exerts a wholesome influence on him and tries to urge him to work from nature to renew himself in a closer contact with nature. But the fame machine turns round inexorably and everybody gets richer and more heartless.

I fervently hope this separation won't mean giving up my contact with you which I value so highly. I hope, too, that you will soon make the acquaintance of Charles [Leirens]. He is leaving for America on the 7th of October to finish his courses in photography at the New School. I was supposed to have accompanied him but I have no visa. I was told at the American Consulate that an enquiry has to be made regarding my associations with Chagall who is a "Communist." Isn't it infuriating? To describe Marc as a Communist is really very funny. You know how virulently he attacks the Soviets whenever he can. But he signed the Stockholm appeal.

The Stockholm Appeal of 1950, calling for world peace, was initiated by the French Communist physicist and Nobel Prize laureate Frederic Joliot-Curie. It attracted many humanistic intellectuals in Europe and was signed by over 273,000,000 persons (including the Soviet adult popluation).

my father: Sir Godfrey Haggard was head of the Department of Anglo-American relations in the British Foreign Office.

I can only console myself by thought of Charlie Chaplin's possible smile from the USA! I really wouldn't care at all if it were not for the fact that I must help Charles with the moving of all his possessions because he has a weak heart and can't possibly do it himself. I still hope I will get my visa because my father and a Belgian lawyer friend of Charles in New York are trying to pull strings. If I do, it will be lovely to see you again.

Do write to me soon, please, and tell me if I shall have a chance of seeing you.

Love from Virginia

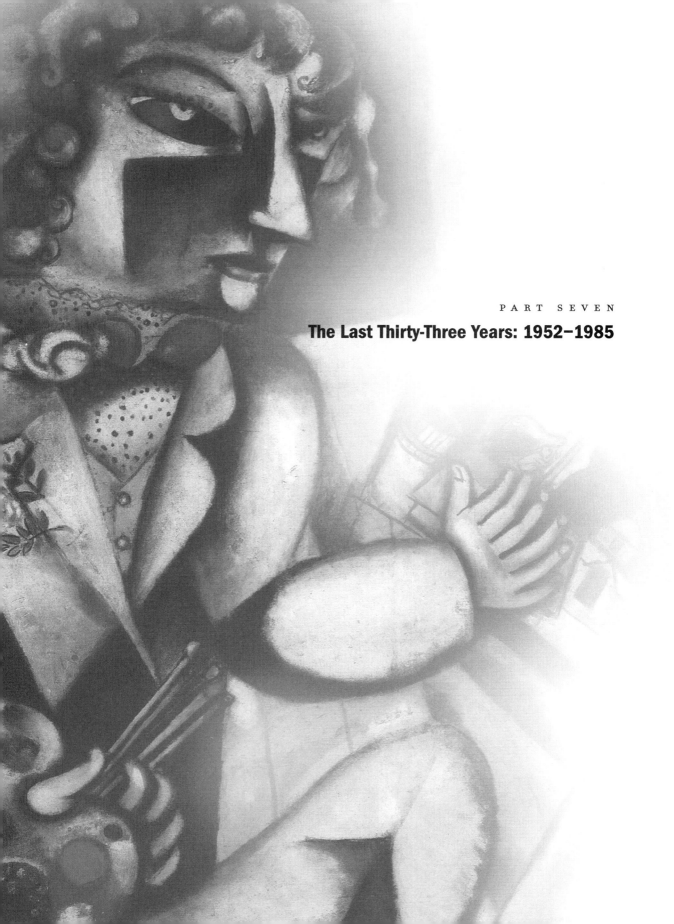

CHAPTER TWENTY-ONE **Life with Vava: 1952–1956**

Life with Vava Brodsky

The seven years with Virginia ended abruptly, causing much pain to Chagall. Virginia left for London on April 16, 1952, and the very same day (!) "the two Idas" (Chagall and Bourdet) brought a housekeeper "to rescue me from sadness alone in the house," as Chagall explained. Ida assumed it would be a temporary arrangement, just a stop-gap measure, but on July 12, Marc Chagall (sixty-five years old) and Valentina (Vava) Brodsky (forty-seven) were married. In a letter to Daniel Charny (1957), Chagall writes: "I have another wife (the third) from the Brodsky family itself from Kiev," referring to the famous Jewish sugar magnates. The Brodsky name among Russian Jews was something like "Rothschild" in the West, but it was also a common name. Some contemporaries doubted whether the distinguished pedigree was correct. As the quote shows, Chagall considered Virginia a wife in every respect, and he was deeply hurt by her sudden departure.

Henceforth, Marc and Vava would be inseparable. The marriage gave him a sense of home and security. Vava always traveled with him, conducted his correspondence, and took care of him as the other women in his life had done. Yet Vava increasingly controlled his mail and his visitors, took charge of the busi-

Chagall and his third wife Vava, in Vence, 1952.

ness affairs previously handled by Ida, and eased his son David out of the house. At one point, Marc and Vava secretly divorced in a small village, only to remarry half a year later on much better terms for Vava. This was illegal, because people affected by the terms have to be notified beforehand, and Ida had no idea of it.

Not many details about Vava are known. Her past was shrouded in mystery, and she appeared before Chagall as a *deus ex machina*. The general outlines may be reconstructed as follows: Valentina (Valya) Brodsky was born in 1905 in Russia (according to the FBI documents: in Kiev, but she was probably the ultimate source of that determination). After the Revolution, her family fled to the West, perhaps to Berlin, and eventually settled in London, where she grew up and became a milliner. She apparently knew Russian and some English as well as French, and she wrote most of Chagall's business letters in French, indicating that she lived in France for several years (as did her brother Michel Brodsky).

Chagall boasted to his Jewish friends that now he had a Jewish wife, which felt to him like a relief from the differences in mentality between him and Virginia. But Michel Gordey insisted (in an interview with me) that Vava had converted to Christianity while still in London. This information came from his aunt and cousins in London, with whom he had close relations, and "after all, the Russian émigré community in London was very small and they all knew each other." If this was the case, she hid it carefully from Chagall, and since neither of them practiced religion, the problem did not arise. Yet Yiddish correspondents complained that she limited access to him and would not show him Yiddish letters or the Yiddish newspapers, which were his lifeline to the Jewish world and to current information about Israel (because "they would upset him"). An American publisher of art books asked Chagall to illustrate the Passover Hagaddah (the kind of classical Jewish texts he had always dreamed of being commissioned to do), and the response came from the Maeght Foundation: Chagall does not want to be known as a Jewish painter (What else could he be?). Yet on major issues, Chagall prevailed, and they traveled to Israel several times, even for his ninetieth birthday.

There is a puzzle: Vava's mother died in Berlin, and Vava went to the funeral without Chagall (he always refused to go to Germany). Was her mother a Christian? Russian or German? If not, what would she have done in Berlin? Did she survive the Holocaust there? In any case, Vava buried Chagall in the Christian cemetery in St.-Paul de Vence; Chagall apparently refused to talk about death and could not possibly have wanted that.

Soviet Anti-Semitism

Another blow, although of different dimensions, was the betrayal of the Soviet Union, especially Stalin's cruel and irrational anti-Semitism. Soviet Jewish culture and its leaders were physically liquidated; the campaign against "Cosmopolitans" targeted assimilated Jews who were prominent in Russian literature and culture; and the show trials in Prague in 1952 accused Rudolf Slansky, Secretary of the Czech Communist Party, and other Czech Communists, of "Zionism" (a euphemism for "Jew"). Nothing else undermined Chagall's trust in human nature as much. When he talked of Jewish destiny, he lost any rational ground and reverted to a folklorized, pan-historical perception of Jewish suffering, irrespective of country or political system.

The Vision of "Love"

In many of his public statements, Chagall embraced the abstract vision of "Love" —first invoked in his panel "Love on the Stage" in the Moscow Yiddish Theater, where any Jewish cultural sign disappeared and the dancing bodies almost melted into the transparent shapes and colors. Now "Love" became identified with "Color" and "Truth" and was transformed into the "biblical message" the Jews gave the world. This theme recurs in various statements about Israel, in speeches on art, in private letters, and in paintings for his museum in Nice, founded by the French government and named National Museum: Marc Chagall—The Biblical Message. This was a "universal" message, and Chagall could now be seen as a universal painter, rather than as a parochial portrayer of Jewish Eastern Europe. Indeed, the "biblical message" was a message from within, from the painter who lived the biblical narratives in his own childhood, to the world of Christian Europe. His work for churches only complemented this spiritual vision. Yet Chagall did not betray his past: Images of the Jewish masses and the *shtetl* which had fallen into an abyss appear on the margins of the towering biblical figures, that are full of joy and power.

The Fictional Worlds of Literature

Such abstract concepts as "Love" and "Color" are, of course, too fuzzy for a concrete art and too dangerous for a representational artist. Chagall was honest in the images he depicted, even when he distorted and reshuffled their coherence, or when they became stereotypical. His sense of Jewish identity never left him, whether it was detrimental to his art or not. He evoked in his paintings a world based on images he knew intimately and on the "documents" he painted in Vitebsk and Lyozno after 1914 directly from "nature": the characters, mores, and landscapes of Russian provincial Jewry. He created a mythological space called "Vitebsk," which consolidated his images into one fictional universe, often deformed and desentimentalized in his whimsical compositions.

But when he was cut off from Jewish Vitebsk—as early as 1922—and couldn't replenish its imagery ("Vitebsk was over," he said at the end of his first autobiography), and again when it was wiped off the face of the earth in World War II, he reduced his stock images to abbreviated conceptual emblems. The Russian Revolution, the Exodus from Egypt, the "burning town," and the Holocaust were just such general concepts, with which he could evoke his schematic mass scenes. The image of Jesus Christ as the symbolic suffering Jew helped him individualize that immense experience, as no earthly individual figure could, and to identify with it personally.

But when he lost touch with a world of his own, what saved Chagall from poster art or repetitive kitsch were the fictional worlds of great literature he illustrated. Here, he did not have to tell his own story any more; his story had been exhausted long ago. Though he did some fresh and vibrant paintings from French nature,

The cover of Vitebsk, a collection of memoirs and historical studies in Hebrew, published by the
Association of Immigrants from Vitebsk and Vicinity, Tel Aviv, 1957. Chagall signs his names in
the Hebrew (not the Yiddish) spelling (MRK ShGL), yet hints at Yiddish by adding a tentative second
V in the name of the city (VViTBSK).

they did not add up to a private, total "Chagallian" world. The source of his original strength—the insistence on a peculiar Chagallian universe, composed of modular units repeated time and again in various transformations, which created a private language and an authentic impact—became a burden, a trite repetition of himself. What was initially a strong counterpoint—between presented "reality," on the one hand, and disjointed and decontextualized forms and colors, on the other—lost its edge when the presented "reality" itself grew emblematic and trivialized, when both the grotesque and the defiance of gravity turned sentimental and smooth. Now the figures were no longer flying above the ground but floating in the air, in a groundless space of the canvas. The tensions that had informed his early masterpieces—tensions between the boundaries of colors and objects, representational figures and geometrical forms—subsided, and Chagall was in danger of becoming a sweet colorist, covering ready-made spaces with bright colors.

Illustrating the fictional worlds of others gave Chagall free rein to express his full powers: in the etching technique, in the celebration of colors, in figures from his own world inserted into the margins of others, and in the combination of original insights and whimsical subversions of the serious. Gogol, La Fontaine, Eluard, Pushkin, "Daphnis and Chloe," the Circus, Boccacio; the Yiddish poetry of Hofshteyn, Sutzkever, and Lyesin; work for the ballet and opera—all provided Chagall with stages for his own dance.

The "Biblical Message"

The Bible seemed to be the culmination of it all. The Bible brought together the basic antinomies of Chagall's painting and consciousness: It merged the Jewish and the universal; it bridged the gap between the learned and the popular; it combined the presentation of nameable individuals (King David) with spiritual abstractions (national dignity, Love and Music). It also resolved the problem of what Abram Efros called the "three times" (past, present, future)—raised and yet curtailed in the Jewish theater murals. The Bible was both a historical mythology and the imaginary world of his childhood; it conflated the earliest stories a Jewish child heard with impressions of modern Israel. It was a concrete book to be illustrated in the present, and the vision of a naïve, utopian, prophetic future for Israel (in Jerusalem) and for all humanity (in Nice)—all at the same time.

This bridging of opposites rather than exposing the cracks, this "unconsciously conscious," joyful and optimistic, nonintellectual art was at odds with the mainstream of Modernism. It was not understood by the new art of the modern, quite non-"Jewish," secular state of Israel; the mere use of traditional Jewish emblems (Tablets of the Law, Menorah, the Wailing Wall, and so on) was seen as narrative painting, religious sentimentalism, tourist art, or kitsch. Those who understood him in Israel, who were not ashamed of the simple, straightforward, eternal Jewish emblems, and who saw him as the greatest living Jewish artist, were Diaspora Jews themselves, like the President of Israel, Zalman Shazar, or the Speaker of the Knesset, Kadish Luz, who were not involved with the adventures of modern art but of building a Jewish state. With them he immediately found a personal rapport and corresponded in Yiddish and sometimes in Russian. And in France, this biblical retrospection-cum-vision could be perceived as a spiritual, religious, even Christian message. André Malraux, the writer, scholar, and French Minister of Culture under Charles de Gaulle, who commissioned Chagall to paint the Paris Opera ceiling, believed in the spiritual function of art.

Expanding the Genres of Art

In the last third of Chagall's century, the insatiable artist kept expanding his field of activity. It was a period of classical consolidation of a formerly "crazy," deviant artist. He obtained large, functional bodies to paint on—the realization of his call; "Give me a wall!"—as he screamed both as a Commissar in the "People's" Vitebsk and ever after the Moscow Yiddish Theater murals. Now he got

Chagall working on a stage set. His son David is reading.

walls, monumental windows, and ceilings: at the Paris Opera, the Metropolitan Opera in New York, the Hadassah Synagogue and the Knesset in Jerusalem, and the Cathedrals of Reims, Metz, and Mainz.

Chagall always strove to expand his art to new media. To the painting and drawing he learned from Pen and Bakst, he added mass decorations of a city in Vitebsk, theater murals in Moscow, etchings and lithographs in Berlin. And after World War II he spilled over to new genres and media: ceramics, lithographs, sculpture, stained glass windows, and tapestries. The same world of Chagallian images expanded to the other media and acquired a fresh look. To execute such works, he collaborated—literally, interacted every step of the way—with some of the best French artisans in those media, notably the master lithographer Charles Sorlier and the stained-glass master of Reims, Charles Marq. In his old and frail years, his designs were executed by others, the best masters in each field. His major activity now was as a French master, yet most of the communication was oral: Chagall did not trust his written French, and proximity did not require correspondence. Nevertheless, many short messages to both Charleses were preserved, and a selection is included in this book (chronologically).

Jewish Correspondents

At the same time, he continued to correspond almost to the end with many Yiddish writers and Israeli friends, mostly in Yiddish, and sometimes in Russian. Handwritten by Chagall himself, those letters were personal, full of warmth and concern, totally different from the dry business letters typed by Vava or a secretary and signed by Chagall. Sutzkever in Tel Aviv received over seventy Yiddish letters from Chagall; many letters were preserved by Leon Leneman, Mendel Man and Yosef Schein in Paris; Gavriel Talpir, Moshe Mokady, David Giladi, and Kadish Luz in Israel; and many others in the Jewish domain.

Chagall did not really read and understand the development and sophistication of modern Jewish culture, literature, and ideologies in the twentieth century; and in these letters, he fell back onto his parents' primitive and stereotypical views. When he liked or disliked a book printed in Israel, he automatically generalized, praising or accusing Israel itself; while in the West, he knew very well that the state did not dictate the actions or guarantee the quality of individual museums or publishers. When the American Zionist women's organization, Hadassah, commissioned windows for a small synagogue attached to their hospital in Jerusalem and he didn't like the size of the building, it was "Israel's" fault and reflected the State's attitude toward Chagall. Yet he could not get rid of his attraction to and perennial ambivalence toward Israel or the Jews.

Leon Leneman wrote in his book on Chagall that in later years, Vava did not show Marc Yiddish letters or newspapers, ostensibly to protect him from excitement and to suppress his image as a "Jewish" artist. The hundreds of letters to Chagall mostly written in Yiddish (Virginia referred to a trunk full of them in their house Les Collines) apparently disappeared.

To be sure, Chagall's own tendencies to dissociate himself from a blatant Jewish image, and thus be accepted as a Russian or French artist, were evident quite early. Yet he himself knew well that removing his Eastern European Jewishness would obliterate Chagall: even the biblical message wouldn't survive without the prism of his childhood world, in which it was refracted.

The Recluse

Chagall was not satisfied with having his works of art in museums and galleries. He also wanted public, simple art on display for the masses. On the other hand, throughout his life, he expressed the wish to stay isolated, somewhere in nature (in Zaolshe, High Falls, or Les Collines). Like the Hasidic Rebbe Menakhem Mendel of Kotsk (whose image he often alluded to), he would close himself off for the last twenty years of his life and receive food through a small aperture in the wall. That also closed him off from new images and impressions and endowed his art with an aura of repetition and sentimentality. Gregarious Chagall, joker and entertainer—but also workaholic—achieved that peace of mind in his last years, when he was increasingly protected or "imprisoned" (his own word) by Vava.

Marc Chagall in Vence to Abraham Sutzkever in Tel Aviv

"Les Collines" Vence (A.M.), August 11, 1952

[Yiddish] Dear friend Sutzkever,

Please forgive me for not writing for so long. I am used to always getting new things from you: both a letter and your thick collections with your young and brilliant poems, and as always, your very Jewish book of poetry. If I could I wouldn't have been silent and would have talked so much about you (and perhaps about myself), let us say, like recently in Israel, where I was beside myself with happiness. And you probably know: how strange the one who made me [un]happy (after Bella), the English woman, that blond one, who inexplicably left me with my son David. I am still jitery, though I was forced to get married to another one (a Jewish woman), so that I wouldn't go berserk alone in the huge house, and still be able to work a little. I cannot write about it in a letter, but I am not the same person you knew (somewhere not the same). You know what it is. For I was already once "jittery" after the holy departure of Bella (no comparison), and by the way, I am happy to hear that her two books will be published, I think with Schocken, perhaps toward the anniversary of her death in September, and I would be happy if, in your-our Yiddish journal, you could remember my holy bride, poor soul, who lies alone in America and left two most Jewish books like pictures. I hope the Hebrew translation will be poetic. Who knows, you will tell me. And how is your *Siberia*?

Are you really coming to France? It goes without saying, I will be so happy to see you in Vence, and meantime I kiss you warmly,

As ever, your/Marc Chagall

Marc Chagall in Vence to Yosef Opatoshu in New York

Vence 1952

[Yiddish] Dear Opatoshu, just received your letter from Israel. I am glad that you're having a good time there. I would like so much to know your impressions, later. And now: we are leaving for Italy tomorrow—for Rome, and spend there about a week and a half, from there we travel to Greece. I have to see the country (I have to make a book "Daphnis and Chloe"). I hope to return but I don't know whether I'll be back precisely in the beginning of October when you are returning to France, i.e., the 6,7 October. So what and how shall we do it? My address in Italy:

American Express, Rome, Italy

Your devoted/   Chagall

Ida Chagall in Gordes to the Opatoshus in Paris

[Stationery: Gordes (Vaucluse)]

17/X/52

[English] Dear Friends

I see, by your letter to father that you are in Paris. And I am so sorry that I cannot see you, speak to you. And have my husband meet you both.

How are you? How was the trip to Israel?

Father is still in Italy. I have very little news, but expect them at the end of the month. Where will you be by then?

not recovered yet: From the break with Virginia.

We went through hell. Father has not recovered yet. Morally and physically it will take more time than he thinks. We could not tell him how bad were the (his own) cardiograms. Only time and peace can cure him. I am sorry that you could miss seeing him and meeting Valentine. I cannot imagine you not liking her. She is a golden heart. She adores father and in so many ways I cannot help thinking of mother. Father's instinct pushed him to marry her, so that she should remain, but his eyes are seeking still Virginia, that poor, poor, fool who was more cruel than if she were bad.

All my love, my regrets not to receive you and kiss you / Yours

Ida

Marc Chagall in Vence to the Opatoshus in New York

"Les Collines" / Vence / A.-M.   1952, 14 November

[Yiddish] Dear friends, I was happy with your letter from the ship. I hope you'll be able to rest from all your travels. I was so happy to see you in Vence, though I was saddened that Adelye was not with you. It is good that you made the voyage [to Israel]. Only with your own eyes can you see—what goes on in a land that is so dear to us. Your letter saddened me. You with your love for me (and sometimes the old love for her [Virginia])—nevertheless you saw her twice. She has, bless God *different kinds* of talk for "everyone separately." One thing is clear, that she has to "denigrate" me, me (as God knows), unfortunately the . . . innocent, to justify her leaving me. I agreed a bit with your way of seeing her, for I thought that as a writer you were confused, when "something" in our artistic life is not clear to us. But unfortunately I think that it is anyway not clear—neither for you nor for me—the "tragedy" as you call it.

It is clear that I loved her and she didn't understand what it demands—neither my art nor my life nor my child . . . (and her daughter)

May God save her from downfall, may she have some pleasure in her life, though she threw me into a strange pit. I am waiting and waiting for months to cool off, to heal, to find the taste of life (and even art), and to get closer and closer to the woman who came to me—to be near me and help. You saw her. And though I am "innocent," I believe in a God of some kind who will not want me to finish my life in bitterness.

Every woman and man has the right "to leave," though it is tragic—but this should and can be done in a nicer way. (Thus, for example, Ida and her first husband Michel parted and remained such good friends.) But she, mercilessly, frivolously sullied my house when I lived with her and worked with my ideal in my heart. For years, she plotted something. Brought an old Goy——it was not nice for everybody, for her, for me, and even now to talk about that——

May at least the boy David be happy someday—with or without me.

If you want, *send me her letter*, which she wrote to Adelye (I will send it back to you) to know what she accuses me of. Don't be afraid of me.

I think that a little exhibition of mine is now open in the gallery Curt Valentin.[1] Those are the [illustrations to] *LaFontaine* which I made during my life with Bella—the Holy One—and the latest ceramics and sculptures—till very recently.

How are you? How did you find your house, and your friends? And how is Adelye now?

I kiss you both warmly. / *Your devoted Chagall*

I know that it is painful for Adelye. I shall be happy to get a word from her.

Marc Chagall in Vence to Yosef Opatoshu in New York

28 novembre   Vence 1952

[Yiddish] Dear friend. Got your letter. I shall try to do something [= paint] but God knows what may come out of it. You left and I remained here alone. Though I ask God (in my way) that I may become a human being, it is hard going.

How is [Chaim] Greenberg? And Leyvik? Give them my love and best wishes. Don't forget to send me either a translation of her [Virginia's] letter or the original, I promise to send it back to you. I am looking for means to recover. Did you see my small exhibition in Valentin gallery [in New York]?

you left: Opatoshu visited Chagall in Vence in mid-October, on his way back from Israel, after Chagall's return from a trip to Greece and Italy.

I kiss you both, your devoted

Chagall

And what does Mr. Dvorkin, the husband of Yehoash's daughter, think about my house.

Dvorkin: Dvorkin apparently took charge of selling Chagall's house in High Falls.

Marc Chagall in Vence to Abraham Sutzkever in Tel Aviv

Vence, Nov. 28, 1952

I wanted to write to you so many times, but it isn't easy. I wanted to tell you of my great satisfaction with the publication of your book.[2] I think that technically it is very fine indeed. It seems to me that it is a great achievement in Israel, the page-drawings came out perfect, even better than the famous *Verve*. Soon the editor of

Verve [Tériade] is coming to me and I shall boast to him about the work done in my Israel. Well, I think that perhaps the typography, the letters, could be more harmonious. But please tell Goldberg and Gordon, I shall write [to them]—I hope it is really beautiful.

Now I would like them to send a book to Ida and perhaps a few to me. If it will be in English (?) I shall someday show it to my dear son———

My dear, how are you? Oh, how I'd love to talk to you, even in Israel. Oh, how I'd love to bathe in the sea of our Jewish tears and worries with all of you. My God, what is happening to me? I kiss you and the air around you.

Your/Marc Chagall

Goldberg: Owner of a printing house in Jerusalem.

Gordon: Moshe Gordon, Director of the Mossad Bialik Publishing House.

Vava Chagall in Vence to Virginia Haggard in Brussels

"Les Collines"/Vence/(A.-M.)   1.12 [December] 1952

[English] Dear Madame,

Thank you for your letter.

I am very sorry not to be able to take David for Christmas, but we have already made other arrangements for this winter.

Marc is very happy that David is working well.

Of course I will send you the toys, theaters, and books at the end of January.

Best wishes for a very nice trip.

V. Chagall

Marc Chagall in London to Yosef Opatoshu in New York

what "terrible" news: "They are our enemies"—in this case, Stalin's Russia.

last drop: The major Soviet Yiddish writers were shot in Moscow on August 12, 1952. The "Prague trial" of Robert Slansky and other leading Czecho-slovakian Communists stressed their Jewish (called "Zionist," hence "Nazi") nature, and shocked the Jewish leftist world (what remained of it).

London 1953   8/1 [January]

[Yiddish] Dear Opatoshu, a few words from London. I remain here a few more days and return soon to Vence where I must finally work so much. Thank you for the news you're sending me.

About the exhibited etchings from Dr. Loewe. Please apologize to Dr. Loewe that I haven't yet written to him. He is so nice to me———

Here in London it is so gray looking out of the window that Vence seems from afar like the last Garden of Eden. Though every day of the new year we are wait-ing [to hear] what "terrible" news they will throw our way. Thank God, some 3 or 4 months ago I resigned as Honorary President of M.R.A.P. in Paris. They try to hush it up. The last drop went over [the rim] (even before the Prague trial). I be-came (as I was) a Jew from Vitebsk, like our fathers, prepared for suffering———

We feel "good": they're doing evil to us. It is not we who are doing it—
Greetings for the New Year

We feel "good": When persecuted, we are in our Jewish element.

Your devoted   Marc Chagall

Marc Chagall in Vence to Yosef Opatoshu in New York

Chaim Greenberg (1889–1953) was a thinker, an essayist, and a leader of the New York Yiddish cultural, anti-Communist milieu. A charismatic personality, he was considered a moral and intellectual authority among Yiddish- and Hebrew-speaking Jews. He came to the United States in 1924, and from 1932 until his death, he edited the *Yidisher Kemfer* (*Jewish Fighter*), a high-standard Zionist-Socialist and literary weekly. He was the director of the Culture Department of the Jewish Agency. Chagall knew him in New York.

19/III   1953   "Les Collines"/Vence/A.-M.

Dear Opatoshu, just received your letter about [Chaim] Greenberg's death. I attach a few words (of course, with several spelling mistakes in Yiddish), please give it [for publication]. It is in Ida's name too, and even in Bella's name. I find no words. I resent that I am so far away from all of you. I would so much like to be among Jews for a while, and America has a lot, a whole sea of them. When it is not good in your heart . . . it is "good" to melt into that sea. Ach, this is not good either. One has to work, one has to know how, one has to have strength, one must not be as crazy as I am. But not everyone is as wise as our great and dear Chaim Greenberg was . . . I felt that I miss him. But it is late [at night]—have a good Passover. Eat a *kneydl* [matzo ball] for me, drink *Pesakh* wine and be happy.

Love to both of you/ Your devoted

Chagall

Marc Chagall on Chaim Greenberg's Death

19/III   1953   "Les Collines"/Vence/A.-M.

[Yiddish] *On Chaim Greenberg's Death*

When a President dies, one can substitute another one. But sometimes, when a "simple" person dies—you find no place to hide. There is no one to substitute for him. And sometimes you feel that you are out of air to breathe—

Greenberg was such a person—a man of love, being in love, a special nuance without which life or art are not full (whole).

We shall lament him: the Jews are orphaned.

Warm greetings to his family and friends.

Marc Chagall/   and my daughter Ida

Marc Chagall in Vence to Yosef Opatoshu in New York

"Les Collines"/Vence/A.-M.   [July 12, 1953]

I'm sitting at the desk: The following associative chain in his letter is pure Sholem-Aleichem: Tevye the Milkman's monologues.

such a false human being: Virginia.

for the first time: Since the separation.

a son: Piet Marc Meyer was born on July 10, 1953.

[Yiddish] Dear Opatoshu, thank you for your letters. I'm sitting at the desk, quite tired. And today is my day, our day, the 12/7 [July 12] when Valya became my wife—and it seems she is happy and I have a very nice friend for my life. Though only God knows how my life is twisted, and it seems, tortured, and when you imagine, through such a false (?) human being without any soul (?) and a pity for the little Dovid'l, that you have to have a lot of strength not to see it (just recently I saw him for the first time), that who knows whether he remained a Jew in that dark village school. How are you? And how is Adelye? Well, I became a grandfather. Ida has a son. She is in Zurich now. I think we shall go there. I wrote you that I saw your Dovid [Opatoshu] here in Vence. He was not alone, I couldn't talk much with him. But it is always a pleasure to see him. In Torino my largest exhibition in Palace Madame had just closed. I hope they will start publishing the Bible [with Chagall's etchings]. I hope the difficulties will straighten out. But I think I would rather see you personally. Are you coming here? You know, I have a little house at the side, for guests. For the two of you. Yes, I keep thinking and want to ask, if I am not mistaken, Mr. Bernstein to help me save Dovid from her paws one way or another. And in the meanwhile I get sad about the chicken in High Falls. I would like to sell it and the money perhaps to put aside in *David's name*, for he was born there, though he is not Chagall (my name). And how she tried frivolously time and again to "doubt" whether he is "entirely" my son. If I could only find the strength: not just to forget her (this is much easier) but to endure the boy's plight.

Please try, nevertheless, to ask about selling the house. Bernard Reis has the keys and the right to sell. Perhaps one should put *ads* in *Woodstock* (the artists' colony there, not far from High Falls). Please write to me.

In the meantime, I send my warm regards to both of you.

Your devoted Chagall

Valya always sends her love

Ida and Franz Meyer in Zurich to the Opatoshus in New York

27/7/53

Zurich

[English] Dear friends,

Thank you so much for your nice cable.

Here is Piet. And we had the joy of Vava and father's visit. Father was quite proud of his little grandson.

All the best to you both.

Yours

Ida & Franz

Marc Chagall in Paris to Yosef Opatoshu in New York

[Stationery: "Pont-Royal Hotel/7, Rue Montalambert. Paris"]

22 Oct. 1953

[Yiddish] Dear friends. Received your letters and it is my fault that I write rarely. But I am so preoccupied, and not just work. I came here to take Valya out for a rest. But it's all the same, we don't get to it at all. Just visits and eating. I hope you both are well and as fresh as ever (as I saw you in Vence). At the request of Vinaver, I did the title page for [the Anthology of] Jewish Music[3] (in Greenberg). I restrained myself not to cause too big expenses in printing, by adding one more color. But I still wanted to add a *red* color for the *king's* coat and I'd like to paint it in before the printing.

Dear Opatoshu, please help me somehow to sell the house in High Falls. Let it be Dvorkin, not to lose too much. One has to sell, otherwise it will decay in the winter. (I want to put the money away for Dovid.) He lies on my "stomach."

Please send me what you read in *Commentary* about the book with Skira.[4] Poor Clement Greenberg. I shall try to get you an album.

Warm greetings from me and Valya

Your devoted

Marc Chagall

Vence (A.M.) France

And Reis has the keys to High Falls and can close the sale when it happens.

Vinaver: Chemjo Vinaver (1900–?), conductor and composer of Jewish religious music, born in Warsaw, was chief conductor of the temple in Berlin until 1933, then in New York. He must not be confused with Chagall's early mentor Maksim Vinaver, who died in 1926.

Greenberg: Chaim Greenberg was director of the Culture Department of the Jewish Agency. Apparently, the Anthology of Jewish Music was supported by the Jewish Agency.

Clement Greenberg: The influential art critic Clement Greenberg published a rather unpleasant review of Chagall in *Commentary*, October 1953.[5] It seems that for him, Chagall was too Jewish (and certainly too figurative and nostalgic). He praised Chagall, however, as a great etcher and lithographer.

Marc Chagall in Vence to Yosef Opatoshu in New York

"Les Collines"/Vence/A.-M.   19 Nov. 1953

[Yiddish] Dear Opatoshu. First, I want to thank you for your letters. I would like so much to see you and even be with you in your pleasant apartment where I often sat and was "innocently" happy (in a different way). And how is Adelya? Why doesn't she write a word, I [love] to read her. But perhaps she has other things on her head. And how is Dovid [Opatoshu]. I was so glad to see him. And now, listen. Of course, we must sell the house in High Falls, for it will melt after the snow . . . Let the money remain for my poor little (not very happy) Dovid'l, who is still far [from me]. I want Dvorkin to take care of it and let him address himself to Reis (he can prepare the official papers and is *very* friendly. Do you know him?) And let it be over. I don't know about the price. Tell me yourself what one can get over there. I would like not to lose "too much." Reis knows the details of the house. The house is near *Woodstock*, where artists live. It may be advisable to place an ad in the *shtetl* too. I attach a few words for Mr. Dvorkin and I shall write to Reis too. Thank you for sending me the clipping about the album (I shall send it if you don't have it) and what he writes. It's a pity [?] that he [Clement Greenberg] saw me a few times in N.Y. at Madame Busch Meier-Graefe, since then— but the world turns anyway.

Vava will write to you. She was happy to get your book. We were in Paris. Circled there. One has to work so much. I hope that the Bible will appear by next year. Near Paris saw the boy [David]—poor child. But he is in a village. I hope maybe he'll come here for a few weeks at the end of the year.

I don't know how the cover for Vinaver's book *Jewish Music* will come out. I thought perhaps making [King] David in red (the coat). Give my love to Mrs. Greenberg when you see her.

I kiss you both/Your devoted

Chagall

Regards from Valya

P.S. I would like Dvorkin to be in touch with Reis: Bernard Reis, 252 E. 68 St.

Marc Chagall in Vence to Yosef Opatoshu in New York

Vence 1954   12/1 [January]

[Yiddish] Dear Opatoshu. Thank you for your letter and received your book but the Jews in Israel are apparently decaying. Rarely do they have taste. My drawing

shtetl: The small town of Woodstock.

Mrs. Greenberg: The widow of Chaim Greenberg.

decaying: Chagall diagnoses the decay of the Jews because his drawing was placed outside the frame! In the Hebrew society of Israel, a publishing house of Yiddish books was marginal and far from representing the culture of the country.

is outside [the frame] and the cover of the book is wild. But don't upset your heart. You know that the most important thing is our [Jewish] consciousness and you (and Adelye) have it. I would like to come to you someday and sit at your table (in the meantime I am unsettled about) [last sentence crossed out].

One gets older and maybe younger. I sent you the Skira album. Valya sent you a short letter. She writes rarely. I "work" as far as I can. Some people in Paris make my exhibit in June. Though I myself would like to disappear somewhere in a *pension* with my sack and stick . . . Your mind gets turbid when you read the news in the papers. But people say that I don't look bad . . . Yes, I would so much like the little one [Chagall's son David], wherever he is wallowing, to become a *mench* [a decent human being] . . . and this will give me peace. We shall leap over to Paris and London.

my sack and stick: The image of the Wandering Jew in exile.

And maybe there will be news about my house in High Falls. Please ask Dvorkin to take care [of it]. I think this should interest *artists* for it is not far from Woodstock.

I thank Adelye for her letter. Please write to me about everything. What is new in Jewish life in America? How do the Jews live over there?

I kiss your devoted

Marc Chagall

Marc Chagall in Vence to Yosef Opatoshu in New York

Vence 1954 26/4

[Yiddish] Dear friends

I sit in the middle of the night to write you, so you won't believe your little doubts: [he's] cross and things like that. Simply, I rarely find time myself. So "caught up" am I by nothing and by everything. Work, people, Dovid'l (who is with us for the Passover days). And more and more. And the "older" I am the more screwed up, can hardly pull myself together and take pen in hand. I should have written long ago. People are waiting, but I lack discipline.

Now listen—but I cannot forget that my Bella's (10th?) anniversary is approaching and it isn't [?] because when I think that nothing is being done for her (by us). One should have a little book with her sweet writings and find some other things of hers with my love drawings. I see only a person like you with your taste (I remember your own little books of this kind). I have no high demands. I am even prepared to make an original lithograph frontispiece for this, both in Yiddish and English. But when [who?] would move in to help realize it?

Opatoshu wanted Chagall to illustrate classical Jewish books, but Chagall had no publisher to support it. BeShT (acronym for Ba'al Shem Tov, a magician), was the founder of Hasidism and an author of orally transmitted parables. Bratslaver is Rabbi Nahman from Braslav (Bratslav), the founder of a Hasidic sect and author of allegorical stories.

Your project about the Bratslaver or the BeShT is, of course, fine, but I would be calmer if [a book] were published of her writings along with my drawings for her 10th anniversary. For she was a fine artist in Yiddish word-images, so she deserves it. I think. What do you think, my dear? Or as Vinaver promised me—I sent him a cover for the Music Book, he works in the [Jewish] Agency, if I'm not mistaken—promised me to do something in her name, for I rescinded the honorarium (and he has the original too) in order to use it for Bella. And I accepted his commission, because he reminded me of Chaim Greenberg. I would be glad if you found *something* out.

I work a lot because my large Paris exhibition is being prepared for June, and on the Bible too, which I hope will appear in 1955. Thank you for sending me your Mlava book, thank you for the letters, also from Adelye. Thank you for your Passover *seder*—remembering us. When Dovid'l will really be with me, I will also conduct a *seder*, for the time being I am waiting. But further details I shall write to you later. Vava always greets you. She is filled with Jewish manners. And in yet another while, I shall be like everybody else.

Please write, I warmly kiss both/Your

Marc Chagall

your Mlava book: Mlava (Polish: Mława), was Opatoshu's home town. He is referring to a memorial book for the Jewish community of Mlava.

Jewish manners: Meaning: motherly, warm, a good homemaker.

Virginia Haggard in Brussels to Adele Opatoshu in New York

May 10th [1954]

[English] Dearest Adele,

Your letter made me very happy. I'm so glad there's no ill feeling, in spite of what happened and what must have hurt you a lot. Fortunately Marc now sees David regularly and they are more and more attached to each other. David is going to spend all the summer with his father. I'm so pleased that at last they are reunited and that all the vicious stories people spread no longer influence Marc.

Please forgive me for not writing sooner. I thought of you a lot since your let-

vicious stories: Stories doubting that Chagall was David's father.

ter and I am so sad for you in solitude. Perhaps you can find a moment to give me news of your David & his family & tell me how you are putting up with life. My children are both very well and happy, doing good work at school & turning out to be even nicer than I ever hoped. My poor husband is still completely bed ridden (two years now) and it will still be a long while before he can get on his feet again. I do photography in his place & I find it extremely interesting. I am beginning to earn quite well. But as I am a nurse to my husband & have to look after the household as well that doesn't leave me much time.

on his feet again: In fact, he never did recover. Charles Leirens died in 1963.

I shall leave you now. Don't forget, I'd love to have news of you some time. Tell David [Opatoshu] I know he has become a successful movie actor. I'd love to have news of him. Do you know that Ida has three children now, a boy & two little girls? They are all *beautiful*. I have only seen photos, of course. The man who photographed them showed me lots of photos of the whole family (David included). One of them will shortly appear in an album. David seems to be going to develop with [?] He has a wonderful disposition.

> Much love, dear Adele
>
> Your friend, as ever,
>
> Virginia

Marc Chagall in Vence to Yosef Opatoshu in New York

16/9 Vence 1954

[Yiddish] Dear friend Opatoshu. How many times I wanted to write you. But time goes by. A day after a day. I have become perhaps even lazier than before, and if I do work, it goes very slowly. Not as I would like and should have. But I want to know how you are. You are so good to me as always—you write and send me the books—your stories of Mlava are simplicity itself (one must learn from you). And Dubnov's book in Russian—thanks. Yesterday I got the article from you—Lerner. He visited me here. He seems to be a clever man; how profound he is and how "great" . . . his Jewishness is, I don't know. I think he is too preoccupied with general politics to be steeped in culture, art. But he is a very nice man—a realist.

Dubnov's book: The historian Simon Dubnov's memoirs, *Kniga Moyey zhizni* (*The Book of My Life*) republished in Russian, New York: Chekhov Publishing House, 1954.

Recently, because of my exhibition, I was in Paris and then travelled to London (with Valya). There I saw Sholem Asch several times. I was not overjoyed to see him. He is not aging well. And as you know, he is still one of those whom the world "owes" something. If he hadn't been (as he thinks and writes) also preoccupied with God—it would have been more "normal." So I just got from his friend and publisher a request to illustrate one of his books. But it's impossible.

How are you? How is Adelye? When will you be here? Or when will I visit you?

My God, at the end of the year, there is the 10th anniversary since my Bella left. She lies alone over there in your country. And nothing came out yet about her, about her things. It is my fault. Perhaps someone will remember her [publicly] in your place. I could perhaps send a Jewish drawing for sale for an institution or Yiddish writers or something else in her name. Think about it. And I shall start thinking—perhaps publish her books in three separate small books, illustrated by me: 1) Vitebsk 2) Holidays 3) Love. You will advise me. You have great and fine experience. Write to me more often about yourself, your children, and Jewish life in America.

In my life—Valya keeps the house—well. I become—I hope—calmer, though I may never see little Dovid'l again. He is 8 years old and one has to decide (for his sake) that he should not be in 3 "homes" with 3 fathers—either with me here or with her there. That's what I heard from her. But she has an English head, turned upside down even more than in my paintings. I want to get strength to overcome this too.

I kiss you warmly

Your devoted

Marc Chagall

Marc Chagall in Greece to Adele and David Opatoshu in New York

[On the death of Yosef Opatoshu]

Athènes (Grèce) 1954 24 Oct

[Yiddish] Dear friends Adelye and Dovid,

Your letter, forwarded from Vence, threw me here in Greece into a deep mourning. I did not believe my eyes. Reread your lines several times and understood that my great, very great friend left us. I did not expect this. I cannot imagine your pain. How sad it is that I was not near him in recent years and near you—my dear ones.

my great friend left us: Yosef Opatoshu died in October 1954.

I cannot find the words to convey my pain—to lose such a unique friend. I cannot even write anymore. But—write to me—how did he leave the world. Not an old man at all and full of life. How? Please describe it for me. Was he sick the last days? And what are you doing, Adelye? Keep yourself together and be well. You have such a fine son (with his wife and son) that is unique. I love all of you. But I shall always keep in my heart the treasure—my friend Opatoshu. I know—he loved me too (and Bella, who lies not far from him). And through him, I loved Yiddish literature and Yiddish writers, among whom he was the finest star.

Ay, how great is our loss. The great Jew, the great Jewish artist. The rare friend. And left us early. I kiss you from my heart and please convey—my Jewish—wrapped in tears, greetings to his—my—friends, Yiddish writers who were left alone without him—to swim in the sad sea of life. For when he was, the world was illuminated with such a light and never did the death of a friend evoke such a desert in my heart . . . Why—I don't know.

Yours as always devoted

Marc Chagall

P.S. Vava—my wife sends her greetings./I shall write the sad news to Ida./Don't forget me—write.

Virginia Haggard in Paris to Adele Opatoshu in New York

54 Avenue Simon Bolivar   Paris 19e   May 28th {1955}

[English] My dear Adele,

I heard quite by chance from Marie Katz the sad, sad news of Oppen's death and I was terribly upset. And in spite of the chill that has come over our friendship since the letter I wrote to you confidentially and which Marc was given to read, I still feel the same about you and the loss of Oppen is as much of a sorrow as ever it would have been before. Also the terrible loneliness that you feel makes me doubly sad, for I know how hard it must be for you to live without him. Please, dear Adele, if you still have *any* feeling left for me, write and tell me so. I am very unhappy about the many misunderstandings, for that is what they are, in reality. Friends as far away as America have heard all kinds of untrue stories about me and about the problem of David [Virginia's son] and if you knew all the truth, I'm sure you would be less hard on me. In any case, I find it hard to understand how such very close friends as we used to be can suddenly become bitter enemies. You must have changed every opinion you ever had of me and consider me absolutely monstrous. I thought real friendship was more understanding, more ready to weigh the circumstances carefully and without prejudice before turning away once and for all in condemnation. All your signs of affection which surround me still, the bracelets, books and other things you gave me (I wear the Mexican bracelet Oppen gave me almost every day of my life) make the sorrow even deeper and I can't keep silent. I must tell you what Oppen's death means to me, even though he didn't love me any more.

Yours, as ever, in friendship

Virginia

Ida Chagall in Paris to Becky Reis in New York

35 Quai de l'Horloge, Paris 1e   June 25, 1955

[English] Dearest Becky,

Thank you so much for your sweet letter. I am always delaying to write to you because you cannot read my handwriting . . .

How are you darling? I heard about your party from Stern. He wrote that it was fabulous.

children: Ida's three children: Piet and the twin girls Bella and Meret.

Here, our house begins to be so crowded with children that we will be obliged to do some thing. But I am sticking to this house anyway. Franz has accepted the post of Director of the Kunsthalle of Bern, which will mean commuting and if so I prefer to arrange for a house with a garden in Bern where to put our little zoo, rather to leave them here.

The girls are all right now. I am feeling better too. I stayed for more than three weeks at the clinic, because of a bad operation which nearly finished tragically, and with all its stupid consequences. Now, there is so much to do on all fronts that one has to feel better.

We do need your help very much: Franz has signed with the German publisher of the Klee book (Harry Abrams Editor [= publisher] for the States) for a big "Chagall." Please, whenever you see a painting of importance, could you ask the collectors for a photograph with sizes? Chagall titles seem to change from one collector to an other and it makes such a mess as I can not tell you. When I think that Mrs Kandinsky was offended that the Curt Valentin Gallery lately

Barbara: The Reis's daughter.

"dared" to call three Kandinsky—"compositions." If Barbara knows of Chagalls, it would be wonderful.

Leymarie: Director of the Museum of Modern Art in Paris, curator of the major Chagall exhibition in 1969, held in the Grand Palais and the Bibliothèque Nationale.

All this does not tell you that we would love to visit things with you, to laugh together and to have some good time. I asked Jean Leymarie if he saw your back at your party! And he answered of himself: "Oh, it is a beautiful back!" . . .

Love. Love to you both. We are really longing to see you.

Your Ida

Marc Chagall in Vence to A. Glanz-Leyeles in New York

"Les Collines"/Vence/A.-M.   16,17 sept. 1955

[Yiddish] Dear friend Glanz.[6] I thought for a long time about you over there. Especially when our great friend, the unique one [Opatoshu], has left us. It became so sad, so sad. I can imagine your loneliness. And nevertheless I didn't write. Not so much that I am lazy, and I lack organization. And suddenly the little book about your wife and her poems that you sent me, as from the Other World.[7] Which reminded me of mine too, who lies not far in N.Y.—thank you. It is always such a strange feeling to read poems by people who have left us: their style grows even deeper, lonely, and we have to listen carefully to hear their sigh, which we had no "time" to hear when they were alive . . .

I want to hope that in the New Year, perhaps it will become a little more joyful and perhaps the friends of Opatoshu will not forget me, so that I know once in a while what is happening in our Jewish world. I miss the Jews, and indeed, the American Jews where I lived almost ten years ago. Please give my greetings to those who love me or believe in me, except for the bad ones (among the Jews) (i.e., not real Jews).

Like Opatoshu, you will never believe [the rumors] and doubt my Jewishness, as one among you (Gl).[8] It is false. So if I have time and strength, we shall speak. Greet Adelye and Dovid and everybody.

> Happy New Year/ Your devoted
>
> Marc Chagall

Marc Chagall in Vence to Bernard and Becky Reis in New York

"Les Collines"/ Vence /A.-M.   16 January 1956

[French] Dear friends Bernard and Becky,

Thank you very much for letting us know how you are from time to time.

I wrote to you to inform you of a plan relating to a kind of museum for biblical murals which is to be built in Vence.

An architect, Mr. Rosenauer, an Englishman born in Austria—he built Richard Strauss's house and the building for Life-Time in London—spent his vacation in Vence. We met him. He saw some sketches I made for chapels which won't be done since we are thinking of making a museum. The mayor of Vence is giving the land and Mr. Rosenauer has made a plan.

At present, Mr. Rosenauer is in America, where he has asked me by telegram for a list of my friends. The first idea that came into my mind was to give him your address, for you are the one who knows me best. Ida also advised me to send Mr. Rosenauer to you so that he can get in touch with you, so that you can see what he has done, and so he can inform you completely. Advise me on something that may be very important as long as I have the strength to realize it.

I hope that, despite the few details I am giving you, you will understand me and that, after you see Mr. Rosenauer and the plan that he has made, you will give me your idea.

built in Vence: This became the Musée National Message Biblique Marc Chagall in Nice.

Of course, if this plan is accepted, it may undergo certain changes, if necessary. For the moment, we are thinking of doing it in three parts:

Biblical, Song of Songs, and modern times

And now I leave to you and our friends, if possible, the care of seeing and thinking about this.

I hope that you are well and I am still thinking that we will see each other. I would like to talk to you,

See you soon,

Marc Chagall

Lithographs

After the war, Fernand Mourlot became the major force in reviving the old art of lithography in France. Almost concurrently with his work in ceramics, Chagall plunged into the art of making lithographs in Mourlot's workshop. From 1950 to 1952, he regularly attended Mourlot's atelier in Paris and studied all technical aspects, under the guidance of Charles Sorlier and the printer Georges Sagourin. Sorlier became a close friend of Chagall's and produced all his lithographs for several dozen years. Chagall nicknamed him "mon petit Charles" despite his impressive height and bulk (in Yiddish a diminutive may indicate not size but endearment), to distinguish him from the other Charles, Marq. Sorlier called Chagall "le Patron" and wrote several books about him.

According to Sorlier, Chagall "became an absolute master of the technique."[9] For four years he worked on the illustrations to *Daphnis and Chloe*, making about a thousand plates in twenty to twenty-five colors each: "This book marks the summit of polychrome lithographie."[10] Chagall's meticulous, demanding attention to every detail can be seen in the brief notes he wrote to Sorlier between one visit and another. After 1966, Chagall did almost no painting and devoted himself to engravings on copper and lithography, as well as stained-glass windows.

Working on lithographs. From left: Charles Sorlier, Marc Chagall, Georges Sagourin, Eugène Degave.

Marc Chagall in Vence to Charles Sorlier in Paris

"Les Collines"/Vence (A.M.)/June 9, 1956

[French] Dear Charles,

Thank you very much and Georges (Sagourin), too.

I have just received your package of lithographs, and anxiously opened it . . .

You ask for information about the back of the "Green Banquet"; in my opinion, the color doesn't reach. Maybe that will have to be reworked?

The angel on the red background makes me think of the devil, but I don't know too much about it. I find it too brutal, especially after the blue cover. On opening, it is going to be cold and hot. It is a problem.

Agreed about the violet for the back of the Warriors.

Agreed about the pink, plate of the "Rivals." For the spots, we will see when I come, in July.

I am happy with the whole, except for the angel.

If retouching is necessary, I will be able to work on it only in July when I come to Paris. I will get in touch with you.

I hope that you will be able to send me the copies of the forms of *Verve*.

Regards to Georges.

Cordially, wishing you good health and good work.

Marc Chagall

Louis Stern in New York to Ida Chagall in Bern

June 14, 1956

[English] Dear Ida:

As you can well imagine, I have been swamped with things that have been neglected during my four months' absence and I am struggling hard to catch up on the mail.

First, let me thank you for your kindness and courtesies to me while in Paris and Berne. That has become an established thing with you.

I am enclosing a copy of a letter that I am sending to the *Vence Branch* of the Chagall Family, which speaks for itself. I want you to read and consider it carefully—first to determine whether you want to disclose that I sent you a copy of this letter, or whether to see if your father tells you about it. At any rate, I am trying to be candid, open and "above board." I would like to have your opinion on the subject. I am sincere in this whole enterprise. If it involves more money than I can comfortably afford, I will have to give it up, for I do not want to question or deprecate the value of your father's work. On the other hand, you have expressed it better than I could when you said that I am paying for merely a loan of these pictures, since my time on this earth is more or less limited and I am definitely and unqualifiedly leaving my Chagall collection to a Museum or public institution. At any rate, please do not hesitate to express your opinion frankly.

Khrushchev and Bulganin: Nikita Khrushchev was Secretary General of the Communist Party; Nikolay Bulganin was Prime Minister of the Soviet Union.

I have just spoken to Dorothy Miller of the Museum of Modern Art. She tells me that Alfred Barr is with Picasso now working on the next Picasso show, which I learned is not to be open until next May and to continue on until October, 1957. Alfred has been in Moscow. Just how successful he was in persuading Messrs. Khrushchev and Bulganin to lend the Museum of Modern Art their wonderful Picassos, I don't know.

I am anxious to get this letter off to you so that you will receive your copy at the same time that your father receives the original, hence I will close without further ado.

I still regret that I didn't see the twins, but if the negotiations with your father go through and I have to be in Vence to be reproduced in the form of a billy goat, a rooster or a donkey, then I will have another chance to see you and your troika.

troika: Trio in Russian; Ida's three children.

With best to Franz and you, I am

As Ever,　[Louis Stern]

Louis Stern in New York to Marc and Vava Chagall in Vence

June 14, 1956

[English] Vava and Cher Maitre Chagall:

I have been home for two weeks and am still struggling with catching up with a number of things that have accumulated during my four months' absence. Up to this writing, I haven't as yet opened all the mail.

I want you to know how deeply I enjoyed the week-end with you in Vence. It was agreeable and stimulating. I appreciate the courtesy and hospitality very much indeed.

I am all excited about the various phases of my Chagall Collection and I am impatient to have our plans put into operation. So as to have the various aspects of conversations reduced to a definitive state, I will take the liberty and the time to jot it down here. As I understand it, it consists of three parts:

One relates to the big picture now in Vava's room, which is to take the place of my big wall where I originally intended to have a mural.

Two, a group of small pictures to be selected from those I picked.

Three, the portrait which we discussed, which is to be more or less of a double portrait. I am more than keen about that. I want it to be a characteristic Chagall rather than a likeness of myself; although I prefer to have myself sufficiently identified so as to make it a Louis Stern Chagall, rather than anyone else's Chagall.

On all those three phases I am in accord and anxious to bring it to a head. For the purpose of the portrait, I will be prepared to come to Vence for a sufficient length of time to satisfy the necessities. There is but one phase—and it is an important one—and that is the amount of money it will involve.

I don't need to tell you that in speaking of the material side of this problem, I do not have in mind the value, for the whole thing would be priceless to me and posterity. However, my means are more or less limited and I have long ago decided that while I am an ardent collector and love pictures, especially my Chagalls, I should not involve myself financially in such a way as to cause me worry. For that purpose, I wish you would discuss the matter and go over it thoroughly, and indicate to me approximately how much I should be prepared to expend. Please do not hesitate to be frank. Our relations are such that I would not take offense at any proposition you may have to suggest. On the other hand, I would expect you not to take umbrage at anything I might have to say on the subject.

I will await with a great deal of interest for your reply to this single phase.

Incidentally, if you want to send me the little picture of the crucifix with the click, I would very much like to have it as soon as possible. I cannot shake the memory of it from my mind.

Will you please discuss the whole subject fully and frankly and let me hear from you.

Until then, I am with warmest regards and renewed appreciation and thanks,

As ever,   [Louis Stern]

Ida Chagall in Bern to Louis Stern in New York

[Stationery: 23 Herrengasse, Berne]

June 23, 1956

[English] Dear Louis

Thank you so much for your nice letter. I did not expect anything so quickly as I could well imagine how busy you were coming back. How is Alice?

I must congratulate you for your letter to Vence. I find it extraordinary fine, clever et political. Probably by now you have an answer from them. I did not hear about it as from the time of my last visit to Vence I am no more busy with father's affairs. This was notified to me there, just when the children were in the car and I was saying good-buy. It is so much better like that, but I would hate if the "deal" with your big painting is not as I would have wanted.

So far I did not mention in my letters that I know about your letter. As I am seeing them soon, I will see. Anyhow I could have known all this just from your visit too.

I do hope that you will come back. Vava was enchanted from your visit also. She told how touched she was that you complimented her on the bath-room and the house and so forth.

I learned that you were surprised that Skira had an ektachrome of your Purim . . . How a poor memory you have . . . Did we not take ektachromes in your house? . . . The Skira book will be fine I believe. With things not too known. The exhibition in Basel opens on August 24th, and I think that you are going to be asked for your "Dans la Nuit."

I am sincerely sorry that you did not see the Giacometti show that Franz has. Compared with Arp, it is a thousand time better. Perfect and free. Excuse me to

father's affairs: Ida was managing various affairs of her father's, including organizing exhibitions, relations with Maeght, and the sales of paintings, for which she apparently got a commission. Now Vava pushed her out of this business.

say: a sort of exhibition that Sweeny would have liked. Do not think that I am too conceited, but really the exhibition is wonderful. The catalogue is not unfortunately. Giacometti was here, for a few days, he came in advance, worried, and then did not change a single thing. He stayed in his rooms, pleased and happy not wanting to see anything else or any other work of art.

I learned also that Barr was in Moskow, and have been told that he asked also about father's things. How successful he was I do not know.

Do let me hear about things so if I can help.

With best to you from us both

your Ida

Louis Stern in New York to Marc Chagall in Vence

June 25, 1956

[English] Cher Maitre Chagall:

Thank you for your letter of June 15th and also for the snapshots of the small pictures which you showed me.

You may tell Rudlinger that he can have DANS LA NUIT for the Exhibition if he wants it, or any other of my Chagalls.

Rudlinger: Arnold Rudlinger, a friend of Franz Meyer's, curated Chagall's exhibition in Zurich and later took over Meyer's position as Director of the art museum in Bern.

Skira's photographer was here some time ago and they made Ektachromes (color plates) of the DANS LA NUIT and PURIM. Mrs. Fields, Skira's representative, had authority only for DANS LA NUIT. I pointed out to her that that picture has been reproduced so often and so much, whereas PURIM which, in my opinion, is definitely one of your *great pictures*, has not been reproduced. She cabled Skira and received authority to have color plates of PURIM also. She tells me that they are now working on the cuts. As soon as proofs are received here, she will come to compare the color. This, I understand, is the usual procedure.

Since my return here, I have been quite busy with a number of things which ordinarily do not come on top of one another. I was rather amused with your appeal to God to help you paint good pictures, and especially our double portrait. I think by this time you can depend on your own power and ability; although maybe with me intervening, you will need God's help. I am thinking of our project continuously and hope that we can work it out as discussed.

I remember that you had the invitation to go to Amsterdam and I am sure that you will enjoy your visit both to Holland and to Italy. When you view the Rembrandts, take a good look at the little picture "The head of a Man," which is owned by the Boyman's Museum in Rotterdam. If I had a choice, that is the one I would take for my collection.

I don't know of anything important to add at this time, so I will close with the usual warm regards to you and Vava.

As ever,

[Louis Stern]

Vava Chagall in Vence to Louis Stern in New York

[Stationery: "Les Collines" / Vence (A.M.)]

10.7.56 [July]

[English] My dear Louis,

We are off today to Amsterdam via Paris.

Ida, Franz, Michel will be there too.

Marc asks me to tell you: *1st* that he thinks a lot about your portrait. *2nd* that he prefers to talk with you about the picture in my room when you will be here again in Vence. And we hope it will be soon!

Do write when you can come.

All my love and Marc's too—

Yours Vava

Louis Stern in New York to Ida Chagall in Bern, Switzerland

July 10th, 1956

[English] Dear Ida:

Your letter of June 23rd has been on my desk with the hope that I would have heard from your father. Up to this writing, I have had no word from him. By the time you read this, your father and Vava most likely will be in Amsterdam where they are supposed to attend some function on the 14th.

I am stumped for I do not know what my next move should be. It is my present notion that I should wait until I hear from your father and that I should not write again to urge him to give me a reply. What do you think? While I know that your father will go to Italy from Holland there was no indication as to how long they planned to be away. At all events, please let me hear from you your ideas in the matter. Perhaps, by this time, they will have been in touch with you.

I haven't heard a word from your friends in Basel with respect to the Chagalls they want for the Exhibition from me, but you can tell them that they can have

DANS LA NUIT. With respect to the Ektachrome of PURIM, I didn't know that I was "surprised." I remember that you had a photographer here but this is the first that I hear that PURIM was one of the pictures. Incidentally, they did make another Ektachrome here but no one has come back as yet to compare the colors.

Since you mention Sweeney, I am wondering whether you know that Laura Sweeney has been ill. I do not know much about the nature of her illness. I thought I ought to mention it to you in case you want to write.

I am glad and pleased to hear about Franz' Giacometti Show and wish that I could have seen it.

New York has not been too bad so far and I am making the usual rounds of week-end trips and not having a bad time of it. If you have a minute to spare and you can add anything to the mystery of your father not answering, drop me a line.

With love to you and the children and best to Franz, I am,/As always

[Louis Stern]

Ida Chagall in Bern to Louis Stern in New York

[Stationery: 23 Herrengasse, Berne. July 12, 1956]

[English] Amazing, I got so quickly your letter that I cannot help answering as soon!

We were in Vence for the weekend of July 7th (father's birthday). Seldom was I *so impressed* by his late work. It is fantastic! How is it possible that he did all this lately.

Vava seemed perturbed by answering to you by letter! She wanted to tell you that when you are coming you would all together discuss it!—They are in Paris. Tomorrow I am flying to meet Franz and the family in Amsterdam. There is a small chance that after Basel, Franz may take a part of the exhibition—things done after 1950—for Berne. But it depends on Sandberg.

If it is so, will you come? Here are greetings from the children, so that you should come!

Yes, I know that Laura Sweeney was sick. I saw her in Paris.

The Miro exhibition at Maeght is a sensation, by the way.

Please *do not tell* the Reis I have written, as I have had not a minute to write to them.

Sandberg: Willem Sandberg, Director of the Stedejlik Museum in Amsterdam.

With love

Ida

After Amsterdam the Chagall's are coming back to Vence, with David until the end of Sept!

Louis Stern in New York to Ida Chagall in Bern

July 17, 1956

[English] Dear Ida:

Your letter of July 12th with the snapshots of your "troika" was a very welcome surprise. If you are considering propositions, I hereby declare myself in love with Bella. Mered [= Meret] and Piet resemble each other markedly, although off-hand it seems to me that they all have the same eyes. Whatever the situation is, you can well be proud of such lovely children. I, of course, look forward to the time when I will meet them in the flesh.

On the same day that your letter arrived, a card, dated July 7th (your father's birthday) came from Vava. In substance it does not answer the one question which I asked, and that you will remember was how much money it would involve. All that Vava tells me is that your father wants to discuss with me the large picture. I suppose she means the price. This has put me in a quandry, for the one thing I don't want to do is to get into a discussion of prices, comparisons, valuations, etc. etc. However, I suppose I will have to handle it sooner or later if the thing we were discussing is to be realized.

I note what you say with respect to the Reis'. Don't be concerned about that for I hardly ever see them and am not likely to get into a discussion with either of them.

I do not exactly know how to plan because while, Vava, in her note, urges me to come over soon, she doesn't indicate when they will be back in Vence and in the last letter from your father, he said definitely that they plan to be in Italy after Amsterdam. Will you please write to me after you know when your father will be back in Vence. I assume, also, that they will be going to Basel when the exhibition opens.

Incidentally, I heard from Mr. Rudlinger and I am writing him today that I am willing to loan DANS LA NUIT.

Wittenborn, the art book shop is sending out literature with respect to the Chagall Bible. Who is looking after my copy? Please let me know.

Have you seen Issue No. 7, 1956 of the XX Siecle? It would be of special interest to you for it has articles on all the people that you and Franz are interested in.

I cannot think of anything else at the moment, so I will close with affectionate regards to all of you.

As ever,/   [Louis Stern]

Ida Chagall in Bern to Louis Stern in New York

[Stationery: 23 Herrengasse]

July 23, 1956

[English] Dear Louis

We are back from Holland where we had quite a wonderful time. The Chagaux were there too as you know.

Just as I wrote you in my last letter, they are going back to Vence, in fact to marrow [sic] with David. They will stay there until Sept anyhow. In Sept may be father will have to come to Paris to sign the Bible etchings. And it is only in October that they planned to go to Italy for the cure.

I do not think that they will go to the Bâle [Basel] opening. I know it is quite bothering for you to discuss the thing of the picture en presence. But may be, if you plan to come it will turn for the best. They are not people to write clearly or to decide by letter.

Do not worry about your Bible copy. You will have from the party that has the best No. for you, that means the No 6. We do not know yet into which lot it will fall.

Meyer Shapiro wrote a really outstanding article for the Verve-Bible.[11] It is wonderful and at last something important on father. If you see him, tell him that we both quite thrilled by it.

Franz extended [the] Giacometti [exhibition] until next Sunday. Henry Clifford lunched here yesterday, telling about his Russian trip and tomorrow the Leigh Blocks are here.

Will come for Basel? Later at the end of October Franz will present a Chagall show, but from 1950 on only, with ceramics and sculptures.

Have a nice month now and all our best wishes to you.

With love

Ida

The girls are beginning to walk and it is quite touching.

Louis Stern in New York to Ida Chagall in Bern

August 2nd, 1956

[English] Dear Ida:

I hope you will not mind receiving letters from me so frequently. This letter is to tell you that my DANS LA NUIT has gone off and by the time this reaches you, it will probably have arrived in Basel.

I must assume that Museum Directors are a special species of homo sapiens. It is difficult for me to understand why DANS LA NUIT, which has been shown all over Europe and at every Exhibition in the United States and is reproduced in almost every book on Chagall, should be wanted for the Chagall Exhibition in Basel; whereas PURIM which, to my knowledge, is not reproduced anywhere and has never been shown, is left out. I have always had a theory that Exhibitions should have a certain amount of news value. To merely repeat over and over again the same statement is, to me, somewhat monotonous. Among the Chagalls which I have, which is not reproduced anywhere and has never, to my knowledge, been shown, is the one which I call WAR. This is one of the most delicate and exquisite pictures. The PURIM, incidentally, I consider the equal of anything that Matisse has done. Yet, neither one of these pictures have ever been requested for Exhibition or shown. So much for that.

In my last letter I asked you to let me know when your father is definitely back at Vence. Since he and Vava seem to change their plans from day to day, I want to make sure about where they are. Will you let me know? I am still in a quandry as to what to do about my "Chagall Collection." The inquiry which I made touching the amount of money it will require, was not an academic question. There is no point to my flying over to Vence if in the end it proves that the amount of money required will be beyond my means. Let me hear from you with all your ideas on the subject.

I have been spending my summer very pleasantly by visiting friends for week-ends. Tomorrow, Friday August 3rd, I am leaving for Margate which is a few miles south of Atlantic City, right on the ocean, where I expect to visit with friends for a few days. The following week-end, August 10th, I will spend with a very good friend of mine, a former professor at Princeton, who has a home in Bucks County, Pennsylvania, in the hills, not far from the Delaware River—and so it goes—So far, there have not been any hot days and it has been most pleasant here.

Until the next time, with warm regards to Franz, I am

As ever,

[Louis Stern]

Louis Stern in New York to Marc and Vava Chagall in Vence

August 23rd, 1956

[English] To Marc and Vava Chagall:

I will address myself to you, Vava, since it is so much easier for me to correspond with someone who has the command of the English language as you have. I do not understand why you have Marc write to me in French when your English is so good.

I am writing this letter primarily to clarify the situation in which I find myself. Under date of June 14th, I wrote a rather extended letter about our conversations in Vence when I was your guest. To that I did not receive any reply other than your card saying that Marc wants to talk to me. My inquiry about the material side was made largely because I wanted to know how to prepare myself. Added to all this is the confusion about the time when I should travel to Europe and visit with you so that the portrait could be painted.

If I am to travel to Europe and spend some time with you in Vence I must know when it will be timely and convenient. From the letters received and my recollections of the discussions, I know that you had planned to be in Holland to visit the Rembrandt Exhibition (which has been done). I know further that you plan to go to Italy some time or another, and that Marc has to be in Paris in connection with the "Bible." What I want to know now is, when you will be back in Vence to stay and whether Marc still wants me to come to Vence for the purpose of having the portrait painted.

You realize, of course, that I will have to have some notice so that I can arrange my affairs. While I would have preferred to get some idea of the financial angle so as to make preparations to meet the obligations, I am willing to wait until I get to Vence and we can then discuss it. Will you therefore, as soon as you have had a chance to read this carefully, discuss it with Marc and let me have a prompt reply.

Until then, I am with warm regards, / Sincerely

[Louis Stern]

Marc Chagall in Vence to Bernard and Becky Reis in New York

"Les Collines"/ Vence (A.M.)

10 décembre 1956

[French] Dear Bernard and Becky,

As always, I am happy to get your letters. How are you? When will we see each other again? I think of the happy times spent together . . .

I am working "very hard," as they say, that is, it's not going well. Every painting is harder than giving birth to a child and when the child comes out . . . you saw what there was at the exhibition.

Like gypsies, the exhibition is transported from Basel to Bern, to Franz, then to Amsterdam, to Sandberg. Of course you will receive the catalogue. I did not go to the opening. Then, the paintings will go to Brussels, to the Palace of Fine Arts. But I won't go to the opening there either.

Thank you for all those people you had to see. As you advise me, I agree that they should take some biblical proofs there, not too many. They will have to state that those proofs are part of the Bible published by Tériade.

I think you must have received the issue of Verve. The word Bible does not appear on the cover, the American publisher didn't want it. The original of the Bible is going to appear here soon, no doubt next month.

Thank you for talking to Mr. Kootz. I do want to see him, but I will not promise anything without writing to you. Time is passing and I am getting older and I believe that nothing will be done since nothing has been done up to now.

Attached and duly signed is the document you asked me for.

Both of us embrace both of you.

Cordially,

Marc Chagall

Second Visit to Chicago: 1957–1958

Professor John Ulric Nef, Chairman of the Committee on Social Thought at the University of Chicago, was a long-time admirer of Marc Chagall. He invited Chagall to lecture at Chicago in March 1946 and now again in 1957. Because of Chagall's past association with institutions that were later perceived as Communist front organizations, he was denied a reentry visa to the U.S. in 1951 and 1952. In 1957, however, a complex correspondence ensued (only a selection of several of the letters are reproduced here), and the final positive result was obtained with the help of the White House. John Nef and his second wife Evelyn S. Nef became close friends of Marc and Vava Chagall. They spent some time together in the summers on Cap d'Antibes, exchanged gifts, spoke French with one another, and corresponded frequently. In the late 1960s, Chagall was invited to lecture in Professor Nef's new Center for Human Understanding in Washington, D.C. and to build a mosaic in Nef's garden, which was completed in 1971.

Marc Chagall, 1957.

John Nef in Chicago to Marc Chagall in Vence

February 4, 1957

Dear Marc,

My good friend, William Wood Prince, who is very active on the Committee on Social Thought, shares our admiration for your work. The other day, we were talking about you and about the possibility of inviting you once again for a short stay with the Committee on Social Thought. I am thinking of two or three weeks with two or three talks with students and a small audience here in Chicago.

 We have an overall sum of $4,500.00 which would be at your disposal if you (and Vava of course) could come either next autumn or in the spring 1958, either by ship or by plane.

 All the advantages would be on your side; I am simply writing to know if you are interested.

 Much affection to you and Vava.

John Nef

Professor

University of Chicago

Marc Chagall in Vence to John Nef in Chicago

Les Collines/ Vence, A.M. March 6, 1957

Dear John,

Returning to Vence after almost two months in Israel, Switzerland, Belgium, and then in Paris, we found your letter of February 4, for which we thank you very much.

 You are inviting us to visit the Committee on Social Thought next autumn or in the spring of 1958. If God gives us strength, we would like very much to accept . . .

 But since we hope very much to see you again this summer, as usual, we will use the occasion to talk about the details. Before that, the subjects and the nature of the lectures I will deliver has to be specified.

 Vava asks to be excused for not being able to write you: she has just lost her mother in Berlin and has just returned from there.

 Both of us send you our warm regards.

Marc Chagall

Marc Chagall in Vence to Charles Sorlier in Paris

"Les Collines" / Vence (A.M.) / March 12, 1957

My dear Charles,

Look, I don't forget you and I hope that you haven't forgotten me either.

All those books, those catalogues and reviews are coming close and walking all over me; but I hope that the studio is busy with me.

Will you send me the proofs; I will return them immediately.

We haven't yet received the box of lithographs. We're longing to have it.

Tell me how you all are. My regards to you, everyone around you, and Georges.

Cordially, see you soon.

Marc Chagall

Marc Chagall in Vence to Charles Sorlier in Paris

"Les Collines" / Vence (A.M.) / June 3, 1957

Dear Charles,

A few quick words.

I was happy to talk to you in person, but I am very sad to learn that your wife is ill. I hope with all my heart that she will recover very soon and that everything will be back in order with you.

I sent an express package to Maeght. It contains small lithographs for the invitation. I added a few modest colors; you know that technique.

It also contains a self-portrait lithograph—made by me right now. Hoping, if it is accepted, to enhance it with a few colors.

And also a drawing—whose paper is very fragile, be careful—on a lemon yellow background. I used it to make the poster, with bold black, varied, points, thin lines: in short, a nice dish you know very well . . . For the colors: strictly what is there on the background and preserve the indented whites, reds. Everything, except the bad folds of the paper. All that on condition that you and Maeght choose the best for the poster.

There, my dear, is what I wanted to tell you.

I understand that you have an enormous amount of work with this damned season, those damned exhibits; not to mention the poster that the Bibliothèque Nationale is also doing. I don't know with whom. I think they chose an engraving-lithograph "Peace on Earth."

If you have a free moment, write me about those posters.

I saw Tériade recently. He is restored but he is sighing. I told him that after that flood with Maeght and the books, we would start the lovers "Daphnis and Chloe" over again.

I hope to be in Paris about June 20.

My best wishes,

Marc Chagall

Marc Chagall in Switzerland to Daniel Charny in New York

30/8 1957 [Yiddish] I am here for a few weeks and will soon go to Italy

Burgenstock Hotels Lucerne Suisse *My address: France Vence (A.M.)*

Dear Charny. I was so happy: suddenly a letter from you. I read and re-read with joy and sadness. So many memories arose. But I am happy simply that you are alive . . . In our time whoever "feels like" goes away from the world—I don't like it, you have to live as you can and . . . work, and didn't I tell you once: *write*. I wish I could give advice to myself. Now that's how it is, I don't know what happened, according to my passport I am indeed 70, so it must be true what I overheard as a "boy" how my parents worried about Moshka, his impending *prizyv* [military draft] and apparently lengthened [the time] between me the older and my younger brother David—perhaps by 2 or 3 years. So I become naturally or unnaturally 70, according to my passport, which is not all the same. I still [like] to love, eat, work, I still believe in "many things" I even finished my Bible [illustrations], I daubed pictures, I travelled here and there. I [have] another wife (the third) from the Brodsky family itself from Kiev, and I am often sad about our Jewish news and even about Jews themselves. And about some who are not ashamed to talk (and even write) about me (especially those who are no poets and think they are).

So you can imagine with what pleasure I would love to tire you out—talking to you, especially since I learned from your letter that you still love me . . . And dear Charny, I beg you not to be a pessimist. Life is always beautiful even though it is sad: good people and some close to us leave us . . . My situation is such: I am often sad about Dovidl because I rarely see him, I give him (that is, I pay for) an education in a good French school. Things go well for Ida, she has a nice husband from Switzerland and 3 beautiful children. And I hope I shall have the strength to come to New York for a month. I am invited to speak at Chicago University about this and that. And shall perhaps be a couple of weeks in New York and would try to see you (I still don't know when) but in the meantime be well. And thanks for the article you want to publish about my life.[1] Tell me [when it appears] so I can close accounts with you on your own "day."

close accounts: A Yiddish way of teasing by saying a nasty thing and meaning its affectionate opposite.

John Nef in Chicago to Vava Chagall in Vence

21 November 1957

[French] Dear Vava,

What good news! Your letter of 13 November crossed mine of 15 November which we sent to Vence, with the official documents of the university about your entrance into the United States. Yesterday I sent a copy of those documents to your address in Paris to be sure that you will have them right away.

Phillips Brooks:
Director of Library
Services at the U.S.
Information Service in
Paris; he apparently
was in charge of
screening visas.

Moreover, I wrote to Mr. Phillips Brooks of the cultural services of the American Embassy, asking him to expedite your visa; in this case, too, I sent you a copy of my letter.

If there are any difficulties about the visa, write to me, please, right away, airmail: I am sure I can arrange everything. Our ambassador in Paris was in my regiment in 1914 for several weeks and we often saw each other after the war at Harvard. I will contact him directly if there is the slightest trouble. I am eager that both of you have a perfect voyage.

Elinor: The first wife
of John Nef and an
admirer of Chagall.

Mrs. Shaw, president of the Arts Club of Chicago is a great friend of Elinor and me; she asks me to ask you if there is a film about Marc and if there will be a way of getting hold of it to show it to the members of the Arts Club during your stay here.

I am very eager to see you. I often dream about those days and one of my dreams is to return to France on the same ship as you and Marc.

My very affectionate regards to both of you,

John U. Nef

Ida Chagall and Franz Meyer in Bern to Bernard Reis in New York

[Stationery: 23 Herrengasse, Berne]

Nov 26 1957

[English] Dear, dear Bernard

A full month of sikness by the grippe, the famous one and all the hectiveness that resulted from the loss of time, prevented me from writing to you before. Thanks dear friend about the thrift account. Of course every thing you do is OK with me and I am only too grateful for your help and advice.

I just wrote quite at length to Becky about Vava suddenly telling me to send you the Bible [Chagall's illustrations]. But when she told me so I was quite sick and unable to attend to it at the bank vault. I did send you copy No 28 which is the lowest I have. It is so nice that you want to donate a copy to the Museum of Modern Art. No. 145 comes from father, as I told him I could not spare 2 copies (but of course if you want one for Barbara there is no problem). Let me know, as I will be back in Paris in 10 days.

On Dec 2 there will be a sale of just 3 old pictures of father's Ch. & Bella flying over Witebsk, which is a fantastic picture, a nude (page 88 of the Lassaigne book on father at Maeght) and a third one also from 1914.

Mother (and I . . .) (Chagall was already in Berlin) mother took those pictures with 15 others belonging to a Russian collectioner who wanted to deliver these pictures to his brother in Paris. This brother died and the remaining 3 pictures— all the rest he did sell—will be dispersed on Dec 2nd. You will get a catalogue.

those pictures: Chagall left Moscow for Berlin in the spring of 1922; Bella and little Ida followed about six months later, when she apparently transported the collector's Chagalls.

How are you? Your health and mood?

What do you think of all the events, down and above?

Love love love and love and love

Ida and Franz

Vava Chagall in Paris to John Nef in Chicago

7.12.57

[French] Dear John,

I was at the Consulate again about our visas. They told me that, unfortunately, they have to ask Washington, for in 1951 and 1952, when Marc wanted to renew his emigration visa—they refused him. They were very nice at the Consulate and they told me that they telegraphed to Washington and that they have informed you about the matter. So we have to wait!—

Thank you for your letters and your friendship. Of course, we are in agreement on Chicago, that is, the arrangements (if the visa comes).

We are staying another 10 days in Paris, where Marc is working.

I will write you as soon as I know anything.

Regards from both of us,

Vava

John Nef in Chicago to Phillips Brooks in Paris [Excerpt]

December 9, 1957

[English] Dear Mr. Brooks,

[. . .]

The most important subject is of course the visas for Mr. and Mrs. Marc Chagall. I assume from your having quoted Mr. Cohen to the effect that "the visa will be issued," this means that the visas will be issued in time for them to come to the United States on the SS LIBERTE which sails from Le Havre on February 12, I think.

The University has arranged a number of important events in connection with Chagall's visit, and we have scheduled several meetings and luncheons and also an exhibition of his paintings. It would be most unfortunate for our cultural relations, as I wrote you earlier, if the voyage had to be abandoned on account of the visas, and it would be almost as serious if the Chagalls were to be offended and pull out as it would be if they were actually refused the visas.

Not having heard from you, but having received a longhand note from Madame Chagall to the effect that the authorities had asked further questions in connection with the visas, I wrote a further letter to Miss Speyer, of which I enclose a copy. As you will know the whole visit is backed by Mr. William Wood Prince, the President of Armour & Company, and a number of people in Chicago are going to be very much disappointed if anything goes awry. Mr. Hermon D. Smith has told me since I wrote to Miss Speyer that he would be glad to write to Mr. Houghton.

May I therefore appeal to you again for guidance, my dear Brooks? Please let me know as soon as you can if there is anything I ought to do now which I have not done. And please tell me if anything goes wrong after I have written.

With much gratitude for your help.

Yours very sincerely,

Mr. Phillips Brooks

Director of Library Services

The Foreign Service of the United States of America

1 Place de l'Odéon, Paris 5, France

Miss Speyer: Darthea Speyer of the U.S. Information Service, American Embassy, Paris.

Hermon D. Smith: John Nef's childhood friend, President of Marsh and McLennan.

Houghton: U.S. Ambassador to France.

Phillips Brooks in Paris to John Nef in Chicago

United States Information Service
Centre Culturel Américain
Bibliothèque Benjamin Franklin
1 Place de l'Odéon, Paris-6

December 17, 1957

[English] Dear Mr. Nef,

Thank you for your letter of December 9th. [. . .]

Vis-à-vis the affaire Chagall: I trust that my letter of December 4th may have helped somewhat to relieve the anxiety which I know you feel on this score. I have been in touch with Mr. Cohen in the matter. This has taken, principally, the form of a long cable to the [State] Department, pointing out the delicacy of the situation, and urging action at the earliest possible moment.

Since decisions of this kind, as I understand it, are always made in Washington, I believe this is all that can be done from Paris for the time being. However, Mr. Morrill Cody, our Public Affairs Officer and chief of the U.S. Information Service for France, has also impressed upon the Embassy the urgency of the case from a public relations viewpoint. This, combined with the efforts of Darthea Speyer and my own small contribution, I am sure has had the effect of underscoring the importance of the case as we see it here.

Mr. Cohen tells me that there is a serious backlog of such requests to the Department, and that there has been a delay of some three to four weeks in the processing of visas in general. All this, I understand, he has communicated to M. and Mme. Chagall, who apparently have decided to await the final decision before accepting your invitation.

Since this affair has now been going on for some time, I would imagine that a reply should be available in the not too distant future. I can only repeat at this point Mr. Cohen's private assurance that, in his opinion, a visa surely will be issued. If it becomes necessary for any further action to be taken, we shall certainly let you know.

Very best regards,

Phillips Brooks

Director of Library Services

Darthea Speyer in Paris to John Nef in Chicago

U.S. Information Service/The Foreign Service of the United States of America
American Embassy, Paris

December 18, 1957

Mr. John Nef
The University of Chicago
Committee on Social Thought

Dear Mr. Nef:

I was depressed to receive your letter and to know that the Chagalls were having difficulty about their visa. I immediately discussed at length the subject with Phil Brooks and the Consul in the Visa Section and they assured me that everything possible is being done to hasten the mechanics of this case.

We all realize how important it is for Chagall to receive his visa as quickly as possible, both for Franco-American relations and as far as your University is concerned. However, I do not think that there is anything further that we can do here at this moment. It seems almost certain that it will be only a matter of a few weeks until Chagall has his visa but the Visa Section is absolutely unable to give me a definite date when the visa will be granted.

I am meeting Jim for Christmas in Istanbul and very excited about the prospect.

With kindest regards and best wishes for the holidays and the hope the Chagall matter will be settled at once. On my return, January 6, I shall immediately look into the matter again and write to you.

Sincerely,

Darthea Speyer

Exhibitions Officer

Telegram from John Nef in Chicago to Henry Villard in Washington, D.C.

[English] (To be charged to Elinor Castle Nef Foundation)

Western Union

December 1957

Many thanks for your telegram which I will share with William Wood Prince Dutch and James Douglas. As Chagall is very famous and as his integrity and fondness for the free world and the United States are widely known, refusal of entry would damage our foreign relations at the same time that it would prevent carrying out program planned at the University of Chicago where his visit is regarded as perhaps the most important educational event of the year. We are grateful for what you are doing. Please keep us informed. Warm regards.

John Nef

(sent from Beliard home in Lake Forest)

Telegram from Harry Villard in Washington, D.C. to John Nef in Chicago

Western Union

1957 December 27

[English] Chagalle visa application undergoing security check owing previous communist background Paris embassy has requested special waiver to enter country immigration authorities alerted investigation expected be complete about January 3rd [h]ave requested action be expedited and will follow up regards=

Harry Villard = =

Telegram from Harry Villard in Washington, D.C. to John Nef in Chicago

Western Union

1958 Jan 6

[English] Chagall security check still not finished one more source remains to be checked will gladly notify you as soon as action completed =

Harry Villard =

John Nef in Chicago to Maxwell Rabb at the White House

Maxwell Rabb:
Secretary to the
Cabinet in the
Eisenhower White
House.

January 8, 1958

[English] Dear Mr. Rabb,

Mr. William Wood Prince has suggested that I write you at once concerning Mr. Marc Chagall, whom he is helping to bring to the University of Chicago and to the Committee on Social Thought, of which I am the chairman. I think that the information you need is contained in the following passages from a letter I wrote yesterday to Ambassador Houghton [in Paris]:

"Marc Chagall comes from a very poor Jewish family in Vitebsk, Russia where he was born about seventy years ago. He began to paint as a child and was supported in Paris by a rich Russian for a number of years before the First World War. He went back to Russia, I think it was on the eve of that war. When the Russian revolution came he was exploited, as I understand it, by the Bolsheviki who made him some kind of subcommissar for art, although I don't imagine he could possibly run an office for five minutes. He told me the story some years ago. As nearly as I can remember he soon became disgusted, deserted from the office, and fled the country with his wife and small daughter. They settled in Paris and he lived in France until the Second World War. After the invasion of France, he came to this country where he lived about four years. His first wife, Bella, died in or near New York, I think in 1945. He returned after that to France with a re-entry permit to the United States, which I think he told me he was unable to renew in 1950 or 1951. He is entirely dedicated to painting, and in so far as he has any political views at all, they are very strongly hostile to the Soviet regime. Indeed I think he told me that, not only would it be impossible for him to return to Russia, after his having fled the country, but that he would certainly be persecuted if the Russians were to get possession of any country in which he happened to be. In this matter, he is as different from Picasso as it is possible to be.

"As you probably know better than I, he is a painter of very great distinction. The University of Chicago has made extensive arrangements to bring him here and have an exhibition of his works in February and early March.

"He and his second wife, Vava, applied for visas either late in November or early in December and were told by the Embassy in Paris that it would take some time but they were sure that visas would be granted. From Harry Villard with whom Dutch Smith and I have communicated in Washington (at Dutch's suggestion) we learn that the security inquiry into his case is nearing completion. But Billy Prince, Dutch and I all feel that in view of the importance of the case, it would be unfortunate if he were not given assurances within the next few days so that he can prepare for his journey. He should leave France about February 10 at the latest in order to meet his engagements here. He and his wife take journeys rather hard, even short journeys in Europe, and that is why we don't want to run the risk of his feeling that he is not wanted and giving up the project of coming."

If there is any further information that you need, please let me know. Mr. Prince and I will greatly appreciate anything you can do which will enable us to cable to Chagall, in a few days if possible, telling him that he and his wife will have their visas in time to leave.

Yours sincerely,

The Honorable Maxwell Rabb

The White House

Washington, D.C.

The Immigration and Naturalization Service in re: Marc Chagall

United States Department of Justice
Immigration and Naturalization Service

Jan 13, 1958

Application: Temporary admission pursuant to Section 212 (d) (3) of the Immigration and Nationality Act, despite his inadmissibility under Section 212 (a) (23) of that Act.

The applicant is a citizen and resident of France, born at Vitebsk, Russia on July 7, 1887. He is a prominent painter who has been invited by the University of

Chicago to act as visiting professor to Committee on Social Thought during February 1958.

The ground of inadmissibility arises from affiliation with Communist front groups and Communist inspired peace movements.

The American Embassy at Paris France advises that although the applicant is an artist of world renown he appears to lack political astuteness and seems to fall prey to all requests for his signature in support of organizations and movements, especially when appealed to through his extremely orthodox religious feelings; that the listing of his name of [= on] letterheads of red front groups is more an indication of his having been duped than of militant Communism on his part. That Embassy has no evidence that applicant ever joined the Communist Party. It is added that applicant's works of art would be exhibitioned in this country, and the United States Information Service expressed interest in featuring applicant on the radio after arrival in the United States. The Embassy is of the view that the applicant's admission into this country would be in the public interest and recommends favorable action.

extremely orthodox: Though a good excuse, Chagall had neither religious nor orthodox feelings, let alone "extremely" orthodox ones. He did have strong sentiments of Jewish identity, especially in solidarity with Jewish suffering, but in the sense of Jews as a national community rather than a religion.

The Department of State informs us that checks completed of its records and of a security agency have disclosed no further derogatory information than that furnished by the Embassy. Moreover, that Department stated reference was made for another security agency regarding such agency's memorandum of January 3, 1958, setting forth activities of the applicant with Communist front movements in the United States. That information is in the records of this Service and confirms such activities. The Department of State is of the opinion there is no reason to believe the applicant's entry would endanger the safety and security of the United States and concurs with the favorable recommendation by the responsible Embassy.

IT IS ORDERED that the application be granted, subject to revocation at any time and conditioned upon application for admission being made within thirty days.

J. Williams
ASSISTANT COMMISSIONER
EXAMINATIONS DIVISION

Visits to the United States

Similar language was used by the FBI and the INS on several other occasions. Thus, Chagall was allowed to enter the U.S. in February 1958 as a visiting professor at the Committee on Social Thought, University of Chicago; in May–June

1960 to receive an honorary degree at Brandeis University; in April 1963 to participate at a meeting in Washington, D.C.; in November 1966–January 1967 "to install some of his paintings in the Lincoln Center, New York City"; in October 1971, to unveil his mosaic in Washington, D.C.; and in August 1974 to unveil his mosaic at the First National Bank in Chicago.

Ambassador Houghton in Washington, D.C. to John Nef in Chicago

Department of State/Washington

January 14, 1958

Dear Dr. Nef:

Ambassador Amory Houghton has asked me to write to you stating that a visa has just been authorized for Marc Chagall. Mr. Chagall should apply for his visa within thirty days.

    The Ambassador wanted to write you personally about this matter but was so tied up here in the Department before leaving that he did not get the opportunity to do so. However, he wanted to be sure that you received this news urgently.

Sincerely yours,

Matthew J. Looram

Cable: John Nef in Chicago to Marc Chagall in Vence

Western Union

January 14, 1958

CHAGALL

VENCE

FRANCE

Visa favorably settled through William Prince. You will be notified in time. We are overjoyed that you are coming. Love

John

John Nef in Chicago to Marc and Vava Chagall in Vence

15 January 1958

[French] Very dear friends,

As you already know from my cable, your visas are guaranteed. It is the White House that decided today and now there can be no more difficulties. I do not know exactly when the Ambassador in Paris will inform you, but I can guarantee that it will be well before your departure. I am in communication with our Ambassador, who was in my regiment in 1914 and is currently in Washington. It is a very happy conclusion and your visit will be even more precious because of these events.

If I understood your last letter, dear Vava, you have your tickets on the Liberte, which leaves from Le Havre on February 12 and arrives in New York on the 18th; I would like to send you train tickets from New York to Chicago, with a little check in dollars that you can cash in New York for your expenses in that city. Where should I send it, to Vence or to Paris? Write me a note, please, to tell me and I will send them to you immediately after.

I hope that you will find conditions here in the house satisfactory for work; I am arranging matters so that the first four days of your stay will be free of any engagements, except a few meetings with close friends, like the Wood Princes who have prepared this stay; so we will prepare together the talks that will take place later.

What joy to see you, my friends! I send you my very affectionate regards, and this time, I can say without any hesitation: see you soon

John U. Nef

U.S. Embassy in Paris to Director, FBI

THE FOREIGN SERVICE
OF THE
UNITED STATES OF AMERICA

American Embassy
Paris 8, France

Date: January 16, 1958
To: Director, FBI
From: Legat, Paris (105-770)
Subject: MARC CHAGALL, aka Moiss Chagall
IS - R & FR

XXXXX Visa Section, U.S. Embassy, Paris, on 1/15/58 advised that a waiver had been secured to issue subject a visa to go to the United States.

Subject's file reflects that he is a prominent and well known painter, who has been affiliated with some Communist front groups. He was born on 7/7/87 in Russia. He will be accompanied by his second wife, VALENTINE BRODSKY, born 11/16/05 in Kiev, Russia, a British national.

Subject's file reflects that he has been invited by the University of Chicago to act as Visiting Professor on Social Thought during the month of February 1958. Professor XXXXX [= Nef] of the University of Chicago is planning an exhibit of subject's paintings at the Museum of Modern Art, Chicago. The file also reflects that XXXXX [= Rudy Bing] of the New York Metropolitan Opera, is a family friend of the subject. "Look" Magazine in its issue of 11/26/57 ran an article on the subject.

Museum of Modern Art, Chicago: There is no such museum; it is apparently the Art Institute of Chicago.

The Visa Section will advise this office when a visa is issued.

Two extra copies of this communication are being provided for possible transmittal to the Chicago office.

Maxwell Rabb in the White House to John Nef in Chicago

The White House
Washington

January 21, 1958

[English] Dear Dr. Nef:

I am delighted that you were so pleased with the news about Mr. Chagall. I was, indeed, happy to have been of assistance to him.

With kind regard,

Sincerely,

Maxwell M. Rabb

Secretary to the Cabinet

U.S. Embassy in Paris to Director, FBI

MEMORANDUM—UNITED STATES GOVERNMENT
To: DIRECTOR, FBI   Date: 3/5/58
From: SAC, NEW YORK (100-87783)
Subject: MARC CHAGALL, wa
Mark Chargal
SECURITY MATTER—C

On 1/14/58, this office was advised by the Immigration and Naturalization Service (INS), 70 Columbus Avenue, New York City, that captioned subject, born

7/7/87, in Russia, was authorized to enter the United States to act as visiting professor at the University of Chicago during February 1958, under condition he apply for admission within thirty days.

By letter dated 2/19/58, INS advised that captioned individual, an alien, arrived at the Port of New York on 2/17/58, and was admitted as a non-immigrant until 5/17/58.

He is destined to the University of Chicago for three weeks and then he will stay at the Essex House, New York City.

A review of the subject's case file reflects that he has for the past few years resided in France. It is further reflected that he had previously resided at High Falls, New York.

No investigation is contemplated, and the above is submitted for the information of the Bureau.

Louis Stern in New York to Ida Chagall in Bern

March 26, 1958

[English] Dear Ida:

I am writing this note an hour or two after the S.S. LIBERTE sailed with your father and Vava aboard. I want and hope this letter reaches you before you see them on their return.

I can report to you that your father's visit to the United States was *socially* a great success. The Chagalls were tead, dined and wined in Chicago and New York, and your father stood the test with surprising grace. I do not remember the names of the people who entertainted in Chicago—your father and Vava will more than likely tell you about that. In New York, however, I can give you particulars and details. The outstanding social event, for my point of view, was the dinner party for about twenty people given by Mr. and Mrs. Nelson A. Rockefeller. He, as you know, is Chairman of the Board of The Museum of Modern Art. Next in importance, all for my point of view, was the cocktail and tea party given by Mr. and Mrs. Gilbert Chapman (she, as you know, is the former Mrs. Goodspeed of Chicago). Of my affair, I cannot very well speak; you will have to get the report from the Vence branch of your family. In numbers, in food and drink, in attire, the soiree staged by me should compare favorably. There were, of course, other social events of which you will hear, but which carry no significance with me.

I cannot speak with any authority on the impression your father made as a lecturer, other than that Professor Nef reported to me of a most favorable impression your father made on the audience.

From an art standpoint, the trip was a nullity and, if anything, was consider-

the Lejwas: Mr. and Mrs. Lejwa, owners of the Chalette Gallery in New York, claimed that they represented Maeght and organized a Chagall exhibition without his consent.

ably marred by the disgusting behaviour of the Lejwas, who persisted in staging a Chagall exhibition notwithstanding your father's express wishes. There were some strange behaviourism on the part of your and your father's friends. In view of my knowledge of your extraordinary kindness to the Max Lerners, their conduct towards me and towards your father is difficult to explain. The Sweeneys, also, did not come up to normal expectations. Due to my diplomatic intervention, there was a rapprochement made between your father and Sam Salz. He extended an invitation to your father and Vava to come to his house, which they did one morning, which gave Sam a chance to tell me how wonderful he, Sam Salz, was, and what great pictures he, Sam Salz, has! Never, for one moment, apologizing or withdrawing some of the nasty remarks which he has been making about your father during the past twenty years, but that is true to his type.

I had hoped to send you some photographs taken the evening of my party, but they have not been developed as yet. If and when they are, I will send you some of the photographs. As I am dictating this, I am looking at the photograph of your three gorgeous children, on the score of which I sincerely congratulate you.

After you have had a report from your father and Vava and you have time, I will appreciate a word from you. Until the next time, I am, with affectionate regards to all of you,

[Louis Stern]

Stained Glass Windows: 1958–1964

Marq: The following summary is based on two interviews with Charles Marq and on Chagall's letters to him.

In 1957, the French government bureau in charge of Historical Monuments invited Chagall to design two stained glass windows for the Metz Cathedral. In the Spring of 1958, upon his return from the United States, he met with Charles and Brigitte Marq, the proprietors of the Jacques Simon Glass Works in Reims. Marq caught the spirit and the intentions of Chagall, which were often expressed in gestures and feelings. The Marqs, devout Christians, were impressed by Chagall's spirituality, and a close collaboration ensued.

Marq describes his relationship with Chagall as that of an actor to a scriptwriter, or of an orchestra conductor to a composer. Together, they created a series of famous works, combining the effects of glass, light, and many shades of color. These included more stained glass windows for the Metz Cathedral; the Twelve Tribes of Israel windows in the synagogue of the Hadassah Medical Center in Jerusalem; eight windows for the Union Church of Pocantico Hills, New York, commissioned by the Rockefeller family; the "Peace" window at the United Nations in New York; four blue windows in the Art Institute of Chicago; a window for the Musée National Message Biblique Marc Chagall in Nice; a stained glass window for the Cathedral at Reims; and several windows for the Cathedral in Mainz, Germany, finished by Marq after Chagall's death.[1]

Charles Marq personally supervised the installation of Chagall's windows in Jerusalem, unveiled on February 1962. These were Chagall's first windows on such a large scale; furthermore, they required special security glass. In June 1967, the windows were taken off to protect them during the Six-Day War, and some pieces of glass broke. Marq himself went to Jerusalem to take care of the damage.

Chagall's correspondence with Marq is all typewritten; it is often short and cryptic, relating to things discussed during personal meetings, making arrangements for work on projects or appointments, as well as personal greetings. "All that was exchanged between us," says Marq, was in oral conversation and short reflections while we worked together." Only a selection of the letters is presented here, with some annotations that benefited from Marq's personal recollections.

Marc Chagall in Vence to Charles Marq in Reims

The gothic Cathedral in Metz suffered a great deal from bombardments during World War II; an important part of the old windows was destroyed. In 1958, Robert Renard, Chief Architect of the Metz Cathedral, asked Chagall to create several of the windows, a project that expanded over time. The work was accomplished between 1959 and 1968.

[Stationery: "Les Collines" Vence (A.M.)]

19 August 1958

[French] Dear Marq,

Thank you very much for your letter. I was so happy with it . . .

Of course, the difficulties raised by the Historical Monuments made me sad. But the letters of Dupont, Renard, and you give me courage.

Dupont: Jacques Dupont, Inspector General of Historical Monuments, which specialized in movable objects, including stained glass windows, tapestries, and furniture.

I am glad that you were beginning to work for me, on those mockups for which I made such a great effort.

I am waiting impatiently for your visit to Vence. Moreover, I want us to stay in touch and to meet often, for we have to realize a masterpiece [the windows for the Metz Cathedral].

Three important exhibitions are being prepared, two in Germany and one in Paris. It would be good if we could exhibit there, at least part of those mockups.

I give both of you a warm handshake, and see you soon.

My wife joins me in sending you our best.

Marc Chagall

Ida's Worries

Ida Chagall in Bern to Louis Stern in New York

[Written across the top:]   *CONFIDENTIAL, please destroy after reading*

[Stationery: 23 Herrengasse, Berne]

Aug 25th [1958]

[English] Dear Louis,

Since months, since April, I want to write to you, and it is only now in the clinic where I am since nearly 3 weeks that I find the long lost peace of mind. You must be cross at me or maybe you guessed how was the atmosphere of my dear family coming home. I shall start from the beginning.

We were at Le Havre, meeting them as there was a general strike preventing passengers to reach Paris if one did not have a car. Immediately I was faced with quite disagreeable accusations as concerning my former managing father's affairs in NY. They did not find papers (which are in Vence) in NY and it was the first report I got instead of telling us about their good time. Vava told me how she cried every night because it was so difficult for her to repair all the moral damage I did to father before in the States! She was very happy of her result, thank goodness.

This return was quite a shock.

In May father got violently sick all of a sudden, happily in Paris. He asked me to call our old friend-doctor [Dr. Camille Dreyfus], which I did. The doctor wanted to take father to the hospital as he was fearing an intestinal occlusion. It was a battle to bring father there, as Vava did not know this doctor and therefore did not trust him. Finally father was brought in. A nightmare of 4 days and 4 nights began. Doctors—I succeeded to get several top ones—gave us no more than half an hour to accept an operation. Father was vomiting blood (which he kept doing so for 4 days after the operation). The diagnosis was appendicitis with peretonitis and intestinal occlusion. They found afterwards a dark brown stone in father's appendicitis! Vava again did not want to accept the operation. Thank goodness Franz was there and he pushed.

The result: father is OK now. It was very long and he suffered terribly all kinds of complications. For 4 days he was in great danger. When it was over, Vava told: "These cattle-dealers (meaning the doctors) would not have been able to save him if he really had all they wrote he had." So the official version is that father had just an appendicitis with complications due to bad treatments! And it is final.

I do not care to make a battle over diagnosis. I don't and really do not see the importance of it. But the atmosphere is worse than ever before.

Father is much weaker now of course than before and the only thing I can do for him is to act as if nothing concerns me. But it gave me this damn ulcer.

It is only for this reason that *I beg* you not to tell anyone what I am writing to you. As long as I can I do not want to be the one that "speaks against."

Since nearly 3 weeks I am here after a [?] hemorrage which stopped in the clinic. I hope in one week to be able to go down to the Italian Riviera to join the children and relax and to forget stupidities.

Did you get Odilon Redon's catalogue? Franz did quite a good job. Unfortunately without the Redon's [sic] in America.

Dear Louis, I wrote you all this too long letter so that you should know why I kept silent, and please do not be cross. When are you coming? What did you do this summer?

Hentzen: Dr. Alfred Hentzen had introduced Chagall's exhibition in Hannover in 1955. From February 6 to March 22, 1959, he curated a major Chagall exhibition of 403 works in the Kunstverein in Hamburg, Germany.

Tomorrow in the hospital, I am seeing M. Hentzen from Hamburg about father's big shows. I believe you got letters too? But I do not know your reaction.

Excuse my handwriting. I am writing in bed. Write to me if you can.

The address in Sept will be:

Casa Eugel—Via Privata Repellius 23A / Sta. Margharita—Ligure—Italia

Are you well? / With fond regards,

your Ida

Marc Chagall in Vence to John Nef in Chicago

Les Collines / Vence (A.M.)

October 15, 1958

Dear friend,

I hope you are well and are currently in Chicago.

It is now my turn to write you to ask you a favor, for a change.

I would like to ask you to intervene with the Chicago Art Institute to accept the loan of the big old painting, "The Birth," as well as the "White Crucifixion" for my exhibitions. Both of them are very important for their period. Moreover, I am in a hurry to have the answer because the catalogue has to be done.

I hope that your friendship for us will help you and allow you to get a positive answer.

You also need to intervene with Mrs. Culbert [sic], whom you know and who has already lent her paintings for my exhibition in Chicago, during my stay with you. Since "Anywhere Out of the World" is biographically very important in my work, I would be very disappointed if it could not be part of my exhibitions.

In addition, I have already written myself to the Museum and to Madame Culberg [sic], but I am convinced that your intervention will surely be decisive.

I await news from you on all fronts . . .

Vava joins me in sending you all our good wishes and thanks.

Marc Chagall

Marc Chagall in Vence to Louis Stern in New York

"Les Collines"/Vence (A.M.)   5 novembre 1958

[French] Dear friend Louis,

I have received your letter of November 2. And see how quickly I answer your questions!

In fact, Mr. Hentzen has not yet told me of your agreeing to lend "PURIM" and "LA GAZETTE DE SMOLENSK." Thank you very very much for agreeing to part from them.

But, because of our friendship, and since you know me, allow me to tell you how much I like these retrospective exhibitions to be underlined by the fantastic and unreal; and you have precisely that painting "Okh, Bozhe" . . . Think whatever you want of me, but I can't resist asking you to lend that painting so that it can also be shown. I would be so grateful to you.

Okh, Bozhe: "Oh, God" in Russian.

As for my health, it is much better now—touch wood.—I am trying to work and I am finishing "LA CREATION DE L'HOMME" so that it can be exhibited at the exhibitions that are now being prepared. I am also preparing another big work.

As you know, Daphnis and Chloe was presented in Brussels, but very hastily. The management insisted on showing it in spite of everything. That ballet will be performed at the Opéra in Paris, in December, with SKIBINE who is replacing Lifar. He is the one who played in my ballet Aleko, in New York. He is going to redo the choreography of Daphnis and Chloe and I think that afterward it will be good. I hope very much that you will see it someday.

The book of Daphnis and Chloe will be done next year. Tériade is beginning to prepare the text for it. I think it will be very good, like everything this great Tériade undertakes.

Do you have the colored Bible album? And the album published by the Vent d'Arles, drawings reproduced by Jacomet with a preface by Jean Cassou?

Despite all that, I am "*meshuge*" enough.

I am trying not to annoy Vava too much (and such a letter is written during her absence).

We have not gone on vacation this year and we kept David with us, then he went to Ida. At the moment, he is not a brilliant student.

I don't know why, but these exhibitions torment me as if I were a boy of 17, especially the one in Paris.

Too bad I can't talk with you. You would tell me what I am.

I remember your secretary very well. She is very nice. She saw my stained glass windows for Metz. And she gave a hand in the other windows; I thank her for it. She is sensitive for Chagall and for Stern.

Write to me and give me your opinion about the painting "Okh Bozhe." And let Hentzen know if you agree.

Meanwhile, warm regards. / Your

Marc Chagall

Marc Chagall: "When will you come, my hour"

[Yiddish]

When will you come, my hour,
When I shall go out like a candle,
When will I reach you, my distant one,
And when will my rest come?

I don't know if I'm walking,
I don't know who I am,
I don't know where I stand,
My head and my soul—where they are.

Look, my dear mother,
At your son going down,
Look, my dear crown,
How quiet and deep my sun sets.

Louis Stern in New York to Marc Chagall in Vence

November 12, 1958

[English] Cher Maitre Chagall,

Your letter pleased me very much. It made me feel as if we were talking to one another. As you must know, I am in full sympathy with anything that you want to accomplish, and I am ready to assist in any way possible.

I note what you say about "Okh Bozhe," and I am willing to lend it, for I understand your point of view precisely. The difficulty arises that Hentzen did not ask for this particular picture. The other pictures that he asked for are "Dans la nuit," "L'auge" and your self-portrait of 1914. Do you have any objection to write to Hentzen, or perhaps to ask Ida to write to Henzen (I don't know exactly what the situation is with respect to Ida's participation in these exhibitions)? At any rate, as soon as Hentzen will ask me for "Okh, Bozhe," I will comply.

Now, it occurs to me that, perhaps, you would be willing to lend me a few of your small pictures, or perhaps the large one, while my Chagalls are away for a year. Don't you think that would be a fair exchange?

I have heard of the album the Bible in color, but I haven't seen one. I would, of course, like to have a chance to examine the album, although, frankly speaking, I have always entertained considerable doubt as to the propriety of having the Bible in color. I have not forgotten the explanation you gave me on the day of the Vernissage [= opening] at the Bibliotheque Nationale, when I was commenting on the difference between the plates of "Les ames mortes" and those of the Bible. Your explanation to me was short and to the point. You said, in illustrating the Bible, you had a two thousand year tradition to deal with, whereas, in "Les ames mortes," you were completely free to use your knowledge and imagination. Notwithstanding, I would very much like to see the album, and perhaps—since I have an almost complete collection of your books—to add the album to my collection.

You will recall that, in the summer of 1957, I met the lady who manages LE VENT D'ARLES, and her Turkish boyfriend or husband—I don't know which. My understanding was that she promised to have a copy for me. Can you, or will you speak to her about it? At any rate, if it can be bought, I would like to have a copy.

I am delighted to hear about your state of health, and that you are apparently full of energy to do so much work as you are doing. I would certainly enjoy seeing the opera with your decors of "Daphnis et Chloe." I assume that the musique is by Ravel, which appeals to me most strongly. Perhaps I will arrange to come to Paris when your exhibition is on, with the hopes that "Daphis et Chloe" will be given by the Opera company at that time.

I am somewhat mystified about the "La creation de l'homme." Is it an oil painting, or what?

I could prolong this letter, but I do not want to tire you out. I will conclude as I began—that you can rely on me to cooperate in every way with the forthcoming Chagall exhibitions.

[Louis Stern]

Marc Chagall in Vence to Louis Stern in New York

November 20, 1958

[English version] Dear Friend Stern,

Thank you very much for your letter of November 12. I knew very well that I could count on your friendship, and I thank you with all my heart for your kind reply.

I relay to Hentzen all that you tell me about the pictures; he will be contacting you.

If you want the album "BIBLE" in color, I must tell you to ask it from Tériade; concerning the album "COULEUR AMOUR," you should ask it from the woman editor of VENT D'ARLES, 39 Blvd de Port Royal—Paris (13e), for I do not own these albums.

I wish I could have loaned you a painting while yours will be away at the exhibitions . . . Alas, I have been asked to contribute in such proportions that there will be nothing or almost nothing left at home.

I do not know yet when the ballet "Daphnis et Chloe" will be played. No definite date has been set yet.

I thank you again for your great understanding, and I send you, as well as from Vava, our very cordial memory.

Chagall

Louis Stern in New York to Dr. A. Hentzen in Hamburg

November 30, 1958

[English] Dear Dr. Hentzen,

Your letter dated November 26, concerning Chagall's self-portrait in my collection, presents a complicated problem. By this time, you must have heard from Chagall that he has been in touch with me directly, asking my help for your exhibition—apparently not knowing that you had written to me, asking for certain definite pictures, and that I had agreed to send "Purim" and "La gazette de Smolensk." Curiously enough, he asks that I contribute but one picture, and that is the one with the Russian title: "Okh Bozhe" which, translated, means "Oh God." I immediately replied to Chagall, advising him of my agreement to lend "Purim" and "La gazette de Smolensk," and telling him further that, before I could agree to send the picture which he wants, "Oh God," I would have to receive a request from you. And now, you come asking for the self-portrait.

In replying to Chagall, I suggested that he might lend me some of the small Chagalls of which he must have a multitude in his studio, whereupon Chagall replied that I would be hearing from you, but that he would not be willing to lend me any of his pictures, since, as he wrote:

> I have been asked to contribute in such proportions that there will be nothing or almost nothing left at home.

Chagall's attitude makes me feel that I wished I had not agreed to lend any of my pictures. This is not my first experience with Chagall, and I am almost fed up with his expecting everything from me and unwilling to do anything for me. I am not even certain of Ida's attitude towards me, for it has been questionable. Under the circumstances, I am not in a position to give you a definite answer on the self-portrait. If Mr. Obersteg's experience with Chagall is similar to mine, I am not surprised that he refused to lend—I wish I had the courage to do the same.

Sincerely yours,

[Louis Stern]

P.S. I have no objection to your showing this letter to Chagall or Ida, or both.

Louis Stern in New York to Ida Chagall in Bern

December 18, 1958

[English] Dear Ida,

I have postponed writing you in acknowledgement of your letter dated November 30th, first to make it possible for me to tell you that the matter of the Chagall pictures which I am lending to Professor Hentzen has been definitely determined, and second, to be able to furnish Franz a photograph of the little gouache, "The Raising of Lazarus." The photograph is enclosed herewith.

As you will note, I granted Dr. Hentzen's request for your father's "Self-Portrait," so that I am loaning three pictures:

"Self Portrait"

"La gazette de Smolensk"

"Purim."

I have no hesitation in saying that your Vence relatives do not deserve the consideration which I am showing them. I do not want to enter into a lengthy correspondence about my grievances. Some day, when we meet again, I am bound to tell you, for it weighs heavy on my mind.

I am sorry to hear about your father-in-law's illness, and I hope he has a complete and speedy recovery. He was most courteous to me on the occasions when I saw him. I will never forget the great courtesy which he extended to me when he came to the Kuntz Museum in Zurich to meet me and take me to his home for lunch. That was the act of a true gentleman, which I always found him to be.

Thanks for the snapshots of your lovely children. They are growing nicely.

Until the next time, I am always/Sincerely

[Louis Stern]

Marc Chagall in Vence to Charles Marq in Reims

[Stationery: "Les Collines" Vence (A.M.)]

March 20, 1959

[French] Dear Marq,

I was very glad to read your letter in Vence today when I returned from a trip to Switzerland.

Thanks for the good news about the glasses. It is a great joy to know that you have the range of colors necessary for those stained glass windows. I hope to see them when I come to Paris.

June exhibition: "Marc Chagall," Musée des Arts Décoratifs, Paris, June–October 1959; 185 paintings.

It would be good if we could have something for the June exhibition in Paris. Of course, on condition that it doesn't force you to rush.

See you soon, I hope.

My wife joins me in sending both of you our very cordial regards.

Marc Chagall

P.S. If you aren't working on two mockups at the same time, perhaps you might give one to Monsieur Berlin René, 231, rue de Belleville in Paris (19th) (tel. Bol. 80-79). He promised me to redo the canvas backing of the mockups, since the first was defective. That, of course, if your work won't suffer from it.

P.S. Our best to all the nice staff of the studio. I do not forget how lovingly they all worked and helped at the Pavillon de Marsan.

Ida Chagall in Berne to Pierre Matisse in New York

April 12, 1959   Herrengasse 23 Berne

[French] Dear Pierre,

The photostat notebook of Colten photos is very precious to me and to thank you for it is not enough. You will see in the overly long list of proofs that I am asking you for—most of them because I lack them or because the publisher considers the non-Colten proofs not good enough. But I ask you urgently and I think that we agreed about that at Saint-Jean Cap Ferrat that your photographer was to send me directly the bill not only for the photostat of the notebook, but also for the proofs. Please, don't forget. All the same, I hope that those costs for the photos will be returned in the expenses for the publisher, for we should not have any scruples, especially since you know very well that it has nothing to do with my gratitude at receiving all this material.

I am returning from Munich where the exhibition this time didn't go as "harmoniously" for the hanging as in Hamburg. Perhaps it is the proximity of the Baroque that demands that. In any case, the exhibition is good, even bigger than Hamburg, it is the gigantic scale of the Hitler style of the "Haus der Kunst" that probably demands it. There were 3600 people at the opening, it is their largest number since Van Gogh and I suppose that our "Papa" must be secretly satisfied or rather officially amazed that there were fewer visitors at the opening of Picasso at the same "Haus der Kunst."

Your "Blue Horse" stands out magnificently well but I hope that you will forgive me for removing the frame leaving the casing which was below. I hadn't even noticed that it wasn't signed. Papa didn't come to Munich. I doubt that he will come there. But I suppose that the picture will go to the third stage which is the Museum of Decorative Arts [in Paris] and there, I have no doubt that Papa will do it. In any case, I will make sure that it is not forgotten. But I think he would be thrilled if you would send him a little card to that effect, reminding him to add the date of 1948. Recently, my stepmother is less appreciative of things that come from me. So I don't want her to be insulted about that. But I think that you will understand that family complication.

Thanks again with all my heart, dear Pierre, very affectionately yours,

Ida

P.S. I have just received the Soviet visa and I plan to leave alone on the 22nd [April]. Do you need anything? Skira is going to try to give me color proofs to correct. But do you need black and white photos? I suppose that it is childish of me to ask you and that you have everything. Answer me in Paris where I shall be until the 22nd.

"Haus der Kunst": Haus der deutschen Kunst (The House of German Art) in Munich, where, in 1937, Hitler inaugurated the "Great Exhibition of German Art" as a contrast to the "Degenerate Art" exhibition (which included Chagall).

"Blue Horse": Chagall's painting "The Blue Horse" (1948). Matisse loaned it to the Munich Exhibition.

I doubt that he will come there: Chagall avoided traveling to Germany after the Holocaust, even for his own exhibitions.

Marc Chagall in Vence to Charles Marq in Reims

[Stationery: "Les Collines" Vence (A.M.)]

May 15, 1959

[French] Dear Marq,

Thanks for your nice letter.

I am glad to know that you are glad . . .

Of course, it would be necessary to be strong enough to come see all that in place; but how to do that? I have wings but I don't have legs. I pray to God that you and your wife, feeling and loving, would convey all that to the stained glass windows so that not only our friends, but also our "enemies" feel it.

Of course, I would very much like it to be exhibited at the Pavillon de Marsan; will you get in touch with Monsieur Mathey about that?

I really don't understand if, in two weeks, you are thinking of coming to Vence or to Paris. As far as I am concerned, I will be here until the end of May and afterward in Paris.

Thanks again, see you soon.

Cordially,

Marc Chagall

Pavillon de Marsan: The wing of the Louvre along rue de Rivoli, where the Musée des Arts Décoratifs was located.

Mathey: Francois Mathey, Chief Curator of the Pavillon de Marsan.

Marc Chagall in Paris to Charles Marq in Reims

Paris, June 9, 1959

[French] Dear Marq,

Thanks for your letter; thanks also for understanding me so well.

On Wednesday, I will also come to the Museum and perhaps we shall meet.

I hope that with the help of the God of your very beautiful cathedral [the cathedral of Reims], we will do very good work together.

My wife joins me in thanking you for the lovely day spent with you.

My compliments to you and yours,

Marc Chagall

P.S. Our best to all the nice staff of the studio. I do not forget how lovingly they all worked and helped at the Pavillon de Marsan.

Ida's Trip to Russia

After the Chagalls left the Soviet Union in 1922, they did not see their homeland until Ida's visit in 1959 and Marc and Vava's visit in 1973. Now, as Franz Meyer was about to finish a major biography of Chagall, aided by Ida and the family documents and photos, Ida had a double incentive to go, observe, make connections, and find pertinent documents. Khrushchev's political "thaw" created a somewhat more lenient climate, and a tourist could speak to local people and see relatives without endangering their lives.

Ida Chagall in Bern to Becky and Bernard Reis in New York

5.8.59 [August]

[English] Dearest Becky and Bernard,

I am so sorry I could not write you before, but life was just too hectic and wonderful, of course, in the same time. I wonder where this note will reach you. I hope it will be forwarded to you. We are leaving next week for Gordes, where we plan to stay and to go only to Vence. Franz wants absolutely to finish the greater part of his Chagall work and not to move anywhere else. But we may come to Paris between the time that you will be there, so please, please let us know.

Yes, maybe you have learned that I was able to get some of the pictures from Russia. It was the most exciting event, an adventure I ever went through and as long as I live I will never forget it. Of course, I did not get all the pictures I wanted, but still it is very important and both in meanings and who knows maybe it will go from the cellar to the first floor in the Museums. I have heard that they are so thrilled now of the Chagall success in Paris that they gave orders that the big Jewish [theater] murals be restored. I just cannot believe it. My staying there for 25 days was the most enchanting and wonderful thing of my life. Not only did I see all the people I wanted to see among the most "forbidden" people, also the family, both of fathers and mothers, but I found such friends as I never had. Well, what is the use of telling you, you know yourself what kind of wonderful people the Russians can be when they are just plain Russian people. Do enjoy your vacation and, if possible, please phone or cable and let us try to meet.

> *not to move anywhere else*: Franz Meyer worked on his comprehensive biography of Marc Chagall in collaboration with the painter. Hence, it would be valuable for him to work near Vence.
>
> *from the cellar*: The Chagall treasures in Russian museums, along with other "modernist" (unrealistic and decadent) art, were hidden in the museum stores.

With our love and fond, fond wishes for a happy summer, / Yours devotedly,

Ida

Ida Chagall in Gordes to Louis Stern in New York

Gordes 8/9/59 [September]

[English] Dear Louis

I was happy of your letter and in the same time perturbed. Do you really intend to operate yourself? There are today so many medecine for better circulation. Is not rest safer than the weakness and trouble of an operation? I am really sorry of these bad news, though I hope it is not too serious as you are writing of swimming pool week ends. Do let me know about yourself, and please do not forget that *you have* a friend in me and I wish I could do something. My father in law who was so critically ill is now better and getting along—*quietly* though—with medecines. I was operated so often myself that I am now afraid for others.

Thank you for all the nice things you are writing to me personally. Father's gratefulness?! It is quite another chapter. I should be grateful, they think, for having the honor to do things!—Russia? I went there for my own fun so to say. Learn about mother's and father's relatives still alive and thought it is better to go

the sky is clear: An allusion to the years of Krushchev's "thaw."

while the sky is clear, the relatives alive and the documentation on the big Chagall of Franz still unclosed. As far as their documentation is concerned I brought back amazing things. It is really worth the trip to see them! Dozens of photographs of pictures all over, including Erevane in Armenia, and the *Metricheskoe Svidetelstvo* [birth certificate] of father's family where the 1887 date stands firm! When leaving—I did not believe that I would get the pictures (I got *only* those from Moscow) but there I did it as a sport and had from that a "cover" also which helped me to see all those I wanted. (Mikhoels's widow, etc.) I saw more people than I ever did in my life, and it was due to a miracle, to a help, I will tell [you] one day, but not by letter. When I went I thought I will meet Pasternak. And there I

my visit will not spoil things: During the Stalinist regime, people suffered for having relatives abroad or for meeting foreign tourists, and Krushchev's "thaw" was quite precarious.

forgot about him. And this due to this "miracle." I hope my visit will not spoil things for them one day. Meanwhile I keep receiving letters and documents on Chagall (such as copies of letters he wrote from 1909 to artists and writers, copy of his "bourse" [scholarship] of 15 roubles he got in Petersburg). We are having "dates" finally . . .

I spent a lot of time with the families. It is difficult to speak about father's one, except that he is without doubt a great artist, but that it took also to be a genius to get out from that family.

Mother's side is different. With one brother of her and family I had little contact (though fascinating: a cousin is a big mathematician, and it is thrilling to see how they live intensely), but with the older brother of mother who was the dean of the law faculty of Leningrad who had his regular 12 years of deportation, but came back serene, intelligent, and adorable, I had the most unexpected wonderful contact. As if mother was with us. She was his beloved sister and it was the same with her, this much I knew. I came back craving for his tenderness, gentleness—without any sentimentality. I felt so at home and confident, without words. I hope I will be able to see him again. I left friends there and I admire and respect their work in these dreadful conditions. Especially for Jews.

I did not see Barr there. He lectured after my departure. We did not meet Clifford lately. I wish I could come over and see museums and exhibitions—could you have sent to me the list of the late Museum of Modern Art publications? We are dreadfully behind on them, and I would like to order some.

You are writing "mazel tov" about father's remarriage. It is certainly *not* a Mazel Tov [good luck] for me. I learned about it through the press, though it is quite hush-hushed. Afterwards father refused to speak about it with me saying that *"Ya ne mogu, ya ne mogu"* [Russian: "I cannot, I cannot!"]. I learned afterwards that they were divorced on last March 5, 1958 (so before your party . . .) and remarried in Sept. while I was in Italy. So it means that when father nearly died [hurt?] by car they were divorced.

For some years, a remariage after a divorce, with a different marriage contract is permissible [in France] under the express condition that it does not spoliate a possible heir. This is the reason why it had to be so secret. So that I should not learn about it. It was the reason also of the American trip I am sure. To be away from their domicile. You are asking me about it, so I am writing to you. This ugly affair had a very good result for me, morally. Before I suffered from Vava's hatred, now that it is such a Balzac story, I do not feel mixed in it, and care *much less*.

such a Balzac story: An issue involving family intrigues and money.

Anyhow, if father would have told me about it, asked me, I would have said "Do what you please." And I feel like it always. I knew these last years, that I am robbed by Vava, but he apparently likes it, or is quickly satisfied with the big "consolation," that I need nothing, but that he needs his peace, which he does not even sell any more, but gives away everything for.

If you speak about it all (it is not secret, as it was in the press, but people think that it was due to a bad marriage formality before, or so on, and few people do know the real reason. If you speak, do *not* quote me only as the one that gave you the detail.) The whole thing was cooked by a great, dangerous lawyer here, and he was father's witness also.

It was hard to work for Hentzen, Hamburg afterwards. But I had promised him this 3 years previously and do not like to fail. Vava is a great "stratege" and to say that she is dangerous is not enough, but he is amused maybe by all this and anyhow respects it. It is difficult to say but I have the feeling that one pays for each thing in its way.

What is hard is for Franz to keep on with the big book.

Our relationship with the family is polite, social. I wish you could be here, as I am preparing few papers in case and I would have appreciate your advice. But we have time, of course. Write to me on your reactions. I prefer that you would write by hand, without secretary's mixed.

Troika: Ida's three children. The word *troika* (in Russian, "the trio") is used for three horses harnessed in a carriage.

Here are some photos of the Troika. They grow up nicely meanwhile. Father barely sees them. I brought them to Paris in June, for the ballet. I wanted Piet to remember.

15 years since Bella is gone!

Franz sends you his greetings. His Matisse show is *fantastic*. Ask Pierre [Matisse] about it. He came with Patricia and was pleased.

Be well. *Take care of yourself.* There are not many good people around, Louis!

Love,/   Ida

Marc Chagall in Vence to Charles Marq in Reims

In June 1959, Dr. Miriam Freund, National President of Hadassah in the U.S., and Joseph Neufeld, the architect of the Hadassah–Hebrew University Medical Center in Jerusalem, saw the first Metz Cathedral windows exhibited in Paris. They commissioned Chagall to produce twelve windows for the small basement synagogue in the new Hadassah Medical Center in Jerusalem. Charles Marq executed Chagall's designs.

[Stationery: "Les Collines" Vence (A.M.)]

8 September 1959

[French] Dear Marq,

I am enclosing a letter from Monsieur Neufeld, the architect of Hadassah, as well as the plans that are attached to it.

I hope that someone will be able to translate all that for you [From English].

As you can see, Monsieur Neufeld wants to get the mockup you spoke of in your last letter, which we sent to him.

I advise you, on studying the attached plans, to decide if the new ventilation proposed won't be ugly and risk detracting from the composition of the stained glass. I would like to know your opinion on this very important point.

I will not be able to see you in Paris this month as planned; my wife is a bit tired and I have to go to Italy with her for her cure. But we will come in the autumn and I will let you know.

The stained glass windows for the Hadassah Hospital synagogue in Jerusalem, installed for an exhibition at the Musée des Arts Décoratifs, Paris, June 1961.

   To speed things up, it may be good for you to be in direct relations with Monsieur Neufeld.

   My wife joins me in sending both of you our cordial regards.

Marc Chagall

P.S. Thanks for your letter and for the two palettes I have just received.

Marc Chagall in Vence to Charles Sorlier in Paris

"Les Collines"/Vence (A.M.)/31 October 1959

[French] Dear Charles,

Thank you for your letter which gave me great pleasure.

I have had a lot of work here in these last weeks. But, in spite of everything, I always think: "What to do to satisfy all those good publishers."

I have certainly received the proofs of Daphnis, Verve, and Mourlot's big lithograph. I would certainly like to talk about all that in person with you, and to retouch those proofs. Since I will soon be there, wait for me before undertaking the final printing.

I promise to be very nice and not too demanding . . .

I will call you as soon as I arrive.

I delight in seeing you again and talking with you.

See you soon. / Yours, / Marc Chagall

Ida Chagall in Bern to Louis Stern in New York

[Stationery: 23 Herrengasse, Berne]

22.11.59

[English] Dear Louis,

Did I ever answer your long and nice letter? I was really happy to know that your health is not worrying you and that it is no more question of an operation. If your secretary is back and it does take you less time, drop a line about you and your health. I read in the paper controverses about the Guggenheim Museum but I would love to have your point of view.

Is it really improper for painting? Is it really a beautiful piece of sculpture? I am really sorry for not being to see it meanwhile.

I am deep in the Chagall documentation that I keep receiving from Russia. It is amazing. Articles that he wrote while he was "Comissar." All kinds of information about unknown exhibitions and whereabouts and, as I jokingly said to my father this morning at the phone, if it will go on, we will learn that he is born in 1877! I am not sure he understood the joke.

As far as this documentation goes, I would love very much to receive a black and white photograph of your little "Over Vitebsk." You see, Louis, that I am very Chagallish to ask you a favour in a letter like that, but I cannot help it. I discovered in Russia, in Leningrad, a small little gouache of "Over Vitebsk" and I would like to compare yours with that one. But I am sure you will understand my motives. I am so deep in that documentation work that I cannot think of no plans of travelling. I would have loved to stay a little bit in New York, but I believe Brandeis University, as you know, will have the privilege of greeting the Chagalls . . . —nor can I think meanwhile of my dream to go back to Russia. Maybe it is better, so dreams remain.

controverses: The controversy about Frank Lloyd Wright's design for the Solomon R. Guggenheim Museum in New York.

1877: Instead of 1887.

Vava and Marc Chagall with Miriam Freund, President of American Hadassah under Chagall's windows in the Hadassah Hospital synagogue in Jerusalem. Photo by Boris Carmi. Courtesy Rubin House, Tel Aviv.

My troika is growing up. You should see them at dance lessons—rhythmic. How both girls show me how a little bird goes. I am just melting.

Franz is in good shape, working hard, and does not need me at all anymore—I mean for his work!

Lots of love/   Ida

John Nef in Chicago to T.S. Eliot in London

January 15, 1960

My dear Tom,

I have just received a letter from my friend Marc Chagall in which he expresses the hope that you may be prevailed upon to write a very brief preface for a set of lithographs, about a hundred, which he has done for the Bible. I quote in French the paragraph that is relevant:

> [French] I would like to ask for your cooperation: Tériade is doing a series of biblical Verve for which I have made about a hundred lithographs. I thought that the preface might be done by the poet Eliot. One poem, even a very short one, would be enough. Recalling that you are on very good terms with Eliot, I thought you might get in touch with him. It would make me very happy. If you tell me that he tends to accept, Tériade will be in contact with him.

I am writing to tell him that I should be overjoyed if you did this, but after all you will make your own decision independently of me. I am suggesting that he write to you directly.

You know of course that I have a long standing friendship with Chagall, which goes back to the period just after he lost his first wife and came for a lecture under the auspices of the Committee on Social Thought. More recently he came again, and he and his second wife, who is a very nice person indeed, spent rather more than two weeks with me.

This is a poor excuse for a letter. I was deeply touched to have the beautiful Christmas card from Valerie and you. You both fortified me by your presence. In a way you are still here. I am happy to say that so far as I know things go no worse with me than when I last talked with you.

With profound affection to you both.

Yours ever,/   [John Nef]

T.S. Eliot responded on January 27, 1960:

My dear John,

I have your letter of January 15th. It is, of course, flattering that Chagall should want me to do a preface for a book of lithographs, but I don't feel that I am really qualified for this task. I have many requests to write prefaces, but I have to be very careful to consent only where I am obviously the right person, and where I am not simply offering my name without being able to speak with authority. I do hope that he will understand and forgive me. It is a matter of both modesty and

Chagall speaks at the dedication of his stained glass windows in the Hadassah Hospital synagogue in Jerusalem. Photo by Boris Carmi. Courtesy Rubin House, Tel Aviv.

prudence, and I feel that there are others who could embellish his publication more effectively than I. [. . .]

Yours ever affectionately,

Tom

John Nef in Chicago to Marc Chagall in Vence

January 15, 1960

My dear Marc,

I am deeply touched by your wonderful letter of January 9. I have the impression that you have done well to devote yourself to your work. It would have been quite imprudent, especially because of your flu, to come to Brandeis University in the middle of winter for a visit that would have been quite fatiguing.

You will never be able to give me enough work of the sort that you propose in your letter. It is a pure pleasure if I can be useful to you. I hope that my intervention with my good friend Tom Eliot will not be without influence. He is a true friend. He and his wife came in November to spend several days in my apartment, as you and Vava did two years ago. They are two other lovers and, since for me, only love consoles us in life, it is an immense joy to offer them a lodging.

However, I am afraid that it will be rather difficult to persuade Eliot without your cooperation. Under separate cover, I am sending you a copy of the letter I am writing to him. In my opinion, you should now write him a letter explaining to him, from one artist to another, exactly what you want. I know that Eliot is very difficult about a collaboration. To justify it, I entrust you with a recent case which I ask you to keep confidential. Stravinski [sic] and his wife recently tried to convince him to collaborate with them on an opera. Despite Eliot's appreciation for Stravinski's work and despite his rather friendly relations with him and his wife, Eliot hasn't yet come round. He may yet find a poetic text that he wants to write himself and that may serve the plan of the great musician. In short and in all friendship, I advise you to be very flexible about the small collaboration you want to ask of Eliot. He can write something that he wants to write by himself. I may be wrong, but I have the impression that he is interested in a biblical poem. If that is true, and I am not at all sure, it will be wise to play your cards so that he makes you the offer himself, for example, you might ask him if he is currently composing a biblical poem he would allow you to use as a preface to your lithographs.

Would that be published in English? This is another rather important question, in my opinion. As you know better than I, it is very hard to translate poetry. I know that Eliot has a French translator he trusts, but I have the impression that he only translates prose.

Chagall (center) with his friend Joseph Boxenbaum (left) and Mayor of Jerusalem Teddy Kollek in a development town in
Israel, 1962.

I hope to see you and Vava soon, my dear Marc. I need you and your advice,
especially your friendship. It would help me if I knew your schedule during the
winter. I have a lecture in New York on February 8, almost two years after our
very happy meeting on the "Liberté." It will give me the necessary strength if I
know that you and Vava will be with me again on February 8.

With great affection and brotherly warmth.

Marc Chagall in Vence to John Nef in Chicago

Francis Bellamy, an editor at University Publishers in New York, suggested pub-

lishing a collection of Chagall's essays and lectures. Before the negotiations were over, he moved to another publisher and the project did not materialize. Chagall, of course, was aware of the major problem: His texts were dispersed, not easy to find, and most were in Yiddish.

His texts were dispersed: The essays were finally collected, translated, and published in *Marc Chagall on Art and Culture.*

Les Collines/Vence (A/M)

January 30, 1960

Dear John,

Thank you for your letter.

In principle, I agree to the publication of my lectures by Bellamy. If that gentleman really intends to do that, I must seek and translate the texts written in Jewish, Russian and French. For French, that will be easy, but not for the texts in the other two languages.

written in Jewish: Chagall writes: "en juif" ("Jewish," i.e., Yiddish), yet Nef, in his letter to Bellamy, suppressed the disparaged Yiddish and mistranslated it as "Hebrew."

However, Mr. Bellamy should get in touch with me about that, for it always takes a long time to realize such a project.

In any case, after the appearance of "My Life" [in English], it will be possible for him to publish that book.

Thanks again for all your attention to my business.

Warmly,

Marc Chagall

Marc Chagall in Vence to Charles Sorlier in Paris

"Les Collines"/Vence (A.M.)/30 April 1960

Dear Charles,

Thank you very much for your letter.

I have received the package of lithographs for the catalogues: four items in black and white, two items in color.

The circus dancer, whose colors are good, can be printed.

As for Paris-Notre-Dame, don't print it yet. It needs corrections that I will indicate in person.

When I come, we will also talk about the black and white lithographs and their fate . . .

I read with pleasure that the Verve Bible as well as Paris is going well. Very happy that Daphnis is finished.

I will come to Paris on May 15, and will stay only a few days. Will you get in touch with me on the 16th so that we can work together. And please prepare as many things as possible so that I will be happy when I come.

See you very soon.

Cordially,

Chagall

INS in Germany re: Marc Chagall

Immigration and Naturalization Service
American Consulate General

Frankfurt/Main, Germany   May 5 1960

IN RE: MARC CHAGALL

FOR CONSIDERATION OF: Temporary admission pursuant to Section 212 (d) (3) (A) of the Immigration and Nationality Act, despite inadmissibility under Section 212 (a) (28) of that Act.

The subject is a citizen of France, born in Vitebsk, Russia, on July 7, 1887. He has been found by the American Embassy at Paris to be ineligible to receive a visa because of his having affiliation with Communist front groups and Communist inspired peace movements in passed [sic] years. There is no evidence that the applicant ever joined the Communist Party and although he is an artist of world renown, the American Embassy in Paris has reported that he appears to like [sic; should be: lack] political astuteness and seems to fall prey to all requests for his signature in support of organizations and movements, especially when he is appealed to through his extremely orthodox religious feelings.

He desires to enter the United States for a period of approximately three weeks to be present at Brandeis University in Waltham, Massachusetts, to receive an honorary degree at the end of the Spring term. He intends to arrive in New York by an unknown air line about June 1, 1960.

The subject's temporary admission was previously authorized on January 13, 1958 and again on January 19, 1960; however, he did not enter the United States as a result of his last authorization. There is no indication that he violated the terms and conditions of his previous admission. Security checks made by the American Embassy have disclosed no additional derogatory information and that office recommends that temporary admission again be authorized.

his last authorization: Chagall postponed his trip to Brandeis University.

IT IS ORDERED that the application be granted, valid for a single entry into the United States at any time prior to July 31, 1960, subject to revocation at any time.

Joe F. Staley

Officer in Charge

OFFICIAL COPY FOR:
Federal Bureau of Investigations
Washington, D.C. May 13 1960

From SAC, New York, to Director, FBI, Washington, D.C.

FBI

Date 6/3/60
Via: AIRTEL
To: DIRECTOR, FBI
From: SAC, NEW YORK (100-87783)
Subject: MARC CHAGALL
SM - C

For the information of the Bureau and Boston, INS advised that captioned individual, born 7/7/87, in Vitebsk, Russia, presently a French citizen, arrived in NY on the SS LIBERTE on 5/2/60, and was admitted B-1 until 8/26/60, under waiver Section 212 (d) 3.

Subject was destined to Brandeis University, Waltham, Massachusetts.

Waiver of 212 (a) (28) was granted.

No further action contemplated by the NYO. Above is for the information of Boston and the Bureau.

Marc Chagall in Vence to Abraham Sutzkever in Tel Aviv

Vence. Oct. 9, 1960

Dear Sutzkever,

I received your letter and a few days ago I received *Siberia* [in English] (a sample, for the other books are not yet ready) and I was amazed. I know that you, from far away, are not guilty, but the publisher (Abelard-Schumann) has no taste. Such a book can do no good either to you or to me (Woe to the "money" he may give you_) first, the blue cover, which didn't come from me. And on the cover and on the second page of the inside cover, it says: *"with original lithographs by Chagall"* . . . this is *not true.* Those are *drawings* and so it was printed in the *Yiddish publication* in Israel (which was so beautifully printed).

The blue cover on both sides of the book, smeared with lines à-la Chagall around the cock with blue daubing is most tasteless, and naturally, I am responsible for the *entire* artistic aspect of the book. The publisher asked somebody (apparently he was afraid to ask me . . .) to daub in the *titles* and *numbers* of the poems in my name. And somebody printed it tastelessly while I am responsible for the public. Let alone that my name on the cover is ten times bigger than yours, which is not nice to you, for my name stands first. You know well that I am used to art being art, and the publisher thought about something else. The way the book looks will bring honor neither to me nor to you. It will actually cause damage to me and my publishers who publish books *with lithographs*—and they will be most hostile.

And I am not even talking about the fact that he printed my letter or speech about you as a "Preface"—it is false, it should have said: a letter.

In short, I wrote to him that he must *throw out* the blue cover and everything that was not made by me and simply print: *drawings*, that's enough.

I shall say it again, personally I would have loved to draw a cover and small titles, if he had asked me, but as it is it must not remain. *Those are not lithographs* (bad) and would confuse the true lovers of lithographs and the publishers. I am writing to you about it as a friend. I know how you feel everything and you know how lovingly I drew for you. Please *write* about it all and believe me, as a poet abroad you will only gain from a *modest and simple* look of the book (with the word: *drawings* and without any other tasteless daubing). As to the money, he will probably cheat you anyway.

This is how I illustrated: Paul Eluard, Ivan Goll, and others.

I am writing in a hurry, because I am about to go to Paris and Copenhagen and wish you all the best for the New Year. Please write to me.

With best regards/Marc Chagall

P.S.

Let the "publisher" not hurry and correct everything as I wrote. Let him not be afraid to lose "his money" and do as an artist tells him (my publishers, more venerable than he is, listen to me) and when it is as I wrote, perhaps I shall have strength to come to an event devoted to your book, as he, the *smearer*, asked me.

Ida Chagall in Bern to John Nef in Chicago

22/8/61

Dear Mr. Nef my friend,

The big book on Chagall [by Franz Meyer] that we planned for so long is under press and at the last second I see that I do lack few informations.

First I do hope that you will agree to have your gouache "The Bath" reproduced in it? In this case, which mention of the collectioner's name would you like to have in it? Your name or "Private coll[ection]"?

Also, to my great shame, I see that I do not have the measures of your gouache! Could you be so kind and mail them to me? In a few days I must be back to the printer with the last information and I feel dreadful about it! Thanks a lot again and with

cordial greetings,

Ida Meyer Chagall

Marc Chagall in Vence to John Nef in Chicago

The stained glass windows made for the Hadassah synagogue were exhibited in Paris and New York before they were shipped to Jerusalem. The exhibition, "Marc Chagall: Windows for Jerusalem," in the Pavillon de Marsan (a wing of the Louvre in Paris) took place June 16–September 30, 1961. Apparently it was prolonged for two more weeks. The windows were subsequently shown in the Museum of Modern Art in New York, and then installed in Jerusalem.

Les Collines / Vence (A.M.)

September 13, 1961

Dear friend,

I received your long letter of August 19 and thank you very sincerely. As always, you know, I would like to wish you lots of luck, calm, and I don't know what else . . .

I think the exhibition of stained glass windows that is closing here [in Paris] at the end of September will leave for the Museum of Modern Art in New York shortly after. But I am worried about the windows. I do not want that ensemble to be theatrical. If a special wing cannot be created, they should at least be exhibitioned as paintings, not very high.

The publisher of your books asked me for a few words about you. I am busy preparing that and will send it to him without delay. I am glad if that pleases you.

That's all for the moment!

Vava and I send our very warm regards.

Marc Chagall

Marc Chagall in Vence to Charles and Brigitte Marq in Reims

[Stationery: "Les Collines" Vence (A.M.)]

14 October 1961

[French] Dear Charles and Brigitte,

I know that the exhibition ends officially tomorrow and, officially, seriously, you will be there to prepare for the departure of the stained glass windows [to New York].

I am calm when I think that you are going to do all that with love, like all the artisans of your studio to insure the good preservation of the whole.

I don't yet know the exact date we will be in Paris.

We are leaving in two or three days, for a week, so that Madame Chagall, who is tired, can have a change of air.

Then, we will come to Paris, but perhaps you will have already left for America. Yet, I do hope that we will see you before that.

In spite of everything, I wish you in advance a good return, hoping that there, despite their extremely political concerns at the moment, the exhibition will be calm, distinguished, not too Hollywoody . . .

You will be my visible and invisible inspector and censor there. I am counting on you. Write me a little, will you?

Vava asks me to attach the contract you spoke to her about.

She also wishes you much good and we embrace you.

Marc Chagall

Marc Chagall in Vence to Bernard Reis in New York

"Les Collines" / Vence (A.M.)

November 11, 1961

[French] Dear Bernard,

Thank you for your letter, which I found on my return from my trip to Italy where we went to rest for a few days. Unfortunately, I got sick and couldn't come back until today.

I hasten to reply to you.

Please tell Dr. Gerstenfeld that I absolutely refuse to duplicate the stained glass windows of Jerusalem. That is not done and, anyway, I do not have the right to do it.

If he wants other original stained glass windows, let him send me the plans with the size of the windows, the distance between each of them, the subject; let him also indicate if there will be other stained glass windows or only the five made by me.

Then I will see if I can do it.

Thank you very much for your letter.

I hope that you are well and that Becky and the children are too.

Vava joins me in sending you our very cordial memory.

Marc

Vava Chagall in Vence to John Nef in Chicago

"Les Collines"/Vence (A.M.)

January 22, 1962

Dear John,

Thanks for your letter of January 7.

We left for a few days in Switzerland before leaving again for Jerusalem.

Marc is a little worried about the setting of the stained-glass windows there and the arrangements after the experience of the exhibition in New York.

After these few days of rest, he is going to throw himself wholeheartedly into work. No doubt we will have quite a battle in Jerusalem. But what do you want, people are becoming less and less serious in their work.

I liked the plan for your Center [for Human Understanding, in Washington, D.C.], we will have to discuss that. I hope very much that we will have the chance to see each other this summer and talk about this in person.

We are happy about the publication of your book and hope it will have the success it deserves.

Marc joins me in sending your warm regards,

Vava Chagall

Vava Chagall in Vence to John Nef in Chicago

Les Collines/Vence (A.M.)

March 2, 1962

Dear John,

Thanks for your letter of February 11. We have finally returned [from Israel] to Vence, very happy to be home after all those weeks of travelling.

The stained-glass windows are set. It is not too bad, but not altogether satisfying either. What to do with people who don't know anything about art!

Well, we hope that things are going to work out; they promised.

For the moment, we are thinking of staying in Vence and not budging, except, perhaps, a few days for Easter to avoid the crowd.

I am very happy that your book has appeared and I hope that it will be well presented. If possible, send me a copy of it, that will please me.

Write me from time to time.

Marc joins me in sending you warm regards,

Vava Chagall

Marc Chagall in Vence to Charles Marq in Reims

> Chagall and Marq worked on several projects simultaneously. Marq outlined the form of the windows on Arches paper (*papier d'Arches*, paper made of "pure rag," used for wash drawings, gouaches, etc.) on a scale of 1:10; then Chagall would make his painting in watercolors, thus creating a mock-up on the same scale. In his mock-ups for the Hadassah synagogue windows, he wrote some biblical phrases in Yiddish (from the Yiddish translation of the Bible he used), yet in the final window he used only Hebrew words. The Hadassah windows are 11 feet high and 8 feet wide, much larger than Chagall had done ever before. They are also very wide, to avoid the effect of a Christian, Gothic cathedral. In addition, the synagogue is built underground, close to the cleansing facilities for dead bodies, and from the outside the windows are on the street level, exposed to blows, hail, or stones. For that reason, special plates of protective glass were placed outside the stained glass windows; they are invisible from the inside.

[Stationery: "Les Collines" Vence (A.M.)]

5 April 1962

[French] Dear Charles Marq,

Thank you very much for your letter which I have just received.

I am glad that the work continues at your place even though you had to limit your kind staff, as you put it.

I am currently very involved in work, but I hope to come to Reims to work there, even though I don't know exactly when. At the moment, unfortunately, I cannot tell you precisely.

Thank you for wanting to make me the layout on Arches paper, in the same quality as that of the mockups of the first two windows of Metz, not too big nor too fine.

I am going to try to send you the package of paper on which you can cut out the Arches paper, in order to cut it afterward.

As for Mr. Renard, I have received one or two very loose letters from him in which he talks to me of the work and tells me, somewhat strangely, without talking to me about it, of his plan to do an exhibition of future works. You can imagine my opinion on that subject, I for whom an exhibition is a torment, a torment that has barely ended with the stained glass windows of Israel. It really is too much!

As for the safety glasses for the Jerusalem synagogue, I am still waiting and God knows if the stained glass windows will really be safe! There are people who tell me that they aren't safe. What do you think?

Farewell for the moment. All the best to Brigitte and your whole family.

Chagall

Marc Chagall in Vence to Charles Sorlier in Paris

"Les Collines"/Vence (A.M.)/11 May 1962

Dear Charles,

Thank you for your note.

I am happy that Sauret's book is done. Let us hope that everything will go well and properly with him.

I am glad that the work for Tériade is also going well.

Derrière le Miroir: A special Chagall issue of the journal of modern artists with original lithographs, published by Maeght.

Now, considering the exhibit that Maeght insists on having, I am going to prepare some lithographs for Derrière le Miroir. As I discussed with Fernand [Mourlot], I insist that this be done by you. I will also make a cover in black and white and a double page inside that will be colored later.

I am also going to try to do a poster, at least to sketch it here.

That takes time, alas. And since, naturally, Maeght wants the exhibit for the season, that means soon, I am going to sit down to prepare all that.

And you, my dear friend, you will have to make an effort to carry it out, with your usual care.

I am curious to see my room around you. Is there already an atmosphere in the studio with all the smells that accompany it and that I love so much.

Write me how the work is going.

Cordial greetings from me and Madame Chagall. Hello to everyone around you.

Marc Chagall

Marc Chagall in Vence to Kadish Luz in Jerusalem

Kadish Luz (Lozinsky; 1895–1972), Speaker of the Israeli Knesset, was born in Bobruysk, Byelorussia, the capital of a neighboring province, south of Vitebsk. He studied social sciences and agriculture in St.-Petersburg, Odessa, and Tartu (in Estonia). A soldier in World War I and an officer after the Revolution, he was a Labor Zionist leader in revolutionary Russia and came to Israel in 1921, where he joined a *kvutsa* (small kibbutz), "Degania B." Luz was Speaker of the Knesset from 1959 to 1969 (in Hebrew: "Chairman"; Chagall addressed him as "President," as in France).

When Chagall visited Jerusalem in 1962 for the opening of the stained glass windows in the Hadassah Hospital synagogue, Luz persuaded him to create tapestries and mosaics for the newly planned building of the Knesset, the Israeli parliament. An elaborate process of negotiations ensued, and a friendship developed with a long correspondence in Yiddish and Russian between those two lapsed ChABaDniks; Marc and Vava visited the Luz home in Kibbutz Degania B, and so did Ida. The first letters were formal and brief, typed or handwritten in French by Vava and signed by Chagall. Then Chagall took over and wrote his emotional, associative letters in Yiddish, heedless of mistakes.

"Les Collines" / Vence (A.M.)

22/7 1962
[in Chagall's handwriting]

[Yiddish] Dear President and friend

The memory of my stay in Jerusalem is so strong that I permit myself to call you thus. In your eyes, and in those of your collaborators, I read a friendship which touched me.

I received the model of the Knesset in wood, but I don't understand much about it, though there are some explanations in Russian.

Diener: Marcus Diener, a Swiss architect and major Chagall collector.

I have here a friend from Basel (Switzerland), Mr. Diener, an architect (also a collector of my paintings) who will write [to you] as a specialist about things not clear to me.

May all of you remain healthy and happy,

Your devoted
Marc Chagall

Marc Chagall in Vence to Charles Marq in Jerusalem

[Stationery: "Les Collines" Vence (A.M.)]

14 September 1962

[French] Dear Charles Marq,

Thank you for your letter which I found only today on returning from Switzerland.

You can imagine how sorry I am that you did not find me before your departure [for Israel].

I hope that you will be able to oversee the installation of those glasses which are to protect the stained glass windows.

I am happy that you are there to make sure.

I think that you will give them all the instructions they may need.

I am sorry that I could not give you a letter of introduction to the Members of the Knesset, but I am adding a card to my letter. Please give them my most cordial compliments.

In Switzerland, I saw Madame Gad who is taking care of the interior decoration of the synagogue. It's not bad.

With my best wishes, see you soon. / Cordially,

Marc Chagall

John Nef in Washington, D.C., to the Ford Foundation in New York [Excerpts]

November 20, 1962

Mr. Matthew Cullen
International Affairs Program / The Ford Foundation
477 Madison Ave. / New York 22, N.Y.

Dear Mr. Cullen,

Thank you for your kind letter of November 14, which my secretary forwarded to me in Washington. I am much pleased by Mr. Stone's suggestion for two Travel and Study Awards.

If you wish to reach an immediate decision in the matter, I shall be happy to conform to your and his wishes. But I ought to tell you that I am in communication about the bringing of foreigners to our meeting with my friend James H. Douglas, who is a trustee of the Fund for the Advancement of Education, as well as an associate of our Center for Human Understanding, and who was planning I think to talk over the whole matter with Mr. Faust. Indeed I had supplied Mr. Douglas two weeks ago with the draft of a letter which he might wish to use in this connection. [. . .]

P.S. The foreigners we perhaps need most for the meeting are Marc Chagall and his wife. Like the other two couples I have mentioned they are inseparable and have to be brought together. Their interests in this meeting of our Center (of which he is now a member) and in its future development are great. As the Chagalls travel by boat, we should have to provide $5,000 for their visit.

Marc Chagall is perhaps, after Picasso, the most widely admired painter alive. Knowing that the Ford Foundation is interested in the development of art in the United States, I am wondering if there may not be some branch of the Foundation that would be able to put up this money, in addition to that Mr. Stone is so generously offering. The Chagalls came five years ago to the Committee on Social Thought, when a private citizen put up the necessary $5,000. Their visit then did much for the appreciation of art and gave much encouragement to young persons sensitive to beauty. If they came to us again (as he would like to his health permitting) this would do at least as much again, because his reputation has been enhanced by his stained glass windows. His coming to the May meeting will serve one of the principal aims of the Center which is to demonstrate the importance of relating beauty to all sides of life and thought.

Maybe you and Mr. Faust can find a way of handing this request over to the appropriate department.

Yours sincerely, / John Nef

Marc Chagall in Vence to Shmuel Izban in New York

[Stationery: "Les Collines"/Vence (A.M.)]

1963, March

[Yiddish] Dear Shmuel Izban, thank you for your books you sent me: "Queen Jezebel." In the meantime, I have read the text. It is great. One needs a lot of strength to connect to our Jewish history. But how much Jewish pleasure it provides! Especially if one is just steeped in being Jewish and writes for ourselves. It is only a disaster that they torment us in the world. And people don't want to take our Jewish life as an example, and let us live.

I wish you all the best. Regards to all around you.

Marc Chagall

P.S. Perhaps I shall come soon to America for a while on an invitation. I hope so.

Immigration and Naturalization Service in re: Marc Chagall

United States Department of Justice
Immigration and Naturalization Service

12th and Pennsylvania Avenue, N.W./Washington 25, D.C.

April 18, 1963

In re: Marc CHAGALL aka Moise Chagall

Application: Temporary admission to the United States pursuant to Section 212 (d) (3) of the Immigration and Nationality Act, despite inadmissibility under Section 212 (a) (28) of the Act.

The applicant was born in Vitebsk, U.S.S.R., on July 7, 1887, and is a citizen and resident of France. The Department of State has found that he is ineligible to receive a visa because of his close association with Communist-front groups and Communist-inspired peace movements. He is a prominent painter who seeks to enter the United States for 1 month to visit the University of Chicago at the invitation of the Committee on Social Thought for the purpose of making lectures. While in this country, his activities will include participation in a meeting to be held at the Meridian House, 1630 Crescent Place, N.W., Washington, D.C., from May 2–4, 1963.

Previous orders authorizing admission of the applicant have been entered by the Service on two occasions. There is no evidence to indicate that he violated the conditions of those admissions. Partial security checks made by the Department of State have disclosed no additional derogatory information. Notwithstanding that security checks are incomplete, that Department and the consular officer at Paris recommend that admission be authorized because of the alien's age, his status as a world-renowned painter, the purpose of his proposed entry, and the wide interest evidenced in his trip. The Department believes that refusal of a visa would result in a strong negative public relations reaction, and finds that there is no evidence to indicate that the applicant's entry would be prejudicial to the public interest. The Department further recommends that the applicant be admitted to the United States on multiple occasions for a period of 2 years.

IT IS ORDERED that the application be granted, subject to revocation at any time, valid for the entry of the applicant into the United States on multiple occasions for a period of 2 years from the date of this order.

LEWIS D. BARTON

DISTRICT DIRECTOR

Marc Chagall in Vence to Bernard and Becky Reis in New York

"Les Collines"/Vence (A.M.)

October 12, 1963

[French] Dear Friends,

I received your letter of October 9.

In fact, Mr. Robbins asked me to collaborate on a show about Sholem Aleichem. I was very sorry not to be able to do sets and costumes for it, as he wanted, because I was busy. I informed him on time by telegram.

I am amazed that Mr. Robbins, who is a great artist, can consider using my drawings against my will.

> Jerome Robbins (1918–?) was a choreographer and director of musicals on Broadway. This refers to Robbins's production of *Fiddler on the Roof*, which opened in the autumn of 1964. The fiddler on a roof was a Chagallian key image, appropriated by Robbins for a musical based on a work by Sholem-Aleichem.

In fact, I would certainly have wanted to work with him, for I respect him and I appreciate what he is doing; but it isn't possible since I can't commit myself. And I do not consent at all to his use of my drawings without my cooperation. It isn't a financial question, but only an artistic question, for I cannot be responsible for something I didn't take part in personally.

I sincerely hope that he will not carry out his plan for I absolutely cannot permit anyone to use my work and my name without my permission.

Vava and I send all of your family our affectionate memory.

Marc Chagall

Marc Chagall in Vence to Charles Marq in Reims

[Stationery: "Les Collines" Vence (A.M.)]

16 October 1963

[French] Dear Charles,

I don't know what has become of you! I don't hear from you anymore. One would say that you have vanished into thin air. Which would be unfortunate because there is still work to do.

there is still work to do: According to Charles Marq, he did not communicate with Chagall for the whole of two weeks.

Could it be that that damned Lassaigne brought you to Canada for another conference.

Take an example from me; look, despite all temptations, I haven't gone to Japan because I have to work.

Lassaigne: Charles Lassaigne, art critic and editor of Skira, was Chagall's friend and wrote a book about him.

Write me or phone me. Tell me if you are working.

The UN representative came here; I showed him the sketch. He liked it. So there will be work on a stained glass window for that.

I hope to be in Paris in early November.

the sketch: For the "Peace" window at U.N. headquarters in New York, unveiled on September 17, 1964.

But before that, it would be nice if you would send me a line. How is Brigitte and the whole family?

Greetings from both of us,/   Marc Chagall

Vava Chagall in Vence to Charles Sorlier in Paris

"La Colline"/St. Paul de Vence/12 August 1964

Dear Charles,

Thank you for your card, and thank you also for your letter which we received and which moved us very much.

We haven't written to you because, ever since we came to Vence, we have been taken up with the Chagall hall at Maeght's, then by the opening of the Foundation, and by a lot of people at our home and around us, as you can imagine.

Then Bierge came with Paul. They brought the little ceiling which Mr. Chagall has meanwhile finished. Paul left for Paris, but Bierge is still in Saint-Paul.

Meanwhile, we learned from the newspapers and from Mr. Anthonioz that they have begun to put up the ceiling. This work will be finished on August 23. We plan to be in Paris on the 26th of next month because the scaffolding remains until September 1, which will allow Mr. Chagall to do retouching if he wants to.

The small ceiling will be lined on September 1; but there is another scaffolding for that, which will also allow Mr. Chagall to rework, if he thinks it useful, but that will be on the 3rd or 4th of September.

That is our plan. There is no question of rest!

I hope that you are resting and that you and all of yours are taking advantage of your vacation.

Friendly greetings to all three of you, / Vava Chagall

the little ceiling: A mock-up for the Opera ceiling in Paris.

The Louis E. Stern Collection

Upon Louis Stern's death in 1962, his collection was bequeathed to the Philadelphia Museum of Art, his art library to Rutgers University, and additional items to the Brooklyn Museum and the Museum of Modern Art; the correspondence went to the Archives of American Art, Washington, D.C. In 1964, the Philadelphia Museum of Art organized an exhibition of the Louis E. Stern Collection and published a catalogue. We reproduce here the first page of the price list of Stern's collection used to probate his estate.

Collection of Louis E. Stern   Paintings

Artist	Painting	Medium	Value
Bonnard	After the Shower	Oil	$20,000.00
Bonnard	Hommage A Maillol	Oil	15,000.00
Bonnard	Vollard with Cat	Etching	100.00
Boudin	Seascape	Oil	1,500.00
Braque	Nude	Drawing	1,500.00
Braque	Still Life	Oil	10,000.00
Brooke	Nude	Oil	1,500.00
Bruce	Italian Landscape	Oil	400.00
Cassat	The Letter	Colored Aquatint	600.00
Cezanne	House on the Hill	Water Color	7,500.00
Cezanne	Olympia	Water Color	3,500.00

Cezanne	Portrait of Mme. Cezanne	Oil	50,000.00
Cezanne	Self-Portrait	Lithograph	250.00
Chagall	By the Window	Gouache	1,500.00
Chagall	Le Dur Désir de Durer	Drawing	300.00
Chagall	In the Night	Oil	7,500.00
Chagall	Over Vitebsk	Gouache	1,500.00
Chagall	Purim Feast	Oil	5,000.00
Chagall	The Resurrection of Lazarus	Gouache	500.00
Chagall	Self-Portrait	Oil	1,500.00
Chagall	La Tortourelle	Gouache	2,500.00
Chagall	Study in Red	Water Color	250.00
Chagall	The Trough	Oil	7,500.00
Chagall	Oh God	Oil	3,500.00
Chagall	War Across the Table	Oil	3,500.00
Chagall	Crucifixion Scene	Drawing	500.00

Marc Chagall in Vence to Kadish Luz in Jerusalem

Vence 1964 [September]

[Yiddish] Dear President and friend

Thank you for your friendly letter. I hope that now you are in good health. I want to write you that I finished the *third* model for the triptych of tapestries I want to create for the Knesset. The first model is with the government at the Gobelins—where a sample was made. And now I bring to Paris the third (and last) model, so that the Minister of Culture and Gobelins will start to weave, all three at the same time (a work like this may take some years . . .). Let the Jewish Ambassador Eytan get in touch with me.

Gobelins: The French government factory of tapestries.

I am going to Paris where the government officially installs my ceiling in the Opera on September 23. But first I have to go to New York, where my great stained-glass window, "Memorial," was sent to the UN—a memorial for Secretary Hammarskjöld and others who fell for peace.

Hammarskjöld: Dag Hammarskjöld (1906–1961), Swedish statesman and United Nations Secretary-General (1953–1961). He died in a plane crash in Africa while on a mission to the Republic of the Congo.

This will be on September 17. So you have to pray for me to the Jewish God—

With warm regards to you and your wife

Devoted   Marc Chagall

Varian Fry's Aggravation: 1964–1969

Varian Fry, head of the Emergency Rescue Committee in Marseille during 1940–1941, had rescued Chagall from Nazi Europe. He now worked for the International Rescue Committee in New York. Its Executive Director in New York was Charles (Carel) Sternberg (1911–2003), who had worked on Fry's team in Marseille, and its public chairperson was Mrs. Kermit Roosevelt (daughter-in-law of President Theodore Roosevelt).

The Committee planned to publish a portfolio of lithographs by famous artists to commemorate its wartime activity and support its current work. The artists who initially agreed to participate included Picasso, Max Ernst, Alberto Giacometti, Jacques Lipchitz, André Masson, and Joan Miró. As a theme for the portfolio, the sculptor Jacques Lipchitz suggested the T.S. Eliot reference to Aeneas as "the original Displaced Person."

Fry tried to get Chagall to contribute a lithograph. He went to France, pulled all strings possible, including Chagall's daughter Ida, her ex-husband Michel Gordey, and the Jewish Theological Seminary (JTS) in New York (which agreed to offer Chagall an honorary doctorate). One of Fry's connections was André Malraux, who was in Vichy France after the surrender. Fry had put Malraux in touch with General de Gaulle in London in 1940. As French Minister of Culture, Malraux invited Chagall to paint the ceiling of the Paris Opera (unveiled on September 23, 1964). He also endowed a national museum for Chagall in Nice.

Fry could not believe Chagall's reluctance to participate in the portfolio for the International Rescue Committee and became obsessed with it for three years. He wrote several dozen letters (only a few are selected here), yet Chagall remained evasive. After Fry's death, Chagall finally delivered an unsigned lithograph, produced by Mourlot.

Varian Fry was almost crippled by bursitis and died in his home in Connecticut in September 1967, at the age of 59. The portfolio appeared in 1970, on the 30th anniversary of the rescue operation, with contributions by Chagall, Lipchitz, Lam, Masson, Miró, Motherwell, Calder, and other artists.

Diary-Report of Varian Fry in Paris to the International Rescue Committee in New York

[English] *Chagall*, Marc

20.10.64   Saw Chagall. He refused to commit himself. He said that big books don't sell as well as they used to, because the publishers have published too many of them; what the Committee does is all very well, but it is only "une goutte dans la mer"; he would have to consult his dealer and his publisher to see if he is free to make a gift, etc.

6.1.65   According to Jacques Lipchitz, we *must* have Chagall. "I will get him. You get Malraux to write the preface and make sure he mentions in it Chagall as one of the many artists the Committee saved. I will send a copy to Ida (Chagall's daughter) with a letter of my own saying 'Quelle honte si votre père sera le seul parmi ceux nommés par Malraux qui n'aura rien contribué!'" [What a shame if your father were the only one of those named by Malraux who won't have contributed anything!"]

23.1.65   I had an appointment with Giacometti at 6 o'clock and had just begun to explain my mission when a young woman came into his studio. I thought at once that she looked remarkably like Ida Chagall but Giacometti didn't introduce me and she didn't apparently recognise me. Giacometti apologised for having made two appointments at the same hour for two different people and asked me if I could return at the same hour the next day. I said, of course, and left.

24.1.65   I saw Giacometti again at 6 o'clock today. He said it was Ida Chagall who had come in the day before and that after I had left she told him not only what I had done for her mother, her father and herself, but also for other artists. In fact Giacometti's whole attitude had been changed by what Ida had told him. When I said I would like very much to see Ida, and asked whether she was staying in Paris, he said that unfortunately she had already left for her home in Bâle [Basel, Switzerland].

26.1.65   I wrote Ida at Bâle telling her how sorry I had been that we had not had a chance to talk and asked if I might hope to see her soon.

3.2.65   Ida Chagall called me and invited me to her apartment, 35 quai de l'Horloge, for drinks at 6.30. There I told her about the plans for the anniversary album. She asked if her father had agreed to contribute a lithograph, and when I told her he had not done so, she said she was ashamed of him. She spoke very frankly and openly about her step-mother, who she said was a mean and grasping woman who completely dominates her father. Nevertheless, she said, she would do all she could to help me get a lithograph for the album from Chagall. She also offered me the house at Gordes which now belongs to her for the whole summer, rent free, explaining that she would not be using it, and that she would be very happy indeed to have me and my family enjoy it. Two or three days later I received from Bâle an envelope containing a postcard view of Gordes with the little old house circled in red, and the following message on the back: "This house will be happy to have its larder open for you. Fond greetings. Ida Meyer-Chagall."

9.2.65   At Bert Jolis's suggestion I saw Dr Camille Dreyfus, 2 Avenue Hoche, and asked him if he could help. He explained that when Bella, Chagall's first wife and Ida's mother, was alive the Chagalls and the Dreyfuses were very close friends, but that since Chagall's second marriage he seldom sees them except professionnally. Nevertheless he promised to do what he could to persuade Chagall that he must not fail to contribute a lithograph to the album. He said he would probably have to work with Ida on the problem in order to get a chance to speak to Chagall when Madame Chagall was not present. He said that Madame Chagall doesn't care to have her husband do anything which does not bring him money. "Anent Chagall: perhaps Ida Chagall, who seems to have fond recollections of meeting you in

Dreyfus: Chagall's doctor since the 1930s.

1940, will open the door Malraux cannot open for us." Charles Sternberg, memo of 29.1.65.

23.2.65   Had a drink with Michel Gordey (Ida Chagall's first husband) at the Café de la Paix. He said the only way to get a lithograph from Chagall is to work through his present wife, and though they have millions of dollars—not francs, but dollars—she is so greedy she won't even let him give his grandchildren drawings any more. Instead, she buys them cheap toys. She had also stopped Chagall from supporting his illegitimate son; So Ida now has to take care of the boy, with no help whatever from the boy's father. In short, Michel left me with the impression that getting Chagall to do a litho will require a kind of "chantage"—a threat to embarrass him if he refuses.

Varian Fry's Notes on Visiting Chagall in Vence

[Two tiny pieces of paper with handwritten notes, apparently jotted down on the spot, October 20, 1964]

Chagall

The sweat on his face, and the other signs of his anxiety, when I saw him at Vence: he was embarrassed not to be able to promise a litho and afraid his second wife would make a scene.

He took out his pencil to sign the Hungarian lithos, but his wife forbade him to: "Non, Marc, tu ne peux pas. Elle sont déjà dans le catalogue." "Ah, oui, oh oui."

Varian Fry in Paris to Jacques Lipchitz in New York

[Stationery: International Rescue Committee, 35 Boulevard des Capucines, Paris 2e]

Copies to Charles Sternberg [New York] and Yvan Super [at the Paris office]

re: Ida Chagall/   4 February, 1965

[English] I think I told you that I missed seeing (or, rather, talking to) Ida Chagall the first time I called on Giacometti. So I wrote her, at Bâle, telling her how sorry I was not to have ignored my perhaps too strict upbringing and have asked her if she were not Chagall's daughter.

Anyway, she telephoned me yesterday and invited me to visit her at her apartment, 35, Quai de l'Horloge. This, of course, I did. She was extremely warm and cordial, and when I told her what I am in Europe for, she asked if her father had promised a lithograph for the album. When I told her what had happened during my one visit to the Chagalls in Vence, she was horrified. She told me that she does not like her stepmother at all, that her stepmother is a grasping woman, and that she had even, at one point, persuaded her father to divorce and then remarry her with a new and (to her) more favorable marriage contract.

She said that she agreed entirely with me about the house her father and step-mother are living in at Vence: that it has all the appearance of a very wealthy épicier en gros [wholesale grocer] whose wife has employed a decorator, given him a large sum of money with which to decorate the house, and said she wants to have some Chagall originals on the walls. She added that the house her step-mother is now building somewhere between Vence and St. Paul will be even worse.

She promised to do everything she possibly could to get her father to do a lithography [sic] for the book, and just now she has telephoned me to offer me her house at Gordes for the entire summer (for my whole family) and to say that she has decided to get Malraux to work on her father for the lithograph and will do so.

She also told me just now that what her father had told me about his contract with Maeght possibly preventing him from donating a litho was a lie: he has no contract with Maeght. He does have a contract with Tallandier, publisher of art books, but she is going to make sure that Tallandier gives him pleins pouvoirs [plenty of authority] to create and donate a litho.

In short, we have in Ida our best possible ally, and I shall keep in close touch with her until her father's litho has been printed and signed.

Ida even said, last night, and again this morning on the telephone, that if it had not been for me, her father almost certainly would have died in an extermination camp more than 20 years ago. She added that it would be a disgrace *to him* if the collection should appear without any contribution from him.

Marc Chagall in St. Moritz to Charles Marq in Reims

[Stationery: Hotel Villa Suvrette, St. Moritz]

February 6, 1965

[French] Dear Charles,

We were very happy to have your little card. We have been here for two weeks where we thought of resting and where I thought of working on Mozart's Magic Flute. But alas, Vava broke her leg skiing and unfortunately has to stay in bed without moving for at least three weeks.

How are you? I hope that the whole family is well. As you know, we wanted to return home on about February 15. But once more alas, we are forced to stay here

Magic Flute: Chagall designed the stage sets and costumes for the Metropolitan Opera in New York.

until the end of the month. I am writing that to you to tell Paul so he won't come early. I would write as soon as the doctor will allow us to leave.

How is the work going? I am sure it will be good, I trust you. What a dream for me to come to your studio in Reims.

Meanwhile, best wishes,

Marc Chagall

Varian Fry in France to Charles Sternberg in New York

19 February, 1965

[English] Last night, I met, at a late supper party in the flat of an American photographer here (Gene Fenn), the wife of a correspondent of FRANCE PRESS who is now in Saigon.

His wife told me that Ida Chagall's first husband (who has now changed his name from Rappaport-Chagall to Gordey, and is a reporter on the staff of FRANCE SOIR) has more influence on Chagall than does Chagall's own daughter. I am therefore going to telephone Gordey and ask for his help in getting Chagall not merely to promise but actually to do a lithograph for us.

Vierny: Dina Vierny was born a Jew in Odessa and changed her last name (Vierny means "faithful" in Russian). As a young woman, she was the model of the sculptor Maillol in his old age and active in the resistance during World War II. She owns and directs the Maillol Museum in Paris.

This morning, on the way to the office, I met Dina Vierny in front of St. Germain des Prés. She said she had met Ida Chagall (who seems to travel a great deal) "chez le Général de Gaulle" [at General de Gaulle's] and that Ida had told her she would consider it "une honte" [a shame] if Chagall failed to contribute a lithograph to the album. They agreed to work together to persuade Chagall that he must do so.

Yesterday, I dictated a letter (in Bert Jolis's office) to André Malraux. I explained that I would soon have to leave France myself and that therefore I might not be here when Chagall comes to Paris to receive the highest order of the Légion d'Honneur (a ceremony to which, you remember, Malraux promises to "convoke" me). So I asked him to talk to Chagall about the album himself if he has an occasion to do so.

I shall almost certainly have to return to Nice, because I left a lot of things there, including all the Hungarian lithographs, when I flew home for Christmas, and Yvan Super seems to have forgotten his promise to send them to me. But I very much doubt that Mme. Chagall will permit me to see her husband again myself, because she now knows what it is I want from him, and Ida has told me that her step-mother is opposed to his doing anything which does not bring in lots of money. She even tried to prevent him from agreeing to do the ceiling for the Opera, according to Ida.

If I do have to return to Nice, you may be sure that I shall *try* to see Chagall again. But I think Ida, her first husband and Malraux will almost certainly be able to convince him that, in view of the fact that I got him out of jail in Marseille by threatening the Prefect with world-wide publicity as "le plus grand con du monde" if he did not release him immediately, and that we then shipped the whole family safely in the U.S., he *must* contribute a litho. As Ida said, if it had not been for us, her father would almost certainly have disappeared into one of the gas chambers at Auschwitz more than 20 years ago.

Copy to Jacques Lipchitz

Varian Fry in Paris to André Malraux in Paris

22 February 1965

Monsieur André Malraux
Minister of Culture / 3, rue de Valois / Paris 1er

[French] Dear André Malraux,

Since I had the pleasure of seeing you again a few weeks ago, I have also had the pleasure of seeing Ida, Chagall's daughter, again. She asked me if her father had agreed to contribute a litho for the album I am preparing for the International Rescue Committee, and I was forced to explain to her that, on the contrary, he had given me several reasons why he couldn't tell me immediately whether he would do it or not. Ida answered that it would be shameful for the album to appear without a contribution from her father, especially considering what the Committee did for him and his family, and she promised me to persuade her father to agree. However, she did convey to me that she had seen her father less since his marriage.

Consequently, I would be very grateful to you if you would talk to him about our plan the next time you should meet him. You very kindly offered to invite me to be present when Chagall receives his medal of the Legion of Honor; but unfortunately I shall most likely be forced to return to the United States before Chagall comes to Paris for that ceremony. In any case, one word from you will be worth a hundred of mine!

Cordially,   [Varian Fry]

Varian Fry in Paris to Charles Sternberg in New York

24 February, 1965

[English] I had drinks at the Café de la Paix with Michel Gordey (formerly Michel Rappaport-Chagall, the first husband of Ida Chagall, Marc Chagall's only daughter and now a foreign-affairs expert on the staff of *France Soir*) last night.

Michel said that the only way to get a lithograph from Chagall is to persuade his present wife to let him do one for us.

He spoke at least as frankly about Chagall's present wife as had Ida. He said she was an incredibly greedy woman, and he cited facts to prove it.

For instance: he said that, after his first wife's death, Chagall had a long affair with a young English girl named Virginia. Virginia bore him an 'illegitimate' son. Until he remarried, Chagall supported his son. But his second wife persuaded or forced him to stop doing so, and it is now Ida who takes care of the boy—with no help from her—and the boy's father—at all.

Until his remarriage, Chagall used to send his grandchildren small watercolor drawings he did specially for them. Since his remarriage, Chagall's new wife has persuaded or forced him to stop doing this: Chagall originals are too valuable to waste on grandchildren. In their place, Chagall now sends small toys selected by his new wife, apparently with a view to economy.

"They have millions and millions of dollars—not francs, dollars," Michel said, "and yet she is never satisfied: she wants still more millions. There are such people in the world. What can you do? Nothing. Chagall is completely dominated by her."

I have written André Malraux to ask him to put pressure on Chagall if he can. In the letter in which he explained that he could not write the preface, Malraux added: "Mais si je puis vous être utile ailleurs, vous savez qui j'en serais heureux" ["But if I could be useful to you in some other way, you know that I would be glad to do so."] This is one place where he can perhaps be "utile ailleurs" ["useful in some other way"].

I have also written to Ida (as I believe I have already reported), thanking her for the offer of her house at Gordes for the summer, telling her that I shall almost certainly not be able to accept the offer, and repeating my request that she do everything she can to get her father to contribute a litho.

Copy to Jacques Lipchitz

Mrs. Kermit Roosevelt in New York to Marc Chagall in Vence

[Stationery: International Rescue Committee, 460 Park Avenue South, New York 16, N.Y.]

15 June 1965

[French] Dear Monsieur Chagall,

Twenty-five years ago, the Emergency Rescue Committee sent a young man to Marseille whose mission was to help artists, writers, and politicians to escape from the South of France and the clutches of the Gestapo. We are proud to be able to say that, in those dark days, we were able to help several representatives of the high artistic and humanitarian traditions of Europe, including Marc Chagall. In this respect, therefore, our work can be considered as being part of the Resistance. This is why we feel a very deep satisfaction on learning that you were about to be named Commander of the Legion of Honor by André Malraux.

Last autumn, Varian Fry went to France again on behalf of the Rescue Committee to get contributions to an album of lithographs that we are planning to publish to commemorate the twenty-fifth anniversary of the beginning of our work.

To avoid duplication, I list in alphabetical order the names of the artists who have promised to collaborate in this album: Max Ernst, Alberto Giacometti, Oskar Kokoschka, Jacques Lipchitz, Andre Masson, Joan Miro, Henry Moore, Pablo Picasso and Graham Sutherland. M. Lipchitz has finished his lithograph and I am sending you a reproduction of it in black and white (I hasten to add that it is only a pale reflection of his very beautiful work); Miro's lithograph will soon be finished.

But the present list could not be considered complete, either artistically or historically, if the name of Marc Chagall did not appear on it. This is why I take the liberty, on behalf of the Rescue Committee, to join with Mr. Fry in soliciting your consent and expressing the hope that you will grant it to us.

Please accept my highest respect, dear Monsieur Chagall.

Mrs. Kermit Roosevelt

Varian Fry in Connecticut to Charles Sternberg in New York

Ridgefield, Conn., Aug. 5, 1965

[English] SUBJECT: Chagall

[In response to Sternberg's note suggesting that Chagall "wants out."]

Chagall doesn't exactly 'want out.' He's never been in. Unfortunately, he's one artist who may not be impressed even by Picasso—if we get P. to do a litho for us before he dies of old age. You remember: Madame asked what artists had already agreed to contribute lithos. I mentioned P. 'Pas un artiste,' said this ex-millinery saleslady, with a contemptuous downsweep of her right hand.

Ordinarily, one would not have any control over what the TIMES cuts. But I thought you said the wife of someone on your staff works for the MAGAZINE?

I too doubt that they will cut the Chagall paragraph *unless* they do so because to them it seems merely to repeat what has so recently been reported in TIME.

Our present hope, then lies in the NEW YORK TIMES MAGAZINE, so far as Chagall is concerned; if he is really 'more attentive to his public relations in the States than in France,' that should impress him.

Marc Chagall in Vence to Kadish Luz in Jerusalem

Vence 1965

[Yiddish] Dear friend and President,

I hope you are well. The mosaist Dodo Shenhav visited me and I gave him my big sketch for the mosaic—the floor of the Knesset. I assume you will see him. We discussed it at length and I explained to him how to execute it. It must be as light as clouds in the sky, not to interfere with the future tapestries. What came out in my work is like 12 clouds or our hosts[1] for the 12 tribes—I think perhaps he should try to make one small cloud as a sample and then we must see it.

I think that when the work starts, one should perhaps ask other countries: perhaps one could get pieces of marble stones from them, of yellow, red, blue, and green. (Through our ambassadors to those countries.) I sent your artisan to Paris to see my other mosaist, who has done a lot of good work for me. I hope we shall be able to come to the Land later.

With warm regards. Be healthy,

Marc Chagall

Marc Chagall in Paris to Varian Fry in Connecticut

20/October 1965 Paris

[French] I received your letter and its content, which was sent to me by Monsieur Maeght, and I thank you as well as the Jewish Theological Seminary for their very great and friendly attention to me. It is with much pleasure that I would like to accept the honor that is offered me, but right now, I do not see the possibility of coming to America to attend the ceremony on November 14.

I hope that I will soon have to make the trip to the United States for my work for the Metropolitan Opera, and perhaps at that time it will be possible to grant both things . . . In any case, the Metropolitan Opera will be informed of my possible arrival.

Of course I have not forgotten the lithographs for the album you are planning, and I will speak of that with Monsieur Mourlot.

With very cordial memories, I remain your

Marc Chagall

attention to me: The JTS offered to award Chagall an honorary degree in the presence of the President of the United States.

Varian Fry in Connecticut to Charles Sternberg in New York

96 Main Street, Ridgefield, Connecticut, Oct. 26, 1965

[English] SUBJECT: Chagall and the Art Project

Prepare yourself for a pleasant surprise. Then read the enclosed copy of a letter I have just received from Marc Chagall.

I looks as though I had managed to trap the old rogue into a commitment after all!

I leave it to you to spread the news to the proper persons. If you want to borrow the original of the letter, in order to make more (and cleaner!) photocopies of it, just let me know and I'll send it on to you.

I'll let you know the minute I know exactly when Chagall will be in New York, so we can have the delegation call on him. It seems to me to be a good idea to have the delegation call on him and thank him for his extraordinarily generous offer. I don't see how we can have Mrs Roosevelt write him a letter just now, do you? But she could perhaps be among those who call on him to thank him when he is here.

Varian Fry in Connecticut to Ida Chagall in Paris

96 Main Street   Oct. 26, 1965

[English] Dear Ida

See what the postman brought me today!

It looks as though my complicated strategy had worked!

Affectionately,   [Varian Fry]

had worked!: The joy was premature: Chagall dragged on for another two years or more.

P.S. The Jewish Theological Seminary will be delighted to arrange a special convocation in honor of your father whenever he can be in New York to attend it. I shall so write him. The only problem is that the JTS must know at least two months in advance of the date exactly when it can count on his presence. One does not, for instance, invite the President of the United States at the last moment!

V.F.

Marc Chagall in Paris to Kadish Luz in Jerusalem

1966 2/2 Paris

[Yiddish] My beloved, dear friend and President Luz,

A long time has passed since I was in your (our) country, how happy I was, and began to work for the Knesset. I hope you and your dear wife are in good health.

Melana: Chagall's mosaic specialist.

Now, the following: Melana will prepare the material here—more beautiful stones which we need for the floor. And I beg you, when he sends his letter, please see that they help get the necessary material in Israel—I made a new *model* for the remaining small wall (in the big hall)—a mosaic representing—I asked you for advice—the Wailing Wall and a large Menorah, which burns for our past "Diaspora." And it will all be made of marble stones of King Solomon in the

stones of King Solomon: The "King Solomon mines" near Elath, at the Red Sea.

Land. I hope it will be beautiful and in garmony [sic] with the other things in this hall. And now I would like to ask you to watch carefully the 12 drawings, and I would like to get a letter from you that it will be well preserved in the Knesset, because unfortunately such things get stolen to sell in galleries, who knows what.

I sent Mr. Friedman a letter with Melana, and I hope he will show it to you. You must do as much as possible to make the work easier, as he writes.

With our warm regards—for both of you/Your devoted

Marc Chagall

Kadish Luz in Jerusalem to Marc Chagall in Vence

[typewritten] Jerusalem, March 2, 1966

[Yiddish] Dear friend Marc Chagall,

I received your letter of February 2 and I thank you for the great interest you show for the building of the Knesset. All your drawings, the models and the stones you selected as samples of colors as well as the films are all preserved in an iron safe in a room of the Knesset guards, who are on duty day and night.

I showed your letter to Mr. Friedman [Director of the construction of the Knesset], who told me that he wrote to you about everything concerning the building.

I wish you and your wife health and happiness, and hope to see you soon.

With devotion,

Kadish Luz

Marc Chagall in Vence to Charles Marq in Reims

[Stationery: "Les Collines" Vence (A.M.)]

April 4, 1966

[French] Dear Charles,

Thanks for your letter.

Don't worry, don't be sad. We don't have time, because we are right in the middle of moving.

In addition, we have to get ready to go to America for the mural.

I am glad that you are preparing all you can.

I have in hand the mockups of the stained glass windows of Michael to redo them for the 8th.

I hope that after my trip I will be free to come to you and we will be together.

You write to me about the stained glass windows of Metz. As always, the administration is asleep, except for the taxes! Tell them that if they go on like that I will offer them to another place.

The weather is very lovely now but I am unhappy because Vava is busy with all sorts of work for the move.

I know that Brigitte is looking at all the flowers; tell her that she is admiring them for me who no longer has the time.

Regards to all of you

Chagall

moving: The Chagalls gave up their house "Les Collines" in Vence and moved to a house "La Colline" in St.-Paul de Vence near the Maeght Foundation.

mural: Two large murals, "The Sources of Music" and "The Trial of Music," for the Metropolitan Opera House in New York, were made for its opening on February 19, 1967, with Mozart's *Magic Flute*, also decorated by Chagall.

for the 8th: A reference to the eighth window Chagall made for the Church at Pocantico Hills, New York, funded by the Rockefellers. This window, "Crucifixion," is in memory of Governor Nelson A. Rockefeller's son Michael, who died in New Guinea.

Metz: The last part of Chagall's windows for the Metz Cathedral, installed in 1968.

Maxwell Rabb in New York to John Nef in Washington D.C.

Maxwell M. Rabb
61 Broadway/New York 6, N.Y.

June 6, 1966

Dear Mr. Nef,

This past week-end in Washington was a very exciting one for me, and the unexpected meeting with you heightened the pleasure.

I cannot tell you what a deep feeling of satisfaction I experienced to learn that you were the initiating force in bringing the famed Marc Chagall episode to a successful conclusion. As I told you, I had kept this story very much to myself, but it was one of the great gratifications of my life that I was instrumental in overcoming a stupid bureaucratic obstruction that would have had unwarranted and destructive repercussions. Marc Chagall is, of course, one of the great fig-

Chagall episode: A reference to the difficulties involved in getting a visa for Chagall in 1957–1958.

ures of our time, and I am proud that you, William Wood Prince and I were of assistance to him. As you so rightly indicated, this was an occasion where right triumphed. Of course, I stand ready to help Mr. Chagall in the future in any way that I can in line with our discussion.

With warm regard,

Sincerely,/   Maxwell M. Rabb

Marc Chagall in Vence to Charles Marq in Reims

[Stationery: "Les Collines" Vence (A.M.)]

30 June 1966

[French] Dear Charles,

Thank you for your note.

As time passes, we are deeper into moving [to the new house in St.-Paul de Vence]. I'm not the one who is working, but Vava. And the more tired I am!

I wonder how things are with you, in Reims?

I am morally preparing to pay you a visit for a "general inspection," as they say.

While waiting, it occurred to me that I should have in hand the architectural sketches that we created together for the "biblical message" project and for the foundation in New York, your remarks, etc. . . . which you talked to me about and showed me.

I think I can talk about it with the architect on July 18, when he will come here for an official proceeding.

Even if it isn't yet well formed, be nice and send me those plans and ideas, preferably typewritten.

The house is gradually emptying out, but I will be the last to leave or perhaps the one before the last.

Greetings to you and all of yours,/   Chagall

"biblical message" project: The future Musée National Message Biblique Marc Chagall. At Chagall's suggestion, Charles Marq became the first director of the museum.

Marc Chagall in Vence to Kadish Luz in Jerusalem

1966 St. Paul de Vence [Stamp: received on 15.7.66]

Dear president and friend, Thank you for your letter. I recently returned, indeed, from America, where I installed the murals for the foyer of the new Opera in New York. And I always ponder: how is it going in the Knesset and how will it look when the whole Hall is complete. I hope so, and know that you are dream-

ing of it too, with all your sympathy and love. I received the photos of the work
on the mosaics and feel that it is good. And the wall will and should give a specific feeling. And the content comes from you . . .

  meanwhile, regards to you and your dear wife from both of us

Your devoted

Marc Chagall

P.S. We changed the house and the address

INS in Washington, D.C. re: Marc Chagall

[. . . similar to earlier letters]

November 16, 1966

The Department of State and the consular office at Paris recommend that admission be authorized because of the applicant's advanced age, his status as a
renowned painter, and because the purpose of his proposed trips are considered
to be in the public interest. [. . .]

Marc Chagall in St.-Paul de Vence to Charles and Brigitte Marq in Reims

> A new commission came from Lady Rosemary d'Avigdor-Goldsmid in England.
> Her daughter Sarah had been enthusiastic about Chagall's Jerusalem Windows,
> which she saw in Paris in 1961. Two years later, she tragically drowned in the sea
> along with her fiancé. Grief-stricken Lady d'Avigdor-Goldsmid commissioned
> Chagall to make a stained glass window in her daughter's memory in their village
> chapel in Tudeley, Kent. The window was completed during 1966–1967. Eventu-
> ally, twelve windows were made between 1967 and 1978.

[Stationery: la Colline, quartier les Gardettes, 06—Saint Paul]

18 November 1966

[French] Dear friends Charles and Brigitte,

I was glad to hear about you through your phone conversation with Vava.

stained glass windows:
For the Rockefeller
family chapel in
Pocantico Hills,
New York.
I am happy that you were going to New York to install the stained glass windows. God knows how they will look. I perspired and sighed pretty good; and you too!

Try with the help you will have there to place them in the order of the shades as you have it. I think that the colors placed like that will be very harmonious and won't disturb the majestic collages.

I think of what you told me about protection for it will be placed very low and someone might even touch it. We saw that in Jerusalem.

Write me when you are there to tell me how the work is going and to give me a general impression once it is in place.

go to Lincoln Center:
Chagall is worried
about the murals at the
Metropolitan Opera
House in New York.
You will surely have a moment to go to Lincoln Center. You will see up close if the colors aren't too frozen or if they have wept in my absence.

I don't know what else to tell you. All that's left for me to do is to embrace both of you. And I also embrace your charming children.

With all my heart I wish you a good journey and also the joy of seeing you again.

All the same, we must also do something for that unfortunate English woman [Lady Rosmary d'Avigdor-Goldsmid] and I am preparing my strength for the *Hermann:* André
Hermant, the
architect of the
Chagall museum
in Nice. biblical message. I am waiting for news of the architect Hermann [= Hermant].

Cordially,

Marc Chagall

Varian Fry in New York to Mr. and Mrs. Chagall in St.-Paul de Vence

[Telegram]   [undated]

International Rescue Committee—460 Park Avenue South, New York, N.Y. 10016

joy: Even this joy was
premature.
[English] Cannot exaggerate the joy with which I learned through the committee that the lithograph for the album has been completed and given to Mourlot stop if my health permits I hope to see you soon in Paris.

Varian Fry

Marc Chagall in St.-Paul de Vence to Kadish Luz in Jerusalem

[January?] 1967 [Stamp: received 25.?.67]

[Yiddish] Dear friend and President K. Luz

I haven't heard anything new in a while—from you, from the Land. Perhaps it is my fault. We are always guilty ourselves . . . I am upset that I was not at the Opening of the Knesset, but I couldn't come. Though in my soul I am anyway with you, among you . . . always—this is my destiny to be far away—but I remember you so well, and your wife, and cannot forget your goodness and Jewishness and your sympathy toward me when I was in the Land and worked. And my dream lies with you, in the Hall, and I think about and work on the tapestries. Naturally, I would not like "My Hall" and my work in that hall to be "at the expense of Rothschild" (as some think)—well, I don't know them, and let people know that it goes only from [my heart]

[second page missing]

> "At the expense of Rothschild," or "at the expense of the Baron," is an Israeli saying, derived from the settlements of the end of the nineteenth century, funded by Baron Rothschild, implying that a rich patron, the government, or an institution pays, and the person need not worry. In this case, it was not a proverb; the Rothschilds really did contribute to the Knesset building. Chagall is offended, for, unlike similar, well-paid commissions, he claimed he gave the tapestries as a gift to the Knesset.

Kadish Luz in Jerusalem to Marc Chagall in St.-Paul de Vence

February 1, 1967

[Yiddish; typewritten] Dear friend Marc Chagall!

I was very happy to get your letter. I have not heard from you in a long time, though we mention your name all the time, for we call the great hall with the mosaics "Chagall's Hall." I am very touched by your good words about me and my wife, and even more so by your words: "always—this is my destiny to be far away—but I remember you . . . And my dream lies with you." Perhaps unwittingly you write a poetic phrase very similar to the phrase of our great poet of the Spanish age, Yehuda HaLevi: "My heart is in the East and I am at the end of the West."

We are all upset that you couldn't come to the Opening of the Knesset building, but we consoled ourselves that you will soon visit us. We agree among ourselves that the second inauguration of the building will occur when you bring us the long-awaited tapestries.

Since the opening of the Knesset, we have had over 120,000 visitors. When I

"My heart is in the East . . .": Opening line of the "Zionide," a Zionist poem in Hebrew written by Yehuda HaLevi (c. 1075–1141), a great Hebrew poet in Spain. Chagall alluded to HaLevi earlier, too. Of course, Spain was "the end of the West" in the known world of the time.

speak to larger groups of visitors, I always stress that the building is not yet finished and it will be entirely complete when you bring us the tapestries.

I always stress that both the mosaics and the tapestries are a pure gift from you and have no relation at all to Rothschild's gift or to the share of the government.

I have arranged to send you two air tickets so you can come at any moment when it may be possible, and I think that Passover is the proper time to visit Eretz-Israel.

> Warm regards from me and my wife to you and your dear wife,
>
> Shalom, shalom!/Devoted to you!
>
> Kadish Luz

Varian Fry in Connecticut to Ida Chagall in Paris

27 February, 1967

[English] Dear Ida

S.O.S.! As I told you, your stepmother telephoned the New York office of the International Rescue Committee to say that Chagall had delivered his lithograph for the committee's album to Mourlot before leaving for New York.

I suggested that the New York office ask the Paris office to check with Mourlot. The Paris office has had a good many dealings with him, because he has already done the Masson and the Miro lithographs for the album.

We have just had the cabled reply: Mourlot denies that he has received anything from Chagall for the committee, but reports that Pignon has completed his lithograph, and that he awaits only the bon a tirer [ready for print] on that one.

Can this mean that your father sent Mourlot a lithograph without saying for whom it was intended? Does it mean that your step-mother anticipated a little, just to get rid of all the telephone messages, written notes, etc.?

Whatever your conclusion, the question in my mind now is, what should I do? Or can you do it for me while you are in Paris? Please telephone me before you leave: UNiversity 5-5193.

> Affectionately,

[hand written] 1/III/67 Ida says Vava is the one to believe: Mourlot may not know it is for I.R.C., or may have received Vava's permission to say so. So reported to Carel (VF)

Marc Chagall in St.-Paul de Vence to Charles Marq in Reims

[Stationery: "La Colline" St. Paul de Vence]

April 17, 1967

[French] Dear Marq,

I just received your letter. How nice of you to write me.

I am glad that you saw M. Hermant and please continue to see him. If you find something interesting, so much the better!

continue to see him: Concerning the building of the Chagall museum in Nice.

I have to see him soon, either in Nice or in Paris.

In any case, try to see him about that work as often as possible. Moreover, he is very favorable to these meetings with you.

As for the idea of the windows, I think it wouldn't be bad. Of course, the windows mustn't be too wide, for that would be too decorative and would compete with the biblical paintings. On the other hand, we must also try to avoid things that are too narrow and Gothic.

Who knows, I will be able to do something all the same. We'll see.

The paintings left today for the exhibition in Zurich and I want to hope that you have kindly done what is necessary for the stained glass windows to be exhibited in Zurich too.

Of course, I would like it very much if you could make a little trip there.

I would also like to ask you to send me by registered mail, to St. Paul, what you have left of the mockups for Rockefeller, especially the collages (seven, I think). It would be nice to do that for me because I want to show them to him.

I hope that you and all of yours are well.

My poor Vava fell down yesterday and hurt her leg. I don't know why, I feel guilty as always.

Love to all of you./Yours,

Marc Chagall

Mrs. Kermit Roosevelt in New York to Marc Chagall in Paris

9 May 1967

Mr. Marc Chagall/13 Quai d'Anjou/Paris 4/France

[French] Dear Mr. Chagall:

Just recently, the French government awarded the Cross of the Legion of Honor to Varian Fry. It was the work he did in Marseille a quarter of a century ago that earned him that decoration. In fact, he contributed to saving the lives of several artists, scientists, and writers who were trying to flee Europe.

The collection to which Varian Fry has devoted so much effort during the last two years and to which you have so generously agreed to make the gift of a lithograph will constitute a worthy testimony to the work done at that time.

Allow me to take advantage of this occasion to thank you once more for your generosity and to express the hope that it will be possible for you to finish the lithograph soon so that this remarkable collection of art works can be presented to the public.

All my best regards,

Mrs. Kermit Roosevelt

Marc Chagall in St.-Paul de Vence to Kadish Luz in Jerusalem

This was written one week before the Six-Day War broke out on June 6, 1967. At the time, the atmosphere in Israel was very tense, and the tension was magnified in the international press. The very existence of the Jewish State was threatened by hostile Arab armies amassing their troops on her borders in overwhelming numbers. Eighty-year-old Chagall was agitated and wrote to Kadish Luz.

31/5 St. Paul de Vence 1967

[Stationery: "La Colline"/St. Paul de Vence; Stamp: received 5.6.67 (June)]

[Yiddish] Dear friend and President K. Luz

With great pain I listen to the tumult and outrage that our enemies want to commit against our country. With what pleasure would I have given my last years [to be] with all of you to defend the Land with all the young and old.

Unfortunately, I am far away, but part of my soul is with you. I kiss you with all my heart. I believe in your greatness. Though we [the Jews] are alone—

I hope we shall see each other in joy, for in our heart is justice. Your devoted

With warm regards   Marc Chagall

Marc Chagall in St.-Paul de Vence to Charles and Brigitte Marq in Reims

[Stationery: "La Colline," St. Paul de Vence]

12 June 1967

[French] Dear Charles and Brigitte,

I was glad to receive your letter about your trip.

I am happy to know that you returned safely from your dangerous trip. I am relieved.

We are leaving Wednesday for Paris, but I would like to remind you to be kind enough to think of that stained glass window for the main entrance to the exhibition of the Biblical Message.

I hope that you will be able to go give them a hand to install it as it should be. I send both of you from both of us our affectionate regards.

Chagall

dangerous trip: Marq made a trip to Israel to secure the stained glass windows at the Hadassah Hospital synagogue in Jerusalem, which were removed on the eve of the Six-Day War. Marq flew back to France on the morning the war started.

main entrance: The Chagall museum in Nice.

Kadish Luz in Jerusalem to Marc Chagall in St.-Paul de Vence

June 21, 1967

Dear friend Chagall,

I got your letter of May 31 on Monday June 5.

Hearing on the radio that a war broke out on the Egyptian border with Israel, I intended to answer your letter right away. But suddenly I heard the sound of cannons firing, the Jordanian army began a bombardment of Jerusalem, and I had to start arranging everything for the war situation. The Knesset members and employees assembled in the Knesset shelter. That day we had to approve two meetings. I decided to conduct them in the assembly hall of the Knesset. I felt it imperative that the speeches delivered in the Knesset be heard over the radio by the whole Israeli society.

In those two meetings we passed three laws related to the needs of the war and heard the Prime Minister's [Levi Eshkol] speech about the military victories. All the parties (except for the Communist Party) were united in support of the government and in favor of every effort to win the war, and they also accepted the Prime Minister's proposal to enlarge and strengthen the government with three new ministers from the former opposition parties—Messrs. Begin, Dayan, and Yosef Sapir.

I don't have to tell you what transpired in the ensuing weeks. The whole world knows about our great victory. Many generations of the Jewish people believed

opposition parties: Since the beginning of the state, the Israeli government was dominated by the Labor Party. Now, at a time of danger, a Government of National Unity was formed, with the major opposition party, Likud (including the former Labor leader, General Moshe Dayan).

in miracles; our generation was lucky enough to see real miracles with its own eyes. Every hour we got reports about the events and the unfolding of the war and we felt as if we were dreaming.

We are now envisioning a big political struggle to ensure the peace, and we hope that in this struggle, too, we shall prevail. We have decided to be strong and to realize a new miracle.

Before this last war, I read in a newspaper that the world will soon celebrate your 80th birthday. I am sure there will be a big celebration in France. I congratulate you on reaching the Age of Courage and wish you long long years, health, and rich artistic work. I shall allow myself to remark that it would be splendid for you and for the Jewish people if we could also celebrate your birthday together with you in Israel.

Age of Courage: In Hebrew, eighty is called the age of *Gevurot*, the Heroic Age, or the Age of Courage.

> With love and warm regards,
>
> Kadish Luz

Marc Chagall in St.-Paul de Vence to Kadish Luz in Jerusalem

Paris   25/6   1967

[Yiddish] Dear friend and President K. Luz,

Now [after the Israeli victory in the Six-Day War], my heart is relieved. I would like to know how you are, what is happening.

Though I am older, I feel "stronger" with the strength of Israel.

Just don't let them "push her back" from the territories.—I am happy that my 12 tribes windows [in the Hadassah Hospital synagogue] remained unscathed. As did the symbolic wall and floor in the Knesset.

Warm regards to you and your wife and all the people around you. (And from my wife.)

> Your devoted   Marc Chagall

Marc Chagall in St.-Paul de Vence to Kadish Luz in Jerusalem

1967   13/xii

[Stationery: "La Colline" St. Paul de Vence]

[Yiddish] Dear President and friend,

I was so happy to get your letter. I had not heard from you in a long time. Like all the Jews in the world, I was always thinking (now too) about Israel. I hope that, with our Jewish energy, we shall come to a well-deserved peace.

As for the tapestries, one is ready, the others are advancing . . . And I am happy (a rare thing).

The Minister [of Culture, André] Malraux wants to exhibit them in Paris when they are ready. At my great exhibition which he is planning.

Obviously, you should and must be present at the moment when I, God willing, will bring them to the Knesset. Because you initiated it and you inspired me.

But I still hope somehow to get to Israel with my wife.

Warm regards to you and your wife from both of us

Devoted   Marc Chagall

P.S. You probably know the history of the 12 stained-glass windows of the Hadassah synagogue, which do not fit there.

Marc Chagall in St.-Paul de Vence to Mordekhay Tsanin in Tel Aviv

When his stained glass windows of the Twelve Tribes of Israel were installed in the small underground room of the Hadassah Medical Center synagogue—hardly the size of a cathedral—Chagall was furious, broke chairs (as he had done in the Yiddish Chamber Theater half a century earlier), and took a long time to calm down. However, he had been well aware of the synagogue dimensions in advance, and designed the windows to almost cover the whole walls. Yet, rage aside, he was also skeptical about moving the windows to a larger place.

Mordekhay Tsanin was a Yiddish writer and Bundist from Warsaw who settled after the Holocaust in Tel Aviv. For many years, he edited the major Israeli Yiddish newspaper *Di Letste Nayes*. Chagall's speech in the Knesset was published in that paper in its original Yiddish.

[Stationery: "La Colline" St. Paul de Vence]

13 December 1967

[Yiddish] Dear friend Tsanin, I saw you just once and felt close to you immediately. Many others probably feel the same way about you. Thank you with all my heart for your letter and your article, written with so much sympathy. I value the things you wrote and said to important persons about the 12 stained-glass windows in the Hadassah synagogue. But no matter what—I don't want it moved and a *big* synagogue built, where the stained-glass windows will be transferred. I think they should be in a more intimate place (with space, let's say, for about 200 people). Otherwise, they'll get lost or worse, be surrounded with various "art decoratif"——

In any case, I must first see the plans, and nothing should be done without my consent.

Sometimes I think that near the Knesset (where my mosaics are, and where hopefully the tapestries will arrive later—in a special hall)—is not bad.

But enough for now—the Land [of Israel] surely has other, great worries, and God knows how it will all go.

Regards, your devoted   Marc Chagall

Charles Marq in Reims to Marc Chagall in St.-Paul de Vence

On the context of this letter, Charles Marq writes: "At that moment I was realizing the important ensemble of windows for the tritorium of the Metz Cathedral. Chagall had made splendid mockups, representing bouquets of flowers flying across the windows. 'Your flowers' refers to those mockups, enlarged tenfold, which Chagall saw on the windows of the atelier" (letter to B.H.).

31 January 1968

[French] My Dear Chagall,

Time passes silently, but I am in constant conversation with you, with your flowers, projected in a big bouquet on the wall of the studio. It is so beautiful, so real that I have a lot of trouble maintaining the lightness and mad freedom of all that. I am trying to be strong without being heavy, hoping that the light is going to help me.

I think that, by the middle of March, a good part will be ready to paint, a quarter or a third of the whole, the rest naturally following.

For the other projects, I will go to Saint-Paul as soon as it is useful, you know that. During out last phone conversation, you seemed not to need me right away, so I am waiting patiently . . . We hope especially, Brigitte and I, that health and work progress as you wish, and that despite your great responsibilities you and Vava will be able to get a change of air.

The Studio of Reims has demanded a lot from us, we are also working for our-

The opening of the Jerusalem tapestries in the Gobelins factory in Paris, 1968.

selves a little [painting], all that makes a very full life that you know better than us. Benoit and Charlotte understand their parents [the Marqs] well . . . and their spiritual grandparents [the Chagalls]. They send you regards.

> With my loyal affection, sincerely, for you and Vava.   [Charles Marq]

Marc Chagall in St.-Paul de Vence to M. Tsanin in Tel Aviv

[Stationery: "La Colline" St. Paul de Vence]

St. Paul 1968

[Yiddish] Dear friend,

Thank you for the book you sent me, which I read with pleasure and seek in it the mood of the Land and its people.

I remember your visit.

When I pick up a newspaper here, I primarily seek news of the Land.

All the "nice" people and our enemies mainly want Israel to "return" the land, for Israel cannot and must not win a war, as other nations have done in the past. She must be "punished" for it, and naturally not be recognized . . .

Warm greetings to you and everyone

Marc Chagall

P.S. Thank you for the clipping of "To the Slaughtered Artists."

"To the Slaughtered Artists": A reprinting of Chagall's long poem in Yiddish, "To the Slaughtered Artists," about the Jewish artists in France who were killed by the Nazis; see p. 719.

Rachel and Kadish Luz in Degania B to Marc Chagall in St.-Paul de Vence

1968 [Stationery: "Speaker of the Knesset"]

Degania B. 16.9.

[Yiddish] Dear friend Marc Chagall,

We were overjoyed to get live regards from you and Vava through your daughter Ida. She visited us in Degania and told us that you are well and are working a lot with the greatest success. It pleased us very much. She also said that the tapestries would be ready soon. It will be a great joy for all of us, for the Jews of Eretz-Israel as well as for the hundreds of thousands of Jews coming to see us and spending each more or less time. Every one of them comes to the Knesset to look at your creations as well as the building itself. I hope there will be no special difficulties to bring the tapestries to Israel.

This year, 243,000 people visited the Knesset. And all of them look at the mosaics and the great wall, and when they hear that the whole wall will bear your tapestries, they swear they must come again to see them.

We hope you will come soon to visit us and we are waiting impatiently for your visit.

We wish you a happy, healthy, and creative New Year. And we wish us in Israel Peace Peace Peace! / Happy New Year,

With love and admiration   Rachel and Kadish Luz

U.S. Embassy in Paris to Director, FBI

UNITED STATES GOVERNMENT MEMORANDUM   10/7/68 [October]

To: Director, FBI
From: Legat, Paris
Subject: Marc Chagall
Re Paris let to Bureau 1/18/67

The Visa Section, Embassy, Paris, advised on 10/7/68 that the captioned French national, of Russian origin, a well-known artist (painter) has requested visa to visit the United States leaving between November 5–15, 1968 to visit friends. His contacts were furnished XXXXXXXXXXXXXXXX Washington D.C. and Hotel Plaza, New York City.

The Visa section advised that he is ineligible because of association with Communist and Communist fron organizations (see Paris let 3/24/66), but will undoubtedly be issued a waiver.

Kadish Luz in Jerusalem to Marc Chagall in St.-Paul de Vence

[Stationery: "Speaker of the Knesset"]

Jerusalem 25.11.1968

[Russian] Dear friend Marc Chagall

I was very sorry I was not able to see you during my trip to France. Back in Israel, before my departure, I learned that you had gone to America.

All the members of our delegation visited Gobelins and observed your tapestries for a long time and with enthusiasm. I talked to Mr. Antonioz, and he told me of the difficulties of transferring the tapestries to us for the Knesset. I asked Ambassador Eytan to arrange a meeting with Minister Malraux.

Before I left, I met Malraux, and he told me that when they negotiated with you, it was clear to them that the pictures would become the property of France, and this would be the compensation for the value of the work and materials. French law forbids giving tapestries as a gift. Now they learned that the pictures would not be their property, and are therefore asking for a payment of $250,000. He added that there is a theoretical possibility of lending us the tapestries, on condition that they remain the property of the French government, but that depends on the Finance Minister, and he does not advise appealing to him under the present circumstances. My answer was: when I return to Israel, I will ask our Prime Minister Eshkol and Finance Minister Sherf to

Antonioz: Bernard Anthonioz was, as a young man, a courier of the French underground, connecting France with de Gaulle via Switzerland. Now he was de Gaulle's son-in-law, and in charge of major enterprises in the Ministry of Culture.

include the required sum in the budget, and I hope it will be done, despite the financial difficulties.

I hope we shall soon be able to celebrate a big event: the arrival of your tapestries in the Knesset. This will be a great holiday for you and for us.

I wish you good health and creative satisfaction. Regards and best wishes to your wife Vava. My wife Rachel greets you and Vava. Your Kadish Luz

Marc Chagall in Paris to Kadish Luz in Jerusalem

Paris 1968 11/xii [Stamp: arrived 16.12.68]

[Russian] My dear friend Kadish Luz

I returned from America and found your letter about the situation concerning the transmission of the tapestries to you.

You can imagine how flabbergasted and upset I was when I learned from you and now also from Mr. Antonioz, that they have to charge you for the transmission of the tapestries.

I don't know what to tell you. I can only assure you that I never knew about it. From the very beginning, even before I wanted to give you my tapestries as a gift, I was told that one copy (that is, a triptych) *is due me*. Believe me, I had nothing to do with it, that it upsets me terribly, and I went to see our Ambassador Eytan in this matter and told him my feelings and opinion. I hope soon to write you more.

Be well and healthy. Warm greetings to your wife, regards from mine.

Your devoted

Marc Chagall

Marc Chagall in Paris to Kadish Luz in Jerusalem

[Stationery: "La Colline" St. Paul de Vence]

30 - 1 1969

[Yiddish] Dear friend Kadish Luz,

No Jew can feel safe now, when innocent people—Jews, are being shot, as before by the Nazis. I send you these few lines from the depth of my heart. As always, I am with you, even though from afar. I kiss you and the whole nation.

Your devoted   Marc Chagall

Kadish Luz in Jerusalem to Marc Chagall in St.-Paul de Vence

Jerusalem 12.2.69 [February]

[Yiddish; typed] Dear friend Marc Chagall,

I was very moved when I got your short letter. We are in a serious and complicated situation, and yet we are proud and calm. We are only worried about the fate of the Jews who are in Arabic hands. It seems to me that the Jewish people has never been so united around Israel as in recent years. Jews feel that if not for Israel, the Jewish nation would have gradually disappeared under the present conditions of assimilation on the one hand and persecution on the other. *Aliya* [immigration] to Israel has increased and many Jews come to us from France, America, and other countries.

Be well and strong. I wish you good, creative work. Warm regards to your wife from me and my wife.

What is new with the Gobelins?

With warmest greetings and best wishes.

Yours   K.L.

Marc Chagall in St.-Paul de Vence to Kadish Luz in Jerusalem

[Stationery: "La Colline" St. Paul de Vence]

21/4 1969

[Yiddish] Dear friend Kadish Luz,

I am happy—got your letter. Like many thousands of Jews, every day I think about you, our country.

—As you know, the triptych, the three tapestries, is ready. I hope they will soon come to you—meanwhile for some time—[they were created] because of you. But they must come back for the greatest exhibition [of Chagall's work] the government organizes in the "Grand Palais" of Paris—which opens in late November this year.—I will be happy to see you at the Opening.

This will be the first (and last) time the tapestries will be exhibited outside the Knesset.

I shall be happy to get a word from you. / With best regards for you and your wife

From us/   Your devoted   Marc Chagall

CHAPTER TWENTY-FIVE   **The Grand Palais and Other Glories: 1969–1985**

From December 1969 through March 1970, the French government staged a most comprehensive retrospective exhibition, "Homage to Marc Chagall"—474 works displayed on three floors of the recently renovated Grand Palais. It was organized by Jean Chatelain, Director of the Museums of France, and Jean Leymarie, Director of the Museum of Modern Art in Paris, who became the General Commissioner of the exhibition.

Director of the Museums of France in Paris to Pierre Matisse in New York

Ministère des Affaires Culturelles
Arts et Lettres
Réunion des Musées Nationaux
Palais du Louvre, Paris Ier   June 4, 1969

[French] Sir,

Within the framework of national homage paid to the greatest contemporary artists, the Ministry of Cultural Affairs has assigned the Union of National Museums to organize a retrospective of the work of Marc Chagall.

This exhibition will be presented in the newly arranged galleries of the Grand Palais and will last from December 1969 to March 1970.

The General Comissioner of it will be Monsieur Jean Leymarie, head curator

Marc Chagall with French Prime Minister Jacques Chaban-Delmas at the opening of the Chagall retrospective at the Grand Palais in Paris, 1969.

of the National Museum of Modern Art, who wishes to illustrate the various aspects of the genius of this artist in the most complete and representative fashion possible.

This is why I allow myself to ask you if you would agree to part for some time with the following pieces, whose importance and quality make them truly necessary for the full success of this show:

The Blue Horse—1948
The Rider—1966
The Little Concert—1968
The Big Circus—1968

It is understood that the greatest care will be taken both for the presentation and for the safety of the objects entrusted to us and that all costs of packing, shipping, and insurance will be paid by the Union of National Museums.

I allow myself to send you the corresponding forms and I would be grateful if you would return them to me filled out and signed, if, as I hope, your response is positive.

Thanking you cordially in advance for the assistance you will agree to give us, please accept my sincerest feelings.

Director of the Museums of France

Administrator of the Union of National Museums

P.O. Inspector General of the Museums

[Hubert Landais]

Marc Chagall in St.-Paul de Vence to Kadish Luz in Jerusalem

[Stationery: "La Colline" St. Paul de Vence]

10/6 1969 [June]

[Yiddish] Dear friend Kadish Luz,

Recently I got your letter. Thank you. I had to go to Paris right away with my many tasks—work I have to do and the exhibit in Paris which the government prepares in the Grand Palais on three stories. I saw our dear Ambassador Eytan. He too conveyed to me your wish that I come to the Opening of the three tapestries for the Knesset. It is first of all your holiday—so I shall master all my "youthfulness" and come to you with my wife Vava and accompanied by her brother—Michel Brodsky.

We shall leave, I hope, on June 17 from Nice directly to Tel Aviv. I think there is only one airplane a day.

So we shall finally see each other. You can imagine our joy: to be at least several days in our biblical Land, among brothers.

With my warmest regards to you, your wife, and friends

My wife sends her greetings. Your devoted   Marc Chagall

Marc Chagall in St.-Paul de Vence to Kadish Luz in Jerusalem

[Stationery: "La Colline" St. Paul de Vence]

1969 [Stamp: received 30.6.69]

[Yiddish] Dear friend Kadish Luz,

Dear friend K. Luz, We came back and I would like to thank you for your dear friendship—how [well] you organized the celebration with a splendid ceremony.

Chagall's grandchildren at the painter's major retrospective at the Grand Palais in Paris, 1969.

You and your wife—from a distance your life and world and your relationship appear as something from another world. This is our Jewish world. And I shall never forget how good and deeply friendly you were toward me and toward the work for the Knesset.

With our warmest regards

Your devoted/   Marc Chagall

Vava greets you both

Marc Chagall in St.-Paul de Vence to Kadish Luz in Jerusalem

[Stamp: received 22.8.69]

[Yiddish] Dear friend, we were happy with your letter, and how could one "forget" the time we spent with you around the Knesset . . . I feel your love and your Jewish heart—I am happy that the tapestries fit well in the Hall, together with the floor and the wall mosaics. And my joy, that all that was created "with you" . . .

And now you write that there is a need to make an album (and postcards) or a little book with colored reproductions of the tapestries (as well as of the floor and wall). I understand that thousands of people would like to have such a souvenir. I agree to it in principle. But I want to be shown a "model" in advance, how it will look. And I must give my "OK" to every reproduction and content.

You know that the great exhibit is being prepared in the "Grand Palais" (opening, end of November), I hope you will make an effort so that the three tapestries will arrive in time for the Paris exhibition (leaving time to hang them properly), and then we shall be able to make good colored photos right here for the planned album and I shall see it. By the way, I have a friend here, a good artisan printer, Mourlot, with whom I always work.

You also have some materials—large drawings I made for the floor and a sketch for the wall—those can serve as additional documents for the album-book.

Please send a letter to the Commissar of the exhibition later on.

Well, I wrote a long letter. I hope you have some time to rest, and your dear wife too.

Commissar: Chagall got his worlds mixed up; he means "Commissioner."

> With my best wishes for you and the whole Land
>
> Your devoted/   Marc Chagall
>
> Regards from Vava

Marc Chagall in St.-Paul de Vence to Thomas Messer in New York

T. Messer was Director of the Guggenheim Museum in New York.

[Stationary: "La Colline," St Paul de Vence]

29 September, 1969

[French] Dear Monsieur Messer,

As you certainly know, a very big and important exhibition of my work is being prepared at the Grand Palais as well as at the Bibliothèque Nationale, in Paris, and I would very much like the paintings, "The Green Violinist" and "The Birthday" to be part of it.

You must have received a letter from the Director of the Museums of France, Mr. Chatelain, as well as from the Director of the Museum of Modern Art, Mr. Leymarie, curator of the exhibit organized by the government, beginning next November 25.

Fernand Mourlot and Marc Chagall.

At the time of that retrospective, the stained glass windows, the tapestries, the sculptures, and the ceramics will also be presented, the engravings being exhibited at the Bibliothèque Nationale.

That loan by the Museum would be an encouragement for me and a sign of sympathy that I would particularly appreciate.

I would be happy if you would answer me as well as the Directors of the museums, Mr. Chatelain and Mr. Leymarie.

Please accept my best regards,/   Marc Chagall

Ida Meyer-Chagall in Basel to Thomas Messer in New York

4.10.69 [October]

Dear Tom,

I wanted to write to you since a lot of time. But, but so many things happened since that visit in New York que la main ne se levait pas [that the hand refuses].

I do hope that I will still see you here or in Paris (35, Quai de l'Horloge, Paris Ier, Tél. ODEon 40-68) and I will be able to give you some good hours in our old Europe, though you don't need me for that.

I know that Jean Leymarie has written to you about the Chagall Exhibition in Paris. I know all what one can think about the exhibition arrangements in Paris. But, I wanted you to know that I am so impressed by the new, exceptional set-up in the Grand Palais on three floors which is going to be opened for Chagall, that I cannot help telling you that I cannot imagine this exhibition without your "Paris [through the Window]."

"Paris [through the Window]": The Guggenheim Museum refused to lend this early masterpiece.

Please, if there is a way to think it over, I would like you to know that I will be more than grateful, if you lend the pictures. I cannot imagine. Je ne visualise pas cette exposition without the Chagall-Guggenheim pictures.

Forgive me if I am intruding. Time is getting frightfully short and please help that the exhibition should be a success.

To your wife and yourself, all my friendly souvenirs

Yours/   Ida Meyer-Chagall

Marc Chagall in St.-Paul de Vence to Kadish Luz in Jerusalem

Paris 10/10 1969

Gamzu: Chaim Gamzu, Israeli art critic, Director of the Tel Aviv Museum.

Shazar: Zalman Shazar, President of Israel.

[Yiddish] Dear friend, I hope you are well and your wife too. I did not forget the splendid days with you recently in the Knesset (how can one forget it). You must have received my letter approving your idea about a book: "The Knesset Tapestries"—an excellent idea. And I am willing to help and oversee. It may include your speech, mine, and perhaps a text by Gamzu. And the beautiful speech by Shazar, recently published in Sutzkever's [journal] *Di Goldene Keyt*.

Fernand Mourlot, Marc Chagall, and Charles Sorlier at the Atelier Mourlot.

The great exhibition in the Grand Palais is being prepared on 3 stories. As always, I am "nervous." This is the first time that a government makes such an exhibition (by a Jew) and I hope you will do everything to bring the three tapestries on time. The opening is on December 5, and they have to get into the catalogue and must be hung on time beforehand in a special hall.

And I hope you will come with your wife.

Meanwhile, be well and regards to both of you

Devoted   Marc Chagall

Evelyn Nef in Washington, D.C., to Vava Chagall in Vence

January 30, 1970

Dearest Vava:

This is to report that I went to New York and took Mary Carswell to see what New York calls Marc Chagall's *Magic Flute*. It was wonderful. I had forgotten how truly beautiful all the sets and costumes and animals were. The cast was a good one despite lots of cast changes at the last minute, and Tamino was sung by a handsome young negro with a beautiful voice; he was the best of all with a perfect Mozart understanding. The only change I noticed, and it wasn't really a change, was that several of the ladies had their skirts slit, with underskirts of the right color underneath so that they could move up, down and around, the raised circle in the middle of the stage. They have been doing the *Magic Flute* often, you will be glad to know, and getting good notices. For the first time in my memory the Metropolitan isn't sold out for every performance. Because of the strike many people turned in their subscriptions, and people are so used to having it sold out that they don't try for tickets. The situation is improving, but Rudy Bing certainly is having his difficulties.

Rudy Bing: Artistic Director of the Metropolitan Opera.

Mary also reported that she had seen Marc's newly designed *Firebird* and not unnaturally found it thrilling, beautiful, an "experience." I will try and see it too before the season is over, but I am working at the moment for the Steuben Glass people, and also at the Corcoran Gallery of Art as a docent and research writer, so my days are full. John is in *pleine forme*.

How did you manage to live through the Grand Palais openings? The papers and magazines were full of news of it—how we wished we could see it.

Kate Carswell, who is two years old, now speaks in sentences and is as precocious as she is beautiful. We all send you our love, to you and Marc.

Marc Chagall in St.-Paul de Vence to Kadish Luz in Jerusalem

[Stationery: "La Colline" St. Paul de Vence]

3/2 [February] 1970

[Yiddish] Dear friend K. Luz, I have not heard from you in a long time. How are you? Like thousands of Jews around the world, I always think about you. If we have a God . . . But I am a firm believer in Jewish strength. And now, your tapestries from the Knesset are displayed on the walls of the Grand Palais, and who has not seen them! And always when I am near them, I remember you, my dear friend. Without you, they would not exist. I hope you'll write me how things are with you, and what you are doing now. May God give me strength to be able to go and see what is happening in your place. Your strength over there also gives me strength to persevere and still work as much as I can.—I kiss you and send you my warm regards, Your

Marc Chagall   And Vava

Marc Chagall in St.-Paul de Vence to Kadish Luz in Jerusalem

[Stationery: "La Colline" St. Paul de Vence]

10/11 [November] 1970

[Yiddish] My dear friend Kadish Luz, I have not heard from you in a long time. But if you are healthy, that's good. I was in bed a whole week—grippe—and one has to work. I am writing the day the General [de Gaulle] left. Such a sadness has descended, I don't know, though to me personally he was good—

> Charles de Gaulle died on November 9, 1970. Chagall personalized his relationships. As a Frenchman, he admired de Gaulle and was grateful for the Legion of Honor and the invitation to paint the Paris Opera ceiling, which he received from de Gaulle and Malraux. Yet he felt guilty about it because of de Gaulle's negative attitude toward Israel and his reference to the Jews as "that intransigent people."

How are you and your wife, what are you doing, I shall be happy to hear how life is for you. About the Land, I read in the newspapers and I hope as always that our God will not abandon us. From a distance, I can see and feel our youth.

And what is happening at the Knesset, are the tapestries getting along well with the mosaics? I thought you wanted to publish an album or something for the audience that comes to see. How is it going?

You surely know that many large sketches for the mosaics are lying in the Knesset. (They must not get spoiled.)

How are you? You are surely writing [a book]. Good luck

Kadish Luz in Degania to Marc Chagall in St.-Paul de Vence

14.12.1970

[Russian] My dear friend Marc Chagall,

Several days ago I wrote you about myself. Now I am writing about the forthcoming World Jewish Conference to express our solidarity with Soviet Jewry. Yesterday I returned from Tel Aviv where I participated in a meeting of the Preparatory Committee. We were told in detail about tens of thousands of Jews who applied for permission to emigrate to Israel, about hundreds who signed their names and addresses on collective petitions, asking for permission to go to Israel, in spite of the antisemitic incitement. Those few who succeeded in getting here say that not only in the Baltic countries and Bessarabia, but also in Moscow, Leningrad, Kharkov, Minsk etc., the Jewish youth, up till now alienated from Jewishness, are spiritually returning to their people and are studying the Hebrew language and Jewish history in semi-underground conditions. Textbooks in those fields are being copied by hand and are snatched up. An unusual renaissance of Russian Jewry began, in spite of the repression and arrests.

The Baltic countries and Bessarabia were annexed to the Soviet Union in 1940, occupied by the German army in 1941, and again liberated by the Soviets in 1944. Thus, they had now been under continuous Soviet rule for only twenty-six years, and still remembered Jewish culture and Zionist longings, whereas the bulk of Soviet Jewry had been under the Communist regime for over fifty years since the Revolution of 1917.

It is the duty of the Jewish people, in particular those from Russia, to do all they can to let the whole world know, and especially the Soviet authorities, that we will strive to enable our brothers to live as Jews, educate their children as Jews, and unite with us in Israel.

It was the unanimous request of all participants in the meeting to ask you to participate in the Conference to be held in Brussels on February 23, 1971. The conference will be attended by most prominent representatives of Jewry in public life, science and art. I was given the task of asking you to give this unusual phenomenon—the revival of Russian Jewry—a graphic image-symbol that would rise on all public events related to the situation of the Jewish people in the Soviet Union. Who better than you can immortalize the renaissance of Russian Jewry, which holds your name so close to its heart.

Awaiting your answer.

Your devoted   Kadish Luz

In the past, Luz had succeeded in getting Chagall to create major public works of art—tapestries and mosaics—for the new Israeli Knesset. The emblem Luz asked Chagall to create now was to fulfill a symbolic and mobilizing function similar to Picasso's dove in the peace movement. No doubt, Chagall felt very strongly about the lot of Soviet Jewry, yet in his response, he reverted to his old excuses.

Marc Chagall in St.-Paul de Vence to Kadish Luz in Jerusalem

St. Paul de Vence   18/xii   1970

[Russian] Dear friend,

As soon as I returned from Paris I got your two letters. Thank you. I am always so happy to have any news from you. I would like first of all to answer the second letter, received today—concerning the unfortunate Jews in Russia. But my trouble is—I have several sisters there with their families—they live in Leningrad and you understand how I have to—alas—restrain myself in many ways, in order not to "harm" them . . . I have "restrained" myself like this for 50 years. What can you do!

I was asked about it here too, and I answered the same thing. Of course, these words of mine must not get into the newspapers . . . But I rely on the power of world Jewry. I am dreaming of having the possibility of getting to you. This would give me a little strength, to see what is close to my heart.

For the "goyish" New Year, I wish you and your wife and family and Israel all the best and good health. My wife sends her greetings.

Your devoted
Marc Chagall

[Yiddish] P.S. Forgive me for writing in Russian. Especially about such a terrible problem . . . one cannot write in Yiddish——

Marc Chagall in St.-Paul de Vence to Charles Marq in Reims

[Stationery: "La Colline" St. Paul de Vence]

August 21, 1971

[French] Dear Charles,

I confirm what I told you on the phone this morning.

During a visit to the construction site of the donation in Nice, we discussed the various modifications to be planned with Mr. Chatelain who was kind enough to come and deal with all those issues himself.

The most urgent issue at present seems to me to be the lighting for the paintings.

I talked about that with Mr. Chatelain and Mr. Hermant, for the frames and the glasses that were offered me do not suit me.

Trusting in your experience in this area, I suggested to Mr. Chatelain that you might help us resolve this problem. Consequently, I ask you, knowing your taste

Chatelain: Jean Chatelain, Director of the Museums of France.

Chagall in his eighties at the Atelier Mourlot.

and considering our long artistic collaboration, to get in touch with Mr. Chatelain to advise us as well as for other problems concerning the donation.

Hence, will you get in touch with Mr. Chatelain on my behalf.

Cordially, / Marc Chagall

Evelyn Nef in Washington, D.C., to Vava Chagall in Vence

September 22, 1971

Dearest Vava,

Today the workmen began to dig in the garden, and we begin to feel the reality of the possibility of a finished wall with a Chagall mosaic in its center. The prospect is glorious!

Here are a few snapshots of the summer. I love the one of you and have had a copy made for myself to keep in my work study upstairs for inspiration. When I get tired or depressed, one look at your smile and remembering your example should renew me completely.

John is going to try and get help from his friend, Senator Percy, to smooth the path for Marc's visa.

Bless you both, keep well and remember that you have always the loving devotion of your friends, John and [Evelyn]

John Nef to Marc Chagall at the Unveiling of the Washington Mosaic

Ceremony honoring Maître and Madame Marc Chagall at the dedication of his mosaic created for the garden of Evelyn and John Nef, Monday, November 1, 1971.

My dear Maître,

For Evelyn and me, your work is the greatest gift and the greatest testimony of our lives. We thank you with all our heart, you and your wife, for bringing your colors into this garden. Thanks to your genius, they are the colors of Provence—of St. Paul, Biot, Cap d'Antibes. Thus, through this mosaic, you bring a piece of France to the United States in the most harmonious and brilliant way. But much more: you bring your unique imagination. It is neither French—your adoptive country—nor American—the country of your asylum during the war—nor even altogether Russian—the country of your birth. It is universal.

The message of hope and unity (the combination you have created with Orpheus, Gluck's music, with compassion for emigrés, and with passionate love that Stendhal baptised the miracle of civilization), this message is uniquely yours. The two of us—Marc and I—make syntheses. The four of us (Vava and you, Evelyn and I) share hope in beauty and hope in love.

The recognition and support of such efforts, such hopes, are unique to France. The four of us are not French by birth. Nor is the good Lino Melano who carried out this mosaic for you. Neither is Colden Florance, the architect of this wall. But it is the French who, for about fifty years, have granted me as well as you, an understanding and esteem that have raised our confidence and helped us undertake new enterprises.

Now, it is thanks to French universality, interpreted perfectly by Charles Lucet, that this meeting is taking place today in Georgetown. We offer the Ambassador and his country the friendship and affection that are the motivating forces of our lives. Thanks to him, thanks to all of you, for coming. Thanks to the authorities of Georgetown and Washingtown for accepting this mosaic masterpiece of Marc Chagall.

John Nef

Pierre Matisse in New York to Vava Chagall in Paris

16 November 1971

[French] Dear Vava,

What a shame that you and Marc couldn't stay in New York a little longer. Those few days went by so fast that you seemed to come and go on a draft. So fast that I didn't have time to talk to you about a plan proposed by Mr. Bing Broide for the Jensen House in New York. Here is the copy of his letter. This House is part of an industrial empire, the Kenton Corporation, which you will find a glimpse of in the attached brochure.

If I have not made more of an effort to write to you about this, it is because I knew you were coming, then here I felt that you had a lot of other, more interesting things to do, like re-viewing the painting, the "Fiancés." In any case, to put my mind at rest, I insist on informing you. This Mr. Broido is going to write to you at length about it after I told him that you were too busy to examine the project in New York, that you would examine it in the Midi.

You must suspect how the idea of an exhibition in the spring obsesses me. I think of it constantly and it urges me to go to the Midi to rush to you to see the new crop. It was always like that, that impatience and eagerness to see the new harvest.

Yet I cannot help being a bit disturbed by the idea of two simultaneous exhibitions in Paris and New York. Obviously, where resistance is the strongest, it is necessary to make a deliberate and strong expression, without seeming to.

We have begun with an exhibition of paintings that is sensational for its density, its variety, and its "deep" shock quality. Then we did the gouaches in the same vein, finally the watercolors and drawings, lighter and more relaxed, although some were extremely "deep." What we should have re-done with a new formulation is the first exhibition, remaining, as we discussed, in medium and even small dimensions, but very dense. Perhaps half paintings and half gouaches!

In sum, what I fear about doing this kind of exhibition is that there aren't enough works to support two exhibitions, especially since the New York one has to be started in January. For that purpose, I have found a marvelous printer in Geneva who will be able to come do his photographs in St. Paul and have the works ready for corrections (very important). In short, my dear Vava, think of all that, the "Iron Pot," Paris and the "Clay Pot," New York—an unequal contest!!

Here is the check for thirty thousand francs for the "Cock on a black background."

I hope you both had a good trip and are resting in Paris before returning to La Colline. My love to both of you and all our affection.

[Pierre Matisse]

    1 check
    1 copy of a letter
    1 brochure

Evelyn Nef in Washington, D.C., to Vava Chagall in St.-Paul de Vence

September 25, 1972

[English] Dearest Vava:

Some days ago I sent newspaper clippings and dinner programs from the very grand Wood-Prince dinner in Chicago. It was meant to be impressive and it was. The best part of it was the exhibition of Chagalls from the Art Institute and local collectors!

At lunch with the Wood-Princes I launched the idea of giving a painting to the National Gallery (since the Art Institute already has several marvelous ones) and they were delighted. I offered $25,000.00 toward the purchase of a painting to be given in Marc's name and Billy immediately offered $50,000.00. He thought if the two families alone could manage the cost it would be best. It will certainly be simpler. I had in my mind the splendid painting of the arrival of the Queen of Sheba from the last Matisse show, which is impressive in quality and size. Pierre Matisse told me the price was $100,000.00 and if that is the one that is decided on we can raise the extra $25,000.00. Do you both approve?

Next I went to see Carter Brown who was charmed with the idea and immedi-ately thought of wanting an *early* Chagall, but I told him you and Marc must not be bothered and we wanted to simply buy and give a painting. This was to protect you—naturally if you have any other ideas we would be guided by your desire. By the end of our interview Carter said he thought the Queen of Sheba might be most acceptable but that it would be polite to ask his curator of 20th century painting before the decision to accept was made. I am to call him before the Wood-Prince leave for Europe so they can bring word to you of our progress. At his request I left the catalogue of the Matisse show with Carter. It would be splendid if it could really be arranged so neatly. When I saw the painting in New York I said to Pierre Matisse that I would like to see it in the National Gallery thinking we might get David Lloyd Kreeger or someone like him to buy it.

Carter Brown: John Carter Brown, Director of the National Gallery in Washington, D.C.

Darling I hope all this won't be one more *souci* for you.

I finished my book. The publishers are pleased and want me to do another one, and I will. Our mosaic gives us and our friends incredible joy and keeps your image fresh, lively and as always much loved.

John joins me in a warm embrace to you both.

CC: Thomas Alcock, Esq.

Our mosaic: John and Evelyn Nef moved from Chicago to Washington, D.C., and Chagall made a mosaic on the wall of their garden.

Vava Chagall in St.-Paul de Vence to Pierre Matisse in New York

"La Colline," St. Paul de Vence   10 October 1972

[French] Dear Pierre,

I have just received your letter of 6 October, as well as the press clippings which gave Chagall great pleasure.

You are very nice to take care of all these requests to do original lithographs. But you know that Chagall doesn't do that outside of Mourlot.

Moreover, we are limiting to the maximum that kind of request for right now there is a craze for lithographs. Everybody wants to do them and we don't appreciate this proliferation!

I hope you got back well and that everything is going well for you and Patricia.

Marc and I send both of you our best, / Vava

John Nef in Washington, D.C., to the National Gallery of Art in Washington, D.C.

December 21, 1972

Mr. John Carter Brown
Director
National Gallery of Art
Constitution Avenue at Sixth Street, N.W.
Washington, D.C., 20565

Dear Carter:

It gives me much pleasure to make over to the National Gallery of Art herewith (through our attorney Thomas H. Alcock) 800 shares of Castle and Cook stock. It is understood that at the beginning of the new year (1973) we will add a further contribution bringing our total contribution up to the value of $18,984.00. Of this sum $18,334.00 is designated as our 1/3 share (the other 2/3 coming from Mr. and Mrs. William Wood-Prince) in the purchase of the 1917 oil painting of Vitebsk by Marc Chagall, the painting you and Evelyn have discussed. Our remaining gift of $650.00 is for the purchase for the National Gallery of *Verve Magazine* devoted to Chagall's work.

You have made it a most agreeable experience, dear Carter, dealing through you with the National Gallery, and we thank you for your unfailing courtesy and discretion.

With all good wishes for the new year to you and your wife from Evelyn and

Yours faithfully,/　John Nef

Marc Chagall in St.-Paul de Vence to Friends in Israel

[May] 1973

[Yiddish] My dear friends. As you all celebrate in your heart the twenty five years of our Land—I want to send you from afar my distant joy. And when I say distant—you can feel my dreamy sadness, that I am not with you. But I always felt that I live among you.

For a long time now, Vitebsk has left my soul. Though in my paintings some distant ghetto dreams still appear.

Count me as a neighbor of yours who lives somewhere not far from you. And my pictures look at you. On the twenty-fifth anniversary of the new Land—please accept my blessing, for at my age I can already make such a blessing.

You and the youth have shown and will show the world the biblical will and strength to live in our own Land, with friendship to all other peoples and countries.

Marc Chagall

to friends in Israel: This letter was written for publication in the Hebrew daily *Maariv*, at the request of David Giladi, then editor of the literature and art section, and author of a Hebrew book on Chagall.

Pierre Matisse in New York to Jean Leymarie in Paris

31 May 1973

Mr. Jean Leymarie
Musée National d'Art Moderne
Paris

[French] My dear Jean,

Pursuant to our conversation, here is how the Chagall project appears:
    A dozen marbles
    Three stones, one big one and two small ones
    Five or six bronzes
    About fifteen paintings
    About ten gouaches
This is the first time that the marbles, bronzes, and stones are exhibited in America and Chagall is taking a great interest in that. It is going to make a dense exhibition which seems very lively and good. For a man of Chagall's age, it is quite good.

The catalogue which is not yet completely set will include the color reproduction of the marbles, bronzes, and stone, plus most of the paintings and gouaches; in all about forty color plates. It will be printed in Lausanne at the Impriméries Réunies.

As you know Chagall's work thoroughly, I thought and hoped that you might undertake this little job. A text of the importance of the one you did for Balthus's drawings, which was so successful. The fee for the text has been set at $1,000 (cash).

I strongly hope that your many commitments will allow you to consider our proposal, which would give me the great pleasure of having a text by you in our collection.

I leave Sunday and after 48 hours in Paris, I will be in St. Jean, working with Chagall. In any case, we will see each other at the Message Biblique, but give me a sign to reassure me. The text would be needed by the end of July.

My best wishes,/[Pierre Matisse]

Marc Chagall in St.-Paul de Vence to Thomas Messer in New York

16 July, 1975

[French] Dear Mr. Messer,

My wife had a telephone conversation with someone announcing an exhibition titled "The Jewish Experience in the Art of the Twentieth Century,"[1] which was to take place in October 1975 at the Jewish Museum in New York.

This person also told her that works by me would be requested from the Solomon R. Guggenheim Museum.

Not having been consulted in advance, I cannot give my consent. Moreover, I do not understand why someone plans to exhibit my works under such conditions.

If it is possible, I would be grateful to you if you could make sure that your museum does not agree to loans for this show.

Thank you in advance. My best wishes,/   Marc Chagall

Pierre Matisse in New York to Vava Chagall in St.-Paul de Vence

4 November 1975

[French] Dear Vava,

I am sending you the catalogue of the exhibition of the Jewish Museum. Naturally I saw the exhibition and despite our apprehensions, the exhibition is altogether not too bad. Naturally, there are a lot of names that one does not know, pictures that are not such horrors but that are totally lacking in interest. But, all the same, there is a group among which your husband is very well represented, which makes a great impression. You have to read Mr. Avram Kampf's text and you will know in what spirit the pictures were chosen. That is why Pascin and Modigliani are represented by so few works.

In any case, the exhibition is very well attended and has attracted a great deal of attention. Altogether, in short, it is not as bad as that.

Affections to both of you, / [Pierre Matisse]

Vava Chagall in St.-Paul de Vence to Pierre Matisse in New York

"La Colline"   13 November 1975

Dear Pierre,

I was very happy to hear from you.

Even though you didn't tell us, I presume that you are well and so is Tanna.

Marc was happy to get the catalogue. I see, in fact, that there was a great deal of Chagall.

As you say, the exhibition doesn't look too bad, but I detest those exhibitions designated Russian or Jewish or other art . . . It is a pretext to exhibit bad painters. Of course, they have to live, but not like that! Nevertheless, it is not serious.

We are both quite well. Chagall is working a lot. He is now preparing a book with a text by Malraux. That gives him a lot of work and cares. So he is very busy but he feels that he needs it.

The weather is all right, but all the same, we enjoy very nice, still warm days.

As always, there is a coming and going of visitors with more or less honest proposals.

This is the latest news.

Best wishes from Marc and me to both of you,

Vava

Ida Chagall in Paris to Pierre Matisse in New York

35, Quai de L'Horloge, Paris, 1er   23 April 1976

[French] Dear Pierre,

I have just received your very nice letter and I am panic-stricken . . . I wrote you a letter from the Midi on 15 April, by hand, it is true, with an illegible writing, but in which I tried to explain to you why I intervened in that exhibition only so belatedly. Otherwise, you know very well that you would have been the first I would have asked for help.

And now that it is on the front burner, I am the one who is burning and I have no idea how to get out of it. The only one who is not going to burn is obviously Chagall. But help me, please, so that those he loves and who love him are in the forefront of all of Papa's shows.

This letter is clumsy, but it is only to make you understand that if I didn't write to you about this at the beginning of the year, it is for good reason . . .

Keep a little friendship for me, for I have a great deal for you and help me once more.

Affectionately,

Ida Chagall

Pierre Matisse in New York to Jean Leymarie in Paris

11 March 1977

Mr. Jean Leymarie
Musée National d'Art Moderne

[French] Dear Jean,

Here are the photographs of my Chagall exhibition, for which I still hope very strongly that you can write the preface of the presentation under the same conditions as last time. The text might be from 1000 to 1200 words.

The aim of the exhibition, on the occasion of Chagall's 90th birthday, is to juxtapose our first exhibition of 1910–1939 with the years 1960–1977. It is also a kind of celebration.

Shortly before the war, I had been to see Chagall in Paris with the idea of making an exhibition for him in New York. I had met him at his 1924 exhibition at the Gallery Barbazanges where I was working at that time.

The Paris house was full of marvelous paintings that I would have certainly liked to exhibit. They formed the other and much more thrilling aspect of the pictures that were generally seen in New York. (The pictures in the Guggenheim collection were not yet visible to the public.) It was the "wild" side that attracted me in what I saw on the walls. But, for one reason or another, it turned out that the pictures were not available and my plan failed.

In June 1941, with the exodus [from Europe], Chagall arrived in New York, where he settled in September. We met again and I became his "dealer." An exhibition was immediately planned for the following December and my dream came true. The marvelous pictures that I had seen in Paris were hung on the

French Prime Minister Jacques Chaban-Delmas awarding Chagall the Grand Cross of the French Legion of Honor, January 1, 1977. Chagall's daughter Ida is in the center.

walls of the gallery in a breathtaking exhibition. To establish the historical nature of these facts, I intend to publish in our catalogue the complete photos of the exhibition of 1941, as well as all the works exhibited, eight of them in color.

And that's the problem. The exhibition opens on May 17 for four weeks. I am lighting a candle and praying for my preface.

Marc Chagall in St.-Paul de Vence to Pierre Matisse in New York

"La Colline" St. Paul de Vence   23 April 1977

[French] Dear Pierre,

I appreciate your attention in organizing a small retrospective of my works in honor of my birthday.

That stirs in me the memory of the 40s, when, thanks to the American museums, I was in New York with other artists from Europe. I met you there; that was the beginning of our collaboration and it continued throughout the war.

After an interruption of some years, we resumed contact. And since 1966, you have constantly shown me your friendship by exhibiting my works.

I hope that the show of this year will bring you much satisfaction and I regret not being able to express my affection to you in person.

Marc Chagall

Ida Chagall in Paris to Pierre Matisse in New York

35, Quai de L'Horloge, Paris, 1st   13 June 1977

[French] Dear Pierre,

You can't know how happy you made me with the marvelous photos of your even more marvelous exhibition.

Your hanging seems to have been done in the very grand style which probably doesn't exist anymore.

On all sides, I hear only praise. And I am happy that this "celebration" is a homage of your talent to Papa's youth.

I cannot thank you enough for that joy.

Affectionately, / Your Ida

Ida Chagall

Robert Carswell: John Nef's son-in-law.

Robert Carswell in Washington, D.C., to Marc Chagall in St.-Paul de Vence

The Deputy Secretary of the Treasury
Washington, D.C. 20220

March 11, 1978

[English] Dear Marc:

Dobrynin: Anatoly Dobrynin, long-time Soviet Ambassador to the United States.

This week Mrs. Mondale, the wife of our Vice President, and Carter Brown, the Director of the National Gallery, visited Ambassador Dobrynin in Washington to enlist his aid in trying to get the Soviet Government to agree to lend modern paintings stored, but not exhibited, by the Leningrad Art Museum. They would like to have an exhibit of those paintings at the National Gallery. I understand that among the paintings are a number that you executed early in your career.

Both Mrs. Mondale and Carter Brown have seen the paintings and think they are marvelous.

Apparently, the Soviets are reluctant to lend the paintings. I gather that it might be helpful in convincing them that the time has come for them to do so if you could write a letter along the lines of the enclosed draft. If you are prepared to send a letter, obviously you should correct the draft in any way you like.

I would hope you will see your way clear to sending the letter as we all think it would be splendid to have your paintings on exhibit here. And I would appreciate your letting me know if you have written.

Mary joins me in sending you and Vava our very best regards.

Sincerely,/   Robert Carswell

[Letterhead of Marc Chagall]

Dear Mr. Ambassador:

I understand that the National Gallery in Wahsington, D.C., is trying to arrange for the loan of paintings owned but not presently exhibited by the Leningrad Museum for the purpose of an exhibition at the Gallery. Among those paintings are a number that I painted early in my career. They are based on traditional Russian themes and represented my attempt as a young artist to depict life in his country.

I would be pleased if it were possible for these paintings to be made available for the exhibit. I think it could only help the cause of cultural understanding and world peace.

Sincerely,/   Marc Chagall

His Excellencey

H.E. Anatoliy F. Dobrynin

The Ambassador of the Union of Soviet Socialist Republics

1125 16th Street, N.W. Washington, D.C. 20036

Vava Chagall in St.-Paul de Vence to John Nef in Washington, D.C.

18 March 1978

[French] Dear John,

I have received your note and immediately afterward Bob Carswell's letter about the paintings that are in Russia.

Unfortunately, Marc does not think it opportune to sign the letter. I will provide the reasons for that decision this summer when we see each other.

We were happy to hear from you.

Regards from both of us to both of you,

Vava

Vava Chagall in Vence to the Nefs in Washington D.C.

"La Colline"/St. Paul de Vence   July 3, 1978

Dear friends,

We are always happy to hear from you. Thanks for the very beautiful photos of the Mosaic and the garden. It is really very beautiful now.

Marc thanks you for your congratulations. As the day [of his birthday] approaches, he does not like to talk about it very much, you know him.

We have made two trips. One in Italy, to Florence, where there was an exhibition at the Pitti Palace and where we stayed only a few days, and the other to Switzerland for the opening of a small rose window that Marc did for Fraumünster; we used the opportunity to see the doctors.

We are very happy to be back in St. Paul, even though the weather isn't very nice.

We are preparing an exhibition of French Roman sculptures of Toulouse. We are very hopeful that this exhibition will be a success. In the Biblical Message in Nice.

Hoping that you are both well, our sincere friendship.

Love,/   Vava

Vava Chagall in St.-Paul de Vence to Pierre Matisse in New York

"La Colline" St.-Paul de Vence   20 February 1980

[French] Dear Pierre,

I received your letter of 11 February as well as the letter that Tana sent me, with those of the schoolchildren, which gave Marc a great deal of pleasure. I sent them a little card to thank them.

As for Mr. Shanks, I am going to thank him for his article.

For the journal of the Anti-Defamation League, Chagall agrees completely that they can reproduce a work by him on the cover of their program. He asks you to choose a picture and, if you agree, one of those you have. Thank you in advance.

I did not answer the questions you asked me.

As for the picture, "Le Matin," it is with the publisher H. Abraham [Abrams].

As for the mosaic for the University of Wichita State, Marc does not feel up to undertaking such a work.

As for the 250 unsigned copies made for the International Rescue Committee, they are already mentioned in the catalogue raisonné of lithographs as *unsigned*. So it will be impossible to sign them now.

For the exhibition, Chagall wants to think a little bit. I will write to you again about that.

Marc is well. Working a lot. It is already spring here. I am not very well, I don't know why, but I have made a big decision, I will go see a new doctor on Wednesday.

Marc and I send you both our good wishes.

Vava Chagall

Laurence Chalmers in Chicago to Marc Chagall in St.-Paul de Vence

Chalmers was President of the Art Institute of Chicago from 1972 to 1986.

The Art Institute of Chicago
Office of the President

Maitre Marc Chagall/"La Colline"/Avenue Henri Matisse/St. Paul de Vence (A.M.)/France   March 31, 1980

[English] Dear Maitre Chagall:

Once again we are enormously excited by the prospect of yet another great work of art by the greatest living artist in the world today. Your mosaic at the First National Bank Plaza begins to come alive as thousands of people respond to the arrival of spring by spending more time out of doors. Your stained glass windows at the Art Institute are admired and enjoyed by more than four thousand visitors every day of the year except Christmas—and now we look forward to the prospect of another great lithograph poster. It is almost too much to expect.

I write to assure you that we are prepared to handle all of the details and costs of printing and marketing the lithograph poster, and that we will return to you, for whatever purposes you deem appropriate, one-half of all profits from the sale of your next great work.

Vava, Marc Chagall, and Ida at the Maeght Foundation in St.-Paul de Vence, 1981.

As has been true so many times before, we at the Art Institute and indeed all Chicagoans are indebted to you for your great artistic genius and generosity.

Sincerely yours,

E. Laurence Chalmers Jr.

President

Marc Chagall in St.-Paul de Vence to Laurence Chalmers in Chicago

Mr. E. Laurence Chalmers Jr./The Art Insitute of Chicago/Office of the President

Saint-Paul, April 15, 1980

[French] Dear Sir,

I have just received your letter of March 31, 1980.
    All that you write to me about the Chicago mosaic pleases me very much.

As for your friendly proposal to make posters, I would ask you to be a little patient. I must consider and consult the staff of the museum.

Yours sincerely,

Marc Chagall

museum: Musée National Message Biblique Marc Chagall in Nice.

Mailgram from Evelyn and John Nef in Washington, D.C., to Marc Chagall in St.-Paul de Vence

On Chagall's ninety-third birthday.

07/03/80 [July]

Your wonderful mosaic lightens our way and draws us ever closer to you in loving admiration and gratitude

Evelyn and John

Marc Chagall in St.-Paul de Vence to Abraham Sutzkever in Tel Aviv

1980

Dear friend Sutzkever,

Thank you for your letter. I understand—you would like to see me. But now it is difficult for me.

You want to write about me. May God help you. I feel your mood always and your Jewish sensibility.

And everything that comes from our holy Land is dear to me. One thing causes me grief—that I cannot come again to the Land.

With my warm regards/   Marc Chagall

Cable from Laurence Chalmers in Chicago to Marc Chagall in St.-Paul de Vence

7/6/82 [July]   11:30 AM

Congratulations on your 95th birthday. May you celebrate many more in good health and great happiness.

Vava Chagall in St.-Paul de Vence to Charles Marq in Reims

During 1977–1984, Chagall made six stained glass windows for the choir and later three for the transept of St. Stephan's church in Mainz (Mayence), Germany. Marq presented the three grand windows to him in St.-Paul de Vence in mid-November 1984, when Chagall was ninety-seven years old, and he was "very happy." These were his last windows, and they were inaugurated in Mainz a short time after his death. According to Marq, Chagall never went to Germany, and refused to go, though he said he understood that there should be a rapprochement. The Mainz windows were the only ones he made for that country; he was reluctant to do it, but was persuaded by his wife, window by window. Eventually, Charles Marq himself completed the remaining windows.

[Stationery: "La Colline," 06570 St. Paul de Vence]

28 November 1984

[French] Dear Charles,

Thank you sincerely for your letter. You are the only person who has understood Marc's condition and what he is thinking at this time.

Even though he is surrounded by cares and affection, he suffers because, as he says, he is imprisoned; but as in life, one doesn't have a choice, you have to accept things as they are, and this applies to us too.

At any rate, we were very happy to have seen you at our home and especially, we both found that the windows were very successful. We hope that they will have as much success in Mainz.

Regards from both of us./I embrace you

Vava

Epilogue

On March 28, 1985, Marc Chagall died at his home in his ninety-eighth year. He was buried not in the Jewish cemetery in Nice but in the Christian cemetery of his own village, St.-Paul de Vence. The Mayor himself gave Chagall a place in his family lot. At the funeral, a lonely voice recited the Jewish Kaddish (a prayer for the dead). A big cross loomed above Chagall's grave, to the chagrin of his Jewish friends, but it was subsequently removed. It is hard to imagine Chagall making that choice, but given the information we have on Vava's clandestine conversion to Christianity, the matter seems clear. Ida, apparently, had no say on the matter or was confused herself.

Vava continued some relationships, notably with Charles Marq, who completed the work on the windows for St. Stephan's Church in Mainz. One of her last letters follows.

Vava Chagall in St.-Paul de Vence to Charles Marq in Reims

[Stationery: La Colline, 06570 St Paul de Vence]

April 27, 1992

[French] Dear Charles,

Thank you for your kind letter, I was happy to read it and to hear how you are.

I am very glad to learn that you and yours are well. I wish you a belated happy Easter.

Nevertheless, I always get news from the curate of Mainz and I know that the work on the stained glass windows is proceeding, which pleases me very much because I think that the church of Mainz is truly a remarkable work.

Everything is fine at the museum of Nice, I think, although I don't go there because it is hard for me to move now.

Cordially,

Vava Chagall

Vava Chagall died on December 24, 1993. The estate was transferred to her brother Michel Brodsky, who died a lonely bachelor and bequeathed it all back to the Chagall family.

Ida Chagall, who devoted her life to her father's work and kept the voluminous records of Chagall's life and art, died in her home in Paris in 1995.

*

Chagall was one of the most popular painters of the twentieth century. In the last third of his life, his lithographs and prints could be found everywhere and his paintings fetched high prices. He was known as a painter of joy and optimism, a flamboyant colorist, a dreamer and poet in painting. Many art critics, fascinated by the formal innovations of Modernism, did not think highly of him, yet many intellectuals, including such figures as Apollinaire, Walden, Malraux, Eluard, Aragon, admired him as one of the great and original artists of the modern age.

A radical change in the understanding of Chagall occurred after the collapse of the Soviet Union, when the treasures of the artist's early period emerged from hiding. After Chagall left the U.S.S.R. in 1922, he was considered a traitor and was rarely mentioned. His early works held in Russian museums had been kept in the cellars and were never shown. When the Yiddish State Theater was demolished in 1948, its Art Director Jacob Tyshler carried Chagall's murals on his back at dusk to the Tretyakov Gallery, where they were stored in a damp cellar of a closed little church. During Khrushchev's "thaw," in 1973, Chagall was allowed to visit the Soviet Union (but not his native Vitebsk) and was asked to sign his murals. Although this gave them added value, they were still not shown to the public.

Finally, in 1987, on Chagall's 100th birthday—sixty-five years after he left Russia—a Chagall exhibition was mounted in Moscow and a book was published in Russian, inspired by the poet Andrey Voznesensky.[1]

At last, in 1991, the Yiddish Theater murals came to the West. The canvases were meticulously restored by a team in the Tretyakov Gallery in Moscow and mounted on new frames; yet the paintings themselves were not touched, and there are still many creases and areas were the color was washed out. Unlike some recent Italian work, the theory of the Russian restoration team was to let the ravages of time remain as they are. This is a highly respectable and restrained approach; the problem is that these ravages were caused by a murderous regime. The murals were first shown in Switzerland, at the Fondation Pierre Gianadda, Martingy (which financed the restoration). Subsequently, the murals and many early works were shown around the world—at the Schirn Museum in Frankfurt, at the Guggenheim Museum in New York, at the Musée d'Art moderne de la Ville de Paris; in Jerusalem, St.-Petersburg, Rome, Finland, Spain, Japan, and so on.

Chagall was never paid for his work. Because of their size, he could not take the murals with him when he left for the West, and they became the property of the Yiddish Theater in Moscow. That Jewish theater was ransacked in Stalin's pogrom. Now the Tretyakov Gallery in Moscow leases it to Western museums.

An entirely new Chagall has appeared. We can now see the foundations of his later work and the sweeping originality of his beginnings. Yet his early work, "Surrealist" as it often looks, is steeped in multicultural allusions and subtexts, the ground for which we tried to explore here.

Reference Matter

NOTES

PREFACE

1. My earlier publications on Chagall include "Marc Chagall: Painting, Theater, World" (in Hebrew), *Alpayim*, No. 8 (1993), pp. 9–97; "The Role of Language in Modern Art: On Texts and Subtexts in Chagall's Paintings," *Modernism/Modernity*, Vol. 1, No. 2 (April 1994), pp.51–87; "Les vitraux de Jérusalem à la lumière de la poétique chagallienne" (in French), in *Marc Chagall, Hadassah, de l'esquise au vitrail*, Paris: Musée d'art et d'histoire du Judaisme, 2002, pp. 119–129; English version: "The Jerusalem Windows in the Perspective of Chagall's Poetics of Art," in *Marc Chagall, Hadassah, From Sketch to Stained Glass Windows*, Paris: Musée d'art et d'histoire du Judaisme, 2002, pp. 119–129.

2. Virginia Haggard, *My Life with Chagall: Seven Years of Plenty with the Master as Told by the Woman Who Shared Them*, New York: Donald I. Fine, 1986.

INTRODUCTION

1. Franz Meyer, *Marc Chagall*, New York: Abrams, 1961.

2. See Sylvie Forestier, *Au coeur d'un chef d'oeuvre: Résistance, Résurrection, Libération de Marc Chagall*. Rennes: Édition Ouest-France, 1990.

3. See several speeches of that time in *Marc Chagall on Art and Culture*.

4. See Chagall's optimistic article, "The New Dawn in Poland," published in April 1945 (see English translation in this book, p. 555).

5. Lionello Venturi, *Chagall*, Paris: Skira, 1956.

6. See *Language in Time of Revolution*.

7. Chagall was admitted to this Russian school in 1900, at age thirteen; studied for four years, repeated one year, and according to the school records never graduated (information obtained by Aleksandra Shatskikh). Chagall himself wrote in his resumé of 1921 that in 1907 (when he was twenty years old), he finished a city high school, but there is no confirmation for this from any other source.

8. The "Cendrars Notebook" was left by Chagall in Paris when he went to Berlin and Russia in 1914; it was found in his room by his friend Blaise Cendrars and preserved by his daughter Miriam Cendrars (see p. 190). Some excerpts were translated into French in *Marc Chagall: Les années russes, 1907–1922*, Paris: Paris Musées, 1995, pp. 234–235.

9. See Benjamin Harshav, "The Jerusalem Windows in the Perspective of Chagall's Poetics of Art," *Marc Chagall, Hadassah, From Sketch to Stained Glass Windows*, Paris: Musée d'art et d'histoire du Judaisme, 2002.

10. Nevertheless, Chagall's Yiddish spelling is not as unruly as it looks at first glance; his seemingly obvious "mistakes" are quite systematic. In his youth, there was no standardized or generally accepted Yiddish spelling, but after the Revolution, such a standard was created in Soviet Russia, and he tried to follow it. His deviations are of several clearly defined kinds: (a) He tried to overcompensate for his local Yiddish dialect. Many words where standard Yiddish says *oy*, Lithuanian Yiddish has *ey* (*broyt*/*breyt*) but not vice versa; many Lithuanian *ey* remain so in standard Yiddish. To "correct" his dialect, when Chagall heard *ey* he often spelled *oy*, even when it was wrong: He spells *shoyn*, *moyn*, *goyn* instead of Lithuanian and standard Yiddish: *sheyn*, *meyn*, *geyn*. He spells *oyntselner*, *oygentum*, *Loyvik* (instead of *eyntselner*, *eygentum*, *Leyvik*) and he writes to the Yiddish poet A. Lyesin: "*hob ikh dem gantsn zumer geloynt* [= *geleynt*] *ale ayere bikher*"; "*ayer moynung*" [= *meynung*]. Sutzkever, who knew him well, told me that Chagall never spoke like that, he just spelled the sound *ey* as *oy*. (b) Chagall spelled most words of Hebrew origin phonetically, as instituted in the Soviet reform of Yiddish spelling. For example, *vos sayekh* [= *shayekh*], rather than ShYKh. However, when he tried to do it in Hebrew proper, as was the norm in non-Soviet Yiddish spelling, he showed his ignorance of Hebrew. (c) In the last example, we also see the Yiddish Lithuanian confusion of *s* and *sh*, which works both ways: *folkshtimlikh* [= *folkstimlikh*], *khots* [= *khotsh*]. (d) There are also vestiges of premodern ("Germanic") spelling, as practiced in Yiddish books at the time.

11. See J.-P. Crespelle, *L'Amour, le rêve et la vie*, Paris: Presses de la Cité, 1969.

12. *Chagall by Chagall*, ed. Charles Sorlier, trans. John Shepley, New York: Abrams, 1979.

13. Franz Meyer, *Marc Chagall*, Bibliography: Works by Chagall #47, p. 712.

14. See *The Meaning of Yiddish*. Chapter 4: "The Semiotics of Yiddish Communication."

15. Virginia Haggard, who had left him a year earlier for another man.

16. Marc and Virginia's son, David McNeil.

17. See *The Meaning of Yiddish*, pp. 102–107.

18. Abram Efros, *Profili (Profiles)*, Moscow: Publisher Federatsiya, 1930, p. 289.

19. I discuss this multicultural personality in my introduction to the collection of Chagall's speeches and essays, *Marc Chagall on Art and Culture*.

CHAPTER 1

1. See below, p. 64, "When and Where was Chagall Born?"

2. Alexandra Shatskikh, "When and Where Was Chagall Born?" in *Marc Chagall: The Russian Years 1906–1922*, ed. Christoph Vitali, Frankfurt: Schirn Kunsthalle, 1991, pp. 21–22.

3. The Russian Futurists painted their faces only after 1910, in order to shock—"épa-

ter la bourgeoisie"—whereas Chagall's was a pure narcissistic move, pronouncing his originality.

4. See Benjamin Harshav, "Chagall: Postmodernism and Fictional Worlds in Painting," in *Marc Chagall and the Jewish Theater*, pp. 15–64.

5. See *Language in Time of Revolution*.

6. Isaac Deutscher, "From Vitebsk to Eternity: The Jewish Vision of Marc Chagall," *Jewish Observer and Middle East Review*, December 31, 1965, p. x.

7. Translated in *Marc Chagall On Art and Culture*.

8. See Chagall's essay "My Meeting with Max Liebermann" (1935), p. 356 (below).

9. See p. 33.

10. See below, p. 740, letter to the Opatoshus, February 28, 1951.

11. This high figure may perhaps include many bilingual Jews, or persons whose mother-tongue was Yiddish though they spoke Russian in the present. Declaring Yiddish rather than Russian was also a matter of national pride. Yet the overwhelming majority still lived their daily lives in Yiddish.

12. Thus, an article on the Uzbekistan photographer Max Penson states: "Penson was born in 1893 in the Belorussian village of Velizh, near the ghetto where another talented Jewish boy, Marc Chagall, was growing up at the same time." (Stephen Kinzer, "Chronicle of an Upheaval," *New York Times*, January 25, 1998.) However, Velizh was not a village but a town and capital of a district; it had over 12,000 inhabitants, half of them Jews; it had two Jewish colleges for men and one for women; and it hosted a branch of Chagall's Vitebsk Art College. Nor was there ever a ghetto in Vitebsk.

13. The confusion comes from the fact that in Yiddish, *shtetl* (town) is a diminutive from *shtot* (city), i.e., "small city," derived from the Polish categories: *mjasto/mjasteczko*. Chagall and others automatically translated the pair into French as *ville/village*, though "village" is not really a town. In English writings, even in Jewish memoirs, one often finds the mistaken term "village" for a small Jewish town, although no matter how small, poor, or unpaved a *shtetl* was, it was not occupied with farming, and its inhabitants were never bought or sold, as the peasants were.

14. The statistical information is from *Evreyskaya Entsiklopediya*, the Russian-language Jewish encyclopedia published just before and after the Revolution. The statistics are primarily based on the comprehensive Russian census of 1897 and other sources.

15. I owe this observation to Sam Kassow. Even today, if you go to Vilnius (Vilna), for example, you see how many baroque and nineteenth-century churches dominate the streets of the so-called Old City, formerly Jewish neighborhoods.

16. Only a few big cities, such as Warsaw and Odessa, had a much larger Jewish population.

17. Moshe de Shalit, "On the Fire Watchtower," in *Sefer Vitebsk*, ed. B. Krupnik, Tel Aviv: Organization of Immigrants from Vitebsk in Israel, 1957.

18. During 1772–1815, between the time Vitebsk was incorporated into Russia and the end of the Napoleonic wars, the city population in Vitebsk Province grew threefold; however, the Jewish city population grew sixfold, whereas the Gentile population did not even double. See Yakov Leshchinsky, "Vitebsk and Province in the Nineteenth Century" (Hebrew), in *Sefer Vitebsk*, ed. B. Krupnik.

19. A Soviet lexicon of 1930 states about Chagall: "born [. . .] in a family of a small tradesman"—certainly not a socially reliable class. *Entsiklopedichesky slovar' Granata*, Vol. 49–50, (1930), pp. 32–33.

20. See Aleksandra Shatskikh, *Vitebsk: The Life of the Arts, 1917–1922* (in Russian), Moscow: Yazyki Russkoy Kultury, 2001.

21. In a "List of the Employees of Vitebsk People's Art College," at least twelve out of the eighteen names are unambiguously Jewish, and among them six out of the nine professors. (See reproduced photocopy in *Marc Chagall: The Russian Years, 1907–1922*, Frankfurt: Schirn Kunsthalle, 1991, p. 70.) In a photograph of Chagall's master class, all students were Jews (see p. 246).

22. Of special interest is the name of the oldest sister. In the document, she is registered as Chana-Berta, yet Chagall records her name as Bella-Anna. "Chana" is, of course, "Anna" and "Berta" becomes "Bella," as in the name of his fiancée; but among the siblings she was called Anyuta or Nyuta, diminutives of "Anna" in Russian.

23. The name Bella was probably inspired by Bella Naumovna Germont, the daughter of Attorney Goldberg's father-in-law, whose house in Narva Chagall lived in before going to Paris. In a letter to his sister Nyuta (around 1910), Chagall writes: "Don't be shy to visit them. They are dear people. You will get friendly with them forever. Bella Naumovna, though an effete young woman by birth, is interesting and super-good, and is no provincial." ("Cendrars Notebook," p. x.)

24. Berta, apparently, spent several years in Moscow but it is not clear whether she actually attended a University, for Moscow University was almost closed for Jews.

25. Blaise Cendrars (Switzerland 1887–Paris 1961), a friend and promoter of Chagall.

26. See Benjamin Harshav, "The Role of Language in Modern Art: On Texts and Subtexts in Chagall's Paintings," *Modernism/Modernity*, Vol. 1, No. 2 (April 1994), pp. 51–87.

27. It is probably derived from the German *Hausierer* (peddler), who goes from house to house to sell his merchandise rather than having a store. Some books erroneously refer to a Yiddish idiom, "to go over the villages." But this is not an idiom, just a sentence, which may be used for peddlers who indeed go from village to village to trade their merchandize or sartorial skills; there is nothing metaphorical about it. On the other hand, "to go over the houses" is an idiom, meaning to be a beggar or a pauper, even if he goes nowhere. The painting clearly shows no villages, but it carries a realization of the metaphor.

28. Translated from Yiddish by Benjamin and Barbara Harshav.

29. Words in Yiddish with a penultimate stress have a final neutral vowel, sounding like *e*: *Móshke*, *pokróvske* ("street"), etc. To be user-friendly, we spell such words with *a*: *Moshka*, *pokrovska*; in a Slavic reading, it would be *a* anyway.

30. See reproduced photocopy in Franz Meyer, *Marc Chagall*, New York: Abrams, 1961, p. 25.

31. Chagall signed his letters from Paris to Alexandr Romm in St.-Petersburg between 1912 and 1914 "Moysey," and a postcard of 1920 from Moscow (to her parents?) was signed by Bella in Russian "Berta, Moysey, and daughter."

32. See letter from the Russian Ministry of Interior, September 30, 1908 (p. 181).

33. See Chagall's letter of May 9, 1937, p. 467.

34. Copies of the wall paintings were published by El Lissitzky in the Yiddish art his-

tory journal *Milgroym* (and its Hebrew counterpart, *Rimon*): "The Synagogue of Mo-hilev," *Milgroym*, No. 3., Berlin, 1923. The synagogue itself burned down during World War I.

35. Ida Chagall brought this and other documents back from her first trip to Russia in 1959, just before her husband Franz Meyer finished his biography of Chagall. Many of them were copied for Ida Chagall on a typewriter by the prominent Jewish Russian lit-erary scholar Ilya Samuilovich Zilbershteyn. In a letter to Louis Stern of September 8, 1959 (see p. 871), Ida describes the documents and jubilantly exclaims: "and the [birth certificate] of father's family where the 1887 date stands firm!"

36. *Di Ershte Bagegenish* (*First Encounter*), New York, 1947, last chapter, "The Birthday."

37. A similar story was told by Chagall's teacher Yehuda Pen in his published child-hood memoirs, which Chagall prodded him to write. The memoirs begin thus: "When I was born and how old I am—I don't know, and even my Mama cannot remember it for her head is turned by more important things, she has to supply bread for her ten mouths." (Yehuda Pen, "The *Heder* Years," *Shtern*, Minsk, Vol. 2, No. 2–3 (5–6) (March 1926), p. 22. Since Chagall was personally close to Pen and repeatedly encouraged him to write his memoirs, it is possible that Chagall borrowed Pen's anecdote (or vice versa).

38. Even in Bella's account, to whom Marc told the same story, the figures don't match. He overheard Mother saying that his sister Chanka (Anyuta) will soon be seven-teen and needs a husband, and he is two years older, hence he must be nineteen (the age when he left for St.-Petersburg), which is in line with the official registration. If he were two years younger, he would be born together with his sister, and all dates of the family had to be changed. It may be possible for a father not to report a birth and register his son at a later date, but to predate a birth two years earlier and report it four years later (when David was born) would be illegal and makes no sense. Perhaps what Marc over-heard was the opposite: that they registered David belatedly, to give him a four-year dis-tance from Moyshe, which is possible, because David was registered two years after Anyuta, and she two years after Moyshe—large gaps in that environment.

39. See the reproduction in Franz Meyer, *Marc Chagall*, p.25.

40. The document does show an almost four-year difference between the brothers (ages twenty and sixteen), with one sister between them, eighteen years old.

41. New York State Department of Health, Division of Vital Statistics, Certificate of Death. "Place of death: State of New York, County: Franklin, Town: Altamont, Mercy General Hospital. Date of birth: December 15, 1895. Date of death: September 2, 1944. Immediate cause of death: Diabetes Mellitus. Age: 48 years, 8 months, 17 days. Duration of Condition: 2 years. Date of Burial: September 6, 1944."

CHAPTER 2

1. Lunacharsky's review of May 14, 1914 (p. 213). Lunacharsky made a plural of a unique situation. But he caught the spirit of Chagall's narrative art.

2. Guillaume Apollinaire (1880–1918), influential French avant-garde poet and art critic. Promoted Chagall and wrote a poem about him (see Chapter 4). Ricciotto Canudo, editor of the avant-garde journal *Monjoie!*, host of Friday gatherings of young avant-garde artists; promoted Chagall. Blaise Cendrars (1887–1961), French avant-garde poet,

friend of Chagall. Herwarth Walden (1878–1941), German expressionist writer and theoretician, founder of the gallery and journal *Der Sturm* (The Storm) in Berlin.

3. A. Efros and J. Tugendhold, *The Art of Marc Chagall* (in Russian), Moscow: Helicon, 1918. German translation: *Die kunst Marc Chagalls*, Potsdam: G. Kieperheuer, 1921. English translation by Barbara and Benjamin Harshav in *Marc Chagall on Art and Culture*.

4. See a French translation in, *Marc Chagall: Les année russes*, p.246.

5. Also known by its Yiddish title, "Bletlakh." See English translation in *Marc Chagall and the Jewish Theater* and in *Marc Chagall on Art and Culture*.

6. *My Own World*, esp. the opening of Chapter XVI, p. 162. Actually, only his parents and brother David died. The sisters moved to Leningrad, but he had little contact with them.

7. Dovid Hofshteyn, "Troyer" ("Grief"), Kiev: Kulture-Lige, 1922. Title page, cover, and six drawings by Marc Chagall.

8. Pavel Ettinger wrote, in March 1923, that Chagall had read some chapters from his autobiography "a year ago," i.e., in 1922, to a small circle of friends in Moscow. "Note by P. E.," *Sredi Kollektsiyonerov* (*Among Collectors*), March–April 1923, p. 37.

9. Here, the published book *My Life* is weakened and blurred; it ends: "I am tired . . . I shall come with my wife, my child. I shall lie down near you. [Whatever that means!] And, perhaps, Europe will love me and, with her, my Russia."

10. *The Lithographs of Marc Chagall*, Introduction by Marc Chagall, Notes and Catalogue by Fernand Mourlot, Monte Carlo: André Sauret, New York: George Braziller, 1960.

11. Marc Chagall, *Mein Leben: 20 Radierungen*, Berlin: Paul Cassirer, 1922/1923. Portfolio. 110 numbered copies.

12. *Di Tsukunft* (The Future) March–July 1925, pp. 158–162, 211–214, 290–293, 359–361, 407–410.

13. See the French translation of both volumes *Khaliastra: Revue littéraire Varsovie 1922 Paris 1924/la bande*, Paris: Lachenal & Ritter, 1989.

14. The typescript of the Yiddish version (80 pages) is preserved in the archive of *Di Tsukunft*, at the YIVO in New York (version A), thoroughly edited in longhand (version B).

15. This was conclusively demonstrated by Nikolay Borodulin at the YIVO in New York, based on comparisons with other manuscripts by the same authors.

16. Yet the chapter published in Markish's journal was in version A, i.e., in Markish's translation, unedited by Chagall.

17. Marc Chagall, *Ma vie*.

18. Even many years later, when Bella wrote her own memoirs in Yiddish, her style was sweet and sentimental, without the vigor, rough edges, gaps, and concrete complexity of Chagall's hand.

19. Like the Russian of Babel's Jewish characters, it had a heavy Yiddish subtext.

20. Franz Meyer, "At Bakst's," *Marc Chagall*, New York: Abrams, 1961, p. 600, note 3.

21. See the complete text of the Bakst essay in Chapter 3.

22. The English edition, *My Life*, has even further problems. It transcribes Russian names as in French or German: *moujik* (instead of *muzhik*), *Penne* (*Pen*), *Baal-Machschowes—Eljascheff* (*Baal-Makhshoves—Elyashev*). Suddenly, a "pope" appears in Lyozno: "Pope or no pope, he smiles as he passes by," where what is meant is a Russian village priest (in Russian: *Pop*).

CHAPTER 3

1. The artists' league *Peredvizhniki* was founded in St.-Petersburg in 1870. Many prominent Russian artists of the late nineteenth century belonged to it.

2. Franz Meyer, *Marc Chagall*, New York: Abrams, 1961, p. 49.

3. Chagall uses this number (one and a half) elsewhere, such as in announcing that he is going to Palestine in 1931 "for a month and a half," when he actually went for three months (March 1–June 5).

4. Published in *Razsvet (L'Aube)*; "Social-Political and Literary Weekly, Devoted to Jewish Interests," a Zionist-Revisionist (radical right-wing) journal published in Russian in Paris; Editors V. Jabotinsky and M. Berchin. Paris, January 30, 1927.

5. See my interpretation of that painting in *Marc Chagall: Les années russes, 1907–1922*, p. 166.

6. Written in 1927, i.e., counting from 1889, which Chagall often assumed was his birth year.

7. Yiddish: "Good morning." Apparently Pen spoke Yiddish with his pupils (how often?).

8. He means Pen's school, which he left in 1907. Chagall did see Pen again during 1914–1920 in Vitebsk.

9. All the information is drawn from the protocols of the Pedagogical Council of the Imperial School for the Encouragement of the Fine Arts and from the monthly reports on payment of salaries.

10. The teacher Bobrovsky disliked Chagall and criticized him constantly. According to Franz Meyer, when Bobrovsky said Chagall wasn't capable of drawing a knee from a live model, Chagall left the school without even collecting his scholarship. Well, he would have hardly left for a badly painted knee! But in his early, unexpurgated autobiography (see Chapter 2) he quotes Bobrovsky: "What kind of a *behind* do you have?"—referring to his own parts. This adds to several other possible homosexual connotations in his autobiography. The event happened in July 1908; yet the correspondence with Director Roerich concerning Chagall's draft deferment lasted into September.

11. Exemptions are described in S.M. Goryaninov, *Ustavy o voinskoy povinnosti (Regulations on Military Duty)*, St.-Petersburg 1913, 12th ed., paragraph 61. Among them were "persons who completed their studies in artistic-industrial colleges [. . .] who are sent abroad for further studies." Students in secondary and higher-level schools may defer their military service until age twenty-four or twenty-seven, respectively, for purposes of completing their education.

12. Franz Meyer calls him Annenkov (p. 52). Antokolsky is clearly the name of a Jewish dealer, probably the nephew of Marc Antokolsky. As elsewhere, Chagall supplied Meyer with information that looks less Jewish.

13. *The Oxford Companion to Twentieth Century Art*, ed. Harold Osborne, New York: Oxford University Press, 1988, p.39.

14. Excerpts from Y.L. Obolenskaya, "In the School of E.N. Zvantseva, Directed by L.S. Bakst and M.V. Dobuzhinsky (1906–1910)," lecture at the Academy of Art Sciences, Moscow, 1927 (typescript). The author herself was a student during the whole period Bakst directed the school. We selected only a few passages, relevant to Chagall.

15. Published in Russian in *Razsvet*, Paris, Vol. XXVI, No.18, May 4, 1930, with author's note: Chapter of a book to be published by Stock in Paris, in the translation of the artist's wife and André Salmon. Simultaneously, the book will be published by Pieper in Germany.

16. The text between the double asterisks and triple asterisks is similar to the pages in *My Own World*, with various changes.

17. In *My Own World*, it was Bakst who lifted the paintings from the floor.

18. This may be a later "modest" and ironic remark. In 1910, Chagall worked as an assistant to Bakst, preparing the decorations for Chereprin's ballet *Narciss and Echo*.

19. The Italian poet D'Annunzio lived in Paris at the time and was a theater critic. Rumors had it that "no pleasure was alien to him." Indeed Nijinsky was homosexual and the lover of Diaghilev, the director of the Ballets Russes.

20. About Chagall's attempts to exhibit in those places, see Chapter Four.

21. I am most grateful to Mme. Miriam Cendrars for allowing me to read this valuable and hitherto unpublished text.

22. There is a curious feature in Chagall's Russian text. Before the Revolution, Russian spelling had an obligatory "hard sign" (ъ) mandatory after all words ending in hard consonants; this letter indicated no sound, was obviously superfluous, and abolished after the Revolution. Thus, Chagall wrote his uncle's name: Shagalъ (in "The Barber of Lyozno," 1912). Yet, in the "Cendrars Notebook," the hard sign at the end of words is consistently omitted. Was his poetry copied after the Revolution? But Chagall used the old spelling consistently for two other "superfluous" letters: yat' (ѣ) and izhitsa (i), which were abolished after the Revolution. Furthermore, the messy drafts of letters in the same notebook belong to 1910–1911. There can be no doubt that the notebook was written in 1910 and found by Cendrars in Chagall's bedroom in 1914. The only solution to this puzzle seems to be that Chagall, or someone who corrected his spelling in St.-Petersburg, followed the demands of several progressive linguists to abolish the superfluous end-sign. Thus, I.A. Baudouin de Courtenay, the founder of Phonology, omitted this letter in his book *On the Relation of Russian Spelling to the Russian Language* (*Ob otnoshenii russkogo pis'ma k russkomu yazyku*), St.-Petersburg, 1912, and in earlier writings. See V.V. Vinogradov, ed., *Obzor predlozheniy po usovershenstvovaniyu russkoy orfografii (XVIII–XX vv.)*, Moscow: Nauka, 1965, pp. 65, 480.

23. Most poems have dates. They are: Peterburg: twice 09; thrice February 1909; February 14, 09; April 8, 1909; May 10, 09; Vitebsk: thrice June 1909; June 8, 1909; August 6, 09; August 09; thrice September 09; twice September 15, 1909; Lyozno: twice September 09; Vitebsk: October 20, 09; October 24, 09; Peterburg: November 8, 1909; November 15 1909; December 28, 09; Narva-Vitebsk: June 910; Narva: twice July 1910; Peterburg: August 1910. And a long prose poem *Love*, Vitebsk 1909. We may assume that he went to Vitebsk for summer vacations in June–August 1909, returned to St.-Petersburg for school on September 1, fled to Vitebsk and Lyozno in mid-September until late October 1909. Between September 15 and October 24 he was in Vitebsk and on November 8 he was already in St.-Petersburg. In June 1910 he took farewell of his family in Vitebsk, but left for Paris in August or later.

24. I am grateful to Nina Rudnik for this reference.

25. Aleksandr Blok, *Sobraniye Sochineniy v shesti tomakh*, Leningrad, 1980, Vol. 2, p. 55.

26. Published in *Razsvet*, Paris, October 24, 1926.

CHAPTER 4

1. Abram Borisovich Kozlov (Berkovich), born in Ukraine, lived and studied in Paris and exhibited in the Salon d'Automne, left Paris for Russia around 1910 and returned in 1919; later, painted scenes from the Jewish past in Ukraine.

2. Published in *Iskusstvo*, Moscow, 1928, Nos. 3–4.

3. Tugendhold was then twenty-seven years old, Chagall was twenty-three.

4. See Chagall's essay on Bakst, p. 186.

5. A year later he was accepted, but was later rejected again.

6. This letter seems to precede the following one, in which case one of the dates is mistaken, unless they were sent through parallel channels. In any case, it had to be written before the exhibition in February 1912.

7. Less modest pictures were the nudes he painted at that time.

8. Collection of N. V. Ilyin, Frankfurt am Main. Not previously published.

9. This letter seems to be written after the previous one; if so, it was written in early 1912, because the exhibition was in February 1912. Another explanation could be that one was inserted with the paintings, and the dates are correct.

10. An exhibition of works by students of the Zvantseva Art School, April 20–May 9, 1910, on the premises of the Symbolist journal *Apollon*. (See the photo of a contemporary caricature depicting the walls with two paintings by Chagall in Meyer, p. 28.)

11. From *Selected Writings of Blaise Cendrars*, ed. Walter Albert, New York: New Directions, 1966.

12. Ida Chagall, using reliable sources in Russia, identified Sillart as Tugendhold. Published in *Apollon*, May 1914, No. 5, pp. 30–33.

13. The article was written in Paris and published in Russia in *Kiyevskaya Mysl'* May 14, 1914, No. 73.

14. Bernier, George, and Monique Schneider-Manoury, *Robert et Sonia Delaunay*, Paris: J.C. Lattes, 1995, p. 124.

15. Translated from German by Barbara Harshav.

CHAPTER 5

1. During World War I, Chagall participated with many works in several exhibitions. According to Franz Meyer, those were: "The Year 1915" (Moscow, March 1915, twenty-five works); the avant-garde Salon of the Rayonists, "Jack of Diamonds" (Moscow, November 1916, forty-five works); Dobychina's gallery in Petrograd (April 1916, sixty-two works; and November 1916, seventy-three works; 1917, seventy-four works; 1918, thirteen works); the Exhibition of Paintings and Sculpture by Jewish Artists (Moscow 1917, forty-three works).

2. N. Shebueva, "Impressions . . . ," *Obozreniye teatrov*, Petrograd, April 10–11, 1916, Nos. 3066–3067.

3. Published in the newspaper *Russkiye vedomosti*, Moscow, March 29, 1915, No. 71.

4. A Futurist movement in Russian avant-garde painting, founded in 1912 by Laryonov and Goncharova.

5. Exhibition of three artists at the Dobychina gallery in Petrograd, April 3–19, 1916, where Chagall got a room to himself with sixty-two works. Published in the newspaper *Rech'*, April 22, 1916, No. 109.

6. Published in *Literarishe Bleter*, Warsaw, June 9, 1939, No. 16 (779).

7. Chagall exhibited twenty-five works in a Moscow gallery on March 23, 1915.

8. This was written in 1939, when Chagall was close to the Communist line and apparently saw Elyashev's views as not politically correct.

9. Owner of The Art Office (Khudozhestvennoe Byuro), Chagall's gallery in Petrograd during World War I. Dobytshina mounted five large Chagall exhibitions in 1916–1918.

10. Sweden is across the sea from Petrograd.

CHAPTER 6

1. Abram Efros, "Ends without Beginnings (Art in the Revolution)," *Shipovnik*, Moscow, 1922, No. 1, p. 115.

2. During the 1930s, when Bukharin was liquidated by Stalin, the street was ironically renamed after the newspaper he had edited, Pravda (Truth) Street.

3. I prefer the name "college" (for *utshilishtshe*) to the common translation "academy" (*Akademiya*) because the latter may be confused with the "academic" art Chagall opposed. Indeed, *utshilitshche* is a professional college, not an academy.

4. See *Sefer Vitebsk* (*The Book of Vitebsk*, in Hebrew), ed. Barukh Karu, Tel Aviv: Organization of Immigrants from Vitebsk in Israel, 1957, especially pp. 306–307. Also the Vishnyak family tree, written by Jesse Cherry, courtesy of Naomi Schiff of Oakland, California.

5. On Chagall's views on the nature of Revolutionary Art and the relationship between Revolutionary Art and the political revolution, see his published programmatic essays (English translation in *Marc Chagall on Art and Culture*). In the present volume, we include only those articles that contain concrete descriptions of Chagall personally and the school's activities in his time.

6. *News [Izvestiya] of the Vitebsk Province Soviet of Peasant, Workers, Red Soldiers, and Farm Laborers' Delegates*, August 23, 1918, No. 178.

7. *News [Izvestiya] of the Vitebsk Province Soviet of Peasant, Workers, Red Soldiers, and Farm Laborers' Delegates*, September 20, 1918, No. 202.

8. *Vitebsky Listok*, September 26, 1918, No. 988.

9. *Vitebsky Listok*, October 8, 1918, No. 1000.

10. Article by Grebenik, member of the editorial board, published in *News [Izvestiya] of the Vitebsk Province Soviet of Peasant, Workers, Red Soldiers, and Farm Laborers' Delegates*, October 19, 1918, No. 226.

11. Ya. Tugendhold, *The Art of the October Epoch*, 1930, pp. 17–18.

12. *Vitebsky Listok*, October 22, 1918, No. 1014.

13. *Vitebsky Listok*, October 28, 1918, No. 1020.

14. *Vitebsky Listok*, November 2, 1918, No. 1025.

15. The weekly *K oruzhyu* (*To arms!*), Organ of the Vitebsk Military Commissariat, November 11, 1918, No. 6.

16. Published in *Vitebsky Listok*, November 16, 1918, No. 1038. The article is unsigned, but as suggested by A. Shatskikh, its content and style indicate Chagall's authorship.

17. *Vitebsky Listok*, November 22, 1918, No. 1044.

18. *News [Izvestiya] of the Vitebsk Province Soviet of Peasant, Workers, Red Soldiers, and Farm Laborers' Delegates*, December 5, 1918, No. 264.

19. *Vitebsky Listok*, November 7, 1918, No. 1030. English translation in *Marc Chagall on Art and Culture*.

20. *Vitebsky Listok*, December 8, 1918, No. 1959.

21. *Vitebsky Listok*, December 9, 1918, No. 1961.

22. A similar address-and-debate was scheduled again in February; see *Vitebsky Listok*, February 6, 1919, No. 1120.

23. Written during Chagall's official voyage to Petrograd and Moscow and published in *Iskusstvo komuny* (*Art of the Commune*), Petrograd, December 23, 1918, No. 3.

24. It is not clear what caused the cancellation of Chagall's address-and-debate planned for December 7, 1919. See the documents preceding this article.

25. Written on a calling card in the new Soviet spelling. OR GRM, Moscow, f. 115, unit 338, p. 1. Not previously published.

26. *Vitebsky Listok*, January 8, 1919, No. 1091, p. 1. The article was written after Chagall's return from Petrograd and Moscow.

27. Yu. P. Annenkov, a prominent graphic artist, did not go to Vitebsk, in spite of his initial promise to Chagall.

28. The Winter Palace of the Tsar in St.-Petersburg. In 1917, it was the seat of Kerensky's government in Petrograd; its conquest signaled the victory of the Bolsheviks.

29. According to an announcement in the *News* of January 3, 1919, No. 2, registration has opened to four classes of the Art College: Radlov—drawing; Chagall—painting; Tilberg—sculpture; Lyubavina—preparatory class. Radlov apparently never came to Vitebsk.

30. Published in the section "Orders of the Local Government" in *News [Izvestiya] of the Vitebsk Province Soviet of Peasant, Workers, Red Soldiers, and Farm Laborers' Delegates*, January 16, 1919, No. 11.

31. G. Grilin, *Vitebsky Listok*, January 30, 1919, No. 1113.

32. Published in the section "Orders of the Local Government" in News *[Izvestiya] of the Vitebsk Province Soviet of Peasant, Workers, Red Soldiers, and Farm Laborers' Delegates*, January 31, 1919, No. 23.

33. This resolution has provoked a sharp open letter by the Society in the Name of Y.L. Peretz (devoted to Yiddish secular culture), accusing the Subdivision of artistic dictatorship, and a rebuttal by Ivan Punyi in the name of the Collegium of Graphic Arts.

34. *News [Izvestiya] of the Vitebsk Province Soviet of Peasant, Workers, Red Soldiers, and Farm Laborers' Delegates*, February 6, 1919, No. 28.

35. *News [Izvestiya] of the Vitebsk Province Soviet of Peasant, Workers, Red Soldiers, and Farm Laborers' Delegates*, March 6, 1919, No. 52.

36. *News [Izvestiya] of the Vitebsk Province Soviet of Peasant, Workers, Red Soldiers, and Farm Laborers' Delegates*, March 9, 1919, No. 55.

37. *News [Izvestiya] of the Vitebsk Province Soviet of Peasant, Workers, Red Soldiers, and Farm Laborers' Delegates*, April 16, 1919, No. 84.

38. *News [Izvestiya] of the Vitebsk Province Soviet of Peasant, Workers, Red Soldiers, and Farm Laborers' Delegates*, April 24, 1919, No. 88.

39. *Vitebsky Listok*, May 10, 1919, No. 1209.

40. *News [Izvestiya] of the Vitebsk Province Soviet of Peasant, Workers, Red Soldiers, and Farm Laborers' Delegates*, June 29, 1919, No. 139 (192).

41. *News [Izvestiya] of the Vitebsk Province Soviet of Peasant, Workers, Red Soldiers, and Farm Laborers' Delegates*, July 31, 1919, No. 169.

42. Written in July 1919, summarizing the first academic year of the school. Published in *Shkola i revolutsiya* (School and Revolution), Vitebsk, 1919, Nos. 24–25, the last issue of a weekly jointly published by the Executive Committee of Vitebsk Province and City, the Soviet of Student Deputies, and the Committee of the City Union of Socialist Students.

43. This exhibition was open between June 28 and July 20, 1919, in the building of the Art College. The best works were included in the museum of the school.

44. See Aleksandra Shatskikh, "Marc Chagall and Kazimir Malevich" in *Chagallovskiye Dni v Vitebske*, special issue of *Vitbichi*, July 1992, nos. 3–5.

45. *News [Izvestiya] of the Vitebsk Province Soviet of Peasant, Workers, Red Soldiers, and Farm Laborers' Delegates*, September 19, 1919, No. 210.

46. Twenty-five of Chagall's letters to Ettinger were published in Russian by A.S. Shatskikh, "Marc Chagall's Letters to Pavel Ettinger (1920–1948)," *Soobshcheniya Gosudarstvennogo Muzeya Izobrazitelnykh Iskusstv im. A.S. Pushkina*, No. 6, Moscow: Sovietsky Khudozhnik, 1980, pp. 191–218.

47. About sixty works done in 1914–1915, after Chagall's return from Paris, mostly oil on paper or cardboard, depicting family members, neighbors, relatives, landscapes, and scenes of daily life, which Chagall subsequently called "documents."

48. The chronicle in the Vitebsk journal *Shkola i revolutsiya* (School and Revolution), 1919, Nos. 24–25, mentions 600 registered students, but only 300 attending.

49. The first was held at the end of the first academic year, June 28–July 20, 1919, and the second, in December 1919. The First State Exhibition of Local and Moscow Artists in Vitebsk included some major artists from the capitals (Kandinsky, Malevich, Falk, etc.), yet half of the forty-one participants were students in Chagall's school.

50. Perhaps a one-act play by Calderon.

51. Never materialized.

52. In August 1919, the idea of a local museum was realized; throughout 1919 and 1920, paintings by major masters, such as Falk, Malevich, Chagall, Pen, Yudovin, Goncharova, Laryonov, and Kandinsky, were received from the Central Museum Foundation in Moscow.

53. They weren't on speaking terms, because El Lissitzky had been a self-declared follower of Chagall and became a renegade, having switched over to Malevich's Suprematism.

54. The International Art Office at the Division for Graphic Arts of the People's Commissariat of Enlightenment (Narkompros). On July 14, 1919, Chagall asked the Bureau to protect his art works that remained in Berlin and Amsterdam. On August 12, the Bureau

responded, explaining that it took measures to protect Chagall's art through the German Soviet of Workers' Deputies in Moscow and their representative in Berlin Ludwig Baer.

55. K. Malevich, *On New Systems in Art*, Vitebsk, 1919.

CHAPTER 7

1. See my study and the translations of "Texts and Documents" in the Guggenheim Museum catalogue, *Marc Chagall and the Jewish Theater* (1992).

2. Max Reinhardt (1873–1943) was one of the pillars of the modern German theater.

3. Excerpt from "The Artists of Granovsky's Theater," *Iskusstvo*, 1928, Vol. 4, books 1–2, p. 74. English translation by Benjamin and Barbara Harshav in: *Marc Chagall and the Jewish Theater*, p. 153.

4. Written on the Yiddish Theater's tour of Western Europe. Published in *Di Yidishe Velt: Monthly for Literature, Criticism, Art, and Culture*, Vilna: Kletskin, May 1928, No. 2. The published Yiddish text is translated from Russian, but the original is lost.

5. Chagall bought something called "Dutch sheets," which he sewed together; he painted his murals on them.

6. The invitation could not have come before the government decision to move the theater to the new capital, Moscow, in the summer of 1920. Yet Chagall repeatedly mentions 1918 as the date of this invitation.

7. Some scholars assume that Chagall painted the ceiling as well, but there is no evidence for it in this description or in the description of his theater murals in his resumé of 1921. It was apparently confused with the long frieze, just under the ceiling.

8. In the original: "I couldn't not go"—clearly a mistake.

9. Aleksey D. Diky (1889–1955) was a well-known Soviet theater director. In Chagall's time, he worked in the First Studio of Stanislavsky's theater MKhAT (Moscow Art Theater).

10. A hall for public events, where F.T. Marinetti lectured when he visited Russia in 1914.

11. See "In Memory of My Friend Baal-Makhshoves" in Chapter 3.

12. IZO NKP is Division of Graphic Arts, People's Commissariat of Enlightenment; at the time, it was headed by the artist David Shterenberg.

13. Published in the official Yiddish newspaper *Der Emes* (*The Truth*), Moscow, September 16, 1921.

14. Twenty-five years since Pen founded his art school in Vitebsk.

15. Typescript in the Vitebsk Province State Archives, f. 1947, op.1, d.47, 1.320 (original was not preserved). It was published in an abbreviated and edited version: "An Artist-Laborer (On the 25th anniversary of Yu. M. Pen's artistic activity): Article and regards from Marc Chagall," *Vechernaya Gazeta*, Vitebsk, September 24, 1921, No. 18, p. 4.

16. See review by A. Romm, "The Anniversary Exhibition of Yu. M. Pen," *Izvestiya Vitebskogo Soveta Rabochikh, Krestianskikh i Krasnoarmeyskikh Deputatov*, Vitebsk, September 7, 1921, No. 202, p. 4.

17. Ettinger had good connections with the relevant authorities, or so Chagall thought.

18. A literal translation of a Yiddish expression, meaning busy and confused.

19. Chagall's wife and daughter joined him several months later.

CHAPTER 8

1. See *Royter Shtern* (Red Star), Vitebsk, January 1923, No. 11, p. 13.

2. On Chagall in Berlin, see Werner Schmidt, "Chagall und Berlin" in *Berliner Begegnungen: Ausländische Künstler in Berlin 1918 bis 1933*, Berlin: Dietz, 1987, pp. 272–275.

3. Published in the newspaper *Otkliki*, Vitebsk June 24, 1922, No. 12, p. 3. The original has not been preserved.

4. Chagall's portrait of Pen was given to Pen as a gift and used to hang in his workshop. Its traces disappeared after Pen was murdered; a copy is reproduced in Franz Meyer, *Marc Chagall: Life and Work*, New York: Abrams, 1962, Classified Cat., 276.

5. Perhaps under Chagall's influence, Pen published autobiographical essays in the Minsk Yiddish journal *Shtern*: "The *Heder*-years: Memoirs of an Artist," *Shtern*, Minsk, 1926, Nos. 2–3; "Memoirs of an Artist," *Shtern*, 1926, No. 4 (signed Yehuda Pen), reprinted in *Vitebsk Amol*, New York, 1956, pp. 363–390. In interviews with A. Shatskikh, Pen's pupils, in particular the architect M.M. Lerman, told of Pen's extensive memoirs, which they had read in the 1930s in Vitebsk. If those went beyond the published chapters, their whereabouts are unknown.

6. "With the Jewish Artists in Vitebsk," *Royter Shtern*, Vitebsk, January 1923, No. 11, p. 13. The same section had an article on Y.M. Pen and on the artist Sh. Yudovin.

CHAPTER 9

1. Chagall addressed his friend as "Opatoshy," as pronounced in the writer's Polish Yiddish dialect (here we restored the correct spelling). His close friends also called him by his nickname, "Oppen."

2. Published in *L'Art vivant*, December 15, 1927, 3, No. 72, pp. 999–1011. The first part of the article, omitted here, is a discussion of Chagall's art by Jacques Guenne. We include here the interview itself.

3. Typical of Chagall, confusing dates: The invitation to work for the Yiddish Theater came in 1920, as the theater was preparing to move from St.-Petersburg to Moscow in November of that year.

4. The full name was The Yiddish Chamber Theater, founded in Petrograd in June 1919. Typically, Chagall obfuscates its Jewishness.

5. HaBimah was a Hebrew theater founded in Soviet Moscow in 1917. It went on a tour in Western Europe in 1926.

6. Gustave Coquiot bought the canvases from Blaise Cendrars, who saved them from Chagall's room in La Ruche, which Chagall had closed with a piece of string before leaving for Berlin in June 1914.

7. The second Exhibition of Independent Artists and Engravers, Barbazanges-Hodebert Gallery, Paris, 1924.

8. Chagall worked on the illustrations during 1923–1925; he produced ninety-six full-page illustrations, eleven inserts, and eleven end-engravings. The book did not appear in Vollard's lifetime.

9. In the nineteenth century, only parts of the book were published in French; the first complete translation, by Henri Mongault, was published in Paris in 1925.

10. *L'Album des peintres-graveurs* (Album 3), Paris: Vollard, 1924. Not published.

11. In Berlin, Chagall produced thirty etchings, over thirty lithographs, and five engravings on wood. Twenty etchings were published in *My Life*.

12. Fifty works exhibited at Gallery Le Centaure, Brussels, March 22–April 2, 1924.

13. Abraham Walt (A. Lyesin), *Lider un Poemen (1888–1938) (Poems and Long Poems)*, New York: Forverts Association, 1938, three volumes, with thirty-four drawings by Marc Chagall.

14. H.D. Nomberg (1887–1935), a Yiddish writer, lived in Berlin at the same time as Chagall.

15. Sholem Asch (1880–1957) was a prominent Yiddish novelist.

16. Y. A. Leyzerovich (1883–1927) was a Yiddish writer and journalist who lived in Paris from 1923.

17. Only twenty engravings were published.

18. Not so fast! The French translation was published only in 1931. André Salmon, Chagall's old friend who tried his hand at it, concluded that Chagall's Russian was not Russian and the thing was untranslatable. Whether or not there was a German translation is unknown.

19. "The Work of Marc Chagall 1908–1924," Gallery Barbazanges-Hodebert, Paris, December 17–30, where Pierre Matisse, who worked there, first met Chagall.

20. As usual, Chagall exaggerates the dates; he left Paris in June 1914 and returned in September 1923—nine years.

21. *L'Art d'aujourd'hui, Fascicule d'hiver*, Paris: Albert Morancé, 1924. This publisher produced 105 deluxe issues, including Christian Zervos, "Marc Chagall," and Chagall's etching, "Bare Woman with Fan."

22. The International Exhibition of Artistic-Decorative Arts opened on April 28, 1925 in Paris, including a Soviet-built pavillion.

23. Chagall managed to get his paintings out of Russia in 1922; but he could not take his large murals, which were still hanging in the theater studio. They were left with the theater by default, though they were never paid for.

24. It was, nevertheless, published in two columns, as the normal *Di Tsukunft* layout.

25. The Society of Independent Artist-Engravers included many prominent artists of the Paris School and French masters, such as Ottakar Kubin, Duffrense, Dufy, Marie Laurencin, Pascin, Picasso, Segonzac, and Vlaminck.

26. Made for the opening of the Moscow Yiddish Chamber Theater on January 1, 1921. Chagall hoped somehow to get them out of Russia, but to no avail.

27. *Catalogue des Tableaux Modernes, composants la collection de Mme X...*, (A Catalogue of Modern Paintings including the collection of Mrs. X), Paris: Hotel Drouot, March 12, 1928.

28. The braces are in the manuscript; they indicate dates inserted in pencil by another hand, perhaps Adele Opatoshu's. These dates are usually very reliable. Whenever Chagall does write a date, it is in the European manner: day followed by month; whereas here it is mostly (not always) the other way around, in the American fashion, i.e., month followed by day. Roman numerals, however, always indicate the month (as in this case).

29. Yosef Opatoshu's nickname.

30. Opatoshu was a journalist on the New York Yiddish daily *Der Tog*.

31. The Reinhardt Gallery in New York held a Chagall exhibition, including 110 works,

January 9–30, 1926. An illustrated catalogue was published with a preface by the curator Christian Brinton. This exhibition is mentioned in several of the letters that follow.

32. The journal edited by Lyesin is in Yiddish, but Chagall addresses him in the language of high "culture," Russian.

33. Here and elsewhere, Chagall spells the name of the New York Reinhardt gallery in the Russian manner, substituting G for H, and often skipping the final *t*.

34. For the book, Marcel Arland, *Maternité*, Paris: Au Sans-Pareil, 1926, with five engravings by Chagall.

35. He means Marcel Arland and spells the last name the Russian way: Orlan. See the previous letter, dated 21/X/25.

36. Samuel Margolin (1893–1953), a theater director and critic, wrote reviews of the Moscow Yiddish and Hebrew theaters and the brochure *Chronicle of HaBima* for its European tour. HaBimah went on to the U.S. and Palestine, but several members returned to Russia, among them Margolin, who carried Chagall's letter.

37. The engravings are now in GMII, the State Museum of Fine Arts in Moscow.

38. Jean Giraudoux et al., *Les sept péchés capitaux*, Paris: Simon Kra, 1926. Includes fifteen etchings by Chagall.

39. Nouvelle Revue Française in Chagall's French spelling. It apparently never materialized.

40. The exhibitions were: (1) "30 Canvases by Marc Chagall," Paris, Gallery of Katia Granoff, June 14–July 5, 1926; (2) "Marc Chagall: Summer Works," same gallery, November 22–December 11, 1926.

41. Benois, then Director of the Hermitage Gallery in Leningrad, left the Soviet Union on a trip to Paris in 1926 and settled there. Yet unlike Chagall, he could go back on a visit.

42. Chagall doesn't understand that he was "unmentionable" in the Soviet Union. Yet it is also true that the Russian émigrés in Paris did not see Chagall as a Russian artist.

43. A series of nineteen gouaches, later called "Vollard's Circus," 1927.

44. Marcel Arland, *Maternité*, Paris: Au Sans-Pareil, 1926. Bibliophile edition. Includes five engravings by Chagall.

45. Opatoshu went to his home town Mlava (Mława) in Poland and to the Soviet Union in September 1928. On his way back, he stopped in Paris.

46. *Humash (Pentateuch)*, New York: Tanach, 1926, two volumes. Volume 1 includes the first two books of the Bible, which Chagall used for his engravings of 1930–1931. Subsequent volumes were published in 1927, 1929, and 1936. Later, Opatoshu sent him additional volumes.

47. Affectionate, "vocative" form of the name.

48. Henri Serouya was a French philosopher, born in Palestine, who went to America. Chagall recommended him to Lyesin in a letter of November 3, 1928 (not included in this book).

49. In matters of poetry, the modern artist Chagall was a generation behind. He felt, apparently, that Lyesin was not a modernist, but succumbed to the masterful "Russian" meters and sentimental charm of Lyesin's verse, which abounds in narrative poems from all periods of Jewish history and martyrdom, as well as nostalgic poems about the "old home" in Eastern Europe.

50. A prestigious literary newspaper of worldwide Yiddish literature, published in Warsaw during 1924–1939. He refers to the long poem *A Letter From America to a Distant Friend* (1927), *Complete Works by H. Leivick*, Vol. I (*Ale Verk*), New York: H. Leivick Jubilee Committee, 1940, p. 383–396.

51. In Chagall's folk-mind, it is a case of considering the Jews as undignified prey. Specifically, he has in mind his attempts in Berlin in 1923 to sue Herwarth Walden and recover the paintings he had left with Walden in 1914.

52. Avrom Vevyurka was a Soviet Yiddish literary critic; in 1921, he praised Chagall's style in the work he did for the Yiddish Chamber Theater in Moscow.

53. *Sélection*, No. 6, Antwerpen (April 1929): Special Chagall issue, 152 pp.

CHAPTER 10

1. See *Marc Chagall on Art and Culture*.

2. The text of Chagall's address is published in *Marc Chagall on Art and Culture*.

3. Written for the YIVO Conference of 1929, published in Yiddish in *Journal for Jewish Art*, published by the Art Museum of the Jewish Scientific Institute, Vilna: YIVO, No. 1, November–December, 1936.

4. A person with a stoic attitude, not easily excitable, accepting reality as it comes.

5. The exhibition "Chagall's La Fontaine," Gallery Bernheim Jeune, Paris, February 10–21, 1930. Vollard's introduction: "I publish LaFontaine's *Fables* and select Chagall as the illustrator."

6. This excerpt of a letter, as well as most information on Rebay, is from Joan M. Lukach, *Hilla Rebay: In Search of the Spirit in Art*, New York: George Braziller, 1983.

7. Published in *Di Tsukunft* (*The Future*), vol. XL, May 1935, No. 5, pp. 282–283.

8. H. Ostwald, *Das Liebermann-Buch*, Berlin 1930, p. 218. I thank Walter Cahn for this anecdote.

9. In 1921–1922 Chagall lived and taught in a Jewish orphanage in Malakhovka near Moscow.

10. Apparently someone's retelling of the stories.

11. Chagall is apologetic and aggressive, but the Jewish cultural establishment in Yiddish, wandering around the globe, was quite poor and lost most of the rich and the young to assimilation into the major cultures.

12. *Di Tentserin—The [woman] Dancer / Around Grand Street / A Novel / A Piece of Jewish Life in the Years 1910–1911* (in Yiddish), Vilna: B. Kletskin, 1930.

CHAPTER 11

1. See Tami Katz-Freiman, "Founding the Tel Aviv Museum, 1930–1936," *Tel Aviv Museum Annual Review*, January 1982, pp. 9–48.

2. Interview with Neta Weinstein, *Doar HaYom*, Jerusalem, March 15, 1931 (Vol. XIII, No. 134).

3. At that time, "Palestinians" were the Jews who carried (British) "Palestinian" passports. They called the land "Palestine" (as well as A"I = Eretz-Israel), and the local Arabs were simply called "Arabs."

4. See p. 351.

5. Allusion to his political troubles as commissar of art in Vitebsk.

6. See below, p. 375, "Chagall on Palestine: An Interview in Paris with Ben-Tavriya."

7. Hermann Struck (1876–1944) played a crucial role in Chagall's development as an artist (in Berlin, 1922–1923) and was his natural ally in matters of the proposed Tel Aviv Museum.

8. "Our Teacher Moses," an affectionate epithet of the biblical Moses.

9. In Russian, *Komandirovka*, a document sending a person on some official business. Here he means: to the West.

10. The exhibition was realized only in 1935.

11. Namely, Chagall, Fleg, and Orloff.

12. This echoes the slogan, "For a Revolutionary Society—a Revolutionary Art," launched by Chagall in Soviet Vitebsk.

13. Indeed Chagall, Fleg, and Bialik traveled together on the ship *Champollion* from Marseille to Beirut, and by train to Palestine.

14. Sholem Asch (1880–1957) was fifty years old.

15. "Paintings by Chagall," Demotte Gallery, New York, November 10–December 6, 1930; seven paintings and twenty watercolors.

16. The essay "On Modern Art" was published in Hebrew; see the English translation in *Marc Chagall on Art and Culture*.

17. There were several Aronsons in Chagall's orbit. This may be Khil Aronson.

18. The Chagalls went on a trip to Palestine for three months, from March 1 to June 4; The figure "1 1/2" is a Chagallian figure of speech.

19. In a letter to a Soviet addressee, he would not mention the "Colonialist" and "Zionist" country, Palestine.

20. The first book publication of Chagall's memoirs, translated by Bella Chagall, *Ma vie*, Paris: Librairie Stock, 1931.

21. Aleksandr Benois, "Book Illustrations" (in Russian), published in the Paris Russian newspaper *Posledniye novosti*; republished in the book *Aleksandr Benois Reflects*, Moscow, 1968.

22. Here, Chagall dates his real beginning as an artist at 1907, when he decided that he had gotten enough from Pen and left his school for St.-Petersburg. His lucky number was 7, he was presumably born on 7/7/87, and it was also the date of the October Revolution (November 7, 1917). Yet later, he saw his beginning as an artist in 1908, when he painted the "Dead Man."

23. Speech by Marc Chagall at a Reception of the Hebrew Writers Union for the French Jewish poet Edmond Fleg, the Hungarian Hebrew writer Yoseph Patai, and Marc Chagall in Tel Aviv. Published in *Moznayim* 48 (98), April 16, 1931. Chagall's response in Yiddish is preserved only in this Hebrew publication.

24. Der Tunkeler (The Dark One), pseudonym of Yosef Tunkel (1881–1949), was a well-known Warsaw Yiddish journalist. The allusion is not clear.

25. Published in *Razsvet*, Vol. XXVII, No. 24, Paris, June 14, 1931. The journalist's opening and impressions of Chagall's home and environment have been omitted.

26. The date in the letter is "1921"—clearly a mistake.

27. Chagall's personal letter to Ben-Yishay was published in Hebrew, accompanied by a long reply from Mayor Dizengoff, both in the Jerusalem newspaper *Doar HaYom*,

September 11, 1931, and the literary-cultural weekly *Ktuvim* in Tel Aviv, No.38-9 (28-9), September 11, 1931. Dizengoff's reply was also published in Russian in *Razsvet* in Paris, November 1, 1931, with a new reply by Chagall.

28. *Razsvet*, Vol, XXVII, No. 44, Paris, November 1, 1931.

29. Standard Yiddish: *mónefshekh*, from Ashkenazi Aramaic: *mimo nafshekho*, meaning "either/or, make up your mind." Since England is near Paris, "it" should invite him.

30. March 12–April 3, 1932.

31. A group exhibition with Derain, Kissling, and others, January 20–February 15, 1932.

32. It did not materialize.

33. The same day, he wrote similar letters to Paul Ettinger in Moscow and Leo Kenig in London.

34. "Kosher le-Pesakh" (Kosher for Passover) is the Hebrew label on rabbinically certified wine and food for Passover, as Chagall used it on his fresco for the Moscow Theater murals. What Chagall means here is Passover greetings ("Have a kosher Pesakh").

35. A Zionist ideal, as opposed to what was perceived as the parasitic and unproductive Diaspora life.

36. He refers apparently to the book *A Day in Regensburg* (New York: E. Malino, 1933), with Chagall's drawing.

37. Because he won't get the daily newspapers.

CHAPTER 12

1. The original date is 1923, obviously a mistake.

2. *A tog in Regenspurg un Eliyohu Bokher (A Day in Regensburg and Elija Levitas)*, New York: E. Malino, 1933. Deluxe edition printed on parchment in 100 numbered copies. Drawing by Marc Chagall.

3. He means: bibliophile.

4. Kunsthalle, Basel, Switzerland, November 4–December 3, 1933; 172 works.

5. Ida was eighteen years old at the time.

6. *Di Tsukunft* was founded in 1892 and is published to this day. Chagall refers to twenty years of Lyesin's editorship, which started in 1913.

7. Published in Hebrew on the 25th anniversary of the founding of the first Jewish city, 1909–1934, in *Yediyot Iriyat Tel-Aviv (Tel Aviv City Hall News)*, edited by A.Z. Ben-Yishay. Here translated from the manuscript.

8. Not available. He probably never wrote it.

9. Opatoshu published his first story in 1910.

10. In Bella's handwriting, found in the historical archives of the city of Tel Aviv.

11. A Yiddish phrase within the Russian text.

12. A *minyan* (=ten) is the minimal number of Jews required for prayer in public.

13. A Yiddish phrase within the Russian text.

14. See Chapter 10. Chagall's programmatic speech of 1935 is published in *Marc Chagall on Art and Culture*.

15. Wilno was the Polish name of Vilna; today: Vilnius, capital of Lithuania.

16. The letter of Dr. Karl Schwarz of June 24, 1935. Not in this collection.

17. "Peintres instinctifs. Naissance de l'Expressionisme," Paris, Gallerie Beaux-Arts et Gazette des Beaux-Arts, December 1935–January 1936; thirty-four works.

18. In 1927, Chagall sent a series of his illustrations for *Dead Souls* to the State Tretyakov Gallery, with an inscription: "A gift for the Tretyakov Gallery, with all my love of a Russian artist for his homeland, this series of 96 engravings I made in 1923–925 for Gogol's *Dead Souls*, for the publisher Ambroise Vollard in Paris. Paris 1927 Marc Chagall."

19. Published in *Heftn far Yidisher Kunst* (*Journal for Jewish Art*), Vilna: YIVO, No. 1, November–December 1936. Dr. Otto Schneid was appointed Scientific Secretary of the Art Commission at the YIVO in Vilna and editor of the new *Journal for Jewish Art*.

20. This idea was later developed in Chagall's poem "My Land," written on his first visit to Europe after World War II in June 1946. See below, p. 583.

21. Published in *Heftn far Yidisher Kunst* (*Journal for Jewish Art*), Vilna: YIVO, No. 1, November–December 1936.

22. As usual, Chagall announces something before it is finished, or continues working on it after the closure. The published poem contains a section on the death of Yury Pen, who was murdered on March 1, 1937, thus it could not have been finished in 1936.

23. Published for the first time in *Shagalovskiye dni v Vitebske* (*Chagall Days in Vitebsk*), supplement to the weekly *Vitebsky Kurier*, Vitebsk, July 3, 1992, No. 2, p. 2.

24. According to a Byelorussian scholar, there has been no decisive solution to the crime; see Alexander Lukashuk, "Who Killed the Artist Pen?" *Starozhil*, Vitebsk, 1990, No. 2, pp. 4–5. Yet a lack of documentary evidence for that period, when most witnesses were liquidated, can be no argument, and no other explanation was offered.

25. Published in the Yiddish journal *Oktyabr*, Minsk, March 1937; Byelorussian translation in *Zvyazda*, Minsk, April 5, 1937. A Russian translation in *Shagalovskiye dni v Vitebske*, supplement to the newspaper *Vit'bitski*, Vitebsk, July 3–5, 1992, p. 5.

26. On May 21, 1937, Dr. K. Schwarz answered this letter: "Obviously, the Museum will organize the exhibition by itself. The Museum assumes all expenses, shipping, publicity, catalogue, advertising posters."

27. Chagall's paintings were exhibited in the Jewish Pavilion of the International Exhibition in Paris 1937.

28. This poem was published in Yiddish in two journals simultaneously: *Di Tsukunft*, Vol. XVI, No. 12, New York, December 1937; and *Literarishe bleter*, No. 9, Warsaw, February 25, 1938. Chagall's manuscript of the *Tsukunft* version is in the YIVO; the order of the strophes, however, is confused. We have used the New York manuscript and printed text but restored the order of the stanzas according to the Warsaw version. In the New York *Zamlbikher* (edited by H. Leyvik and Chagall's friend Opatoshu), No. 5 (1943), Chagall published several separate sections (but not the whole poem) with titles like "My Father," "My Mother," etc., later reprinted in *Di Goldene Keyt*, Tel Aviv, No. 60, and translated as separate poems into French and other languages.

29. Yehuda Pen, founder of the Vitebsk school of Jewish painters, was murdered in his home in Vitebsk on March 1, 1937, apparently by the secret police (which Chagall may not have known at the time). Hence, at least this part was added in 1937.

30. No. of Decree 2637534.

31. The letter is preserved in Documentation du MNAM—CCI, Musée national d'Art moderne, Centre Georges Pompidou, Paris.

32. Chagall's last name was really Shagal. But the problem lies in official Russian documents. In the family birth certificate, it appears as Shagalov, and the first name was always Moses (in Russian: Movsha or Moysey), while Marc is his private invention. In the letter of September 20, 1908, from the Russian Ministry of the Interior, the name is registered as "Moysey (Movsha) Shagal (Shagalov)." Chagall preferred a less obviously Jewish name. (See the discussion of his names in Chapter 1, p. 63.)

33. *Zamlbikher*, Vol. 2, January 1937.

34. International exhibition, "Art and Technology in Contemporary Life," Paris, May 24–November 23, 1937.

35. Picasso's "Guernica" was painted for the Paris Exhibition.

36. "Chagall's Gouaches," Paris, Gallerie Renou et Colle, October 26–November 13, 1937.

37. See *Ershter Alveltlekher Yidisher Kultur-Kongres (First World Yiddish Culture Congress), Paris 17–21 Sept. 1937: Stenographic Report*, Paris: Central Board of the World Yiddish Culture Alliance (YIKUF) Paris–New York–Warsaw, 1937, 372 pp.

38. Delegates came from the United States, Poland, Lithuania, France, England, Austria, Belgium, Estonia, Latvia, Romania, Palestine, Denmark, Czechoslovakia, the Netherlands, Switzerland, Canada, Italy, Argentina, Uruguay, Brazil, South Africa, Mexico, and Cuba.

39. Characteristically, organizations dominated by the Socialist Bund, such as the YIVO in Vilna or the Yiddish school organization CYShO in Warsaw, did not officially participate, for, as Opatoshu put it, the Bund did not believe in a Jewish world nation; in that sense, the Communists were closer to the nationalists. Of course, most Zionist organizations were pro-Hebrew and would not openly support Yiddish culture, yet there were at the conference many individual Zionists as well as a delegation from the Yiddish-oriented Left Labor Zionists in Palestine.

40. Yoseph Opatoshu, "The Great Competition" (from a speech held in New York and other cities about the Cultural Congress and YIKUF)," *Literarishe bleter*, No. 26 (737), June 24, 1938, pp. 431–433.

41. That would be 1923 in Berlin, when he intended to finish it, but Cassirer waited in vain and published the illustration only.

42. "A Conversation with Yoseph Opatoshu" (in Yiddish), *Literarishe bleter*, No. 39–40, October 21, 1938, pp. 640–642.

43. He probably refers to "The White Crucifixion," which responds to the Nazi Kristallnacht of November 1938.

44. A. Lyesin died in 1938 at the age of sixty-six, and his poetry was published posthumously in 1938 in three volumes by the Forward Association, the publisher of both the daily *Forverts* and Lyesin's literary journal, *Di Tsukunft*.

45. Editorial Secretary of *Di Tsukunft*.

CHAPTER 13

1. Meyer, *Marc Chagall*, p. 431.

2. Daniel Charny, *Family Chronicle: Memoirs, Part I: Childhood Years, 1888–1901* (in Yiddish), Vilna: B. Kletskin, 1927.

3. Letter of May 31, 1983, to Cynthia Jaffee MacCabe, curator of the Hirshhorn Museum in Washington, D.C. (reproduced by courtesy of the U.S. Holocaust Memorial Museum Archives).

4. This account is based on archival material at the Rare Books and Manuscripts Library of Columbia University, the archives of the YIVO and MOMA in New York, the Solomon R. Guggenheim Museum, and the U.S. Holocaust Memorial Museum in Washington, D.C., as well as material received from Professor Walter Meyerhof, Elizabeth Berman, Annette Fry, and interviews with Michel Rapaport-Gordey, Dina Glance, and Lillian Opatoshu.

5. For example, Ezra Korman, poet and editor of a landmark historical anthology of Yiddish women poets, collected $100 in Detroit: two persons contributed $1.00, five persons $2.00, twelve persons $5.00, the "Sholem Aleichem Reading Circle" $10.00, and so on.

6. Letter of the Fund for Jewish Refugee Writers, signed by Sholem Asch, Hon. Chairman, on November 5, 1942, to Judge Matthew M. Levy, Bronx, New York.

7. Interview with Lillian Opatoshu, daughter of Aaron Weinberg, New York, January 1998.

8. The letter was written while the Chagalls were still in Marseille.

9. See *International Herald Tribune*, May 24–25, 1986.

10. This list of persons processed by the American Relief Center in Marseille (*Liste Complète des Clients du Centre Américain de Secour*, 2nd list) contains over 2000 names in alphabetical order, sometimes mentioning the spouse in the same entry (e.g., "Rapaport, Michel and Ida"). Not all of them went through, but on the other hand, many persons whose passage was facilitated by Fry's people (such as Heinrich Mann or Franz Werfel) are not mentioned in the list. Thus, if we include family members, the total may reach 4000 or 5000 individuals.

11. See Varian Fry, *Surrender on Demand*, New York: Random House, 1945, and the archive of his manuscripts at Columbia University. An exhibition of Fry's mission was held in the Holocaust Museum in Washington, D.C., and the Jewish Museum in New York.

12. See *New York Times*, July 17, 1935.

13. Michel Rapaport-Gordey, in an interview with Benjamin Harshav in February 1998, also thought that Chagall hesitated. He probably both wished to get out and was afraid to go at the same time.

14. The American Federation of Labor sent Dr. Frank Bohn with long lists of European labor leaders to be rescued.

15. Fry, *Surrender on Demand*, p. 219.

16. Fry, op. cit., p. 101.

17. Sidney Alexander quotes André Chastel who mentioned only 800 pounds; see Sidney Alexander, *Marc Chagall: An Intimate Biography*, New York: Paragon House, 1978; paperback, 1989, p. 327.

18. According to Cynthia Jaffee-MacCabe, "The German Embassy ordered customs to impound the crates, which are released after intervention by a Prado curator." The source of this information is not clear.

19. Claude Kirschen and her mother paid $700 and Victor Brombert $1000 on the same ship. It probably depended on when and where the tickets were bought.

20. The information about the voyage of the *Navemar* is based on detailed interviews with Michel Rapaport-Gordey in Paris and Claude Lopez (formerly Kirschen) in New Haven, Connecticut.

21. The Bernsteins did not want to leave Europe because their son, who served in the French army, was taken by the Germans as a French prisoner of war. With the help of friends, they went to Barcelona and all three survived the war.

CHAPTER 14

1. This date is according to the Immigration and Naturalization Service (Memorandum for Visa Division, Department of State, July 7, 1942). Thus, the accepted date of June 23 is wrong. The Chagalls arrived in New York on the same evening when the Germans invaded the USSR. That happened at 5:00 a.m. on June 22, 1941, which would be 9:00 p.m. June 21 in New York.

2. *Aleko*, a ballet in four scenes; argument by Léonide Massine and Marc Chagall, based on A. Pushkin's Russian long poem, "Gypsies." Choreography by Léonide Massine; sets and costumes by Marc Chagall; music by Tchaikovsky. Main roles: Georges Skibin and Alicia Markova. Performed on September 8, 1942, in Palacio de Bellas Artes, Mexico; and October 6, 1942, in the Metropolitan Opera House, New York.

3. The information in this section is based on the Chagall files of the Pierre Matisse archive in the J. Pierpont Morgan Library in New York.

4. See the letter from Pierre Matisse to Jean Leymarie, March 11, 1977, below, p. 947.

5. Thus, on December 1, 1941, Chagall was paid $1317, on November 18, 1942— $1280. The price of a gouache or watercolor was determined by size: A—$26.67, B— $20.00, C—$13.34. The important early painting "To Russia, the Donkeys, and Others" was priced at $6000 in October 1945. The values kept rising and in 1977 "Time is a River Without Banks" of 1930–1939 was assigned an insurance value by MOMA of $250,000 (MOMA letter of March 17, 1977).

6. In March 1949, Matisse returned many paintings and gouaches with Ida and in June 1950 with Anne-Marie (Busch) Meier-Graefe.

7. U.S. Department of Justice/Immigration and Naturalization Service/Memorandum for Visa Division, Department of State: Application for Reentry Permit P-1345461, July 7, 1942. Stamped by Federal Bureau of Investigation July 10, 1942.

8. In the FBI documents, obtained through the Freedom of Information Act, certain parts are erased and marked here by a series of crosses: [XXXXX].

9. This probably means not Chagall but his lawyers. Chagall's visa was issued.

10. A Hungarian-born conductor who arrived in the U.S. in 1941.

11. The premiere of the ballet *Aleko* was on September 8, in Mexico City.

12. Bella Chagall, "Yom Kippur: a chapter from a volume of memoirs, forthcoming, with drawings by Marc Chagall," *Idisher Kemfer*, September 18, 1942.

13. See FBI Report on Marc Chagall, later in this chapter.

14. "Revolution," 1937–1941. "Marc Chagall: Paintings, Gouaches," October 13– November 7, 1942, Pierre Matisse Gallery, New York.

15. Bella Chagall, *Brenendike likht (Burning Lights)*, with drawings by Marc Chagall, New York: Book League of the Jewish People's Fraternal Order, IWO, 1945; and *Di ershte*

bagegenish (*The First Encounter*), 1947. English edition: *Burning Lights*, New York: Schocken Books, 1946.

16. Report of the California Committee of Un-American Activities, 1947.

17. In 1951–1952 Chagall, then in France, applied for an American visa and was rejected, mainly on the basis of this secret report.

18. This information is based on two articles in the Communist newspaper *The Daily Worker* of January 22 and 28, 1944.

19. Chagall refers here to his long poem *My Distant Home* (see p. 460). He places its inception during his visit in Vilna in 1935. Indeed, only after his participation in the YIVO conference in Vilna did Chagall begin writing poetry in Yiddish.

20. See p. 500.

21. Chagall visited Vilna in 1935, in peacetime, but the poem is clearly written from a distance, and during the Holocaust.

22. Yiddish idiom for bad conditions to go out in the street: either cold weather or a god-forsaken place: "You won't even find a dog [in the street]."

23. James Johnson Sweeney, Curator of the Chagall exhibition at MOMA in April 1946.

24. Virginia Haggard, *My Life with Chagall: Seven Years of Plenty with the Master as Told by the Woman Who Shared Them*, New York: Donald I. Fine, 1986, pp. 23–24. Virginia Haggard wrote her book from notes she kept throughout the years. The authenticity of her descriptions and quotations is corroborated by letters she wrote at the time of the events and did not see again for fifty years. Often the same words reappear in her old letters and the retrospective book. Of course, her information is colored by the way Chagall presented things to her, especially on sensitive "Jewish" topics.

25. Sidney Alexander, *Marc Chagall: An Intimate Biography*, New York: Paragon House, 1978; paperback, 1989, p. 364.

26. Ida's letter of March 27, 1945, to her cousin Bella Rosenfeld in Paris.

27. Marc Chagall's introduction to Bella Chagall's book, *Di ershte bagegenish*, p. 6.

28. Bella Chagall, the two books mentioned above.

29. There are two handwritten versions of this text, which Chagall sent to Opatoshu. One is written in an extremely disturbed handwriting, probably right after Bella's death; then, an expanded clean copy. The text here combines both versions. An abbreviated version was published at the beginning of Bella's book in Yiddish, *Burning Lights*.

30. As we know today, this is a mistake: Bella was born in 1888 or 1889. According to the INS, the date was December 2, 1895. But this was Chagall's information.

31. These were probably seminar papers for some institution of higher learning. There is no evidence that Bella studied at Moscow University; it was extremely difficult for Jews to get in there. In the family dynamics, however, she was the intellectual.

32. Chagall is mistaken: They came to Paris in September 1923, though they left Russia for Berlin in 1922. In wartime, he may have been reluctant to mention a sojourn of over a year in Germany and omitted this fact, here and elsewhere.

33. See the catalogue, *The Louis E. Stern Collection*, Philadelphia: Philadelphia Museum of Art, 1964.

34. André Seligmann was a French painter living in New York during the war.

35. Dorothy H. Dudley, Registrar of MOMA to Daniel Catton Rich, July 22, 1946.

36. Published in *Eynikeyt*, New York, April 1945.

37. See the Yiddish journal *Oyfsnay*, published in Paris in 1945.

38. The MOMA exhibition was April 4–June 23, 1946; the same exhibition was held at the Art Institute of Chicago on November 14, 1946–January 12, 1947.

39. Lionello Venturi, *Marc Chagall*, New York: Pierre Matisse, 1945.

CHAPTER 15

1. From a letter by Chagall written in the late 1940s to Mrs. John Nef. Quoted in the Foreword to the catalogue *Marc Chagall: Paintings and Graphic Works*, University of Chicago, Committee on Social Thought, The Renaissance Society, February 15–March 8, 1958.

2. Virginia Haggard, *My Life with Chagall: Seven Years of Plenty with the Master as Told by the Woman Who Shared Them*, New York: Donald I. Fine, 1986, p. 13. A recent book on the Haggard family is Victoria Manthorpe, *Children of the Empire: The Victorian Haggards*, London: Golancz, 1996. As the book points out, the Haggards had Jewish ancestry from Central Europe, but Virginia probably didn't know it at the time.

3. This observation was made by Sidney Alexander in his book, *Marc Chagall: An Intimate Biography*, New York: Paragon House, 1978; paperback 1989.

4. "The Works of the Mind," Chicago: University of Chicago Press, 1947; reprinted in *Marc Chagall on Art and Culture*.

5. The painting was acquired by the Art Institute of Chicago in 1937. In the questionaire the museum sent him, Chagall wrote: "Nationality: French."

6. For Marc, it began as an affair with a housekeeper that developed into a serious matter; furthermore, it was an "illegitimate" child with a married woman. He might also have been uncomfortable—despite the "progressive" ideology of Chagall and his friends—because Virginia was not Jewish.

7. Yosef Opatoshu's novel, *In Polish Woods*, 1921 (English edition, 1938).

8. In letters to the Opatoshus, the dates in braces are added in the original, often in pencil, perhaps by Adele Opatoshu. While Chagall puts the month after the day, in the European style, here, usually (but not always), the month precedes the day, in the American manner. When in doubt, we have reconstructed the month from the context and indicated that in words.

9. A character from Opatoshu's story "In the Saloon," collected in his book *Untervelt* (*Underworld*), New York, 1918 and later editions.

10. Haggard, *My Life with Chagall*, p. 51.

11. Chagall's retrospective at the Museum of Modern Art opened on April 4, 1946.

12. James Johnson Sweeney, *Marc Chagall*, New York: Museum of Modern Art, 1946.

13. Martin Chauffier was a French writer, moralist, and humanist. A member of the Resistance, he was sent to German concentration camps and wrote a book about it, *l'Homme et la bête* (1947).

14. For the full text, see in *Marc Chagall on Art and Culture*.

15. Published in *Parizer Shriftn* (*Paris Writings*), organ of the Federation of Yiddish Cultural Organizations in France, September 1946, No. 4, pp. 15–17. English translation in *Marc Chagall on Art and Culture*.

16. The history of the poem is as follows: (1) Chagall wrote the poem in Yiddish some

time in June 1946 or just before his speech on July 8; it was published in *Parizer Shriftn*. (2) In 1947, Chagall himself translated the poem into Russian, slightly romanticizing the rougher Yiddish surface, and arranging it in neat, four-line strophes. (3) In 1948, he sent the Russian text to Sutzkever in Tel Aviv for publication. The date "1947" (of the Russian version) was crossed out and corrected to the original "1946"; the title "Mayn land" and his signature were added in Yiddish. (4) Sutzkever translated the Russian poem back into Yiddish, but the language seemed too fancy and literary to Chagall. (5) Chagall himself "retranslated" or restored the poem from memory in Yiddish, using some of the changes of the Russian text. (6) Sutzkever published Chagall's version in Yiddish with Chagall's other poems (*Di Goldene Keyt*, No. 60), and with the changed title, "Toward High Gates" (which fits Sutzkever's symbolism more than Chagall's earthy language).

It seems that the additions in the Russian text (2) were made to fill in the neat strophes with words from Russian Symbolist poetry at the beginning of the century: They have some sentimental and symbolic overtones, foreign to the straitforward Yiddish text. We followed here the original text of version (1) and the structure of Chagall's second Yiddish version (5).

17. In later versions, the line reads: "My own streets stretch out inside me."

18. See my interpretations in *Marc Chagall: Les années russes*.

19. In the first, newspaper version (1), this line was missing, perhaps a typo. We restored it from the later versions (6).

20. In the later versions, this line is missing.

21. The last stanza is in the second Yiddish version, yet omitted in print.

22. Clement Greenberg, "Two of the Moderns: Review of *Chagall* by Jacques Lassaigne and *Soutine* by Ramond Cogniat" in *The Collected Essays and Criticism*, Vol. 3, Chicago: University of Chicago Press, p. 158. Originally published in *Commentary*, October 1953.

23. Yosef Foshko (1892–?), a New York artist, illustrated books of Yiddish literature. The article in Yiddish is "Chagall's Fantastic World: On the Retrospective Exhibition of Marc Chagall's Painting in the Museum of Modern Art," *Di Tsukunft*, June 1946, Vol. LI, No. 6, pp. 444–448.

24. Neighbors of Irish origin.

25. Chagall arranged the publication of Bella Chagall's memoirs in a French translation. It appeared as *Lumières allumées*, translated by Ida Chagall, Geneva: Editions des Trois Collines, 1948.

26. He thought he was unable to send money because of currency restrictions after the war.

CHAPTER 16

1. Franz Meyer lists the date of October 17; see Meyer, *Marc Chagall*, New York: Abrams, 1961, p. 734 (#976). Indeed, there were invitations for that date, but the opening had to be postponed because of a strike. See Chagall's letter to Virginia, October 24, 1947, p. 622.

2. See Marc's letter of November 3, 1947, p. 624.

3. English title, *Arabian Nights: Original Color Lithographs by Marc Chagall for Four Tales of the Arabian Nights*. New York: Pantheon Books, 1948.

4. *Poésie de mots inconnu*. Paris: Le Degrée 41, 1949; one engraving by Chagall.

5. Paul Eluard, *Le dur désir de durer*, Paris: Bordas, 1946; frontispiece and twenty-five drawings by Marc Chagall.

6. Paris: Editions J. Budry, 1926; four drawings by Chagall.

7. Paris: Editions André Delpeuch, 1926; three drawings by Chagall.

8. Abram Markovich Brazer (1892–1942), a sculptor and artist, lived with Chagall in La Ruche during 1912–1914. He was active in the art life of Vitebsk from 1918. He was shot by the Germans in Minsk in 1942, and most of his works were destroyed.

9. An artist at La Ruche; in 1930, he left for the Soviet Union and disappeared.

10. Natan Altman (1889–1970), a major Soviet painter and stage designer, lived in Paris in 1910–1912.

11. James Johnson Sweeney, *Marc Chagall* (catalogue of the exhibition at the Museum of Modern Art, New York) lists the date of Chagall's birth as July 7, 1889, rather than 1887, probably in coordination with Chagall.

12. Ben-Zion Goldberg (1895–?), born in Vilna Province and immigrated to the U.S. in 1907, was a prolific journalist in Yiddish and English, as well as a cultural activist on the left. One of the founders of YIKUF.

13. Joseph Braynin was the son of the prominent Hebrew literary critic Reuven Braynin (1862–1939), who shifted in his later years to Yiddish and was a spokesman in America for the Jewish autonomous region in Birobidjan (in the Soviet Far East). Joseph was at different times both a pro-Zionist and pro-Soviet journalist and a cultural activist in New York.

14. Published in *Yidisher Kemfer*, May 7, 1948.

15. According to Virginia Haggard, the house rental did not materialize, but the wedding did take place (personal information).

16. As far as we know, this was Chagall's last letter to Ettinger, who died in Moscow on September 15, 1948, at the age of eighty-two.

17. See the letter from Stern to Virginia Haggard of August 16, 1948, p. 648.

CHAPTER 17

1. The International Workers Order (IWO) later renamed the Jewish People's Fraternal Order (JPFO), organized many Yiddish schools, summer camps, and publications in the U.S.

2. The most extensive collection of Sutzkever's work in English is Abraham Sutzkever, *Selected Poetry and Prose*, selected and translated by Benjamin and Barbara Harshav, Berkeley, Calif: University of California Press, 1992; includes *Siberia*, with reproductions of Chagall's illustrations.

3. Charles Sorlier, *Chagall, le patron*, Paris: Librairie Séguier, 1989, p. 132.

4. English translation appears in *Marc Chagall on Art and Culture*.

5. *Brenendike likht (Burning Lights)* and *Di ershte bagegenish (First Meeting)*.

6. See P. Novik's letter to Sholem Asch of July 5, 1949, p. 680.

7. Raïssa Maritain, *Marc Chagall*, New York: Editions de la Maison Française, 1943. Her book in French was published in New York during the war and republished as *Chagall ou l'orage enchanté*, Geneva: Editions des Trois Collins, 1948.

CHAPTER 18

1. "How I Got to Know Peretz" in *Marc Chagall on Art and Culture*.

2. This is a handwritten draft. The typed letter was not preserved, but Chagall answered on April 1, 1950.

3. See Sylvie Forestier and Meret Meyer, *Les céramiques de Chagall*, Paris: Albin Michel, 1990.

4. See the letter of February 17, 1950, to Lionello Venturi, p. 699.

5. The following page is headed "p. 2," but it is not clear whether it is a continuation or part of a new letter.

6. In the original typescript: "now"—clearly an error.

7. *YIVO-Bleter* vol. XXXIII, p. 220–224.

8. An unclear allusion; perhaps a mistake in the name.

9. Chagall's album of etchings for *My Life* was published by Paul Cassirer in Berlin in 1923, in an edition of 110 copies.

10. Collister Hutchison, *Toward Daybreak*, New York: Harper & Row, 1950; four drawings by Marc Chagall.

11. Susanne Tenand, *Portrait de Chopin,* Paris: Editions Comité National de Centenaire, A l'Enfant Poète, 1949. One drawing and cover design by Marc Chagall.

12. See *The Art Collection of Gershon Fenster, Tulsa, Oklahoma* and *Judaic Treasures from the Gershon and Rebecca Fenster Gallery of Jewish Art*, Tulsa, Oklahoma, 1973.

13. Afraid of their criticism, especially because he represents the Diaspora "ghetto Jews."

14. *Vitebsk Amol* (*Vitebsk of the Past*): *History, Memoirs, Destruction* (in Yiddish), New York, 1956; and *Sefer Vitebsk* (*The Book of Vitebsk*), with a frontispiece by Marc Chagall (in Hebrew), Tel Aviv, 1957.

CHAPTER 19

1. See "Lithographs" in Chapter 21, below, p. 827.

2. Written in Russian, published in French, English, and Hebrew in very liberal translations. This is a new translation from the original Russian.

3. Statement published in *News of the City of Tel Aviv-Jaffa*, Vol. XXI, No. 3-4, August– September 1951.

4. Chagall's poem "For the Slaughtered Artists," written as an introduction to H. Fenster's book commemorating the perished Jewish artists who lived in France, was now reproduced in the New York *Tsukunft* with an introduction by H. Leyvik. See the English translation, above, p. 720.

CHAPTER 20

1. The Yiddish *Algemeyne Entsiklopedye* (*General Encyclopedia*) was begun just before World War II in Paris, continued in New York, and never finished. Three volumes, titled *Yidn* (*Jews*), were published separately and contained valuable synoptic studies of the major aspects of Jewish history and culture: Vol. A, Paris: Dubnov Foundation, 1939; Vol. B, Paris: Dubnov Foundation, 1940; Vol. C, New York: Dubnov Foundation and CYCO (Central Yiddish Culture Organization), 1942.

2. Dr. Rochl Vishnitser-Bernstein, "The Historical Development of Jewish Art," *Algemeyne Entsiklopedye*, *Yidn B*, pp. 467–536. Chagall met Rachel Vishnitser in Berlin, Vilna, and New York.

3. February–March 1952.

4. A note in English indicates the site of Bella's grave: Westchester Hills Cemetery, Mount Hope, New York (on the Saw Mill River Parkway), Grave no. 19 plot no. 792.

5. See Virginia Haggard, *My Life with Chagall: Seven Years of Plenty with the Master as Told by the Woman Who Shared Them*, New York: Donald I. Fine, 1986, p. 166.

6. Despatch No. 2400 of March 12, 1952, obtained through the Freedom of Information Act. The relevant excerpts from the document are presented here.

7. Haggard, op. cit.

8. Ibid., p. 173

9. Haggard, op cit.

CHAPTER 21

1. Curt Valentin Gallery, New York: Sculptures, Ceramics, Etchings for the *Fables* of La Fontaine, November 18–December 13, 1952.

2. *Siberia*, with drawings by Marc Chagall (Yiddish and Hebrew versions), Jerusalem: Mossad Bialik, 1953.

3. Chemjo Vinaver, *Anthology of Jewish Music*, New York: Edward B. Marks Music Co., 1955. Frontispiece by Chagall.

4. Jacques Lassaigne, *Marc Chagall*, Geneva: Skira, 1952.

5. See Clement Greenberg, *The Collected Essays and Criticism*, vol. 3, ed. John O'Brian, Chicago: University of Chicago Press, 1993, pp. 157–160.

6. A. Glanz (the Yiddish Introspectivist poet A. Leyeles, 1889–1966) and his family were close friends of the Opatoshus. See a selection of his poetry and criticism in English in Benjamin and Barbara Harshav, *American Yiddish Poetry*, Berkeley: University of California Press, 1986.

7. A. Leyeles, *Fanye* (book of poetry in Yiddish), New York, 1953.

8. Apparently, the poet and critic Jacob Glatshteyn.

9. Charles Sorlier, *Chagall, le patron*, Paris: Librairie Séguier, 1989, p. 140.

10. Ibid.

11. "Chagall's Illustrations for the Bible," in Meyer Shapiro, *Modern Art—19th & 20th Centuries: Selected Papers*. New York: George Braziller, 1979, pp. 121–134.

CHAPTER 22

1. Daniel Charny, "Marc Chagall (1887–1957)," *Der Oyfkum*, vol. 13, No. 1–2, New York, January–February 1958, pp. 16–18.

CHAPTER 23

1. For a full description and reproductions of Chagall's stained glass windows, see: Sylvie Forestier, *Marc Chagall, L'oeuvre monumental: Les vitraux*, Milan: Jaca Book, 1987.

CHAPTER 24

1. The text is not clear; it could also read "gifts," but what would that mean?

CHAPTER 25

1. This exhibition took place at the Jewish Museum in New York; it was curated by Avram Kampf. See his book, *Jewish Experience in the Art of the Twentieth Century*, S. Hadley, Mass.: Bergin Garvey, 1984.

EPILOGUE

1. Audrey Voznesensky, *Shagal Vozvrashtshenie Mastera* (*Chagall: The Return of a Master*) (Moscow: Sovetsky Khudozzhnik, 1988). In 1989, the first Russian book reproducing Chagall's early work was published in the West: Aleksandr Kamensky, *Chagall: The Russian Years 1907–1922* (New York: Rizzoli International Publications, 1989).

INDEX OF NAMES

Names are listed according to the name most frequently used in the text. Variants are supplied. **Bold** indicates where a name or term is described; *en* indicates a note in the Notes section; *fn* indicates a footnote; *mn* indicates a margin note.

INDEX OF WORKS BY MARC CHAGALL
MENTIONED IN THE TEXT

mn indicates a marginal note; *fn* indicates a footnote; *en* indicates an end note.

INDEX OF LETTERS AND DOCUMENTS

All the letters included in the book are listed here alphabetically by correspondent; within each correspondent, in chronological order. The dates are all converted to the American system: *month.day.year*, whereas the original letters reproduced in the book often use the European system: day/month/year. Thus 12.3.56 means December 3, not March 12. Other documents—poems, articles, interviews, etc.—are listed separately, below. The sources of the documents are indicated by a code, explained at the end.

FBI AND STATE DEPARTMENT [FOIA]

CHAGALL'S POEMS

GLOBAL PERMISSIONS

[Paris] Comité Marc Chagall in Paris: permission to publish the complete book, as described by me. Additional permission to publish all the archival material and the family photos which I found in the Chagall home archives, located in the house of Chagall's daughter Ida Chagall. Signed by Meret Meyer-Graber (Chagall's granddaughter) for the Estate of Ida Chagall in Paris.

[Haggard] Virginia Haggard-Leirens, Chagall's second, common-law wife: permission to publish her profuse correspondence, which I found in different archives.

[YIVO] YIVO Institute for Jewish Research in New York: permission to publish all the Chagall correspondence as well as his Yiddish writings and manuscripts, stored in their archives. This is valid for letters to Lyesin, Nigger, Opatoshu, Bickel, and Glanz-Leyeles and to Chagall's autobiography.

[AAA] Archives of American Art (Smithsonian Institution, Washington D.C.): the correspondence with Louis Stern and Bernard and Rebecca Reis.

Congress for Jewish Culture, New York: permission to publish Chagall's autobiography and poetry published in their journal *Tsukunft* (1892–present). The same material has been republished by Marc Chagall in the Tel Aviv journal *Di Goldene Keyt*, edited by A.Sutzkever (see next entry).

[Sutzkever] The poet A. Sutzkever (born in 1913), editor of the Yiddish literary Quarterly *Di Goldene Keyt*, Tel Aviv.

[Jerusalem] Dr. Rafael Weiser, Director, Archives of the National and University Library, Hebrew University, Jerusalem: the correspondence with Leo Kenig and others, available in their archives.

[Guggenheim] Solomon R. Guggenheim Museum, New York: permission to publish the letters in their possession between Chagall, Hilla Rebay, T.Messer, and Solomon Guggenheim.

[Art Institute] of Chicago: correspondence with and concerning Chagall.

[FOIA] Public Citizen Litigation Group, Washington D.C.: permission to publish all documents obtained for me through the Freedom of Information Act, including FBI and the State Department.

[Fry] Permission by the widow of Varian Fry and the Fry family to publish the correspondence with and concerning Chagall. The Fry papers are kept in the Special Collections of the Columbia University Library.

[Luz] Permission by Prof. Zvi Luz to publish Chagall's correspondence with his father, the Speaker of the Israeli parliament Kaddish Luz.

[Genazim] Permission by The National Institute Genazim in Tel Aviv to publish letters found in their archives.

[Mokady] Permission by Nina Mokady-Hayon, daughter of the painter and director of the Culture Division in the Israeli Ministry of Education and Culture to publish the letters and texts which she sent me.

[Shatskikh] Permission to publish the material she prepared for this volume, including her edition of texts and annotations to Chagall's letters to P. D. Ettinger.

[Tel Aviv] Correspondence between Dizengoff, Chagall, and the Tel Aviv Museum. City Archive of Tel Aviv.

SPECIFIC SOURCES

[Bibliothèque] Bibliothèque nationale de France, le Fonds Jean Grenier.

[Chicago] University of Chicago Library, Special Collections.

[Grenier] Permission by Alain Grenier.

[Harel] Permission by Shulamit Harel in Tel-Aviv to publish Chagall's letters to her father, A .Z. Ben-Yishay.

[Knesset] Archive of the Israeli parliament.

[Kornfeld] Eberhardt Kornfeld, Bern: permission to publish two letters to a publisher and the copy of a hand written page of Chagall's memoirs.

[Leloup] Permission to publish Chagall's letters to Coquiot in his possession.

[Marq] Charles Marq gave me Chagall's letters to him specifically for this publication and corresponded with me about the text and footnotes.

[Morgan] J.Pierpont Morgan Library Archive, New York: letters to Pierre Matisse.

[Philadelphia] Philadelphia Museum of Art: letters to Fiske Kimball and L. Venturi.

[Pompidou] Viviane Tarenne at the National Museum for Modern Art, Centre Georges Pompidou in Paris.

[Rosenfeld] Bella Rosenfeld-Zitter, the niece of Chagall's first wife, gave me this letter for publication.

[Tériade] Alice Teriade gave me Chagall's letters to her husband for publication.

[Tsanin] The writer M. Tsanin in Tel Aviv gave me Chagall's letters for publication.

[Walter] Falguiere-Walter: permission to publish a Chagall letter to Dennoyer de Segonzac.

[Yale] Yale University, Beinecke Rare Book and Manuscript Library: Chagall letters to Sedykh and Veynbaum.

[Lebouc] Yves Lebouc: permission to publish Chagall's letters to Charles Sorlier.

ILLUSTRATIONS

SOURCES OF THE IMAGES

AL: Abraham Lyesin, illustrations to the work of the Yiddish poet
CR: Carmela Rubin, Director of the Rubin Museumm Tel-Aviv
DB: David Brainin, son of Yiddish activist Yosef Brainin
EK: Eberhardt Kornfeld, Bern, Switzerland
G: Guggenheim Museum
GP: Musée national d'art moderne, Centre George Pompidou, Paris; Cabinet d'art graphique. Curator: Viviane Tarenne
HU: National and University Library, Jerusalem
IM: Israel Museum, Jerusalem, Visual Resources dept., Tanya Zhilinsky
LB: Yves Le Bouc, bouquinierre de l'Institut, Paris
MM: Meret Meyer-Graber, from the collection Ida Chagall in Paris
NV: Nathalie Vofsi, daughter of Solomon Mikhoels
OP: David Opatoshu, grandson of Chagall's friend
PC: prerevolutionary postcards (supplied by A. Shatskikh, Moscow)
VH: photos given by Virginia Haggard